SPORT PSYCHOLOGY Interventions

Shane M. Murphy, PhD
Editor

Human Kinetics

Library of Congress Cataloging-in-Publication Data

Sport psychology interventions / [edited by] Shane M. Murphy.
p. cm.
Includes index.
ISBN 0-87322-659-3
1. Athletes--Mental health. 2. Athletes--Mental health services.
3. Athletes--Counseling of. 4. Sports--Psychological aspects.
I. Murphy, Shane M., 1957-
RC451.4.A83S66 1995
616.89'008'8796--dc20 94-10390
CIP

ISBN: 0-87322-659-3

Developmental Editor: Mary E. Fowler; **Assistant Editors:** Sally Bayless, Hank Woolsey, Karen Bojda, Erik Dafforn, and Jacqueline Blakley; **Copyeditor:** Tom Plummer; **Proofreader:** Pam Johnson; **Indexer:** Joan K. Griffitts; **Production Manager:** Kris Ding; **Typesetter:** Sandra Meier; **Text Designer:** Keith Blomberg; **Layout Artist:** Tara Welsch; **Photo Editor:** Karen Maier; **Cover Designer:** Jack Davis; **Illustrator:** Craig Ronto; **Printer:** Braun-Brumfield

Printed in the United States of America 10 9 8 7 6 5 4

Human Kinetics
Web site: www.HumanKinetics.com

United States: Human Kinetics, P.O. Box 5076, Champaign, IL 61825-5076
800-747-4457
e-mail: humank@hkusa.com

Canada: Human Kinetics, 475 Devonshire Road, Unit 100, Windsor, ON N8Y 2L5
800-465-7301 (in Canada only)
e-mail: orders@hkcanada.com

Europe: Human Kinetics, 107 Bradford Road, Stanningley
Leeds LS28 6AT, United Kingdom
+44 (0) 113 255 5665
e-mail: hk@hkeurope.com

Australia: Human Kinetics, 57A Price Avenue, Lower Mitcham, South Australia 5062
08 8277 1555
e-mail: liaw@hkaustralia.com

New Zealand: Human Kinetics, Division of Sports Distributors NZ Ltd.
P.O. Box 300 226 Albany, North Shore City, Auckland
0064 9 448 1207
e-mail: info@humankinetics.co.nz

CONTENTS

PREFACE

Sport in the United States is in serious trouble. Front page stories in the sports section of any metropolitan newspaper describe a pattern of turmoil and discontent.

- At a Little League baseball game a father argues angrily with the umpire over an *out* call on his son. After the game another argument breaks out, and the umpire is stabbed and seriously wounded.
- A feature story describes the experiences of a former professional female tennis player who burned out and retired from the sport at age 17.
- Another story presents the startling statistic that 40% of children leave competitive sport every year. The story includes interviews with parents and teachers describing the pressure of competitive sport and what can be done about it.
- Three starters on a Division I football team are arrested and charged with the gang rape of a college student.
- An aging professional comes back from retirement twice in one season and is arrested on a charge of cocaine distribution. He explains that his gambling debts were so large that he "couldn't see any other way out."
- A promising young Olympic athlete is arrested after the car she was driving crashes, killing a passenger. The Olympian's blood alcohol level was .12, and she later pleaded guilty to manslaughter.

Such stories tempt the jaded observer to question whether sport itself produces these problems. The answer is probably that such problems are a reflection of society as a whole but that the intense scrutiny that accompanies high-level sports competition in our society produces greater publicity when athletes are involved. *Sport* is still synonymous with *play* and is meant to be fun. But in professional and elite sport environments, there is often little fun.

This book is about ways of helping athletes cope with the special circumstances of committed sports involvement. The focus is on psychological interventions—ways to produce change in the individual athlete. Several other texts have been written that discuss psychological interventions aimed at increasing athletic performance. Performance is not the focus of this text. Instead, the underlying philosophy here is that athletes who can learn to manage their lives successfully, who can grow and develop as individuals, and who can experience sport as a positive learning process will enjoy their participation more and perform better.

Sport Psychology Interventions is written for all helping professionals who are working with or interested in helping athletes. It addresses the practical concerns that are typically encountered by physicians, athletic trainers, psychologists, counselors, and health care professionals working with athletes. Because understanding the psychology of sport, competition, and training is critical to the effectiveness of any intervention with athletes, this book is a necessity for all helping professionals who work in sport, but it also will interest anyone—athlete, coach, parent, or fan—who wants to understand sports participation and how to gain the maximum positive benefit from being an athlete.

In editing this book, I turned to the top professionals in the field of sport psychology. Knowledge in an applied area grows in proportion to the number of professionals working in that area, and the application of the science of psychology to athletics was still in its infancy a decade ago. Fortunately many professionals throughout the United States now are working with athletes and sport organizations to help improve the athletic experience for participants, and it is that group with whom I began this venture. Thus this book is written by authors familiar with the struggles of athletes.

Part I presents a variety of models of intervention in sport, encompassing systemic, educational, cognitive-behavioral, and marital therapy, with each model examined in the context of application to a specific sport group. In this way the issues specific to a variety of athlete populations are addressed for the first time in the sport psychology literature. Intervention issues in working with elite athletes are described along with issues specific to helping female, competitive, recreational, student, and child athletes.

In Part II, experts address issues commonly encountered by helping professionals in the sport setting. Injury, alcohol and drug use, eating disorders, career transitions, and overtraining are discussed, and interventions are described.

Each chapter in this book contains extensive case-study material, allowing the authors to use real-life illustrations of the issues they address. The case studies help focus the book on applied issues and prevent the discussions from becoming too theoretical. You will find that the case studies bring the chapters to life in an exciting and enriching manner.

Sport Psychology Interventions presents a new philosophy of helping athletes, recognizing that athletes face special challenges and sometimes unique problems. As editor, I am pleased to present the stimulating and thoughtful ideas of some of the nation's leading sport psychologists on how to tackle these issues. I believe that the ideas we discuss can profoundly change the sporting experience in this society. I hope this book will serve all of us who care about sport and about athletes.

Shane Murphy

ACKNOWLEDGMENTS

Many people assisted in the development of this book, and I would like to publicly thank them.

First, all the chapter authors, who met their deadlines and suffered my continual questions with gentle patience. Their expertise is highly valued.

The sport psychology staff at the United States Olympic Committee, who helped me continually refine my ideas, especially Sean McCann, Chris Carr, Bob Swoap, Frank Perna, Megan Neyer, Suzie Tuffey, Kirsten Peterson, Shirley Durtschi, Mike Greenspan, Doug Jowdy, Vance Tammen, Michael Lesser, and Alan Budney.

My ever-patient and always smiling secretary, Sally Bowman.

My developmental editor at Human Kinetics, Mary Fowler, for all her patient help. And many, many thanks to Rainer Martens, whose personal vision for sport psychology inspired this book.

The staff of the United States Olympic Committee, whose dedication to helping athletes reach their potential serves as a wonderful model for the sporting community, and in particular Harvey Schiller, Charles Davis, Jim Page, Jay T. Kearney, Tom Crawford, Steve Fleck, Sarah Smith, Leonard Jansen, Sheryl McSherry, and Peter Van Handel, who all have taught me so much.

Rob Woolfolk, who supported my interest in sport psychology from the very beginning.

All the athletes I have known over the years—those many wonderful people I have learned so much from.

Jerry May, who has been a wise and valued mentor.

My wife, Annemarie, and my children, Bryan and Theresa, for their support and patience through the missing weekends and long nights.

And lastly, my father, Tom, and mother, Nola, who taught me everything I know about being a good sport, the thrill of participating, and the love of the game. With that training, is it any wonder I became a sport psychologist?

CHAPTER 1

INTRODUCTION TO SPORT PSYCHOLOGY INTERVENTIONS

Shane M. Murphy, PhD
United States Olympic Committee

The effect sport has on our lives and how individuals adjust to sport are topics that have been too long ignored in the psychological community. Using psychological interventions to help athletes manage the stresses of intensive sport involvement is a relatively new enterprise. It differs from the more traditional *sport psychology* that mainly seeks to understand and optimize athletic performance.

You might wonder if the subject of psychological interventions with athletes deserves an entire book. I argue that it is important to explore how people can develop healthier, more productive athletic lifestyles. Professional sport is a pervasive feature of American society. For good or bad many Americans, young and old, identify strongly with sports figures. Recreational athletic activity has never been more actively promoted, as an aging population grapples with its lifestyle choices, preventive medicine, the costs of health care, and the quality of life. Sport and exercise are integral to our lives and deserve no less serious attention by health care professionals than our work and relationships.

Psychological interventions are required with sports issues such as treating the emotional effects of athletic injury, preventing overtraining and burnout, helping athletes with eating disorders, attacking drug and alcohol abuse in sport, heightening awareness of gender issues in sport, and assisting athletes who are making the transition out of competitive sport into the business world. We discuss these issues in *Sport Psychology Interventions*. Before describing these sport psychology interventions, however, we must first review the broader history of sport psychology.

WHAT IS SPORT PSYCHOLOGY?

The term *sport psychology* has developed two separate, entirely different meanings, resulting in a great deal of confusion and even stress in sport psychology organizations. One meaning relates to the practice of psychology by professionals who specialize primarily in working with athletes in a variety of sport settings. After World War II, the practice of psychology flourished (see Napali, 1981 and Pryzwansky & Wendt, 1987, for a history), and subspecialties began to appear, such as clinical psychology, school psychology, industrial-organizational psychology, and rehabilitation psychology. These subspecialties were defined primarily by setting and type of clients: Thus school psychologists work in school settings with students, and industrial-organizational psychologists work with employers and employees in companies and organizations. Similarly, as some psychologists began to specialize by working with athletes in sport organizations they called themselves sport psychologists.

Most psychologists who practice in the area of sport have received little formal education in a content area called sport psychology. There is a clear reason for this situation: Few psychology training programs offer formal course work in the sport area. The study of the psychological issues confronted by athletes is almost nonexistent in graduate psychology programs. This situation has characterized other specialty areas: in the early years of school psychology, its practitioners received their training in other specialties, such as clinical or counseling psychology. As the demand for psychologists grew in school settings, training programs were developed to prepare psychology students for working in schools. It remains to be seen whether a similar growth will occur in sport psychology. (I will return to this issue later.)

But a second, very different view of sport psychology emerges if we examine the development of the academic discipline known as sport psychology, usually found in university departments of sport science, human movement, or physical education. Here the study of sport psychology is "concerned with both the psychological factors that influence participation in sport and exercise and the psychological effects derived from that participation" (Williams & Straub, 1986, p. 1).

Many universities in the United States offer courses and programs in sport psychology, and many of the faculty in these programs call themselves sport psychologists. Yet the training and interests of this group of sport psychologists differ greatly from the first group's. It is tempting to say that a major difference between the groups is that the first works in the applied area—the practice of psychology in sport settings—whereas the second group is academically based, working with research issues, theory development, and education. Although this might have been true in the past, it no longer is. In the last decade interest has grown in applying the knowledge gained from academic sport psychology in the sporting arena. Books like *Applied Sport Psychology* (Williams, 1986) and *Psyching for Sport* (Orlick, 1986) demonstrate this growing interest. Simple generalizations do not work in the complex, rapidly evolving area of sport psychology. We need to take a closer look at the historical development of both strands to understand the rope known as sport psychology.

TRACING THE HISTORY

The history of psychologists working with athletes is more difficult to trace than the development of academic sport psychology, because practicing psychologists usually experience less pressure to publish than their academic colleagues. I have traced the development of practice with athletes through presentations, professional publications, and occasional books. The development of the academic discipline of sport psychology, described as "the youngest of the sport sciences" (Williams & Straub, 1986, p. 11), was traced more directly through the publication of foundational works in the field.

Psychologists in Sport Settings

It seems that before the 1960s few psychologists specialized in working with athletes.

Courtesy USOC

Those who did seemed to be "isolated individuals without any recognizable training who applied techniques such as hypnosis to sport without any special rationale" (Nideffer, 1987, p. 2). In the 1960s and 1970s, however, a small group of psychologists became interested in the practice of psychology as it relates to athletes. The publication of such books as *Problem Athletes and How to Handle Them* (Ogilvie & Tutko, 1966) and *The Madness in Sport* (Beisser, 1977) and such articles as "The Psychologist's Contribution to Sport Organizations and the Athlete" (Butt, 1979) indicate that the psychological concerns of athletes were seriously addressed during this period.

A major factor in the increasing involvement of psychologists with sport organizations has been the increasing professionalism of sport itself. The advent of two factors in the 1960s and 1970s transformed the face of sport in America: sports television and sports sponsorship. Money was the common element. As networks paid organizations to air their competitions and as companies paid them for the right to associate products with star athletes, the profitability of sport organizations grew. Athletes in turn began to receive substantial sums for their sports participation. This trend was evident across all areas of major sport: professional, collegiate, and Olympic. Although many lament the demise of "playing for the love of the game," the influx of money into the sporting arena was inevitable. Sport organizations began to view athletes as valuable assets. Without great athletes, success was out of reach—success that bred bigger television contracts and bigger sponsorship deals. An organization that had spent years developing a scouting and coaching system to create successful athletes was averse to losing them, especially to factors perceived as psychological problems. Thus psychologists were hired as consultants to work with athletes, in a sense protecting the investment of the organization. Although some might decry this analysis as overly economic, ample evidence suggests it is a viable model that explains the development of sport over the past 20 years (in particular see the analysis of the development of the Olympic movement in *The Lords of the Rings* by Simson and Jennings, 1992).

The result for psychologists has been increased opportunities to work in sport settings, a blessing for those who love sport and who enjoy helping athletes. Individual psychologists have been hired to work with professional sport organizations and national

Olympic sport organizations and by college counseling centers to work primarily with college athletes. Many of the contributors to this book work in such settings. Overall, however, the opportunities remain few. Compared to other areas of professional specialization in psychology, sport psychology is too small to warrant subspecialty status. The future of the field remains a mystery.

One indication that an interest area is becoming a subspecialty is the development of professional organizations to address the needs of professionals in that area. As more psychologists worked with athletes over the long term, a move began in the national organization of psychologists in the United States, the American Psychological Association (APA), to develop a separate area for psychologists interested in sport and exercise. In the early 1980s, APA instituted a freeze on the development of new subareas, called divisions of APA, so psychologists interested in sport formed a special interest group. Thanks largely to the tireless efforts of leaders such as Steve Heyman and William Morgan, APA approved a new Division of Sport and Exercise (Division 47) in 1985; it is one of the fastest-growing divisions in APA. Division 47 has addressed many professional concerns in the field and has published a small pamphlet for students interested in careers in sport and exercise psychology, describing the opportunities available and the training required for different career tracks.

Academic Sport Psychology

The beginnings of the academic discipline of sport psychology were *Psychology of Coaching* (1926) and *Psychology of Athletics* (1928) by Griffith. The publication record shows a long gap until the appearance of another *Psychology of Coaching* in 1951, by Lawther, but by the 1960s a variety of research was published in journals such as *Research Quarterly for Sport*. In 1967 a group of teachers and researchers formed the North American Society for the Psychology of Sport and Physical Activity (NASPSPA), the first sport psychology organization in the United States. It took another decade for the first separate sport psychology journal, the *Journal of Sport Psychology*, to appear, but the 1980s witnessed an explosion of interest in the area. Wiggins (1984) has written an excellent history of the development of academic sport psychology.

Sport psychology grew in the 1980s as a result of increasing interest in its applied aspects. Although it is difficult to infer a causal relationship in such matters, the publication of an important article by Rainer Martens in 1979 seemed to signal the growth of interest in applied issues. "About Smocks and Jocks" criticized much of contemporary sport psychology research for being conducted in artificial laboratory settings and contained a call to arms for researchers to emphasize field research, which is directly relevant to athletes and coaches. The article also emphasized that new multivariate theories that would not assume unidirectional causality would need to be developed in sport psychology. The increase in methodologically sound field research in the following decade seemed to answer Martens's call for action.

It thus became logical to study the impact of educating athletes and coaches about this body of knowledge. For example, if research indicates that certain factors might promote team cohesion, a logical follow-up line of inquiry is to determine if structuring the team to promote those factors increases cohesion. As researchers began working with sport groups, interest grew among coaches and athletes in understanding the psychological factors involved in their sporting vocation. As consumer demand for information grew, it was filled by educators formally trained in the academic discipline of sport psychology. What distinguished them from the psychologists just described is that few were graduates of psychology training programs or were licensed psychologists. Thus an entirely separate group of professionals interested in applying the principles of psychology to sport came to be identified as "sport psychologists" in the eyes of the public. Given the age-old instinct of territoriality, it was inevitable that clashes between the two groups would occur.

The transformation of academic sport psychology to include application as a major focus can be seen in the advent of books, journals, and organizations centering on the topic. The journal *The Sport Psychologist* began publication in 1987 and was followed by the appearance of the *Journal of Applied Sport Psychology* in 1989. Perhaps most significantly, an organization devoted entirely to applied issues, the Association for the Advancement of Applied Sport Psychology (AAASP), held its first conference in 1986 at Jekyll Island, Georgia. AAASP was the first in the new field to attract a representative mixture of professionals from both university psychology departments and the sport sciences. Almost from the first, however, members intensely debated whether the proper focus of sport psychology was primarily educational, focusing on performance issues, or psychological, focusing on personal development of athletes. As would be expected, individual training was often the decisive factor in determining on which side of the issue members stood.

THE CURRENT STATUS OF SPORT PSYCHOLOGY

As you might expect from this history, considerable confusion exists in the field of sport psychology concerning its nature, goals, and priorities, primarily because two groups of professionals regard themselves as sport psychologists. However, because of their different educational experiences and training, these groups see many issues from different perspectives, and hostility can arise when one group perceives the other as imposing its worldview on an issue.

The sport psychology literature is filled with debate over basic questions: Who is a sport psychologist? What are the boundaries of sport psychology? How should sport psychologists be trained? What services should sport psychologists supply? (Brown, 1982; Clarke, 1983; Danish & Hale, 1981, 1982; Dishman, 1983; Gardner, 1991; Harrison & Feltz, 1979; Heyman, 1982; LaRose, 1988; McAuley, 1987; Monahan, 1987; Newburg, 1992; Nideffer, DuFresne, Nesvig, & Selder, 1980; Nideffer, Feltz, & Salmela, 1982; Rejeski & Brawley, 1988; Silva, 1989). As the debate has evolved, some basic concerns have been addressed repeatedly. For sport psychology to develop as a profession, at least the following issues must be resolved.

- *Competency.* A specialized area of practice assumes that the professionals working in it are competent to practice. There are several ways to address competency of practitioners, including requirements for minimal educational qualifications and competency-based exams or practice reviews.
- *Knowledge base.* Practitioners should agree on the general knowledge base that guides their practice. This might be based on research, be based on a set of codes or rules, relate to a body of experiential knowledge, or represent a combination of these.
- *Training.* Those wishing to enter the profession must participate in a recognized training experience that adequately prepares them for practice. Such training usually involves both academic study at a university and a structured practical experience under the guidance of recognized professionals.
- *Ethics.* All professions have their own set of ethical guidelines that guide proper

and appropriate practice. Each of the previously mentioned issues might involve various ethical questions. For example, an ethical guideline on competency could be that professionals practice only in areas within their competency. Professions have varying procedures for ensuring adherence to ethical guidelines.

These issues have been debated again and again in the literature but have not yet been resolved. Some, for example, argue that sport psychology services should not be provided because not enough is known about the psychological factors that affect sport and exercise participation; others feel that sport psychology should be a separate profession with its own structure and specialized training. I will deal with these issues again when I examine the future of sport psychology. But at this point I will examine the nature of the issues and concerns that professionals typically encounter when working in the area of applied sport psychology, however it is defined.

ISSUES IN THE PRACTICE OF SPORT PSYCHOLOGY

It does not matter whether one's professional training is in the sport sciences or in psychology; the concerns of athletes are the same in either case. Most issues or problems that lead athletes to seek assistance from a sport psychology consultant are related to the environmental stressors that committed athletes inevitably face in a modern sport context. At the Olympic Training Center in Colorado Springs we have kept records for 6 years on more than 1,000 athletes seeking consultation with our sport psychology staff, and more than 60% of the identified issues leading to consultation involve performance concerns. Typical concerns include anxiety at competitions, concentration during performance, lack of motivation in the face of grueling training schedules, worry over whether success will be gained and efforts rewarded, and problems communicating with a coach or fellow athlete.

Discussion of interventions for such issues is infrequent in the applied sport psychology literature. In reading the major books in the applied sport psychology area, one is struck by their uniformity of approach. Typically these books take a mental-skills-training approach to working with athletes, an approach that has grown out of the cognitive-behavioral model in psychology. The mental-skills approach assumes that sport performance is managed largely by athletes' thought processes and emotional states. Athletes are taught these "effective" ways of cognitively managing their performance in the expectation that these methods will lead to better performance. Much of this literature assumes that athletes have few problems and that their primary concern is simply better performance. Williams and Straub, for example, state that "some data suggest that over 90% of all athletes are very stable psychologically" (1986, p. 9). This assumption can be dangerous, as it leads practitioners toward a complacent attitude that few athletes have serious problems. Given the extent of the problems facing sport, as any casual reading of a newspaper sports section will indicate, this view is naive. The reality is that athletes operate in a stressful world with challenges that few of us can imagine. Athletes encounter a variety of problems in their sports participation, and the interventions described in this book have grown out of a need to help athletes with these problems.

Also strikingly uniform in the applied sport psychology literature is the common focus on techniques. Every applied sport psychology book has chapters on techniques such as visualization or imagery, relaxation, concentration, and goal setting. Little attention is paid to the wide variety of concerns athletes in different performance settings encounter. Consider, for example, the different needs and concerns of athletes in the following situations:

- Youth sport athletes
- Recreational adult athletes
- Collegiate female athletes
- Masters athletes
- Minority athletes in high school sports
- Professional athletes
- Olympic hopefuls
- Collegiate athletes in revenue-producing sports

This sample list indicates how much the concerns and issues of athletic participants can vary. Some issues are common to all athletes, but even the meaning of a common problem, say injury, will be different for a first-year pro than for an active 60-year-old masters participant. In this book, the issues faced by different levels of sports participants are addressed for the first time.

THE FUTURE OF SPORT PSYCHOLOGY

It is perilous to look into the crystal ball for revelations about a professional area as young as sport psychology. Yet the brief historical overview of the field presented earlier includes many issues that remain unresolved and demand further discussion. Resolution of these issues will require much debate among those working in this field, but it is possible to predict some resolutions based on current trends. This final section of this introduction deals with possible developments in the sport psychology areas discussed previously.

Academic Sport Psychology

In some ways the future of the sport science subdiscipline known as sport psychology looks bright. There exists a great and still growing interest in the psychological processes related to athletic performance and the effects of sports participation on individual athletes. Research in this area will continue to grow, and it is natural to expect it to be conducted in sport science or physical education departments. These faculty have the keenest interest in athletes and sport, and the results of their research directly impacts their teaching. Funding for such research may expand as society commits some of its resources to tackling some of the problems associated with sports involvement: on-the-ice and off-the-field violence, cheating, blood doping and drug abuse, sex-related problems, and academic–sport conflicts. On a more positive note, the benefits of athletic participation and exercise will also have a higher research priority as society strives to find ways to encourage everyone to be fit and to adopt healthy lifestyles. As the baby boom generation ages and a greater percentage of the U.S. population reaches the senior years, a focus on the benefits of a preventive approach to containing health care costs will be critical.

Yet there might be storm clouds on the horizon of this optimistic outlook, and indeed the first signs of a coming tempest might have appeared. As interest in applied sport psychology has grown, more and more students have enrolled in sport psychology programs at both the undergraduate and graduate levels. This could cause problems if students graduating from these programs wish to enter careers in applied sport psychology and find few job possibilities. This career issue was addressed at length in a recent AAASP presidential address by Michael Sachs (1992). Problems can arise for students if (a) few job openings that fit their training are available when they graduate and (b) if the available job openings are more likely to be filled by graduates of other types of training programs.

The first situation apparently already exists. Typically, the most appropriate type of position for sport psychology graduates is a teaching and research appointment at a college or university. As has occurred in most university areas, the number of teaching positions in sport psychology has steadily decreased over recent years; at the same time student enrollment in sport psychology graduate programs has increased. Combine this situation with the apparent preference of many current graduate students to enter primarily applied careers and it is clear that a discrepancy exists between student expectations and job possibilities.

The second situation is a potential problem because many jobs that require direct intervention with athletes are likely to be described as "psychologist" positions, because they require applicants to have a state license to practice psychology. This is true of positions such as counselor or clinician for a sport organization or university counselor, and certainly anyone working in private practice as a "sport psychologist" must be licensed. Graduate student frustration can result if job positions are perceived as going to graduates with less training in sport psychology.

The immediate implications of this development for graduate training programs in sport psychology are twofold. First, students must be clearly educated about potential careers in sport psychology when they enter a program. Second, administrators of graduate programs must reexamine their priorities and determine if changes need to be made in areas such as the number of positions available for incoming graduates, the curricula offered, and the types of training experiences made available to students. The content of appropriate training programs for students interested in applied sport psychology careers is examined on page 10.

The academic discipline of sport psychology is in a turbulent period. Even as new opportunities emerge, several prominent physical education programs have been merged with other departments or closed down entirely. As several leaders of the field have noted (Bunker & McQuire, 1985; Silva, 1989), the discipline might have to undergo dramatic structural changes to keep pace with the changing demands of sport, students, and society.

Psychologists in Sport Settings

As this book makes clear, many psychological issues and problems encountered in the athletic domain are unique to sport. Psychologists practicing in this area without an adequate understanding of these issues are likely to experience many problems. Yet the current sport psychology literature does not often address these practice issues, and until this book's publication the practicing psychologist had no place to seek information on issues such as injury concerns among professional athletes, challenges to confidentiality in sport settings, approaches to drug education in sport, ethical issues encountered in working with a sport organization, and so on.

It is interesting to speculate on reasons for this apparent lack of interest on the part of the psychological community toward the problems of athletes and exercise participants. That a possible negative bias exists toward the serious study of sport in psychology is indicated by a comment made by the head of a clinical psychology program in response to a survey by LeUnes and Hayward: "The idea that one should devote one's life to 'bringing out the best' in sports performance is repulsive to me . . . it's a sign that we have a lot of misordered values in our society" (1990, p. 18). A personal anecdote also gives some measure of the extent of the problem. When I was in graduate school I chose a sport psychology topic for my dissertation research, only to have a senior faculty member take me aside and caution that I was "wasting my time" in sport psychology because "there are no careers" in this area.

The basic problem with the study of sport in psychology departments seems to be that because sport is a form of play, it is widely viewed as frivolous or trivial. Yet Freud himself said that life is made up of three essential elements, "love, work and play." Although courses on the study of love and relationships and on work and business can be found in all psychology departments, LeUnes and Hayward (1990) found that just 10 psychology programs of 102 respondents offered any type of graduate course work in the psychology of sport. Further, 92% of respondents indicated they had no plans to create such a course in the future. Although some of the paucity of courses on the psychology of sport might be explained by the existence of such courses in physical education departments, it is clear that there is little drive toward establishing the study of the athletic domain as a serious specialty for future psychologists.

The growth of sport as an area of serious study in psychology looks much less promising than it does in physical education. Without student interest, course offerings, and career possibilities, there is simply no impetus to establish applied sport psychology training in existing psychology programs. Instead, the study of the types of issues described in this book might become a postdoctoral specialization for psychologists who are interested in expanding their practice to include working with athletes. Evidence for such a trend is given by the popularity of continuing education courses in sport psychology that I have offered at the last several meetings of the APA. According to the APA continuing education staff, the sport psychology workshops are always among the first to be filled, and many more people apply than the 40 who are accepted each year. It is likely that the two major applied sport psychology organizations, AAASP and Division 47 of APA, will begin in the near future to offer more extensive and coordinated continuing education courses in sport psychology to conference attendees.

The future of psychologists in sport settings is uncertain. It remains to be seen whether enough psychologists will continue to practice in the sport world to warrant serious attention to issues concerning the profession and its practice. It is the hope of all the contributors to the present volume that our work is of enough concern to stimulate much more research.

Training Programs in Applied Sport Psychology

Some leaders in the sport psychology community have argued that to accommodate the interests of students in applied issues graduate programs should change to incorporate more applied training experiences. Silva, for example, recommends that "the training of future sport psychologists who wish to practice or apply their specialization should be differentiated from that of research specialists by the formal establishment of intervention observation, supervised experiences with interventions, and structured internships" (1989, p. 269). Likewise, Feltz argues that the future of graduate education in sport psychology will be tied to more integration with mainstream psychology departments, but she argues strongly that the courses and faculty in sport psychology should stay in human movement or sport science programs (1987).

The issue of what constitutes proper training for a consultant in sport psychology has been tackled head-on by the AAASP. In 1990 it finally published, after several years of deliberation, a set of certification criteria by which applicants would be judged qualified for the designation *Certified Consultant, AAASP*. In publishing these criteria, AAASP noted that several benefits are to be gained by establishing a certification program, including increased accountability, more recognition for individuals and the field, enhanced credibility, increased public awareness, and further definition of appropriate professional preparation. With respect to the last point, the AAASP certification materials note that the process ". . . will provide colleges and universities with guidelines for programs, courses, and practicum experiences in the field of sport psychology."

Because they represent the culmination of intense debate among many leaders in the field of sport psychology, the AAASP certified consultant criteria are important and are worth examining closely. The criteria follow:

1. A doctoral degree
2. Knowledge of scientific and professional ethics and standards
3. Three courses in sport psychology
4. Courses in biomechanics or exercise physiology
5. Courses in the historical, philosophical, social, or motor behavior bases of sport
6. Course work in psychopathology and its assessment
7. Training in counseling (e.g., course work, supervised practica)
8. Supervised experience with a qualified person in sport psychology
9. Knowledge of skills and techniques in sport or exercise
10. Courses in research design, statistics, and psychological assessment

(At least two of the following four criteria must be met through educational experiences that focus on general psychological experiences rather than sport-specific ones.)

11. Knowledge of the biological bases of behavior
12. Knowledge of the cognitive-affective bases of behavior
13. Knowledge of the social bases of behavior
14. Knowledge of individual behavior

Several points concerning these criteria should be noted. First, in order to meet all criteria, a graduate student currently in training would probably have to take courses in at least two, perhaps more, different departments in the university. Few graduate training programs could currently offer all the necessary courses and practica to a student to ensure certification. Second, the criteria heavily emphasize training in two areas: psychology and sport. Except for Criteria 3 and 4, the guidelines do not emphasize a sport science background. Third, there remains some ambiguity in the criteria. For example, exactly what constitutes a qualified person in sport psychology?

It remains to be seen whether the AAASP criteria will be widely accepted by the sport psychology community, by universities and colleges, and by the general public. If the existing criteria (or some modified version) can be agreed on by other groups, such as Division 47 of APA and NASPSPA, then the chances of long-term success for the endeavor to establish criteria are probably greater. The criteria have not existed long enough to accurately judge whether they will have the hoped-for impact on the types of curricula offered by sport psychology training programs.

Potential Opportunities in Applied Sport Psychology

Having been a full-time sport psychologist in the most applied sense of the word for the last 7 years, I would like to conclude this introductory chapter with my own thoughts on resolution of the issues I have raised in this chapter. I would like to thank the many colleagues whose discussions have stimulated the thoughts expressed here, but I take sole responsibility for the opinions expressed.

It might be possible to resolve an issue that is currently receiving a lot of attention, namely, whether those interested in the application of sport psychology principles should abandon the term *sport psychology* entirely and adopt a new title, for example, *performance enhancement consultant* or *life skills specialist*. I believe the opposite, however—that the term sport psychologist is more relevant today than ever. This is true because (a) the term accurately describes the nature of the profession and (b) it is recognized as meaningful by the public.

Some of those who recommend that the term *sport psychologist* be abandoned argue that those who intervene with athletes and performance issues draw from many disciplines: ". . . the consultant reaches into an ever-expanding tool kit. In this tool kit are ideas from the world of psychology, as well as many other tools, such as philosophy, coaching strategies, interpersonal skills" (Newburg, 1992, p. 23). The argument has also been put forward that sport psychology is fundamentally different from other areas of psychology. "In most cases psychologists are helping unhappy, dysfunctional people to be normal. That is not what we're trying to accomplish at all" (Rotella, cited in Newburg, 1992, p. 16). Yet when a separate field of *performance enhancement* is promoted, the descriptions of this field end up being descriptions of psychological interventions:

> "What I do is teach people to think good thoughts, to think effectively. We spend a great deal of time talking about having a free will." (Rotella, cited in Newburg, 1992, p. 16)

> "We usually are working on human potential in an athletic setting. This work includes dealing with the athlete's attitudes, thoughts, and beliefs. . . . We help them learn life skills that match their situation. Maybe the best way to say it is we teach self-management." (Halliwell, cited in Newburg, 1992, pp. 17-18)

> "When it comes to performance, they need a myriad of tools to succeed, to even take the first step. They need the right thoughts, mechanics, execution, attitude, commitment, intentions. And then throw in their feelings, affect. They need connection, immersion." (Ravizza, cited in Newburg, 1992, p. 17)

Psychologists and educators will recognize each of these approaches as variants of various psychological theories drawn from the work of such theorists as Ellis, Beck, Frankl, Perls, and Meichenbaum. It seems unwise to deny the historical and theoretical roots of such approaches. The danger of "reinventing the wheel" is apparent. As this book illustrates, there is much more to be gained from recognizing the intellectual roots of the field and drawing on them in fresh and creative ways. The variety of intervention models described in this book are a testament to the vibrancy of the field of psychology and to the opportunities for incorporating a variety of approaches into the applied practice of sport psychology.

As well, it is not necessary or advisable to change the meaning of sport psychology or to come up with a new descriptor of the field, because the present term already has a well-accepted meaning in the eyes of the public. This was brought home to me forcefully at a recent sport psychology conference when a young college athlete was asked to comment on whether his coach could also be his sport psychologist. The athlete pondered this question carefully and researched his answer. He concluded that it would be acceptable for his coach to teach him visualization techniques, to set goals with him, and to teach him how

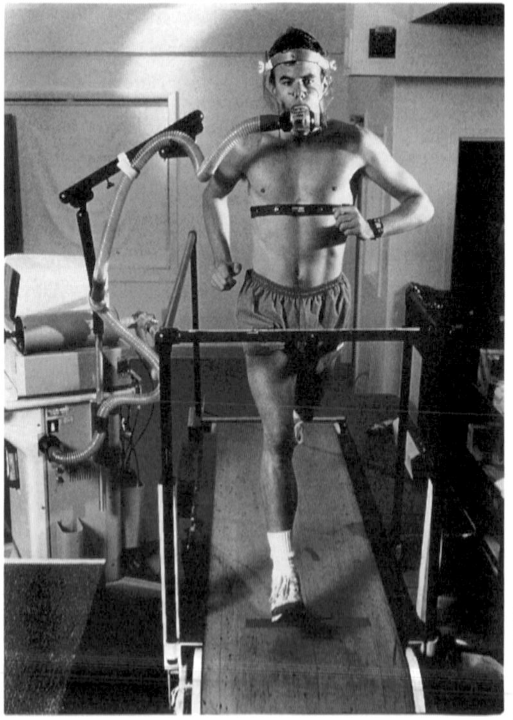

to relax under pressure. But in one area the athlete believed that the roles of coach and sport psychologist were incompatible: "If I had a problem in performance, I couldn't go to my coach to talk about it. I couldn't say 'I'm having a problem at the free throw line in the last five minutes of a game.' The coach would yank me from the game at the end. I would have to go to a sport psychologist to get help for a problem like that" (Walker & Griess, 1992). This athlete clearly delineated the important role that athletes expect a sport psychologist to play in the athletic setting.

So the term *sport psychologist* is an accurate descriptor for applied practitioners of sport psychology, and the term has a clear meaning to athletes, coaches, and the public. Yet the field itself is in a state of confusion, beset by questions of competency, identity, education, and practice. How can the field meet these challenges and continue to move forward as an applied profession? My own belief is that the education of future sport psychologists is the critical issue facing the field. The important issue is not where students receive their training, but the nature of the training they receive, the skills they develop, and the impact they can have on the fields of sport, exercise, and recreation. As the AAASP certification criteria suggest, current education programs in sport psychology are inadequate and do not properly prepare students to be practitioners in this field. Yet there is a tremendous interest on the part of students in applying the principles of sport psychology in the real world of sports.

A potential solution to this problem is to restructure graduate training programs in sport psychology, much along the lines suggested by the AAASP certification criteria. Such programs would give students a strong background in both sport and psychology. Such programs should continue to be housed in academic departments of sport science, physical education, and human movement. The reason is simple. As explained previously, it is only in these departments that sport is taken seriously as an area of study. Psychology departments are unlikely to ever devote the resources necessary to investigate the myriad of psychological dimensions of sport. However, sport science programs will have to develop strong relationships with companion departments of counseling or clinical psychology. Training in counseling, psychotherapy, and abnormal psychology together with supervised training in practicum settings will require a far larger psychological component to graduate education programs in sport psychology than has ever existed. The rewards should be great, producing well-trained people who are adept at applying psychological interventions in a variety of sports and athletic settings.

Should these sport psychologists of the future be licensable as psychologists? A strong case could be made for arguing the affirmative. As licensed psychologists, these people would have a greater variety of career paths open to them, a bonus in the present workplace environment. Additionally, they could legally use the term *sport psychologist* in offering their skills on a fee-for-service basis. To gain the types of experience that would prepare them to use most of the intervention models described in this book, students would meet most training criteria required of licensed psychologists. It would not, therefore, be an onerous extra requirement to meet the criteria for licensing. Such an attitude on the part of programs of sport psychology would require some psychology departments to relinquish some control and cooperate with programs preparing psychologists outside psychology departments. This battle has been won before, for example, by school psychology and educational psychology programs. This attitude also would require some sport psychology programs to adopt a new role, that of preparing professional practitioners rather than academic educators and researchers. Such changes will probably require enormous effort on the part of individual leaders in the field of sport psychology.

CONCLUSION

The field of sport psychology is in a controversial period in its history. Yet it is also an enormously exciting period. New areas of investigation are constantly being explored and new knowledge in the applied area is constantly being acquired. Many of the chapters in this book break new ground in the areas they tackle and the intervention models they present. We hope that the research and ideas presented in this book help many professionals assist athletes in enjoying and benefiting from their sports experience. Sports involvement can be a positive experience for all participants, but only if the experience is properly structured with the physical and psychological needs of the participants in mind.

REFERENCES

Beisser, A. (1977). *The madness in sport*. Bowie, MD: Charles Press.

Brown, J.M. (1982). Are sport psychologists really psychologists? *Journal of Sport Psychology*, **4**, 13-18.

Bunker, L.K., & McQuire, R.T. (1985). Give sport psychology to sport. In L.K. Bunker, R. Rotella, & A. Reilly (Eds.), *Sport psychology: Psychological considerations in maximizing sport performance* (pp. 3-15). Ann Arbor, MI: McNaughton & Gunn.

Butt, D.S. (1979). the psychologist's contribution to sport organizations and the athlete: An example. In P. Klavora & J.V. Daniel (Eds.), *Coach, athlete, and sport psychologist* (pp. 74-81). Champaign, IL: Human Kinetics.

Clarke, K. (1983). US Olympic Committee establishes guidelines for sport psychology services. *Journal of Sport Psychology*, **5**, 4-7.

Danish, S.J., & Hale, B.J. (1981). Toward an understanding of the practice of sport psychology. *Journal of Sport and Exercise Psychology*, **3**, 90-99.

Danish, S.J., & Hale, B.J. (1982). Let the discussions continue: Further considerations on the practice of sport psychology. *Journal of Sport Psychology*, **4**, 10-12.

Dishman, R.K. (1983). Identity crises in North American sport psychology: Academics in professional issues. *Journal of Sport and Exercise Psychology*, **5**, 123-134.

Feltz, D.L. (1987). The future of graduate education in sport and exercise science: A sport psychology perspective. *Quest*, **39**, 217-223.

Gardner, F.L. (1991). Professionalization of sport psychology: A reply to Silva. *Sport Psychologist*, **5**, 55-60.

Griffith, C.R. (1926). *The psychology of coaching*. New York: Scribner's.

Griffith, C.R. (1928). *The psychology of athletics*. New York: Scribner's.

Harrison, R.P., & Feltz, D.L. (1979). The professionalization of sport psychology: Legal considerations. *Journal of Sport and Exercise Psychology*, **1**, 182-190.

Heyman, S.R. (1982). A reaction to Danish and Hale: A minority report. *Journal of Sport Psychology*, **4**, 7-9.

LaRose, B. (1988). What can the sport psychology consultant learn from the educational consultant? *Sport Psychologist*, **2**, 141-153.

Lawther, J.D. (1951). *Psychology of coaching*. Englewood Cliffs, NJ: Prentice Hall.

LeUnes, A., & Hayward, S.A. (1990). Sport psychology as viewed by chairpersons of APA-approved clinical psychology programs. *Sport Psychologist*, **4**, 18-24.

Martens, R. (1979). About smocks and jocks. *Journal of Sport Psychology*, **1**, 94-99.

McAuley, E. (1987). Sport psychology in the eighties: Some current developments. *Medicine and Science in Sports and Exercise*, **19**, 95-97.

Monahan, T. (1987). Sport psychology: A crisis of identity? *Physician and Sportsmedicine*, **15**, 203-212.

Napali, D.S. (1981). *Architects of adjustment: The history of the psychological profession in the United States*. Port Washington, NY: Kennikat Press.

Newburg, D. (1992). Performance enhancement: Toward a working definition. *Contemporary Thought on Performance Enhancement*, **1**, 10-25.

Nideffer, R.M. (1987). Applied sport psychology. In J.R. May & M.J. Asken (Eds.), *Sport psychology: The psychological health of the athlete* (pp. 1-18). New York: PMA.

Nideffer, R.M., DuFresne, P., Nesvig, D., & Selder, D. (1980). The future of applied sport psychology. *Journal of Sport Psychology*, **2**, 170-174.

Nideffer, R., Feltz, D., & Salmela, J. (1982). A rebuttal to Danish and Hale: A committee report. *Journal of Sport Psychology*, **4**, 3-6.

Ogilvie, B., & Tutko, T.A. (1966). *Problem athletes and how to handle them*. London: Pelham Books.

Orlick, T. (1986). *Psyching for sport: Mental training for athletes*. Champaign, IL: Human Kinetics.

Pryzwansky, W.B., & Wendt, R.N. (1987). *Psychology as a profession: Foundations of practice*. Elmsford, NY: Pergamon Press.

Rejeski, W.J., & Brawley, L.R. (1988). Defining the boundaries of sport psychology. *Sport Psychologist*, **2**, 231-242.

Sachs, M. (1992, October). *AAASP Presidential Address*. Paper presented at the annual meeting of the Association for the Advancement of Applied Sport Psychology, Colorado Springs, CO.

Silva, J.M. III. (1989). Toward the professionalization of sport psychology. *Sport Psychologist*, **3**, 265-273.

Simson, V., & Jennings, A. (1992). *The lords of the rings: Power, money and drugs in the modern Olympics*. London: Simon & Schuster.

Walker, A., & Griess, A. (1992, October). Dual roles: The coach/sport psychologist—conflict or compatibility? Symposium conducted at the annual meeting of the Association for the Advancement of Applied Sport Psychology, J.M. Silva, Chair, Colorado Springs, CO.

Wiggins, D.K. (1984). The history of sport psychology in North America. In J. Silva & R. Weinberg (Eds.), *Psychological foundations of sport* (pp. 9-22). Champaign, IL: Human Kinetics.

Williams, J. (Ed.) (1986). *Applied sport psychology*. Palo Alto, CA: Mayfield.

Williams, J.M., & Straub, W.F. (1986). Sport psychology: Past, present, future. In J. Williams (Ed.), *Applied sport psychology* (pp. 1-13). Palo Alto, CA: Mayfield.

PART I

MODELS OF INTERVENTION

CHAPTER 2

PSYCHOLOGICAL INTERVENTIONS: A LIFE DEVELOPMENT MODEL

Steven J. Danish, PhD
Virginia Commonwealth University
Al Petitpas, EdD
Springfield College
Bruce D. Hale, PhD
Staffordshire University, United Kingdom

This chapter describes Life Development Intervention (LDI), a framework for the practice of sport psychology based on a psychoeducational-developmental perspective. Following an explanation of the concept of critical life events (the concept that serves as a structure for understanding the life course of an athlete), we will present a number of LDI strategies and techniques. We define a *technique* as a specific procedure or method and a *strategy* as a detailed plan to reach a goal. Within a strategy several techniques might be used (Danish & D'Augelli, 1983). A number of techniques will be mentioned but will not be described in detail, due to space constraints. Throughout the chapter we use a specific case study to provide examples of how the life-event perspective applies to sport psychology and how LDI is used.

We will also delineate the training and roles necessary for an LDI specialist to practice sport psychology. At the outset it is important to clarify that the LDI framework, although multidisciplinary, borrows heavily from psychology. Whereas most sport psychologists seem to equate the term *psychologically trained* with clinical psychology (LeUnes & Haywood, 1990), a number of "psychologically trained" sport psychologists are actually trained in counseling psychology. The differences between clinical and counseling psychology can be considerable, depending on an individual's training. Perhaps Super (1977) delineated the differences most succinctly:

> It is the difference between developmental and remedial help, between education and medicine, between pathology and hygieology. Clinical psychologists tend to look for what is wrong and how to treat it, while counseling psychologists tend to look for what is right and how to help use it.

Though the distinctions between counseling and clinical psychologists might not be as great as they once were, the contrast between a focus on proactive versus remedial interventions still exists. Proponents of LDI design and implement both proactive and remedial interventions, although the proactive predominates.

■ *THE CASE OF CHUCK* ■

Chuck was a highly recruited middleweight wrestler in high school. He earned all-state honors his last 3 years and was state champion twice. Chuck's father, a national-caliber coach, pushed him to excel, and his younger brother, just 2 years his junior, also was an excellent wrestler who had won all-state honors. Chuck accepted a scholarship to a top-ranked collegiate wrestling program with a goal of becoming an NCAA champion.

Even though Chuck had been a *B*-student in high school, school was not particularly important to him. His dreams and goals revolved around wrestling. He knew he would have to work harder in college to succeed academically, but his energy and concerns had little to do with school. He would do what he had to in the classroom to please his mother and his counselor. However, his main focus was on what happened in the wrestling room, not the classroom.

Early in his first year Chuck began to experience disappointments. It became evident almost immediately that he was not the best wrestler on the squad; he was uncertain whether he was even the best freshman. He was continually being decked by upper-class middleweights. No one had ever taken him down so easily. He began to lose confidence and doubt his abilities. His schoolwork suffered, and his girlfriend from home broke off their 2-year relationship. He competed intercollegiately just twice his first year, winning once.

During his second year Chuck had to deal with the first of two potentially debilitating injuries that were turning points in his development. A chronic shoulder weakness would not allow him to wrestle, and surgery was required. He spent a "redshirt" year rehabilitating his shoulder and trying to redevelop his psychological strengths. As it turned out, this injury was a catalyst for his future development as a wrestler and student. During his rehabilitation Chuck enrolled in a sport psychology class, where he learned many mental skills that improve sport performance, including goal setting, stress reduction, imagery, and positive self-talk. He also learned how to apply these same skills in non-sport-related areas, such as school, work, home, interpersonal relationships, and even coping with injuries.

As a result of his sport psychology class Chuck came to realize how important his early training with his father and brother had been and how what he had learned during these formative years had contributed to his success as a wrestler. Chuck also recognized how he had failed to understand the role some of these mental skills played in his success. It seemed as if he thought he could win in college by strength and quickness, yet in his previous successes his ability to concentrate, plan, and be positive had been critical to his success. He began to refocus on using and strengthening these and other mental skills he learned, and he began to apply these skills in school. The psychological skills Chuck learned during this period helped him to earn a starting position, and during his third and fourth years he earned All-America honors.

In Chuck's fifth year, when he was a senior, an acute bout of mononucleosis a month before the NCAA championships seriously jeopardized his final attempt to attain his goal of being a national champion. Chuck began to panic. He temporarily forgot how to apply some of the psychological coping skills he had learned in the sport psychology class and in subsequent consultations with the LDI specialist. Chuck felt weak and quickly became fatigued when he tried to maintain his fitness level for the championships. He was frustrated, angry, and on the verge of quitting on his goal of becoming national champion. The LDI specialist reminded him to apply the goal-setting model to his short but critical daily workouts. It was important to view an increase of a minute longer on the stationary bicycle as improvement and a successful step toward his ultimate training goal. Focusing on his end result and his inability to train at the desired level would have been counterproductive. But with small, progressive training steps Chuck was able to regain his fitness level by the tournament date. His confidence level was revived, because he could focus on his successes no matter how small they were. As a result of his refocused efforts, he won his weight class in the regional tournament and attained All-America status for the third time.

Another critical life event occurred when Chuck was about to graduate. While on work-site practicum, he realized that he had probably made the wrong career choice and did not want to become an investment counselor. First, he wanted to try out for the Pan-American Games team (he ended up not qualifying for the team, as he had a reoccurrence of mononucleosis). Chuck also needed to choose an alternative career. Initially he was somewhat confused and unsure about the next step, but by applying the life skills he had learned, he used the decision-making process and decided to pursue his interest in sport and communication. Chuck obtained an interview and ultimately a job in the advertising office at a major television network (where he recently received a promotion).

LIFE-SPAN DEVELOPMENT: A FRAMEWORK FOR INTERVENTION

The LDI model described in this chapter is based on the perspective of human development. The major assumption of this framework is its emphasis on continuous growth and change. To understand both we must examine several disciplines, namely, the biological, social, and psychological. Thus the study of behavior, development, and change is multidisciplinary and should be considered against the backdrop of prevailing norms and present environment. Furthermore, because change is sequential it is necessary to consider any stage of life in the context of both past and future events. Finally, although changes in one's life might result in problems or crises, these are to be viewed not as pathological but rather as critical life events (Baltes, Reese, & Lipsett, 1980).

In the case study of Chuck we can see the changes he encounters and the effects they have on many of his life domains. The problems he faced when he first entered college were difficult for him, and it could be said that he was "in crisis." Despite how we commonly interpret the word *crisis*, it is not synonymous with being mentally ill and in need of psychotherapy. The word is derived from the Greek word meaning *decision*. The Random House *Dictionary of the English Language* defines crisis as "a stage in a sequence of events at which the trend of all future events, especially for better or for worse, is determined; turning point."

Most of us do not like change in our lives, because change disrupts our routines and relationships with others and can result in stress. We like continuity without having to confront life decisions and change. Systems, like families, teams, and work units, resist change for the same reasons (Watzlawick, Weakland, & Fisch, 1974). For this reason a change resulting from life situations has been called a critical life event. We experience many such events throughout life. In the year he applied to colleges, Chuck had to decide to attend a certain college, to leave the security of his home to go away to school, to change the nature of his relationship with his girlfriend (who still had a year of high school left), and to commit himself to work harder in school. Yet despite his willingness to make these decisions, several other decisions (crises) were thrust upon him. Perhaps the most important was the result of his failure to immediately live up to his own expectations as a wrestler. This sense of personal failure was the event that gave Chuck the most difficulty during his transition and first year in college.

Sometimes an individual anticipates a change but it does not take place. These nonevents can also result in considerable stress (Schlossberg, 1984). An example of a nonevent for Chuck in the sport domain was his realization that he would not make the starting team during his first season.

Although we often regard *events* as occurring in a discrete moment of time, critical life events are really processes that begin before and continue well after "events." Critical life events, then, have histories—from the time we anticipate them, through their occurrence, and until their aftermath has been determined and assessed.

Coping With Critical Life Events

As noted earlier and as discussed in detail by Danish and D'Augelli (1983), Falek and Britton (1974), Haerle (1975), and Mayer and Andrews (1981), among others, critical life events are not the same as crises. As depicted in Figure 2.1, critical life events can result in debilitation or decreased functioning; they might result in little change in one's life; or they might result in increased opportunities for growth.

Which result occurs is dependent on a person's resources before the event, level of preparation for the event (preoccurrence priming), and past history in dealing with similar events. For example, Chuck was able to overcome his mononucleosis, despite some difficult times, because he had experienced similar events (his shoulder injury) and had developed resources through the mental skills learned in the sport psychology course he took and because he worked individually with the LDI specialist to cope with the difficult situation.

All critical life events are similar to each other. If an athlete has handled past critical life events successfully and knows how it was done, being able to cope with a present event will be easier due to feelings of confidence and anticipation of success. In Chuck's case, because he had not been pampered in high school and college by his teachers, coaches, and parents and because he had been expected to make his own decisions, he was better able to cope with new events as they arose and to benefit from his ability to have successfully encountered past events.

THE STRATEGIES AND TECHNIQUES OF LDI

The central strategy of the LDI approach is the teaching of goal setting as a means of

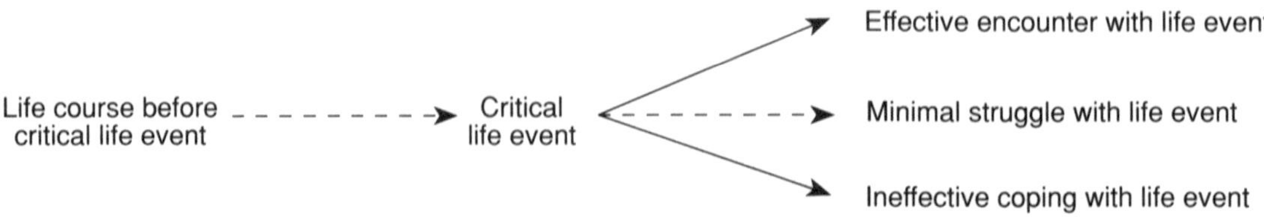

Figure 2.1 People have three basic ways to cope with critical life events.
Note. From *Life Development Skills* (p. 3) by S.J. Danish and A.R. D'Augelli, 1983, New York: Human Sciences Press. Copyright 1983 by Human Sciences Press, Inc. Adapted by permission.

empowerment. In this section we will begin with a discussion of goal setting. Other strategies and techniques that enable a person to learn skills to successfully encounter critical life events will be considered as well.

Setting Goals

Proponents of a life-span development framework assume that individual behavior is intentional. Thus people shape rather than respond to their environments. Goals are the source of energy that motivates people to action. A person without goals is like a computer without a program. The key to developing *personal competence*—defined as the ability to do life planning, be self reliant, and seek the resources of others (Danish, D'Augelli, & Ginsberg, 1984)—is to be able to identify, set, and attain goals. When people can set and attain goals they are able to gain control over their lives, because they feel able to direct their future. As a result, they feel empowered (Rappaport, 1981) and have a greater sense of self-efficacy (Bandura, 1977). Once people are able to accomplish this step they can then acquire the necessary interpersonal and intrapersonal skills. *Interpersonal* skills are those used to communicate with others in a variety of situations. *Intrapersonal* skills include both physical and mental skills; however, in LDI this term usually refers to what Vealey (1988) has called psychological skills. Interpersonal and intrapersonal skills are useful in the athletic domain but are not strictly athletic related. They are life skills.

By *goals* we mean actions undertaken to reach some desired end, not the end itself. Goals are different from results: Goals are actions over which the participant has control. For example, when Chuck chose to reconsider his career objective and focus on identifying the skills he had learned in sport that are transferable to the workplace, he was working on attaining a goal. If Chuck had chosen as a "goal" to secure a non-athletic-related job, he would actually have chosen a result. Similarly, when Chuck was in rehabilitation following his shoulder injury or mononucleosis, developing a rehabilitation plan was a goal; wanting full recovery and the ability to wrestle was a result. People have control over their goals and only partial control over the results they want.

Three other elements are crucial for effective goal setting:

- Setting goals that the goal setter is motivated to attain
- Making sure the goal is stated in positive terms
- Having a specifically defined goal

Having people set goals for themselves is critical. If a goal is more important to others it is unlikely to be achieved. Unimportant goals rarely are. Goal statements that include words like *should* or *ought to* inspire lower levels of commitment than goal statements including words like *want*. Therefore, to increase the energy level invested in attaining a goal it is important to help a person ascertain whether goals are *should* or *want*, to change *should* goals to *want* goals, or to identify *want* goals.

When goals are not positively stated, the focus is on the negative and considerable energy is wasted trying not to do something. Setting a negative goal almost always produces a negative result. Goal statements that include words like *not, avoid, less than*, and *limit* should be changed to positive statements so the image of the goal is something to be achieved and worked toward. Having a positive goal means being able to identify the actions that must be done to reach the goal.

The goal should also be behaviorally stated and defined clearly. Goals that include vague terms such as *do better* or *improve* do not allow the goal setter the satisfaction of truly knowing whether or not the goal has been attained.

When the lack of clear feedback about goal attainment occurs, frustration and loss of motivation usually result and often lead to quitting. A rule of thumb when developing behaviorally stated goals is to answer this question: How many times, when, and under what conditions will the action occur?

Being willing to take an active role in setting a goal is one thing; being able to reach or attain the goal is another. There are roadblocks to reaching goals, whether athletic goals (improving concentration when attempting takedowns), career goals (making a decision about what to do following graduation), or personal goals (learning to be a better public speaker). The four major roadblocks are a lack of skill, a lack of knowledge, the lack of ability or courage to take appropriate risks, and the lack of adequate social support. In the case study, Chuck had many roadblocks throughout his career. He lacked knowledge of the therapy regimen he could undergo to strengthen his shoulder; he lacked the skill of talking positively to himself when he first came to college and experienced some setbacks; and when he became disaffected with his major he had to risk failure to find an alternative career.

Intervention requires that roadblocks be removed to enable people to work toward their goals. Removing roadblocks can become a goal in itself. Much of what the LDI specialist does is to teach or coach others, individually or in groups, to set goals, identify and overcome roadblocks, and reach their goals—by developing new skills, acquiring new knowledge, learning to take risks, and developing effective social support systems.

Attaining the goal involves developing a specific plan, a *goal ladder*, to reach the goal. Developing a goal ladder involves breaking the goal down into achievable, small steps. Too often people try to reach the goal all at once. If the goal can be broken down into 8 to 10 steps, the likelihood of achieving it increases tremendously. For example, Chuck's goal ladder for reaching his goal of rehabilitating his shoulder is depicted in Table 2.1.

Goals are identified and plans developed to help people encounter critical life events successfully. The fact that athletes are accustomed to goal setting is both a help and a hindrance. The familiarity with goals allows athletes to feel comfortable during the intervention process. However, because athletes are often taught or encouraged to set outcomes (results) as opposed to goals, some relearning might be necessary.

Developing LDI Strategies

As noted in our discussion of the life-span development framework, development is continuous. Critical life events produce a state of imbalance that precedes change and growth and might actually make growth possible. Consequently, the major focus of LDI becomes optimizing rather than remediating performance so that change is viewed as a challenge rather than a threat. Critical life events, whether sport- or non-sport-related, will occur; helping enhance or enrich a person's ability to encounter the event constructively through goal setting and other strategies is an empowering act (Danish & Hale, 1981; Danish, Petitpas, & Hale, 1990). In other words, the LDI specialist must help the person prepare to encounter the event, contend with the event during its occurrence, and cope with it following its occurrence (Danish, Smyer, & Nowak, 1980). Thus it is essential to consider the timing of the intervention in determining what strategies are to be used.

For the LDI specialist, the emphasis is on growth. Life events are considered processes that include anticipation, actual occurrence, and aftermath. Interventions occurring before an event are considered *enhancement* strategies; those occurring during an event are *supportive* strategies; once an event has

Table 2.1 Goal Ladder

End result

To rehabilitate my shoulder by the end of spring semester so that strength and flexibility measures equal or surpass what they were last fall before my injury

Goal

(Performance goals): Be able to military-press 175 lb; be able to clench my hand behind my back by reaching over my shoulder

Process-oriented

Physical skills: New exercises for strength and flexibility

Mental skills: Goal-setting plan for rehabilitation, exercises, and kinesthetic imagery for shoulder moves on takedown

Knowledge: Ask the trainer about progressive resistance exercises and flexibility program

Risk taking: None

Social support: Talk with trainer and coach about feedback

Steps	Progress	Problems or roadblocks
Ask trainer for information about rehabilitation exercises for my shoulder	January 15	
Develop daily rehabilitation training program with trainer for the semester and begin a journal	January 20	
Record training sessions and have trainer evaluate once a week	January 21-April 21	Spring break means I will be at home for 1 week
Attend practice at least 3 times a week to watch demonstrations and coach freshmen	January 15-March 15	
Spend 15 min 5 times a week imagining takedowns, escapes, defenses	January 15-April 15	Will I get frustrated and lose my motivation?
Learn new mental images for coping with injury, work with trainer and LDI specialist to become confident that my shoulder can handle the stress	April 1	
Begin regular strength training with Nautilus and free weights 5 days a week	April 1	Might be too sore
Be able to military-press 160 lb	April 30	
Meet with coach to assess strengths and weaknesses and plan summer workouts	May 1	
Test my performance goals with trainer	May 15	

occurred, interventions are considered *counseling* strategies (see Figure 2.2).

Enhancement Strategies

Enhancement interventions are designed to prepare people for future events by

- helping them anticipate normative events,
- assisting them in recognizing how skills they have acquired in one domain apply to other life areas, and
- teaching skills that enhance their abilities to cope with future events.

Helping Anticipate Life Events. Understanding the nature of the future events that are likely to occur and having confidence in these strategies to cope with the future event increases self-efficacy. With this increased self-efficacy comes a sense of predictability and control that translates into lower levels of stress (Meichenbaum, 1985).

When life events are examined to determine their effect on a person, three characteristics are usually considered: the timing of the event, the duration of the event, and the contextual purity of the event. The *timing* of the event refers to the congruence of the event with either the personal or societal expectations of when the event should occur (Neugarten, 1968). For example, Chuck's failure to make the Pan-American Games team following graduation and his subsequent retirement from competitive wrestling is an instance of an off-time event.

When we experience events that are on time we usually have the support of informal and formal networks to help us through the transition. When the event is one that is experienced by most or all people there also exists an opportunity for *preoccurrence priming* (Schlossberg, 1984). This form of anticipation

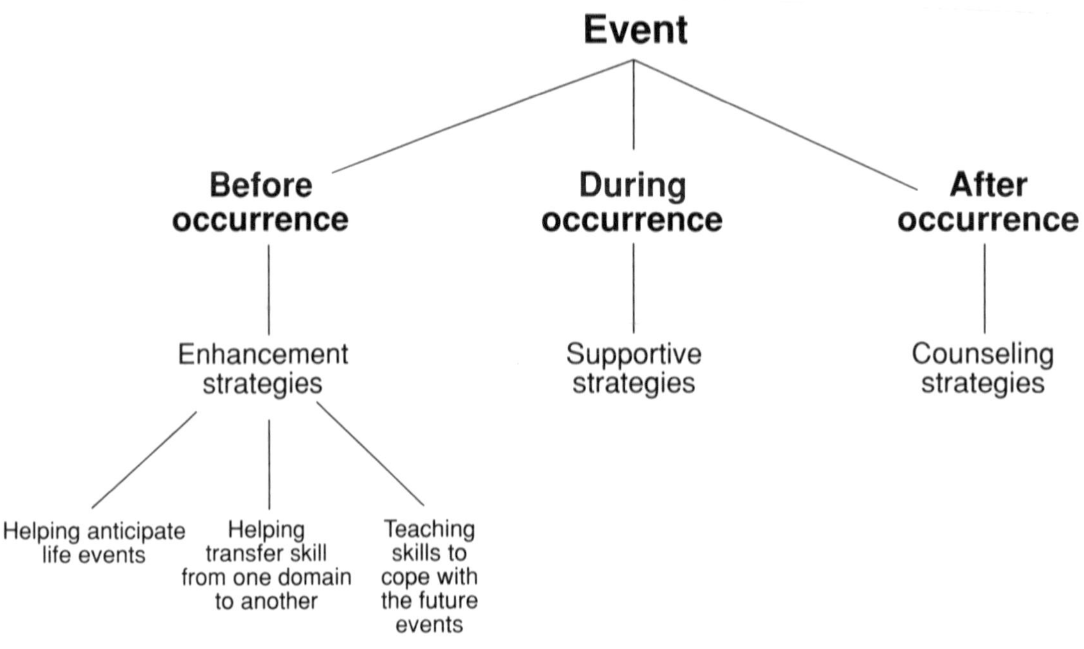

Figure 2.2 The type of intervention used must be related to the timing of the intervention.

Courtesy University of Illinois Sports Information

provides a rehearsal period (an opportunity to try out different responses to the event). However, when the event is off time, such as athletic retirement in one's 20s (Baillie & Danish, 1992), coping becomes more difficult. A greatly off-time event, such as a sport injury that forces retirement before most athletes are ready, does not allow any preparation time for adaptation and teammates and coaches tend not to offer the social support that is essential in coping (Pearson & Petitpas, 1990). Moreover, when athletes retire as a result of injury they tend to feel unfulfilled, making the retirement process more problematic (Kleiber, Greendorfer, Blinde, & Samdahl, 1987).

Retirement from sport is not the only event athletes experience that can involve timing problems. The adulation, the time demands of practice, the loss of a normal childhood, and the expectations of success thrust upon young national-level elite athletes are all off-time events for adolescent athletes.

The *duration* of an event relates to its perceived length. Life events can be perceived as temporary, permanent, or uncertain and evaluated as positive, negative, or mixed (Schlossberg, 1984). A person's interpretation of a life event affects the type and severity of emotional and behavioral responses. For example, during Chuck's rehabilitation from injury and recuperation from illness he was often confused and anxious. However, as with other athletes in similar situations (McDonald & Hardy, 1990), once he believed that his condition was temporary and that he was making progress toward recovery, he became more goal directed and his emotions returned to normal. Had his injury been permanent, he probably would have experienced a more severe and protracted grief reaction (Rotella & Heyman, 1986). There is evidence that managing life events with uncertain durations produces the most stress (Chodoff, 1976). It should also be noted that perception of duration is often colored by the value one places on an event. As a sophomore Chuck knew he was redshirting, and he was able to design a more long-term recovery plan for his shoulder; his reaction to mononucleosis was panic, and his recuperation was probably slowed by his failure to manage the anxiety and to adhere to a carefully designed recovery program.

Contextual purity refers to the number of events being experienced simultaneously. Events usually don't occur in isolation. The more events being experienced simultaneously, the more difficult the adjustment. Events can be divided into a number of domains, such as familial, occupational, biological, or psychosocial. For example, as Chuck was learning that other middlewight, higher-class wrestlers were stronger and more experienced (biological domain), he experienced a loss of confidence and self-esteem (psychosocial domain), his grades suffered (career domain), and he and his girlfriend broke up (family and interpersonal domain). Although the latter event might not have been related to the others, it occurred at the same time and made coping more difficult. Thus even with a single event other issues intercede. Therefore, successful coping involves dealing with the perceived primary event as well as other events.

Athletes face many critical events in their careers. Injury, the annual team selection process, and forced retirement are but three of the events that can rob athletes of their prime sources of identity. These events typically occur much earlier in life for an athlete than they would in the career of a businessperson or medical professional. Assisting athletes in anticipating these events is but one of the goals of intervention programs like the United States Olympic Committee's (USOC) Career Assistance Program for Athletes (CAPA) (Petitpas, Danish, McKelvain, & Murphy, 1992) or the Ladies Professional Golf Associations' (LPGA) Preparing for Future Careers Program (Petitpas & Elliott, 1987).

The LPGA program was designed to assist members of the tour to prepare for their transition off the tour. The main goals of the program were to (a) provide athletes with a supportive environment where they could share their concerns; (b) help identify their values, needs, interests, and skills; (c) assist them in understanding and implementing a life-work plan; (d) enhance their self-confidence to assure successful career transition; and (e) establish peer and tour-alumni support groups.

Helping Transfer Skill From One Domain to Another. A second enhancement strategy is helping athletes recognize and use skills in other life areas that they have acquired through sport. The NCAA and other sport governing bodies have widely promoted the belief that sport is good preparation for life. This notion is true only if skills acquired through sport generalize to other life domains. Research on generalizability of skills indicates that skills acquired in one domain do not automatically transfer to other domains (Auerbach, 1986; Meichenbaum & Turk, 1987). For skills to generalize, many factors must be present:

- A belief that the acquired skills and qualities are valued in other settings.
- Awareness of current skills, both physical and psychological.
- Knowledge of how and in what context skills were learned.
- Confidence in the ability to apply skills in different settings.
- A willingness to explore nonsport roles.
- The desire and ability to seek out sources of social support.
- The ability to adjust to initial failures or setbacks. (Danish, Petitpas, & Hale, 1992)

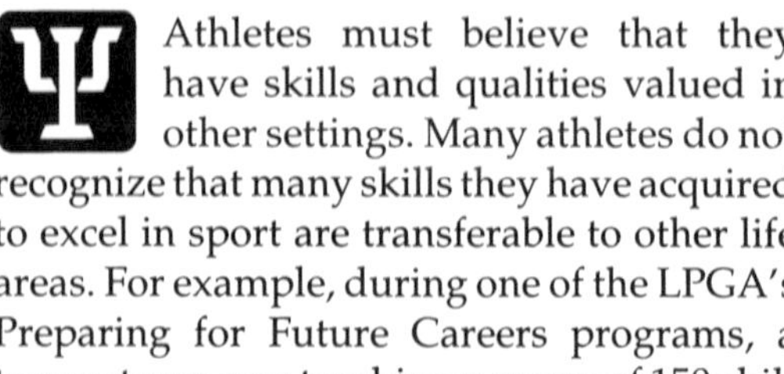

Athletes must believe that they have skills and qualities valued in other settings. Many athletes do not recognize that many skills they have acquired to excel in sport are transferable to other life areas. For example, during one of the LPGA's Preparing for Future Careers programs, a tour veteran was teaching a group of 150 children and adults the basics of the golf swing using towels to demonstrate the proper mechanics and tempo. Her audience consisted of a large number of English-, French-, and Spanish-speaking people. She instructed and told stories in all three languages. The group was alive with laughter and enthusiasm. After this 90-min lesson, this same golfer was asked about her career plans. She immediately responded by stating, "I have no skills, the only thing I know how to do is hit a golf ball." Yet it seemed that the athlete had a number of skills and qualities that have considerable value in nonsport environments. Unfortunately, because she did not recognize that these qualities have value they will not transfer.

Athletes must learn that they possess both physical and psychological skills. There is a lot more to sport than just throwing a ball or running fast. Athletes plan, set goals, make decisions, seek out instruction, and manage arousal levels as a routine part of their athletic participation. Without mental skills it is unlikely that a person can qualify for elite levels of participation. When Chuck recognized that the mental skills he possessed had been a key to his success as a high-school wrestler and then committed himself to applying these skills in college, he became a much-improved wrestler. However, if athletes do not recognize that they possess mental skills it is unlikely that they will be able to use these skills in other nonsport domains.

For athletes, it is not enough to know that they possess physical and mental skills. They must also know how and in what context these skills were learned. Both types of skills are learned in the same fashion. For example, skills can be acquired through formal instruction. A skill is named and described and a rationale for its use is given. Then, the skill is demonstrated so the athlete can observe correct and incorrect use. Lastly, the athlete is given numerous opportunities to practice the skill under supervision to insure continuous feedback.

Skills can also be learned by trial and error. People practice skills they observe in the playground or on television. They attempt to imitate these skills on their own, and with continual trial and error they acquire their own version.

It is helpful for athletes to understand why they wanted to learn the skill and whether they have tried to use the skill in different contexts or settings. If they have tried to use the skill in other settings, it is helpful to explore levels of success. In Chuck's case, he had learned how to set goals in his sport psychology class. When he later needed to apply this skill for his injury rehabilitation he was confident he knew how. If athletes have not attempted to use the skill in other settings, it might be helpful to explore what has held them back.

Athletes can lack confidence in their abilities to apply skills in different settings. They might fear failure or "looking bad." For example, when Chuck came to college his father chose Chuck's initial major. His father chose a "safe" major because Chuck was unwilling to examine his career interests and skills at the time. If athletes lack understanding of a new setting, this fear of the unknown can add to their hesitancy in attempting a skill. The LDI specialist can help by providing information about the new domain and coach the athlete through the process of preparing for and implementing the skill. By providing domain-specific information the LDI specialist can help to reduce the unknown and lessen the anxiety that can block an athlete from using a skill.

Some athletes have so much of their personal identity tied up in sport that they have little motivation to explore nonsport roles. They view themselves as successful athletes, not successful people. This mind-set can rob them of their confidence and prevent them from exploring nonsport roles. If they do not think they can be successful in other settings they might choose not to explore other options.

In addition, many athletes have internalized the belief that to succeed they must "give 110%" to their sport. This view can block athletes from investing time and energy in nonsport pursuits. It can also promote a narrowness of self-esteem and a lack of confidence in the ability to function effectively in other domains.

An LDI specialist can assist athletes by helping them understand that they possess valuable, transferable skills. The specialist can also promote the notion that having alternative activities can help generate a freshness and enthusiasm for sport that can protect against staleness and burnout and improve quality and concentration.

If a fear of failure blocks an athlete from trying the skill in another setting, the athlete and the LDI specialist should examine the perceived costs and benefits of the action. If the perceived benefits of the action outweigh potential costs, it is likely the athlete will risk the new behavior. If the perceived costs outweigh the benefits, the costs must be minimized and the benefits raised for the athlete to feel safe enough to take the risk. LDI specialists can teach risk-taking behavior using the process outlined by Danish and D'Augelli (1983).

Athletes might have difficulty seeking out sources of social support necessary to help them transfer their skills. Some athletes view seeking assistance as a sign of weakness. They might avoid opportunities to test out their skills in new settings, preferring to concentrate on their sport. Other athletes might not know the types of support they need or the best resource to supply the support. For example, Chuck did not realize that the LDI specialist could help him deal with the psychological reactions he experienced as a result of his mononucleosis and help him develop a rehabilitation goal. Too often coaches are viewed as the primary source of many types of support for athletes. Unfortunately, coaches are not always good sources of emotional support, and many coaches are not supportive of activities that, in their opinion, might detract emphasis from sport.

LDI specialists can assist athletes by teaching them how to identify types and sources of support. They can also help athletes understand the importance of support in the overall framework of personal competence so that they view seeking support as a sign of strength, not weakness. Two models of teaching how to identify the types and sources of support and how to seek out such support are outlined by Danish and D'Augelli (1983) and Pearson (1990).

Athletes can have difficulty adjusting to initial failures or setbacks in attempts to transfer skills to different settings, even though these skills are valuable in many nonsport settings. Such initial failures might be due to the lack of information and experience necessary to quickly adapt these skills into larger strategies required in new settings. This domain-specific knowledge might take some time to acquire and athletes who are used to elite levels of performance might become frustrated with their progress in new settings. In addition, plateaus and setbacks in skill attainment are common, and athletes might view these events as failures and begin to doubt their abilities. The slow pace of Chuck's recovery from mononucleosis was difficult for him, as he was used to more rapid success in other endeavors.

LDI specialists can assist athletes by preparing them for the pace of skill transfer by initiating a goal-setting procedure that may insure some initial success experiences. Using the goal-ladder process described earlier, the LDI specialist can help athletes plan out realistic time tables for skill transfer and plan strategies for overcoming any roadblocks to skill attainment that emerge. In addition, LDI specialists can use a relapse-prevention model to assist athletes in coping with any plateaus or setbacks that develop (Meichenbaum, 1985). The LDI specialist should also help athletes recall the time and processes involved in becoming elite athletes. Too often, athletes have short memories of the efforts they have expended in reaching elite-athlete status.

Teaching Skills to Cope With Future Events. Another type of enhancement strategy is teaching life skills that augment a person's ability to cope with future events. We have referred to these skills as life skills (interpersonal and intrapersonal skills); Vealey (1988) calls them psychological skills. Among the skills Vealey includes are arousal management, attention control, decision making, goal setting, positive self-talk, stress management, and time management, among others. These skills can be used in a number of life areas such as life-work planning, self-exploration and self-appraisal, and preparation for competition.

ATHLETES' VALUABLE LIFE SKILLS

To perform under pressure
To be organized
To meet challenges
To handle both success and failure
To accept others' values and beliefs
To be flexible to succeed
To be patient
To take risks
To make a commitment and stick to it
To know how to win and how to lose
To work with people you don't necessarily like
To respect others
To have self-control
To push yourself to the limit
To recognize your limitations
To compete without hatred
To accept responsibility for your behavior
To be dedicated
To accept criticism and feedback as a part of learning
To evaluate yourself
To be flexible
To make good decisions
To set and attain goals
To communicate with others
To be able to learn
To work within a system
To be self-motivated

Psychological skills can be taught through a series of interactive steps (Danish & Hale, 1981). The skill is described in behavioral terms, and a rationale is given for its use. This step is critical in assuring that people not only understand what the skill looks like but also have some faith that it can improve their performance. If athletes question the utility of a particular skill, it is doubtful that they will invest sufficient time and energy to acquire it. Once athletes understand how and why a particular skill can improve performance, the skill should be demonstrated. Many people must see both successful and unsuccessful attempts at using the skill to learn to differentiate the two and refine their mental picture of what is necessary for successful execution. From this point athletes are ready to attempt the skill, and with continual feedback based on their progress they can establish reasonable levels of mastery. Homework assignments and in vivo practice with continual supervision from the LDI specialist further enhance skill mastery.

Once athletes have reached adequate levels of skill attainment, LDI specialists can provide information on how individual skills fit into larger intervention strategies. For example, mastery of dribbling will not insure excellence as a basketball player. Acquisition of domain-specific strategies requires knowledge and understanding of the norms, processes, and structures of the new environment (Martin, 1990). LDI specialists assist people in acquiring this knowledge by providing information and experiences in the new domain as they provide support and feedback.

Supportive Strategies

Interventions that occur during an event or transition are called support. Some people require types of social support that cannot be provided by their natural system of family and friends. For example, the USOC has developed CAPA (referred to earlier), a service for present and transitional national-sport-team athletes. The goal of this program is to enhance participants' abilities to engage in the career-development process. Feedback from many CAPA participants indicates that one of the most significant elements of their experience was the ability to share feelings and concerns with other athletes "who really knew what we are going through" (Petitpas et al., 1992). The support groups that developed out of the CAPA workshops validated feelings, brainstormed job-hunting strategies, and supported both self-exploration and career exploration.

Chuck also commented that the life-skills course he took in his first year of college was critical for "helping me get back on track" during that year as well as for his future development. Although he believed that some of the skills he had learned were valuable, he commented that knowing other athletes experience some of the same feelings and worries about the future put him at ease. Until then, he worried that what he was experiencing was not normal.

Support can range from regular team meetings to group sessions for injured athletes. An LDI specialist can provide considerable personal support for transitional athletes through active listening and other aspects of rapport building. Other types of support would include

- organizing support groups for normative and paranormative transitional events such as injury or retirement;
- assisting in the development of personal support networks by assessing support needs and organizing resources;
- identifying potential mentors and role models;
- linking people to appropriate organizational resources;
- educating people about their own support-person roles; and
- advocacy.

In providing these services the LDI specialist becomes an important part of a person's support network.

An example of a support-based intervention now being conducted is the Going for the Goal program for the U.S. Diving Federation. This program involves having high-school–aged divers who have qualified for Junior Nationals teach a life-skills program for younger, less-experienced divers. It is expected that in addition to teaching skills, the older divers will serve as positive role models and mentors to the younger athletes.

Counseling Strategies

Another type of intervention, counseling strategies, takes place after a life event has occurred. These strategies help people to cope with difficulties confronting the impact or aftermath of a life event. The goal of counseling is to enable people to grow through a life event.

Unfortunately, many people experience emotional difficulties as a result of life events (Ogilvie & Howe, 1986). Often this occurs because a person's strategies for coping with the difficulty have now become the problem. For example, an athlete who was having difficulty managing his emotions due to a career-threatening injury was given pain medication to help manage the physical discomfort. The athlete soon realized that increased doses of the pain killer would also deaden the emotional pain. Quickly the athlete adopted a self-defeating pattern of self-medication that gave him short-term pain relief, but at the cost of commitment to his rehabilitation. In addition, his increased dependence on various types of medication superseded his need for family and friends. The end result of the athlete's attempts at managing his emotional pain was a substance-abuse problem.

Counseling interventions in an LDI framework attempt to assist people in identifying and developing resources to more effectively cope with significant life events. The approach is more educational than remedial. The first goal of counseling is to understand the problem from a person's perspective. This includes identifying the original intent of any maladaptive self-cure strategies. The second goal is to assess the coping resources, sources of support, and domain-specific variables. The third goal is to mobilize existing resources and teach new skills. The fourth goal is to give opportunities to practice the new skills in vivo with continual feedback, support, and follow-up. The fifth and last goal is to plan for future events and terminate the counseling relationship. A more inclusive example of the LDI counseling perspective as it relates to injury rehabilitation is presented in chapter 11.

In sum, LDI is designed to enhance personal competence in dealing with a number of life domains, both sport- and non-sport-related.

THE ROLE OF THE LDI SPECIALIST

As noted in the previous section, the strategies employed relate to the timing of an intervention vis-à-vis the occurrence of a critical life event. The education, training, and skills needed by LDI specialists are dependent on what strategies (enhancement, supportive, or counseling) are used. In this section we provide a general perspective on the requisite knowledge and skills needed by LDI specialists depending on the interventions and strategies they wish to implement.

Listening and Understanding

LDI specialists, regardless of what strategies they intend to implement, must be good listeners and be able to develop an understanding of the person or persons receiving the intervention. Understanding the critical life event from another's perspective is a difficult but necessary prerequisite. Too often we assume that we understand others and their problems and then rapidly begin the problem-solving attempt. When we initiate a problem-solving approach prematurely, we impede development of rapport, curtail self-exploration, and run a high risk of failure.

Attempting to solve a problem before it is fully understood can happen if the LDI specialist lacks training in sport sciences and misses or ignores important data about the athletes' experience (e.g., the centrality of sport in the athlete's life); has extensive experience in sport and assumes that this experience is identical to the athlete's; or uses the same methods in all situations due to the lack of a range of intervention skills or strategies.

Listening to and understanding others is the first essential phase of the helping process. LDI specialists must have such training. There are many effective listening-skills programs. These programs include *Helping Skills: A Basic Training Program* (Danish, D'Augelli, & Hauer, 1980), *The Skilled Helper* (Egan, 1986), and *Intentional Interviewing and Counseling* (Ivey, 1983).

Effective helpers, however, must not only understand the individual skills involved in listening, such as reflection of feelings and paraphrasing, but must understand the larger strategies of building rapport and gaining a commitment to action. Ineffective helpers come with a few skills and tend to force them on their clients. They do not understand the sport and intervention domains and assume that the few skills they have will work with everyone. LDI specialists must possess specific knowledge about both sport and the helping process to enable them to understand the unique dynamics presented.

The Training of the LDI Specialist

Although developing rapport with an athlete or group of athletes is a necessary first step, it is not sufficient if the goal is to enhance athletes' life development or athletic development. LDI specialists must have training to work with athletes experiencing a variety of critical life events. The training will differ depending on whether the intervention is implemented prior to, during, or after the event and whether the target of the intervention is an individual or group. Whereas other chapters in this book cover some of these topics in greater detail, we discuss several training issues here only briefly. As a preface for this discussion it is important to note that other sport psychologists, especially those trained as psychologists, might disagree with this perspective.

Courtesy Jeff Miller and the University of Wisconsin

Organizations such as the USOC and the Association for the Advancement of Applied Sport Psychology (AAASP) have developed guidelines for identifying the training needed for sport psychologists. The USOC has developed the Registry for the Psychology of Sport; AAASP has developed a certification system. One of the major distinctions underlying both credentialing systems is the discipline in which the sport psychologist is trained. Sport psychologists trained in physical education are viewed as educators; those trained in psychology are viewed as clinicians. What seems most important to us is whether a person has the requisite skills and knowledge to implement the intervention (strategy or technique) chosen; has the understanding of potential consequences, both intended and unintended, of the intervention; and has an understanding of human behavior (individual development, personality theory, abnormal behavior) so as to put both person and personal reactions into social context. Other necessary requisite knowledge and skills pertain to the area of sport. These include a knowledge of sport psychology subdisciplines, biomechanics, history and sociology of sport, physiology of exercise, motor learning, coaching strategies, and training and supervised practice working with athletes to enhance athletic performance. Additionally, people preparing to work in this field need experience in working with the coach–athlete relationship as well as with athletes who are training and participating in competitive sports.

From the LDI perspective, when the intervention occurs prior to the event, the major task of the LDI specialist is to teach life skills. To be an effective life-skills teacher requires a knowledge of how skills are taught and how learning takes place. Additionally, knowledge of the cognitive-affective and social bases of behavior as well as an understanding of human behavior (as detailed previously) are necessary. Regardless of what kind of intervention is being conducted, such knowledge is essential. This knowledge can be gained from a variety of sport- and psychology-related courses. The intervention agent must also have training and supervised practice in how to teach skills. We have described such a process earlier in this chapter as well as in other works (Danish & Hale, 1983; 1981). Gould (1983) has also delineated this process in considerable detail.

When the intervention occurs during an event, the focus of the intervention becomes threefold: to provide support; to help the person or group deal with the potential negative emotions and reactions being experienced as a result of the event; and to teach the new skills to encounter and, if possible, to grow from the event. The knowledge and skills required of an intervener providing support are diverse. In addition to the knowledge delineated above, knowledge of the social support and crisis intervention processes is critical. A *crisis* as we are referring to it here is something different than the denotative meaning of a turning point; it is the connotative meaning and is synonymous with emergency. Crises occur when an event has a sudden onset, is of great intensity, and represents a threat to important life goals (Danish & D'Augelli, 1983). When an event is being experienced, the LDI specialist must be prepared to contend with a crisis and its accompanying disorientation, confusion, and distraught emotion, even though these do not always occur.

Lastly, when the intervention occurs after the event, counseling becomes the intervention of choice. Although as we noted earlier an LDI perspective is different than a remedially oriented approach, the intervener must be knowledgeable about life-skills development as well as psychopathology. To understand normal development, one must have a knowledge of abnormal development and functioning. Training in counseling, both on a one-to-one basis and in groups, should be gained. The intervener should have supervised practica with an appropriate client population. For the intervener to be fully prepared to function in this context, training as a psychologist will most likely be needed. Such training, specified by the American Psychological Association, requires a doctoral degree in either clinical or counseling psychology. The application of psychological principles to sport is also essential.

In this section we have only touched on the issue of professional training. The topic is fraught with emotion, and we hope that these comments stimulate a reasoned discussion of the educational needs of a specific kind of sport psychologist, one who has training in two disciplines—physical education and psychology—and practices as an LDI specialist.

CONCLUSION

In this chapter we have described an educational-developmental model for the practice of sport psychology. We believe that the model provides a framework in which individuals trained in both psychology and physical education can design, implement, and evaluate a wide range of interventions with a variety of athletic populations. These athletes might be young or old, active or retired, able or disabled, or recreational or professional athletes; because of the emphasis on life-span development and the critical life events encountered throughout life, athletes at all levels can be considered. The primary focus of LDI is enhancement and social support, yet in some cases postevent adjustments might necessitate more clinically oriented strategies.

More importantly, an LDI perspective emphasizing optimization and the acquisition of life skills provides a framework for the practitioner to evaluate why, how, and for what purpose interventions are attempted. The LDI model recognizes that development is multidimensional. Change occurs in a variety of domains and affects not only the person but the system in which the person exists. By understanding the biopsychosocial context in which the person functions, the LDI specialist is less likely to rely on interventions targeting individuals when system-level problems exist. Additionally, having an LDI focus allows the specialist to be better able to identify the conditions that build character and enhance personal competence.

We recognize that other models for the practice of sport psychology exist. They must be shared so that appropriate roles and functions can be delineated. Following an examination of the various models, sport psychology will be able to begin the process of establishing itself as a unique discipline and profession.

REFERENCES

Auerbach, S. (1986). Assumptions of crisis theory and a temporal model of crisis intervention. In S.M. Auerbach & A.L. Stolberg (Eds.), *Crisis intervention with children and families* (pp. 3-37). Washington, DC: Hemisphere/Harper & Row.

Baillie, P.H.F., & Danish, S.J. (1992). Understanding the career transition of athletes. *Sport Psychologist*, **6**, 77-98.

Baltes, P., Reese, H., & Lipsett, L.P. (1980). Life-span developmental psychology. *Annual Review of Psychology*, **31**, 65-110.

Bandura, A. (1977). Self-efficacy: Toward a unifying theory of behavioral change. *Psychological Review*, **84**, 191-215.

Chodoff, P. (1976). The German concentration camp as a psychological stress. In R. Moos (Ed.), *Human adaptation: Coping with life stress*. Lexington, MA: Heath.

Danish, S.J. (1991). *Assessing the impact of a mentoring program to teach life skills*. Proposal submitted to the United States Olympic Committee, Sports Medicine and Science Committee.

Danish, S., & D'Augelli, A.R. (1983). *Helping skills II: Life development intervention*. New York: Human Sciences.

Danish, S., D'Augelli, A.R., & Ginsberg, M. (1984). Life development intervention: Promotion of mental health through the development of competence. In S. Brown & R. Lent (Eds.), *Handbook of counseling psychology* (pp. 520-544). New York: Wiley.

Danish, S.J., D'Augelli, A.R., & Hauer, A.L. (1980). *Helping skills: A basic training program* (2nd ed.). New York: Human Sciences Press.

Danish, S.J., & Hale, B.D. (1981). Toward an understanding of the practice of sport psychology. *Journal of Sport Psychology*, **3**, 90-99.

Danish, S.J., & Hale, B.D. (1983). Teaching psychological skills to athletes and coaches. *Journal of Physical Education, Recreation, and Dance*, **57**, 11-12, 80-81.

Danish, S.J., Petitpas, A.J., & Hale, B.D. (1990). Sport as a context for developing competence. In T. Gullotta, G. Adams, and R. Monteymar (Eds.), *Developing social competency in adolescence: Vol. 3* (pp. 169-194). Newbury Park, CA: Sage.

Danish, S., Petitpas, A., & Hale, B. (1992). A developmental-educational intervention model of sport psychology. *Sport Psychologist*, **6**, 403-415.

Danish, S., Smyer, M.A., & Nowak, C.A. (1980). Developmental intervention: Enhancing life-event processes. In P.B. Baltes & O.G. Brim, Jr. (Eds.), *Life-span development and behavior: Vol. 3* (pp. 339-366). New York: Academic Press.

Egan, G. (1986). *The skilled helper: A systematic approach to effective helping* (3rd ed.). Monterey, CA: Brooks/Cole.

Falek, A., & Britton, S. (1974). Phases in coping: The hypothesis and its implications. *Social Biology*, **21**, 1-7.

Gould, D. (1983). Developing psychological skills in young athletes. In N. Wood (Ed.), *Coaching science update* (pp. 4-10). Ottawa, ON: Coaching Association of Canada.

Haerle, R. (1975). Career patterns and career contingencies of professional baseball players: An occupational analysis. In D.W. Ball & J.W. Loy (Eds.), *Sport and social order* (pp. 461-519). Reading, MA: Addison-Wesley.

Ivey, A.E. (1983). *Intentional interviewing and counseling*. Monterey, CA: Brooks/Cole.

Kleiber, D.A., Greendorfer, S.L., Blinde, E., & Samdahl, D. (1987). Quality of exit from university sports and subsequent life satisfaction. *Journal of Sport Sociology*, **4**, 28-36.

LeUnes, A., & Haywood, S.A. (1990). Sport psychology as viewed by chairpersons of American Psychological Association—Approved clinical psychology programs. *Sport Psychologist*, **4**, 18-24.

Martin, J. (1990). Confusions in psychological skills training. *Journal of Counseling and Development*, **68**, 402-407.

Mayer, T., & Andrews, H.B. (1981). Changes in self-concept following a spinal cord injury. *Journal of Applied Rehabilitation Counseling*, **12**, 135-137.

McDonald, S.A., & Hardy, C.J. (1990). Affective response patterns of the injured athlete: An exploratory analysis. *Sport Psychologist*, **4**, 261-274.

Meichenbaum, D. (1985). *Stress inoculation training*. Elmford, NY: Pergamon Press.

Meichenbaum, D., & Turk, D.C. (1987). *Facilitating treatment adherence: A practitioner's guide*. New York: Plenum Press.

Neugarten, B. (1968). *Middle-age and aging*. Chicago: University of Chicago Press.

Ogilvie, B., & Howe, M. (1986). Trauma of termination from athletics. In J.M. Williams (Ed.), *Applied sport psychology: Personal growth to peak performance*. Palo Alto, CA: Mayfield.

Pearson, R. (1990). *Counseling and social support: Perspectives and practice*. Newbury Park, CA: Sage.

Pearson, R., & Petitpas, A. (1990). Transitions of athletes: Developmental and prevention perspectives. *Journal of Counseling and Development*, **69**, 7-10.

Petitpas, A., Danish, S., McKelvain, R., & Murphy, S. (1992). A career assistance program for elite athletes. *Journal of Counseling and Development*, **70**, 383-386.

Petitpas, A., & Elliott, W. (1987, November). *Preparing for future careers*. Presentation at the Annual Sponsor's Meeting of the Ladies Professional Golf Association, Pine Isle, GA.

Rappaport, J. (1981). In praise of paradox: A social policy of empowerment over prevention. *American Journal of Community Psychology*, **9**, 1-25.

Rotella, S.A., & Heyman, S.J. (1986). Stress, injury, and the psychological rehabilitation of athletes. In J.M. Williams (Ed.),

Applied sport psychology: Personal growth to peak experience (pp. 343-364). Palo Alto, CA: Mayfield.

Schlossberg, N.K. (1984). *Counseling adults in transition: Linking practice with theory.* New York: Springer.

Super, D.E. (1977). The identity crisis of counseling psychologists. *Counseling Psychologist*, **7**, 13-15.

Vealey, R.S. (1988). Future directions in psychological skills training. *Sport Psychologist*, **2**, 318-336.

Watzlawick, P., Weakland, J., & Fisch, R. (1974). *Change: Principles of problem formation and problem resolution.* New York: Norton.

The authors appreciate the comments and suggestions of Patrick Baillie, Britt Brewer, Jennifer English, and Douglas Jowdy.

CHAPTER 3

CHILDREN IN SPORT: AN EDUCATIONAL MODEL

Maureen R. Weiss, PhD
University of Oregon

From 1930 until the early 1950s, the "experts" governing children's school and community athletic programs in the United States strongly urged the discontinuance of competitive sport for children of elementary and junior high school age (Wiggins, 1987). In particular, physical educators, health directors, and school administrators concluded that interscholastic and agency-sponsored competition among children and young adolescents was harmful for their developing bodies and minds. The experts instead recommended that these youngsters be involved in physical education and intramural programs, so as to maximize the positive physical and psychological benefits of participation in physical activity.

These recommendations had a strong impact on the prevalence of competitive sport programs in the elementary schools but had little effect on the community- or agency-sponsored programs governed outside the schools. Picking up the slack where elementary schools left off, agency-sponsored sport organizations at the national, regional, and local levels flourished. Organizations such as the YMCA, Catholic Youth Organization (CYO), and Boys and Girls Clubs stepped up the pace that they started earlier in the century. Little League Baseball was founded in 1939, and the number of nonschool programs continued with Biddy Basketball, American Youth Soccer Association, USOC developmental programs, and millions of local organizations in every sport imaginable. In the end, the real experts prevailed—the youngsters themselves, their parents, and their coaches, who in many cases were also parents. In short, the overriding belief that sport contributes positively to children's physical, psychological, and social development has resulted in the participation of nearly 25 million children in nonschool-agency–sponsored competitive sport programs (Martens, 1986).

Despite the popularity and success of youth sport programs today, the debate continues regarding the potential benefits and costs of organized competitive sport for children. The key word in all these discussions is *potential*. The potential benefits of sport include physical development, such as skill learning and fitness, development of psychological characteristics, such as positive self-esteem and the ability to cope with stress, and development of social qualities, such as empathy for others and the development of lifetime friendships. However, these benefits are not automatically transmitted through mere participation in games and matches.

Rather, both positive or negative attitudes and behaviors are potentially taught in the sport setting by significant adults and peers and are learned by young athletes over time. If the physical, psychological, and social benefits available through sport are to occur, they must be purposely planned, structured, and taught as well as positively reinforced. This does not always happen.

This chapter provides knowledge about the development of children's self-perceptions, enjoyment, and motivation through sport experiences. Knowledge comes from theory, research, and personal experiences, and all are targeted at helping the practitioner maximize the probability of positive experiences and minimize the negative ones in the youth-sport competitive setting. Special attention is given to developmental or age-related differences in children's perceptions of their competence, of their coaches' and parents' feedback, and of their own performance outcomes. The objective is to determine how to structure the sport setting so that it develops youngsters physically, psychologically, and socially. If children sustain their activity involvement, then the value of sport in terms of self-confidence, enjoyment, and friendships will be optimally realized.

The chapter is organized into several sections. First I introduce three young athletes who serve as case studies to make developmental concepts and particular sport experiences more vivid as they are discussed. Next I describe a philosophy for understanding children's development through sport, with particular emphasis on an integrated sport science approach. Third, I review the literature on children's psychosocial development, emphasizing motivational theories and research and the salient characteristics influencing motivated behavior in children and adolescents. In the fourth section I focus on methods for enhancing psychological skills in children using a skill development model that describes the relationships among competence, self-confidence, and motivation. These constructs are further addressed using a psychological methods model that emphasizes the essential links among observation of behavior, instructional responses, and personal reflection of behavioral changes. I conclude the chapter with a return to the case studies and explore the intervention possibilities suggested by the information in the chapter.

■ *THE CASE OF LAURA* ■

At 14 Laura was an outstanding rhythmic gymnast who excelled in all of her events as well as at ballet. She had competed since she was 8 years old, and her coach's high expectations of her future in the sport were justified by scores in competitive meets and her improvement each season. Just after the start of one season Laura's coach contacted me, a sport psychology consultant, and expressed concern over Laura's decline in self-confidence, strength, and endurance during tricks and routines, and her subsequent overall performance decrements. Moreover, Laura was now self-conscious and constricted in her body movements and artistic expression, as exemplified by her wearing oversized T-shirts during practice. Laura's mother told me that Laura had grown several inches over the previous year and had gone through numerous physical changes in height, weight, and sexual development. Talking to Laura confirmed the observations of her coach and her mother. In particular, she expressed self-doubts and anxiety about upcoming meets and questioned her commitment to her sport in light of preparations for high school. New opportunities, such as academic courses, more time with friends, and specializing in ballet and theater, were becoming more and more attractive. Her parents and brother were extremely supportive in whatever route she decided to take. Despite Laura's attempts to understand that the reasons for her performance decrements were due to normal maturity changes, she decided to withdraw from rhythmic gymnastics and pursue other interests.

■ *THE CASE OF RAUL* ■

Raul's love for sports was unmatched among his 9-year-old peers. He loved all sports—basketball, track and field, baseball, swimming, and wrestling. In spite of his undying love for sports, he wished he could be as good an athlete as Roberto, his older brother. Roberto was one of the best football and baseball players in his high school. But Raul was small for his age, especially for football. And he wasn't as good in baseball as his brother, who was already being approached by college recruiters. Although Raul tried not to lose enthusiasm, it was clear that sibling comparison weighed heavily on his mind, and he wondered whether his parents, coaches, and friends would continually compare him to Roberto. Then one year at a summer sports program, the wrestling instructor observed Raul's enthusiasm and motivation as well as definite performance potential for the sport of wrestling. His size did not matter—he could be matched with similar-sized boys for practicing moves and competing in simulated matches. His instructor encouraged Raul to join a local USA Wrestling club, which he did, and he continued his involvement in wrestling at the middle school level. By the time Raul entered high school, he was still small for his age, but he was an accomplished wrestler with lots of room for improvement. He continued to improve steadily throughout his high school years, culminating in a district championship in the 136-lb (62-kg) class his senior year. During the summers of high school years, Raul often returned to the sports program to help teach children in the wrestling room, where he served as an excellent role model for youngsters much like him.

■ *THE CASE OF JULIA* ■

Julia, an 11-year-old, had competed for a gymnastics club since she was 6 years old. Her father drove her 45 mi (72 km) to practice each day so she could benefit from the best instruction in the state. For some time Julia had been distressed because her coach was *encouraging* her to practice harder, try more difficult moves, and generally "go for it" even when she did not feel confident that she could execute a trick. Competition against teammates, rather than participation with them, escalated when the coach started to encourage intrateam rivalries and to offer or withhold affection and attention based on the outcomes. What made matters worse for Julia was an ankle injury that did not seem to be healing; this affected her performance and self-confidence. Julia used to enjoy gymnastics because it gave her a sense of being good at something and allowed her to be with her friends, but lately the sport had turned from play to work. Thoughts of quitting gnawed at her, but she often heard her coaches and teammates call former gymnasts "quitters" and "losers." Moreover, she knew how proud her parents were and how they loved to show off about her talent, and she did not want to let them down. What should she do? She did not want to continue going to gymnastics, but she didn't want to quit either. On the long drive each day, she repeatedly rehearsed telling her father about her desire to quit, but she could not seem to get the words out. The anxiety of practice and the unrealistic demands of her coach were stressful, but so was the thought of telling her father she wanted to quit. Haunted by the anxiety of indecision, Julia finally made a choice. At practice one day, she purposely overshot a trick and twisted her knee on landing. Her self-imposed injury put her out for the season: she could avoid the stigma of being called a loser because she could claim that she had been "forced to discontinue gymnastics participation."

A PHILOSOPHY FOR UNDERSTANDING CHILDREN'S PSYCHOLOGICAL DEVELOPMENT THROUGH SPORT

My philosophy of working with children and understanding their development in sport settings revolves around three major themes. Personal development and a healthy lifestyle through positive sport experiences are the primary focus, with performance enhancement a secondary goal. More specifically, positive self-perceptions, intrinsic motivation, enjoyment, positive attitude toward the value of physical activity, ability to cope with stress, and sportspersonlike attitudes form the core of characteristics that provide the justification for children's competitive sport (Wiggins, 1987). However, little substantive evidence supports this claim. Instead, many parents and coaches come to expect that these personal qualities and skills will emerge as a result of mere participation and exposure to the rigors of competitive play. But if we are to claim that sport builds character then we must purposefully target these areas in our consulting with parents and coaches and especially help them structure sporting experiences to maximize the probability that these positive outcomes will occur.

Another theme of my philosophical approach with children in sport is the notion of a theory-to-practice and practice-to-theory perspective. That is, both the developmental and sport-psychology literatures provide tremendous insights about the nature of children's self-esteem, motivational orientations, and cognitive abilities as they relate to motor skills and behaviors. The solid knowledge base about children's cognitions and perceptions can help us in understanding and explaining their sport participation and performance. However, just as important are children's expressions of their own experiences, which can provide unique information not found in books and journals. Together, the empirical and experiential knowledge about children and adolescents provides a rich source of information for helping practitioners understand children's perceptions of sport experiences and the selection of appropriate intervention strategies for influencing positive changes.

Lastly, I have found it useful to adopt an integrated sport science approach to understanding children's attitudes and behaviors in sport settings. An integrated approach combines scientific knowledge from such areas as sport psychology, sport sociology, motor behavior (development, learning, control), exercise physiology, and biomechanics to describe, explain, and predict participation behavior and performance. It thus describes the interaction among biological, psychological, social, and physical differences in the social context of the developing child in sport. Such an approach should help to explain more of the variance in sport participation behaviors as well as provide practitioners with information that they can use to solve sport-specific problems, such as attrition from sport programs, effects of game and rule modifications, and readiness for sports competition.

The logic and rationale of such a multidisciplinary perspective can be seen with our three case-study athletes, Laura, Raul, and Julia. Before Laura entered an intense growth spurt at age 12, she was by far the best performer in her club. Her routines were exceptional in the rope, ball, hoop, ribbon, and clubs events. As a result of biological and physical changes associated with her maturation, mechanical and neuromuscular constraints influenced her ability to execute well-learned tricks and techniques. Having to adjust to her new body parameters to execute routines affected her psychologically, especially in terms of self-confidence, anxiety, and enjoyment. In addition, expectations of her coach and the elite structure of rhythmic gymnastics elevated feelings of anxiety and doubt about further performance. The combination of biological, psychological, and physical factors along with important social influences by family and coach influenced her eventual decision to quit gymnastics.

Raul's small size as a result of being a late-maturing youngster was a barrier to pursuing football as his brother had done, and his skills in baseball were not as good as Roberto's. But his extreme enthusiasm and motivation for sports kept him involved and determined to achieve in his own way. Strong encouragement from his instructors and coaches, a desire to excel in a unique area of achievement, and his physical size combined to make him a perfect match for wrestling. His successful experiences and positive feedback from peers and adults motivated his desire to excel in the sport, resulting in superior achievements at the high school level. Thus we again see that physical, biological, psychological, and social environmental factors influenced participation behaviors and performance in sport.

Lastly, we have the negative experiences and outcome for Julia. When Julia began her gymnastics participation, it was fun for her because of all the opportunities to learn new skills and to be with friends. As she got older and more talented in the sport, her own self-imposed demands as well as those of her parents and coach resulted in less enjoyment and the propensity for injury. The injuries had both physical and psychological consequences, which in turn affected the quality of her performance. The potential stigma of being called a quitter by significant adults and peers only made matters worse. She neither enjoyed her participation nor found a way to discontinue the sport without significant harm to her self-esteem. Her only way out was to incur an injury that gave her no choice but to withdraw from competition. The influence by significant others and the structure of sport in combination with individual differences along physical, social, and psychological lines contributes to our understanding of Julia's final decision.

An integrated perspective provides a holistic way of explaining children's participation and performance in sport. By considering the range of biological, physical, psychological, and social individual difference factors influencing the child as well as environmental factors, such as significant adults and peers, the particular level or structure of sport, and one's ascribed attributes, such as gender, race, and culture, researchers and practitioners alike can maximize their understanding of children's experiences in sport. Moreover, pinpointing the various influences in a child's life in sport can help practitioners decide on what psychological skills and methods should be chosen.

The focus on an integrated sport-science approach to understanding children's participation and performance in sport lends itself well to a focus on personal development and lifestyle skills. *Personal development* refers to the psychological skills or qualities to be attained through experiences in sport and physical activity, whereas *psychological methods* refer to the techniques or strategies for ensuring that these skills are developed (Vealey, 1988). Psychological skills can infer either those characteristics needed to facilitate optimal performance or those needed to maintain a positive attitude toward and enjoyment of physical activity. The psychological skills that I emphasize in my work with children along with strategies for developing them appear in Table 3.1.

The focus of my presentation on developing psychological skills in young athletes is on self-perceptions, affect, and motivation. In order to understand antecedents, correlates, and consequences of these characteristics in children's lives, I will review the social, developmental, and sport psychology literatures on motivation theories and research. Following this presentation, I will derive from this literature intervention strategies or psychological methods for influencing positive self-perceptions, affect, and motivation.

PSYCHOSOCIAL DEVELOPMENT IN CHILDREN: REVIEWING THE LITERATURE

The research on participation motivation and attrition, although largely descriptive in nature, has provided a wealth of data on why children and adolescents participate in sport

Table 3.1 Psychological Skills and Methods in Working With Children in Sport

Psychological skills	Psychological methods
Positive self-perceptions	Environmental strategies
Intrinsic motivation	Skill development methods
Interpersonal skills	Structure of practice and competitions
Positive attitude toward value of physical activity	Game and rule modifications
Coping with competitive stress	Motivational climate
Moral development and sportspersonship	Parent and coach education
Positive affect	Communication styles
	Social reinforcement principles
	Leadership effectiveness
	Expectancy effects
	Modeling techniques
	Individual control strategies
	Imagery
	Goal setting
	Relaxation
	Self-talk

(Gould & Petlichkoff, 1988; Weiss & Chaumeton, 1992; Weiss & Petlichkoff, 1989). Several common themes for participation reasons have emerged based on the number of studies conducted. These include

- competence (learning and improving skills),
- affiliation (being with and making friends),
- team identification (being part of a group, team spirit),
- health and fitness (getting and staying in shape),
- competition (excitement, demonstrating skills), and
- fun.

The reasons cited are primarily intrinsic, rather than extrinsic, in their orientation. Less consensus exists about reasons for discontinuing involvement. Early research efforts identified lack of playing time, reduction in fun, dislike for the coach, and an overemphasis on competition as predominant reasons for discontinuing involvement. Subsequent studies reported reasons such as "conflicts of interest," time demands, and "other things to do" (Weiss & Chaumeton, 1992). An encouraging finding of the few studies that were specifically designed to follow up on athletes who withdrew from a sport was that the large majority are not permanent dropouts but rather that they often transfer to another sport or to the same sport at a lower intensity (Weiss & Petlichkoff, 1989). Nevertheless, a common theme of these findings is that reasons for leaving a sport are often linked to issues related to perceptions of competence, dissatisfaction with the social environment (e.g., coach, competitive emphasis), or no longer enjoying participation.

Although the research on participation motivation primarily tells us what reasons predominate for athletes' participation in sport, the underlying processes explaining *why* these reasons exist and how they are developed in the young athlete are not as clear. To understand the underlying social and cognitive mechanisms that might explain why athletes participate or discontinue sport involvement, I will review the developmental and social psychology literatures. Most of these theories have been supported primarily in the academic domain, but recent research in sport psychology strongly suggests that they are also valid when applied to physical achievement situations.

Children's Motivation According to Harter

Harter's competence-motivation theory (1978, 1981) emphasizes an understanding of children's psychological development as they strive to demonstrate competence in a particular achievement domain. According to competence-motivation theory, children are motivated to become competent in their social environments and do so by engaging in mastery attempts. When these efforts are successful in the child's eyes, perceptions of competence and internal locus of control increase, resulting in heightened positive affect and the maintenance of competence motivation. Thus the person continues to be motivated toward seeking challenges that will result in competent performance accomplishments.

Harter identifies other salient components that contribute to the development of these self-perceptions, affect, and motivation. In particular, the child's socialization history in the form of modeling, feedback, and reinforcement from significant adults and peers in response to performance plays a large role in psychosocial development. Moreover, adoption of a reward system and standard of goals are shaped through the quality of communication received from these significant others. Children who are reinforced for independent mastery attempts and encouraged to try harder, to persist in the face of skill barriers, and to use self-referenced information to judge competence (e.g., skill improvement, enjoyment of sport) will likely develop an intrinsic motivational orientation in which a self-reward system and mastery goals are embraced. In contrast, the child who is encouraged to view competence primarily in relation to the performance of others will most likely adopt an extrinsic motivational orientation, where a dependence on external rewards and the adoption of outcome goals predominate.

Relation of Perceived Competence to Affect and Motivation

The relationships among several of the salient components in Harter's model have been strongly supported by research in both the academic and sport domains (Weiss & Chaumeton, 1992). For example, Klint and Weiss (1987) found a strong relationship between perceived competence and motives for participating in competitive youth gymnastics. Specifically, athletes high in perceived physical competence indicated that skill development reasons were most important for their participation, whereas those athletes who registered higher perceived peer-acceptance scores identified affiliation and team aspects as most salient for their participation. Thus children were motivated by reasons related to opportunities for demonstrating their competence in the competitive sport setting and, in turn, perceptions of competence contributed to continued motivation.

Several studies have substantiated consistent relationships among perceptions of competence and control, affect in the form of enjoyment and anxiety, and intrinsic motivation. For example, Weiss and Horn (1990) were interested in children's accuracy of perceived competence and its relation to achievement characteristics. They found that children who underestimated their abilities (i.e., their perceived competence scores were considerably lower than teachers' ratings of their actual competence) indicated higher trait anxiety, an external locus of control, and lower challenge-seeking behaviors in comparison to their accurate- and overestimating peers. Weiss, McAuley, Ebbeck, and Wiese (1990) found a strong relationship between self-perceptions and causal attributions for performance in the physical domain. Specifically, children who were higher in perceived competence made causal attributions for perceived success that were more internal, stable, and personally controllable than did those lower in competence perceptions. Lastly, Weiss, Bredemeier, and Shewchuk (1986) investigated the relationships among perceived competence, perceived control, intrinsic motivation, and physical achievement in children participating in a variety of sports. Results revealed that children higher in perceived competence demonstrated higher achievement scores and a more intrinsic motivational orientation than children low in perceived competence.

Taken together, the results of these three studies (Weiss et al., 1986; Weiss et al., 1990; Weiss & Horn, 1990) suggest that children with high levels of physical competence perceptions follow a pattern of functional achievement behaviors, reflected by success perceptions, appropriate causal attributions for success and failure, an intrinsic motivational orientation, and positive affective outcomes. Conversely, children who evidence low (or inaccurate) perceptions of competence are characterized by psychological characteristics describing a more extrinsically oriented individual: low in challenge-seeking behavior and high on negative affect such as anxiety, inappropriate attributions for performance outcomes, and low future performance expectations.

Sources of Competence Information

A particularly interesting and insightful line of research testing Harter's predictions has been the investigation of developmental differences in the sources of information children use to judge their competence in the physical domain. Horn and her colleagues (Horn, 1991; Horn & Hasbrook, 1986, 1987; Horn & Weiss, 1991) have conducted several studies to investigate the developmental nature of preferences for sources of information. This research indicates that younger children (ages 8 and 9) prefer the use of adult feedback and evaluation; as children get older (ages 10 to 14) preference for adult feedback declines and reliance on peer comparison and evaluation becomes dominant. The later adolescent years are characterized by a tendency toward the use of multiple sources of criteria to judge competence, particularly a decline in the use of peer comparison and evaluation, and an increase in the use of internal criteria, such as goal achievement, self-improvement, speed, ease in learning new skills, and enjoyment of the activity.

Research has also found a relationship between sources of competence information and patterns of self-perceptions in children and adolescents. Specifically, Horn and Hasbrook (1987) found that children who were low in perceived competence and high in external perceptions of performance control indicated a preference for external sources of information, such as parental feedback and evaluation. Conversely, children high in perceived competence and internal locus of control were more likely to prefer internal sources of criteria to judge their physical competence, such as degree of skill improvement, ease in learning skills, and effort. These relationships were found in children 10 to 14 years of age, but a nonsignificant relationship between information sources and self-perceptions was found for the 8- to 9-year-old group, indicating that a certain developmental level of cognitive sophistication, socialization history, or both must be in place for these relationships to unfold.

Dimensions of Self-Esteem

Another developmental finding in Harter's framework concerns the differentiation and salience of dimensions of self-esteem in early childhood through adolescence. Factor analyses have determined how self-esteem dimensions are integrated or differentiated with increases in maturity. More specifically, children younger than 8 years old do not distinguish between cognitive and physical competence, which load together on one factor, nor between social acceptance and behavioral conduct, which load on a second factor. Children in middle childhood (ages 8 to 12 years), however, clearly differentiate among five salient domains: scholastic competence, athletic competence, physical appearance, peer acceptance, and behavioral conduct. With adolescence, four unique dimensions emerge: close friendships, romantic relationships, job competence, and morality. Thus, with cognitive and physical maturity changes come concomitant changes in the importance of various competence or behavioral domains.

Accuracy of Children's Perceived Physical Competence

The accuracy of children's estimates of competence also exhibit a developmental shift. With increasing age, children show both a decline in levels of perceived competence and an increase in the accuracy of these judgments. Both Harter (1978, 1981) and Nicholls (1984) contend that accuracy of perceived competence increases as a function of two developmental phenomena: (a) children's cognitive ability to analyze the causes of performance outcomes in terms of ability, effort, and task difficulty, and (b) a shift in the sources of information used by children to judge performance capabilities. This phenomenon was demonstrated in an investigation by Horn and Weiss (1991). They found that perceived competence declined and accuracy increased over the age range of 8 to 13 years based on correlations between ratings of perceived competence and teachers' ratings of actual competence. The greatest differences in accuracy were between children 8 and 9 years of age with those 10 to 13 years old. These accuracy differences in age were associated with changes in the criteria children used to judge competence. Older children indicated a reliance on peer comparison and evaluation as preferred sources of information, whereas younger children were more dependent on parental feedback and evaluation.

In addition to accuracy judgments as a function of age, Horn and Weiss (1991) were interested in the relationship between accuracy of perceived competence and sources of information preferred by children. Children were divided into groups representing underestimators, accurate estimators, and overestimators, based on discrepancy scores between perceived and actual competence ratings. Results revealed that differences in accuracy estimates of physical ability were strongly related to preferences for competence-information sources. Underestimators and accurate estimators indicated primary reliance on peer comparison and evaluation, whereas overestimators scored highest on self-comparison sources such as skill improvement and effort exerted.

These findings are of great interest in light of their possible implications for consultants and practitioners. Although it is reasonable to understand that accurate estimators were influenced by peer-comparison and peer-evaluation sources of information, this same source was found for the children who seriously underestimated their physical competencies. What could be going on here? One interpretation is that a different standard of reference in peer comparison was used for the underestimators compared to the accurate estimators. It is possible that those who were low and inaccurate were comparing their abilities to a more select and talented group of peers, such as the star fourth graders or the best athletes in the class, whereas the accurate estimators were using a more similar group of peers (i.e., teammates in the program or age-mate peers of similar ability and experience).

Coaching Behavior Influences

Given the important role of the coach in youth sport, it is surprising that just a handful of studies have examined coaching behaviors on psychological development. Two studies were specifically designed within Harter's framework to examine coaches' influence on self-perceptions, affect, and motivation in young athletes. Horn (1985) was particularly interested in whether observed coaching behaviors would contribute to self-perceptions above and beyond improvement in skill level, using a sample of female junior-high-school softball players ages 13 to 15. Results revealed that skill improvements accounted for the most variance in self-perceptions of ability, but certain coaching behaviors also significantly contributed to these changes. Specifically, players who received more frequent positive reinforcement scored lower in perceived physical competence, and players who received higher frequencies of criticism were found to be higher in competence perceptions.

At first glance, these results directly contradict predictions based on Harter's competence-motivation theory. However, Horn (1985) observed that positive reinforcement statements frequently were given to lower ability players, often unconditional to their skill behaviors. That is, praise was frequently given in the form of "good job" or "way to go" without specific reference to the desirable skill technique or strategy displayed or combined with informational feedback on how to improve. Therefore these athletes might have inferred low performance expectations conveyed by the coach and this influenced perceptions of competence. In contrast, the criticism given for skill errors usually was directed at the high-ability players and contained skill-relevant information on how to improve on the next attempt (e.g., "Use two hands when you are trying to catch a pop fly!"). These results are important in demonstrating that the quantity of reinforcement and the mere use of positive statements is not sufficient to effect changes in ability perceptions and motivation. Rather, the quality of coaches' communication, specifically the contingency to behavior and the appropriateness of the information provided, are crucial for influencing children's perceptions about skill capabilities.

A recent study conducted by Black and Weiss (1992), using athletes' perceptions of coaching behaviors, also found that coaches' contingent feedback and reinforcement responses affected self-perceptions, affect, and motivation in youth swimmers. For children 12 to 18 years of age, perceptions of coaches' use of praise plus corrective information following performance successes were associated with higher perceptions of success and competence, higher enjoyment levels, and higher intrinsic motivation in the form of optimal challenge seeking. Similarly, athletes' ratings of their coaches' frequent use of encouragement plus corrective feedback in response to unsuccessful performances were also associated with more positive self-perceptions and intrinsic motivation.

In sum, Harter's (1978, 1981) theory of competence motivation provides a useful framework for understanding the development of children's self-perceptions and motivation in achievement domains. The findings reported here strongly suggest that there are consistent and strong relationships among self-perceptions of competence and control, affect, and motivation. Children who are high in perceived physical competence show functional achievement behaviors in the form of an internal locus of control and appropriate causal attributions for performance, greater enjoyment toward their participation, and higher intrinsic motivation in the form of challenge-seeking and mastery attempts. Second, sources of information for judging physical competence vary developmentally, from early childhood through adolescence, and this shift in information sources helps explain the decline in perceived competence or increase in accuracy with age. Lastly, significant others such as coaches (as well as parents and peers) can directly influence perceived physical competence, affect, and motivation, primarily through the quality of feedback and reinforcement they provide for performance outcomes.

Children's Motivation According to Nicholls and Dweck

An alternative approach to Harter's competence-motivation theory is the view from achievement-goal theorists such as Nicholls (1984, 1989) and Dweck (1986; Dweck & Elliott, 1983; Elliott & Dweck, 1988). These theories focus on children's motivation as a function of the types of goals adopted toward achievement and the way in which ability is construed as a result of this goal orientation. Like Harter, these achievement theorists strongly believe that the demonstration of competence is the central issue for understanding and explaining children's motivation and self-perceptions in achievement domains. Although the terminology used by these theorists is different from Harter's, I strongly believe that their theories and approaches are more similar than different. Therefore, after discussing these theories, I

Courtesy Colonial Bread

will summarize their commonalities to identify interventions that would comply with both approaches.

According to both Nicholls and Dweck, children interpret their performances based on two goal perspectives. The first is a task, or learning-goal, perspective in which people rely primarily on self-referenced information to judge their level of competence. In this perspective, mastery of personally challenging goals is the focus, and sources such as effort, positive affect, learning, and improvement are used to judge level of ability. With a task, or learning-goal, perspective, individuals who are high or low in perceived competence are hypothesized to choose moderately difficult challenges, exert effort and persistence to attain these challenges, show task interest and enjoyment, and use effort attributions to maintain progress toward meeting goals as well as to respond to unsuccessful performances. When these mastery-oriented people encounter failure, they view it as a temporary setback and a cue to increase effort or to determine what factors they can modify to maximize the probability of future success.

In contrast to the task, or learning-goal, perspective, Nicholls and Dweck describe the ego- or performance-goal-oriented person as one who seeks to maximize the display of high ability and minimize the display of low ability. These people define competence in relation to the performance of others and thus primarily depend on social comparison and evaluation to judge their abilities. According to Nicholls and Dweck, the ego- or performance-goal-oriented person who is high in perceived competence should evidence the same types of achievement behaviors as the task- or learning-goal-oriented person: selection of optimal challenges, intrinsic interest, effort, persistence, and enjoyment. However, the ego- or performance-goal-oriented person who is low in competence perceptions avoids moderate challenges so as not to risk demonstrating low ability. Such people (labeled as helpless-oriented by Dweck) choose very easy or very difficult tasks to protect evaluation of their ability: Easy tasks guarantee success and the demonstration of ability, whereas failure at difficult tasks would not necessarily signify low ability. In addition, the ego–low-confidence person is expected to exert little effort and persistence, thereby increasing the probability of low performance attainments. The helpless-oriented person experiences little enjoyment and low levels of intrinsic motivation and attributes negative outcomes to low ability, which is viewed as predictive of future failures.

Achievement-goal theorists also state that goal perspectives vary as a function of situational and individual difference factors. Situations that emphasize interpersonal competition, public evaluation, and normative feedback are likely to invoke an ego or performance-goal orientation, whereas situations characterized by a focus on learning, participation, skill mastery, and problem solving increase the probability of invoking a task, or learning-goal, orientation. Goal perspectives also vary as a function of individual differences, such as disposition, gender, culture, and age. Dispositional goal orientations, as well as those that are gender and culture related, are largely the function of childhood socialization experiences (Duda, 1987, 1992). Specifically, studies by Duda (1985, 1986) have shown that white males tend to be more ego involved in their sport-related achievement goals than black, Hispanic, and Navajo athletic participants. Similarly, males are more likely to emphasize ego-involved goals in the form of competitive outcomes and social comparison than females, who show a preference for skill mastery and self-comparison sources of information.

Developmental Trends in Goal Perspectives

The adoption of task and ego-goal perspectives also follows a cognitive-developmental pattern (Duda, 1987; Nicholls & Miller, 1983). Developmental differences revolve around children's ability to differentiate the concepts of ability, effort, and task difficulty in analyzing performance outcomes. Up until about age 9, children hold an undifferentiated view of the concept of ability, where effort is viewed as equal to ability in explaining successful performance. That is, children believe that a person who tried hard and succeeded has displayed high ability. At about age 9 through 11, children's cognitive ability to analyze the causes of performance becomes partially differentiated. That is, children come to understand that athletes must be highly skilled to be successful in a challenging competition, regardless of the level of effort exerted. But children do not employ this reasoning systematically. Lastly, at the completely differentiated view of ability, which is attained at about ages 11 to 12, children view ability as a capacity, where additional effort on a task might have limited impact on performance outcome, depending on the level of ability a person possesses.

According to Nicholls and Dweck, once children attain the cognitive maturity to view ability as a capacity that limits the effect of effort on performance, they can adopt either the undifferentiated or differentiated conception of ability. The undifferentiated view is consistent with the notion of a task, or learning-goal, orientation, with its focus on effort to attain personal mastery and use of self-referenced criteria to judge competence. The differentiated view is consistent with an ego, or performance-goal, orientation, with its emphasis on maximizing the demonstration of ability in comparison to others and use of normative criteria for self-ability judgments. These developmental findings in relation to achievement-goal perspectives have implications for the types of feedback and goals used with children in the competitive sport setting. For example, Horn (1987) cautions that using effort attributions in response to skill errors with a young child might result in a perception of low ability, whereas with an older child or adolescent, who can differentiate ability from effort as causes for performance outcomes, effort attributions should imply that with greater effort, attention, and strategy selection the child might be successful.

Nicholls's and Dweck's theories of achievement motivation have been widely supported in the academic domain (Elliott & Dweck, 1988; Nicholls, 1989), and the concepts and relationships these theories provide are intuitively appealing for application to the sport domain. However, testing of the relationships posited by achievement-goal theories among attributions for success and failure outcomes, goal perspectives, task choice, effort and persistence, and affect is scarce in the developmental sport psychology literature. The few published research studies have been primarily conducted with adult populations (Duda, 1992). However, given the support of achievement-goal theories in the academic domain and the competitive sport setting to date, I believe interventions that logically derive from such theoretical predictions definitely are important.

Consolidating Knowledge

Although Harter's competence-motivation theory and Nicholls's and Dweck's achievement-motivation theories take slightly different approaches to the understanding of children's development of self-perceptions and motivation, their similarities far outweigh their differences. For this reason, I propose an integrated model of motivation that takes into consideration the common constructs and relationships found in these theories (see Figure 3.1). This consolidation will provide the framework for identifying intervention strategies that can be used with children in the context of the competitive sport setting (Weiss & Chaumeton, 1992).

Each of the theories distinguishes the child who is mastery- as opposed to performance-outcome-oriented in his or her motivational perspective. Both types of motivated children seek to demonstrate competence (e.g., learning and improving skills, attaining goals) and this is the central construct for explaining reasons for participating in sport. When demonstration of competence takes the form of mastery attempts followed by successful or unsuccessful outcomes, reinforcement by significant adults and peers helps to establish a standard of goals and a reward system. If independent mastery attempts and the skill learning process are encouraged and rewarded, the child tends to use internal or self-references criteria (e.g., skill improvement, effort) to judge ability and adopts a self-reward system and task or learning goals as a standard. If performance outcome (e.g., winning, performing better than others) is emphasized and rewarded by significant others, the child is expected to become dependent on external or normative criteria (e.g., peer comparison and evaluation) and adopt an extrinsic reward system and ego or performance goals as their preferred motivational orientation.

These motivational orientations, in turn, influence perceptions of competence and performance control, affect, and motivated behavior. The mastery-oriented child will derive positive perceptions of competence and an internal locus of control (or adaptive attributions for success and failure) and enjoyment and pleasure, and will choose optimally challenging skills and display maximal effort and persistence. Ultimately, high levels of personal performance achievement will be attained. The performance-outcome-motivated youngster, in contrast, will be susceptible to negative perceptions of competence and an external locus of control (and maladaptive attributions) and negative affect

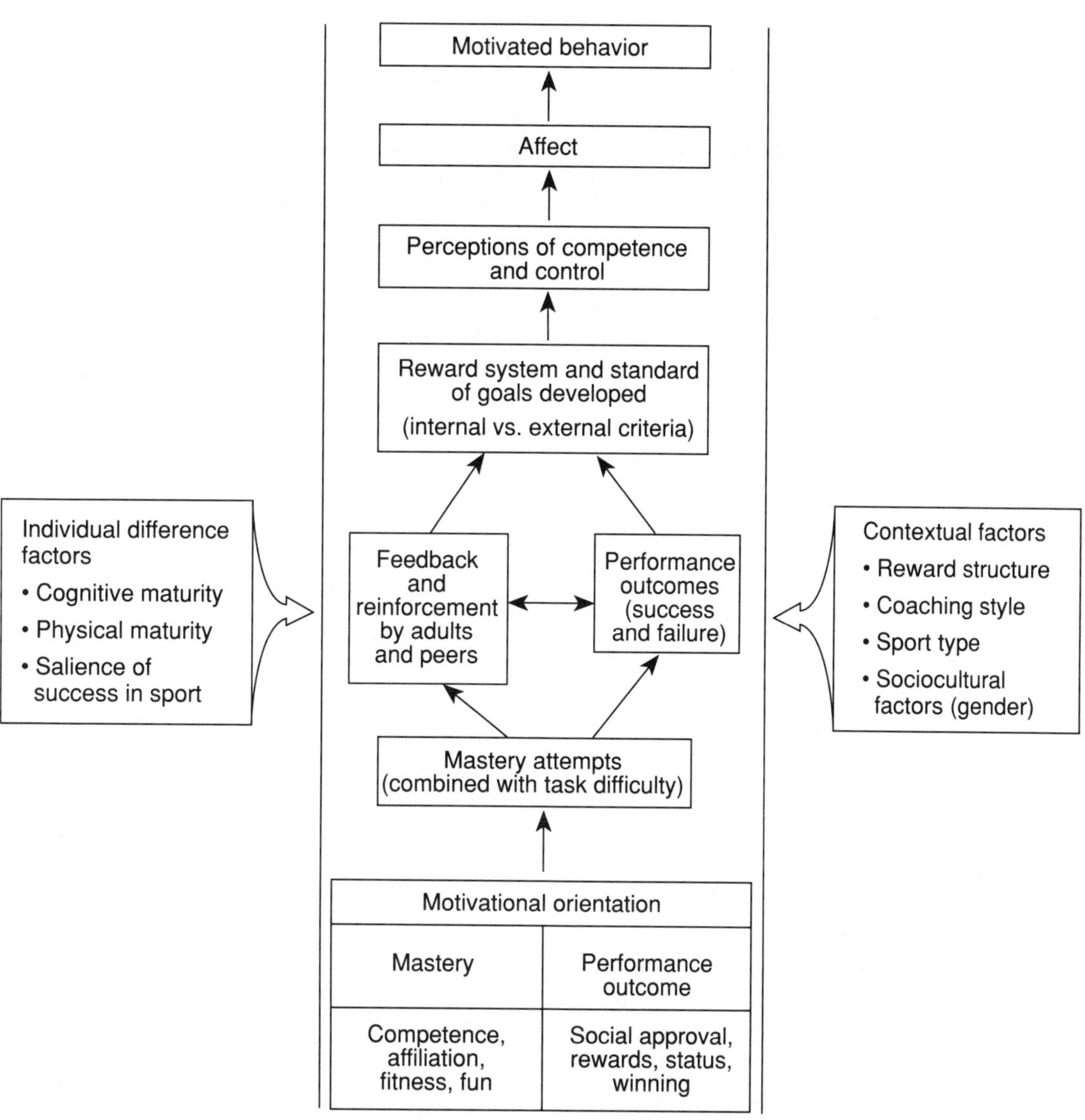

Figure 3.1 A proposed integrated model of sport motivation.
Note. From "Motivational Orientations in Sport" by M.R. Weiss and N. Chaumeton. In *Advances in Sport Psychology* (p. 90) by T.S. Horn (Ed.), 1992, Champaign, IL: Human Kinetics. Copyright 1992 by Human Kinetics. Reprinted by permission.

in the form of anxiety and embarrassment, and will choose easy or difficult tasks and display little effort and low-persistence behaviors. This orientation should result in less-than-optimal personal performance.

In addition to the major relationships among motivation and self-perception constructs, each of the theories suggests that developmental differences exist in children's perceptions of competence, their preference for internal and external sources of criteria to judge their ability, and their ability to analyze the causes of performance outcomes. Research indicates that children's perceptions of competence steadily decline, on average, but become more accurate with age. Thus younger children are more likely to be higher and less accurate in their judgments of competency than older children. These differences were associated with age-related differences in preferences for sources of competence information: younger children preferred parental feedback as criteria for judging their abilities, older children primarily relied on peer comparison and evaluation, and adolescents used internal standards (self-set goals, effort, improvement) more frequently.

Children also vary in their cognitive abilities to distinguish ability, effort, and task difficulty in their attempts to analyze performance outcomes. Specifically, Nicholls's theorizing contended that younger children (up to about age 11 or 12) cannot fully differentiate the concepts of ability and effort. However, a child capable of a differentiated conception of ability can separate the contributions of effort and skill in relation to the challenge of mastering a task. Thus younger children might deem themselves successful based on effort and simple task mastery, whereas older children are more likely to perceive success when their ability compares favorably with similar peers. After becoming capable of taking a differentiated view of ability (at about age 11 or 12), a child might choose to adopt a task or ego motivational orientation. The orientation choice has implications for subsequent motivated behavior and psychosocial development.

The information gleaned from motivational theory and research provides a number of recommendations concerning intervention techniques for enhancing intrinsic motivation, self-perceptions, and performance in the youth-sport setting. Each theory suggests that environmental factors (e.g., significant others, competitive emphasis) as well as individual difference factors (e.g., age, intrinsic vs. extrinsic orientations) influence motivation and performance in social achievement settings such as competitive sport. The next section focuses on psychological methods that consultants and practitioners can incorporate to maximize the probability of developing psychological skills in children, primarily via strategies for nurturing in sport the intrinsically oriented child (i.e., a child who displays positive self-perceptions, affect, and motivated behaviors).

ENHANCING PSYCHOLOGICAL SKILLS IN CHILDREN

The emphasis on a developmental approach to positive achievement behaviors in youth leads naturally to the selection of particular psychological skills or personal qualities to be gained from participation in sport. These skills represent those needed for optimal enjoyment and performance in competitive sport settings. Specifically, I focus on the psychological skills of self-perceptions of competence and control, positive affect, and intrinsic motivation. The psychological methods I advocate include strategies categorized as environmental, or social, influences and individual control, or self-regulated, learning strategies.

Environmental Influences

Based on motivational theories and research, coaches and parents significantly influence children's formation of favorable or unfavorable self-perceptions and subsequent motivated behavior. Their verbal and nonverbal behaviors in the form of modeling, feedback and reinforcement, and emphasis on mastery or performance-outcome goals strongly impact children's motivational orientation toward sport participation. The objective of our work with children is the development of mastery-oriented youngsters who are characterized by positive perceptions of competence and an internal locus of control, enjoyment, and pleasure with sport participation, and behavior in the form of optimal challenge-seeking, maximal effort, and persistence in the face of skill obstacles.

A key practical implication for consultants in the area of environmental strategies is providing educational workshops to coaches and parents about the importance of demonstrating appropriate attitudes and effective behaviors in response to children's performance in sport settings. To provide a systematic way of effecting changes in children's self-perceptions and motivation through mediating coach and parent behaviors, two models are presented. One model (see Figure 3.2) is a schematic representing the relationships among competence in meeting skill challenges, self-confidence (perceived competence and control), and motivation as suggested by theory and research (Bressan & Weiss, 1982). Thus self-confidence is seen as both a consequence of successful mastery attempts as well as a mediator of task choice, effort, and persistence. The diagram reveals that increases in skill competence with optimal challenges result in heightened self-confidence that, in turn, positively influences intrinsic interest and task persistence. Sustained effort or persistence increases the probability of further performance gains and the demonstration of competence in meeting skill challenges. I call this the skill development model.

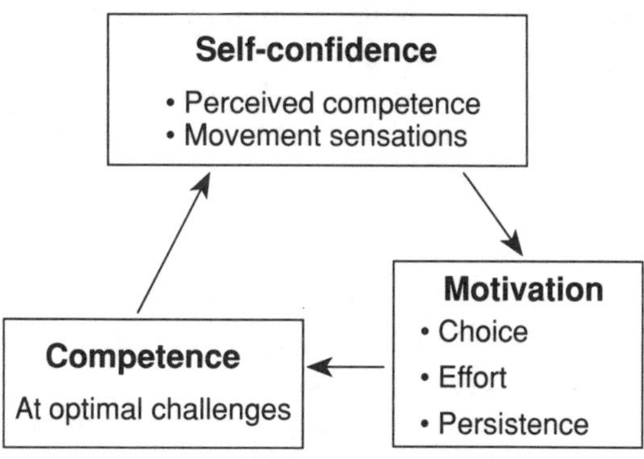

Figure 3.2 The skill development model describes the interrelationships among competence, self-confidence, and motivation.

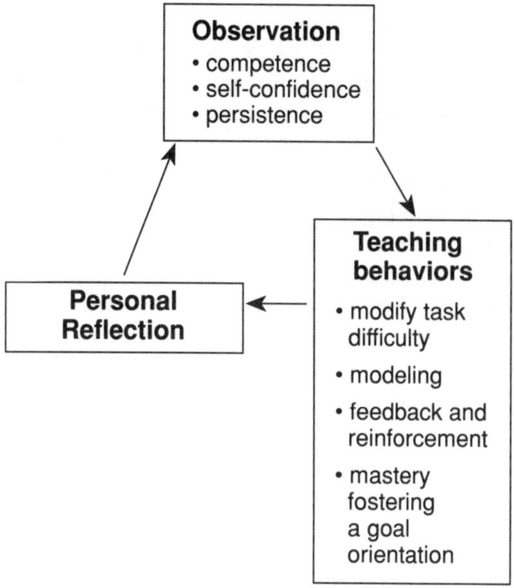

Figure 3.3 The psychological methods model describes the interrelationships among observation, teacher behavior, and personal reflection.

The skill development model highlights the specific skill components for which instructional guidelines should be established. The consultant, through coach and parent education workshops, can systematically provide information on methods for positively influencing competence, self-confidence, and intrinsic motivation in the youth-sport setting. Another schematic, which I will call the psychological methods model (see Figure 3.3), identifies the essential skills of observation, teacher (instructional) behavior, and personal reflection for effecting changes in skill competence and psychological development of youth (Barrett, 1977). This model describes the process by which coaches and parents can effectively promote the development of an intrinsically motivated child in sport, primarily through the use of specific strategies designed to focus the child's efforts on mastery attempts for moderately difficult tasks and enhance perceptions of competence and performance control. For intervention strategies to be successful, coaches and parents must be made aware of or observe for competence, self-confidence, and persistence, respond with appropriate instructional behaviors, and personally reflect or evaluate whether the method chosen to implement change achieved its purpose.

Observation Skills

Careful observation of what is going on in the learning environment is the critical first step to initiating behavioral change in the youth-sport setting. Coaches and parents must realize that they need to purposefully and systematically search for verbal and nonverbal behaviors that convey information about children's levels of competence, self-confidence, and persistence behaviors. Competence pertains to both the child's actual skill capabilities in meeting certain task demands of a sport and the child's knowledge base related to declarative (facts), procedural (rules), and conditional (when to apply facts and rules) features of successful sport execution. The actual demands or challenges of the sport situation are also important in being able to accurately assess actual competence levels. Assessment methods that outline accurate sport techniques and strategies can be used to determine children's demonstration of competence.

Self-confidence refers to perceptions of competence and performance control manifested by the performer in relation to task demands. Parents and coaches can infer high levels of confidence when children verbalize a positive attitude toward participation, convey optimism about learning a sport skill, approach opportunities for trying challenging skills, demonstrate effort and persistence while struggling to approximate proper skill technique, and make personally controllable attributions, such as effort or incorrect strategy for unsuccessful performances. In contrast, children with low levels of self-confidence typically manifest avoidance behaviors, give up easily when trying to learn new skills, set unrealistic performance standards (too low or too high), and adopt strategies to avoid the demonstration of low ability (e.g., make excuses).

Self-confidence in executing sport skills might also be considered in relation to anticipated positive or negative sensations that might be experienced. These movement sensations include effects such as the physical contact in taking a charge in basketball, the disorienting vertigo when performing a flip on the trampoline, and the tension of entering a cold swimming pool. Behavioral manifestations of expected sensory effects can provide coaches and parents with indices of self-confidence in youngsters. For example, the eagerness of trying new physical skills and strategies, seeking out repetitive practice opportunities, and positive affect in the form of excitement and curiosity might indicate positive sensory anticipation and high self-confidence. In contrast, hesitation or avoidance of skill patterns, inappropriate fixation or attention to single elements in the performance environment (e.g., the trampoline bed), extraneous or protective movements, and facial expressions of uncertainty and fear might exemplify negative sensory perceptions and low self-confidence.

Observation of persistence behaviors is also critical for determining children's levels of self-confidence and motivation and thus the appropriate selection of intervention methods. The element of persistence is one of the prime indices of mastery or performance-outcome motivational orientations. Thus accurate determination of this psychological characteristic in children will convey important information about underlying cognitions and perceptions. Siedentop (cited in Bressan & Weiss, 1982) suggested that high levels of persistence can be inferred when children maintain their efforts on learning and performing skills under the following conditions: (a) instruction comes from indirect sources (e.g., videotape, workout sheet) rather than directly from the coach; (b) the athlete is not under direct coach supervision (e.g., coach is working one-on-one with another athlete); (c) athletes are willing to work toward deferred rather than immediate rewards (e.g., refining a technique or strategy rather than reverting to an old habit that usually results in successful outcomes); and (d) athletes continue to work toward skill mastery despite the frustrations and setbacks incurred from unsuccessful performance.

Coaches, parents, and consultants must be able to identify by observation behavioral indicators of competence, self-confidence, and persistence as outlined in this section. These observations provide a baseline from which the practitioner can establish levels of positive or negative physical skills (e.g., sport ability) and psychological skills (e.g., perceptions of competence, locus of control) in children. Once competence, confidence, and motivation levels can be ascertained, recommendations for implementing psychological methods for enhancing these skills can be made. These recommendations target instructional behaviors on the part of coaches and parents that are consistent with theoretical notions of developing intrinsic motivation.

Instructional Behaviors

The skill development model can be set into motion by first targeting changes in physical competence to meet skill challenges. According to developmental motivation theories and research, performance accomplishments based on mastery attempts are critical to forming positive self-perceptions and subsequent motivation. Harter, Nicholls, and Dweck concur that successful performance at moderately difficult or "optimal" challenges has the greatest chance of heightening perceptions of competence, perceptions of performance control, and intrinsic motivation. Consequently, consultants should facilitate coaches and parents in modifying the task difficulty for the purpose of challenging young learners at a level that is difficult but attainable. I like to view this concept of optimal challenges and modifying task difficulty as fitting the activity to the child, not the child to the activity.

Modifying Task Difficulty. To optimally challenge child athletes one must be able to carefully analyze what physical skill elements are necessary for successful performance. For example, coaches need to outline developmental progressions for each sport skill, so that the most simple tasks precede and transfer to more difficult executions. Learning to perform a dive from the side of the pool, for example, requires a progression of teaching steps to maximize the probability of performance success, enhanced self-confidence, and continued efforts to attain the skill. USA Wrestling developed the "Seven Basic Skills" (proper execution of body position, mobility, changing levels, penetration, lifting, back step, and back arch), where each skill depends on proficiently learning the skill preceding it. Other strategies for modifying task difficulty include providing physical guidance under conditions where athletes will not attempt the skill (e.g., a new trick in gymnastics), physical prompts (e.g., spotting belt), and physical aids (e.g., sliding pads for baseball; volleyball spike-it). It is important that use of these external aids is gradually eliminated so that athletes are performing the skill on their own and can attribute performance success to their own ability and effort.

The modifications of equipment, facilities, and rules to match the developmental capabilities of athletes also comprise ways of modifying task difficulty. For example, an 8-ft (2.4-m) rather than 10-ft (3.0-m) basketball goal, a Size 4 soccer ball, an "incrediball" rather than a hardball, and narrower and shorter fields increase opportunities for children to practice specific skills, receive informational feedback, and be reinforced for positive performances. Modifying task difficulty combined with ample practice opportunities in a positive social climate will enhance children's chances of increasing their competence in meeting skill challenges and thus positively influence self-perceptions and motivation.

Instructional behaviors can also directly target the area on the skill development model depicting self-confidence, which includes such characteristics as perceived competence, perceived control, and attributions for performance. Educational support strategies refer to those behaviors that can modify the performer's perceptions of the challenge inherent in the movement situation or their feelings of confidence about their chances for success (Bressan & Weiss, 1982). According to motivational theory and research, variables that directly or indirectly influence perceptions of competence and self-determination in the sport setting include modeling; feedback and reinforcement by adults and peers; and the nature of the climate (mastery or performance outcome). Each of these influential variables infer prescriptions for intervention methods in the youth competitive environment.

Modeling. *Modeling* refers to the cognitive, affective, and behavioral changes that occur as a result of observing adults and peers, whereas *models* are persons whose behaviors, verbalizations, and nonverbal expressions serve as cues for subsequent modeling (Schunk, 1989). Thus modeling can serve both an informational and a motivational function, and these functions have been strongly supported in the sport psychology and motor behavior literatures (McCullagh, Weiss, & Ross, 1989; Weiss, Ebbeck, & Wiese-Bjornstal, 1993). Adults can affect children's self-perceptions of ability through verbal (e.g., positive self-talk) and nonverbal (e.g., behaving calmly in a tight situation) behaviors that denote confidence and individual control in the sport setting. More importantly, peer modeling strategies have been found to be highly successful in affecting self-confidence and motivation in observers (Schunk & Hanson, 1985; Schunk, Hanson, & Cox, 1987). For example, same-age, or same-gender, or same-age-and-gender peers represent similarity between the model and observer, thus maximizing attention and motivation of learners. Similar models are likely to invoke the perception that "if she (he) can do it, so can I," and encourage mastery attempts. Coping models initially verbalize and demonstrate the same fears and hesitations of observers but gradually overcome uncertainties and perform the skill successfully. Coping models can influence self-confidence and motivation through both an informational function, conveying strategies for overcoming fears and performing successfully, and a motivational function, by invoking perceived similarity and bonding between observer and model. Thus coaches can be taught how to be aware of their own modeling behaviors as well as how to use teammates as effective models for children low in self-confidence for learning certain athletic skills.

Feedback and Reinforcement. Feedback and reinforcement by adults and peers provide salient sources of information to children and adolescents about their abilities. Younger children (under age 10) primarily rely on adult feedback and evaluation, while preference for peer comparison and evaluation becomes predominant from ages 10 to 14. Lastly, use of social comparison sources decline and preference for self-referenced criteria emerge among 14- to 18-year-old adolescents. Although preferred sources of information show developmental trends, it is important to remember that individual differences in age level also exist. This was seen in the study by Horn and Weiss (1991) where children between ages 8 and 13 who were low and inaccurate in their estimations of ability indicated preference for the use of peer comparison and evaluation. It is also important to remember that although one or more sources might be preferred by youngsters of particular age levels, many other sources are also available and used to some extent by children and adolescents. Based on these findings, then, consultants need to educate coaches and parents about the importance of using contingent and appropriate feedback in response to children's performance successes and errors as well as the need to de-emphasize the frequent use of peer comparison during the middle childhood years. That is, because children are prone to stacking up their skills against those of similar age or gender, it can be easy for them to fall into a rut of only defining success in peer-comparison terms. Adults can facilitate positive self-perceptions and motivation in youngsters by emphasizing improvement in personal performance capabilities rather than outcome-related goals.

Horn (1987) recommends three major guiding principles for developing positive self-perceptions in young athletes through coach and parental communication. These are (a) contingency and quality of praise and criticism; (b) frequency and contingency of skill-relevant feedback; and (c) appropriate attributional feedback for performance outcomes. These principles are strongly supported by intervention and correlational research in both the academic and sport psychology literatures (see Horn, 1987; Horn & Lox, 1993; Schunk, 1989). More specifically, contingent praise provides children with information about their competence, the performance standard they are expected to reach, and the criteria (i.e., winning or skill mastery) by which their competence will be evaluated (Horn, 1987). Appropriate use of praise means providing reinforcement in proportion to the difficulty of the skill attained. If children succeed at a simple task or demonstrate only mediocre performance, excessive praise for these behaviors might convey negative information and expectations. It is not the quantity of positive reinforcement that makes a difference, but rather the quality of the content in terms of contingency and appropriateness.

Another principle, providing appropriate skill-relevant feedback, is a crucial one for influencing perceptions of competence and performance control in children. In the area of competitive sport, the opportunities for committing skill errors are numerous and have the potential for being negatively evaluated by young athletes as indicants of low ability. However, research in the academic domain consistently shows that when unsuccessful performances are viewed as temporary setbacks or a natural part of the learning process by teachers and students, then perceptions of performance control are increased and competence perceptions are not negatively affected. More specifically, when coaches and parents respond to children's skill errors with encouragement and corrective instruction, self-perceptions of ability and control are enhanced, and effort and persistence increases.

Lastly, attributional feedback plays a large role in the formation of self-perceptions and motivation. Effort attributions made for performance errors in the sport setting are likely to enhance perceptions of control and motivation, because effort is usually a temporary quality and one that is under the young athlete's control. However, it is important to note that children must perceive that they have the requisite skills to eventually achieve success; otherwise, greater effort will not be perceived as effective. To do this, coaches and parents can make effort attributions for unsuccessful performance and combine them with instruction on how to modify the skill technique on the next attempt. Age differences in the capacity to distinguish ability and effort as causes of performance outcomes must also be considered. Young children who hold an undifferentiated view of the concept of ability might best benefit from effort attributions for success, whereas ability attributions for success might likely be more credible and effective for older children and adolescents.

Fostering a Mastery-Goal Orientation. Fostering a mastery-goal orientation is another educational support strategy that can be employed to positively influence psychological development. According to achievement-goal theories, children are more likely to develop self-confidence, positive affect, effort attributions for performance failures, intrinsic task interest, and persistence when they adopt a mastery- or learning-goal orientation to participation rather than a performance-outcome goal orientation. The central focus of a mastery-goal orientation is on learning and developing skills, and information about competence is primarily self-referenced. The child asks questions such as, How can I get better than I was before? and What strategies will help me improve from my unsuccessful performance? The performance-outcome goal orientation is concerned with social comparison criteria as the main indicant of achievement (Did I win? Was my performance better than the rest of the class?). In the setting of competitive sport, it is difficult to avoid at least some orientation toward performance goals, with emphases on competing against others and striving toward the goal of winning. But Ames (1986; 1992; Ames & Archer, 1988) suggests that coaches and parents can learn to stem the tide of a highly competitive emphasis and foster a mastery-goal orientation in their young athletes.

One strategy for fostering a mastery-goal orientation is an emphasis on individualistic, rather than competitive, reward structures. Ames (1986) defines a competitive-goal structure as one in which athletes work against each other for a reward or recognition (e.g., coach's praise, starter role), whereas an individualistic-goal structure is one where athletes work toward independent goals (e.g., personal skill improvement, attainment of a technique). Ames contends that goal structures provide performance information and influence attributions, cognitive strategies, and affective outcomes. More specifically, a competitive-goal structure invokes the use of social-comparison criteria to evaluate ability and encourages an emphasis on the achievement outcome (e.g., winning). Attributions for failure revolve around inadequate ability, resulting in negative affect and a decline in motivation. An individualistic-goal structure is likely to invoke the use of self-referenced information for judging ability (e.g., effort, improvement) and encourages an emphasis on the process of learning skills. Effort attributions for unsuccessful performances predominate, resulting in perceptions of control and motivation to persist on the part of the athlete.

Despite the obvious benefits for employing individualistic-goal structures to influence psychosocial development, competitive sport by its nature maximizes the likelihood of invoking a competitive-goal structure, where winning and being number one are highly valued. However, competitive-goal structures give added salience to the natural use of peer comparison cues while decreasing the salience of self-referenced cues. If praise and criticism for children's performance are given primarily for the outcome of an event or competition, young athletes are likely to adopt peer comparison and evaluation as a primary source of judging ability. But if adults also praise the quality of performance success, provide corrective instruction in response to performance failures, and encourage the use of effort attributions, then children also learn to use internal sources such as self-improvement, degree of effort, and quality of skill technique to judge their competence.

Ames and Archer (1987) found that mothers' beliefs about the role of school learning could be classified as mastery- or performance-oriented, and these orientations were related to children's beliefs about the role of ability and effort in academic competence. Thus significant adults in the sport setting can help balance the child's motivational or goal perspective by emphasizing individualistic-goal structures in the context of competitive youth sport.

Similar to the notion of goal structures is the nature of the motivational or psychological climate of the classroom (Ames, 1992; Ames & Archer, 1988). Athletic "classrooms" are the gymnasiums, natatoriums, and the fields where daily practices and competitive events are held—where learning takes place and performance is demonstrated. According to Ames, there should be a positive relationship between a mastery climate and positive motivational characteristics (e.g., attributions, intrinsic task interest, persistence). Ames and Archer (1988) tested this notion by examining children's perceptions of classroom climate in relation to a number of motivational indicators. They defined a mastery-goal climate as one in which success is defined as improvement or progress (versus high grades and high normative performance): Value was placed on effort and learning; the teacher was oriented toward how students were learning (versus performing); errors were viewed as part of the learning process; and evaluation criteria were focused on absolute standards or individual progress (versus normative standards). Results revealed that students who perceived mastery goals as salient in their classroom preferred challenging tasks, had a more positive attitude toward the class, and had a stronger belief that success follows from one's effort. Students who perceived performance-goal orientations in their classroom focused on their normative ability, evaluated their ability negatively, and attributed failure to lack of ability. Thus adoption of a motivational climate that focuses on learning, improvement, and individual goal attainment is more likely to result in adaptive motivational patterns on the part of athletes than would emphasis on normative criteria for determining one's level of sport ability.

Personal Reflection

The selection of particular instructional strategies to influence changes in competence, self-confidence, and motivation included task modification, modeling, contingent feedback and reinforcement, effort attributions for failure, and emphasizing a mastery motivational climate. These methods require that consultants, coaches, and parents subsequently engage in personal reflection. Personal reflection entails the judgment and monitoring of the effectiveness of one's teaching or intervention methods (Barrett, 1977). That is, it requires that change agents actively compare what is happening in the learning environment with what was intended by the particular psychological method of intervention. Did the use of contingent feedback and reinforcement result in higher competence perceptions and continued motivation? Did a coping model effectively reduce anxiety induced from anticipated negative sensory experiences and motivate the learner to attempt the skill? Did an emphasis on self-referenced criteria to judge competence influence perceptions of performance control? In sum, personal reflection completes the psychological-methods-model cycle by comparing whether interventions used in response to observations about competence, self-perceptions, and motivation resulted in positive changes.

Individual Control Strategies

Consistent with a focus on developing mastery-oriented young athletes, the emphasis of this section is on identifying strategies that will help children and adolescents in competitive sport become self-regulated learners (see Zimmerman & Schunk, 1989). According to Schunk (1989), self-regulated learning occurs from children's self-generated behaviors that are systematically designed to maximize attainment of their goals. Thus children are active agents in their choice, control, and achievement of specific goals. Children who are effective in using self-regulation strategies to guide motivated behavior are characterized by favorable self-perceptions, high perceived performance control, accurate estimation of their abilities, steady progression toward self-set goals, and a tendency to thrive under a cooperative leadership style (McCombs, 1989; Schunk, 1989). The combined knowledge from motivational theory and the empirical research on self-regulated learning lends itself nicely to the view that consultants can work directly with young athletes on developing self-regulation skills.

Self-regulated learning is comprised of three subprocesses: self-observation, self-judgment, and self-reaction (Bandura, 1986), which are highlighted in Table 3.2. Self-observation entails monitoring one's behaviors regularly and proximally through some means of self-recording. Self-observation serves both an information function by showing progression toward goals and a motivational function by encouraging behavior change as a function of increased awareness through behavioral recording. Self-judgment is a process where learners compare present

Table 3.2 Components of Self-Regulated Learning

Component	Description	Acquisition strategy (for all 3 components)
Self-observation	• Monitors behaviors • Shows progress toward goals and encourages behavior change through increased awareness	Modeling Attributional feedback Social comparison
Self-judgment	• Compares present performance level with desired level	Reward contingencies Goal setting
Self-reaction	• Positive or negative evaluations of progress toward goals	Self-monitoring progress Strategy training Self-instructional talk Attribution retraining Anxiety management

performance level with desired goals. This process can be influenced by the types of goals adopted (e.g., mastery versus performance outcome); specificity, task difficulty, and proximity of goals; the importance of goal attainment; and attributions made for one's performance outcomes. Lastly, self-reaction refers to positive or negative evaluations concerning progress toward goal attainment. Positive evaluations of acceptable progress raise self-perceptions and motivation, whereas negative evaluations need not deter motivation if people believe themselves capable of improving in the future. Self-reaction can include evaluations from sources of information provided by self-reinforcement or external rewards and feedback.

Schunk (1989) provides a comprehensive literature review on the development and acquisition of these self-regulatory skills. Interventions include social influences such as modeling (e.g., peer models, coping models), attributional feedback, social comparison information from similar others, and reward contingencies. These methods were discussed previously in conjunction with educating coaches and parents on the content and quality of their communication with young athletes. Consultants working in the competitive youth sport system can employ these strategies one-on-one with athletes to help develop self-regulatory skills and subsequently enhance self-perceptions and motivation. (Because these topics were discussed on pages 57-62, they will not be repeated here.)

Other intervention techniques for developing self-observation, self-judgment, and self-reaction skills include athlete-centered or control strategies such as self-monitoring progress, goal setting, and strategy training. Strategy training can include such areas as self-instructional talk, attribution retraining, and anxiety-management skills. Goal-setting skills have been discussed extensively in the academic, industrial, and sport psychology literatures (Gould, 1986; Locke & Latham, 1990) and emphasize the importance of setting specific and measurable, moderately challenging, mastery rather than performance, and short- and long-term goals. Developmental considerations in the use of goal setting center on children's accuracy in making self-ability judgments and thus their ability to determine if progress is being made. As seen in developmental research, younger children tend to be higher in perceived competence and less accurate than older children and adolescents. Thus it becomes imperative for consultants and coaches to provide accurate feedback concerning children's progress toward skill-learning goals.

Self-instructional talk and attribution retraining go hand in hand because of their emphasis on modifying cognitions and thus influencing performance and motivation. Self-instructional talk has been primarily examined through the use of strategy verbalizations by children in attempting to achieve goals. These strategy verbalizations often take the initial form of overt self-talk, then proceed to faded and finally covert self-instruction. Considerable research by Schunk (1989) has shown that strategy verbalization skills enhance self-efficacy, performance, and ability attributions for success. Attribution retraining is a strategy recommended and used by Dweck (1986; Dweck & Elliott, 1983) to encourage children with maladaptive behavior patterns to view performance failures in a different light. Specifically, this technique involves training children to make effort—rather than ability—attributions for failure, and thus come to see future performance as changeable and under their personal control. Dweck has found that attribution retraining has positively influenced children's persistence on challenging tasks, in comparison merely to guaranteeing success experiences and not providing opportunities for dealing with failure.

Lastly, young athletes can be taught to monitor cognitive appraisals and physiological arousal before competition and to employ anxiety-management skills. These skills include progressive and cognitive relaxation techniques, mental imagery, task- or strategy-oriented rather than worry-oriented self-talk, mastery rather than outcome goals for competitive events, and general coping skills, such as planned alternative strategies in the case of a sudden change of events (e.g., weather, injuries). Again, developmental characteristics that might differentiate younger and older children and adolescents should be taken into account. For example, Ballinger and Heine (1991) recommend that relaxation scripts for children be modified to be interesting, meaningful, and conveyed in understandable language.

INTERVENTION POSSIBILITIES FOR LAURA, RAUL, AND JULIA

A review of the developmental psychology literature reveals that numerous factors directly or indirectly influence self-perceptions and motivation in the young athlete. These factors include cognitive-developmental level, perceptions of success, feedback and reinforcement from significant adults and peers, adoption of a mastery- or performance-outcome-goal orientation, and preference for internal or external criteria for judging competence levels. As a reminder, self-perceptions include the athlete's self-confidence, perceptions of competence, and perceptions of performance control, whereas motivation reflects choice, effort, and persistence behaviors exhibited in the pursuit of competitive sport goals. Taking a closer look at the developmental process of self-perceptions and motivation in each of our case studies will help us understand what dynamics were taking place and decide which intervention strategies were or could have been successfully employed.

Laura

Laura's 6-year participation in rhythmic gymnastics indicates a high level of commitment to the sport. Several developmental and social factors, however, had a bearing on Laura's changed attitude and her eventual decision to withdraw from elite competition. Besides the obvious biological and physical changes affecting her performance of well-learned gymnastic tricks, Laura's cognitive maturity was reflected by changes in the salience of certain dimensions of self-esteem. In particular, physical appearance and close friendships intensify in importance during the adolescent years. For Laura, body changes caused by sexual development, and affective outcomes based on hormonal changes strongly influenced her perceptions of her physical appearance. These perceptions dramatically declined at this point in her life, which led to behaviors such as protecting evaluation of her body through the use of oversized T-shirts and constrained movements during athletic performance.

Anticipation of high-school academic demands and the potential distancing of close friendships due to excessive time demands of gymnastics practice were also influential factors in Laura's negative self-image. These changes in self-perceptions of ability, in combination with the competitive reward structure and the performance-goal climate of the gym contributed to low perceptions of performance control for Laura. Positive social support from her parents and brother as well as her school friends provided the impetus for finally deciding to call it quits after 6 years of committed participation. Although Laura ended up dropping out of highly competitive rhythmic gymnastics, she continued to be physically active, pursued ballet more seriously, and took advantage of every opportunity to cheer her former teammates on during subsequent competitions.

Possible intervention strategies that could have been used to sustain Laura's level of commitment and enjoyment of the sport would include both Laura and her coach. Laura would have benefited by learning about the interacting influence of biological, physical, and psychological factors on performance. Her physical growth and development took her by surprise, and she was never quite sure what was going on with her body, her emotions, and her perceptions of others' evaluations of her physical appearance. Additionally, Laura probably would have been a successful student of self-regulatory skills, especially in the modification of her goals based on her growth and development, anxiety-management skills, and attribution retraining. Retraining her attributions of low ability for unsuccessful performances to personally controllable reasons, such as inadequate practice time or poor strategy selection, would have helped her adapt more realistically to the newly defined internal demands being made on her.

The coach would have benefited by learning from a sport psychology consultant about the multidisciplinary nature of performance changes. This would have helped in the coach's handling of younger girls who would eventually go through the same process as Laura. The coach also needed to learn to become more aware of her reinforcement patterns and to focus on rewarding effort and technique in defining more of a mastery orientation, rather than criticizing lapses in performance and emphasizing skill errors as failures attributable to low ability. Lastly, the coach could have modified the climate of the gym so that athletes felt more comfortable in performing to the best of their ability through maximal effort and persistence, thereby contributing to the development of athletes' mastery motivation.

Raul

Raul was a lucky boy—social and individual control factors positively influenced his motivational orientation, self-perceptions, and sport-achievement levels. First, Raul's social support network, including peers, parents, and coach, provided contingent and appropriate praise for his performances, encouraged his efforts to try wrestling, and employed effective modeling techniques to influence Raul's perceptions of himself as a wrestler. Raul was a late-maturing boy, which accounted for his small size, but his coach had educational training and recognized this individual difference factor and so advised Raul accordingly. Wrestling provided the perfect optimal challenge for Raul—he could be matched in size with other athletes of similar ability and experience. Raul was also fortunate to have participated in athletic environments that encouraged an individualistic-reward structure and a mastery motivational climate. All his coaches at the elementary, middle-school, and high-school levels encouraged the use of self-referenced criteria to judge competence, focused on learning and effort goals, and viewed unsuccessful performances as cues for incorporating new strategies rather than as failures. Lastly, these positive social influences plus a focus on a mastery orientation helped Raul develop into a self-regulated learner, which maximized his self-perceptions of competence and performance control and his motivation to continue participating at moderately challenging levels. Raul's high level of intrinsic motivation guided him to influence others as he had been when he was a youngster; and I hope that his modeling behaviors, positive attitude, and mastery-goal orientation will have the same positive effect on other youngsters.

Julia

The case of Julia is troubling. Neither her social environment nor her own individual skills provided her with opportunities for positively affecting self-perceptions, motivation, and participation in gymnastics. The competitive-reward structure and performance-goal climate of the gym were not conducive to feelings of confidence, control, or intrinsic motivation. The coaches emphasized normative criteria for judging competence, which together with the salience of peer comparison and evaluation common to her age group caused undue levels of anxiety.

The coaches' use of a negative approach to skill learning included constant criticism for skill errors, nonreinforcement for improvements in technique, and frequent disapproval for any off-task behavior in the gym (e.g., talking with friends). As her skill levels improved, the environment did not offer Julia as much fun and enjoyment as it once had. Peer modeling of the labels *quitter* and *loser* had a strong impact on Julia, and this influence from her peers as well as the fact that her teammates were her closest friends made it especially difficult for her to decide to quit. Making matters worse was Julia's perception that she would be letting her parents down if she no longer continued.

All of these factors, combined with her recent injury, negatively affected her perceptions of control, affect, and competence. All were in the negative direction. Julia might be considered what Dweck called helpless-oriented: being performance-goal-oriented, using ability attributions for performance errors, avoiding optimal challenges, and lacking persistence at difficult skills. Her conscious and deliberate attempt to injure herself so that she could leave gymnastics without being called a loser was an extreme action that would have been unnecessary had appropriate intervention occurred.

A sport psychology consultant asked to intervene in this situation would need to proceed on many levels. Julia's support system needed attention and training. Her coaches and parents were, directly and indirectly, negatively influencing her self-perceptions and motivation. They needed to be taught how to nurture a mastery-goal orientation and an emphasis on self-referenced criteria for judging competence levels. Her coaches especially needed intense training on reward contingencies, attributional feedback, and methods of keeping practices fun and enjoyable for young children. Julia could benefit from self-regulatory skills to positively influence the development of self-perceptions and a learning-goal orientation. These would include attribution retraining, realistic goal setting, anxiety management techniques, and strategy verbalizations. Julia was in need of constructive strategies for controlling her own behaviors and performance as well as major changes in her social environment. When children no longer feel they can honestly participate at a level they are capable of because of anticipated disapproval, punishment, negative sensory anticipation, and emphasis on normative criteria, they have no choice but to withdraw. Julia had long ago withdrawn psychologically . . . it was withdrawing herself physically from her sport that she found difficult. She eventually figured out how to do it.

CONCLUSION

Children and adolescents participate in sport for reasons related to developing competence, affirming friendships, enhancing physical fitness, and experiencing fun. I have described a developmental framework of psychosocial growth in children and youth that includes development of positive affect, perceptions of physical competence and peer acceptance, perceptions of performance control, and intrinsic motivation. Empirical research demonstrates that cognitive-developmental differences exist in self-perceptions, that significant adults and peers strongly impact the psychological development of youngsters, and that qualitative differences in motivated behavior are evident based upon the adoption of a mastery- or performance-outcome-goal orientation. With an understanding of the processes involved in developing intrinsically motivated children in sport, I considered many environmental- and individual-control strategies for effecting positive changes in psychological skills. These psychological methods, when made available to coaches, parents, and young athletes, have the potential for developing self-regulated learners who feel in control of their performance outcomes, convey favorable perceptions of their ability, display a positive attitude toward participation in sport, seek optimal challenges in striving for mastery-oriented goals, and show persistence in their pursuit of learning skills and demonstrating competence.

REFERENCES

Ames, C. (1986). Conceptions of motivation within competitive and noncompetitive goal structures. In R. Schwarzer (Ed.), *Self-related cognitions in anxiety and motivation* (pp. 229-245). Hillsdale, NJ: Erlbaum.

Ames, C. (1992). The relationship of achievement goals to motivation in classroom settings. In G.C. Roberts (Ed.), *Motivation in sport and exercise* (pp. 161-176). Champaign, IL: Human Kinetics.

Ames, C., & Archer, J. (1987). Mothers' beliefs about the role of ability and effort in school learning. *Journal of Educational Psychology*, **79**, 409-414.

Ames, C., & Archer, J. (1988). Achievement goals in the classroom: Students' learning strategies and motivation process. *Journal of Educational Psychology*, **80**, 260-267.

Ballinger, D.A., & Heine, P.L. (1991). Relaxation training for children: A script. *Journal of Physical Education, Recreation, and Dance*, **62**(2), 67-69.

Bandura, A. (1986). *Social foundations of thought and action: A social cognitive theory*. Englewood Cliffs, NJ: Prentice Hall.

Barrett, K. (1977). Studying teaching: A means for becoming a more effective teacher. In B. Logsdon, K. Barrett, H. Ammons, M. Broer, L. Halvorson, R. McGee, & M. Roberton (Eds.), *Physical education for children* (pp. 249-287). Philadelphia: Lea & Febiger.

Black, S.J., & Weiss, M.R. (1992). The relationship among perceived coaching behaviors, perceptions of ability, and motivation in competitive age-group swimmers. *Journal of Sport and Exercise Psychology*, **14**, 309-325.

Bressan, E.S., & Weiss, M.R. (1982). A theory of instruction for developing competence, self-confidence and persistence in physical education. *Journal of Teaching Physical Education*, **2**, 38-47.

Duda, J.L. (1985). Goals and achievement orientations of Anglo- and Mexican-American adolescents in sport and the classroom. *International Journal of Intercultural Relations*, **9**, 131-155.

Duda, J.L. (1986). Perceptions of sport success and failure among white, black, and Hispanic adolescents. In J. Watkins, T. Reilly, & L. Burwitz (Eds.), *Sport science* (pp. 214-222). London: E. & F.N. Spon.

Duda, J.L. (1987). Toward a developmental theory of motivation in sport. *Journal of Sport Psychology*, **9**, 130-145.

Duda, J.L. (1992). Motivation in sport settings: A goal perspective approach. In G. Roberts (Ed.), *Motivation in sport and exercise* (pp. 57-91). Champaign, IL: Human Kinetics.

Dweck, C.S. (1986). Motivational processes affecting learning. *American Psychologist*, **41**, 1040-1048.

Dweck, C.S., & Elliott, E.S. (1983). Achievement motivation. In E.M. Hetherington (Ed.), *Socialization, personality, and social development* (pp. 643-691). New York: Wiley.

Elliott, E.S., & Dweck, C.S. (1988). Goals: An approach to motivation and achievement. *Journal of Personality and Social Psychology*, **54**, 5-12.

Gould, D. (1986). Goal setting for peak performance. In J.M. Williams (Ed.), *Applied sport psychology: Personal growth to peak performance* (pp. 133-148). Palo Alto, CA: Mayfield.

Gould, D., & Petlichkoff, L.M. (1988). Participation motivation and attrition in young athletes. In F. Smoll, R. Magill, & M. Ash (Eds.), *Children in sport* (3rd ed.) (pp. 161-178). Champaign, IL: Human Kinetics.

Harter, S. (1978). Effectance motivation reconsidered. *Human Development*, **21**, 34-64.

Harter, S. (1981). A model of intrinsic mastery motivation in children: Individual differences and developmental change. In W.A. Collins (Ed.), *Minnesota Symposium on Child Psychology: Vol. 14* (pp. 215-255). Hillsdale, NJ: Erlbaum.

Horn, T.S. (1985). Coaches' feedback and changes in children's perceptions of their physical competence. *Journal of Educational Psychology*, **77**, 174-186.

Horn, T.S. (1987). The influence of teacher-coach behavior on the psychological development of children. In D. Gould & M.R. Weiss (Eds.), *Advances in pediatric sport sciences: Vol. 2. Behavioral issues* (pp. 121-142). Champaign, IL: Human Kinetics.

Horn, T.S. (1991, October). *Sources of information underlying personal competence judgments in high school athletes*. Paper presented at the AAASP Annual Conference, Savannah, GA.

Horn, T.S., & Hasbrook, C.A. (1986). Information components influencing children's perceptions of their physical competence. In M.R. Weiss & D. Gould (Eds.), *Sport for children and youths* (pp. 81-88). Champaign, IL: Human Kinetics.

Horn, T.S., & Hasbrook, C.A. (1987). Psychological characteristics and the criteria children use for self-evaluation. *Journal of Sport Psychology*, **9**, 208-221.

Horn, T.S., & Lox, C. (1993). The self-fulfilling prophecy theory: When coaches' expectations become reality. In J.M. Williams (Ed.), *Applied sport psychology: Personal growth to peak performance* (2nd ed.) (pp. 68-81). Palo Alto, CA: Mayfield.

Horn, T.S., & Weiss, M.R. (1991). A developmental analysis of children's self-ability judgments in the physical domain. *Pediatric Exercise Science*, **3**, 310-326.

Klint, K.A., & Weiss, M.R. (1987). Perceived competence and motives for participating in youth sports: A test of Harter's competence motivation theory. *Journal of Sport Psychology*, **9**, 55-65.

Locke, E.A., & Latham, G. (1990). *A theory of goal setting and task performance*. Englewood Cliffs, NJ: Prentice Hall.

Martens, R. (1986). Youth sports in the USA. In M.R. Weiss & D. Gould (Eds.), *Sport for children and youths* (pp. 27-33). Champaign, IL: Human Kinetics.

McCombs, B.L. (1989). Self-regulated learning and academic achievement: A phenomenological view. In B.J. Zimmerman & D.H. Schunk (Eds.), *Self-regulated learning and academic achievement* (pp. 51-82). New York: Springer-Verlag.

McCullagh, P., Weiss, M.R., & Ross, D. (1989). Modeling considerations in motor skill acquisition and performance: An integrated approach. In K.B. Pandolf (Ed.), *Exercise and sport sciences reviews: Vol. 17* (pp. 475-513). Baltimore: Williams & Wilkins.

Nicholls, J.G. (1984). Achievement motivation: Conceptions of ability, subjective experience, task choice, and performance. *Psychological Review*, **91**, 328-346.

Nicholls, J.G. (1989). *The competitive ethos and democratic education*. Cambridge, MA: Harvard University Press.

Nicholls, J.G., & Miller, A. (1983). The differentiation of the concepts of difficulty and ability. *Child Development*, **54**, 951-959.

Schunk, D.H. (1989). Social cognitive theory and self-regulated learning. In B.J. Zimmerman & D.H. Schunk (Eds.), *Self-regulated learning and academic achievement* (pp. 83-110). New York: Springer-Verlag.

Schunk, D.H., & Hanson, A.R. (1985). Peer models: Influence on children's self-efficacy and achievement. *Journal of Educational Psychology*, **77**, 313-322.

Schunk, D.H., Hanson, A.R., & Cox, P.D. (1987). Peer model attributes and children's achievement behaviors. *Journal of Educational Psychology*, **79**, 54-61.

Vealey, R.S. (1988). Future directions in psychological skills training. *Sport Psychologist*, **2**, 318-336.

Weiss, M.R., Bredemeier, B.J., & Shewchuk, R.M. (1986). The dynamics of perceived competence, perceived control, and motivational orientation in youth sports. In M.R. Weiss & D. Gould (Eds.), *Sport for children and youths* (pp. 89-101). Champaign, IL: Human Kinetics.

Weiss, M.R., & Chaumeton, N. (1992). Motivational orientations in sport. In T.S. Horn (Ed.), *Advances in sport psychology* (pp. 61-99). Champaign, IL: Human Kinetics.

Weiss, M.R., Ebbeck, V., & Wiese-Bjornstal, D.M. (1993). Developmental and psychological factors related to children's observational learning of sport skills. *Pediatric Exercise Science*, **5**, 301-317.

Weiss, M.R., & Horn, T.S. (1990). The relation between children's accuracy estimates of their physical competence and achievement-related characteristics. *Research Quarterly for Exercise and Sport*, **61**, 250-258.

Weiss, M.R., McAuley, E., Ebbeck, V., & Wiese, D.M. (1990). Self-esteem and causal attributions for children's physical and social competence in sport. *Journal of Sport and Exercise Psychology*, **12**, 21-36.

Weiss, M.R., & Petlichkoff, L.M. (1989). Children's motivation for participation in and withdrawal from sport: Identifying the missing links. *Pediatric Exercise Science*, **1**, 195-211.

Wiggins, D.K. (1987). A history of organized play and highly competitive sport for American children. In D. Gould & M.R. Weiss (Eds.), *Advances in pediatric sport sciences: Vol. 2. Behavioral issues* (pp. 1-24). Champaign, IL: Human Kinetics.

Zimmerman, B.J., & Schunk, D.H. (1989). *Self-regulated learning and academic achievement*. New York: Springer-Verlag.

CHAPTER 4

COMPETITIVE RECREATIONAL ATHLETES: A MULTISYSTEMIC MODEL

James P. Whelan, PhD
Andrew W. Meyers, PhD
Charlene Donovan, MA
The University of Memphis

Some people might consider the term *competitive recreational athlete* an oxymoron. Although *competition* connotes intensity and seriousness, *recreation* suggests play, amusement, and relaxation. Such an apparent contradiction might be unsettling. Some people who might be labeled competitive recreational athletes are quite serious about their sports and might have great difficulty thinking about them as play. These people get up early every morning, rain or shine, to run or swim. They are willing to forgo sleep Saturday mornings to travel several hours to a race, a match, a meet, or a game. These are the sort of people who are conversant with air-cushion soles, carbon fiber, Lycra, a sweet spot, or metal woods. Most of these people do not consider themselves duffers or joggers; they do not refer to their sport as play. They think of themselves as athletes—serious, competitive athletes. They value the health benefits of regular exercise, but they love the competitive goals and experience, even though they might be competing primarily against themselves.

However, we would not argue that the term *competitive recreational athlete* should be abandoned. In fact, the original meaning of the word *competition*, from the latin *com petere*, is to seek or search together. The origin of the word *recreation* is the latin word *recreare*, meaning to restore or refresh. This suggests that recreational competition is a process of self-challenge or self-discovery directed toward restoration. The term also serves a valuable descriptive function. Competitive recreational athletes are different from other athletes considered in these chapters. Their sport involvement is what they choose to do with their free time. Although achievement and excellence in their sports might be valued objectives, training and racing must fit into the rest of their lives. These people typically have spouses, and often children, to whom they have responsibilities. They have jobs with supervisors, customers, deadlines, and obligations. Their self-identity is not solely dependent on their status as athletes.

This group also presents heterogeneous backgrounds, with a variety of athletic achievements and aspirations. Some approach their sports with a long history of athletic involvement; others, with little or no involvement. These competitors possess varying degrees of physical talent, and they have varying amounts of time to devote to training. Unlike elite junior national athletes, collegiate athletes, national team members, and professional competitors, these people compete for reasons other than the ability to perform.

Competitive recreational athletes also offer heterogeneous reasons for sport involvement, such as to establish a social support network, manage stress, moderate mood, control body weight, improve physical function, or combat the aging process. Consequently, competitive recreational athletes face a complex balancing task. Free to select among a variety of activities, they choose to train and compete. This decision must be balanced against the demands of family and work, the limitations of their physical skills, and the feasibility of their athletic and personal goals.

It is important to note that this group of athletes is probably the largest classification of athletes in the United States, and nearly every sport boasts a share of loyal participants. The United States Tennis Association (1990) has about 150,000 people currently playing in its adult recreational leagues, and a survey by the National Sporting Goods Association (1990) found that more than 3 million men and women over age 18 consider themselves to be "very frequent" tennis players (playing more than 30 days a year). According to the National Bowling Council (1990), there are 6 million adult men and women league bowlers in the United States, and the National Golf Foundation (1991) reports that about 10% of adult males and 2% of adult females in the United States play golf. The Athletic Congress, the governing body of track and field in the United States, estimated that over 4 million people participate in sanctioned road-running races each year (Honikman & Honikman, 1991). United States Masters Swimming (1991) records indicate that 25,000 people participated in masters swim meets in 1990. The United States Cycling Federation (1990) licensed over 30,000 competitive cyclists in 1990.

Despite the distinctions between these athletes and other classifications of athletes and between these athletes and nonathletes, the differences within the population of competitive recreational athletes appear greater than the differences between this population and others. We are cautious, therefore, not to propose that psychological intervention for competitive recreational athletes must be unique. Knowledge and awareness of sport, athletes, and sport science is necessary to work with any athlete. But the process of creating change does not appear to be population specific. The available meta-analysis reviews of psychotherapy support the notion that the science of behavior change has not evolved to the point that we can identify particular change mechanisms for particular problems (for a review see Lambert, Shapiro, & Bergin, 1986).

Therefore, in this chapter we adopt a holistic personal enhancement model, similar in nature to psychotherapy, to address the complaints of competitive recreational athletes. We would not argue that therapy can be generically applied without consideration of individual uniqueness. We argue instead that sport participation is only one aspect in the lives of athletes. Directing efforts to resolve athletes' problems based on a snapshot of the athletic context might not be the most effective means of creating meaningful resolution of their complaints.

This chapter provides a conceptual framework for psychological intervention efforts with competitive recreational athletes. We begin by describing three competitive recreational athletes, their presenting problems, the complications that make their sport participation difficult, and how or why they chose to seek consultation from a sport psychologist. These athletes are quite similar to individuals we have treated. Some details about these individuals have been altered to protect their identity to accommodate the needs of this chapter. Next, we briefly discuss the literature on psychological skills training interventions, then place it in the broader context of each athlete's life. The interactions among athletic performance, individual dysfunction, family, workplace, and larger social and cultural issues are presented. Then, returning to our cases, we address assessment and intervention issues for our three athletes. In closing, we highlight some ethical issues of working with competitive recreational athletes. (Note that we use the labels *therapist* and *counselor* interchangeably throughout this chapter to refer to any professional who is adequately trained and credentialed to provide psychological services.)

■ *THE CASE OF JULIO* ■

Julio, a 42-year-old tenured associate professor in the computer science department of the local university, has been actively involved in masters swimming since his mid-30s. Recently he started to experience a disruptive amount of precompetition arousal and anxiety. After reading about sport psychology services available at the university's psychology clinic, Julio called and set up an appointment.

He described his problem as "nerves." Over the last year he had become increasingly anxious in the week before each swim meet. He had difficulty focusing on his workouts and often ended them early; he slept and ate poorly; and he regularly found himself distracted from his university responsibilities. The night before a meet was typically sleepless. By the time Julio's primary race (the 200-m backstroke) was called, he would have great difficulty remembering his race plan, and he either went out too fast and died late in the race or went out too slowly and was out of contention by the last 50 m. In the big long-course meet that ended his summer competitive season, Julio was first at the halfway point of the race, but he faded to finish seventh in an eight-man field in a time slower than his best workouts.

Julio started in age-group swimming at age 7, and by junior high he was a budding star. In high school, at 6 ft, 4 in. and 170 lb (193 cm and 77 kg), he continued to improve, and in his senior year he was the 200-m backstroke state champion. These swimming achievements led to heavy recruitment by many colleges, and he chose an Ivy League school. His first problems appeared there.

Julio's parents and his club and high-school coaches had been easygoing. But his college coach seemed incredibly rigid. Practice workouts were more grueling than he had ever experienced, and there seemed no time for fun or camaraderie. Indeed, the coach appeared to foster an atmosphere of competition among team members. Halfway through his freshman season Julio began to experience "nerves" before competition. This led to increasingly poor practices and meet times and eventually to conflicts with the now-disappointed coach. The season ended with a stern warning from the coach that he "better come back tougher next year."

Julio had hoped that returning to his hometown swim club for the summer would energize him, but instead he found little motivation to work hard. Back at school in the fall he dreaded the beginning of regular practices and after just a few anxious weeks, Julio quit the squad. Then followed a 19-year period—through graduate school, his marriage, and his first academic job—where Julio swam only sporadically. Realizing one day that he weighed more than 230 lb (104 kg), Julio decided to start swimming for fitness and weight control.

Gradually, over the next 4-year period, Julio regained his long-lost physical skills. He eventually returned to competition in small local meets, and by age 40 he was approaching some of his best high-school times. At this point, Julio began to realize that he might be nationally competitive in masters age-group swimming. Later that year his "nerves" returned.

His training journal helped to detail the anxiety response. He described the initial physical experience as a "buzz," almost as if his body was perpetually vibrating. Cognitively, Julio tried to focus on winning, but he obsessed about losing after all the hard training and the compromises that he had to make at work and at home. The journal revealed a good deal of guilt about these sacrifices. He feared his university colleagues would soon realize his "lack of commitment" to his job. Similarly, he was concerned that he was not holding up his end of the marital and family relationships. He had come full circle; he was again considering giving up swimming.

Julio spent a good deal of time preparing for competitions. His daily journal detailed his workouts, his physical and emotional state, and other information that might prove valuable to his training and competitive efforts. The training regimen itself typically involved a gradual increase in training intensity followed by a tapering period before important competitions so that he would be both prepared and rested. Julio usually trained for about 2 hr each morning before work and often did some weight work in the afternoons. However, university or family commitments often forced training-schedule changes.

Julio was married to a 37-year-old lawyer, Maria, and they had a 2-year-old son, Ben. Maria's law career was demanding and involved long and irregular hours. She had no athletic involvement, and though she tolerated Julio's swimming, she was not fond of it. Although they had a housekeeper and relatives lived nearby, and although Ben was enrolled in a day-care center, home and child-care duties were often Julio's. Maria attended the second appointment with Julio, and she reported that he was a devoted father and good companion. Though their career and family demands created a good deal of stress, she believed that the marriage was on solid ground. Maria also noted that she and Julio shared a group of friends with whom both enjoyed regularly socializing.

Although Julio was a tenured associate professor, his research career was at a pivotal point. Continued achievement in the academic community required much hard work and he clearly felt this pressure. Fortunately, his annual evaluations were very positive and he believed that his department chair and his peers valued his contribution. Given this relative stability and support from home and work, Julio viewed his current case of "nerves" as limited to competitive swimming.

■ *THE CASE OF SHERRY* ■

Sherry approached the therapist after the monthly meeting of the local bicycle club. Sherry, the 37-year-old manager of a local bank branch, said she was having difficulty getting motivated for the coming racing season and she wanted to talk. At a first appointment, Sherry reported that after several years of increasingly impressive performances and an eventual ranking as a Category II racer, she had hit a plateau during the past season. Although continuing to perform respectably in local races, she had failed to win any regional races and she had not obtained sponsorship. Even at the local level, her performance was somewhat more inconsistent than it had been in several years, and she was experiencing a number of small, nagging injuries.

Sherry reported feeling "distracted" from her racing and training. This was extremely surprising to her because both the camaraderie and the social world that surrounded racing and training as well as the racing itself were "the most enjoyable" parts of her life. She typically met a group of friends from the bike club for a long (3 hr or more) Saturday morning ride each week. Sherry also worked out with some members of this group on Sunday mornings and Tuesdays and Thursdays after work. On other days she usually worked out alone outdoors, weather permitting, or on an indoor trainer at home or at her health club. All told, Sherry spent 18 to 20 hr a week working out and averaged more than 300 mi (483 km) per week on the bike. Several of her riding buddies had commented that her intensity had been off lately. One even suggested that Sherry see a doctor, "or maybe even a shrink." The suggestion bothered her, so she increased her weekly distance and bought a few subliminal motivational tapes. When both her health and her motivation deteriorated further, her friends told her to give a sport psychologist a try.

She reported feeling lethargic and admitted to moments throughout the day of sadness and tears, all without any obvious explanation. She mentioned that she did not really want to talk to someone like a psychologist, but her husband had begun to insist on it. Sherry's husband, Robert, was a hospital executive, and they had two children, Suzan, 8, and Bobby, 11. Although generally positive about the relationship, Sherry offered little to substantiate the benefits of the marriage or the joys of motherhood. She was not sure what she and Robert had in common anymore. She seemed to find the day-to-day work at the bank enjoyable, but seemed unexcited by her future with the organization. She did not see much room for career advancement—and indeed Sherry had no lofty professional aspirations—but she was pleased that her current job gave her adequate time to train.

Sherry described herself as quiet and somewhat shy. She was the younger of two sisters and viewed her birth family as close but not overly affectionate. Her dominant memories of high school and college involved the struggle to keep her grades up and the challenge and pleasures of varsity cross-country and track. Although her athletic career was not distinguished by titles or school records, Sherry lettered in cross-country and track in both high school and college.

She met Robert soon after taking a management-trainee position with the banking corporation, and they were married 18 months later. Bobby was born less than a year later. Sherry had run sporadically after college, but she hoped that a regular regimen of running after her pregnancy would "relieve some of the tension and lethargy" she was feeling. Unfortunately, an overuse knee injury after 3 months cut short this therapeutic effort. Upon recovering she took up cycling and almost immediately became "addicted." In addition to the pleasure she felt out on the road, alone and in the company of other cyclists, she was attracted to the hardware and technology of cycling. She described bicycles in romantic terms, as beautiful, graceful machines that soared almost silently over the road.

Robert joined a subsequent appointment. He too was puzzled by Sherry's recent behavior. Initially positive about the relationship, he became increasingly caustic and bitter as he described their home life. He was resentful about Sherry's cycling "addiction," and though he thought that Sherry was well-meaning, Robert angered as he detailed the burdens of caring for the children while Sherry was "riding around." He reported that over the last two years he had felt increasingly distant from Sherry and that their sex life had "been dropped from the back of the pack." Robert reported that he had even considered taking a job in another city. Sherry did not seem surprised by this information, but the couple had apparently not discussed these issues openly before.

■ *THE CASE OF PETER* ■

Peter, a 51-year-old lawyer and skilled recreational tennis player, was strongly urged to come in to see a therapist by a close friend and fellow lawyer who was concerned about Peter's explosions of temper on the tennis court. At the first meeting Peter noted that he had always engaged in "John McEnroe–like outbursts" on the court. However, during a recent match this escalated into first a verbal battle and eventually a physical confrontation with an opponent.

Peter appeared to realize the inappropriateness of his actions but saw the event as an isolated occurrence. He was more concerned with the effect his loss of emotional control was having on his tennis game. He reported a number of instances, especially in tournament play, where a close call or errant shot had set him off. Typically, after these eruptions Peter was unable to regain his composure, and he very often went on to lose the match. This was happening with increasing frequency over the past 5 years. He had read articles in the popular media on sport psychology and hoped that a sport psychologist could help him develop the skills necessary to handle these stressful moments.

Peter played tennis at least four times a week and often took a lesson from his club pro on the weekends. For years he had jogged to improve his endurance, but he had given this up to concentrate on tennis. Even at age 51 his tennis skills (though not his match performance) were still steadily improving.

A trial attorney for almost 25 years, he described himself as an intensely competitive and terribly proud man. He had grown up in a poor family; the situation at home had been "harsh." His concentration on his studies and later on high-school baseball was as much to buffer a combative relationship with his father and a somewhat distant relationship with his mother as it was for a sense of achievement. But even so, Peter was extremely proud of his accomplishments. He graduated 7th in his class of more than 200, started 3 years on the baseball team, and dated the captain of the cheerleaders. Peter was not gifted enough to play collegiate baseball, but he continued his academic achievement and eventually graduated from a prestigious Eastern law school. He married Ruth soon after completing his clerkship and taking his first job. They have one daughter, Randy, now 24, who lives more than 2,000 mi (3,218 km) away on the West Coast.

Peter described himself at work as "one tough son of a bitch." He seemed to take pride in his role as an intimidator of young lawyers in his firm and opposing attorneys in the courtroom. He argued that the tough guy image is an appropriate role model for his associate lawyers and the proper role in the courtroom on behalf of his clients.

As part of the assessment and before beginning the performance-related anger-management work, the therapist asked Peter to bring Ruth with him. Peter was adamant that this was not necessary and would not help the therapist to understand his athletic performance problems. In fact, he could not remember the last time Ruth had seen him play tennis. Peter missed his next appointment, and the therapist did not see him for approximately 3 months. He then made an appointment after a particularly embarrassing event at his racquet club. During mixed doubles he had shoved an opponent he said was verbally baiting him—a female opponent. He argumentatively justified his actions but admitted that others who witnessed the situation told him that he had seriously overreacted. Indeed, the club's governing board had given him a formal warning.

When the therapist informed him that any further work would require his wife's involvement, he tearfully admitted that he had regularly "lost my temper" with her. Finally, with a great deal of reluctance, he admitted to regular spouse abuse over the two and a half decades of their marriage. This typically involved slapping and pushing her during arguments that could be initiated by relatively innocuous events. Although he denied any drinking or drug problems, Peter drank regularly and heavily in the evenings. With a great deal of hesitancy and emotion, he agreed to bring Ruth to the next meeting.

VIEWING THE PERSON

Sport scientists compete vigorously for research time and opportunities with the rare, and often elusive, elite athlete. Obversely, the laboratories of sport scientists are filled with non-elite and maybe even nonathlete students from introductory psychology and introductory health, physical education, and recreation classes. Unhappily, we know very little about the psychology of the elite athlete. We know much more about how our clinical and educational interventions function with nonathletes or people who engage only infrequently in athletic endeavors (Whelan, Meyers, & Berman, 1989), but we must cope with the problem of generalizing these results to our athlete populations. The availability and intensity of competitive recreational athletes makes them a more promising test sample for our interventions than the population of first-year college students, yet surprisingly little is known about competitive recreational athletes.

Demographics

The population of competitive recreational athletes is extremely varied and for that reason is difficult to describe. However, we do have data on many athlete groups; this helps us develop an image of this citizen competitor. Perhaps the first such population of serious recreational athletes available to sport scientists came from the running boom of the 1970s, following Frank Shorter's 1972 Olympic marathon gold medal. Investigators have examined the demographics, personality characteristics, and psychological skills of these non-elite but often extremely committed runners.

According to data from the statistics division of The Athletic Congress (Honikman & Honikman, 1991), the average serious male runner is 38 years old, whereas the average serious female runner is 35 years old. Masters runners over age 40 are predominantly married, average 2.3 children, and run five times per week for a total of 27 miles (Okwumabua, Meyers, & Santille, 1987). Freischlag (1981), in a study of 55 marathoners, found that marathoners are usually from large families where boys outnumber girls, are typically first-born children, and rarely attribute their sport success to the influence of others. However, Freischlag reported that peers are most important to the runner's athletic achievement. Interestingly, coaches and parents received "neutral" influence ratings.

Meyers and Okwumabua (1985) found that marathon finishing time was related to many training variables, including the number of weeks spent training for the marathon, the runner's best past race performance, and the strength of the runner's self-efficacy, which in itself accounted for more than 40% of the variance in performance outcome.

Data from other studies suggest that these demographics are representative of competitive recreational athletes in many sports. More than half of triathlon participants are married, with 40% falling between ages 30 to 39. Forty-five percent are college graduates earning an average annual income of $50,100. These athletes reported spending approximately 16 hr per week training, and enter three to four triathlons a year (Whelan et al., 1987a, 1987b). More than half of masters swimmers are male (United States Masters Swimming, 1991), and the United States Tennis Association (1990) reports that a majority of the players in its recreational leagues are male. Most male participants are ages 25 to 34, whereas the highest percentage of female participants are ages 35 to 44. These players are also considered frequent participants, playing more than 30 days during a year. Bowling boasts the most equitable split between the sexes; there are approximately 3 million male and 3 million female sanctioned-league bowlers (National Bowling

Council, 1990). A significant majority of these athletes are married (74.6%) and most are ages 18 to 49. Nearly half of these bowlers have annual incomes greater than $35,000 and more than half attended college. A slightly different picture appears among volleyball players. The highest percentage of adult "frequent" volleyball players are age 18 to 34. More than half of these athletes are female; the majority have household annual incomes of $15,000 to $24,999 (Sporting Goods Manufacturers Association, 1990). This fairly low income figure is probably due to the younger age of the sample.

Personality

Ogilvie (1968) argued for the existence of "athletic" personality traits. This work was based on the assumption that athletes possess unique and definable personality attributes. These attributes are different from those of nonathletes, potentially different from one sport to another, and different across athletic skill levels. Some traits seem obvious: traits of endurance, ambition, and aggressiveness. Other traits that Ogilvie saw as characteristic of athletes include organization, dominance, and deference.

The late 1960s also saw Ogilvie and Tutko's (1966) attempt to integrate psychological assessment and personality theory into sport psychology. Their work marked the first contemporary meeting of clinical psychology and the study of athletic performance. Ogilvie and Tutko concentrated on the development of a personality test that they hoped would allow them to predict the performance of athletes. The success of such testing would facilitate athlete selection, coach-player interaction, and the design of training programs. Perhaps the most intense examination of the athlete personality has occurred with marathon runners. Sport scientists have reported that marathoners are typically more introverted, have lower anxiety levels, and better mood profiles than nonrunners (Clitsome & Kostrubala, 1977; Gondola & Tuckman, 1982; Gontang, Clitsome, & Kostrubala, 1977; Morgan & Costill, 1972; Morgan & Pollack, 1977; Silva & Hardy, 1986; Wilson, Morley, & Bird, 1980).

The work of Ogilvie and other sport "personologists" fell victim to the same problems and criticisms that general personality theory was receiving in the 1960s and 1970s. As Mischel (1968) eloquently argued, global personality traits have been poor predictors of behavior. This is in large part due to the failure of early personality theories to consider both situational contributions to behavior and the interaction among those situational demands and the individual behavioral and psychological skills. Those hunting for the athlete personality had returned empty-handed (Mahoney & Meyers, 1989; Meyers, 1980; Morgan, 1980; Rushall, 1972; Silva, 1984).

At the time personality views were foundering, evidence supporting the efficacy of *mental practice* or covert rehearsal on the acquisition and retention of complex motor skills began to appear (Corbin, 1972; Richardson, 1967a, 1967b). In their review, Feltz and Landers (1983) reported that covert rehearsal, compared to no practice, significantly improved skilled motor performance approximately one-half standard deviation. Then in 1972, Suinn applied a multicomponent cognitive-behavioral intervention to sport performance. He found that training in relaxation and imagery skills combined with a behavioral-rehearsal technique improved the race performances of skilled skiers. Based on Suinn's work, imagery-based mental-practice interventions for performance enhancement became more intricate and began to resemble the growing body of cognitively oriented clinical interventions that had come into favor in the 1960s (Bandura, 1969, 1977; Beck, 1976; Meichenbaum, 1985).

Psychological Skills

The movement away from personality-based approaches to athletic performance enhancement has largely adopted a cognitive-behavioral paradigm. Consistent with this learning-based perspective, investigators and practitioners have emphasized the assessment and development of sport-related psychological skills rather than invariant personality traits.

In a study focusing on collegiate racquetball players, Meyers, Cooke, Cullen, and Liles (1979) found that better athletes were more self-confident and possessed a more structured lifestyle. Imagery skills were also better developed in more skilled and successful racquetball players. Not only did more skilled players report images with more clarity than less skilled players, but the more skilled players also had less difficulty controlling the images. Importantly, the better players were also more skillful in dealing with competitive anxiety than were the less skilled players. The more skilled players reported anxiety at the beginning of matches, as did their less-skilled counterparts. The better players also reported a leveling of and eventual decrease in the amount of anxiety as the match progressed, whereas the less skilled players did not experience the same process. The existing evidence has generally supported the notion that successful athletes employ coping skills that positively influence motivation, preparation, arousal management, concentration, and self-confidence (Feltz & Ewing, 1987; Gould, Weiss, & Weinberg, 1981; Hemery, 1986; Mahoney, Gabriel, & Perkins, 1987).

In addition to these psychological-skill differences, sport scientists have also identified cognitive-strategy differences among competitive recreational athletes. In their work with masters runners over 40 years of age, Okwumabua et al. (1987) found that these athletes were more likely to use dissociative cognitive strategies during a race, concentrating on factors other than those associated with running the race. Younger runners were more likely to use associative strategies and to focus on race-related thoughts, such as performance time and pain level. Differences in strategy might be accounted for in part by differing motivations. Older athletes might run for health and social benefits, whereas younger athletes might focus on performance.

Although it is doubtful that competitive recreational athletes possess unique, sport-relevant psychological skills or cognitive strategies, this perspective presents us with both a framework for understanding the performance of these athletes and a model for psychological intervention. If psychological skills are indeed beneficial to the athlete, then programs to enhance those skills should improve performance.

VIEWING THE PERSON IN CONTEXT

We have described a group of adult athletes who must cope with the physical and emotional requirements of their competitive sports. However, competitive recreational athletes do not live in a sport vacuum; they exist in many worlds, all of which make demands on their time and energy. These various environments require a variety of physical, social, and mental skills for successful performance. Careers, marriage, and child rearing as well as larger community demands place heavy responsibilities on these people. They must meet their obligations and still find time for sport without the support systems sometimes available to elite athletes. Given these burdens or challenges, what motivates the competitive recreational athlete to continue to juggle potentially conflicting demands? As suggested in Figure 4.1, a variety

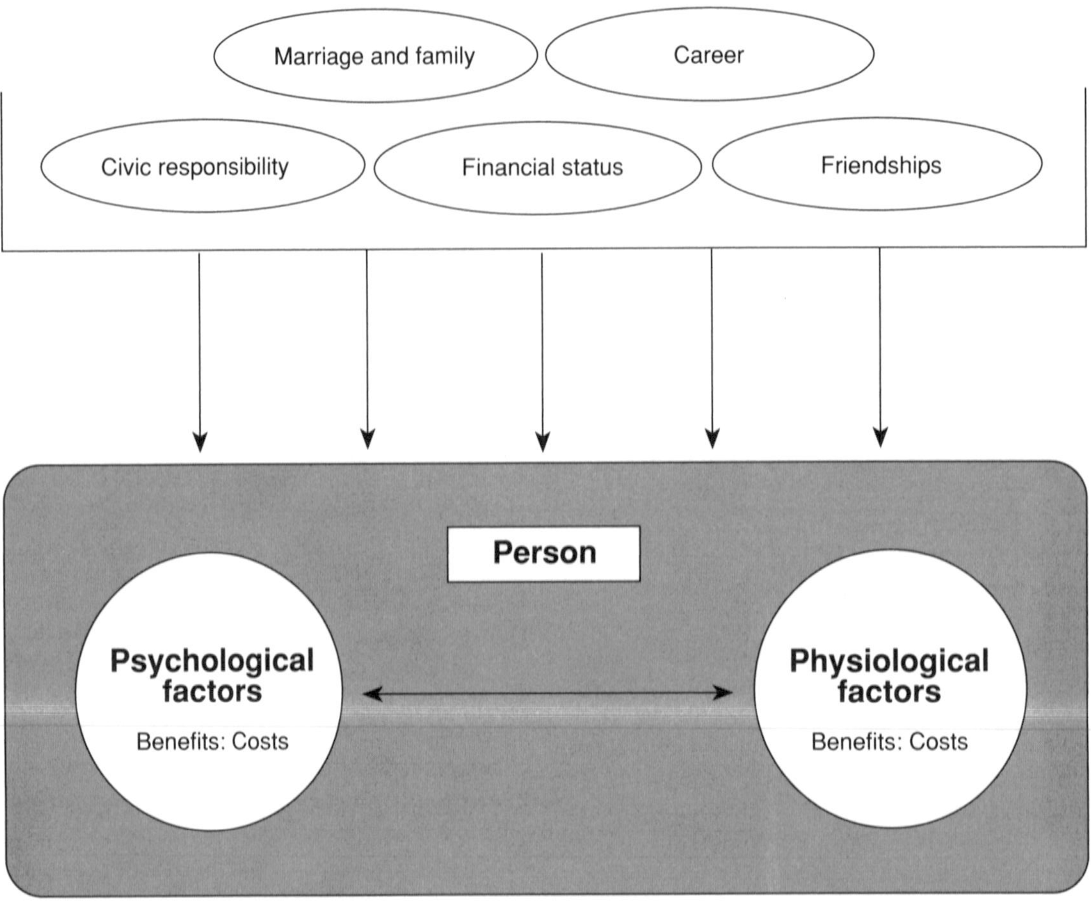

Figure 4.1 Sport and exercise participation has specific psychological and physiological benefits and specific psychological and physiological costs to the person. These benefits and costs are directly impacted by the contextual demands that the person experiences.

of contextual demands can influence the individual athlete's psychological and physical well-being. Unfortunately, no intensive study of the competitive motivation of these athletes has been conducted. The sport literature does, however, detail several promising hypotheses concerning sport participation that may be applicable to the competitive recreational athlete.

Sapp and Haubenstricker (1978) have identified four primary motivators for children's sport participation. Fun is the reason most often given by children for their continued participation in sport, followed by (in descending order of importance) skill improvement, fitness benefits, and team atmosphere. Other motivators include sportspersonship, challenge and excitement, travel, and other extrinsic rewards (see also Gill, Gross, & Huddleston, 1981; Gould, Feltz, Weiss, & Petlichkoff, 1983; Griffin, 1978; Skubic, 1956; Wankel & Kreisel, 1985). These motivators either build self-efficacy or fulfill a social role.

The team as a motivating variable highlights the social and friendship aspects of sport participation. Team membership gives the child a sense of attachment, demonstrated by the team name emblazoned across the uniform. There is shared activity, celebration, and mourning. Success brings a sense of achievement, importance, and public admiration. Failure is often accompanied by the experience of camaraderie, an expression of mutual support in the face of defeat.

Although these motivational issues certainly operate for the competitive recreational athlete, they might not provide a complete picture. Several theoretical models attempt to explain the motivational benefits of exercise. Morgan (1985), in his *mental health model* of human athletic performance, suggested that adults might participate in athletics because of the positive mental-health benefits, increased levels of psychological well-being, and an increased sense of self-efficacy and competence provided by regular physical activity and competition (see also Weinstein & Meyers, 1983). Glasser (1976) has argued along similar lines that runners often manifest an addiction to their sport, albeit a positive one. Their athletic activities offer recreational competitors an element of controllability; athletes are in control of their exercise regime and, we hope, its place in their daily lives. Their developing athletic skills might well bring increased feelings of competence and physical and psychological well-being, the often reported "runner's high" (Sachs, 1984).

The psychological well-being supposedly related to all forms of regular physical exercise has received a considerable amount of research attention. Several investigators (Bahrke & Morgan, 1978; Folkins & Sime, 1981; Raglin & Morgan, 1985) have hypothesized about possible psychological benefits of exercise. Although the scientific debate continues, exercise appears to provide some relief from stress and anxiety. Morgan (1987) has suggested that exercise produces stress reduction through distraction. The distraction model holds that exercise serves to move the person from negative ruminations to physical activity, thus reducing anxiety or depression (Brown, Ramirez, & Taub, 1978; Greist, Klein, Eischens, & Faris, 1978).

Along with the psychological benefits that might provide motivational bases for regular exercise and competition, other hypothesized mechanisms might account for positive addiction. Schildkraut, Orsulak, Schatzberg, and Rosenblum (1983) argued for the existence of a biological basis for the psychological well-being related to regular exercise. They contended that exercise alters one or all of the major brain monoamines. Briefly, when the neurotransmitter norepinephrine, a catecholamine, is experimentally injected into the ventricles of the brain, there is a marked increase in motor activity and other signs of behavioral arousal. Drugs used in the treatment of depression facilitate catecholaminergic transmission in the brain. The result of this facilitation is, among other things, an elevation in mood. These investigators hold that exercise works in ways similar to antidepressant medications by facilitating catecholaminergic transmission and thereby elevating mood.

Another possible biological moderator of the exercise–affect relationship concerns the elevation of body temperature produced during prolonged or intense physical activity. Elevated body temperature has been found to produce a variety of therapeutic effects, and there is clear evidence that deep body temperature is increased in proportion to the intensity of exercise a person performs (Morgan & O'Connor, 1988). This temperature elevation leads to a decrease in muscle tension (Morgan & O'Connor) and might influence the release, synthesis, or uptake of major brain monoamines (deVries, Wiswell, Bulbulian, & Moritani, 1981).

The final proposed biological mechanism for exercise effects on mood involves the relationship between endogenous opioids, such as the endorphins, and regular aerobic exercise (Steinberg & Sykes, 1985). Several studies have concluded that improved mood states following exercise might be stimulated by the release of endorphins, which have a morphinelike effect. However, other investigators examining the role of endogenous opioids in exercise-induced mood changes (Goldfarb, Hatfield, Sforzo, & Flynn, 1987; Williams & Getty, 1986) concluded that even though strenuous exercise stimulates the release of opioids, there is no clear empirical support that these substances are directly linked to exercise-associated mood changes.

From this work, it would appear that competitive recreational athletes might pursue exercise for a variety of reasons, most importantly physical and psychological well-being resulting from both exercise and competitive achievement as well as the social aspects of athletic involvement. Unfortunately, there is little convincing evidence that exercise is causal in improvements in either psychological well-being or the quality of social life. One reason for the dearth of evidence might be that our view of the athlete has failed to include the contextual variables that impact individual well-being, both physical and psychological.

INDIVIDUAL INTERVENTIONS

As we have noted, competitive recreational athletes often have been overlooked in investigations of clinical and educational sport-performance-enhancement interventions. However, we can derive some direction for this population from laboratory and field work with other athlete populations.

There is evidence that cognitive-behavioral interventions can positively impact athletic performance (Feltz & Ewing, 1987; Mahoney & Avener, 1977; Orlick & Partington, 1988; Whelan, Meyers, & Berman, 1989). These interventions have focused on goal setting, arousal management, and precompetition planning. Research in these areas, although not specifically geared toward the competitive recreational athlete, has been summarized by Whelan, Mahoney, and Meyers (1991).

Goal Setting

Locke and Latham (1985) speculated that the positive impact of goal-setting strategies could be applied to athletic contexts. According to Locke (1968), specific, difficult, and realistic goals, as compared to nonspecific, lenient goals or no goals, are associated with improved task performance. These findings have received both support (Barnett & Stanicek, 1979; Hall, Weinberg, & Peterson, 1987; Tu & Tothstein, 1979) and criticism, as many experiments have found no performance differences between no-goal, nonspecific-goal, and specific-goal conditions (Hollingsworth, 1975; Weinberg, Bruya, & Peterson, 1985).

Goal-setting research has also examined the motivational influence of goal orientation (Whelan et al., 1991). People whose achievement goals focus on task mastery rather than competitive superiority might be better prepared to cope more effectively with task demands (Csikszentmihalyi, 1990). Those who desire competitive superiority might seek less demanding tasks to showcase their abilities, whereas tasks that are difficult relative to skills might be perceived as threatening to self-esteem. People who hold task-mastery goals should view difficult tasks as challenges and learning opportunities (Nicholls, 1984; Orlick, 1986). The adoption of task-mastery goals should even serve to buffer the psychological and behavioral effects of task failure (Nichols, Whelan, & Meyers, 1991).

Arousal Management

Physiological and emotional arousal appear to be necessary for optimal response to most competitive demands (Mahoney & Meyers, 1989; Oxendine, 1970). What level of arousal enhances or debilitates performance depends on factors such as task characteristics and individual differences (Landers, 1980; Weinberg, 1989). Evidence indicates that across individuals and situations an athlete's performance can suffer from over- or underarousal (e.g., Fenz, 1975; Fenz & Jones, 1972; Mahoney & Avener, 1977). Arousal modulation, therefore, has become an important target for psychological interventions in sport (Hackfort & Spielberger, 1989).

Efforts to modify overarousal can rely on the anxiety-reduction and stress-management research of clinical psychology (Smith, 1980). Interventions such as relaxation training, biofeedback, and stress-management training (Meichenbaum, 1985; Woolfolk & Lehrer, 1984) have been employed effectively to control overarousal and anxiety in athletes (DeWitt, 1980; Murphy & Woolfolk, 1987; Smith, 1985; Ziegler, Klinzing, & Williamson, 1982). When used with athletes these interventions generally involve skill development, and most packaged skill-training interventions for athletes include at least one such anxiety-management component (Orlick, 1986; Suinn, 1987). In contrast, efforts to modify underarousal have relied on athletes' ability to psychologically ready themselves. The assumption underlying these "psyching-up" efforts is that mental preparation heightens arousal, thereby preparing the athlete to perform (Weinberg, Gould, & Jackson, 1980). The body of work on interventions designed to increase arousal is, however, much less developed than that to reduce arousal.

Precompetition Planning

Precompetition planning (Orlick, 1986) is used to help the athlete devise a general preparation plan for practice and competition. Orlick makes use of goal-setting and arousal-management strategies, but on a more basic level, his planning program enables the athlete to gradually build a process for applying psychological skills and strategies to the competitive task. The plan eventually allows the athlete to identify and refine approaches to preparation for travel; precompetitive routines; interaction with peers, coaches, and family; physical preparation; competitive tasks; the prediction of unexpected happenings; and the postcompetitive experience. It is in this framework that the athlete learns to employ goal-setting, arousal-management, concentration, and refocusing strategies.

MULTISYSTEMIC INTERVENTIONS

Competitive recreational athletes can use these cognitive-behavioral strategies to enhance their competitive performance. But what happens to the athlete plagued by sport performance problems that are influenced by nonsport factors? As we argued on pages 79-80, competitive recreational athletes juggle many responsibilities other than their sports. When family or career do not function smoothly, it is likely that one's sport performance will also be negatively affected. Cognitive-behavioral strategies directed solely at athletic performance issues might be effective, but we adopt the position that these other nonsport stressors must eventually receive attention. Assessment and intervention must consider the competitive recreational athlete's multiple worlds. Family, work, sport, and community demands must be recognized and evaluated. We hope the case studies presented here demonstrate that although sport-related mental-skills training can be useful in some situations, such programs do not completely address the range of presenting problems that competitive citizen athletes bring to the sport psychologist. The level of commitment that these athletes exhibit suggests the need to examine the reciprocal interaction between sport performance and other aspects of the athlete's life.

We do not argue that other athletes are immune to these systemic problems. Indeed, we believe that elite athletes share these same difficulties with competitive recreational athletes. However, elite athletes might have fewer nonsport career complications during their competitive lives (though perhaps more career complications after their athletic disciplines end; see chapter 14) and a more sophisticated support system for dealing with sport demands and life stress. But one of the premises of our argument in this chapter is that the competitive recreational athlete might serve as an appropriate analog for service issues with the elite athlete.

For all athletes, performance is not dependent simply on what happens in training or competition; it is contingent on events in the larger world. One need only to reflect on the tragic death during the 1988 Winter Olympics of the sister of American speed skater Dan Jansen, or the effects of the fall of communism in Eastern Europe on the athletes of formerly communist countries during the 1992 Olympic Games to understand this. What happens to a person in one context certainly and unavoidably influences behavior in other contexts.

This systemic approach to sport performance is equally important when working with competitive recreational athletes. The bridge between unidirectional cognitive-behavioral approaches to sport psychology and a systemic approach to athletic performance is Bandura's (1977) notion of reciprocal determinism (see Figure 4.2). From the unidirectional perspective, behavior is a function of two independent entities, the person and the environmental context. From the reciprocal-determinism perspective, Bandura argued that a person's behavioral skills, cognitive and other internal mediators, and environmental context are in a complex multidirectional interaction. Environmental happenings influence a person's actions and beliefs; beliefs affect behavior and the environment; and actions and their results influence the environment and subsequent beliefs. This interaction cannot be viewed as a linear sequence of events; rather it must be understood as a set of reciprocally interacting feedback and feedforward mechanisms (Mahoney & Meyers, 1989).

This notion of reciprocal determinism has been depicted graphically as a triangle in Figure 4.2 (Bandura, 1978). Behavioral skills, cognitive mediators, and the environmental

Unidirectional perspective

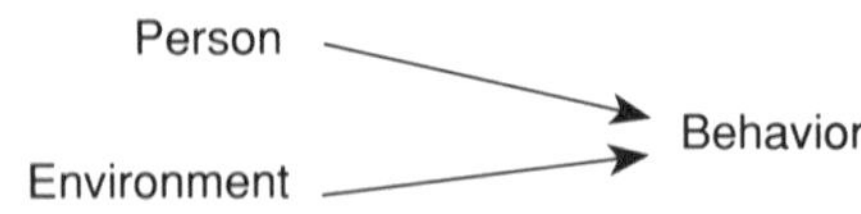

Reciprocal determinism perspective

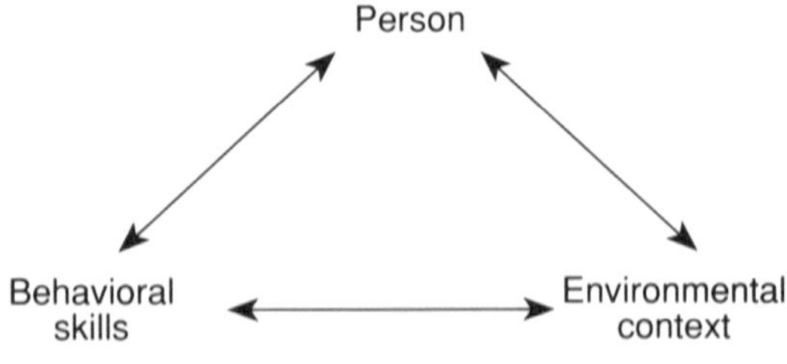

Figure 4.2 Contrasting the relationship of behavior, mediating variables in the person, and environmental context for both unidirectional and reciprocal-determinism approaches.
Note. From "The Self-System in Reciprocal Determinism" by A. Bandura, 1978, *American Psychologist*, **33**, pp. 344-358. Copyright 1978 by the American Psychological Association. Adapted by permission.

context serve as the points of the triangle. The connecting lines demonstrate the reciprocal nonlinear influence that exists; the influence can start at any point and proceed in any direction, not necessarily following the same path in every situation a person might encounter. An event in the environment might influence an individual's behavioral skills, which in turn might impact the person's cognitive mediators. Just as easily, cognitive mediators might influence behavioral skills, which might bring about some environmental change. The key to reciprocal determinism is to remember that events do not occur in a linear sequence, and that an influence can arise from any point of the triangle and affect one or both of the other points.

When a competitive recreational athlete presents with environmental events that are restricted to the areas of training and competition, reciprocal determinism fits very nicely with the application of intervention strategies such as goal setting, arousal management, and precompetition planning, which are directed at enhancing the athlete's sport performance. By addressing the performance issues, which might result in changes in the level of the athlete's behavioral skills, these interventions should also influence both cognitive mediators and the environmental context. These changes should produce more successful sport performance outcomes. In situations where the treatment is limited to sport performance, the educational or cognitive-behavioral skill-building model that constitutes the foundation of current sport psychology intervention efforts should be beneficial. However, as is often the case, people who present with problem issues rarely fit easily into a neat package. When confronted with a person who also happens to be an athlete, limiting the scope of inquiry about environmental events to just those of the sport context might provide a restricted view of the person. This restricted view can lead to the application of interventions that, although useful in some aspects, do not accurately address the broad issues and might result in a lack of progress in therapy.

To avoid the pitfalls of narrow vision, it is necessary to realize that, in reality, people operate in a variety of contexts and that the sport context is only one of many for the competitive recreational athlete. Although the theory of reciprocal determinism deals with only one particular situation at a time, the more accurate picture of influence is gained only when it is understood that environmental events from one situation or context often play a role in other contexts and that keeping the events of one context separate from other contexts is often impossible (see Figure 4.3). If a person has a stressful day at the office, this likely will have an effect on one's actions at home that evening. The person might have less patience for the children's roughhousing or become inappropriately angry with a spouse over trivial issues. Reciprocity not only occurs within a context, but also between contexts. Consequently, when attempting to understand the presenting problems of an athlete, we need to consider

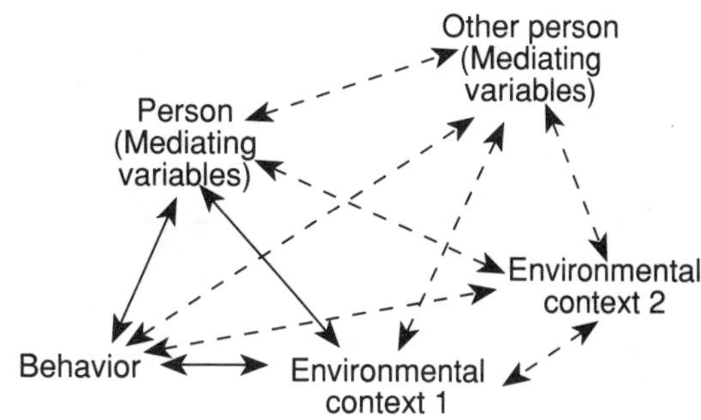

Figure 4.3 The bold lines indicate the reciprocal interaction between behavior, person, and environment when considering a single interaction. The addition of a second environmental context and a second set of person variables that impact immediately on behavior (as shown by the dashed lines) creates a significantly more complex view.

not only the happenings in sport, but also the happenings in other contexts of a person's life. In this example the sport context played no role in the drama, but therapists would not be aware of a stressful work environment if they restricted their inquiries to sport when assessing a presenting problem.

One model for thinking of these interrelated contexts is the multisystemic approach to conceptualizing problems and processes of change. The multisystemic approach (Henggeler & Borduin, 1990) might be seen as a more practical development of Bandura's reciprocal determinism. This approach takes into consideration all areas of a person's world before implementing any interventions. By assessing each of the areas in which the athlete is a participant, the issues causing poor sport performance can be addressed. Taking a systemic approach to the issues presented by athletes allows for a much more appropriately planned strategy for interventions, which should improve not only sport performance but also the level at which the athlete is functioning in other areas of life.

By adopting a multisystemic view of the person, therapists see presenting problems as attempts to handle demands in the contexts of sport, marriage, family, career, and social relations as well as the predictable and the unpredictable changes that occur in anyone's life. Increased marital conflict might be the result when the last child leaves home, leaving the spouses with the task of learning to readjust to being alone with each other. Alternatively, conflict might come about as a response to a career change that requires increased time commitments to work and corresponding decreases in time commitments to family. Not only are these problems attempts to handle stressors and changes, but they also demonstrate the influence contexts have on one another.

To gain a better understanding of the multisystemic perspective, we use a brief overview of systems theory suggested by Patricia Minuchin (1985):

- Systems are organized wholes, and elements within the system are necessarily interdependent. These elements are also bound by predictable relationships with one another. Applying this principle to people is similar to saying that behavior is best understood and predicted when considering as many contextual influences as possible.

- A system is circular, not linear. To conceptualize this principle, consider two people. The actions of Person *A* influence Person *B*, whereas the actions of Person *B* influence Person *A*, and so on. For example, in training for a triathlon, a woman might spend much time away from her family. Her husband might feel she is neglecting them and so might try to nag her into spending more time at home. She might respond by thinking that her husband is selfishly trying to keep her from accomplishing her goals. She becomes angry with him and spends more time training. He nags more, she trains more, and so on. Her actions influence him, his actions influence her; this feedback loop will continue until someone or something disrupts it.

- A system strives to maintain homeostasis, the status quo. The problem with a homeostatic goal is that evolution and change are also inherent in any system. These changes might be brought about by genetic or biological factors (like aging) or by environmental factors. They might be the result of psychological changes, such as confidence following a series of successes or failures. All potential stressors, be they developmental, predictable, or unpredictable, bring about evolution and change. Systems, however, attempt to minimize or resist the change. Although this resistance can be functional and adaptive, it might also have detrimental effects. The tendency to maintain stability, and therefore minimize helpful change, must be kept in mind when dealing with athletes.

• Complex systems are always composed of subsystems. Consider a family as an example. A family is a complex system, but when the family is examined, subsystems can be identified. These subsystems include a spousal subsystem, a parenting subsystem, a sibling subsystem, and perhaps a parent–child subsystem. The subsystems combine to form the system, and it is clear that there is no mutually exclusive membership in any one subsystem. Each subsystem has its own functions and boundaries (Henggeler & Borduin, 1990). The functions of a sibling are different from the functions of a child. Similarly, the functions of a parent are different from the functions of a spouse.

• Subsystems are separated from larger systems by boundaries, and there are implicit rules and structures that govern interactions across boundaries (Wood & Talmon, 1983). These boundaries affect the flow of information to and from systems (Henggeler & Borduin, 1990).

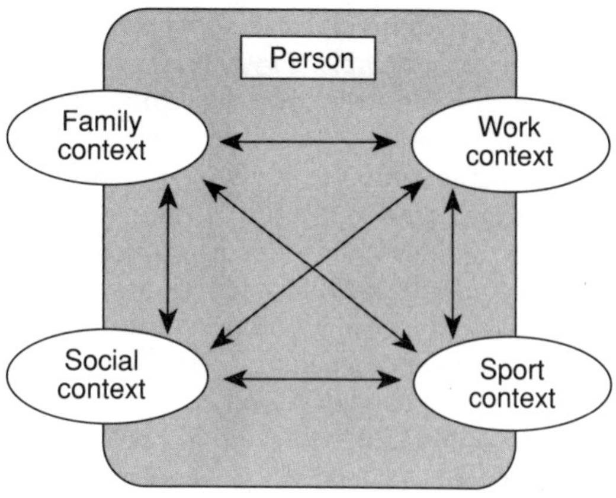

Figure 4.4 The multicontextual model of athletes highlights that individual functioning or performance is the product of reciprocal interactions between several influencing contexts.

The idea of multiple contexts and the workings of multisystemic thought can be depicted as mutually interacting circles (see Figure 4.4). The fact that they do interact makes it clear that influences in one context can readily affect other contexts and can globally affect all contexts. Beyond the contexts depicted in Figure 4.4, or more appropriately the area in which these contexts are embedded, is the cultural context. Society, culture, politics, and economics all influence the athlete.

Stressors and demands impinge on the person in these multiple contexts or systems, affecting not only sport performance but also the ability to function successfully in the family and at work. These demands can be developmental, predictable, or unpredictable. According to Carter and McGoldrick (1988), developmental stressors are those events that, although expected during a normal life span, are often intensely stressful to all members of a particular family system. These stressors usually occur at transitions in a family; that is, instances in which the role of a family member in the system changes dramatically or when a family member leaves the system. Some examples of these transition times include a divorce, the aging of a parent, the birth or death of a family member, or the departure of a child for college. Other developmental stressors can also occur in conjunction with a person's career. For example, a job promotion can significantly impact a person's work context; a new position might demand a significantly greater amount of time to maintain career success. The increased commitment to the work context might require the person to decrease commitment in other contexts, and this decrease might negatively affect performance in these contexts. A career demotion might also produce deteriorating performance in other contexts. Both of these situations carry with them potential for financial changes, and these changes can present additional stressors across many contexts.

These developmental stressors are, for the most part, predictable. However, there are other predictable stressors that are not developmental. An athlete's training season is one example. The training season requires the athlete to reduce the amount of time allotted to family or work. One's spouse must pick up the slack in the family system by assuming more of the caretaking, both of children and home, and both partners are left with less time to devote to their own relationship. In the work context, the athlete might be able to maintain previous levels of job performance, but in the more stressful situation of producing a similar quantity and quality of work in less time.

In addition to these predictable stressors, there are also unpredictable stressors, which might be even more problematic. The competitor has little time to prepare for these capricious stressors and must deal with them as they come. Such stressors might include athletic injuries that affect training or end a competitive season, major health problems experienced by a family member, a financial crisis, or conflicts that appear at work or at home. It is not difficult to imagine how any of these stressors would impact not only their immediate context but also other areas of the athlete's life. Again, understanding the overall impact of any stressor on multiple contexts is central to understanding the issues presented by the athlete. This understanding is necessary to plan useful interventions that target problematic issues, not merely act as bandages for one symptom. Taking a multisystemic approach when dealing with these athletes is possible only after understanding multiple contexts.

Before moving on to look at interventions used with competitive recreational athletes, several important points must be reiterated. Assessment and intervention must take into consideration the importance and influence of multiple systems. When gathering information from the client, it is insufficient to focus solely on sport issues. One must remember that valuable information can also be found in other areas in the athlete's life. The same holds true for interventions. Gearing them toward only a sport issue can lead to failure in treatment if the underlying causes of performance problems exist in other contexts. The interventions should be designed to address the conditions that maintain the problem, so that by positively influencing that area, all other areas will be affected as well. Just as problems reach out and affect other contexts, so will interventions. Elements in a system are interrelated; changing one results in effects throughout the system.

INTERVENTION ISSUES

Creating significant and lasting behavior change requires a clear picture of what needs to be changed, some ideas of how to precipitate that change, and the foresight to predict possible hindrances to the change process. One purpose of assessment is to collect the data to describe and specify the change process (Phares, 1992). The task of the therapist, therefore, begins with a definition of intervention goals. From our perspective, this is not a difficult task. Clients usually arrive with problems, complaints, or questions that they want resolved. Finding satisfactory solutions becomes the goal of therapy. These solutions involve changes in how the person thinks, feels, or behaves. For example, in the case of the anxious masters swimmer, Julio, his therapeutic goal was to overcome his "nerves" during the week preceding a meet and to concentrate on and implement his race strategy. For Sherry, the slumping cyclist, the therapeutic goal focused on developing her motivation to maximize her training and racing efforts.

Courtesy USOC

Not all theories of psychological intervention propose such a direct definition of therapeutic goals. Some traditional approaches to psychotherapy necessitate that goals focus on more characterological or unconscious issues (Weiner & Bordin, 1983; Wolberg, 1967). Presenting problems are seen as symptoms of underlying pathological ways of organizing the world. These are the signs of a deficiency or disease. Resolving the pathology, not just removing the symptom, is seen as the only means of creating an enduring change in the person's life. Thus the pathology must be exorcised and then replaced with something healthier. This change often involves considerable time and money. This is a pathology-focused model of therapy.

Neither the cognitive-behavioral nor systemic theories that form the basis of the multisystemic model explained here view complaints as signs of psychopathology. Rather, problems are viewed directly without resorting to underlying hypothetical constructs (Guttman, 1991; Kanfer & Goldstein, 1986). Problems result from the person's not possessing sufficient or appropriate skills to effectively cope with the present demands (Fisch, Weakland, & Segal, 1982; Kanfer & Goldstein, 1986). In addition, people are often entangled in reinforcing relationships with others that help maintain the problematic solutions or inhibit the implementation of more capable ways of coping. Sometimes the problems are context-specific; other times the problems seen in one context are the result of competent attempts to cope with demands and difficulties in another context. People are viewed as capable as well as vulnerable and as possessing the ability to learn. The goal of therapy is to develop skills or new ways of thinking, behaving, and interacting that will promote resolution of the complaint. This is a problem-focused model of therapy. Although the empirical evidence has suggested that pathology-focused and problem-focused models of therapy produce similarly effective outcomes, the problem-focused models are more economical and time efficient (Lambert et al., 1986).

The Assessment Process

Successful efforts to create change in an efficient and effective manner must depend on a thorough assessment of the person's complaints and primary contexts of life. We propose that the goal of the therapy effort is directly related to clients' complaints but believe that the selection of intervention methods for creating and maintaining change must consider all the factors that impact the individual target problem. The assessment process yields information that the therapist uses to generate hypotheses about the most efficient and effective methods for intervention (Kanfer & Goldstein, 1986; Nelson & Barlow, 1981; Nelson & Hayes, 1986). These hypotheses are based on the therapist's understanding of the client's complaints, awareness of the contextual cues that precipitate and follow the problem situation, knowledge of how the person functions in other contexts, and the interactions in and between contexts that support or promote the problem response.

Assessment begins with a clear statement of the presenting problem or complaint and the client's conceptualization of this complaint. Referred to as "pinpointing" (Patterson, 1974), the aim of this first step is to guide the client to unequivocally define what is wrong, its occurrence, its specific impact on the client's life, and its causes as conceived of by the client. In this way clients define their position about the problem and about change. The clients reveal, in their own language, their view of the world. Their perspective on the problem and expectations for both the therapy and the therapist provide an understanding of whether clients will cooperate with or accept various intervention strategies. Attempts to promote change that begin from the client's worldview and beliefs about potential change are thought to facilitate the therapeutic process (Fisch et al., 1982).

Simultaneously, a functional analysis of the problem can be completed. A functional analysis, in its most basic form, provides a temporal context for the occurrence of the problem by identifying its immediate antecedents and consequences (Kanfer & Goldstein, 1986; Nelson & Barlow, 1981). Antecedents are the discriminative stimuli that provide immediate triggers for the problem response. Consequences are the reinforcing stimuli that serve either to increase or decrease the probability of a future occurrence of the specific problem response. These stimuli can be comprised of thoughts, emotions, and behaviors of the client or interactions in the client's environment that have been found to cue the problem situation. As the therapist tracks the details of the client's problematic situations, antecedents and consequences are identified.

The therapist then assesses the client's functioning in the five primary contexts discussed in the previous section; individual, family, sport, work, and social functioning. The process is not a search for psychopathology, but rather an attempt to clarify how the person functions—successfully and unsuccessfully—in each context. Information pertaining to the strengths and weaknesses in each context helps the therapist develop a balanced understanding of how the person operates in different areas and how these areas interrelate. At the individual level, both psychological and physical functioning need to be considered. Are there any illnesses, injuries, or physical limitations that impact the current level of functioning? Does the person possess physical talent? What is the client's general health status? Similar questions about psychological functioning need to address issues such as intellectual capabilities, perceived ability, confidence, and motivation. Family functioning includes satisfaction and status of the marriage or primary relationship, the impact of the presence or absence of children, and relationships and interactions with the birth family. For the clients presented in this chapter, the strengths and weaknesses of the sport context and athletic performance receive considerable attention. Other contexts, such as work and social relationships, also play a vital role.

Once a clear conceptualization of client functioning in these differing environments is completed, patterns across contexts can be established and interactions between contexts will be more apparent. For example, in the case of Sherry, her submersion in cycling complements her dissatisfaction with her career and her avoidance of marital conflict. The purpose of assessing multiple contexts is to define the issues and generate a set of hypotheses about the causes that have precipitated and maintained the problem behaviors. These hypotheses should subsequently assist in identifying possible venues for change that will alleviate the complaints. Similarly, the information might reveal factors that would impede the process of change. Will the demands in the work setting and those made by family members interfere with an attempt to increase time or energy spent on sport performance?

A variety of methods can be used to complete the assessment. The specific methods used depend on the needs and questions of the particular client and creativity of the therapist. The basis of the assessment is a 1- or 2-hr interview with the client. In this time the primary presenting problems can be defined, a functional analysis initiated, and an understanding of the contextual functioning of the client can be obtained. A week or two of daily diary records of particular aspects of the client's life, such as training habits or cognitions, can help clarify questions and establish baselines. Typically, collateral sessions with significant others help clarify and correct for the client's biased conceptualization. Direct observation is often highly informative, particularly with clients who hesitate to disclose or are less verbally fluent. Pencil-and-paper measures of symptoms are used to secure concrete evidence of particular strengths or weaknesses. The client's permission to complete any assessment that relies on information from others is required, especially with a potentially invasive assessment procedure such as direct observation (American Psychological Association, 1990; Pope & Vasquez, 1991).

Although assessment is emphasized in the first hours of contact, the assessment should be a continuous process (Nelson & Barlow, 1981; Nelson & Hayes, 1986). Regardless of the sophistication or the empirical support of our intervention efforts, verification of effectiveness is essential. At best, research provides a probabilistic statement on the effectiveness of interventions. Evaluation is necessary to identify whether a specific intervention was successful. In addition, continuous assessment provides clear indication to the client and the therapist about the targeted change.

The Intervention Process

The intervention phase of the therapy can begin when two criteria are met. The first is that the therapist is aware of the establishment of a cooperative working relationship. Often referred to as *the therapeutic relationship* or *rapport*, this relationship becomes the vehicle for the change (Frank, 1982; Frank & Frank, 1991; Goldstein & Myers, 1986). Traditionally, this relationship is based on the therapist's communication of empathy, support, and caring for the client. The client, in return, views the therapist as supportive and investing. This allows the client to self-disclose with greater intimacy and trust in the feedback and direction given by the therapist (Goldstein & Myers, 1986; Mahoney, 1991). As a result of this trust, power in the relationship becomes unbalanced, with the client believing in the therapist's intent to protect the client's best interest. The power provides the therapist maneuverability to begin to create change (Fisch et al., 1982). Before intervention begins, the therapist needs to understand these relationship issues to utilize them to promote the client's behavior change.

The second criterion is that the therapist must use the assessment phase to generate ideas about how to precipitate that change. This is accomplished by developing a set of viable hypotheses about the client's complaints and how change might most effectively and efficiently occur (Kanfer & Goldstein, 1986; Phares, 1992). The hypotheses must include a proposal for the change process, foresight to predict what might inhibit this process, and the long-term maintenance of change. There are parallels between being a good therapist and being a good scientist. Like the scientist, the therapist designs interventions to have measurable outcomes that support or disconfirm specific hypotheses. Confirmation of a hypothesis indicates that the interventions should be continued. Disconfirmation indicates the need to shift to a reassessment of the client's position and the selection of an alternate hypothesis. Consequently, the initial assessment phase ends when the therapist has collected enough data to propose a set of viable and testable hypotheses.

The therapist selects interventions that can be implemented by the client, that fit the client's expectations, and that generate information about the value of the therapeutic hypotheses. Although our approach is predominantly cognitive behavioral and systemic, we strive to broaden our intervention techniques beyond those traditionally associated with these approaches. For example, if the client believes in unconscious conflict, the intervention can involve using the language of unconscious processes to allow the client a degree of comfort with the intervention. To ensure a match between the client's view of change and the change strategies, the therapist uses the therapeutic relationship to continually solicit feedback about the acceptability of the intervention (Fisch et al., 1982; Henggeler & Borduin, 1990).

The sessions with the client are used to maneuver the client into a position to accept the interventions and then to use the intervention to initiate change. The change itself begins in these sessions; enduring change depends on the execution of the intervention outside the therapy sessions. The client must enact the change strategy in the targeted context and then perceive that this change occurs. Therapy is terminated when changes have been successfully implemented in targeted contexts.

As evident in the three case studies described here, therapy appears considerably idiosyncratic. The prescriptions for change are tailored to the person's presenting needs. However, a number of similarities should be apparent across all three therapies. All these athletes present with a sport-related complaint. Assessment includes a functional analysis of the presenting problems and careful consideration of the person's functioning across the contexts. The assessment is used both to generate hypotheses about the presenting problem and to gauge progress. Interventions are introduced that consider the nature of the therapeutic relationship and are consistent with the primary hypothesis being tested. The therapist remains highly active throughout the therapy and brings other helping professionals into the treatment as necessary and as permitted by the client.

■ *THE CASE OF JULIO* ■

Julio, the 42-year-old university professor, complained that "nerves" in the week preceding masters swim meets interfered with his functioning at home and work and inhibited his ability to train or execute his race strategy. He believed that this anxiety significantly contributed to slower swimming times during the past 6 months. When asked to explain what "nerves" meant, Julio described physiological arousal cues that "oscillated with increasing amplitude" throughout the week. Symptoms primarily involved motor tension (jitteriness, inability to relax) and autonomic hyperactivity (heart pounding, tingling in hands, upset stomach). Furthermore, sleep and eating patterns were significantly disturbed. He said that he was "not scared, just nervous." When asked what he would do if this could not be remediated, he sighed, "I'd just quit."

A working relationship was easily established. Possibly because of the shared academic affiliation, Julio was immediately trusting and respectful. He seemed to view the therapist as a colleague, or collaborator. He was both receptive to new ideas and interested in understanding as much as he could. From the start, he requested readings that eventually facilitated the therapy work.

Assessment was simplified by Julio's attention to detail and by the training log. The log contained enough information to complete a functional analysis of the "nerves." It revealed that the "buzz" typically began as he started to taper his training for the race, swimming fewer yards less intensely. Consequently, he usually felt that he had a bit more energy. He began to think about the meet, his competitors, how much time he would have between events, and what times he "needed" to swim. These thoughts would lead to growing concerns that he would fail, and failure would mean that all this swimming was a waste of time. As these ruminations escalated he would become irritable and isolated. The consequences included feeling disappointed that he would not swim as well as he knew he could. He would also return to ruminations about the neglect of research or his family. Self-report questionnaires—specifically the Hopkins Symptom Checklist (Derogatis, Lipman, Rickels, Uhlenhuth, & Covi, 1974), the State-Trait Anxiety Inventory (Spielberger, Gorsuch, & Lushene, 1970), the Psychological Skill Inventory for Sport (Mahoney et al., 1987), and the Sports Competition Anxiety Test (Martens, 1977)—supported his propensity to anxiety and concentration problems.

Courtesy USOC

In the second assessment session, Maria, Julio's wife, confirmed his report on the impact of the heightened arousal on his life at home and at work. She noted that although he typically was a good companion and father, these periods of anxiety drove everyone away. Her input placed Julio's self-critical presentation in perspective as she detailed her view of Julio as husband, father, and social companion. His attention to detail apparently often resulted in overly critical self-evaluation across life contexts. She noted that he had always been fairly uptight.

The information from Julio, Maria, and the training log yielded a fairly clear picture of Julio's functioning and his strengths and weaknesses across the various contexts (see Table 4.1). This assessment suggested that Julio is a dedicated, stable, and capable individual. He apparently achieved academically, was supported by family, and maintained a well-developed social network. In most situations, he successfully used his family and friends as a check for his overly harsh self-evaluation. The exception was swimming. Here Julio isolated himself from the relationships that helped him keep his worries in check. He had not developed supportive relationships with other swimmers or a coach. He continued to swim because of what quitting would say about him, not because he enjoyed it. His swim goals appeared diffuse and somewhat unreasonable. He generally lacked concentration.

Two hypotheses were then proposed. First, Julio was not psychologically equipped to manage the demands he faced. His arousal-management skills were severely overwhelmed. Although some arousal increase might be necessary for optimal performance, Julio reported an inability to control his physical response to competition. In turn, this arousal interfered with the execution of his

Table 4.1 Multicontextual Assessment: Julio

Presenting problems: "Nerves," high anxiety before meets, difficulty focusing
Related issues: Motivational lags (swimming; solution to problem is to work harder or get tougher); critical of performance in marriage, family, and job; few connections between swimming and other contexts in his life

	Strengths	Weaknesses
Individual		
Physical	—Healthy and injury free —Physically active life —Maintains nutritious diet	—Physiological arousal cues problematic
Psychological	—Motivated to achieve —Perceives self as capable —Intelligent	—Poor arousal-management skills —Arousal inhibits concentration —Overly self-evaluative —Diffuse, demanding outcome goals —Guilt feelings —Falters in presence of high demands —Anxiety promotes ruminations

	Strengths	Weaknesses
Family		
Marital/ significant other	—Wife says good companion —Wife reports solid marriage —Wife accepts swimming	—Feels he is neglecting marriage —Wife not involved in athletics —Restraints on time for ongoing development of marriage
Children, parents, and family issues	—One child —Wife says good father —Parenting responsibilities are satisfactory —Supportive birth family —Economically secure	—Critical of self as father
Sport	—Talented —Competitive in age group —Solid technical skills —Trains hard	—Competition cues an uncontrolled anxiety response —Diffuse swimming goals —No coach —Race strategy fails when anxious —Fun, camaraderie? —Regrets that he quit swimming
Work	—Tenured —Continued positive achievements —Flexible setting —Support of chair and colleagues	—Pivotal time in career —Wife works long hours
Social/peers	—Supportive friends who share interests with both Julio and Maria	—Peers isolated from his swimming —Undeveloped relationships with other swimmers

training and race strategies. In part, the lack of a coach or training partners placed the responsibility to follow through with a training regimen on him alone. In swim meets, the arousal undermined his ability to concentrate and attend to his race strategies. His personal goals and his strategies for preparing for competition were fueled by his fastidiousness and were consequently overly demanding.

The second hypothesis focused on how Julio separated swimming from the rest of his life. His anxiousness, his self-demanding style, and his attention to detail promoted successful coping in other contexts. He succeeded in a difficult and competitive work context. He capably managed primary child care responsibility. Fortunately, the very characteristics that plagued him in swimming benefited him in other areas. In part, success in these areas depended on feedback from his wife, colleagues, and friends. This feedback was unavailable in his swimming. Potentially, if the sport context were better integrated with his support systems, control would be enhanced.

Intervention

As these two hypotheses were complementary rather than competing, therapy was directed to testing both. Skill building first focused on arousal management. This skill was taught using a variation of David Barlow's integrated cognitive-behavioral treatment for anxiety and panic attacks (Barlow & Cerny, 1988). It is comprised of a rationale and education about anxiety, exposure, and attention to interoceptive or somatic cues; cognitive therapy to identify and challenge rumination or anxiety-producing cognition; and progressive relaxation training and respirator training. Designed for 14 one-hr sessions, this treatment has been found effective under a variety of controlled conditions (Barlow, Craske, Cerny, & Klosko, 1989; Klosko, Barlow, Tassinari, & Cerny, 1990).

The program was altered to highlight the potential value of physiological arousal and the importance of managing, rather than alleviating, this arousal. The treatment was also abbreviated and adapted to de-emphasize issues of psychopathology. In the first intervention session the relationship between anxiety, arousal, and performance was discussed. Julio's "buzz" was redefined as an appropriate bodily response to the need to be competitively aroused. Julio and the therapist discussed the goal of learning to use this response rather than fear it. Julio was encouraged to practice eliciting and controlling the "buzz." To promote understanding, he was given a set of readings about anxiety problems, the sport research on anxiety and on relaxation training (e.g., Lichstein, 1988; Mahoney & Meyers, 1989; Oxendine, 1970). Since Julio planned to race in 10 days, he was directed to monitor his somatic cues of arousal changes, conduct random ratings of the distressfulness of the anxiety, and identify the related cognitive reactions. The next appointment was arranged for the week following the swim meet.

In the subsequent session, Julio reported that he was "a mess" at the meet, but he did collect much data. He then produced a detailed diary of the anxiety response and demonstrated his ability to sense the physiological cues of anxiety and the related cognitive patterns. He had obviously mastered the ability to assess his anxiety response. Using this data, both relaxation training and cognitive therapy were initiated. He was given a daily practice tape of progressive relaxation and controlled breathing exercises, and he was instructed to monitor that practice. The diary provided data to construct a hierarchy of arousing stimulus situations. He was also taught to identify thoughts of catastrophe and use a set of self-statements to deal with the ruminations. Lastly, he agreed that he would find and enter a meet that was 2 to 3 months away.

During the next 6 weeks, Julio progressed through the arousal-management treatment, becoming more comfortable with arousal changes and gaining more control of arousal. Several mock swim meets were arranged to assess skill development and build confidence. His dedication to completing homework assignments made the assessment of progress easy. As gains were made, arousal-management issues received less attention and goal-setting and concentration skills received more. To establish a foundation for these skills, Julio purchased a copy of *Psyching for Sport* (Orlick, 1986). He was instructed to establish controllable effort goals, rather than outcome goals (Burton, 1989), and to strive for specific daily goals that he found challenging and fun. To enhance concentration, Julio's attention to detail was utilized to develop precompetition plans and similar prepractice plans (Orlick, 1986).

To test the validity of the second hypothesis concerning Julio's compartmentalization of his swimming, Maria joined Julio's sessions soon after therapy began. In the first joint meeting Maria's willingness to become more involved in Julio's swimming was assessed. She indicated that she had little interest in listening to the details—times, distances, stroke problems, interval training—but she would do what she could. Together with Julio, the therapist defined her role as "feedback from the real world" and began to involve her in Julio's weekly homework and self-monitoring exercises. Soon, Saturday morning became a family swim outing as Maria and Ben would join Julio toward the end of his workouts and then the family would go to breakfast together. Julio also began to talk with Maria more about his swimming; as long as he controlled the amount of swimming details, she seemed to enjoy providing support and feedback. Although Maria's involvement was only one connection between Julio's swimming and the rest of his life, her frankness and humor appeared to help Julio enjoy the experience and obsess less about his performance.

The outcome of this therapy was positive. Before the next swim meet, Julio still reported the "buzz," but he felt more in control of his week and able to moderate the physiological effects. He noted some ruminations about his performance while at the meet, but felt that the behavioral planning kept him on track. Maria did not attend the meet, which was about a 6-hr drive from their home, but they did talk on the telephone several times. These conversations were not focused on swimming. His performances did not meet his expectations and consequently he was somewhat disappointed. When the therapist asked about the implications of the disappointment, he joked, "Well, at least I don't want to quit."

Following this meet Julio attended two appointments, during which his sport-related psychological skills were honed and his course of treatment was reviewed. It was apparent in these sessions that Julio had a clear command of the skills related to arousal management, goal setting, and competition planning. Julio also realized the impact of encouraging Maria to be more involved in his swimming. The therapy was therefore terminated with the expectation that changes had been initiated and Julio was committed to continuing his efforts. Given his motivation, his attention to detail, and the supportiveness of Maria, the planning for future sessions was left to Julio's discretion. Although he and the therapist never again met formally, the therapist had run into Julio several times on campus. On each occasion, Julio reported that he still was not swimming as well as he would like, but that he was enjoying both his workouts and his meets. In addition, he felt that the "buzz" was under control, and that Maria actually seemed to like her involvement in his swimming. He noted she had become friends with some of the masters swimmers and their families.

■ *THE CASE OF SHERRY* ■

Sherry's presenting problems were "feeling distracted" and "difficulty getting motivated." Furthermore, she related feeling emotional deterioration and fatigue. Although her present training consisted of long, easy "spinning" rides, she detailed a number of nagging injuries. She said that for the first time in years she was dreading the upcoming racing season. She provided details only after considerable hesitation. Finally, Sherry admitted that she was not sure that a therapist could help and that nothing much was really wrong with her.

Initially, relationship building appeared to be difficult. In addition to Sherry's quiet manner, she seemed reluctant, or afraid, to disclose. The therapist's initial impression, substantiated throughout the first few sessions, was that Sherry did not want to reveal any weaknesses or relinquish control. In order to maintain some flexibility as a therapist, the psychologist needed to carefully empower her by addressing her strengths and by deferring to her expertise. The hope was that if the therapist was careful not to fight for control and power, Sherry might begin to trust. Consequently, the therapist reframed the relationship establishing Sherry as the expert athlete and the therapist as an outside consultant.

This reframe proved productive. Sherry identified her main goal as overcoming her motivational slump. This slump included difficulty initiating and completing her workouts. After workouts, she felt feckless; sometimes just sitting in her car crying. Typically, her response to these occasions was to decide to push herself harder tomorrow. When asked about other antecedents or consequences, she said that the one positive consequence of the slump was that her husband left her alone. When asked what her husband would be like if she were to bounce out of this slump, she jokingly commented that he would probably start pestering her again.

Although she denied any problems in her family, work, and social contexts, the joke about her husband opened the door to the initial consultation with Robert. This meeting helped complete the multicontextual assessment (see Table 4.2). Robert related considerable anger toward Sherry and considerable frustration with the marriage. His answer to questions about Sherry's noncycling life was that she tended to avoid and ignore everything except cycling. He felt that he sometimes had to shame her into doing things with the family. He also noted that she hated her job and refused to associate with his friends. He believed that she was depressed. In contrast, Sherry verbalized some dissatisfaction with home and work, but did not relate the tension and conflict described by Robert. She said that she did not hate her job, she just saw it as a dead end. As for friends, she preferred being with people with whom she shared interests, that is, cyclists. Robert provided a better sense that serious problems existed in the marriage.

On the positive side, Sherry's strength, determination, investment in cycling, and supportive network of training partners strongly suggested her potential in other areas. She also seemed quite confident in her sport skills. The shyness she noted in other contexts was not apparent in cycling, suggesting that she possessed valuable social skills that tended to be underutilized.

A number of hypotheses were formulated. The first had already received considerable support, namely, that she was hesitant about seeking this consultation and therefore she was hesitant to trust. To confront the marital and work concerns would only frighten her away. Second, the marital discord was related to themes of control and dependence-independence. Conflict in the relationship pertained to a lack of interaction between spouses on a number of issues. Robert tended to pursue Sherry by confronting her on these issues. Her response was to withdraw in silence. Third, the motivational slump and training injuries resulted from overtraining. It is this third hypothesis that the therapist chose to focus on initially. It was anticipated that if addressed carefully Sherry would approach the marital issues once some confidence and trust was established.

Intervention

Before beginning any interventions, three referrals needed to be completed. Sherry needed to consult a physician. Although the nagging injuries and feelings of lethargy might be psychogenic in nature, a health clearance should be completed before intervention. Like many athletes, Sherry was hesitant to trust physicians because they tend to prescribe rest or greatly reduce the amount of exercise. In fact, she had consulted one physician who lectured her about trying too hard to be a teenager again. So Sherry was referred to a physician who was also an age-group competitive runner. He noted that she was in generally good health, except for a slightly anemic condition, and recommended that she consult a dietician and a coach. The therapist then helped her contact a dietician and the coach, a cycling guru. Sherry was so impressed with the physician that she immediately made appointments to have her diet evaluated and to visit the coach.

Meanwhile, the psychologist's role as a consultant was solidified, but Sherry did not indicate any reason to target issues other than

Table 4.2 Multicontextual Assessment: Sherry

Presenting problems: Difficulty getting motivated to train harder for upcoming season of bicycle racing

Related issues: Feeling distracted, nagging injuries, considerable distance in marriage

	Strengths	Weaknesses
Individual		
Physical	—Exercising regularly	—Small, nagging injuries —Lethargic, often tired —Pushes harder when fatigued —Health status unknown
Psychological	—Determined —Intellectually capable —Enjoys exercise and training	—Mood swings —Typically avoids confrontation —Generally, when the going gets tough, avoid and minimize
Family		
Marital/ significant other	—Married 13 years	—Husband bitter about relationship —Lack of communication on important family issues —Husband dissatisfied with sex life —Couple is disengaged —Unaware or ignoring husband's dissatisfaction
Children, parents, and family issues	—Two children —Reports close relationship with birth family	—Husband resents child care burden —Motherhood is not enjoyable —Minimal contact with sons
Sport	—Long history of running and cycling —Competitive locally —General self-efficacy positively influenced by sport success —Trains hard —Helps overcome shyness —Helps moderate mood and stress	—Recent inconsistent performances —Possibly overtrains —Difficulty maintaining motivation —No coaching
Work	—Job security —Good performance history	—Sees no room for advancement —Does not enjoy job —Works only for financial security

(continued)

Table 4.2 *(continued)*

	Strengths	Weaknesses
Social/peers	—Good camaraderie with training group —Historically has had a larger, more diverse social support network	—No shared social groups between spouses —Disconnected socially from noncycling peers

cycling performance. The focus, therefore, remained on motivation and distractions in training. The next few meetings involved the therapist's listening to the difficulties and frustrations of the last two racing seasons. Attention was drawn to the strength and importance of her drive to succeed despite these frustrations. She was directed to construct a retrospective training log for the last two seasons in an effort to identify her attempts to overcome her competitive plateau. The therapist predicted that she would find patterns of attempted solutions that she repeatedly implemented without success. She was also encouraged to keep a training log to document her pre- and postworkout thoughts and emotional responses. The goal was to reevaluate the problem and try to find a solution that she had not previously tried. Problem-solving skills were taught in session (D'Zurilla, 1988).

Although her meeting with the coach had not occurred, Sherry interpreted her logs as indicating that harder training was not the solution. She was still feeling fatigued and now decided that she needed rest. In order to utilize her general tendency to resist change, the therapist utilized the tactic of telling her not to change (Watzlawick, Weakland, & Fisch, 1974). In discussion the therapist agreed with her comments, noting the need to balance the risk of intense training with periods of recuperation. However, the therapist also expressed skepticism about any changes she might make before consulting a coach, and she was asked to carefully consider the consequences of acting too quickly. She was reminded that if her performance improved Robert's criticisms would return. The psychologist then recommended that Sherry train more and ask Robert to attend the next session so that the therapist could help him to stop his harassment.

The session with Robert concentrated on convincing him to cease his pursuit of Sherry. Robert had again verbalized frustration with Sherry and the marriage. He saw her as disinterested in the family and he was tired of waiting for her to return from her ride so the family could eat together. He was told that he needed to take care of himself and the children and stop demanding that Sherry be a better wife and mother. He was to plan fun family activities, such as a trip to the zoo, during the time Sherry rode. Furthermore, he was not to wait for her at dinner and he was instructed to get a baby-sitter for the children one night per week. These nights he should spend with friends and explore new activities. The intention of these directives was to redirect his pursuit of Sherry. This would result in Sherry's no longer needing to distance herself from him.

In the next few weeks Sherry cut back on her mileage and began asking for ways to better plan her workouts. She was still fatigued but somewhat more motivated. She also became increasingly aware that Robert was acting differently. She stated that he stopped nagging her and that he appeared preoccupied. She speculated that he was having an affair, but knew that most of his time was being spent with the children. Obviously, Robert was complying with the directives given in the collateral session. Although Sherry was talking about the marriage, she had not yet identified it as a therapy issue.

During these sessions the therapist continued to express concern that Sherry was moving too quickly with the training changes, but agreed to discuss goal setting and the contingencies around successful training efforts that might be affecting her motivation. She was encouraged to expand her training log to include daily goals that focused on her effort rather than distance or speed. Stimulus control and contingency management (Rimm & Masters, 1979) were introduced to her preparations for workouts, and she also structured her post-workout time. The training log suggested that she no longer avoided going home but that she still isolated herself when there. The next week Sherry requested a joint session and arrived with Robert. Together they reported a series of conversations during the week. Sherry was riding better but was not any happier. In yet another attempt to do something different, she decided to skip her ride one day and find out what Robert was doing with the children. The afternoon together was tense yet enjoyable. That night Sherry began to cry and asked for Robert's support. This was the first of a series of discussions about the marriage. They realized that these conversations were just the beginning and they began to discuss marital therapy. Unlike many marriages seen in therapy (Guerin, Fay, Burden, & Kautto, 1987), Robert and Sherry presented with a low level of conflict. Their communication had been so severely restricted that any discussion was awkward.

Marital therapy initially targeted increasing the number and frequency of positive behaviors between Robert and Sherry. Behavior-exchange procedures (Holtzworth-Munroe & Jacobson, 1991; Jacobson & Margolin, 1979) were introduced. This procedure involved spouses increasing the frequency of desired behaviors toward each other. The two basic steps involve having each spouse pinpoint specific desirable behaviors that they want from their partner and then increase the frequency of these behaviors. Variations of this exercise used with Sherry and Robert were for each person to identify behaviors the other desired and have each person make specific requests from the spouse. Following a successful week, the behavior-exchange exercises focused on sexual and nonsexual intimacy. Since some uncertainty about sexual intimacy was indicated, sensate-focus exercises were prescribed (Lazarus, 1988). These exercises involved the use of sensual massage to help the couple explore each other's bodies and learn, through verbal feedback, about the effects of this exploration.

As progress occurred, perspective taking and communication skills were discussed and role-played. Particular attention was directed at Robert's resentment over Sherry's spending so much time away from him and the boys. The content of the discussion was on how the couple could arrive at alternatives to overcome these resentments. This strategy for repairing hurt feelings has been described by Sherman, Oresky, and Roundtree (1991). As this discussion occurred, Robert and Sherry were individually interrupted so they could be coached and instructed on basic communication skills such as reflective listening, I-statements, and behavior descriptions of events (Holtzworth-Munroe & Jacobson, 1991). Whenever Sherry would begin to back away from the dialogue or Robert would begin to blame her, the couple were asked to sit apart and attempt to replicate the spouse's perspective on the problem. The couple was then brought back together to verify each of the perspectives.

After 2 months of marital sessions, Sherry and Robert requested an end to therapy. Sherry was racing again. Her performance had improved slightly but was still not at the level she desired. She trained fewer hours per week and spent more time in family activities. Robert reported that Sherry still tended to avoid stressors in the marriage but that he understood her reactions and felt better equipped when approaching her. The issue of Sherry's independence was never fully addressed in the therapy.

In general, this therapy was successful. Sherry's complaints centered on her cycling but were obviously issues in other contexts of her life, especially the marriage. The therapy accomplished several objectives related to the initial hypotheses. First, Sherry's stubborn resistance against change was undermined. By using her hesitation to trust, she was encouraged to examine her difficulties in a novel manner. This examination yielded her decision that training harder was not going to make her better or happier. She abandoned the overused solution of putting her head down and pushing harder. Secondly, by using Robert's frustration in the marriage, a change in how the family system functioned was initiated. Consistent with the homeostatic nature of a system, Sherry had to change to maintain the system. Lastly, as she abandoned the focus on training harder and directed some of her intensity toward the marital issues, she began to perform better. It might have been helpful for Sherry to continue in therapy but initiating the change was the goal.

■ *THE CASE OF PETER* ■

In the initial session Peter, the 51-year-old lawyer and tennis player, presented that his failure to control anger disrupted his tennis game. He disclosed that the anger outbursts were not limited to tennis, but he conceptualized this emotional reactivity as part of his competitive manner. He avoided most questions about his family, work, and social networks, and he refused to have his wife attend an assessment session. The therapist was not surprised when he canceled the subsequent appointment.

The second session, 3 months later, provided a clearer picture of Peter's anger and his life. The warning by the club's board frightened him, which in turn promoted a greater degree of disclosure. Most of the information for the multicontextual assessment was obtained during this session. As is apparent in Table 4.3, angry and abusive outbursts and heavy drinking were the two key individual issues that permeated the problem situations in Peter's life. With the exception of these two behaviors, Peter presented as an intelligent, competent individual.

A functional analysis of these behaviors revealed that the anger and drinking were pervasive and essentially functionally autonomous. Peter noted that he would be angry, intimidating, rude, or demanding throughout a good part of each day. He saw these behaviors as a key part of his personality. It was also apparent that this anger was a key part of his success. When he barked, others tended to cower or react to his anger rather than to the content of his communication. In the adversarial world of law, this demanding, one-up position was adaptive. In addition, he said that most of the time he felt in control of his emotions and that he knew when to use and not use the "personality." However, the cost of this style was considerable. In social, work, and sport contexts people with choices tended to avoid him. About once a month the anger would result in a physical altercation. He felt that his wife was frequently the undeserving target. Usually, he was frustrated about something that happened earlier in the day. Then after arriving at home, he would erupt at some incidental event. He admitted guilt in abusing his wife but was certain that she would not leave the marriage. He felt the marriage was strong. Drinking did not appear to be a reliable antecedent to the abuse.

Peter's drinking consisted of three or fewer drinks about 4 days a week, and about once every other week he would consume about 10

Table 4.3 Multicontextual Assessment: Peter

Presenting problems: Loss of emotional control affecting tennis game
Related issues: Explosion of temper, spouse abuse, alcohol consumption

	Strengths	Weaknesses
Individual		
Physical	—Physically active lifestyle —General good health	—Heavy drinking —Outbursts of anger —Strong potential for harm to others
Psychological	—Intelligent —Competitive and tough —Very achievement oriented	—Poor impulse control —Minimizes temper control problem —Is rewarded for aggressiveness
Family		
Marital/ significant other	—None revealed during assessment	—Physically abuses wife —Several separations
Children, parents, and family issues	—Wants to improve relationship with daughter	—Weak relationship with daughter —Aggression and violence in birth family (father as model) —No relationship with members of birth family
Sport	—Tennis skills improving —Plays frequently	—Angry outbursts have disqualified him for competition —Some trouble finding people to play with
Work	—Very successful lawyer —Economically secure —Drinking has not interfered —Toughness brings in clients	—Frightens and alienates most co-workers —Drinking part of unwinding with co-workers and peers
Social/peers	—Existing friendships are very loyal	—Small social network —Friends overlook aggressiveness

drinks. Other days he would abstain. He noted that drinking helped calm him down and helped him interact in a friendly manner. He thought that he tended to drink more when the demands at work were high or when he was bored. He would usually drink with others at bars or restaurants. Some peers who avoided him during the day would interact with him when he was drinking. He also believed that tennis gave him an alternative to drinking because drinking diminished his proficiency. He avoided alcohol until after he played. The evidence did not suggest that he was severely dependent on alcohol.

The therapeutic relationship with Peter was tenuous, at best. Although disclosing during the second interview, he obviously preferred to be in charge and in control. He wanted to set the agenda, and he was hesitant to deviate from it. As would be discovered later, Peter's information was not always reliable. He initially reported no marital difficulties other than the occasional abuse. Peter's wife, Ruth, later confirmed that they had separated several times and that her commitment to the marriage remained uncertain. Consequently, the therapy needed to be firm, but not confrontive. Although didactic presentation of ideas, especially rational scientific ideas, might be acceptable, Peter needed to make the decisions. He was currently receptive to counseling, but quick changes would be needed to keep Peter engaged and working in therapy.

Peter's descriptions of his drinking and his anger outbursts suggest problems in self-control or self-regulation (Kanfer & Phillips, 1970). He proficiently and successfully used both behaviors to gain control over his world. However, the control was not reliable. When demands were substantial, he tended to lose control over these behaviors. When control was lost, these behaviors became self-defeating and injurious. In such situations his repertoire of alternative coping responses appeared limited. Consequently, it was hypothesized that increased self-control of both the drinking and the anger were necessary.

Intervention

The initial task in therapy was to address Ruth's safety. Ruth accompanied Peter to the third session. Peter was seen first to obtain his consent and support for the therapist's agenda with Ruth. Then Ruth was seen alone, where she detailed both the drinking and the abuse history. Her report suggested that Peter tended to minimize his difficulties but confirmed that the drinking and the abusive anger appeared as separate issues. She was uncertain of her commitment to the marriage but consented to base her decision on Peter's commitment to making changes. Following recommendations from the research on spousal abuse (Bagarozzi & Giddings, 1983; Steinfeld, 1989), Ruth was encouraged to attend therapy with another therapist. This therapy would be directed at empowering Ruth in the relationship, encouraging her to alter her interactions with Peter to further ensure her safety. She agreed to work with the second therapist for the next 6 weeks while Peter would work with the original therapist. At the end of the 6 weeks, both therapists met with Peter and Ruth to discuss the possibility of a series of marital-therapy sessions. Ruth was provided the name of a therapist who had previously agreed to provide this therapy.

Peter then joined the session and was informed about the specifics of the plan. He provided written consent so that his therapist could communicate with Ruth's therapist about his therapy. He also agreed to give written permission to inform Ruth's therapist if he terminated therapy. Peter and the therapist again discussed strategies to ensure Ruth's immediate safety. With her therapist Ruth was able to identify cues that indicated the potentially violent situations and her actions that tended to provoke Peter's anger. She was also able to plan ways of ensuring her safety, including staying with her sister if necessary.

Therapy with Peter then focused on cognitive-behavioral interventions to develop self-regulation skills (Karoly & Kanfer, 1982). The current trend in the treatment of heavy drinking is to view drinking as a disease requiring hospitalization and abstinence. However, the research evidence suggests that heavy drinkers are a heterogeneous group and that the disease model is not applicable to all heavy drinkers (Fingarette, 1985; Miller & Hester, 1986). An alternative treatment model (Sobel & Sobel, 1993) that has received empirical support is based on self-control principles and consequently fits well with Peter's presenting problems. In this treatment (controlled drinking versus abstinence) clients establish their drinking goals, which are reassessed each treatment session. Assessment then begins with the clients' completing a self-evaluation of drinking behaviors including frequency, amount, context, and consequences of drinking. In addition, clients begin self-monitoring drinking behavior and educating themselves about the medical contraindications and social contingencies of drinking. The self-monitoring helps identify particularly problematic or risky drinking situations. Treatment focuses on helping individuals identify and use their own strengths, resources, and preferred coping strategies to avoid excessive drinking. In addition to problem solving, treatment can also include assertiveness training, cognitive restructuring, relaxation training, and self-instructional training.

The most empirically supported treatment for anger has been Novaco's (1975; Bistline & Frieden, 1984) variation of Meichenbaum's (1985) stress-inoculation training. The rationale of this treatment closely fits with the self-control training intervention. The treatment consists of three stages: assessment and conceptualization, skill acquisition and rehearsal, and application and follow-through. Clients learn to think of their anger as controllable. They are asked to assess the parameters of the anger, including the physiological and cognitive antecedents of previously uncontrollable episodes. Working from self-monitoring forms, the anger is viewed as jointly determined by an initial provocation, mediating cognition, the somatic-affective state of the individual, and behaviors that might have the effect of escalating any potentially conflictual encounter. Treatment relies on the development of relaxation skills, coping skills, and use of self-instructional statements. These strategies are learned using imaginal rehearsal of stressful situations that are then applied to actual circumstances. Therapist and client need to be vigilant for interpersonal factors that inhibit the execution of these self-control skills. The application phase attends to feedback from others to alter intervention strategies to produce the most effective outcome.

Therapy with Peter blended these two treatment programs. Initial discussions focused on providing a general self-control model for these problem behaviors and an explanation of the transactional nature of his cognition, emotions, and behaviors. Incidences of both the drinking and anger outbursts were also tracked to educate Peter on how to identify the specific characteristics of provocative situations and interactions. Specific treatment goals were established by Peter. He identified the goal of controlling his drinking so that he would stop at two drinks on any given day. As for the anger outburst, Peter's goals included being aware of his angry reactions and being able to control his expression of anger to avoid "chewing people out" and to prevent physical altercations. Self-monitoring forms were then developed with the initial intention of more clearly defining the problematic contexts and toxic interactions.

Considerable gains were evident in the next two sessions. Using the self-monitoring forms, Peter related a considerably enhanced understanding of both behaviors and the contexts and interactions that precipitated these behaviors. He also appeared more aware of the adaptability of drinking and intimidating others. After the first week of monitoring, he proposed an experiment the following week to determine the effects of changing his drinking patterns. He proposed to go to the bar and drink considerably more some days and less on others while monitoring others' reactions to him. In the next session he seemed impressed by the relationship between his drinking and others' reactions to him. He still argued that the alcohol was a means of relaxing and that he felt somewhat socially isolated when not drinking with his friends. In an effort to provide alternatives to drinking, Peter began to learn progressive and imagery relaxation skills (Lichstein, 1988; Woolfolk & Lehrer, 1984), discuss social skills issues (Bellack & Hersen, 1979), and consider alternatives to socializing and relaxing at the bar.

During this period, Peter had become more aware of the cues that marked the onset of his anger. He was able to reliably identify somatic and cognitive indicators of relatively low levels of anger. He also successfully avoided high levels of anger during the second week of self-monitoring. However, he was frustrated in his attempts to avoid expressing anger. This frustration resulted from his attempt to alter his abrupt, demanding interpersonal style. Although he was warned that this style would evolve slowly, Peter's perception that he had made little progress bothered him. An alteration to the self-monitoring forms was made to help him differentiate angry responses and his intimidating style.

Unfortunately, Peter failed to keep the next appointment. Attempts to contact him failed; he did not return the therapist's telephone calls. Per the therapy agreement, the therapist contacted Ruth's therapist, who detailed that in their last session Ruth appeared on the verge of leaving Peter, at least temporarily. Ruth noted to her therapist that Peter was not drinking, but he was avoiding interaction with her. The lack of interaction bothered her. She felt she needed more support but that he was unwilling to provide it. In the therapy, continued uncertainty about the marriage led to the decision to separate. She thought that she needed time to make personal changes before dealing with the marriage. Ruth's therapist suggested that Ruth propose one conjoint session to discuss her decision. A week later, the therapist received a message that Peter had refused the conjoint session. No further contact with him occurred.

ETHICAL ISSUES

In these case studies we have proposed that competitive recreational athletes be approached from a multisystemic framework. However, we are not suggesting that basic athletic-performance-enhancement interventions are inappropriate—only that such interventions might ignore additional, nonsport factors that influence performance. We are also sensitive to the possibility that the competitive recreational athlete might not desire intervention beyond the sport context. This is the client's prerogative. But it is also the clinician's responsibility to offer the client the most appropriate intervention available.

This discussion brings us to the inevitable ethical issues that arise in work with competitive recreational athletes. Virtually every professional association with members who provide helping services has developed and maintained a set of ethical standards (American Association for Counseling and Development, 1988; American Association for Marriage and Family Therapy, 1988; American College Personnel Association, 1989; American Psychiatric Association, 1989; American Psychological Association, 1990; National Association of Social Workers, 1990). Ethical standards are made necessary by the potential conflict between the interests of the client (i.e., efficient, effective service) and the interests of the professional (i.e., income). These standards assist professionals in becoming aware of issues that might compromise their service delivery and guide their behavior in potentially conflictual situations (Lakin, 1991; Pope & Vasquez, 1991).

Confidentiality

Confidentiality (American Psychological Association, 1990, Principle 5) is perhaps the most obvious ethical issue germane to the multicontextual assessment and intervention described in this chapter. Confidentiality, ethically and legally, is the privilege of the client, not the therapist. The therapist is charged with protecting this privilege because clients are typically not in a position to regulate it and sometimes fail to understand the implications of confidentiality (Benson, 1984; Robinson & Merav, 1976). When nonclients are contacted and involved in assessment and treatment, the issue of confidentiality must be closely monitored. When treatment is directed at more than one person, as is the case in any marital or family therapy, the question of who is the client and who has the privileged and protected communication becomes more confusing (Zygmond & Boorhem, 1989). In each of our cases the therapist met with other family members and could have benefited from contacts with coaches and others (Henggeler & Borduin, 1990). In these situations the counselor must be extremely careful in defining who is the client, securing permission and limitations on communication with others, and clarifying issues of confidentiality with everyone involved.

In each case we defined the client as the individual who has requested assistance. It was the confidentiality of this person's communication that must be protected. Although we argued for permission to contact others, we also clarified with the client what would or would not be said to assess the client's understanding and gain consent for these contacts. When meeting with significant others, the counselor must begin with a clarification of the limits of confidentiality. Specifically, the counselor has a responsibility to alert the informants that promises to withhold information from the identified client cannot be made (though arguments for the value of disclosure can also be made). The paramount issue is the guaranteed confidentiality of the client and clarity of communication to all parties involved in the counseling process.

Competence

A second ethical issue evident in our case presentations was therapist competence. Principle 2A of the American Psychological Association's ethical principles states that "psychologists accurately represent their competence, education, training, and experiences" (1990, p. 391). This principle implies a recognition of the power implicit in the counselor's role. Given this power, counselors must be aware of the limitations of their training and experience, and they adopt an obligation not to misrepresent themselves to their clients. Counselors must also build relationships with other professionals to be aware of available alternative competencies. Finally, counselors should continue training beyond their formal education to maintain the competencies identified by their credentials (Pope & Vasquez, 1991).

Competency limitations were evident in the treatment of both Sherry and Peter. With Sherry, three referrals to other professionals were made because of the possibility that her complaints might be related to issues outside the therapist's area of expertise. The referrals to the physician and dietician were made to address the possible physiological bases of Sherry's presenting problems. Although Sherry was not concerned about her general health or diet, existing evidence supported the possibility that her motivational and mood complaints might have been related to physical health issues.

The decision to refer her to a coach was less apparent but no less important. An examination of her workout log suggested that she was not basing her training plan on her performance or her fitness level. In fact, training was paradoxically related to her performance because indications of overtraining were met with efforts to train harder. Being a cyclist, the therapist fought a temptation to make training recommendations. The therapist was not trained as a coach and the relationship between Sherry and the counselor would have been altered if the counselor adopted both coach and therapist roles. Sherry, giving credence to the counselor's power as a helping professional, might acritically, and possibly dangerously, follow the counselor's advice.

In the treatment of Peter, the therapist was knowledgeable of the self-control treatment of alcohol consumption, but had no experience in providing this treatment. Consequently, to obtain consultative supervision before initiating this intervention, the therapist contacted a psychologist who regularly implemented such treatment. Although a referral was not thought to be necessary in this case, a method to ensure the competency of the treatment was. The supervisor was helpful in providing templates for the self-report assessment instruments, self-monitoring forms, and issues important to maintaining the integrity of the treatment.

Dual Relationships

A third ethical issue evident in the cases presented in this chapter involves the assessment and avoidance of dual relationships with clients (American Psychological Association, 1990, Principle 7). The greatest percentage of ethical complaints about mental health professionals concerns dual relationships (Lakin, 1991). Dual relationships are fairly easy to define; they are much more difficult to recognize. A dual relationship occurs when the counselor maintains another, significantly different relationship with the client that serves to confuse both roles (Pope & Vasquez, 1991). By far the most ethically troublesome exploitive dual relationships involve sexual contact with a client. More commonly, the dual relationship role is quite subtle and might be social, financial, or professional. These relationships frequently evade detection because they develop as purely secondary or appear as inconsequential. The problem with the addition of a second relationship is that it jeopardizes the professional relationship, the therapy process, and possibly the client's welfare (Borys & Pope, 1989; Keith-Spiegel & Koocher, 1985). The dual relationship creates a conflict of interest for the therapist and must be avoided (Lakin, 1991).

Julio's academic status presented an obvious potential for dual relationship. Both Julio and the therapist were employed by the same college in the same university. Although the two had never met previously, the potential for future interactions existed. For example, both client and therapist might be active on the same college or university committees. During the initial session the therapist explored Julio's reaction to this possibility and discussed the importance of carefully considering the impact of counseling on future interactions. Julio's understanding and sensitivity to the dual relationship issues does not alleviate the therapist's responsibility to ensure that future relationships are not negatively influenced by the nature of the therapeutic relationship.

Obviously, other ethical problems require our attention. All ethical issues, including confidentiality, competence, and dual relationships, are complex and often troublesome. They arise at moments when clients are vulnerable and therapists are lax. An understanding of these potential counselor-client conflicts is a necessary component of the counseling process, and a commitment to the highest ethical standards must accompany the therapeutic effort.

CONCLUSION

With the possible exception of high school athletes, there is no larger population of sport competitors than competitive recreational athletes. Their sheer numbers alone make competitive recreational athletes interesting to the applied sport psychologist, and their demanding lifestyles and competitive drive allow them to serve as valuable living laboratories for the sport scientist. Although competitive recreational athletes have traditionally been a relatively homogeneous group, dominated by middle-class males, subpopulations representing virtually all demographic categories can be identified. But common to almost all of these athletes is their voluntary participation in their sport in the face of heavy family and career responsibilities.

Given this, it is not surprising that competitive recreational athletes present to the therapist with psychologically heterogeneous problems and needs. Fortunately, our traditional sport performance enhancement interventions appear to be beneficial for them (Whelan et al., 1989). However, we have proposed here a multicontextual approach to the competitive recreational athlete. This holistic position acknowledges sport as one limited aspect of a person's extremely complex set of interacting spheres of influence. Based on this assumption, our model dictates specific multicontextual assessment and intervention activities that we believe offer the applied sport psychologist a richer, more comprehensive approach to the difficulties of the competitive recreational athlete.

REFERENCES

American Association for Counseling and Development. (1988). *Ethical standards.* Alexandria, VA: Author.

American Association for Marriage and Family Therapy. (1988). *Code of professional ethics for marriage and family therapists.* Washington, DC: Author.

American College Personnel Association. (1989). A statement of ethical principles and standards. Alexandria, VA: Author.

American Psychiatric Association. (1989). *The principles of medical ethics with annotations especially applicable to psychiatry.* Washington, DC: Author.

American Psychological Association. (1990). Ethical principles of psychologists. *American Psychologist*, **45**, 390-395.

Bahrke, M.S., & Morgan, W.P. (1978). Anxiety reduction following exercise and meditation. *Cognitive Therapy and Research*, **2**, 323-333.

Bagarozzi, D.A., & Giddings, C.W. (1983). Conjugal violence: A critical review of current research and clinical practices. *American Journal of Family Therapy*, **11**, 3-15.

Bandura, A. (1969). *Principles of behavior modification.* New York: Holt, Reinhart & Winston.

Bandura, A. (1977). Self-efficacy: Toward a unifying theory of behavioral change. *Psychological Review*, **84**, 919-925.

Bandura, A. (1978). The self system and reciprocal determinism. *American Psychologist*, **33**, 344-358.

Barlow, D.H., & Cerny, J.A. (1988). *The psychological treatment of panic.* New York: Guilford Press.

Barlow, D.H., Craske, M.G., Cerny, J.A., & Klosko, J.S. (1989). Behavioral treatment of panic disorder. *Behavior Therapy*, **20**, 261-282.

Barnett, M.L., & Stanicek, J.A. (1979). Effects of goal setting on achievement in archery. *Research Quarterly*, **50**, 328-332.

Beck, A. (1976). *Cognitive therapy and emotional disorders.* New York: International Universities Press.

Bellack, A.S., & Hersen, M. (Eds.) (1979). *Research and practice in social skills training.* New York, Plenum Press.

Benson, P.R. (1984). Informed consent. *Journal of Nervous and Mental Disease*, **172**, 642-653.

Bistline, J.L., & Frieden, F.P. (1984). Anger control: A case study of a stress inoculation treatment for a chronic aggressive patient. *Cognitive Therapy and Research*, **8**, 551-556.

Borys, D.S., & Pope, K.S. (1989). Dual relationships between therapist and client: A national study of psychologists, psychiatrists and social workers. *Professional Psychology: Research and Practice*, **20**, 283-293.

Brown, R., Ramirez, D., & Taub, J. (1978). The prescription of exercise for depression. *Physician and Sportsmedicine*, **6**, 35-45.

Burton, D. (1989). Winning isn't everything: Examining the impact of performance goals on collegiate swimmers' cognitions and performance. *Sport Psychologist*, **2**, 105-132.

Carter, B., & McGoldrick, M. (Eds.) (1988). *The changing family life cycle*. New York: Gardner Press.

Clitsome, T., & Kostrubala, T. (1977). A psychological study of 100 marathoners using the Myers-Briggs type indicator and demographic data. In P. Milvey (Ed.), The marathoner: Physiological, medical, epidemiological and psychological studies. *Annals of the New York Academy of Sciences*, **301**, 1010-1019.

Corbin, C.B. (1972). Mental practice. In W.P. Morgan (Ed.), *Ergogenic aids and muscular performance* (pp. 94-118). New York: Academic Press.

Csikszentmihalyi, M. (1990). *Flow: The psychology of optimal experience*. New York: Harper & Row.

Derogatis, L.R., Lipman, R.S., Rickels, K., Uhlenhuth, E.H., & Covi, L. (1974). The Hopkins Symptom Checklist (HSCL): A self-report symptom inventory. *Behavioral Science*, **19**, 1-15.

deVries, H.A., Wiswell, R.A., Bulbulian, R., & Moritani, T. (1981). Tranquilizer effect of exercise. *American Journal of Physical Medicine*, **60**, 57-66.

DeWitt, D.J. (1980). Cognitive and biofeedback training for stress reduction with university athletes. *Journal of Sport Psychology*, **2**, 288-294.

D'Zurilla, T.J. (1988). Problem-solving therapies. In K.S. Dobson (Ed.), *Handbook of cognitive-behavioral therapies*. New York: Guilford.

Feltz, D.L., & Ewing, M.E. (1987). Psychological characteristics of elite young athletes. *Medicine and Science in Sports and Exercise*, **19**, S98-S104.

Feltz, D.L., & Landers, D.M. (1983). The effects of mental practice on motor skill learning and performance: A meta-analysis. *Journal of Sport Psychology*, **5**, 25-27.

Fenz, W.D. (1975). Strategies for coping with stress. In I.G. Sarason & C.D. Spielberger (Eds.), *Stress and anxiety: Vol. 2* (pp. 305-336). New York: Wiley.

Fenz, W.D., & Jones, G.B. (1972). Individual differences in physiological arousal and performance in sport parachutists. *Psychosomatic Medicine*, **34**, 1-8.

Fingarette, H. (1988). *Heavy drinking*. Berkeley, CA: University of California Press.

Fisch, R., Weakland, J.H., & Segal, L. (1982). *The tactics of change*. San Francisco: Jossey-Bass.

Folkins, C., & Sime, W. (1981). Physical fitness training and mental health. *American Psychologist*, **36**, 373-389.

Frank, J.D. (1982). Therapeutic components shared by all psychotherapies. In J.H. Harvey & M.M. Parks (Eds.), *Psychotherapy research and behavior change* (pp. 9-37). Washington, DC: American Psychological Association.

Frank, J.D., & Frank, J.B. (1991). *Persuasion and healing: A comparative study of psychotherapy*. Baltimore, MD: Johns Hopkins University Press.

Freischlag, J. (1981). Selected psycho-social characteristics of marathoners. *International Journal of Sport Psychology*, **12**, 282-288.

Gill, D.L., Gross, J.B., & Huddleston, S. (1981). Participation motivation in youth sport. *International Journal of Sport Psychology*, **14**, 1-14.

Glasser, W. (1976). *Positive addiction*. New York: Harper & Row.

Goldfarb, A.H., Hatfield, B.D., Sforzo, G.A., & Flynn, M.G. (1987). Serum beta-endorphin levels during a graded exercise test to exhaustion. *Medicine and Science in Sports and Exercise*, **19**, 78-82.

Goldstein, A.P., & Myers, C.R. (1986). Relationship-enhancement methods. In F.H. Kanfer & A.P. Goldstein (Eds.), *Helping people change: A textbook of methods* (3rd ed.). New York: Pergamon Press.

Gondola, J., & Tuckman, B. (1982). Psychological mood states in "average" marathon runners. *Perceptual and Motor Skills*, **55**, 1295-1300.

Gontang, A., Clitsome, T., & Kostrubala, T. (1977). A psychological study of 50 sub-3 hour marathoners. In P. Milvey (Ed.), The marathoner: Physiological, medical, epidemiological and psychological studies. *Annals of the New York Academy of Sciences*, **301**, 1020-1046.

Gould, D., Feltz, D.L., Weiss, M., & Petlichkoff, L.M. (1982). Participating motives in competitive youth swimmers. In T. Orlick, J.T. Partington, & J.H. Salmela (Eds.), *Mental training for coaches and athletes* (pp. 57-58). Ottawa, ON: Coaching Association of Canada.

Gould, D., Weiss, M., & Weinberg, R. (1981). Psychological characteristics of successful and nonsuccessful Big Ten wrestlers. *Journal of Sport Psychology*, **3**, 69-81.

Greist, J.H., Klein, M.H., Eischens, R.R., & Faris, J. (1978). Running out of depression. *Physician and Sportsmedicine*, **6**, 49-56.

Griffin, L. (1978, April). *Why children participate in youth sports*. Paper presented at American Alliance for Health, Physical Education and Recreation Convention, Kansas City, MO.

Guerin, P.J., Fay, L.F., Burden, S.L., & Kautto, J.G. (1987). *The evaluation and treatment of marital conflict: A four-stage approach*. New York: Basic Books.

Guttman, H.A. (1991). Systems theory, cybernetics, and epistemology. In A.S. Gurman & D.P. Kniskern (Eds.), *Handbook of family therapy: Vol. 2* (pp. 41-62). New York: Brunner/Mazel.

Hackfort, D., & Spielberger, C.D. (Eds.) (1989). *Anxiety in sports: An international perspective*. Washington, DC: Hemisphere.

Hall, H.K., Weinberg, R.S., & Peterson, A. (1987). Effects of goal specificity, goal difficulty and information feedback on endurance performance. *Journal of Sport Psychology*, **9**, 43-54.

Hemery, D. (1986). *Sporting excellence: A study of sport's highest achievers*. Champaign, IL: Human Kinetics.

Henggeler, S.W., & Borduin, C.M. (1990). *Family therapy and beyond: A multisystemic approach to treating the behavior problems of children and adolescents*. Pacific Grove, CA: Brooks/Cole.

Hollingsworth, B. (1975). Effects of performance goals and anxiety on learning a gross motor task. *Research Quarterly*, **46**, 162-168.

Holtzworth-Munroe, A., & Jacobson, N.S. (1991). Behavioral marital therapy. In A.S. Gurman & D.P. Kniskern (Eds.), *Handbook of Family Therapy: Vol. II* (pp. 96-133). New York: Brunner/Mazel.

Honikman, B., & Honikman, L. (Eds.) (1991, September-October). *TAC times*. Santa Barbara, CA: The Athletic Congress.

Jacobson, N.S., & Margolin, G. (1979). *Marital therapy: Strategies based on social learning and behavior exchange principles*. New York: Brunner/Mazel.

Kanfer, F.H., & Goldstein, A.P. (Eds.) (1986). *Helping people change: A textbook of methods* (3rd ed.). New York: Pergamon Press.

Kanfer, F.H., & Phillips, J.S. (1970). *Learning foundations of behavior therapy*. New York: Wiley.

Karoly, P., & Kanfer, F.H. (1982). *Self-management and behavior change: From theory to practice*. New York: Pergamon Press.

Keith-Spiegel, P., & Koocher, G.P. (1985). *Ethics in psychology*. New York: Random House.

Klosko, J.S., Barlow, D.H., Tassinari, R., & Cerny, J.A. (1990). A comparison of Alprazolam and behavior therapy in treatment of panic disorder. *Journal of Clinical and Consulting Psychology*, **58**, 77-84.

Lakin, M. (1991). *Coping with ethical dilemmas in psychotherapy*. New York: Pergamon Press.

Lambert, M.J., Shapiro, D.A., & Bergin, A.E. (1986). The effectiveness of psychotherapy. In S.L. Garfield & A.E. Bergin (Eds.), *Handbook of psychotherapy and behavior change* (3rd ed.) (pp. 157-211). New York: Wiley.

Landers, D.M. (1980). The arousal-performance relationship revisited. *Research Quarterly for Exercise and Sport*, **51**, 77-90.

Lazarus, A.A. (1988). A multimodal perspective on problems of sexual desire. In S.R. Leiblum & R.C. Rosen (Eds.), *Sexual desire disorders*. New York: Guilford.

Lichstein, K.L. (1988). *Clinical relaxation strategies*. New York: Wiley.

Locke, E.A. (1968). Toward a theory of task motivation and incentives. *Organizational Behavior and Human Performance*, **3**, 157-189.

Locke, E.A., & Latham, G.P. (1985). The application of goal setting to sport. *Journal of Sport Psychology*, **7**, 205-222.

Mahoney, M.J. (1991). *Human change processes: The scientific foundations of psychotherapy*. New York: Basic Books.

Mahoney, M.J., & Avener, M. (1977). Psychology of the elite athlete: An exploratory study. *Cognitive Therapy and Research*, **1**, 135-141.

Mahoney, M.J., Gabriel, T.J., & Perkins, T.S. (1987). Psychological skills and exceptional athletic performance. *Sport Psychologist*, **1**, 181-199.

Mahoney, M.J., & Meyers, A.W. (1989). Anxiety and athletic performance: Traditional and cognitive developmental perspectives. In D. Hackfort & C.D. Spielberger (Eds.), *Anxiety in sports: An international perspective* (pp. 77-94). Washington, DC: Hemisphere.

Martens, R. (1977). *Sports competition anxiety test*. Champaign, IL: Human Kinetics.

Meichenbaum, D. (1985). *Stress inoculation training*. New York: Pergamon Press.

Meyers, A.W. (1980). Cognitive-behavior therapy and athletic performance. In C.H. Garcia Cadena (Ed.), *Proceedings of the First International Sport Psychology Symposium* (pp. 131-161). Monterrey, Mexico: Editorial Trillas.

Meyers, A.W., Cooke, C.J., Cullen, J., & Liles, L. (1979). Psychological aspects of athletic competitors: A replication across sports. *Cognitive Therapy and Research*, **3**, 361-366.

Meyers, A.W., & Okwumabua, T.M. (1985). Psychological and physical contributions to marathon performance: An exploratory investigation. *Journal of Sport Behavior*, **8**, 163-169.

Miller, W.R., & Hester, R.K. (1986). Inpatient alcoholism treatment: Who benefits? *American Psychologist*, **41**, 794-805.

Minuchin, P. (1985). Families and individual development: Provocations from the field of family therapy. *Child Development*, **56**, 289-302.

Mischel, W. (1968). *Personality and assessment*. New York: Wiley.

Morgan, W.P. (1980). The trait psychology controversy. *Research Quarterly for Exercise and Sport*, **51**, 50-76.

Morgan, W.P. (1985). Selected psychological factors limiting performance: A mental health model. In D.H. Clarke & H.M. Eckert (Eds.), *Limits of human performance* (pp. 70-80). Champaign, IL: Human Kinetics.

Morgan, W.P. (1987). Reduction of state anxiety following acute physical activity. In W.P. Morgan & S.E. Goldston (Eds.), *Exercise and mental health* (pp. 105-108). New York: Hemisphere.

Morgan, W.P., & Costill, D. (1972). Psychological characteristics of the marathon runner. *Journal of Sports Medicine and Physical Fitness*, **12**, 42-46.

Morgan, W.P., & O'Connor, P.J. (1988). Exercise and mental health. In R. Dishman (Ed.), *Exercise adherence: Its impact on public health* (pp. 91-121). Champaign, IL: Human Kinetics.

Morgan, W.P., & Pollack, M. (1977). Psychological characterization of the elite distance runner. In P. Milvey (Ed.), The marathoner: Physiological, medical, epidemiological and psychological studies. *Annals of the New York Academy of Sciences*, **301**, 382-403.

Murphy, S.M., & Woolfolk, R.L. (1987). The effects of cognitive interventions on competitive anxiety and performance on a fine motor skill accuracy test. *International Journal of Sport Psychology*, **18**, 152-166.

National Association of Social Workers. (1990). *Code of ethics*. Silver Spring, MD: Author.

National Bowling Council. (1990). *Profile of a dynamic market: Bowling*. Washington, DC: Author.

National Golf Foundation. (1991). *Golf participation in the United States*. Jupiter, FL: Author.

National Sporting Goods Association. (1990). *Sport participation in 1990*. Mt Pleasant, IL: Author.

Nelson, R.O., & Barlow, D.H. (1981). Behavioral assessment: Basic strategies and initial procedures. In D.H. Barlow (Ed.), *Behavioral assessment of adult disorders*. New York: Guilford.

Nelson, R.O., & Hayes, S.C. (1986). *Conceptual foundations of behavioral assessment*. New York: Guilford.

Nicholls, J.G. (1984). Achievement motivation: Conceptions of ability, subjective experience, task choice and performance. *Psychological Review*, **81**, 328-346.

Nichols, A., Whelan, J.P., & Meyers, A.W. (1991). Assessing the effects of children's achievement goals on task performance, mood and persistence. *Behavior Therapy*, **22**, 491-503.

Novaco, R. (1975). *Anger control: The development and evaluation of an experimental treatment*. Lexington, MA: Heath.

Ogilvie, B.C. (1968). Psychological consistencies within the personality of high level competitors. *Journal of the American Medical Association*, **205**, 780-786.

Ogilvie, B.C., & Tutko, K.A. (1966). *Problem athletes and how to handle them*. London: Pelham Books.

Okwumabua, T.M., Meyers, A.W., & Santille, L. (1987). A demographic and cognitive profile of masters runners. *Journal of Sport Behavior*, **10**, 212-220.

Orlick, T. (1986). *Psyching for sport: Mental training for sport*. Champaign, IL: Leisure Press.

Orlick, T., & Partington, J. (1988). Mental links to excellence. *Sport Psychologist*, **2**, 105-130.

Oxendine, J.P. (1970). Emotional arousal and motor performance. *Quest*, **13**, 23-30.

Patterson, G.R. (1974). Interventions for boys with conduct problems: Multiple settings, treatments, and criteria. *Journal of Clinical and Consulting Psychology*, **42**, 471-481.

Phares, E.J. (1992). *Clinical psychology: Concepts, methods, and profession* (4th ed.). Pacific Grove, CA: Brooks/Cole.

Pope, K.S., & Vasquez, M.J. (1991). *Ethics in psychotherapy and counseling: A practical guide for psychologists*. San Francisco: Jossey-Bass.

Raglin, J., & Morgan, W.P. (1985). Influence of vigorous exercise on mood state. *Behavior Therapy*, **8**, 179-183.

Richardson, A. (1967a). Mental practice: A review and discussion. Pt. I. *Research Quarterly*, **38**, 95-107.

Richardson, A. (1967b). Mental practice: A review and discussion. Pt. II. *Research Quarterly*, **38**, 263-273.

Rimm, D.C., & Masters, J.C. (1979). *Behavior therapy: Techniques and empirical findings* (2nd ed.). New York: Academic Press.

Robinson, G., & Merav, A. (1976). Informed consent: Recall by patients tested postoperatively. *Annals of Thoracic Surgery*, **22**, 209-212.

Rushall, B. (1972). Three studies relating personality variables to football performance. *International Journal of Sport Psychology*, **3**, 12-24.

Sachs, M.L. (1984). Psychological well-being and vigorous physical activity. In J.M. Silva & R.S. Weinberg (Eds.), *Psychological foundations of sport* (pp. 435-444). Champaign, IL: Human Kinetics.

Sapp, M., & Haubenstricker, J. (1978). *Motivation for joining and reasons for not continuing in youth sports programs in Michigan*. Paper presented at American Alliance for Health, Physical Education, and Recreation (AAHPER) Convention, Kansas City, MO.

Schildkraut, J.J., Orsulak, P.J., Schatzberg, A.F., & Rosenblum, A.H. (1983). Relationship between psychiatric diagnostic groups of depressive disorders and MHPG. In J.W. Maas (Ed.), *MHPG: Basic mechanism and psychopathology*. New York: Academic Press.

Sherman, R., Oresky, P., & Roundtree, Y. (1991). *Solving problems in couples and family therapy: Techniques and tactics*. New York: Brunner/Mazel.

Silva, J.M. (1984). Personality and sport performance: Controversy and challenge. In J.M. Silva & R.S. Weinberg (Eds.), *Psychological foundations of sport* (pp. 59-69). Champaign, IL: Human Kinetics.

Silva, J., & Hardy, C. (1986). Discriminating contestants at the United States Olympic marathon trials as a function of precompetitive anxiety. *International Journal of Sport Psychology*, **17**, 100-109.

Skubic, E. (1956). Studies of little league and middle league baseball. *Research Quarterly*, **27**, 97-110.

Smith, R.E. (1980). A cognitive-affective approach to stress management training for athletes. In C.H. Nadeau, W.R. Halliwell, K.M. Newell, & G.C. Roberts (Eds.), *Psychology of motor behavior and sport—1979* (pp. 54-72). Champaign, IL: Human Kinetics.

Smith, R.E. (1985). A component analysis of athletic stress. In M. Weiss & D. Gould (Eds.), *Competitive sports for children and youths: Proceedings of Olympic Scientific Congress* (pp. 107-112). Champaign, IL: Human Kinetics.

Sobel, M.B., & Sobel, L.C. (1993). *Problem drinkers: Guided self-change treatment*. New York: Guilford.

Spielberger, C.D., Gorsuch, R.L., & Lushene, R.E. (1970). *Manual for the state-trait anxiety inventory*. Palo Alto, CA: Consulting Psychologists Press.

Sporting Goods Manufacturers Association. (1990). *Volleyball: An emerging sport*. North Palm Beach, FL: Author.

Steinberg, H., & Sykes, E.A. (1985). Introduction of symposium on endorphins and behavioral processes: Review of literature on endorphins and exercise. *Pharmacology, Biochemistry and Behavior*, **23**, 857-862.

Steinfeld, G.J. (1989). Spouse abuse: An integrative interactional model. *Journal of Family Violence*, **4**, 1-23.

Suinn, R.M. (1972). Behavioral rehearsal training for ski racers. *Behavior Therapy*, **3**, 519-520.

Suinn, R. (1987). *The seven steps to peak performance: Manual for mental training for athletes* (2nd ed.). Ft. Collins, CO: Colorado State University.

Tu, J., & Tothstein, A.L. (1979). Improvement of jogging performance through application of personality specific motivational techniques. *Research Quarterly*, **50**, 97-103.

United States Cycling Federation. (1990). *United States Cycling Federation rulebook*. Colorado Springs: Author.

United States Masters Swimming, Inc. (1991). *Masters swimming: What's it all about*. Rutland, MA: Author.

United States Tennis Association. (1990). *USTA annual participation report for adult leagues*. Princeton, NJ: Author.

Wankel, L.M., & Kreisel, P. (1985). Factors underlying enjoyment of youth sports: Sport and age group comparisons. *Journal of Sport Psychology*, **7**, 51-64.

Watzlawick, P., Weakland, J.H., Fisch, R. (1974). *Change*. New York: Norton.

Weinberg, R. (1989). Anxiety, arousal and motor performance: Theory, research and applications. In D. Hackfort & C.D. Spielberger (Eds.), *Anxiety and sport: An international perspective* (pp. 95-115). New York: Hemisphere.

Weinberg, R.S., Bruya, L.D., & Peterson, A. (1985). The effects of goal proximity and goal specificity on endurance performance. *Journal of Sport Psychology*, **7**, 296-305.

Weinberg, R., Gould, D., & Jackson, A. (1980). Cognition and motor performance: Effect of psyching-up strategies on three motor tasks. *Cognitive Therapy and Research*, **4**, 239-245.

Weiner, I.B., & Bordin, E.S. (1983). Individual psychotherapy. In I.B. Weiner (Ed.), *Clinical methods in psychology* (2nd ed.). New York: Wiley.

Weinstein, W.S., & Meyers, A.W. (1983). Running as a treatment for depression: Is it worth it? *Journal of Sport Psychology*, **5**, 288-301.

Whelan, J.P., Mahoney, M.J., & Meyers, A.W. (1991). Performance enhancement in sport: A cognitive behavioral domain. *Behavior Therapy*, **22**, 307-327.

Whelan, J.P., Meyers, A.W., & Berman, J.S. (1989, August). Cognitive-behavioral interventions for athletic performance enhancement. In M. Greenspan (chair), *Sport psychology intervention research: Reviews and issues*. Symposium conducted at a meeting of the American Psychological Association, New Orleans.

Whelan, J.P., Meyers, A.W., O'Toole, M., Hiller, D., Stephens, M., Bryant, F.V., & Mellon, M. (1987a, September). *Psychological contributions to triathlon performance: An exploratory investigation*. Paper presented at the Association for the Advancement of Applied Sport Psychology, Newport Beach, CA.

Whelan, J.P., Meyers, A.W., O'Toole, M., Hiller, D., Stephens, M., Bryant, F.V., & Mellon, M. (1987b, September). *Triathlon performances: The role of experience in the athlete's psychological race preparations and responses*. Paper presented at the Association for the Advancement of Applied Sport Psychology, Newport Beach, CA.

Williams, J.M., & Getty, D. (1986). Effects of levels of exercise on psychological mood states, physical fitness, and plasma beta-endorphin. *Perceptual and Motor Skills*, **63**, 1099-1105.

Wilson, V., Morley, N., & Bird, E. (1980). Mood profiles of marathon runners, joggers and non-exercisers. *Perceptual and Motor Skills*, **50**, 117-118.

Wolberg, L.R. (1967). *The techniques of psychotherapy* (2nd ed.). New York: Grune & Stratton.

Wood, B., & Talmon, M. (1983). Family boundaries in transition: A search for alternatives. *Family Process*, **22**, 347-357.

Woolfolk, R.L., & Lehrer, P.M. (Eds.) (1984). *Principles and practice of stress management*. New York: Guilford.

Ziegler, S.G., Klinzing, J., & Williamson, K. (1982). The effects of two stress management training programs on cardiovascular efficiency. *Journal of Sport Psychology*, **4**, 280-289.

Zygmond, M.J., & Boorhem, H. (1989). Ethical decision making in family therapy. *Family Process*, **28**, 269-280.

Support for this chapter was provided by a Centers of Excellence grant from the State of Tennessee to the Department of Psychology at The University of Memphis.

CHAPTER 5

INVISIBLE PLAYERS: A FAMILY SYSTEMS MODEL

Jon C. Hellstedt, PhD
University of Massachusetts–Lowell

The family is the most important influence in an athlete's life. It is where the young athlete develops the life skills and coping mechanisms to meet the demands of competitive sport. The family provides the primary social environment where the athlete can develop an identity, self-esteem, and the motivation for athletic success. Successful athletes often credit their families for encouragement, discipline, valuing achievement, and, above all, love and support.

Unfortunately, a family can also have negative effects on an athlete's development. Parental demands can foster an atmosphere of rigid rules and unrealistic expectations. A poorly functioning or underorganized family system might engender substance abuse, inadequate interpersonal relationships, poor stress management skills, problems accepting authority from coaches, and a lack of internal controls and self-discipline. An athlete's performance can be negatively impacted by either excessive or ineffectual family influence.

The demands on athletes and their families have intensified in recent years. The wealth and glamour of professional sport and the proliferation of youth-sport programs have greatly affected the American family. Berryman, in a historical review of the rise of youth sports for children, states, "Children's sport organizations led to changes in the American family structure and, in many instances, added a new aspect to the socialization of children" (1988, p. 14).

This historical development provides a context for the scene described in the case of the Stanley family (see the case study that follows). This scenario occurs often in other families as well—after ski races, gymnastic events, hockey, and baseball games. The drama involves a talented youngster competing in an athletic event and not meeting parental expectations. The parents, who have put time, money, and emotional energy into their child's athletic development, are disappointed by their son's or daughter's performance. They appreciate the talent their child has but are frustrated by what they perceive as lack of effort. This family drama results in a young athlete's internal conflict (I can't please them so I must be a failure) or tension between parent and child (If they don't lay off, I am going to scream).

■ *THE CASE OF THE STANLEY FAMILY* ■

Amy Stanley was ahead in the semifinal match for 14-year-olds at the regional tennis championships. She was leading, well into the match, when she seemed to get overconfident and she stopped playing aggressively. She lost in a third-set tiebreaker—a match, it seemed, she could have won.

Her parents, Fred and Betty, were watching. Betty was quiet and withdrawn. Fred was visibly upset at Amy's performance and mentioned to Betty, "Why does she always do this to herself? She's so good, yet she doesn't seem to want to win." In the car on the way home from the match, Fred turned to Amy and said, "You didn't seem to really want to win today." Amy was quiet, looked out the car window and said to herself, Maybe you're right.

Fred was concerned about Amy's erratic play and after the most recent match he discussed the situation with Amy's coach. The coach indicated to Fred that over the past year he has observed Amy questioning her commitment to tennis. He has noticed that she doesn't practice with as much intensity as before and lately often needs to be talked into workouts and competitions. The coach acknowledged Amy's considerable talents and told Fred that of all the juniors he has worked with, Amy has the most natural ability. The coach then suggested that Amy talk to Dr. Jane Hawthorne, a sport psychologist who has worked with many tennis players in the area. "She's very good, and she knows a lot about the sport," the coach said. Fred, though somewhat uncomfortable about the idea, talked it over with Betty and Amy and Fred called Dr. Hawthorne for an appointment.

Dr. Hawthorne has an interesting perspective as a clinical sport psychologist. In addition to her skills in using relaxation, visualization, and goal setting to help athletes improve their performance, she also has a background in family systems theory and intervention. During her graduate training she took courses in systems theory, and during her clinical internship she received supervision in family therapy. At many workshops and sport psychology conferences she has learned skills in working with individual athletes, but she is also interested in working with their families. She remembers attending a sport psychology conference where a psychologist who works with elite athletes said that overinvolved parents are often a problem. His policy was to "bar parents from the office" and to work only with the athlete. Dr. Hawthorne felt uncomfortable with that model of intervention. It overlooked an important reality. Parents can't be kept in the waiting room. Family influences are always present, visibly or invisibly, in the athlete's mind and performance.

The Stanley family (a hypothetical composite of several families I have worked with in my clinical practice) and the interactions that form their family system become invisible players and have a direct impact on Amy's performance on the court. As athletics at all levels become more professionalized and as elite athletes compete at increasingly younger ages, the assessment of family-based problems and interventions in the family system become essential skills for the sport psychologist.

REVIEWING THE LITERATURE

Since Rainer Martens (1978) first awakened the consciousness of parents, coaches, and psychologists about the potential emotional risk factors in youth sports, accounts of problems in athlete families have been common in the media. The image of the youth-league parent (or coach) who inflicts emotional (and sometimes physical) abuse on children who fall short of performance expectations is a common theme. Sport magazines, newspapers, and television documentaries have featured stories on young athletes who have been apparent victims of overbearing parents. This media attention raises an interesting question that needs to be addressed with empirical research: What are the positive and negative factors in families of young athletes? Unfortunately, few studies have addressed this issue.

Family Interactions

The research on athlete families underscores the major influence of the family on the developing athlete. For example, studies by both Greendorfer and Lewko (1978) and Sage (1980) found that parents are the major influence on introducing a youngster to youth sport. The role of the father is notable in both studies in that he appears to be the major influence on the sport participation of both male and female children.

Other studies document the major influence of parents. For example, McElroy and Kirkendall (1980) concluded that parents are the primary significant other in the formation of children's (especially males) attitudes toward winning and skill development. Melnick, Dunkelman, and Mashiach (1981) found in a study of Israeli athletes that parents of sport-gifted children held high expectations for their children's performance and offered more encouragement for sport participation than parents of a control group of nonathletic children.

The major influence of the parents is stronger in the early years of development. There is a shift in influence toward peers and other adults when a child reaches adolescence. Higgenson (1985) found that in preadolescent years the parents are the primary influence, but as the child reaches adolescence the influence shifts from parents to coach. During adolescence the influence of the parents is present but more subtle. For example, Berlage (1981), in a study of fathers' career aspirations for their hockey-playing sons, found that fathers of 11- and 12-year-old hockey players have pronounced aspirations for their children to continue in sport. Most of the fathers surveyed hoped their sons would play hockey in high school and college, and almost all fathers believed that continued participation would benefit their sons in adult life. An easy assumption to make is that this type of family environment has a major impact on the attitude of the developing athlete.

Parental stress and pressure are complex issues that are difficult to research. Attempts have been made, however, to determine what factors in the family create a stressful environment for the child. Gould, Horn, and Spreemann (1983) described many sources of stress in the youth-sport environment and indicated a major stressor is the young athlete's fear of failure. Although this fear of failure can emanate from other sources (self, peer, or coach), a major source appears to be parents. In his research on the development of competitive trait anxiety, Passer (1984) has concluded that negative performance evaluation from parents has a major role in the development of high trait anxiety. Conversely, in a study that looked at the other side of this issue, namely, the factors that support positive sport participation, Scanlan and Lewthwaite (1986) found that male wrestlers who experienced positive parental performance reactions and a high level of parental involvement in the sport experienced greater enjoyment than those who did not.

Research on family influences is complex and difficult. Quantitative methodology is often unable to explore the intricacies of the family processes that exist in athlete families. The subtle interactive factors that exist in family life lend themselves more to qualitative methods using interviews and content analysis. In recent years some studies have used this methodology to highlight some of the issues and processes that provide helpful insight into clinical assessment with these families. Among this research are the studies of Bloom (1985), Kesend (1991), and Scanlan, Stein, and Ravizza (1991).

Developmental Events

The work of a research team headed by Bloom studied the developmental events in the lives of exceptionally talented young people. Included in this study were samples of artists, musicians, mathematicians, and scientists, as well as athletes. Bloom's report included studies of Olympic-level swimmers (Kalinowski, 1985), professional tennis players (Monsaas, 1985), and an integrative analysis of their home environments by Sloane (1985). The results of this team of researchers is important to the model developed in this chapter, in that these results provide both a developmental perspective and the system qualities of the home environment.

The developmental process is similar for swimmers and tennis players. Three distinct phases of development occur beginning with early parental influence and ending with the family as an emotional support system for the independently functioning adult athlete.

- In the early years (ages 4 to 12) the child is introduced to a variety of sports mainly by the parents and mostly the father. The emphasis is on playfulness, fun, and family involvement in athletic activity. The parents provide early instruction but soon locate a coaching or instructional program that will expose the child to a higher skill level. Toward the end of this phase, the parents enjoy taking the child to entry-level competitions where the emphasis is on fun rather than on winning.
- In the middle years (ages 13 to 18) there is a shift from fun and playfulness to the development of sport specialization and a commitment to higher levels of training and competition. Both the athlete and the family center their leisure-time activities around the sport. The parents now provide transportation, structure practice time, arrange competitions, and secure the best coaching available. Some problems are reported with parents' negotiating the transition as the coach assumes primary influence on skill development. Conflicts between parents and coaches often develop and coaching changes become frequent (Monsaas, 1985).
- In the later years (ages 19 to late 20s) the athlete separates from the family and moves on to college or independent living. The family is mainly a support system and an emotional refuge from the stress of competition. Monsaas (1985) reports that this stage is negotiated well by most of the parents. Some, however, "missed traveling to tournaments and felt a bit left out in these later years" (p. 265). It is also interesting to note that a few of the fathers continued in the role of coach and traveled with the athletes until they were in their late 20s.

There were similarities in the systemic composition of the families in the study. Sloane (1985) noted three main qualities of the home environment.

- The families shared a strong value system that emphasized success through hard work. This value system was clearly communicated by the parents to the children through verbal teaching and role modeling.
- The families valued the talent area. Both parents, but most clearly the fathers, valued athletic activity as a way to learn important character traits, such as a motivation to achieve and a dedication to hard work.
- The family system willingly organized itself around the athletic activities of the child athlete. Parents forfeited other activities to take the child to the pool or the tennis court. Family vacations were organized around training or competitions. Much time and money was devoted to sport, to the exclusion of other family activities.

Family: A Source of Support or Pressure?

In a study of the sources of stress in the lives of elite figure skaters, Scanlan and colleagues

(1991) demonstrated the multidimensional nature of stress and how the family system is paradoxically both a source of and a refuge from those pressures. They found family influences were a source of both valuable support and stress. On the positive side, most of the athletes reported that family support was essential in helping them cope with the pressures of being competitive athletes. Some athletes, however, reported stressful family interactions, such as performance criticism from parents, precompetition lectures, "backstabbing" from other competitors' parents, and guilt over the large sums of money spent on training. Financial pressures came from parents repeatedly and overtly reminding them of the costs and, covertly, from the athletes' observing their parents working hard to support them.

Another study using a similar methodology was conducted by Kesend (1991). Using interview material obtained from 20 Olympic-level athletes (15 males and 5 females), Kesend examined sources of encouragement and discouragement in the athlete's development. The data showed that the family is the athlete's main source of encouragement. Parents and siblings were more widely cited for providing support than coaches, peers, and members of various sport organizations.

Courtesy University of Illinois Daily Illini

Specific mechanisms for family support were introduction to sport in the early years, support for sport participation, positive role modeling by parents, verbal and nonverbal approval of competitive accomplishments, and emotional acceptance of decisions and ideas about elite-level sport participation.

Parents and family, however, were also sources of discouragement. Parental behaviors interpreted by the athletes as discouraging were suggestions of pursuing alternative careers and parental worry over physical injury. Unrealistic parental expectations also were discouraging to some of the athletes (one athlete had scored 67 points in a basketball game and was criticized by a parent for not playing more aggressively). Overt parental "pushing," however, was not mentioned frequently.

Hellstedt (1990a, 1990b) investigated the parent–athlete interactions in a group of athlete families as they made the transition from the early to the middle stage of athletic development. In a longitudinal study of ski racers and their families, he found that the 12- and 13-year-old elite ski racers perceived their parents as having a strong influence on their athletic development. The specific mechanisms by which parents were influential are parental coaching (teaching and advice giving), off-season monitoring of conditioning and dry-land training, and support and expectations to continue participation in the sport (Hellstedt, 1990a).

In addition, he examined the changes in perceptions of parental pressure that developed between ages 13 and 15 (Hellstedt,

1990b). Parental pressure was measured along three dimensions: general participation in the sport, pressure to continue competing, and performance appraisal. At age 13 there was a substantial group that indicated they were "unhappy" with the amount of parental pressure, especially the pressure to continue participation in the sport. Two years later, however, the athletes perceived less parental pressure and were beginning to perceive the source of this pressure shifting away from parents (particularly the father) to their coach. Figure 5.1 indicates the changes in parental pressure ratings over the 2-year interval.

The data generally showed that these athletes felt positively about the contributions of their parents to their athletic development. However, at least two problem areas were apparent. There was a higher perception of parental pressure in the younger age group, indicating that these years might be a time of higher sensitivity to this type of influence. As well, affective reactions of dissatisfaction were positively correlated with the amount of parental pressure in both age groups (Hellstedt, 1990b). This finding points toward the possibility that anger toward parents can be a factor in sport withdrawal or athlete burnout.

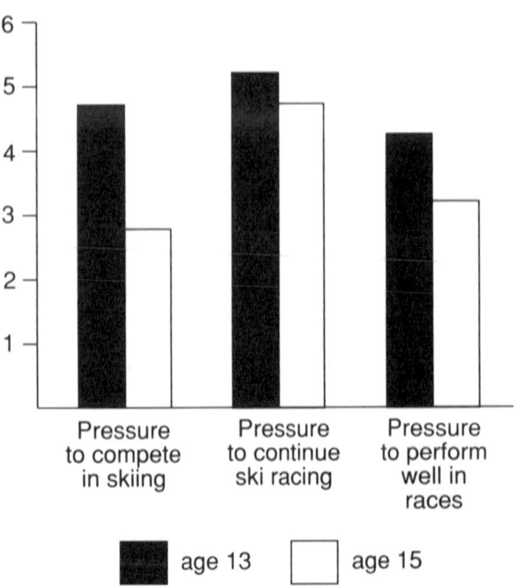

Figure 5.1 Changes in perceptions of parental pressure in a group (N = 67) of developing ski racers. Mean scores on scale of 1 (very little) to 9 (very much).

The Paradox of the Athlete Family

In summary, the research on athletes and their families suggests that though the family might be a source of stress to some athletes, in general the family is an indispensable source of support. Contrary to negative media images of the athlete family, studies on athlete families seem to indicate that for the majority of young athletes the family is a vital social support system that nourishes and encourages their development. The families of successful athletes appear to be tightly organized systems with very concerned, albeit competitive, parents with high expectations for their children. A common denominator in these families is strong parental role models that provide the energy and motivation for the young athlete. These families also value hard work and individual achievement.

It is because of these values that a paradox emerges. The strengths of these families can also be their weakness. What is perceived as a positive encouragement by some young athletes might be a negative, disabling, and damaging experience for others. There is a fine line between positive achievement motivation and excessive pressure. What some young athletes see as parental encouragement might feel like a lack of freedom and breathing space to others.

In addition, the research shows another problem area for families. Perhaps because of the tight organization that develops and the close parent–child relationship, some of these families had difficulty negotiating the transition from one stage of family development to the next. For example, the transition from the parents as the dominant influence on the athlete's training to the teacher or coach was sometimes difficult. Parents and coaches often had conflict over what was necessary for the athletes' skill development.

There is also a developmental process that unfolds in a somewhat predictable course in athlete families. During the early years of sport involvement, the emphasis is on fun and skill development. There is a shift, however, in the commitment stage of development where both the athlete and the family system invest major levels of energy and financial resources in sport involvement. In the later stages of the athletes' development, the athlete separates from the parents and family and is influenced primarily by other adults, such as coaches, agents, and members of athletic organizations. For some families these transitions seem to be difficult and can result in conflict between extrafamilial adult influences and parents. In the next part of this chapter we will more closely examine transitions in the developmental processes of the families.

The balance between healthy encouragement and excessive parental involvement is precarious. When the parents cross over the line they are in danger of becoming too "child focused" (Bradt & Moynihan, 1971). In this process the spousal subsystem in the family loses its vitality, and children's success in sport becomes the emotional center of the family. The result can be marital conflict or family dysfunction during or subsequent to the period of children's active athletic involvement.

A DEVELOPMENTAL MODEL OF THE ATHLETE FAMILY

To fully understand the difficulties facing a young athlete like Amy Stanley, sport psychologists need a model for assessing the structural health and developmental maturity of the athlete family. In this section we will develop a model based on research on athlete families and concepts from family systems theory. We will apply this model to the Stanley family.

Family systems theory developed from the work of therapists and researchers who observed that symptom formation in a person is connected to developmental or structural problems in the family. Although there are many different perspectives and emphases among family theorists, there is basic agreement that the family is an interacting social system in which the component parts affect one another. A useful framework for understanding the structural properties of a family is found in the work of Minuchin (1974). According to this model, the main structural components of the family are the power hierarchy, rules, interactional patterns, subsystems, and types of boundaries between subsystems.

A family is more than structural components, however. A family system undergoes a constantly changing developmental process. A useful perspective on this process of change and the connections between generations as the family develops is provided by Bowen (1965, 1978). Bowen's insights have recently been enhanced by the developmental framework provided by Carter and McGoldrick (1989). This framework is basic to the model developed in this chapter. Following the stage theories of individual developmental paradigms such as Erikson's (1950), Carter and McGoldrick view the family as a social organism that, in much the same way a person does, passes through a life cycle. This is a series of stages in which certain tasks must be accomplished before the next stage of development can be successfully mastered. If these tasks are not completed during early stages there will be problems in later stages of development. The transitions from one stage to the next are particularly stressful for families and are often the interval of time when symptoms are present in individual members or in the family system as a whole.

The demands of athletic competition and training often present unique circumstances that are deviations from the normal family life cycle. For example, a young gymnast's family might experience premature separation brought on by the athlete's leaving home to receive specialized coaching. A swimmer or figure skater must train many hours a day and this absorbs family resources, with great impact on the entire family. A career-threatening injury after years of training will create a grief experience for an athlete and a family to resolve. Such developmental delays, barriers, or impasses can negatively affect the young athlete.

The first three columns of Table 5.1 present the stages and tasks of all families as developed by Carter and McGoldrick (1989). In the last column I have added my own formulation of the unique tasks of the athlete family. The model developed here is limited to intact, middle- to upper-class families, which demographically are no longer the norm in our society. Many athletes emerge from less organized families or families that experience major disruptions, such as abandonment or separation and divorce; these are not specifically addressed in this chapter due to space limitations. The general developmental tasks required of these families can be found in Peck and Manocherian (1989) and Fulmer (1989) and can be adapted to the athlete family system as it is presented in this chapter.

Although the following analysis will demonstrate how the Stanley family is having difficulty negotiating certain developmental transitions and tasks, it is not my intent to "pathologize" this family or athlete families in general. Even though this family is having some difficulty, it is a healthy family with many strengths. It is important to restate what was said earlier in the chapter: that in most cases (including this one) the family is the main source of support and encouragement for the developing athlete.

The Stanley Family: A Developmental Analysis

To an outside observer, the Stanleys are a model family. They are a successful, financially comfortable, professional family with two attractive children who are gifted athletes.

■ *Fred Stanley, age 43, is a lawyer and an avid recreational tennis player. His wife, Betty, 41, is a former school teacher who is currently enjoying her role as a full-time parent to their two daughters, Caroline, 17, and Amy, 14. Both Caroline and Amy are competitive tennis players, and since Caroline was 11 the Stanley family has organized itself around the tennis court. Both girls used to play other sports, but because of their potential and his own love of the game, Fred (with Betty's support) has encouraged them in tennis. At around age 12 each girl chose to specialize in tennis; they are now year-round competitors. Coaches, summer camps, indoor winter training, tournaments, travel, a racquet stringer in the garage, and a station wagon full of tennis gear are visible symbols of the family's avocation. The family used to go on family vacations, but now all family travel is for the girls' tennis tournaments. Fred goes to as many of the tournaments as he can, and both he and Betty attend the local matches.*

A closer look at the course of this family's development, however, reveals some unresolved developmental tasks that are affecting Amy's performance in tennis. We will begin our developmental analysis of this family at the time when Fred and Betty met, dated, and decided to marry.

Table 5.1 Stages and Major Tasks of Athlete Family Development

Stage of family development	Major transitional tasks	General changes needed to proceed developmentally	Athlete family changes needed to proceed developmentally
Single young adult	Differentiate self from parents and family of origin	• Become emotionally and financially independent from family • Develop intimate peer relationships • Establish work and career identity	• Attain psychological peace with own athletic successes, failures, and unfulfilled dreams • Resolve unfulfilled expectations from own parents • View present and future athletic involvement as a mode of self-fulfillment and physical well-being
New married couple	Commit and bond in a new relationship	• Develop internal relationship patterns in commitment, caring, communication, and conflict resolution • Perform external relationship tasks (such as work and recreation) to allow adequate space for marital relationship • Realign family of origin and peer relationships to include spouse	• Maintain boundary around athletic involvement to allow space for spousal relationship • Together with spouse, develop mutually fulfilling athletic and exercise activities
Family with young children (ages 4-12)	Accept children into the family system	• Adjust career and marital relationships to make space for children • Share parenting and household management tasks with spouse • Realign relationships with parents to include grandparental roles	• Introduce children to a variety of individual and team sport environments • Provide or secure quality coaching and safe sport environment for proper skill development • Emphasize fun and skill development and minimize competitive success • Maintain permeable boundaries to allow for nonathletic individual and family experiences

(continued)

Table 5.1 *(continued)*

Stage of family development	Major transitional tasks	General changes needed to proceed developmentally	Athlete family changes needed to proceed developmentally
Family with young children *(continued)*			• Demonstrate family value of hard work and goal attainment by parental example and role modeling rather than verbal persuasion
Family with adolescent children (ages 13-18)	Increase flexibility of family boundaries to allow for gradual independence of children	• Allow for gradual shift from parent to adolescent child in decision making • Develop permeable external family boundary to permit entrance and exits of adolescents and peers to and from family system • Maintain strength of spousal subsystem in the family • Refocus spousal subsystem on marital, midlife identity, and career issues	• Encourage and support commitment of child athlete to sport generalization or specialization, depending on child's skills and desires • Provide financial and emotional support without straining family financial and emotional resources • Encourage permeable boundaries for family and self to allow for nonsport social and intellectual involvement • Allow for increasing independence of child athlete in decision making • Secure safe and productive coaching environment for child athlete • Allow for shift of influence on child athlete from parents to teacher and coach • Encourage and support goal attainment and work ethic through both role modeling and verbal teaching • Maintain spousal identity and relationship apart from athletic activities of child athlete

Launching children (ages 18 to late 20s) and moving on	Accept children as adults and allow entries and exits from family system	• Refocus on spousal system as a dyad • Develop adult-to-adult relationships with grown children • Realign relationships with adult children to include spouses, in-laws, and grandchildren • Accept disabilities and death in grandparental generation	• Allow athlete to gain financial and emotional independence from parents • Continue emotional support and crisis intervention if necessary • Identify family as a refuge from the pressures and rigors of competition • Accept authority of coach and accept lesser role in coach–parent–athlete triangle • Reestablish spousal relationship in absence of direct involvement in athletic activity of children • Continue participation in recreational sport for personal fulfillment and health maintenance • Assist grown child athlete's retirement from competition and transition from competitive athletics to career and work
Family in later life (adult offspring ages late 20s to middle age)	Accept shift of generational roles	• Maintain spousal relationship in face of decline in physical strength • Support a central role in the family system of middle generation • Enjoy grandparental role with youngest generation • Engage in life review and integration • Prepare for and enjoy a fulfilling retirement • Prepare for loss of spouse, friends, and, eventually, one's own death	• Complete unresolved issues over athletic accomplishments of grown children • Assist adult athlete in retirement from competition and emotional resolution of the end of career • Focus on nonathletic activities with spouse and grown children • Participate in recreational sport and exercise for personal fulfillment and health maintenance

Note. From "The Changing Family Life Cycle: A Framework for Family Therapy" by B. Carter and M. McGoldrick. In *The Changing Family Lifecycle* (2nd ed.) by B. Carter and M. McGoldrick (Eds.), 1989, Needham Heights, MA: Allyn & Bacon. Copyright 1989 by Allyn & Bacon. Adapted by permission.

Stage One: The Unattached Young Adult

A developmental analysis of the Stanley family begins with the life experience of Fred and Betty Stanley when they met in college as single, young adults. A genogram (McGoldrick & Gerson, 1985) of this period of the family's development appears in Figure 5.2.

■ *Fred and Betty met during college. Fred, a prelaw student, was a senior. Betty was a junior. Fred's stable, middle-class family encouraged his college education and his entering law school. But Fred had struggled throughout his life for his father's acceptance. His father was an emotionally closed person who had difficulty expressing positive feelings for his son. He owned his own manufacturing company, was a workaholic, and struggled financially at various times when the children were young. Fred's father was set in his ways and demanded a great deal from his children: Although he encouraged Fred to excel in sports and academics he gave him little verbal reward. Fred's mother, on the other hand, was nurturing to her three children. She was not a strong figure, however. She let her husband dominate most aspects of the family decision making. She avoided marital*

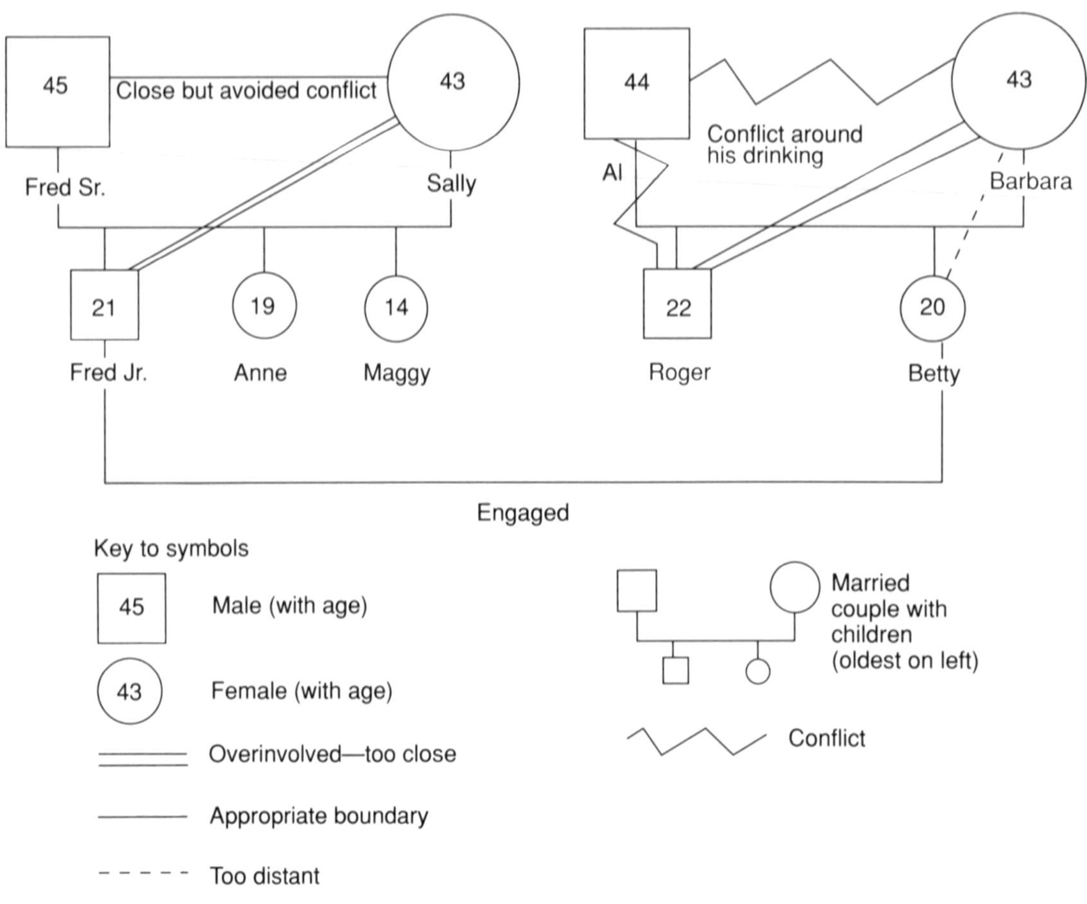

Figure 5.2 Genogram of Fred and Betty Stanley as single, young adults.

conflict and encouraged her children not to challenge their father.

Among the Stanley children, Fred was clearly the star. Throughout school he was a capable athlete and a good student. Fred played baseball, swam, and played tennis at the local club. In high school he played basketball, though he lacked height and often played in a backup role. He also played tennis and was elected team captain his senior year. Fred tried out unsuccessfully for the college tennis team—there were too many talented players at his school. He was frustrated by not making the team but continued to play recreationally.

In contrast to the Stanley family, which was tightly organized and devoid of conflict, Betty's family was quite different. There was open conflict between her parents, Al and Barbara, which centered on her father's drinking and her mother's anger at Al's irresponsibility. Betty's older brother, Roger, was the hero in this family and was often put in the responsible role of taking over many of Al's duties and becoming Barbara's helper. Betty took on the role of peacemaker in the family. The conflict between her parents bothered her, and she would mediate their disputes. Betty became emotionally controlled and internalized pain and sadness that she never expressed to others.

Betty was active in high-school sports. She ran cross-country and track and participated in gymnastics. She was also a solid, hardworking student. Because of her unhappy home life she enjoyed getting away from home, and when she met Fred she was immediately attracted to him.

To the casual observer, Fred and Betty were able to accomplish most of the developmental tasks of this stage of family development, which are

- to establish a sense of self in work and gain financial independence,
- to develop intimate peer relationships, and
- to differentiate themselves from their families of origin (Table 5.1).

At first glance, Fred and Betty looked and acted happy and self-confident. Some unresolved developmental tasks, however, were present that became problems in the development of their own family. Both failed to differentiate from their families of origin; Fred was and is still working to please his father. He is self-centered and fixated on being financially and professionally successful. Betty is a capable person, but she has low self-esteem and rigid emotional control. Her inability to differentiate from her family of origin manifested in a desire to avoid conflict and a need to establish a marital relationship in which Fred was the dominant player.

Athletically, the main task for the young couple was the development of an active and competitive lifestyle. This was relatively easy for both of them, because they were both active in sports. Fred taught Betty to play tennis, and she influenced him to enjoy running for exercise. During their courtship and early marriage they remained active in sport.

Stage Two: The Newly Married Couple

The major task for this stage of family development is to build a strong spousal relationship with an equal share of power. In addition, the couple must develop workable communication patterns, the ability to nurture and express affection for one another, and the mechanisms to resolve conflict (Nichols, 1988). Lastly, the newly married couple needs to establish itself as separate from their families of origin.

■ *Fred and Betty married. Both families were present, though Fred's father and Betty's mother seem to have been the major players in the wedding arrangements and events. Fred had finished his first year of law school, and Betty had graduated from college. They moved to an apartment at Fred's university and Betty began teaching in an elementary school in a nearby town.*

Betty taught school for the first 2 years of their marriage; this helped pay the bills while Fred went to law school. He graduated from school, passed the bar exam, and got an excellent job with a large law firm in the city.

Their marital contract was based on a complementarity of needs. The result was a marital system with an unequal balance of power. In choosing a partner, Betty sought stability; she chose a strong male figure, which she lacked in her own father. She also chose to avoid conflict as a way of making the marital relationship work. Fred, on the other hand, was comfortable with Betty, who was similar to his own mother. He was pleasing his father by being successful and having visibly successful children. He also followed his father's model by becoming a dominant and demanding father figure. Fred's fantasy when he met Betty was that they would create a close family of high achievers. Betty's fantasy was that they would be stable and free of conflict. Their marital roles were also influenced by their complementary sibling positions in their own families. Fred was the oldest and dominant male child, and Betty was the younger subordinate female child.

Fred remained on a successful career path. They were busy during these years. Tennis became a favorite pastime for Fred. He played at the club level and entered local tournaments. Their social life (mixed-doubles events and parties) centered on tennis. They also fell into a pattern of becoming active in activities outside their relationship and began to find little time for each other.

The major task that was not met at this stage was to establish mechanisms for resolving conflict. Betty's desire to avoid conflict and her collusion in the establishment of Fred's dominant role in the power hierarchy became a problem as the family developed.

Stage Three: The Athlete Family With Young Children

In athlete families the main task when the children are young is to introduce them to a variety of sports. In the families studied by the Bloom research team, this was a time of great excitement and playfulness. The excitement of seeing a child learn a sport skill is intense for parents. The child often loves the first encounter with sport because of the playful, noncompetitive nature of the environment.

■ *Soon after Fred began his career as a lawyer, they had their first child. Betty left her teaching position and became a full-time mother. Three years later their second child was born. The children developed without any major physical problems or illness. Fred and Betty stayed active in sports and gradually introduced the children to gymnastics, then soccer, swimming, and skiing. At age 6, Caroline began tennis lessons.*

The Stanleys are typical of athlete families at this stage of development. Parents introduce children to sport and spend time teaching their children sport skills. The family clearly values sport and the parents are willing to spend much family time with lessons and practice. For families who negotiate this stage well the playful and enjoyable quality of sport activity is not lost. Children enjoy the activity and the development of athletic skill.

There are potential problems at this stage of development for athlete families and they have begun to appear with the Stanleys. The main task of a family with young children is to make space for the children. The Stanleys had no problem with this; in fact, they made too much space for the children, who have become an enormous presence in the family.

Fred and Betty have grand expectations for their children and engage in what is called the family projection process (Bowen, 1965), in which one or both parents project their own unfulfilled wishes from their youth onto their children.

Many parents have grandiose fantasies about their children, but in the Stanley family these fantasies developed considerable intensity. Both Fred and Betty had images when their daughters were young (or perhaps even before they were born) that they would be exceptional children and top athletes. Fred's images were the strongest and derived from his relationship with his own father and his inability to be good enough to please him. The pattern of enmeshment with both Caroline and Amy stems from his own family experience. His two daughters have become involved in his need to achieve to please his father.

Another task of this developmental period is that the parents share in the nurturing and care of the children. In the Stanley family, however, these roles have become restrictive. Fred handles the sport role. Betty takes care of most other things.

■ *As the children grew, Betty did most of the parenting in the home and in relationship to school activities. Fred's parenting role largely centered on the girls' sport involvement. Evenings and weekends Fred threw a ball to the girls and took them to the tennis court to practice. As Caroline became more involved in tennis, Fred met her at the club after work and hit balls with her. He became disenchanted with the club pro and soon found another pro to work with her.*

Another unresolved issue at this stage is that Fred and Betty are not able to make adequate space in the family for their own spousal relationship. When too much space is made for the children, the family becomes child focused, and the boundaries in and around the family become rigid because most of the family involvement is in youth sport. They can become a tennis (or hockey, skiing, football, or equestrian) family. The children develop friendships with children in the same sport and don't meet others. The parents neglect their own relationship by focusing too much of their time and energy on the children. This is evident in Fred and Betty's relationship: they were unable to draw a boundary around their own relationship and the level of intimacy decreased.

Stage Four: The Family With Adolescent Children

For many families, adolescence can be the most difficult period of development. It is a time of great turmoil; the child begins to change from being dependent and compliant to being independent and more connected with peer group than family. The authoritative structure of the parental subsystem is challenged and the ability of the parents to adapt to this change is severely tested. If the parents are not able to adapt and retain the respect of the child, the ability of the family to function smoothly is diminished. The main tasks involve a realignment of the boundaries and power hierarchy of the family. The child must gradually be given more power in the family and more involvement in the decision-making processes. For example, Mom and Dad's saying no to a request to stay at a friend's house for the night changes to their asking the adolescent what is a reasonable hour to come home from a party and all agreeing to a mutually acceptable time.

Adolescence is also a difficult time for athlete families because it is during this stage that there is a transition from sports as fun to sports as serious business. Although adolescents in many families drop out of youth-sport programs to pursue other interests (Gould & Horn, 1984), in athlete families the pattern is reversed. The major task for them is to develop a commitment to sport and the role demands of the serious athlete.

Adolescence is also a time where the primary influence on the child athlete shifts from the parents to the coach. The parents' role changes. They become the athlete's support structure. The coach becomes the primary influence for skill and competitive development. Some parents have difficulty with this shift, and diffuse boundaries in the parent–athlete relationship result in conflicts in the coach–parent–athlete relationship (Hellstedt, 1987).

At the same time that the shift in influence is away from them, the parents continue to be influential in the child athlete's development by emphasizing a goal orientation and a strong work ethic. It is critical for parents to strike a workable balance between teaching discipline and determined effort while also fostering a sense of independence in the child athlete.

Adolescence is the stage when the first major derailment from the normal family life cycle occurs in the athlete family. For the child athlete, adolescence is a prolonged or substantially different period than for most of the child's peer group. The demands of athletic training and competition often result in a deprivation of free time, hanging out, and dating. Also, non-sport-related career issues are put on hold as the youngster focuses on the role of athlete. This prolonged adolescence is reinforced by the child's continuing to be dependent on the family for financial support during the early stage of competition. This derailment becomes a moratorium in which the athlete and the athlete's family does not share the experience of summer jobs, peer relationships, or decision making about college choice or career options. Instead, the family continues to concentrate on the young athlete's sport involvement. The result is a developmental impasse.

As shown in Table 5.1, the family can help the athlete through this period in several ways. One is to support, wherever possible, the athlete's sense of independence. A practical way of accomplishing this is for the parents to let the athlete travel and compete without their presence. Another is to let the athlete have major input into decisions about coaching, training programs, and competition schedules. Because they are often sheltered by coaches and sport organizations, some elite athletes need to find from their families the psychological permission as well as the necessary skills to establish independent thinking and decision-making patterns.

The parents' major task is to allow the influence shift from parents to coach by establishing a clear boundary between their roles as parent and coach to their child. This boundary will help the developing athlete view family as a safe and supportive refuge from the pressures of competition and training. Also, the family can encourage the adolescent's social maturity by supporting their efforts to have meaningful relationships with peers. Attending concerts, going to friends' homes for the weekend, and dating are important formative experiences and should be encouraged by parents. A life apart from sport is a healthy present and future resource for the athlete. It helps establish a permeable boundary to the extrafamilial social environment around both the athlete and the family.

The Stanley family has hit some snags at this stage of development (see Figure 5.3). Fred is overinvolved with the two girls. Betty is underinvolved and avoids conflict with Fred. Caroline has accepted the invitation to be overinvolved with her father. She has become so absorbed in competitive tennis that she has had limited peer relationships outside of the sport. She has rarely dated or partied; instead, she has devoted herself to competition and training. Her parents have collaborated in this delayed adolescence by

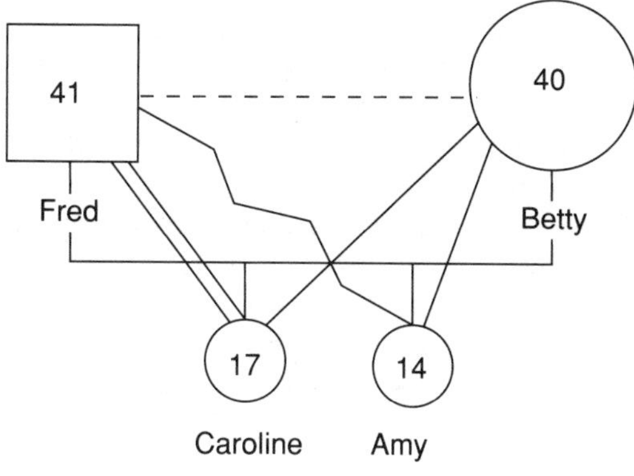

Figure 5.3 Genogram of the Stanley family with adolescent children.

continuing to monitor and supervise her decisions. Career decisions are not important for Caroline or her parents. She has a chance to be a professional tennis player and that has become their goal. She has been granted a college scholarship for her tennis, but the choice of school was made on the basis of the quality of the tennis program and not on academic factors.

Although this parenting approach seems to have worked with Caroline, it hasn't with her younger sister. Amy is uncomfortable with the family script. She wants more independence and is not sure she wants the life of a competitive athlete. Her individual desires are running into conflict with the family values. The crisis that is about to occur has its roots in the failure of the parents and their marital relationship to meet previous developmental tasks.

Amy is about to challenge the family's child-as-athlete focus. She wants more nonsport social involvement and generally more independence in decision making. In addition, Fred and Betty have not developed interests outside of tennis and will have difficulty if Amy pursues other directions. Lastly, Fred has problems with accepting other nonfamily adults as influences on Amy. This leads to conflict with her coaches.

Stage Five: The Launching of Children

The major tasks at the launching phase of family development involve the parents' letting go of their children, developing adult-to-adult relationships with them, and refocusing energy on their own marital relationship. These tasks produce a second major problem area or potential derailment of athlete families from the normal family life cycle.

The normal process is for the young adult (age 18 to 22) to attend college, move away from home, and begin career or graduate training. Marriage and the formation of the adult child's own family might soon follow. Although some young adult offspring will return home for brief periods of time, their goal is to establish independent living apart from the family.

In athlete families the prolonged adolescence of the previous stage results in a launching delay. These families might find they are "out of synch" with other families because their child has put off important life decisions in order to train and compete. There is a trend in many sports for athletes to delay or interrupt college or career preparation to allow them to train more intensively. The launching delay can also result from the parents' maintaining an overinvolved position by managing an abundance of the athlete's life decisions. The emotional separation and letting go of the young adult athlete is hindered by the overinvolvement that might have developed during the previous stages.

If the young adult athlete has committed to sport, the family needs to be aware of and tolerate this delay. Otherwise there will be additional stress or pressure on the young athlete. Athlete families might not have the empty nest that other families experience, so they must tolerate numerous entries and exits from the family caused by the young athlete's leaving home for periods of time to compete and then returning again.

The launching delay can present problems in families where the parents tend toward overinvolvement. The parents might gain emotional gratification from the young adult's delaying independent living, and this might work to the athlete's detriment. For example, in the tennis families studied by Monsaas (1985) two fathers were still actively coaching their young-adult-athlete-offspring well into their late 20s, a process which would likely inhibit the athlete's self-differentiation.

The major task for the athlete family during the launching phase is to perform a delicate balancing act between encouraging financial and emotional independence on the one hand and providing a source of emotional support and refuge from the stress of competition on the other. Finding and trusting a coach outside the family is an essential component in this process.

The Stanleys are in the transition to the launching phase. We can speculate that Fred and Betty will continue to manage Caroline's life and make decisions that will inhibit her growth. It is also possible that Fred and Betty will have difficulty adjusting their own marital relationship without Caroline's (and possibly Amy's) tennis as a focus. The process of separation will be a difficult one for this family.

Stage Six: The Family in Later Life

Later in life the athlete has finished the competitive phase, has retired from sport, and is making the transition to a new career and the establishment of a kinship family. The major issues for the parents are the completion of any unresolved issues about the athletic accomplishments of the adult offspring. It is a time for the parents to enjoy their own spousal relationship and retirement and feel a sense of dignity about their accomplishments as a family. The major issue for them relative to their offspring is to assist and support the athlete around retirement issues and the establishment of a new career and a separate family. A healthy, permeable boundary is appropriate here so that the parents are perceived as supportive but not fused with the adult offspring.

This phase is difficult to predict for the Stanley family. If Fred and Betty are not able to separate from their two daughters and establish their marital relationship as a distinct and valued subsystem, this stage will also be a difficult time for them.

This completes the developmental model. Now we will consider the Stanleys as a family with adolescent children and examine the assessment and treatment issues that emerge when a sport psychologist and family therapist becomes involved with the family.

CLINICAL ASSESSMENT AND TREATMENT

The assessment of the family system of the athlete is an important component to any sport-related assessment procedure. Family processes are often important factors in problems such as eating disorders (Minuchin, Rosman, & Baker, 1978), rehabilitation from injury (Rotella, 1985), burnout and overtraining (Odom & Perrin, 1985), substance abuse (Doherty & Baird, 1983; Krestan & Bepko, 1989), parental overinvolvement (Ogilvie, 1983), and problems in the coach–parent–athlete relationship (Hellstedt, 1987). Even though they present as individual problems, performance blocks or retirement from sport might involve family issues, and a family analysis should be included in the assessment and considered in treatment decisions.

Assessment of the Athlete Family

Based on the model presented in this chapter, two basic questions need to be answered in the process of doing a family-system-based assessment. The first question is, What are the developmental impasses? The second is, What are the structural and interactional strengths and weaknesses of the family?

The best procedure for collecting information is a cluster of interviews with key family members, but all family members do not need to be present for all assessment interviews. It is important, however, to have the principal players in the family together for at least one session to observe the patterns of communication and interaction. A suggested format is to see the athlete alone for a session, the parents together for another session, and the entire family together for one or two sessions. The order in which these sessions take place is interchangeable depending on the circumstances, motivation, and time schedules of family members.

To provide a framework for assessment of the family's developmental and structural characteristics, some assessment categories are helpful. Doherty and Baird (1983) present a succinct assessment formula based on four themes:

1. The level and the source of stress in the family
2. The degree of cohesiveness in the family
3. The ability of the family to adapt to change
4. The interaction patterns in the family

Brief examples from the Stanley family will illustrate these themes.

Levels of Stress

The first task of the clinician in family assessment is to determine the intensity and source of stress in the family.

■ *Fred Stanley called Dr. Hawthorne and asked for an appointment for Amy. "She's a promising young tennis player, but she is easily distracted. And since her last match, which she lost because she lacked the effort, she is talking about quitting tennis and giving up the opportunity to be a top-level player. Her coach suggested I give you a call in the hope that you can sit down and talk with her." Dr. Hawthorne explained to Fred that she likes to do a three- or four-session evaluation, at the end of which she will make treatment recommendations. She explained that the purpose of the evaluation is to get to know both Amy and the family so a treatment contract can be designed to meet everyone's particular needs. Because Caroline would be leaving soon for college, it was agreed that the family would come to the first session together.*

Based on the tone of the telephone conversation, Dr. Hawthorne sensed that Fred Stanley sees the problem as Amy's. He had not defined the issue in a broader context. Dr. Hawthorne speculated that the Stanleys were in a moderate state of stress. No major life crisis faced any family member, but it is likely that feelings of anger, disappointment, and frustration were being felt but not expressed. Their intensity was not as elevated, however, as other athlete families Dr. Hawthorne was currently seeing, such as the family of an elite diver whose mother is dying from cancer during the peak of the diver's career or the family of a gymnast whose father is in the acute stage of alcoholism. Nevertheless, there seemed to be more stress in the Stanley family than Fred acknowledged.

In addition to the degree of stress in the family, it is important to identify the source of stress. Is the source in the family or outside the family system? Internal stressors such as parental pressure on a vulnerable adolescent athlete, financial strain due to a child's training and coaching costs, alcoholism or other substance abuse, death of a family member, or marital conflict and divorce are examples of stressors in the family. Examples of external stressors would be job loss, discrimination and racism, or conflict between the family and a coach or sport organization.

■ *Based on the brief phone conversation with Fred, Dr. Hawthorne formed her initial impression of the source of stress in the family. It seemed to be emanating from a developmental impasse in the Stanleys' transition from a family with young children to one with adolescent children. She also got the impression that Fred's dominance might be a problem in the family and that he might be an overinvolved parent. She would wait and see how they interacted in her office before forming any more impressions.*

Levels of Cohesion

A second dimension for assessing a family is cohesiveness. The main structural element in determining the level of cohesiveness is boundary formation. The rigidity or flexibility of boundaries in and around the family determines the level of cohesiveness in the family. A family that is too cohesive has diffuse boundaries and its members are overinvolved with one another. This would be apparent in a diagnostic interview in which family members think and speak for one another, sit close together, or try to mute the expression of affect. A family lacking in cohesion will have rigid boundaries, evidenced by an unwillingness to look at or speak to one another. This type of family will sit far apart, look distracted or recalcitrant, and not listen when a family member is talking about thoughts or feelings.

■ *In the waiting room Dr. Hawthorne observed that Fred spoke first and introduced the family members to her. Betty seemed quiet and soft-spoken, and Amy seemed sullen and moody. Caroline appeared pleasant and smiled frequently. When they came into the consulting room (with two love seats in an L-shape and the therapist's chair forming a triangle) Fred sat next to Caroline, and Amy sat next to her mother. After some pleasantries Dr. Hawthorne said, "I'd like to hear what each of you likes about your family." Fred was the first to respond by saying, "We have two really outstanding daughters."*

Dr. Hawthorne's initial impressions were that Fred was overinvolved and controlling. He spoke for the other family members and controlled the flow of communication. The cohesion in this family seemed centered on Fred's efforts and agenda. Dr. Hawthorne wondered how the others responded to him.

Adapting to Change

All families need to be able to adapt to changes that are required as the family passes through the stages of the family life cycle. Adaptability implies flexibility in communication, problem solving, and resolving conflict, particularly when a family member asserts a need for change. The impetus for change can come from in the family, such as a developmental change in a member, or from outside the family, such as the death of a friend or relative. For example, the developmental task of the family with adolescent children is to begin to share the authority in the family. The children need to be given more power to make their own decisions. Many families find this difficult to negotiate and the Stanleys are no exception. They have difficulty changing the boundary and power arrangements in the family as the children become adolescents and young adults. A key indicator of the family's adaptability is how flexible the parents are when Amy asserts some independence. A hint of the parents' rigidity emerges early in the interview.

■ *Dr. Hawthorne asked Amy to describe what, if anything, she would like to see changed in her family. Her answer was, "I wish they would let me do more things with my friends and not always want me to be practicing tennis. My wishes don't seem to count." She went on to describe a situation where she wanted to go to a party at her friend's house and her parents wouldn't let her because she had what she described as a "minor" tournament that same weekend. "I don't see why I can't do both," she said in a sullen voice.*

Interaction Patterns

Recurring patterns of interaction form the fourth assessment dimension. Here the clinician looks for communication patterns, ability to tolerate closeness, decision-making processes, time structuring, conflict-resolution patterns, and the mechanisms by which the family accomplishes its daily tasks. Does the family have fun together? Do they spend time apart as well as together? Are they able to negotiate when they disagree on an important issue? Are they able to express intimacy to one another? How do they deal with conflicts between family members?

■ *Betty had been attentive but quiet for the first 15 min of the session. When asked what she liked about the family, she said, "I think we get along pretty well compared to a lot of families." Dr. Hawthorne agreed with her but then went on to ask, "What does happen in the family when you don't agree on something?" Betty indicated that she usually went along with the wishes of others, especially Fred. Amy said, "We don't negotiate; they tell me what to do and I'm expected to do it." Caroline said, "The only two in the family that fight are Dad and Amy. I think they are too much alike. Mom and I get along with everyone just fine." Dr. Hawthorne then asked Fred and Betty what things they do for themselves without the children. They both indicated that right now they have very little time to do things as a couple because they are always going to the girls' tennis matches. They added that the travel and time involved make it difficult to do anything else.*

A week after the interview with the entire family, Dr. Hawthorne met with Amy. In that session she talked about her ambivalence about tennis—her love for the game and the people she had met through the sport but her occasional desire to quit and do other things. She expressed her frustrations about being pressured by her parents to stay with the sport.

■ *Amy told Dr. Hawthorne, "They want me to get a college scholarship just like Caroline did." Amy shared the fact that there are times when she didn't want to train any more but was afraid to say that because her father would be upset. She feels her mother is more understanding but is weak and will not stand up to her father.*

At the end of the session, Dr. Hawthorne asked Amy if she was willing to be involved in family therapy sessions to help improve the communication in the family and establish herself in a more effective way than she had in the past. Dr. Hawthorne explained to her that she would also like to see Amy in some individual sessions to talk about her feelings about tennis, but by working together the family can explore ways they can live together more productively. Amy agreed to participate.

As a final step in the assessment process, Dr. Hawthorne met with Fred and Betty alone. She asked them questions about their own parents and families, how they met, and what their courtship was like, and she obtained a brief picture of the development stages of their own family. She focused on their involvement with tennis, their stance around training, their attendance at matches, and their conversations with the girls before and after competition.

■ *Fred did a lot of the talking, but Dr. Hawthorne skillfully drew Betty into the conversation at key times. For example, when Fred was describing the scene in the car after Amy's last tennis match, Dr. Hawthorne turned to Betty and asked*

"Betty, how did you feel at the time?" Betty said she felt Fred was being a bit hard on Amy, but didn't say anything at the time. "Do you often feel this way and not say anything?" Dr. Hawthorne asked. "Yes, I guess so," Betty replied. "I don't like to have disagreements in front of the kids." "Did your parents fight in front of you?" Dr. Hawthorne then asked Betty. "All the time," said Betty. "I couldn't stand it, and I vowed I would never do that in front of my own children."

Treating Athlete Families

Though some therapeutic insight develops during the assessment phase, most of the change in perspective in the family takes place during and after a treatment contract is negotiated. It is important to involve the family in the treatment whenever possible, depending of course on the extent of family involvement in the level and source of stress and the definition of the problem from the athlete's perspective.

The Treatment Contract

The treatment contract often helps the family reframe a problem from an individual perspective to a broader family perspective. When Fred initially called for an appointment, he defined the problem as Amy's. Dr. Hawthorne's skillful assessment helped the family see Amy's difficulties on the tennis court in a broader perspective.

■ *At the end of the final evaluation session, Dr. Hawthorne explained to Fred and Betty that her experience with athletes has led her to see that the problems they face regarding competition have a direct impact on the family and vice versa. She explained that she believes the families of elite athletes experience unique pressures and stress that many other families do not. She also explained her belief that Amy is facing a personal crisis on two levels. One is her own self-doubt about her ability and desire to be an elite athlete. Another level is how her decisions about tennis impact the family.*

Dr. Hawthorne suggested that treatment must take into account both these levels and asked Fred and Betty if they would be willing to be involved in some family sessions to explore how the family communication and decision-making patterns are related to Amy's feelings about her sport in general and her performance on the court.

Dr. Hawthorne recommended a series of 12 sessions with a mixture of individual, parental, and family meetings. She explained that in the individual work with Amy she will help Amy with competition-related problems of stress and will teach her relaxation and mental imagery skills that will help her performance. In addition, she will give Amy a chance to talk about some of the feelings she has about her self-image, her identity as an athlete, and her goals in the sport. The parental sessions will focus on their ways of dealing with the pressures and stresses of being athletes' parents. The goal of the family sessions will be to help all members of the family communicate with one another and feel that their own needs are being addressed. Fred and Betty agreed that the format makes sense and would be helpful. They began treatment together.

Goals of Treatment

Therapeutic intervention with athlete families has the following goals:

- Assist the family in resolving developmental impasses
- Improve the structural functioning of the family by strengthening boundaries, power hierarchies, communication patterns, and conflict resolution mechanisms
- Develop the support network, both inside and outside the family, necessary for the young athlete's achievement of goals.

To help set her treatment goals, Dr. Hawthorne drew a treatment genogram (see Figure 5.4). This genogram helps her develop strategies for her interventions with the family. She then begins to work with them using the following types of interventions: education and prevention, support, facilitation, and challenge (Doherty & Baird, 1983).

Education and Prevention

The interventions that are aimed at helping the family resolve developmental impasses are often educational interventions. The family needs help in understanding and adapting to the changes that are required as it negotiates the stages of the family life cycle. Educational interventions are geared toward helping the family resolve past and present impasses so they can better meet the challenges that lie ahead. A major impasse is Fred's inability to untangle himself from the drama that he played out as a young man with his own father. In one of the family sessions Dr. Hawthorne helped Fred to see the relationship between his inability to please his own father and his desire for his daughter's prowess in tennis.

■ *Dr. Hawthorne asked both Fred and Betty to talk with their daughters about their own athletic experiences when they were in high school. Betty talked about how little encouragement she received from her parents because they were always involved with her father's drinking. Fred recounted how he felt hurt when his father seldom watched him play. One year he won the high school district singles tournament, but his father hadn't come to see the match. Fred's eyes teared as he talked of how his father later said that he had been unable to get away from the office to attend the match.*

Dr. Hawthorne then asked Fred, "What did you decide at that time about how you would act when you became a parent?" Fred clenched his fist and replied, "I vowed that I would never miss one of my kid's matches. Never."

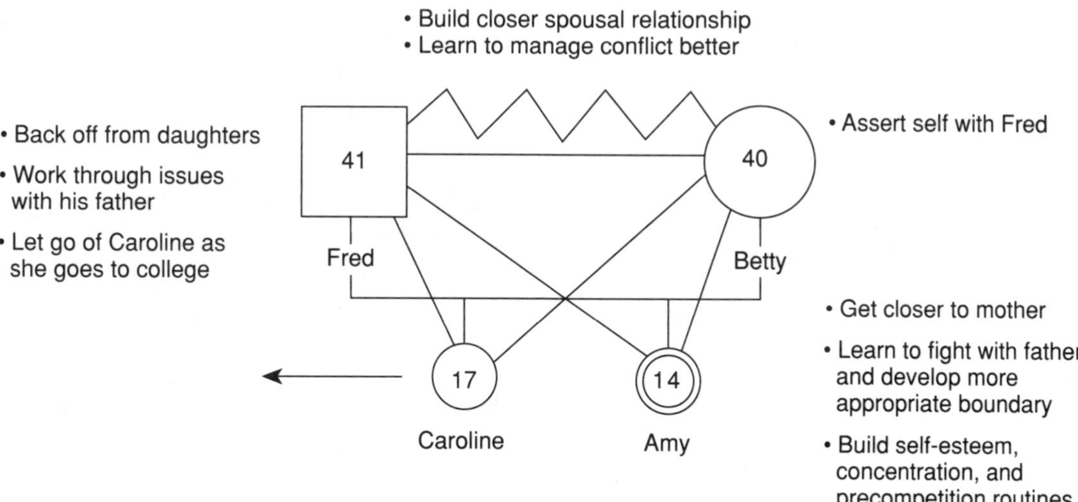

Figure 5.4 A treatment goals genogram of the Stanley family.

Dr. Hawthorne was able to use Fred's connection of past and present to help the family see the need for a change in the boundary between the parents and the adolescent children. She showed her appreciation for Fred's wanting to be at all of Amy's matches, but she was able to help him see the need for Amy to learn to deal with competition pressures without her parents being present. Dr. Hawthorne shared with Fred and Betty an article by a former champion tennis player (Smith, 1990) on how to be an effective tennis parent. One of Smith's suggestions is to attend no more than 75% of the child's matches. Dr. Hawthorne explained the reasons for this suggestion. Then she worked with Fred and Betty in setting up a behavioral change contract to practice during the coming week.

■ *The family agreed that Amy's parents will not attend her next match. When Amy returns home they will ask her, How did you feel about your performance today? Fred and Betty were helped to see that a question such as this shifts the focus from a concern about outcome to a concern for Amy's feelings about her performance. "I believe that the important thing for parents," Dr. Hawthorne said, "is that they not be so concerned about winning and losing, but rather how their child feels about the experience."*

This intervention is educational and preventive in that it helps the family resolve their present impasse and prepares them for the tasks of the next stage of family development. They are about to enter the launching phase; having more flexible boundaries is essential for the successful resolution of that phase.

Support

The athlete family faces a unique set of stressful events and conditions. The win-lose pressures of competitive sport as well as the demands on time and financial resources often contribute to tension in these families. However, these families also have a great deal of strength and their positive qualities need reinforcement. For example, their emphasis on goal attainment and the work ethic is a positive quality. They need to feel understood and supported in what they are seeking to accomplish. In meetings with subsystems of the family, the clinical sport psychologist affirms their struggle to develop the talent in the family.

■ *In one session Fred and Betty shared with Dr. Hawthorne the personal and financial sacrifices the two of them have made to further their daughters' tennis careers. They spoke of the pain that they sometimes felt when Amy didn't appreciate these sacrifices. They also shared how they felt that many of their friends had pulled away, both because of the time commitments to tennis and because they didn't think their friends could relate to the kind of intensity the family put into tennis. "I think many of our friends think we are crazy," Betty said at one point. Dr. Hawthorne listened empathically to these feelings and reinforced them. "You both have to understand that what you are working on is producing 'excellence' in your daughter's tennis, and with that comes a lot of pain and sacrifice. I am sure few people except for other tennis families understand the difficulties you face. Perhaps you need to share more of these feelings, both with one another and with some of your tennis friends."*

Facilitation

One of the main tasks of the clinician in working with athlete families is to open the communication process in the family. This can be done by encouraging the family members to communicate directly with one another. This openness produces meaningful changes in the boundaries and interactional patterns in the family.

■ *In the second session in which all family members were present, the incident that took place in the car after the regional championships was discussed. Dr. Hawthorne asked Fred to share with Amy what he was really feeling after the match. After some hedging he finally said, "I was angry and disappointed. I thought you could have won if you had played harder." Amy responded, "I knew you were angry. I was angry too. I felt like I tried hard [the tears begin to flow]. When I felt the match slipping away, I knew you were over there watching and getting upset. I thought of how you would be disappointed in me during the whole third set."*

Facilitation is more than simply allowing a catharsis to take place. It leads to positive behavioral change. Dr. Hawthorne was able to do this by first commenting that feelings are often communicated without words and that in this case Amy had sensed how Fred was feeling. Then Dr. Hawthorne pointed out that it is better to be direct, so the issue can be talked about and resolved.

■ *At the end of the session, Dr. Hawthorne helped the Stanleys establish a behavioral contract that involves Fred, Betty, and Amy. They agreed that the next time one of them felt anger they would acknowledge it and then state what they saw as the problem and how they would like it resolved.*

Challenge

The family structures that are not working well need to be challenged. A firm nudge often helps a family respond more creatively to the needs of its members. In designing challenging interventions the clinician hopes to rock the boat, shake up the system, and guide it toward reorganizing at a more adaptive level. One of the major areas where the Stanleys need to be challenged is in the area of the power imbalance in the spousal system and the inability of Betty and Fred to deal openly with conflict in their own relationship. Betty needs to empower herself to the point where she is willing to challenge Fred's role in the family. Betty's softer and more understanding approach to problems is an undervalued source of energy in the family.

■ *In a session with Fred and Betty only, Dr. Hawthorne asked them about their fighting style. "We don't fight," said Betty. "What are some issues that you don't fight about?" asked Dr. Hawthorne. "Could you look at Fred and tell him some of the things you have been avoiding?" Betty went on to say that she was really upset with Fred during and after the regional championships, but she didn't say anything, because she "didn't want to start a fight." Dr. Hawthorne suggested they engage in a role play where the car scene is reenacted and the problem is discussed between them. She asked Betty to begin with a clear description of Fred's behavior that she is upset about, and her attendant feelings. Fred was asked to listen, and respond with his own feelings about what Betty has said. The role play went well. A contract was established that the next time Betty feels a strong disagreement with Fred about something she will tell him what the problem is. He will then respond with one of two statements Dr. Hawthorne taught him: either "I understand" or "I don't understand your feelings, please help me."*

Termination

At the end of the 12 sessions the Stanleys terminated their family sessions with Dr. Hawthorne. Amy is feeling better about her tennis and experiences less pressure from Fred and Betty. Betty believes that they are getting their own issues out on the table more openly with one another. Caroline has left for college and they have been able to let go of her. They miss Caroline, but they are not planning to visit her until the fall parents' weekend. Fred agrees with Dr. Hawthorne that he will let Caroline make her own decisions now about tennis and that he will support her choice of direction. Amy agrees, however, to come in for a session once a month to discuss her feelings about her tennis and her decisions about whether to continue or not. They will also continue working on imagery and concentration to enhance her tennis skills. The family also agrees to a follow-up session in three months with all members to assess the changes in the family.

ETHICAL ISSUES IN WORKING WITH FAMILIES

Certain ethical and value issues are more complex when intervening with a family than with an individual athlete. For example, the issue of confidentiality is more complicated when working with multiple family members. The question of whether and when to share information obtained in a separate interview is often a dilemma for the clinician. Corey, Corey, and Callanan (1988) present an excellent discussion of these general ethical issues. This section briefly discusses a few major guidelines that are important to follow when intervening in a family system.

Training and Competence

Working with the athlete's family system is more complex and more difficult than working with the individual athlete. It is important, therefore, that a clinician who takes a family-centered approach with athletes have specialized training in conducting family therapy. The clinician, however, also must have a background in sport psychology and a familiarity with the unique pressures that face a competitive athlete.

The Family as Client

There is a difference in value orientation with a family-centered approach to assessment and treatment. The goal of family treatment is to facilitate change in the whole family, not simply in an individual family member. A basic principle of family system theory is that anything that affects one family member impacts all other parts of the system. It is conceivable, for example, that an individually oriented clinician working with Amy on issues of self-differentiation might provoke a marital crisis between Fred and Betty. Amy might get stronger, but others might get worse in the process. The family-as-client approach allows all family members to negotiate the salient developmental task at the same time.

Avoiding Subsystem Alliances

The clinician must stay out of the triangles, alliances, and entanglements that develop in families as well as between families and coaches and sport organizations. In working with families it is important not to become an advocate of any one member of the family, but rather to remain neutral and be seen as an ally by all members. A basic rule when working with couples or families is that there are no villains and victims, but instead that everyone shares some responsibility for what goes on in the family. Had Dr. Hawthorne become only Amy's advocate (or Fred and Betty's) the family would not have been able to make the changes that it did.

Countertransference

In avoiding the entanglements and unhealthy alliances in families, it is essential that sport psychologists be aware of the role of their own families of origin so countertransference issues do not interfere in their work with client families. Just as we expect overinvolved parents to see their own unresolved issues that they might be projecting onto their children, clinicians need to realize that they too engage in family projection. If a clinician empowers the adolescent athlete at the parents' expense or encourages parents to set limits on a rebellious adolescent because of residues of the clinician's own experience the family will not be helped.

A Model for the Healthy Family

Lastly, the sport psychologist who takes a family-centered approach should base interventions on a model for healthy family functioning that serves as a guide to the complexities of family life. In this chapter I have attempted to present a developmental model, and I hope that this model is a beginning for dialogue and refinement that will lead to an improvement in the quality of life for our young athletes.

An issue that did not come up with the Stanley family but that frequently presents itself in athlete families is whether a young athlete (under age 15) should leave the family home to train in a favorable geographical environment (e.g., warm climate for tennis or mountains for skiers) or with specialized coaching (e.g., tennis, gymnastics, and figure skating). This can be a dilemma for a family-oriented clinician because it presents a conflict between the value of family cohesion against the young athlete's training, coaching, or competition needs.

In keeping with the ethical guidelines of our profession, it is important for the clinician to help the family explore the issues involved in this decision and not impose a predetermined solution or answer. The developmental model can help the clinician and the family assess the developmental readiness of both the family and the young athlete. For example, in one family a dislocation of the young athlete might be appropriate; in another, it might be premature. The important questions for the clinician to help the family answer are What are the major developmental issues in the family now? How have they handled previous stages of family development? Is the young athlete developmentally ready for this kind of move? and How would it affect the various subsystems in the family such as the parents, the siblings, and the extended family? Once a decision is made, the family-oriented clinician can also help the family negotiate the separation so that the negative aspects of the separation are managed as well as possible. Also, during the period of separation the clinician can be of value to the family in helping solve various problems that develop, such as conflicts between the family and the coach or training academy. Lastly, the clinician can be helpful by consulting with sport organizations and academies for which this issue is a frequent problem. The consultant can help the organization both in managing these transitions and in rethinking training and competition philosophies so families can stay together and the athlete's needs can be met at the same time.

THE FINAL SESSION

About 3 months later, Dr. Hawthorne met with the Stanley family and discovered that the family had been able to maintain the changes they made earlier in treatment. They are communicating their feelings to one another; Fred and Betty are discussing their differences and even fighting occasionally. Amy is happier; she is still playing tennis but is taking more time away from the game to have fun with her friends. She is playing in fewer tournaments but with good results. Dr. Hawthorne gave them positive reinforcement for the changes they have made.

Dr. Hawthorne ended the session by asking Betty, Fred, Amy, and Caroline to create a "sculpture" of how they see the family now and the changes that have been made.

■ *Betty started by placing Fred and herself together so they can reach out and touch one another. She put Caroline near the door to the office, indicating her psychological departure for college. Amy is in front of them but standing sideways so she half faces them and half faces the door. When asked if anyone wants to change the sculpture, Amy said she would like to. She walked over to her parents, who faced toward her in the sculpture and moved their heads so they would look more at each other.*

"This is a good place to end," Dr. Hawthorne said. After a family hug, Dr. Hawthorne said goodbye to the Stanley family. She is confident that Amy will be a better tennis player and a happier person as she continues her life's journey.

CONCLUSION

I hope that this chapter has demonstrated that the family is a key player in the athlete's development and performance. The practice of sport psychology is enriched by a family-based orientation to the assessment and treatment of athletes. Creating a workable family system is a challenge for parents, who have many difficult decisions to make and are often without support and direction in making those choices. Sport psychologists can help parents as well as athletes by using family-based assessments and treatment interventions that provide education, challenge, and support to negotiate the tasks and transitions in the family life cycle.

REFERENCES

Berlage, G. (1981, May). *Fathers' career aspirations for sons in competitive hockey programs.* Paper presented at the Regional Symposium of the International Committee for the Sociology of Sport, Vancouver, BC.

Berryman, J.W. (1988). The rise of highly organized sports for preadolescent boys. In F.L. Smoll, R.A. Magill, & M.J. Ash (Eds.), *Children in sport* (pp. 3-16). Champaign, IL: Human Kinetics.

Bloom, B. (Ed.) (1985). *Developing talent in young people.* New York: Ballantine Books.

Bowen, M. (1965). Family psychotherapy with schizophrenia in the hospital and in private practice. In I. Boszormenyi-Nagy & J. Framo (Eds.), *Intensive family therapy* (pp. 213-243). New York: Harper & Row.

Bowen, M. (1978). *Family therapy in clinical practice.* New York: Aronson.

Bradt, J., & Moynihan, C. (1971). Opening the safe—the child-focused family. In J. Bradt & C. Moynihan (Eds.), *Systems therapy.* Washington, DC: Groome Child Guidance Center.

Carter, B., & McGoldrick, M. (Eds.) (1989). *The changing family life cycle: A framework for family therapy.* Boston: Allyn & Bacon.

Corey, G., Corey, M., & Callanan, P. (1988). *Issues and ethics in the helping professions.* Pacific Grove, CA: Brooks/Cole.

Doherty, W., & Baird, M. (1983). *Family therapy and family medicine.* New York: Guilford Press.

Erikson, E. (1950). *Childhood and society.* New York: Norton.

Fulmer, R. (1989). Lower-income and professional families: A comparison of structure and life cycle process. In B. Carter & M. McGoldrick (Eds.), *The changing family life cycle: A framework for family therapy* (pp. 545-579). Boston: Allyn & Bacon.

Gould, D., & Horn, T. (1984). Participation motivation in young athletes. In J. Silva & R. Weinberg (Eds.), *Psychological foundations of sport* (pp. 359-370). Champaign, IL: Human Kinetics.

Gould, D., Horn, T., & Spreemann, J. (1983). Sources of stress in junior elite wrestlers. *Journal of Sport Psychology*, **5**, 159-171.

Greendorfer, S., & Lewko, J. (1978). Role of family members in sport socialization of children. *Research Quarterly*, **49**, 146-152.

Hellstedt, J. (1987). The coach/parent/athlete relationship. *Sport Psychologist*, **1**, 151-160.

Hellstedt, J. (1990a). Early adolescent perceptions of parental pressure in the sport environment. *Journal of Sport Behavior*, **13**, 135-144.

Hellstedt, J. (1990b, August). *The family pressure cooker: Reflections on parents, coaches and young athletes*. Paper presented at the 98th Annual Convention of the American Psychological Association, Boston.

Higgenson, D. (1985). The influence of socializing agents in the female sport-participation process. *Adolescence*, **20**, 73-82.

Kalinowski, A. (1985). The development of Olympic swimmers. In B. Bloom (Ed.), *Developing talent in young people* (pp. 139-192). New York: Ballantine Books.

Kesend, O. (1991). *The elite athlete's sources of encouragement and discouragement affecting their motivation to participate in sport: A qualitative study from a development perspective*. Unpublished doctoral dissertation, The Union Institute, Cincinnati, OH.

Krestan, J., & Bepko, C. (1989). Alcoholic problems and the family life cycle. In B. Carter & M. McGoldrick (Eds.), *The changing family life cycle: A framework for family therapy* (pp. 483-513). Boston: Allyn & Bacon.

Martens, R. (1978). *Joy and sadness in children's sports*. Champaign, IL: Human Kinetics.

McElroy, M., & Kirkendall, D. (1980). Significant others and professionalized sport attitudes. *Research Quarterly for Exercise and Sport*, **51**, 645-653.

McGoldrick, M., & Gerson, R. (1985). *Genograms in family assessment*. New York: Norton.

Melnick, M., Dunkelman, N., & Mashiach, A. (1981). Familial factors of sports giftedness among young Israeli athletes. *Journal of Sport Behavior*, **4**, 82-94.

Minuchin, S. (1974). *Families and family therapy*. Cambridge, MA: Harvard University Press.

Minuchin, S., Rosman, B., & Baker, L. (1978). *Psychosomatic families: Anorexia nervosa in context*. Cambridge, MA: Harvard University Press.

Monsaas, J. (1985). Learning to be a world-class tennis player. In B. Bloom (Ed.), *Developing talent in young people* (pp. 211-269). New York: Ballantine Books.

Nichols, W. (1988). *Marital therapy*. New York: Guilford Press.

Odom, S., & Perrin, T. (1985). Coach and athlete burnout. In L. Bunker, R. Rotella, & A. Reilly (Eds.), *Sport psychology* (pp. 213-222). Ithaca, NY: Mouvement.

Ogilvie, B. (1983). Psychology and the elite athlete. *Physician and Sports Medicine*, **11**(4), 195-202.

Passer, M. (1984). Competitive trait anxiety in children and adolescents. In J. Silva & R. Weinberg (Eds.), *Psychological foundations of sport* (pp. 130-144). Champaign, IL: Human Kinetics.

Peck, J., & Manocherian, J. (1989). Divorce and the changing family life cycle. In B. Carter & M. McGoldrick (Eds.), *The changing family life cycle: A framework for family therapy* (pp. 335-371). Boston: Allyn & Bacon.

Rotella, R. (1985). The psychological care of the injured athlete. In L. Bunker, R. Rotella, & A. Reilly (Eds.), *Sport psychology* (pp. 273-287). Ithaca, NY: Mouvement.

Sage, G. (1980). Parental influence and socialization into sport for male and female intercollegiate athletes. *Journal of Sport and Social Issues*, **49**, 1-13.

Scanlan, T., & Lewthwaite, R. (1986). Social psychological aspects of competition for male youth sport participants: IV. Predictors of enjoyment. *Journal of Sport Psychology*, **8**, 25-35.

Scanlan, T., Stein, G., & Ravizza, K. (1991). An in-depth study of former elite figure skaters: III. Sources of stress. *Journal of Sport and Exercise Psychology*, **13**, 103-119.

Sloane, K. (1985). Home influences on talent development. In B. Bloom (Ed.), *Developing talent in young people* (pp. 439-476). New York: Ballantine Books.

Smith, S. (1990). Are you a good tennis parent? *Tennis*, **26**(3), 42-44.

CHAPTER 6

THE COACH AND THE TEAM PSYCHOLOGIST: AN INTEGRATED ORGANIZATIONAL MODEL

Frank Gardner, PhD
Gardner Consulting Associates, Inc.

Applied sport psychology has undergone a rapid growth in recent years. Increasing membership in such organizations as the American Psychological Association's (APA) Division 47 (sport and exercise psychology) and the Association for the Advancement of Applied Sport Psychology (AAASP) reflects growth and acceptance of the profession. Sport psychology has experienced both increased recognition in print and electronic media and a rise in public acceptance. Individual athletes and sport organizations at the college, professional, and Olympic levels increasingly seek out the services of specialists in the psychology of sport to provide a variety of services in the sport milieu.

Often these services are sought in reaction to specific situations but with little understanding of what sport psychologists can and cannot do. This lack of understanding often leads to failed experiences when clients work with poorly trained professionals or when the team's or individual athlete's needs and the skills of the professional are poorly matched. Typically, the sport psychology literature has described specific services provided to athletes, either in one-on-one or group (team) format. With few exceptions, however, the literature lacks a discussion of the sport psychologist's overall role in the team setting.

One of my goals in this chapter is to clarify how organizational dynamics in team settings influence the way that psychological services are received and provided. A second goal is to give the psychologist a fuller understanding of the athletic environment and how sport psychology fits into this highly specialized and challenging setting. In addition, I present a model for sport psychologists to become integrated into the overall team structure, including relationships with the coaching staff, sports medicine team, and management personnel.

■ *THE CASE OF TEAM BLUE* ■

A Division I collegiate team begins the season expecting a conference championship and hoping for a national ranking and success in the postseason tournament. From the outset of preseason training the coach, an intense, aggressive individual, pushes the team hard and repeatedly verbalizes his expectations. The team is young, having 25% freshmen and 25% sophomores. A year earlier the team had won its regular season conference championship and played consistently well, despite a disappointing (and unexpected) postseason tournament loss. A third of the starting lineup was lost to graduation. Halfway through this season, the team was unexpectedly hovering around .500 (win-loss percentage). At this point the head coach consulted with the team psychologist about what he perceived as "significant problems in team chemistry." The coach felt there was an absence of teamwork, a tendency toward finger-pointing, and a passive approach, both in games and practices.

THE SPORT PSYCHOLOGIST IN THE ATHLETIC ENVIRONMENT

The role of the sport psychologist differs markedly from one situation (i.e., team) to another. One has only to read the variety of descriptions of the role psychologists have in different organizations to realize this (Botterill, 1990; Ravizza, 1990; Smith & Johnson, 1990). That a psychologist's role differs across settings should not be surprising, given the diverse backgrounds of sport psychologists (Taylor, 1991). The relatively recent acceptance of sport psychology as a discipline has been hampered by some confusion as to who sport psychologists are and what they actually do.

Unfortunately, the various roles and job responsibilities that some psychologists have developed can reflect more the differences in their backgrounds and training than the needs of the organizations they serve. The danger is that this confusion about *role* often accompanies a lack of clarity about *goal*. Consequently, psychologists in the athletic arena are vulnerable to being seen as unnecessary, inept, and even as creating problems. As the field of sport psychology evolves and as its nature and purposes and its techniques and principles become clearer, this problem should abate. For now, however, we need to address the danger of sport psychology's being dismissed as trendy or superfluous. We can best accomplish this by staying informed of advances in basic psychological knowledge and technique, being aware of team and organizational dynamics, and by remaining cognizant of the job responsibilities of other professionals working alongside of us.

Organizational Dynamics

The athletic environment is highly complex, and a sophisticated understanding of it is critical for the would-be team psychologist's effectiveness. Nevertheless, little attention has been directed toward organizational dynamics awareness in the sport psychology literature. If the goal of organizational fit is attended to properly and ongoing efforts are made at educating athletic personnel about fundamental psychological principles and their relevance to athletic performance, the inevitable consequence will be more effective working relationships and greater respect for the sport psychologist's value.

It is critical that team psychologists understand that they are working in an organization and need to fully comprehend the organization's rules, administrative systems, goals, values, and reporting structure. These organizational dynamics, recently referred to in the business world as corporate or organizational culture (Schein, 1990), are critical to the success or failure of the team psychologist. Further, the psychologist must be aware that the circumstances of entry into the team and the person or people who brought the psychologist on board directly affect the psychologist's place in the group's organizational dynamics. For example, the psychologist whose entry into the team comes via contact with the coach has a different set of organizational issues than the one who is brought in by the general manager/athletic director. In addition, the previous successes and particular personal relationships of the coach or general manager/athletic director are additional elements necessary for a complete understanding of organizational dynamics. Prior experiences (both good and bad) that key personnel have had with sport psychologists further complicate organizational dynamics for the psychologist. Apart from these issues, the team psychologist must become aware of the roles and interactions of upper management, coaching staff, sports medicine team, media personnel, and so forth. Lastly, to fully appreciate the team culture, the psychologist needs to be clear about

- team goals and overall mission,
- relationship of the team to the larger organization,
- sources of particular pressures (e.g., fans, media), and
- history of the team or organization.

Identifying the Client

When working with an athlete in an individual sport, the dynamics involved are fairly simple. The athlete, possibly some family member(s), and quite probably a coach need to be consulted during the intervention. When these individual sports are at the professional level (e.g., tennis, golf), public relations or sport agents might also be involved and also might be consulted on occasion. This chapter's focus, however, will be on team settings. In the team setting, a multitude of people must be considered:

- The individual athletes who comprise the team—anywhere from 12 to upwards of 40, depending on the sport and type of organization (pro, college, etc.)
- A coaching staff comprised of a head coach and a number of assistants
- A sports medicine team consisting of training and physical therapy staff and team physician(s)
- Management, including general manager/athletic director and staff, scouting personnel, and public relations or sport information staff

Everyone's role must be evaluated and understood for the prospective team psychologist to become integrated into the organization. Figure 6.1 shows a sample organizational chart of a professional team. The team psychologist can realistically expect to be involved in three domains noted: sports medicine (directed by the team physician), team performance (directed by the head coach), and scouting and player development (directed by the director of player development).

In addition, the concept of team psychologist has many potential meanings (Halliwell, 1990; Neff, 1990). In some cases it implies working with athletes on the team for the express purpose of performance enhancement. In other situations it includes both performance-enhancement work (often referred to, incorrectly in my view, as educational service), more traditional clinical service (e.g., psychological counseling of non-performance-related issues, such as family problems, psychopathology, etc.), and even involvement in the player selection process (e.g., predraft psychological testing).

Qualities Necessary for Success

In a recent study evaluating the consulting effectiveness of sport psychologists (Gould,

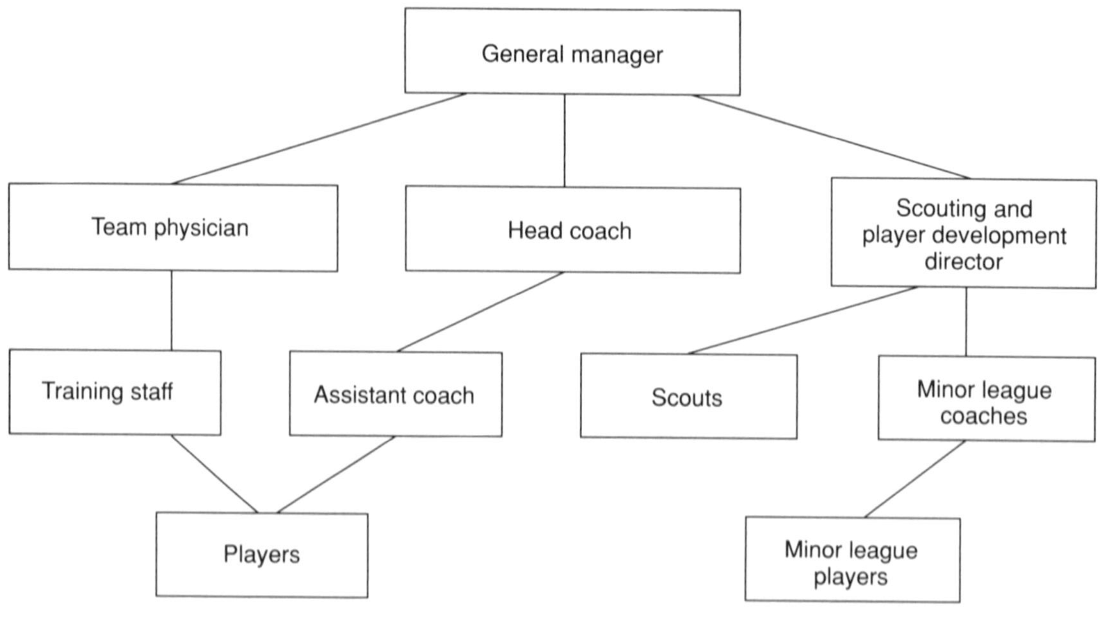

Figure 6.1 An organizational chart for a professional sport team.

Murphy, Tammen, & May, 1991), consultants achieved higher effectiveness ratings when working with individual athletes as opposed to working with teams. Further, consultants themselves reported that working in team situations was more difficult and involved significantly more variables. In addition, when a number of consultant characteristics were rated by coaches, the consultants were given their lowest ratings in ability to fit comfortably into the team environment. The authors suggest that this latter finding might imply a less-than-clearly-defined role for the sport psychologist in American amateur team sports. It might also be reflective of the difficulties in properly matching the skills and interests of the sport psychology consultant to the needs of the client organization. Recent studies have examined the views of coaches and athletes regarding necessary characteristics of effective sport psychologists. Canadian Olympic athletes cited the best sport psychology consultants as those who were likeable, accessible, flexible, and professionally skilled (Orlick & Partington, 1987). In other words, both strong personal skills and sound mental-training skills were viewed as vital to successful sport psychology consultation. Conversely, poorly rated consultants lacked either of those two broad qualities. Similarly, when Canadian Olympic coaches were polled, highly rated sport psychology consultants were rated as positive, confident, capable of working in the sport environment without being intrusive, practical, and knowledgeable (Partington & Orlick, 1987). Once again, both personal and professional skills were implicated. These coaches identified desired services as mental-skills training with athletes as well as staff–athlete communication enhancement and direct consultation about coaching behaviors.

It has been my experience at the collegiate and professional levels that head coaches look to the sport psychologist for help in better understanding the individual athlete whom the coach needs to motivate and with whom the coach communicates regularly. This information (obtained from psychological assessment, observation, and interpersonal interaction) can allow coaches to more adequately perform their jobs. It has not been my experience after working with many coaches that they readily solicit strategies or techniques for team motivation. Coaches at elite competitive levels have their own methods and strategies for this task that they have developed over the years in keeping with their own personalities and experience. Coaches at lesser competitive levels, however, might have different needs and might turn to the team psychologist to help with numerous coaching issues, including team motivation. Further, assistant coaches often seek out the team psychologist for information that could be of value in their work with athletes. Assistant coaches are often more intimately involved in the nuances of the personalities of individual athletes, because these coaches frequently are given the responsibility of working with either one or a small group of players at a time.

Athletes, in my experience, have generally looked to the team psychologist for a variety of services that have included crisis intervention, psychological counseling, mental-skills training for performance enhancement, and relationship counseling. In keeping with the research findings noted previously, my experience suggests that over time the psychological services that athletes are likely to use most will be based on both the interpersonal and the professional talents of the psychologist. The conclusion can readily be made that athletes consider as essential elements in effective consultation the trustworthiness of the psychologist and the psychologist's ability to easily fit into the team environment.

A must, however, for those choosing to work in team settings is a positive, professional relationship with the head coach and coaching staff. The development of a positive working relationship must begin with a full understanding of the team coach's roles and responsibilities.

THE COACH: ROLE, IMPACT, AND PRESSURES

Few jobs in sport, particularly professional sport, possess the pressures inherent in coaching. If we compare for a moment the job functions of a team coach to those of a business manager, there are striking similarities (see Figure 6.2). Traditionally, the business manager is seen as being responsible for personnel selection and utilization, personnel development and training, and strategic planning. This translates in the athletic domain into player selection and recruitment, athletic skills training, and game plan preparation and bench coaching. Another aspect

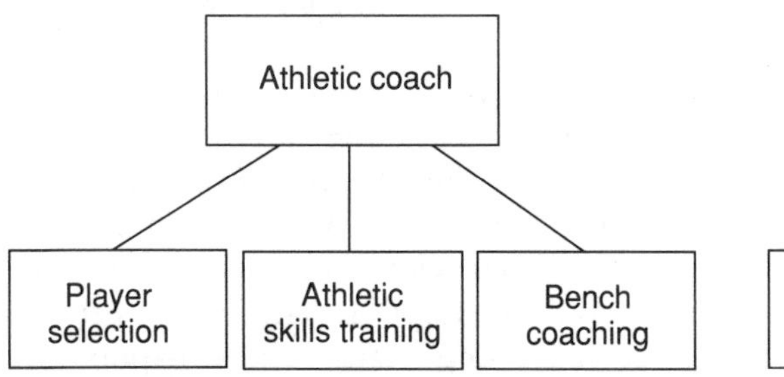

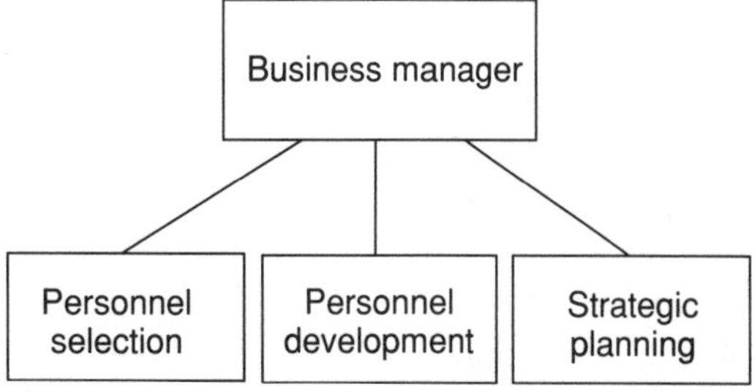

Figure 6.2 Similarities between the responsibilities of an athletic coach and a business manager.

of both jobs is in the development and maintenance of group (team) cohesion, often referred to popularly as chemistry. This is not considered a basic job function of a business manager or athletic coach because it is an indirect activity. That is, group cohesion occurs via a combination of coach and manager behavior, team members' personality mix, and situational variables. We will examine more thoroughly the topic of team cohesion and the role of the coach and psychologist later in this chapter.

Two goals most central to the perceived success of coaches are (a) winning and (b) participant enjoyment and education. The degree to which each one of these primary goals predominates depends on the level of sport participation (i.e., Little League, high school, college Division III, II, I, Olympic, or professional). One can view these two goals as inversely proportional to sport level (see Figure 6.3). As such, the degree to which a coach must focus on fostering enjoyment of sport involvement and is responsible for teaching values and contributing to the athletes' overall development as the primary objective—as opposed to maintaining a primary focus on winning—is similarly inversely proportional.

Some would probably argue that these two goals are not mutually exclusive and in fact can readily coexist—as might be the case in Ivy League sports. As shown in Figure 6.3, there is a point of intersection of these two goals occurring at the college sports level (e.g., Division I, II, or III). Although these two goals can equally coexist to a point, ultimately choices are made; this suggests that one might predominate. For example, Ivy League college teams are at a distinct competitive disadvantage, as they have decided to not offer athletic scholarships. Winning is secondary at these institutions. It is important to note that even as the primary goal of the job changes, the essential job functions of selection, development, and strategic planning remain the same, albeit with different prioritization.

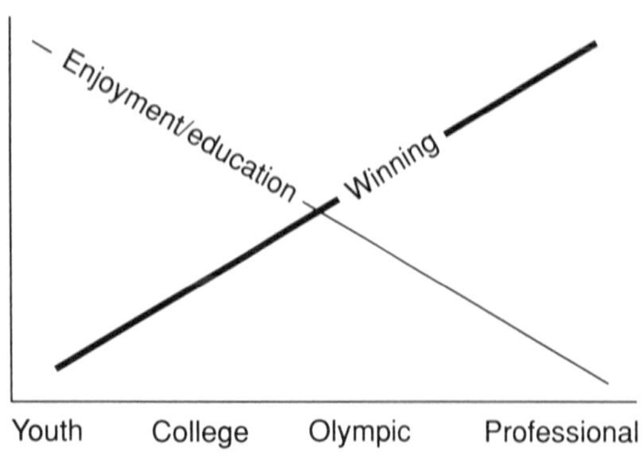

Figure 6.3 Importance at competitive levels.

Martens (1987) has a somewhat similar conceptualization. He considers coaching behavior as falling somewhere along a continuum between highly athlete-centered, where a coach places "the highest regard on the people being coached" (p. 11), and highly win-centered, where a coach places "the highest regard on the outcome of competition." In my view a coach sometimes is clear on the fit between primary personal goals and the primary organizational goals (e.g., organizations such as Ivy League or professional sports), and in other circumstances might not be. This incongruity of personal and organizational goals might be due to a poorly developed or poorly communicated vision about the mission of the organization, as is often the case in college sports. Sometimes a coach might not choose to align personal goals with the stated mission of the organization, as is sometimes the case in youth sports. The influence of these primary coaching goals on a coach's cognitive, emotional, and behavioral process is directly related to the concept of coach burnout (to be discussed in depth later in this chapter.)

It should be pointed out that the achievement of one of the two primary goals—

winning or participant enjoyment and education—ultimately determines the perceived success of the team coach. Next, we must consider the question of which coaching functions contribute to the achievement of the team goal. In answering this question, we once again turn our attention to three general coaching functions: (a) player selection and utilization, (b) skill development, and (c) strategic planning and tactical decision making.

Player Selection

The job function of selection includes both initial selection (or recruitment in the case of college sports) and role determination. When winning is the primary goal, making decisions about team composition is critical. It is not a simple task to select players whose talent (or potential) is at a high enough level, who will fit into a particular style of play, who will interact comfortably with staff, and who can fit in with a particular group of personalities. In some situations (e.g., college sports), this responsibility lies almost exclusively with the coach, as does player utilization and role selection. Role selection involves decisions about playing time and starter–substitute status. At the professional level, player selection is typically the responsibility of the team general manager, often (but not always) with strong input from the coach. Player utilization is clearly the responsibility of the coach at all levels of sport. In situations where participant enjoyment and education is the primary goal, selection might be substantially less important. In youth sports, for example, it is not unusual for all who try out to make the team. Player utilization at this level is often the job function that forces a coach to remain focused on the primary objective. Making sure all players have an opportunity to play—even if doing so leads to a loss—is a difficult challenge for many involved in coaching youth sports.

When winning is the primary focus—in sport as in business—selecting the right people is the first step toward success. Correct selection ultimately simplifies the other tasks of developing both skills and strategic planning. Errors in selection invariably lead to more serious problems down the line. If one looks carefully, what at first glance is often viewed as coaching failure often is actually a failure in adequate player selection.

Athletic Development and Skill Training

Athletic development and skill training is often referred to as teaching. In this function the coach is responsible for developing players' sport-specific skills as well as their capacity to effectively use these skills in game conditions. Drills, practice schedules, and the like are coaching activities that are directed toward enhancing skill development. Included in this conceptualization of the players' skill development is the concept of motivation of players. Being able to get players to put forth maximum effort and to follow the game plan as prescribed is critical to the success of most coaches. Although a full discussion of motivation is well beyond the scope of this chapter, suffice it to say that a coach's effort at motivation has two components. That is, the coach is involved both in activating athletes (i.e., getting them up for athletic performance) and in focusing athletes on a given goal. Sport-specific skill development becomes somewhat less prominent as one moves up competitive levels, whereas efforts at player motivation typically become more central.

Strategic Planning

The last primary job function of the team coach considered here is what the business world calls strategic planning. In the athletic arena, this includes game preparation and analysis, tactical decision making, and so forth. This function remains fairly consistent whether the primary goal is winning or participant enjoyment and education. Of course, the relative importance of this function and thus the pressure coaches feel from their tactical decisions is based on the importance to their organizations of winning.

The nature of the relationship between coach and athlete depends on many factors. What is the primary goal of the organization and coach? Are these goals congruent and are they similarly held by the players? How effective is the coach in performing the basic job functions outlined above?

Does the coach utilize a directive or consensus-seeking style and does this style match correctly with the primary team goal? For example, an organization that holds a primary goal of winning is much more likely to accept (or even require) a more directive coaching style in which the coach is in nearly total control of decision making, whereas an organization that holds participant enjoyment and education as the primary goal might find a directive coaching style less tolerable and might be most comfortable with a coach employing a consensus-seeking coaching style.

How well does the coach understand the personalities of the players? Can the coach respond accordingly? Regardless of a coach's style and personality, the relationship between athlete and coach must be seen as dynamic and highly complex. The coach, in the role of an authority figure (especially for young athletes) must simultaneously

- motivate (i.e., focus the team on clear goals and elicit a consistently high level of intensity in working toward these goals),
- establish clear roles and responsibilities for team members,
- define and maintain team rules and regulations,
- oversee conditioning and injury rehabilitation,
- supervise assistant coaches, and
- be keenly aware of the emotional-behavioral needs, reactions, and problems of players.

An aspect of coach–athlete interactions typically neglected in the sport psychology literature is the athlete's responsibility for the development and maintenance of an adequate relationship with the coach. Although it is universally accepted that successful relationships require effort on the part of all parties involved, the burden for successful coach–athlete relationships is almost always placed exclusively on the shoulders of the coach.

The business world has recognized the duality of boss–subordinate relationships and sport psychology would be wise to incorporate some of the concepts currently used in the business area. For example, in a thoughtful paper written for the *Harvard Business Review*, Gabarro and Kotter (1987) present the notion that boss–subordinate relationships involve a mutual dependence between fallible human beings. They state that although people often place the burden of responsibility on their bosses for the success or failure of their relationships, the fact is that all parties involved need to recognize that both boss and subordinate (i.e., coach and athlete) require the help and cooperation of each other to perform their jobs effectively. Gabarro and Kotter use the term *managing your boss* to describe "the process of consciously working with your superior to obtain the best possible result for you, your boss, and the company" (p. 1).

Having defined the job of team coach and described the complexity of coach–athlete relationships, I now take up the issue of team cohesion.

Team Cohesion

Team cohesion, often popularly referred to as team chemistry, is an issue that all coaches at some time or another must consider. Carron (1982) defines team cohesion as a dynamic process that culminates in a group's tendency to remain united in pursuing its goals and objectives. The two key points in this definition are the phrases *dynamic process* and *united in pursuing goals and objectives.*

In his review of cohesion in sport teams, Carron (1984) suggests that cohesion is a dynamic process because the absolute amount of measurable cohesion fluctuates on an ongoing basis. Many variables appear to influence the development and maintenance of group cohesion. These include team selection, interpersonal attraction or conflict, role formation, acceptance or conflict, coach behavior, and team performance. For example, several studies have suggested that cohesion and performance are interrelated with no unidimensional causative relationship readily inferred (Landers, Wilkinson, Hatfield, & Barber, 1982; Ruder & Gill, 1982).

Studies of work-team effectiveness in industrial-organizational psychology have suggested that the relationship of team cohesion and performance might depend on group norms (Sundstrom, DeMeuse, & Futrell, 1990). Group norms can be defined as standards of work behavior and work output established by team members and managers on the basis of team mission and organizational goals. Stogdill (1972) studied a variety of different work groups and found that work-team cohesion amplified established norms, whether favoring high or low productivity. That is, cohesion can result in enhanced or diminished performance, depending on previously established levels of acceptable work output.

Unity of goal pursuit is also an important phrase in Carron's (1982) definition of team cohesion. Unity of goal pursuit refers to the need for clearly communicated team goals (Zander, 1971) as well as clearly defined individual roles, with the importance of each role in overall team success being understood.

Carron (1984) summarized his exhaustive review of the team cohesion literature with practical suggestions for coaches. These recommendations include

- establishing high norms for productivity through specific, measurable, challenging team goals;
- avoiding, wherever possible, excessively difficult early-season scheduling to promote cohesion via success;
- encouraging activities that enhance social cohesion, intragroup communications, and group identity (e.g., non-sport-related team activities);
- clearly defining individual roles and stressing the importance of those roles to team success; and
- avoiding excessive personnel turnover.

Team cohesion is a natural by-product of team activity and is influenced by factors both within and outside of a coach's direct control. Later in the chapter I will discuss many of these interventions in the context of the case study that was presented earlier. It appears that a coach can be a positive influence in the proper development and maintenance of team cohesion but cannot completely control it. For this reason, I do not list team cohesion here as a primary job function of coaches; rather, it is, at least in part, a consequence of overall coaching behavior.

It has been my experience that at the level of elite-professional team sports, role clarity and team success combine to yield optimal levels of team cohesion (see Figure 6.4). Although players need to understand their roles and how these contribute to ultimate team success, the reality is that elite athletes typically accept a reduced role (e.g., fewer shots, fewer minutes in the game, etc.) only when their team is winning.

Losing breeds unhappiness in several ways. It is difficult to accept the usefulness of a reduced role when you cannot see the

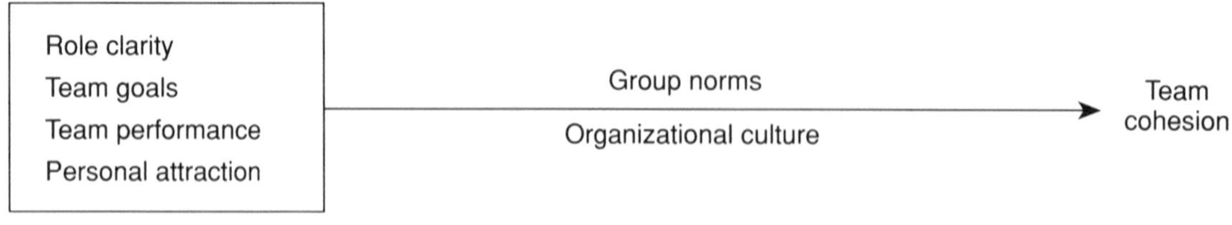

Figure 6.4 Factors affecting team cohesion.

role's leading to ultimate success (i.e., winning). Also, athletes that are competitive by nature naturally believe that the team would perform better if they had a greater role. Lastly, at the professional level athletes are paid for performance. They often (but not always) describe the importance of their roles in winning teams to make a case for higher salaries but cannot do so on losing teams. This increases the pressure for playing time and better statistics. "Playing for numbers," as this is often referred to, tends to have an additional negative impact on team cohesion, as players in losing environments become more and more focused on themselves.

The coach impacts on this process by being the central figure in creating a working environment that either accepts or does not tolerate a deviation from the commitment to team goals. In this environment numbers are viewed only in the context of the achievement of team goals. Thus what is created is an organizational culture that is demanding and challenging (i.e., high-productivity group norms).

In analyzing the job of team coach, we can draw the conclusion that success requires a high degree of sport-specific knowledge, analytic skills, interpersonal communication skills, an awareness of the differences between individual players, and a sensitivity to players' needs and feelings. In addition, the ability to create a vision that the team can strive for is of paramount importance (i.e., the ability to see how individual skills can connect in creating a cohesive team, thus leading to an end product that achieves the established organizational goal). The coach must face the demands from management and administration, the particular requirements for successful performance in the chosen sport, and the emotional-behavioral reactions of individual players. Add to this equation the pressures typically found in high-level competitive athletics (professional, Division I collegiate, Olympic, etc.), such as fan and media pressure, and the job becomes even more difficult. It is therefore not surprising that the issue of coach burnout is often raised in high-level competitive sport.

Coach Burnout

Burnout is a catchword typically used to describe a person's reaction to chronic stress (Freudenberger, 1980). The pressures of coaching at an elite level, including organizational demands, constant expectation to win, frequent travel, maintenance of complex interpersonal relations, and the constant need for attention to a wide variety of detail, place great physical and psychological demands on any person working in this profession.

Smith (1986) brings together research from several areas and discusses the causes, nature, and consequences of burnout within a cognitive-affective model of stress. Taking essentially a social-learning perspective, Smith discusses how interactive situational, cognitive, physiologic, and behavioral components interact in stress and burnout. He places particular attention on an examination of burnout in the athletic arena, although the issue of coach burnout is not a direct focus. Smith suggests that burnout includes physical, mental, and behavioral components and occurs in response to a complex interaction between situational and personal characteristics. He further suggests that the most notable characteristic of burnout is a behavioral withdrawal from previously enjoyable pursued activity.

Burnout also has been described as including emotional exhaustion, depersonalization, and perceived lack of personal accomplishment (Caccese & Mayerberg, 1984). Research has implicated situational variables, such as organizational demands, role incongruence, and lack of social support (Shinn, Rosario, Morch, & Chestnut, 1984). Less attention has been paid to the role of individual (personality) characteristics, such as frustration tolerance, trait anxiety levels, and the like.

In an attempt to examine dispositional (i.e., personality), cognitive, and situational predictors of coach burnout within Smith's model, Vealey and associates (1992) studied 848 high-school coaches who completed self-report questionnaires. Trait anxiety emerged as the strongest predictor of burnout, although perception of role and reward were also predictive. The authors concluded that both dispositional and cognitive factors can be more predictive of burnout than situational and behavioral factors, thus offering some support for Smith's model.

Lastly, considering the literature as a whole, there has been a lack of systematic examination of the scope and magnitude of coach burnout, so this area appears to be fertile ground for future empirical study.

In attempting to understand coach burnout, Dale and Weinberg (1989), in one of the few empirical studies in this area, found that coaches exhibiting a giving, other-oriented, or considerate style of leadership scored higher in frequency and intensity of emotional exhaustion and depersonalization than those coaches displaying an initiating-structuring style of leadership. If this study is viewed as in the context of the winning–participation and education dimension of primary team goal noted earlier, it can be hypothesized that the high-school and college coaches utilized for this study were primarily focused on the participation end of the spectrum, and thus the emotional needs of their players were a high priority. As such, the coaching style utilized might have been particularly draining.

Capel, Sisley, and Desertrain (1987) studied the relationship in coach burnout between role ambiguity and role conflict. They found that although there was a statistically significant relationship between these variables, it accounted for only 14% of total variance. They did, however, suggest that role ambiguity and conflict can be reduced, thereby lowering the probability of coach burnout. Minimization of role ambiguity and conflict might be achieved by delineating the goals of the organization and the standards by which the coach would ultimately be evaluated.

In a study that directly asked 93 high-school and college coaches to describe the most stressful aspects of their jobs, nearly 50% listed player disrespect. Approximately 20% also listed not being able to "reach" their players, that is, not being able to effectively communicate with them (Kroll, 1982). It is noteworthy that 70% of those factors noted by these coaches as being major job stressors are issues relating to the coach–athlete relationship. Only 13% of the factors noted were related to performance issues.

The overview of the job of team coach presented here reveals numerous responsibilities, great pressures, and, from the perspective of the sport psychologist, many areas in which psychological expertise can be of value. However, before a coach can utilize these skills and talents, the psychologist must first fit comfortably into the team environment. In essence, what the psychologist can do is only part of the equation; knowing when and how to offer expertise, that is, knowing how the coach goes about the job, is the other often more crucial variable. Developing sound consulting skills and maintaining an awareness of the psychology of organizations are of paramount importance for the would-be team psychologist. An example of these pressures leading to coach burnout and an approach to intervention can be found in a case study presented later in this chapter.

THE TEAM PSYCHOLOGIST: ROLE DEVELOPMENT

Sport psychologists who desire to work in a team setting must first recognize that in many respects they are on foreign soil. The athletic community (as has been pointed out to me on numerous occasions) has survived for many decades without the need for psychologists. The first task of the psychologist, then, is to convince the organization that (a) applied sport psychology is a legitimate field that can make a real contribution to the achievement of organizational goals and (b) that the psychologist can comfortably fit into the team setting and not be a star-struck person who merely wants to be seen associating with athletes (especially those at the professional level).

Athletic Personnel Perceptions

There appear to be two components to the reluctance of athletic personnel to readily accept psychologists as having a useful contribution to make to the athletic organization. One is basically a lack of knowledge. Athletic personnel frequently do not see psychologists apart from their mental health–psychotherapy function and thus can see no role in sports for psychologists. If (and this is a big if) psychologists understand the sports world, if they can explain logically and without jargon the role of mental factors in athletic performance, if they are knowledgeable and experienced in the particular techniques of mental-skills training, if they are adept at functioning in an out-of-office consulting role and are able to work in the athletic milieu—often without suit, tie, and couch, going to athletes rather than having athletes come to them—then, and only then, do psychologists have a chance to be accepted and valued. The second component relates to the reluctance of athletic personnel, especially at elite and professional levels, to have excessive numbers of people involved with the team. There is often a sense of organizational paranoia as to which, why, and how people become involved with their team. Trust must be developed gradually. It must be pointed out here that as it relates to psychology, this organizational guardedness is particularly strong. The reason for this is understandable. Sports personnel lump all people who are licensed as psychologists, claim to be psychologists, infer themselves to be psychologists, or use titles such as *mental-training consultant*, *performance-enhancement specialist*, and so forth, into one group: psychologists. Many people in these groups are either improperly trained (and thus are at best ineffective and at worst harmful), or make outrageous claims (e.g., guarantee that they can predict who will be injured, or who will become an all-star). As such, professionals legally using the title *psychologist* must prove both their professionalism and their capacity to function in a team setting at a level often beyond that of other professionals. It also appears to be true that the connotation of the sport psychologist as a shrink is still widely held in the sport world, although this appears to be slowly changing.

Functioning in the Athletic Environment

How do psychologists enter and thrive in this seemingly hostile environment? Psychologists must first recognize that their role will in all likelihood evolve gradually and steadily over time as trust in their professional and interpersonal competence rises. As they spend more time around the team and are gradually seen as a natural part of the team, the likelihood of effective utilization increases. It is important to understand that a team is very much like an extended family; outsiders can be welcomed, but only time allows them to be fully accepted into the family. The impact of the psychologist attempting to do "too much, too soon" before the team has accepted the psychologist both personally and professionally can be negative to the long-term relationship with the organization. It is wise to view the development of a program of psychological service to a sport team as an evolutionary process rather than a revolutionary event. Even in the best of all situations, psychologists must remember that their roles are ever changing.

This evolutionary process is not necessarily a simple linear progression. Changes in administration and coaching staff can alter (or even end) psychologists' roles, suddenly and through no fault of their own. This is a fact of life in athletics. Team psychologists evolve from unproven rookies to contributing veterans over time. Their own experiences in this evolution can allow them to understand the hopes and frustrations of athletes, who must go through a similar process. Patience and an understanding that two steps forward might be followed by one step backward is essential. Correctly reading team readiness for advances in the role and responsibilities of the psychologist is critical.

To positively impact on this evolutionary process, sport psychologists must first be honest with themselves about whether or not they possess the necessary training, skills, and knowledge to function in this environment. As well, sport psychologists must be honest with the organization regarding skills, goals, and so forth. In a multidisciplinary field that has itself had some controversy over issues of credentialing, competence, and training (Brown, 1982; Gardner & Heyman, 1982; Silva, 1989), it is especially important that the athletic organization understand from the outset what the psychologist can and cannot do.

Merging Educational and Clinical Functions

I must stress one important point from my own experiences working at the professional level. Athletic personnel for the most part do not distinguish between educational and clinical sport psychologists. As such, there is an expectation that psychologists will be able to deal with not only issues relating to athletic performance, but also clinical issues such as family problems, bereavement and grief, depression, and so forth. If, by nature of training, practitioners of sport psychology cannot ethically, legally, or morally provide such services, they must make that clear from the beginning of employment or risk appearing dishonest or incompetent at best or negligent at worst. The role of a new team psychologist must of course be developed gradually in cooperation with administration and upper management, the coaching staff, the sports medicine team, and player personnel. Lack of clarity about the role of the team psychologist will inevitably lead to a variety of problems:

- Perceived failure of the team psychologist to "get the job done"
- Mistrust by players or staff
- Lack of true responsibility (thus blocking real opportunity)

- A perception that the psychologist has overstepped boundaries and created unnecessary problems for the team.

Defining the Job Function

The team psychologist role can best be conceptualized as an internal consultant. In this regard, my experiences are quite similar to those described by Murphy (1988). Murphy suggests that activities of the team psychologist are broad, involve numerous personnel, and are often difficult to categorize as educational or clinical. Interventions are often brief, informal, and intense. As a team consultant, the psychologist comes to be seen as the primary resource about human behavior, especially relating but not limited to sport. The team psychologist is a full member of the organization who functions as a professional with knowledge and skill that come to bear on a wide range of issues involving the entire scope of organizational personnel. Further, by seeing oneself as an internal consultant and in making an effort to make one's knowledge available to all, the team psychologist cannot easily be cast into the roles of management, coach, trainer, and so forth. This creates a unique positioning that allows for entry and availability all along the personnel continuum with full trust and confidence.

The internal consultant role fosters a positive relationship with all levels of organizational personnel. For example, the coaching staff can utilize the psychologist's knowledge while recognizing that players, administration, and the sports medicine team can also receive valuable service. Thus all members of all subgroups see the psychologist interacting with members of all other subgroups without fear or distrust. The psychologist is expected to consult with all levels of the organization openly and honestly. In establishing this role of internal consultant, issues such as confidentiality must be clearly defined and communicated to everyone early in the consultation process. This important issue will be discussed in greater detail later in this chapter.

The team psychologist potentially has numerous job functions and should have the position's role and job description defined based on personal training and the needs of the organization. The specific services provided by the team psychologist might include psychological testing, performance-enhancement counseling, relationship–team development work, clinical services, and other general consultative services. I will now briefly describe these various services, including to whom the service is most useful, the goal(s) of the service, the role of the coach in the service, the specialized knowledge and training that is required, and the potential obstacles and pitfalls.

THE TEAM PSYCHOLOGIST: SERVICES PROVIDED

One of the most controversial areas of applied sport psychology is the appropriate use of psychological testing. A complete discussion of psychological testing in sport is well beyond the scope of this chapter, and thoughtful discussions have previously been undertaken (Nideffer, 1981; Silva, 1984). Psychological testing has numerous functions in the sport world. Problem identification (i.e., assessment) and intervention planning are often aided by the use of psychometric instruments, such as the Sixteen Personality Factor Questionnaire (Cattell, Eber, & Tatsuoka, 1980), the Test of Attentional and Interpersonal Style (Nideffer, 1976), the Competitive State Anxiety Inventory-2 (Martens, Burton, Vealey, Bump, & Smith, 1990), and the Psychological Skills Inventory (Mahoney, Gabriel, & Perkins, 1987), to name a few.

Generally speaking, psychological testing used in conjunction with interview and behavioral observations can provide useful information for the team psychologist in developing a full understanding of interpersonal

Courtesy USOC

dynamics, individual personality structure, and mental-skills development of player personnel. The information obtained from psychometric instruments can also be used in helping athletes more completely understand the rationale for various intervention efforts. For example, if the team psychologist determines that a player referred for inconsistent performance is experiencing exceptionally high levels of precompetitive anxiety and tends to readily lose necessary attentional focus during big games, it is often useful for the psychologist to see those results psychometrically, not only to possibly corroborate a hypothesis but also to objectively present conclusions to the athlete. As such, the suggested intervention, possibly relaxation training, mental rehearsal, and attention-control training, appear more rational to the athlete.

Although this use of psychological testing has benefits for both team psychologist and athlete, it can also be valuable to the coaching staff and the sports medicine team in allowing them to better understand their players and avoid misconceptions. For example, it can be helpful for medical personnel to recognize the need to more carefully monitor an athlete's injury rehabilitation in cases where the athlete tends toward a somewhat undisciplined approach to rules, structure, and so forth.

Similarly, it is not unusual for an athlete who has some difficulty in attentional focus to be misperceived as being lazy, disinterested, or nonmotivated. Providing a coaching staff with feedback about a player's psychological makeup (i.e., personality) and psychological skill strengths and deficits allows for a more accurate reading of the player and thus aids in coach-athlete relationship development. This team building function of psychological assessment has been described by nearly all the coaches I have worked with as the most useful aspect of having a sport psychologist on board. The testing of team personnel, with feedback first given to the individual players and later to the coaching staff, has been consistently valued by all participants and has consistently had a positive impact. A detailed example of the use of psychological testing in this manner is provided in a case-study presentation later in this chapter.

A few words of caution are necessary concerning the use of testing. First, only licensed psychologists are ethically, morally, and in most places legally able to administer and interpret most psychological tests. This fact is recognized by AAASP in its certification guidelines. Second, any psychologist providing this service should possess substantial specialized training and experience in the particular instruments being used and should have extensive experience in presenting test results to clients. Menu or simplistic score-by-score descriptions of test results or jargon-filled feedback are professionally unacceptable and in fact have contributed to negative attitudes about psychological testing in sports. Further, failure to fully educate the people receiving the feedback as to the nature, uses, and abuses of such information severely compromises the utility of the instruments and the function of assessment itself. The instruments used in psychological assessment often receive a great deal of criticism, whereas the fact that professionals often misuse the instruments typically receive very little. Some practitioners of sport psychology have maintained that athletes are "uncomfortable" about taking psychological tests (Halliwell, 1990). Some authors have suggested that the data obtained from psychological tests are unnecessary (Ravizza, 1990), and in some manner the administration of these instruments might interfere with the development of a personal relationship with players (Dorfman, 1990). Although I believe most people are uncomfortable with the thought of having their psyches explored, it has been my experience that players have not only accepted psychological assessment (if properly presented and utilized), but also that most players have been open to follow-up discussions about the results and their performance and interpersonal implications. Further, it has been my experience that these initial one-on-one feedback sessions are often the first close interaction between team psychologist and player. The sessions allow not only for relevant test results to be discussed but also for the psychologist and athlete to discuss numerous other issues—including the role of the sport psychologist. Thus this process allows for the beginning of both a personal and professional relationship. An adequate relationship between athlete and psychologist requires not only this type of one-on-one contact but also the opportunity for the psychologist to demonstrate professional skill and an approachable personality.

If the psychologist has strong skills in test administration and interpretation and fully understands the numerous issues surrounding test interpretation (Nideffer, 1981), psychometric instruments, particularly personality assessment inventories, are reliable and valid predictors of human behavioral characteristics. If used inappropriately for tasks for which they were not designed, such as predicting a player's likelihood of achieving all-star performance levels or of being injured, they are highly inaccurate (Davis, 1991). It is important to remember that these instruments were not designed to predict performance directly; they were designed for and are effective in describing and thus predicting normal human behavior. It is true that these tests are sometimes used as part of a selection process for professional teams, for example, prior to the yearly entry draft of college- or high-school-age players into the professional ranks. The use of personality tests for this purpose is not unlike testing often performed by psychologists in the business world as part of a corporate screening and selection process. Once again, the important fact to realize here is that the instruments should not be used to directly predict future athlete performance (although it is conceivable that empirical studies will one day make this feasible), but rather to predict how a person is likely to fit into a particular team, the likely interaction with particular coaches, and likely behaviors in a variety of situations (e.g., how athletes might best be motivated, how they are likely to handle criticism, how they are best disciplined, their likelihood of seeking leadership roles, their typical responses to frustration, etc.). This information can then be integrated into a selection process that includes scouting reports, face-to-face interviews, direct observation, and the feedback of former coaches, not unlike the typical selection process utilized in the business world.

An informal form of psychological assessment is often undertaken by scouts who provide reports describing athletic behavior and inferring personality variables such as dedication, heart, mental toughness, and so forth. Formal objective assessment allows for a more complete and accurate understanding of people who have already had their personalities informally evaluated.

The information obtained from psychological testing does not directly predict athletic performance, but is related to numerous performance-relevant characteristics and thus has value to the selection process.

Performance-Enhancement Counseling and Psychological-Skills Training

The function of the team psychologist most typically associated with the field of sport psychology and most often inquired about by students and interested professionals at conferences is performance-enhancement intervention, often referred to as psychological- or mental-skills training. Techniques used in athletic performance enhancement have been thoroughly discussed elsewhere (Williams, 1986), and an in-depth examination of these techniques is well beyond this chapter's scope. The goals of these techniques are typically to help people develop their athletic skills or use existing skills more effectively. These techniques are presented using a psychoeducational intervention model. Skills such as muscle relaxation, attention control, visualization and mental rehearsal, goal setting, and cognitive-control methods are systematically taught as part of a skill-training process. How performance-enhancement counseling and psychological-skills training is administered in a team setting varies across teams, but generally is provided in a lecture-educational type approach typically involving a group of players or in individual one-on-one sessions as needed.

As the team personnel begin to know the psychologist personally and begin to understand the concept of mental-skills training for performance enhancement, players will begin to openly discuss performance-related issues. These discussions are most often conducted in an informal manner, often just prior to or immediately following practice. These discussions may well make use of results previously obtained from psychological testing and will often lead to more formal performance-enhancement counseling. The coaches that I have worked with at first simply tolerated such interventions (it must be recognized that nothing is done with player personnel without full approval by the head coach). These individual sessions occurred when either a player sought out the aid of this psychologist or when a member of the coaching staff believed that an athlete's performance difficulties were frustrating or perplexing enough that they sought out psychological consultation. Later, as the personal relationship between head coach and myself matured and the staff appreciation and respect for the value of a sport psychologist evolved, the coaches began to allow more independence in working with players on my own initiative and finally to incorporate a series of structured mental-skills lectures during training camp. It cannot be stressed too strongly that without the support of the coaching staff, players are not likely to utilize the team psychologist in a performance-enhancement role. Once players see that the coaches value mental-skills training—possibly to the point of even using the language of sport psychology in their own interactions with players—they can feel free to consult the team psychologist without fear of negative reaction. Similarly, the longer the psychologist is involved with the team and the more the psychologist is perceived as a natural part of the environment, the greater the likelihood of adequate utilization of the psychologist's services.

Relationship Enhancement

Maintaining adequate relationships with players is critical to a coach's job. Using information from behavioral observation and psychological testing, the team psychologist can offer insights to the coach to more fully understand players' daily behaviors, motivational needs, and how they are likely to react to specific coaching techniques (e.g., public criticism, positive feedback). This information allows the coaching staff to proactively attend to the relationship with their players rather than to react with postproblem attention. One coach remarked that there is no information that he receives from this process that wouldn't become known to him over time but that the advantage is in being able to avoid the mistakes, confrontations, and misunderstandings that often lead to that knowledge. From this coach's perspective, the team psychologist gave him information that was easily used in enhancing his ability to effectively communicate with his players.

Similarly, understanding player and staff personalities allows the team psychologist to appropriately counsel players in developing effective communication with the coaching staff. Discussions as to how, where, and when to communicate issues and concerns have been reported as valuable by numerous players. In addition, consultation about relationship issues between players has become necessary at times. The team psychologist can have an active role in promoting team chemistry by being a catalyst for effective communication between team members. It is important for would-be team psychologists to recognize that it is not their job to communicate roles, motivate, or impart strategy. Instead it is the psychologist's job to clarify thoughts and feelings and to aid in promoting open lines of communication. In keeping with the conceptualization of coach–athlete relationships noted previously, the team psychologist can aid in their developing a mutual understanding of each other as people as well as in recognizing their mutual dependence. This role is fraught with potential obstacles, and psychologists must continually be aware of the limitations of their roles. Prior organizational consulting experience is highly recommended for persons seeking to do team-building work in an athletic setting. Those interested in team building in organizational settings are referred to the article on effective work teams by Sundstrom and colleagues in the *American Psychologist* (1990), and the text *Building Productive Teams* by Varney (1990).

Clinical Services

The area of responsibility that psychologists are most closely identified with is that of clinical service. The identification, assessment, and treatment of clinical mental health issues such as anxiety, depression, family dysfunction, and so forth, are typical roles for psychologists and might well be expected of team psychologists if within their scope of training. In many respects, these job responsibilities are much like those found in the provision of an employee assistance program (EAP) in which short-term clinical services

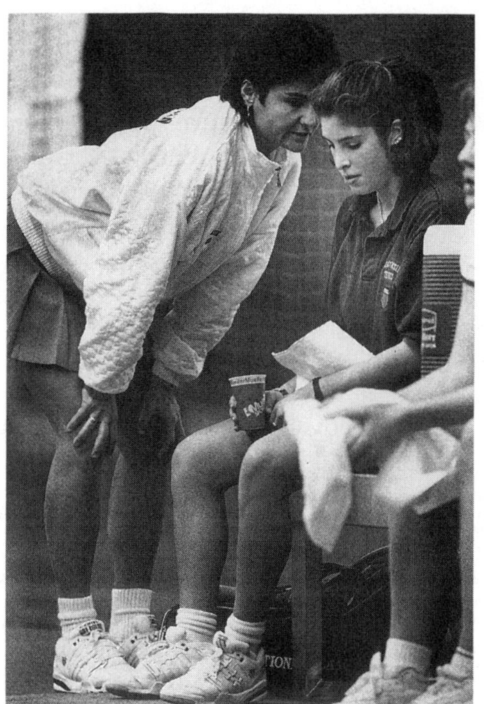

Courtesy University of Wisconsin Women's Sports Information

are readily available to members of the organization (and often their families).

This role may not, however, be required or desired in all settings. For example, in university settings, clinical needs of student athletes or staff are typically addressed by the university health counseling center. The team psychologist in these instances will serve to identify problem areas and assist in referring the person to the proper organizational resource. Further, the team psychologist might at times be required to make outside referrals. Referrals are usually required, for example, in situations requiring intensive or long-term care of drug or alcohol abuse. When outside referrals are necessary, the team psychologist would likely be required by the organization to coordinate or monitor outside treatment efforts. This job function is similar to that of the team physician, who often needs to refer to outside medical specialists while remaining actively involved in the ongoing medical care of the athlete.

In addition to the traditional role of psychological counseling for an athlete (or coach's) mental health needs, clinical services offered by the team psychologist should include active involvement with the sports medicine team concerning psychological aspects of athletic injuries. Injury to athletes is as much a part of sport participation as winning and losing. Psychological reactions to injury range from mild to severe. Variables such as premorbid personality factors, psychological coping mechanisms, severity of injury, level of athletic competition, playing status (starter or substitute, freshman or senior, etc.), and available social support, to name but a few, contribute to the intensity and direction of emotional-behavioral response to injury.

Before reviewing the basic clinical activities that sport psychologists employ in treating injured athletes, it is once again imperative to point out that the team psychologist's role and acceptance by the team will determine actual utilization. In the role of internal psychological consultant, the psychologist must effectively communicate to members of the sports medicine team, coaches, and athletes the psychological factors and reactions involved in the rehabilitation of the athlete's injuries (May & Sieb, 1987; Rotella & Heyman, 1986; Wiese & Weiss, 1987). This allows athletic trainers, coaches, physicians, and even teammates to recognize both expected and extreme psychological reactions to injury.

As the team psychologist becomes intertwined in the day-to-day functioning of the organization, ongoing contact between the athletic trainer and the psychologist will occur. It is most often trainers who not only deal with physical injuries but are first to notice mood and behavioral fluctuations and even hear about significant events in the athletes' personal lives. It is in close cooperation with the training staff that the psychologist truly becomes embedded in the fabric of the team.

As this relationship evolves, the psychologist becomes more intimately involved with the ongoing psychological care of the athlete. In reality, only through regular, direct involvement with the team physician will the psychologist truly be seen as a valued member of the sports medicine team. And only as a member of the sports medicine team can the psychologist be consistently involved, in a structured and meaningful manner, in the psychological care of the injured athlete.

As psychologists, we must again remember that we are in many respects outsiders in the broad area of sports medicine. Our knowledge base regarding psychological aspects of injury and rehabilitation is not typically well known in sports medicine circles. Thus we must be careful not to imply that all answers are within our discipline or that we can somehow predict who will be injured or that we can speed the recovery time for every injured athlete. We must recognize that injury treatment is primarily a physical–medical endeavor, and that psychology can make a unique contribution by offering useful adjunctive services in a consultative model. This will occur, however, only if the professionals offering such services are respected for their knowledge, skill, and interpersonal acumen.

Regular feedback to the trainer or team physician enhances the credibility of the psychologist and further develops trusting collegial relationships. The team psychologist can offer many specific services to the injured athlete and the sports medicine team:

- Assessment of psychological status (Lynch, 1988)
- Pain-control techniques (Singer & Johnson, 1987)
- Cognitive-behavioral interventions for medical treatment adherence and compliance (Meichenbaum & Turk, 1987)
- Stress-management and psychological counseling (i.e., psychological first aid)
- Imagery training and mental practice for facilitating the return to competition (Rotella & Heyman, 1986)
- Facilitation of social-team support (Wiese & Weiss, 1987)

By and large the clinical activities noted here focus on the maintenance and development of the athlete's psychological well-being. It must be pointed out that on occasion coaches or other staff or support personnel have psychological needs that might fit into the team psychologist's domain. There are, as noted previously, many pressures on coaches and administrators in competitive sports. As the previous discussion of coach burnout suggests, coaches and even administrative personnel are prone to severe emotional-behavioral reactions. Team psychologists can, if their personal relationship with the coach has matured properly, offer psychological support and counsel—typically in an informal manner—during periods of intense stress.

Whether or not this service can prevent burnout is essentially an empirical question. However, my own experience suggests that this support function can often allow an appropriate venting of built-up emotions and might not only aid in the coach's psychological well-being but also help insure continued team harmony by removing the need for the coach to act out his emotional reactions onto the team.

General Consultative Services

On occasion the team psychologist is asked to become involved in issues that are time limited and arise out of special circumstances. Examples of these might be

- crisis-intervention work immediately following a personal setback or a significant life event that has struck a team

member and thus impacts the entire team;
- team meetings in the midst of a lengthy slump;
- helping to prepare a team to play against an opponent that it has not defeated for several years;
- helping to prepare motivational videos before the playoffs; and
- offering input as to the role of different practice scenarios on intrateam competitiveness and conflict.

Although the team psychologist can confront these issues with some aid from the literature, they often require creativity and a close working relationship with the coaching staff so that interventions can be developed by consensus. My experience suggests that early in the psychologist's tenure with the team, these issues will not be brought up by the staff. Only as the relationship matures does the staff become comfortable enough to ask for input about these matters. Being asked to become involved in such team issues is arguably a true measure of the psychologist's acceptance by and value to the coaching staff.

This overview of the services provided by the team psychologist presents many opportunities for the psychologist who is both trained in sport psychology and aware of the athletic environment (culture) to make a meaningful contribution. What must be stressed, however, is that the focal point of an athletic team is the coach. It is therefore critical that the team psychologist recognize that the relationship with this person to a large extent determines how or if the psychologist will operate. It safely can be said that without a positive, trusting relationship with the head coach, one cannot fulfill a team psychologist role.

Keeping the coach informed of your activities is necessary. This does not necessarily mean sharing all details of all interactions. Rather, letting the coach know that players are seeking you out for mental-skills training, or that you are in contact with the assistant coach regarding a particular player, or letting the coach know that you are in contact with the sports medicine team regarding an injured player, or simply asking the coach if there is anything or anyone that you can help with goes a long way in building an exceptional working relationship.

There is one last point in this regard. I strongly suggest that new programs or ideas that the team psychologist would like to initiate, for example, the preparation and use of personal highlight videos, be discussed prior to training camp and thus implemented (if agreed upon) early in the year. Coaches at high competitive levels are not likely to initiate new ideas once their season gets under way, due in large part to the overall pressure and enormous day-to-day detail of coaching a team.

ETHICAL CONSIDERATIONS

The team psychologist has many aspects of day-to-day work that require careful attention to ethical principles. First and foremost is the use of the title *psychologist*. The issue of who can legally use the title of psychologist and what background sport psychologists must possess are complex issues that have been discussed in detail elsewhere (Gardner, 1991; Silva, 1989). Suffice it to say that those professionals wishing to function as team psychologists must first face the issue of their own training and credentials. Those practitioners of applied sport psychology that qualify to use the title *psychologist* under state and provincial law are already obligated to understand and follow the American Psychological Association's (APA) ethical standards (1981). Those practitioners who cannot legally use the title *psychologist* and whose educational backgrounds are for the most part in the areas of physical education and sport science have at present no clear ethical guidelines to follow, other than those of APA. Currently, the Association for the Advancement of Applied Sport Psychology (AAASP) is working toward constructing an ethical standard for all those classified by the organization as certified consultants. In understanding how ethical considerations impact on the applied sport psychologist working for athletic teams, I will briefly describe a number of areas mentioned in APA's ethical standards and comment on their relationship to the services previously reported.

Competence

The issue of competence in the area of sport psychology has been addressed in some detail (Gardner, 1991; Silva, 1989; Taylor, 1991). At this point in time it is the responsibility of psychologists seeking involvement in team sports to insure that they possess the necessary knowledge and skill to effectively work in the athletic environment. It is my opinion that organizations like AAASP must take a greater role in establishing guidelines on what training is required to offer what service.

At present the burden of determining competence falls squarely on the shoulders of the practitioner. One caution: In our society it is not unrealistic to believe that should professionals and their respective organizations disregard the need to carefully define issues of competence, the courts ultimately will be asked to make those determinations. I would suggest special caution to those non-psychologically-trained practitioners who offer treatment (i.e., counseling) of clinical problems masked as sport performance problems or utilize psychological (psychometric) assessment as part of their job descriptions.

Public Statements

Essentially, the principle on public statements requires psychologists to honestly and accurately represent their qualifications. This relates to competence, in that initially the psychologist naturally will try to sell services to the team that the psychologist wishes to work for. In all selling there is a temptation to focus on strengths and ignore limitations. Over time the team in question will undoubtedly look to the psychologist for most of the services mentioned in this chapter, so accurate presentation of one's limitations becomes critical to ethical practice. In addition, outlandish claims such as those mentioned earlier involving almost clairvoyant capacity to predict status, injury, and so forth, run contrary to this general principle.

Professional Relationships

As noted throughout this chapter, the team psychologist is required to interact with a variety of staff members responsible for a number of job functions. Maintaining these professional relationships by respecting boundaries and understanding roles and responsibilities of all members of an organization becomes an ethical mandate. Communicating regularly and following designated lines of administrative reporting similarly fall into this category.

Welfare of the Consumer and Confidentiality

Welfare of the consumer and confidentiality are presented as one principle, because in the athletic setting they in effect speak to the same issue. That is, psychologists working in team settings (or any organizational setting for that matter) must make clear to all parties involved the nature of their responsibilities, the purpose and nature of all assessment, treatment, and training procedures, and the limits (if any) of confidentiality. The role of team psychologist presented in this chapter places great demands on the psychologist to adequately fulfill a complex consultative role and simultaneously adhere to these ethical principles.

To walk this line, the psychologist must use judgment and forethought in establishing clear guidelines for all parties involved (administration, coaching staff, and athletes) at the onset of employment. Rules governing confidentiality in psychologist–athlete interactions must be established and understood by everyone involved. It then becomes the responsibility of the psychologist to insure that these rules are respected. What information is the coach going to get about performance-enhancement counseling with athletes or the psychological state of athletes following injury? When utilizing psychological assessment as part of team building and coach-athlete–relationship enhancement, the question arises as to who gets feedback, in what sequence, and toward what end. For example, when working with organizations, I typically establish a format that allows psychometric test feedback to first be given to the athlete. At that time, our discussion includes what information will be provided to the coach in addition to why and how it will be presented. This information is discussed fully until the athlete is comfortable with it. Then and only then do I review the testing material with the coach(es). It should be pointed out that these rules are explained to everyone before initiating the testing–feedback process. Despite the best intentions of the psychologist, not all potential ethical dilemmas can be foreseen. In such circumstances professional judgment, keeping in mind the basic ethical principles, allows the psychologist to effectively and professionally respond to any situation. I have found in my own experience that from top to bottom, athletic organizations respect the psychologist who incorporates ethical concerns into everyday practice. Honest, ethical, and professional behavior leads to trust and respect, which in turn lead to further acceptance.

INTERVENTION IN THE CASE OF TEAM BLUE

As a regular staff member, the team psychologist had an advantage of being involved in the everyday activities of Team Blue before the request for consultation by its coach.

The team psychologist had conducted a series of mental-skills-training lectures in preseason and conducted individual personality assessment utilizing the Sixteen Personality Factor Questionnaire and the Test of Attentional and Interpersonal Style. Detailed feedback, as previously outlined in this chapter, was provided to each athlete during the season. During the season about one third of the team chose to work individually on mental-skills training, one third consulted with the psychologist intermittently, and one third did not avail themselves of sport psychology consultation. Following much discussion with the coaching staff, individual meetings were held with each player, to whom confidentiality was guaranteed.

Based on these meetings, the following issues and problems became apparent:

- A significant portion of the team could not clearly identify their role on the team, did not feel as though they were significant contributors, and were more fearful of making errors than achieving success.
- The freshmen (a significant portion of the team), all former high-school stars used to receiving much attention and playing time, were adjusting poorly to their changed playing status.
- The team members felt they had failed to achieve the coach's preseason goals to that point, their perceptions of a failed season creating high levels of anxiety.
- The team generally felt little pride in its identity and members were more socially isolated from each other than is usual in college teams.

Without identifying particular players, these general themes were presented to the coach, as the athletes knew would be done. It was suggested that a series of meetings between the players and team psychologist be held to begin both a dialogue addressing issues of personal responsibility and commitment and an active effort to use goal setting and imagery training to prepare for practice sessions as well as games.

It was also recommended to the coach that roles and responsibilities might be communicated once again and presented more individually (the coach recalled that roles were discussed once in an early-season team meeting). In addition, to address the issue of mistake-avoidance behavior, it was suggested that discussion of season-long goals (outcome goals) at least temporarily be replaced by individual and team game-performance goals.

Lastly, it was suggested that some social non-sport-related activity involving the entire team be planned (preferably in a situation where the team could be introduced publicly) to help promote a greater social cohesion and sense of team. It was also advised that assistant coaches spend more time with the freshmen to aid in their adjustment to the realities of college sports.

After much discussion, often centering on how these suggestions fit into the coach's philosophy of coaching, all suggestions were implemented. The team psychologist and all players met in several group sessions, the coach arranged for individual meetings between himself and players for role clarification, goals were established on a game-by-game basis, assistant coaches became much more involved with freshmen and sophomores, and the team as a whole began scheduling social activities on a regular basis. Although the team did not achieve the original lofty goals, they did finish the season strongly, won their conference championship, and created a sound foundation for the following year.

THE CASE OF TEAM GREEN

Upon taking over the head-coaching job of a team with a reputation of having numerous difficulties in coach–player relationships, the new head coach consulted with the team psychologist about player personalities and their relevance to issues of communication and motivation.

In this case, a successful and experienced coach joined a team that had in recent years consistently demonstrated not only a losing record but also disharmony and interpersonal strife between players and coaches. The team psychologist brought into the organization by the administration joined the team just after the new coach was hired; after some initial resistance, the team psychologist was accepted by the coaching staff. Similarly, the players were slow to accept the value of the psychologist. Late in preseason, each player completed a psychological assessment battery that included the Sixteen Personality Factor Questionnaire and the Test of Attentional and Interpersonal Style. The assessment process was fully explained to the players in terms of

- its use to them in defining specific psychological strengths and weaknesses that might be further developed for enhanced athletic performance and
- its use in allowing the coaching staff better insight into the athletes' unique personalities.

It was explained that the athletes would receive feedback first and that no information would be presented to the coach without their knowledge and consent. Following these individual feedback sessions (which clearly helped develop the professional relationship between players and psychologist) discussions were held with the coaching staff. Discussed were each player's psychological makeup and how it might relate to previous difficulties as well as what areas and issues need to be remembered in interacting with each player (e.g., sensitivity, authority conflicts, distrust, etc.). Also discussed were specific suggestions as to motivational needs (e.g., praise, recognition, etc.) and suggestions for optimal communication (e.g., private discussion, repetition of verbal instruction due to attentional difficulties, etc.).

The head coach was open to this feedback and was able to readily integrate the information into his coaching style. During the course of the season, he frequently commented to the psychologist about the accuracy of the assessment results and ultimately gave much credit to the assessment process for a successful season that included no significant coach–athlete problems. This led to numerous consultations on a wide variety of issues and a close, long-term professional relationship.

■ *THE CASE OF TEAM GRAY* ■

A coach in the midst of a disappointing season, facing mounting criticism from both inside and outside the organization, and having experienced significant misfortune in his personal life (i.e., family illness), sought out the team psychologist for personal consultation after beginning to exhibit symptoms of burnout.

This head coach had successfully led the team for a number of years in a competitive, high-pressure environment, but at that time was in the midst of a season that had been highly disappointing in terms of wins and losses. As the losses mounted, he was faced with criticism from local print media and from within his own organization.

A hard worker who put in countless hours in preparing for each game and practice, he was confronted with the reality that his team, weaker than in previous years, was not responding to his efforts with improved play. In addition, he had to face a serious family illness that had taken its toll mentally and physically. He had maintained a long-standing professional relationship with the team psychologist, who had provided service to this team for a number of years.

This request for a consultation followed a particularly difficult practice, during which the coach unleashed an intense verbal barrage on the team following a seemingly innocuous error by a player. The coach then ended practice and stormed out.

During the ensuing consultation, the coach reported psychophysiologic symptoms (headache and gastrointestinal distress), sleep disturbance, irritability, and lack of desire to continue coaching. The coach had had a recent physical checkup at which the physician recommended psychological counseling. The coach refused an outside referral at that point. After several meetings in which the psychologist, using a cognitive-behavioral approach, focused on numerous cognitive distortions that the coach exhibited about himself, his overall success-to-failure ratio, external criticism, and his career in general, the coach began reporting symptomatic relief.

Behavior change was accomplished through increased (enjoyable) noncoaching activities and the development of short-term coaching goals. Options for assertively confronting the internal criticism were discussed, as were psychological issues involved in his family crisis. Autogenic relaxation techniques were also taught.

Within 4 weeks (3 to 4 meetings per week) significant reduction of symptomatology occurred and his coaching behavior returned to normal. The coach began to more effectively handle both his team's difficulties and his personal life. By the end of the season the coach once again was committed to remain in coaching.

CONCLUSION

Few jobs in sport carry both the prestige and pressure of head coach. The coach is at the forefront of the team and might as a result get too much credit for producing winning teams and too much blame for losing ones. The coach's job is multifaceted and similar in basic function to that of the business manager. The coach is totally responsible for player development and training as well as strategic and tactical planning. In addition, player selection and recruitment is strongly influenced, if not totally controlled, by the coach. The coach must lead and motivate the team's players to function as a productive, cohesive unit while communicating roles, goals, rules, and strategy. In essence, the coach must understand, predict, and control the sport-related behavior of players.

It is no wonder coaches often exhibit intense emotional and behavioral symptomatology in response to stress. It is readily apparent that the applied sport psychologist has much to offer the coach. In fact, the goals of understanding, prediction, and control of human behavior have often been ascribed to the science of psychology. The sport psychologist can help coaches understand players and enhance communication and relationships with them. The psychologist can offer insights into motivation, group dynamics, and individual behavioral tendencies.

Sport psychology has developed a knowledge base in the psychological foundation of enhanced athletic performance that can benefit the athlete and can offer input into the effects of various coaching behaviors, understand elements of effective leadership, and convey principles of motor learning. The clinically trained sport psychologist can aid in the psychological care of the injured athlete and counsel those whose personal problems are impacting their athletic performance.

For sport psychologists to be given the opportunity to demonstrate their usefulness, they must first demonstrate interpersonal skill, comfort with the sport world, awareness of team culture and organizational dynamics, willingness to be flexible, ability to work informally, and sensitivity to ethical standards. In essence, the team psychologist must demonstrate social skills, knowledge, and professionalism. The model for the team psychologist presented here is that of an internal consultant offering expertise to a wide range of team personnel. The team psychologist must recognize that this role is evolutionary and dynamic, ever changing and slowly developing. There are many potential obstacles, but the successful team psychologist will be acutely aware that this job is a challenging and exciting venture requiring sound judgment, honesty, and an awareness of established standards of professional behavior.

It is my opinion that in the future sport psychology as a discipline must come to grips with the uncomfortable issue of who is trained to provide what services. Ignoring this issue makes it no less important. Confusion both within the field and in the consumer public as a whole requires strong leadership on the part of such organizations as APA Division 47 and AAASP. Failure to address this issue might ultimately have a devastating effect on the continued acceptance of this field. Similarly, these professional organizations must look to create an ethical standard for all practitioners of sport psychology.

For further development of the knowledge base of sport psychology, it is suggested that greater attention be paid to the literature in the field of organizational psychology. For example, a recent special issue on organizational psychology in the *American Psychologist* included the following articles, all of which have clear relevance for sport psychology.

- "Organizational Culture" (Schein, 1990)
- "Work Teams: Applications and Effectiveness" (Sundstrom et al., 1990)
- "Work Motivation: Theory and Practice" (Katzell & Thompson, 1990)
- "Designing Systems for Resolving Disputes in Organizations" (Brett, Goldberg, & Ury, 1990)
- "Power and Leadership in Organizations: Relationships in Transition" (Hollander & Offermann, 1990)
- "Developing Managerial Talent Through Simulation" (Thornton & Cleveland, 1990)
- "Women and Minorities in Management" (Morrison & Von Glinow, 1990)

If we begin to view athletic performance as in many ways analogous to work performance, coaching of athletes as a subset of personnel management, team cohesion as a subset of work team effectiveness, and so forth, we might begin to expand our knowledge base, suggest creative research opportunities, and potentially offer the athletic environment new and exciting insights.

In conclusion, the team psychologist and coach can offer much to each other. With the goals of the team clearly in mind, an effective relationship between the two can yield considerable return.

REFERENCES

American Psychological Association. (1981). Ethical principles of psychologists. *American Psychologist*, **36**, 633-638.

Botterill, C. (1990). Sport psychology and professional hockey. *Sport Psychologist*, **4**, 358-368.

Brett, J.M., Goldberg, S.B., & Ury, W.L. (1990). Designing systems for resolving disputes in organizations. *American Psychologist*, **45**, 162-170.

Brown, M.J. (1982). Are sport psychologists really psychologists? *Journal of Sport Psychology*, **4**, 13-18.

Caccese, T.M., & Mayerberg, C.K. (1984). Gender differences in perceived burnout of college coaches. *Journal of Sport Psychology*, **6**, 279-288.

Capel, S.A., Sisley, B.L., & Desertrain, G.S. (1987). The relationship of role conflict and role ambiguity to burnout in high school basketball coaches. *Journal of Sport Psychology*, **9**, 106-117.

Carron, A.V. (1982). Cohesiveness in sport groups: Interpretations and considerations. *Journal of Sport Psychology*, **4**, 123-138.

Carron, A.V. (1984). Cohesion in sport teams. In J.M. Silva & R.S. Weinberg (Eds.), *Psychological foundations of sport* (pp. 340-352). Champaign, IL: Human Kinetics.

Cattell, R.B., Eber, H.W., & Tatsuoka, M.M. (1980). *Handbook for the Sixteen Personality Factor Questionnaire (16PF)*. Champaign, IL: Institute for Personality and Ability Testing.

Dale, J., & Weinberg, R.S. (1989). The relationship between coaches leadership style and burnout. *Sport Psychologist*, **3**, 1-13.

Davis, H. (1991). Criterion validity of the athletic motivation inventory: Issues in professional sport. *Journal of Applied Sport Psychology*, **3**, 176-182.

Dorfman, H.A. (1990). Reflections on providing personal and performance enhancement consulting services in professional baseball. *Sport Psychologist*, **4**, 341-346.

Freudenberger, H.J. (1980). *Burnout*. New York: Doubleday.

Gabarro, J.J., & Kotter, J.P. (1987). Managing your boss. In Harvard Business Review (Eds.), *People: Managing your most important asset* (pp. 1-9). Boston, MA: Harvard Business Review.

Gardner, F.L. (1991). Professionalization of sport psychology: A reply to Silva. *Sport Psychologist*, **5**, 55-60.

Gould, D., Murphy, S., Tammen, V., & May, J. (1991). An evaluation of U.S. Olympic sport psychology consultant effectiveness. *Sport Psychologist*, **5**, 111-127.

Halliwell, W. (1990). Providing sport psychology consulting services in professional hockey. *Sport Psychologist*, **4**, 369-377.

Heyman, S.R. (1982). A reaction to Danish and Hale: A minority report. *Journal of Sport Psychology*, **4**(1), 10-12.

Hollander, E.P., & Offermann, L.R. (1990). Power and leadership in organizations: Relationships in transition. *American Psychologist*, **45**, 179-189.

Katzell, R.A., & Thompson, D.E. (1990). Work motivation: Theory and practice. *American Psychologist*, **45**, 144-153.

Kroll, W. (1982). Competitive athletic stress factors in athletes and coaches. In L.P. Zaichkowsky and W.E. Sime (Eds.), *Stress management for sport*. Reston, VA: American Alliance for Health, Physical Education, Recreation and Dance.

Landers, D.M., Wilkinson, M.O., Hatfield, B.D., & Barber, H. (1982). Casualty and the cohesion-performance relationship. *Journal of Sport Psychology*, **4**, 170-183.

Lynch, G.P. (1988). Athletic injuries and the practicing sport psychologist: Practical guidelines for assisting athletes. *Sport Psychologist*, **2**, 161-167.

Mahoney, M.J., Gabriel, T.J., & Perkins, T.S. (1987). Psychological skills and exceptional athletic performance. *Sport Psychologist*, **1**, 181-199.

Martens, R. (1987). *Coaches guide to sport psychology*. Champaign, IL: Human Kinetics.

Martens, R., Burton, D., Vealey, R.S., Bump, L.A., & Smith, D.E. (1990). Development and validation of the Competitive State Anxiety Inventory-2 (CSAI-2). In R. Martens, R.S. Vealey, & D. Burton (Eds.), *Competitive anxiety in sport* (pp. 117-190). Champaign, IL: Human Kinetics.

May, J.R., & Sieb, G.E. (1987). Athletic injuries: Psychosocial factors in the onset, sequelae, rehabilitation and prevention. In J.R. May & M.J. Asken (Eds.), *Sport psychology: The psychological health of the athlete*. New York: PMA.

Meichenbaum, D., & Turk, D.C. (1987). *Facilitating treatment adherence: A practitioners guide*. New York: Plenum Press.

Morrison, A.M., & Von Glinow, M.A. (1990). Women and minorities in management. *American Psychologist*, **45**, 200-208.

Murphy, S.M. (1988). The on-site provision of sport psychology services at the 1987 U.S. Olympic festival. *Sport Psychologist*, **2**, 337-350.

Neff, F. (1990). Delivering sport psychology services to a professional sport organization. *Sport Psychologist*, **4**, 378-385.

Nideffer, R.M. (1976). Test of attentional and interpersonal style. *Journal of Personality and Social Psychology*, **34**, 394-404.

Nideffer, R.M. (1981). *The ethics and practice of applied sport psychology*. Ithaca, NY: Mouvement.

Orlick, T., & Partington, J. (1987). The sport psychology consultant: Analysis of critical components as viewed by Canadian

Olympic athletes. *Sport Psychologist*, **1**, 4-17.

Partington, J., & Orlick, T. (1987). The sport psychology consultant: Olympic coaches' views. *Sport Psychologist*, **1**, 95-102.

Ravizza, K. (1990). Sportpsych consultation issues in professional baseball. *Sport Psychologist*, **4**, 330-340.

Rotella, R.J., & Heyman, S.R. (1986). Stress, injury and the psychological rehabilitation of athletes. In J.M. Williams (Ed.), *Applied sport psychology: Personal growth to peak performance*. Mountain View, CA: Mayfield.

Ruder, M.K., & Gill, D.L. (1982). Immediate effects of win–loss on perceptions of cohesion in intramural and intercollegiate volleyball teams. *Journal of Sport Psychology*, **4**, 227-234.

Schein, E.H. (1990). Organizational culture. *American Psychologist*, **45**, 109-119.

Shinn, M., Rosario, M., Morch, H., & Chestnut, D.E. (1984). Coping with job stress and burnout in the human services. *Journal of Personality and Social Psychology*, **46**, 864-876.

Silva, J.M. (1984). Personality and sport performance: Controversy and challenge. In J.M. Silva & R.S. Weinberg (Eds.), *Psychological foundations of sport*. Champaign, IL: Human Kinetics.

Silva, J.M. (1989). Toward the professionalization of sport psychology. *Sport Psychologist*, **3**, 265-273.

Singer, R.H., & Johnson, P.J. (1987). Strategies to cope with pain associated with sport related injuries. *Athletic Training*, **22**, 100-103.

Smith, R.E. (1986). Toward a cognitive-affective model of athletic burnout. *Journal of Sport Psychology*, **8**, 36-50.

Smith, R.E., & Johnson, J. (1990). An organizational empowerment approach to consultation in professional baseball. *Sport Psychologist*, **4**, 347-357.

Stogdill, R.M. (1972). Group productivity, drive, and cohesiveness. *Organizational Behavior and Human Performance*, **8**, 26-43.

Sundstrom, E., DeMeuse, K.P., & Futrell, D. (1990). Work teams: Applications and effectiveness. *American Psychologist*, **45**, 120-133.

Taylor, J. (1991). Career direction development and opportunities in applied sport psychology. *Sport Psychologist*, **5**, 266-280.

Thornton, G.C., & Cleveland, J.N. (1990). Developing managerial talent through simulation. *American Psychologist*, **45**, 190-199.

Varney, G.H. (1990). *Building productive teams*. San Francisco: Jossey-Bass.

Vealey, R.S., Udry, E.M., Zimmerman, V., & Soliday, J. (1992). Intrapersonal and situational predictors of coaching burnout. *Journal of Sport and Exercise Psychology*, **14**, 40-58.

Wiese, D.M., & Weiss, M.R. (1987). Psychological rehabilitation and physical injury: Implications for the sports medicine team. *Sport Psychologist*, **1**, 318-330.

Williams, J.M. (Ed.) (1986). *Applied sport psychology: Personal growth to peak performance*. Mountain View, CA: Mayfield.

Zander, A. (1971). *Motives and goals in groups*. New York: Academic.

CHAPTER 7

PROVIDING PSYCHOLOGICAL SERVICES TO STUDENT ATHLETES: A DEVELOPMENTAL PSYCHOLOGY MODEL

Michael Greenspan, PhD
Arizona State University

Mark B. Andersen, PhD
Victoria University of Technology

Student athletes in the 1990s face more pressure than those of earlier decades to perform well athletically, academically, and socially. Greater rewards as well as greater punishments make extraordinary demands of individual players. Placing so much pressure on people from 13 to 22 years old often causes performance and emotional difficulties. Such problems concern not only student athletes but also their teammates, coaches, physicians, trainers, instructors, advisers, friends, and family members.

The first psychologist to address the specific needs of student athletes from a clinical, or counseling, perspective was Bruce Ogilvie. While a staff member at the San Jose State University Counseling Center, he began in the early 1960s to provide performance enhancement and counseling services to members of several sport teams. Since that foundational work (Ogilvie & Tutko, 1968), clinical sport psychology services for student athletes have developed greatly, with many enhancements both in technique and mode of delivery. Few university athletic departments currently employ psychologists full-time to address the mental health needs of student athletes, but over time psychologists likely will become more involved with university athletic departments as the stakes in major college sports continue to increase.

Although increasing attention is being paid to counseling collegiate athletes (Etzel, Ferrante, & Pinkney, 1991), similar attention to high-school athletes has been lacking. The literature about clinical sport psychology services in high schools is scant. Although some authors (Hellstedt, 1987; Hughes, 1990; Smoll & Smith, 1987) have proposed guidelines for performance enhancement services for younger athletes, to date only the areas of eating disorders and drug education have been addressed. Yet much of the present literature suggests that educational programs in such clinical areas as identity transitions, self-esteem and coping, drug usage, and eating disorders might be more successful at the high-school level than at the college level (Damm, 1991). Ideally, a program would offer developmentally appropriate and coordinated efforts for both the high-school and college levels.

This chapter presents an overview of the major developmental dilemmas facing student athletes and suggestions for the provision and structure of service. It addresses four separate topics: transitions that student athletes face, issues of psychopathology and medical concerns, existing resources at universities and high schools, and the professional and ethical dilemmas that might be encountered in providing services to student athletes.

Courtesy University of Wisconsin Women's Sports Information

■ *THE CASE OF THE PANTHERS* ■

A consulting relationship between a university's counseling center psychologist and the women's golf team was emerging. The psychologist had provided a weekly series of performance-enhancement presentations and had attended practice once or twice weekly for 4 weeks. She had also met one team member for an initial intake regarding low self-esteem, which the golfer attributed primarily to conflict with the coaches and teammates.

After a particularly stormy team meeting, a number of the golfers and the head coach individually sought out the psychologist. Each expressed terrible frustration with others (athletes and coaches) on the team. It gradually became clear that three seniors were in conflict both with other team members (seven freshmen and sophomores) and with coaches. The seniors were clearly concerned with life beyond golf: Each had sustained at least one injury in the last few years, each was involved in a long-term relationship with a nonathlete (one was married and two were engaged), and each planned to retire from golf at the end of the season. The younger team members, who were more openly enthusiastic and team oriented, were having difficulty relating to the seniors. Two of the freshmen were having to adjust to living far away from their parents and in an urban, fast-paced university. Their difficulty in adjusting manifested itself in excessive partying and poor academic performance. On the golf course, however, they were consistently strong. Most of the freshmen were quick to jump into the increasingly polarized situation on the side of the coaches and other younger golfers.

The head coach had always been exceptionally close with her team members, especially the golfers whom she felt worked hard and wanted "it" (success) more. She prided herself on the ability to keep her golfers motivated and "hungry." The coach was having a difficult time figuring out just how far to push the seniors. In turn the seniors believed that everyone was giving them a hard time, and they had difficulty seeing things from the others' perspectives. They reported anger toward certain coaches and team members for what they viewed as favoritism and preferential treatment.

TRANSITIONS FACING STUDENT ATHLETES

The transitions high-school athletes make are most likely to center on developmental tasks, such as identity formulation and developing self-esteem and social competence (Gould & Finch, 1991).

The transitions collegiate athletes face, however, usually can be grouped into one of four diverse categories:

- Making the transition onto a particular team at a particular university
- Making developmental transitions
- Experiencing conflict between the roles of student and athlete
- Making the transition out of competitive sport

Common Realizations

Making the transition to collegiate athletics can involve an awareness that there is much more at stake at the collegiate level than was anticipated. The realization is common that one will likely not play as important a role as previously. Such transitions include a star recruit at a major university who must adjust to all of the attention that comes with being a collegiate athlete or a high-school starter who gets to college and for the first time ever is faced with not starting.

Student athletes, like most other students, at times have a rough semester in school and have to drop a course or two or take an incomplete. They might also, like many young adults, occasionally embarrass themselves in public and possibly even receive a citation from a campus police officer. When it concerns the student athlete, however, such news might appear on the front page of their university's newspaper or on the evening television news. Such heightened visibility is often experienced as tremendous pressure, both on and off the playing field.

A related type of transition is experienced by student athletes who leave a familiar environment to attend college. A college campus might seem a very unfamiliar and confusing environment in terms of size, location, climate, off-campus activities, resources, costs, and social and racial relations. The degree to which a geographical or cultural transition is felt as stressful depends typically on the student athlete's personal resources (self-esteem, ego strength, coping skills), support system (family, friends, advisers, coaches), and experiences as a student athlete (academic and athletic history). A poor combination of these factors can lead to an isolated and troubled person. For example, a basketball player from a low socioeconomic area of a northern city might thrive at a rural southern university if he has a high level of self-esteem, the ability to cope with stress effectively, and the ability to trust and relate to coaches. A high-school teammate with few consistent and effective coping resources and strategies, however, might struggle at a nearby campus, believing coaches do not understand her.

Ethnic and Cultural Transitions

Transitions into college might be even further complicated by issues of ethnicity and culture. Although little research exists on the cultural transitions faced by student athletes,

Anshel (1990) provided an interesting view of the unique needs of black intercollegiate football players in terms of their sport experiences. Although his research was based solely on the experiences of members of one team at one university under one white head coach, Anshel's research is consistent with earlier research by Evans (1978) and Anshel and Sailes (1990) suggesting that black athletes trust white coaches less than they trust black coaches. Research by Cashmore (1982) suggested this mistrust might be due to white coaches' misinterpretation of black athletes' supposed lack of demonstrated intensity (e.g., "virtual absence of verbal assertiveness" before game) as laziness and as reflecting a lack of motivation. Anshel suggested black football players might "take in and respond to environmental demands in a less intense and emotionally demonstrative manner." Anshel's research also suggested clear differences in how black and white football players prepare for competition:

> Rather than demonstrate the proper psychological state with boisterous vocal responses in the locker room, the black players in this study preferred to behave in a calm, low-key manner.

Differences were also noted in black and white football players' degree of affiliation with team goals, in terms of need for individual recognition, motives for participation, and responsiveness to certain coaching communication styles and strategies. For a black student athlete who has rarely or never played for a white coach, a substantial adjustment period might be necessary. Although one might hypothesize that the same is true for white athletes playing for black coaches, no research evaluating that hypothesis exists. We must caution against stereotyping, however, even in the name of cross-cultural sensitivity.

Role Conflict: Student Versus Athlete

Conflict between the roles of student and athlete is not uncommon and is well summarized by Chartrand and Lent (1987). For many people, the conflict seems like a choice between two drastically different sets of expectations, demands, and, most importantly, rewards. Students often see academic studies as demanding, irrelevant, and time consuming, with only moderate potential for reward in the distant future. Athletic participation, on the other hand, is often seen as more enjoyable and as providing more consistent, tangible, immediate, and potentially greater rewards.

According to Chartrand and Lent (1987), conflict occurs when the demands of one role are incompatible with the requirements of another. For those participating in athletics as a means of preparing for professional sports, the role of student might be a perfunctory one that leads mainly to stress and overcommitment (Sack & Thiel, 1985). However, as the research by Mueller and Blyth (1984) shows, many more collegiate athletes expect to play professional sports than reach that level. Much of the conflict between roles typically revolves around time-management and social-development limitations and restrictions.

As commitment to one's sport increases, one's range of possible social and professional options is usually restricted. This reduction in exploratory behaviors contributes to Pearson and Petitpas's (1990) notion of identity foreclosure. Some athletes, as they grow and develop, begin to identify themselves more and more with the athlete role to the exclusion of other potential roles or identities. In a sense, they have foreclosed, or shut out any other identity possibility. Such identity foreclosure places individuals in a tenuous position if their athletic goals are not attained, are interfered with (e.g., by injury), or are not as satisfying as the athlete expected. The role of athlete might be incompatible with many specifics of the student role. Such role conflict has the potential to be academically, interpersonally, and athletically disruptive. It has been our experience, however, that such conflict is typically not a primary presenting problem. More common are academic problems, coach complaints of low motivation, or stress management difficulties. Whenever a referral for such concerns is made, it is important that the issue of role conflict be explored.

Retiring From Competitive Sport

Retiring from competitive sport is usually a difficult transition for student athletes. The degree to which the process is experienced as stressful is likely mediated by a number of factors. Probably most important is how unidimensional the student athlete's identity is. The less one has considered other possible social and professional roles and options, the more likely one is to struggle with the transition. In cases where retirement is due primarily to injury, the severity, acuity, and expectedness of the injury are certain to influence one's coping. The more severe, acute, and unexpected an injury, the less likely the student athlete will have prepared emotionally.

In contrast, a student athlete who has had to deal with a chronically injured and deteriorating knee might resist retirement but should be more prepared for other roles in life. A high-risk situation exists (as it also can in other circumstances) when a student athlete with little in life (present or anticipated future) except sport suffers a sudden, career-ending injury. Most athletes retiring from sport would benefit from a program like the United States Olympic Committee's Career Assistance Program for Athletes (CAPA) program (Petitpas, Danish, McKelvain, & Murphy, 1992); some student athletes, however, need counseling to deal with grief over the loss of a major part of their identity. For those people, the grief process is likely to be remembered vividly for decades.

Intervention in the Case of the Panthers

The case of the Panthers illustrates a number of transitions faced by student athletes that can have profound effects on both their athletic and academic performance as well as on their social relationships. Some younger team members were struggling not only with separation and individuation from their families but also with role conflict (athlete versus student), peer influence (excessive partying and further polarization of the team), sexuality, and the transition from rural areas to an urban university.

The three seniors on the team, however, were struggling with totally different though equally age-appropriate developmental concerns. Their identities were more multidimensional, and they were struggling with identity transitions out of competitive sport and into careers and long-term relationships. Though they had a difficult time recognizing it, these seniors very badly wanted the approval of the coach they reported disliking. Essentially, they were looking for an emotional relationship with a peer, but their coach tended to distance herself when a relationship became too intimate. The seniors then interpreted that as rejection and so viewed the coach as not being there for them when they struggled both on and off the course.

Further exploration suggested that the coach's tendency to get very close to her players fostered a dependency early in the relationship that became a problem when the coach had to discipline her golfers or when the golfers wanted too much intimacy or equality. In the past this pattern of relationships with her athletes had rarely caused the coach problems. These particular seniors, however, were developmentally different than the typical collegiate athlete in that they viewed themselves as women in stable relationships looking for support from a colleague and friend (the coach). Though well intentioned, the coach's managerial style had the potential to exacerbate this situation; thus intervention was important to the team's and the coach's well-being.

The psychologist's interventions involved weekly group meetings with the team and individual meetings with the head coach and some of the players. Continually aware of the fact that she was at times acting as both therapist and team consultant (and constantly processing this seemingly unavoidable situation with her supervisor), the psychologist tried to help those involved understand the validity of others' views without undermining the validity of their own. This, in addition to team process meetings, was intended to reduce some of the conflict and factionalism on the team.

At the same time, support was offered to the coach in de-enmeshing from the team and looking to meet her emotional needs in other ways. This was intended more as an intervention for the coach's present as well as the team's future well-being. Trying to help the coach feel more comfortable with conflict was intended to foster a healthy, appropriate emotional distance from her golfers and to lessen the potential for golfers' becoming too dependent on her. It was agreed that such strategies made actual coaching conflictual at times. Helping the coach with conflict became even more important because some of the sophomores began to sense the distancing and reported feeling like they were losing a friend. Without becoming too enmeshed herself, the psychologist then tried to help those golfers and the coach understand some of the relationship dynamics and the fact that in the long run the changes initiated by the coach were best for the team as a whole.

■ *THE CASE OF NIKKI* ■

Nikki, a female diver at a small southern university, had been attending a process group for athletes composed primarily of swimmers and divers. Group discussions had covered many topics, including adjustment to college life, communication issues, weight control, and appearance concerns. Participation in the group provided part of the impetus to seek individual treatment. The diver was also a nutrition major and in time confided to her favorite professor that she believed she might be developing a problem with her eating behavior. She was referred by the professor to the university's counseling center. She expressed reservations about seeing someone who was not involved in athletics because she felt her problems would not be understood by a nonathlete. The professor eventually was able to locate a counseling center staff member who was a former collegiate swimmer and who had experience treating athletes.

During the initial intake assessment, Nikki revealed that she was the captain of the university's team, and her high GPA showed her to be an excellent student. She had struggled all of her competitive years with perfectionism in and out of the pool and was never satisfied with her athletic and academic performances. Nikki gradually became aware that her mother would subtly withdraw affection if she was not pleased with her daughter's performance. This was a major factor in Nikki's extreme perfectionism.

Nikki reported that she was concerned with her appearance, which she believed correlated highly with her diving scores, and had been restricting her caloric intake. She also used excessive exercise as a means of controlling her weight. She was afraid that she might begin using more drastic measures to control weight, such as vomiting after meals. She had been battling with her weight for several years but stated that her eating-disorder-like symptoms disappeared at the end of each season when she took a break from diving. A brief medical history revealed a recent stress fracture of the ankle, the onset of menses at age 17, and amenorrhea for the last 6 months. She was eating only a small salad and drinking only water at most meals (including team functions), and she was exhibiting increased emotional instability during practices, resulting in several blowups with the coach and other team members.

Nikki's case was discussed at a weekly meeting of the university eating disorders team, which was composed of psychiatrists, psychologists, physicians, and nutritionists. The psychologist from the counseling center presented the case. It was decided to have Nikki see a physician for a complete physical and gynecological exam along with a thorough blood analysis. In addition, the diver was to meet with one of the nutritionists for dietary counseling. It was agreed that because good rapport seemed to have been established between the intake psychologist and Nikki, she should begin exploratory psychotherapy with this psychologist. Psychotherapy focused on helping the athlete gain a better understanding of her perfectionism, her relationship with her mother, and how that relationship influenced her present relationships and behaviors. Counseling progressed favorably over a 9-month period. Despite her emotional progress, Nikki continued to exercise excessively as a means of weight control and experienced another stress fracture in her shin.

PSYCHOPATHOLOGY IN STUDENT ATHLETES

Although we know of no sound epidemiological data, we believe severe psychopathology among student athletes, at least at the university level, is rare. This is most likely due to a type of natural selection process that over time screens out many lower-functioning persons from sport. When difficulties arise, they tend to be mild to somewhat-severe adjustment, mood, eating, and substance-abuse disorders.

Pathogenic Weight Control

One area of pathology with clearly greater incidence among athletes is eating disorders and pathogenic weight-control behavior (see chapter 13). Pathogenic weight control behaviors are more common in sports that stress appearance than in other sports (Borgen & Corbin, 1987). They are also more common among athletes in general when compared to the nonathlete college population (Black & Burckes-Miller, 1988; Borgen & Corbin, 1987) and seem to be more prevalent when coaches tell athletes they are too heavy (Rosen & Hough, 1988). Interestingly, one can apply similar criteria and speculate (sound research does not exist yet) that prevalence differences might be similar for the abuse of anabolic steroids. In other words, steroid use is higher among athletes than nonathletes, is higher in sports emphasizing size and appearance, and is higher when coaches tell athletes they are too small or too weak. Research is sorely needed in this area, however. Because eating disorders are covered thoroughly in chapter 13, we will not go into further detail here except to advocate a university-wide team approach to the treatment of eating disorders.

Injuries and Overtraining

Besides eating disorders, issues arising from injuries and overtraining are the most common problems faced by student athletes. As described previously, transitions due to

career-ending injuries can be terribly stressful and depressing. Non-career-ending injuries, however, might also have an emotional impact and people with such injuries might benefit from support, validation, or stress management throughout the rehabilitation process.

Our experience suggests it is important for injured athletes to maintain a performance-goal orientation. In other words, athletes must be helped to view rehabilitation as a process of small but steady increases and to not try too rapidly to regain preinjury performance levels, because this can lead to recurring or overuse injuries.

The symptoms of severe overtraining, like career termination due to injury, can parallel those of depression. Although the pain of overtraining is primarily of physiological etiology, intervention in both the physiological and psychological realms is suggested. The assessment of overtraining and burnout (presented in chapter 15) is crucial, for if these go undiagnosed, their course is often insidious and destructive.

Effects on the Team

No research exists studying the effects of an individual member's pathology on the team as a whole. The effects can depend on the impaired person's role, the degree to which that person influences teammates, and the type and degree of pathology. We believe pathology such as depression is likely to have little lasting effect on the team beyond temporary impairment of the depressed person's performance and perhaps the team's to a lesser extent. If severe enough (see "The Case of Steven," which follows), though, a team's performance can be drastically altered and teammates can be significantly affected emotionally. Other pathologies, such as eating disorders and substance abuse, have the strong potential to affect other team members if the affected person is an influential team member. Burnout, if present in an influential team member, might slightly affect morale and intensity, but we see little risk of its seriously affecting a team. Until sound research exists, however, we can only speculate about such processes.

■ *THE CASE OF STEVEN* ■

Steven, a freshman football player at a large northeastern university, shot and killed himself at a party attended by some of the other members of the football team. Early the next morning the head coach contacted the athletic department's psychologist and described to the best of his knowledge what had transpired. Other members of the team were informed of Steven's suicide as they arrived for practice.

The head coach asked the psychologist to speak to the team once it was assembled. The psychologist spoke about normal responses to highly abnormal situations, about how emotions are likely to be a mix of sadness, anger, and guilt (among other feelings), that even emotional numbness was a normal response, and that it is OK to have these feelings. The psychologist also discussed what might occur emotionally to the team members over the next several days and weeks. The wisdom of talking with others about what had happened was strongly emphasized. Suggestions were made to speak to teammates, coaches, family, academic advisers, counselors, or psychologists. The team was given information on where services are available on campus.

The psychologist then solicited comments and feelings from team members he knew well and believed would not be uncomfortable disclosing and sharing some personal reactions. The head coach and the head trainer also talked about how they were reacting. The team was then told that the psychologist would be available if they wanted to talk one-on-one or along with a few teammates.

The psychologist had never dealt firsthand with the suicide of a team member and so prior to meeting with the team called in a senior psychologist from the university employee assistance program (who personally knew the head coach) to consult on what might be the best approaches. The senior psychologist made some suggestions and within an hour was on the scene and helped by talking individually to athletes and coaches.

Members of other mental health agencies on campus were then informed of the situation (i.e., the mental health division of the student health center and the university's counseling center). The next day, counseling center personnel intervened in the dormitory where the student had lived and spoke with residents about responses to tragedy, grief processes, and the availability of campus services. Student life and residence life personnel were also debriefed. A memorial service was arranged by the player's academic adviser. Less than one week later, in the conference championship game, the football team played far below par and was easily defeated despite being a 15-point favorite.

The last campus agency to become actively involved in this case was the student mental health center, more than a month after the incident. Three of the teammates who had been at the party where the death occurred were experiencing insomnia, anxiety, confusion, and depression, which significantly impaired their academic functioning. With the cooperation of the head coach, the eligibility coordinator for the athletic department, the athletic department psychologist, and a student mental health psychiatrist, a medical withdrawal from school was arranged that left the players' academic standing and team eligibility unaffected. The players then left the university with the mutually agreed plan to seek counseling at home (future contact confirmed that each player did enter counseling). If they decided to return to the university, they were to meet with the athletic department psychologist and the head of the student mental health center. One of the three reenrolled the following fall and began counseling on an as-needed basis with a counseling center psychologist.

The case of Steven illustrates the widespread effects a tragedy can have on an athletic team and a university community as a whole. It also reveals the extensive resources available at a large university for the management of a critical incident. At small colleges and high schools, such resources are rarely available, but other avenues of crisis management exist. For example, high schools have academic counselors who might have some training in dealing with crises, and many school districts employ a school psychologist who in such a situation should be contacted for consultation. Most school districts also have referral lists of mental health professionals in their areas. Small colleges have at least one advantage over high schools in that there is typically a clinical or school psychologist on the faculty.

Information on the resources available for crisis management or for any other counseling, psychological, or psychiatric concern should be made available to all faculty and staff and be a part of new employees' orientation. The experiences of the psychologists at Steven's university suggest that most educational institutions should have a designated crisis management team with a predetermined procedural plan for use in emergencies.

UNIVERSITY-WIDE RESOURCES

The academic culture of a university or college and the culture of the athletic department, though housed on one campus, constitute two different worlds. Unfortunately, in many cases communication and cooperation between these two worlds are attenuated. Athletic departments take care of their own and athletes often feel uncomfortable going over to the "other" (academic) side where service providers might not understand the special needs, pressures, and concerns of student athletes. Athletic departments usually supply much of the medical and academic counseling services; for scholarship athletes, housing and nutritional needs might also be met. One area, however, in which athletes are underserved is in the realm of psychological services. Only a handful of university athletic departments in the United States offer in-house psychological services to athletes who need them. At other schools the athletes must pursue services on campus but that are on the academic side, something many athletes are reluctant to do. Thus many psychological concerns, some with serious consequences (e.g., severe depression, eating disorders) go untreated for long periods of time.

What is the solution? Most athletic departments are conservative and tend to change slowly, so there is a responsibility for university service delivery organizations (e.g., student health centers, counseling centers, clinical and counseling psychology training centers, exercise science departments) to initiate contact and become involved in a two-way educational process with athletic department personnel. This could involve a wide spectrum of presentations to administrators, coaches, sports medicine personnel, academic advisors, and athletes concerning the different services available, the medical, psychological, and legal aspects of treatment and nontreatment, and ways to help the athletic program become better integrated into the university community.

As one can see from the case study of Steven, the athlete who committed suicide, many university agencies were mobilized, and we hope this will always happen in such exceptional cases. This case, however, is an example of reactive mobilization. The future calls for a proactive, preventive model of interaction between university agencies and athletic department staff, coaches, and athletes.

■ *THE CASE OF KENNY* ■

Kenny, a swimmer at a small midwestern college, came to a psychology professor who was known to have an interest in sport psychology. Ostensibly, the athlete was seeking performance-enhancement services, but it soon became obvious that the athlete had another agenda. Kenny stated that he wanted to improve his performance but would spend whole sessions talking about personal concerns, such as his relationships with his girlfriend and his overbearing father. Kenny felt a combination of ambivalence and fear of engulfment with his current (and first) girlfriend, and he was very resentful of his father's demanding and psychologically abusing nature. This swimmer presented as a very lonely person with low self-esteem who was looking for a loving surrogate parent.

Kenny began making requests of the psychologist for attention outside the sport psychology sessions. The psychologist had attended some swim meets and this greatly pleased the athlete. In addition, Kenny's times appeared to be improving, and he tended to swim particularly well when the psychologist was in attendance. After one particularly good performance that the psychologist witnessed, the coach gave the psychologist some swim team attire (shirts, sweatshirt, and a bag) while discussing how well Kenny was doing. Kenny wanted more attention, however, and began to invite the psychologist out to lunch or dinner and would offer to pay. The psychologist knew that accepting might be in violation of the APA standards on multiple relationships (American Psychological Association, 1992) but temporarily acquiesced with the stipulation that they each pay their own way. Upon further thought, the psychologist tried to cancel the lunch date and attempted to get counseling on a more appropriate track. This led to Kenny's expression of anger through stories about being rejected and abandoned by those he thought close to him.

The psychologist hypothesized that Kenny was likely looking for an ally in his struggles with both his girlfriend and father and that the psychologist had made the mistake, albeit only temporarily, of getting pulled into a therapeutic misalliance (Basch, 1980). In addition, one must wonder if the coach was rewarding the psychologist with team attire for being helpful or, instead, for providing results. Unfortunately, the break in the counseling relationship was severe. Kenny soon left sport psychology services.

ETHICAL AND PROFESSIONAL DILEMMAS

Ethical dilemmas in the practice of applied sport psychology in academic settings might arise in several situations. The two most obvious are working with the student athletes themselves and with coaches. Other likely situations where ethical dilemmas might arise exist in working with parents, administrators, instructors, and recruiters. Ultimately, though, the psychologist is responsible for identifying ethical concerns and preventing negative consequences. We would like to address some of these problem areas and offer some suggestions.

Working With Athletes

A common pitfall in working with athletes is falling into their advocacy too easily. At times athletes will seek out a psychologist to help them with their problems with a coach. The coach might be portrayed as demanding, unreasonable, punishing, and abusive. The psychologist might be too quick to take the athlete's side, an act that easily could backfire. A better approach is to examine the communication patterns of coach and athlete and make suggestions on how to improve coach–athlete interaction. In chapter 6, some useful suggestions are presented for helping athletes take responsibility for managing their relationship with their coach in a positive and direct manner. If possible, it is usually best to meet both the coach and athlete separately at first and then together for clarification of the problem and conflict resolution. Advocacy for the athlete is wonderful, but zeal for protecting the client should not blind the psychologist to the viewpoint, needs, and concerns of another party, in this case the coach.

Working With Coaches

Another common source of ethical problems concerns attempts by coaches to obtain confidential information. There are two main approaches to deal with requests for information. The first is preventive education. A thorough talk with the coaches, at the beginning of a working relationship, about how crucial confidentiality is and the psychologist's code of professional ethics can avoid many future problems. Another path is to ask the athlete, "What would you like me to say if the coach asks me about what we are doing?" For example, the athlete might feel comfortable having the psychologist talk about performance issues but not about family issues.

Another dilemma with coaches is that they might try to enlist the psychologist in selection processes. We believe these practices are questionable and ultimately will backfire. We know of no evidence that psychology can help predict athletic success of student athletes. Only in rare cases might a psychologist's opinion be of value, such as in screening out people with psychopathology. It is seductive for the psychologist to get involved in important decisions like selection, but in general we advise against such involvement.

There are those who advocate that sport psychologists should become members of the coaching team, and in many cases this seems like a good idea. For a psychologist, however, some problems can arise in the form of dual-role conflicts. The psychologist might be an athlete's mental-skills trainer, clinician, companion, and on-site intervention coach. In most clinical situations, this overfamiliarity would constitute a therapeutic misalliance and would be cause for terminating the relationship. This overexposure of the sport psychologist can look suspiciously like dependency fostering. It is not the sport psychologist's job to make him or herself indispensable to the athlete. The answer to the question, "Who is being served?" is "the sport psychologist" and that is the wrong answer. The sport psychologist's job with an athlete is to help empower and encourage independence in the athlete and ultimately to terminate therapy.

Sport psychologists must also carefully manage their public exposure around athletes. Our own preference, developed over time, is for the sport psychologist to actively deflect as much publicity as possible and refuse to talk about any specific athlete-client with any outside sources. The greatest temptation is probably when others, such as the media, are willing to give the sport psychologist credit for an athlete's performance gains. It is essential, however, that sport psychologists continue to encourage the media to attribute such progress to the athletes themselves.

Countertransference

Another source of problems can be countertransference issues. Athletes are in general a very attractive group (socially and physically) and a psychologist's own positive (or negative) countertransference is likely to influence some interventions, just as the athlete's positive or negative transference to the sport psychologist will have an effect on the learning process. This idea is troubling in that only recently has it begun to be addressed in the sport psychology literature (Ogilvie & Harris, 1990).

Working With Administrators

The sport psychologist might also face pressure from administrators and athletes for special academic treatment. An administrator might want a star athlete diagnosed as learning disabled to receive special attention (e.g., more time for tests, testing in special environments, deadline delays). It might be that the athlete has no specific learning disability but is intellectually just slightly below average. An athlete or coach might ask the psychologist to intercede on behalf of the athlete in gaining special consideration for retaking a course or receiving an incomplete. Determining when such requests are legitimate because of extenuating circumstances and when they are just stopgaps for poor preparation may be difficult. Awareness of exploitation should be of concern to a sport psychologist; it is easy to see how the psychologist can be seduced into such misalliances. Our own experiences suggest that guidelines need to be established and clearly communicated early in the relationship and then followed as diligently as possible.

Preventing Dilemmas

The training of sport psychologists in ethical decision making and professional practice needs greater attention. It is not enough merely to know that it is not a good idea to break confidentiality or to become sexually involved with your client. Much more subtle pressures and cues from athletes and others can place psychologists in precarious situations. One dilemma we have encountered is coaches offering us team clothing (shoes, shirts) as an expression of gratitude for our consultation. Little was made of this initially. When we realized the equipment was offered only after athletes we were working with performed well, it became a concern. Although the coaches might have merely intended to thank us or were not aware of any relationship to performance, we still struggle with this topic. Another is the making public of consulting relationships with sport teams. Are consultation clients not to be treated as counseling clients with respect to confidentiality? We never make public statements about our work with individual clients, but sometimes a coach or client may say something even though we encourage them to keep our names out of the media.

More frequently than we would like, the practitioner is put in a double bind. For example, many practitioners of sport psychology services have been trained in physical education or exercise science departments and rightly have been taught that if a client presents with a clinical concern they should refer the client to a qualified professional. What often occurs, however, is that an athlete seeks out a sport psychologist for performance enhancement and then later might bring up more clinical concerns. It might have taken 2 months for the athlete to feel comfortable enough to bring up a sensitive subject, only to be referred to another person. This proper procedure might make the athlete feel rejected. The message, no matter how gently handled, might still be You trusted me with this, but I can't deal with it, and I have to reject you. The athlete might understand the referral on a conscious, rational level but on a deeper level might be hurt. This unavoidable situation argues not against the current role of physical-education–trained sport psychologists but for more broad-based training (assessment, counseling skills, etc.) of future sport psychology practitioners. Andersen (1992) has suggested that in such situations, the sport psychologist refer *in*, that is, bring a clinician into the sport psychology sessions and do tandem treatment. Such an arrangement might help avoid feelings of abandonment and could provide some professional development for both the clinician and the sport psychologist.

CONCLUSION

A psychologist working in an athletic department is often a "stranger in a strange land." Intercollegiate athletics today is often not in the business of education, much less of therapy. It is primarily an entertainment business that is *terra incognita* for most psychologists. The best place to start, as with most newly evolving relationships, is through mutual education. Psychologists need to educate themselves about the structure and function of the athletic organization. Questions such as Who are the key players in the organization? Where might I find allies? Who are the successful innovators? Who is resistant? and What do these people really want? are important to consider. In many cases, the athletic directors and coaches might not know the answer to this last question, and that is where it becomes the psychologist's role to educate the organization as to what services might be offered and what benefits might accrue from the practice of sport psychology and clinical psychology.

For some coaches and organizations, this may be a tough sell. It would behoove most psychologists to wage a campaign of gradually earning the respect of effective internal champions in the organization. In selecting an internal champion, one would be wise to select someone who has successfully introduced and championed an innovative and controversial program. Although it is important to have support at the top of the organization, it has been our experience and is our belief that true innovation more typically happens at a system's lower levels.

This chapter has emphasized that provision of effective services to student athletes requires an understanding of both the developmental issues of the athletes and the systemic issues of the academic organization. Sport psychology consultants working in academic settings will help athlete-clients most if they further their own education and experience in both areas.

REFERENCES

American Psychological Association. (1992). Ethical principles of psychologists and code of conduct. *American Psychologist*, **47**, 1597-1611.

Andersen, M.B. (1992). Sport psychology and procrustean categories: An appeal for synthesis and expansion of service. *Association for the Advancement of Applied Sport Psychology Newsletter*, **7**(3), 8-9.

Anshel, M.H. (1990). Perceptions of black intercollegiate football players: Implications for the sport psychology consultant. *Sport Psychologist*, **4**, 235-248.

Anshel, M.H., & Sailes, G. (1990). Discrepant attitudes of intercollegiate team athletes as a function of race. *Journal of Sport Behavior*, **13**, 68-77.

Basch, M.F. (1980). *Doing psychotherapy*. New York: Basic Books.

Black, D.R., & Burckes-Miller, M.E. (1988). Male and female college athletes: Use of anorexia nervosa and bulimia nervosa weight loss methods. *Research Quarterly for Exercise and Sport*, **59**(3), 252-256.

Borgen, J.S., & Corbin, C.B. (1987). Eating disorders among female athletes. *Physician and Sports Medicine*, **15**(2), 89-95.

Cashmore, E. (1982). *Black sportsmen*. Boston: Rutledge & Kegan Paul.

Chartrand, J.M., & Lent, R.W. (1987). Sports counseling: Enhancing the development of the student-athlete. *Journal of Counseling and Development*, **66**, 164-167.

Damm, J. (1991). Drugs and the college student athlete. In E. Etzel, A. Ferrante, and J. Pinkney (Eds.), *Counseling college student athletes: Issues and interventions* (pp. 151-176). Morgantown, WV: Fitness Information Technologies.

Etzel, E., Ferrante, A., & Pinkney, J.P. (Eds.) (1991). *Counseling college student athletes: Issues and interventions*. Morgantown, WV: Fitness Information Technologies.

Evans, V. (1978). A study of perceptions held by high school athletes toward coaches. *International Review of Sport Sociology*, **13**, 47-53.

Gould, D., & Finch, L. (1991). Understanding and intervening with the student athlete to be. In E. Etzel, A. Ferrante, and J. Pinkney (Eds.), *Counseling college student athletes: Issues and interventions* (pp. 51-69). Morgantown, WV: Fitness Information Technologies.

Hellstedt, J. (1987). Sport psychology at a ski academy: Teaching mental skills to young athletes. *Sport Psychologist*, **1**, 567-568.

Hughes, S. (1990). Implementing psychological skills training in high school athletics. *Journal of Sport Behavior*, **13**(1), 15-22.

Mueller, F.O., & Blyth, C.S. (1984). Can we continue to improve injury statistics? *Physician and Sportsmedicine*, **12**(9), 79-84.

Ogilvie, B.C., & Harris, D. (1990, August.). *Intervention discussion hour: Sexuality in sport*. Paper presented at the 5th Annual Meeting of the Association for the Advancement of Applied Sport Psychology, San Antonio, TX.

Ogilvie, B.C., & Tutko, T.A. (1968). *Problem athletes and how to handle them*. London: Pelham Books.

Pearson, R.E., & Petitpas, A.J. (1990). Transitions of athletes: Developmental and preventive perspectives. *Journal of Counseling and Development*, **69**, 7-10.

Petitpas, A., Danish, S., McKelvain, R., & Murphy, S. (1992). A career assistance program for elite athletes. *Journal of Counseling and Development*, **70**, 383-386.

Rosen, L., & Hough, D. (1988). Pathogenic weight control behaviors of female college gymnasts. *The Physician and Sports Medicine*, **16**(9), 141-144.

Sack, A.L., & Thiel, R. (1985). College basketball and role conflict: A national survey. *Sociological Abstracts*, **33**(5), 1743.

Smoll, F.L., & Smith, R.E. (1987). *Sport psychology for youth coaches: Personal growth to athletic excellence*. Washington, DC: National Federation of Catholic Youth Ministry.

CHAPTER 8

RELATIONSHIP ISSUES IN SPORT: A MARITAL THERAPY MODEL

David B. Coppel, PhD
University of Washington Medical School

This chapter covers the bidirectional association between relationships and athletic performance or involvement. Athletes are involved in relationships both in and outside the sport world. Nonsport relationships—marital, familial, or other—can play important roles in determining emotional adjustment, mood, and, ultimately, athletic performance. Likewise, athletic involvement or performance can influence the quality or outcome of human relationships. General relationship issues, such as independence, identity, security, intimacy, power, control, and communication, can become even more complex in the structure and demands of sport involvement.

Although recognition of the importance of relationships to athletes is not new, little focus has been placed on it in sport psychology. This has been discussed in the context of the role that significant others (e.g., family members) play both in influencing sport involvement (Greendorfer & Lewko, 1978) and in the development of professionalized sport attitudes (McElroy & Kirkendall, 1980) in children; however, little has been written on how relationships impact sport performance or how sport involvement impacts close relationships.

Each of the following case studies illustrates only one direction of this bidirectional relationship. In the first, Mike and Denise deal with how Mike's professional sport involvement has impacted their married life, their moods, and the way they think about or perceive each other. It is clear that Mike feels the distress in the relationship affects his sport performance. In the second case study, Sandra focuses on how her relationship with Dan impacts her training and sport performance; Dan, on the other hand, focuses on how her training and sport involvement detracts from their relationship.

■ *THE CASE OF MIKE* ■

Mike, a professional athlete, and his wife, Denise, are having marital difficulties. Mike and Denise have been married for about two and a half years. They have no children but would like to start a family soon. Mike is in the middle of his second season; he is struggling this year and believes that he is not playing up to last year's level. This disappointment and frustration has caused Mike to experience sleep difficulties, anxiety, depressed moods, and social withdrawal. He is concerned about the possible reduction of playing time and even about his future with the team. He has increased his personal training in hopes of improving his performance. Denise met Mike in college through a mutual friend; over several months of dating they found they had many interests in common and began an exclusive relationship. Denise has been pursuing her interest in a career in interior design by taking courses at a local university. She expresses anger and dissatisfaction with the marriage. She claims that communication is poor and says she does not feel special in the relationship. There is no time for fun together. She has a clear sense of being a lower priority, behind Mike's sport involvement. She has attempted to discuss her feelings with Mike, but this has not helped; it made her feel more frustrated, and Mike believed she was not being supportive of him in his difficult time—in other words, he believed she was adding to his stress. Mike initially told Denise to go to individual counseling to deal with *her* problems; he finally agreed to marital counseling as a couple on two conditions: confidentiality from their families and friends, including other teammates' wives, and an appointment time arranged around his travel and training schedules.

■ *THE CASE OF SANDRA* ■

Sandra is an 18-year-old figure skater who has performed well over the past 2 years and appears to be on the verge of breaking into the top senior women's competition at the national level. Sandra currently lives with her mother, who has been divorced for 4 years. Sandra has a younger sister who is also showing some promise as a skater. Sandra's mother has been intensely involved in Sandra's 8 years of skating. Sandra has also had the same coach for 8 years. Sandra is currently in training for skating, about 6 hr daily at the ice rink. Most of her friends are fellow skaters from the rink. She takes correspondence courses to complete her high-school education. Sandra has been involved with Dan, a 21-year-old ex-skater, for about 1 year. Their relationship has been a source of concern for both Sandra's mother and her coach. They both believe Dan is a bad influence and a distraction. Sandra has altered her training schedule around Dan's schedule to maximize their time together. She has been looking for him during her practices and has even skipped practice to spend time with him. Sandra's training has become quite variable in intensity and motivation, and clean programs have been infrequent (in contrast to her usual skating and training regimen over the years). At times, Sandra appears to be hurrying through jumps, programs, and practice to spend time with Dan. This is Sandra's first boyfriend relationship. Dan has just recently asked Sandra to cut back on her skating and spend more time with him. This occurred as her training for an important skating competition intensified. This request weighs heavily on Sandra, causing her to be distracted and ambivalent. She is torn between her strong feelings for Dan and her desire to compete as a skater. Dan cannot understand her feelings about continuing with skating and focuses instead on the lack of time they spend together. Sandra believes that whatever choice she makes, people will be hurt, and she is confused about what she wants to do. Sandra has been working with a sport psychologist individually for about 8 months, focusing mostly on concentration, enhancing performance, and reducing the stress associated with her sport. At this point in time, Sandra asked Dan to attend a sport psychology consultation session with her to talk about their relationship and its impact on her skating performance.

REVIEWING THE LITERATURE

Research in sport psychology concerning athletes and relationship issues has been almost nonexistent. As sport psychology has become somewhat more aware of the relationship of social supports or resources to mood (Golding & Ungerleider, 1991), to adjustment to retirement from sports (Baillie & Danish, 1992), or to the life stress–injury relationship (Hardy, Richman, & Rosenfield, 1991; Rosenfield, Richman, & Hardy, 1989), the importance of relationships in sport psychology consultation has increased. Significant others and social support are included in some form in most models of sport stress and adjustment, including burnout and sports injury (Smith, 1986; Smith, Smoll, & Ptacek, 1990); thus they should have some place in most intervention strategies. Strategies to enhance social support or minimize marital or relationship distress appear to have the potential to positively impact the athlete in terms of sport performance and personal emotional adjustment. Botterill (1990) included spouses and friends in his consultation program with a professional hockey team, indicating that "these significant others are usually the most important support people in the lives of professional hockey players."

Sport psychology has tended to focus most extensively on athletic performance, with relationship issues in sports, both positive and negative, typically emerging in images created by the media. On the positive side, there might be the supportive friend or spouse during training or recovery from injury, the rock and inspiration during hard times, and the spouse behind the athlete. However, on the negative side, relationships of athletes might be portrayed in the media with images of the angry cuckolded spouse, domestic violence incidents, promiscuity, and insensitivity.

Athletes and the media have also described how social entrances and exits in athletes' lives, such as divorce, remarriage, death, or even a new coach, appear to impact performance and general adjustment. One can observe media reports of inspired and dedicated successful performances traced to relationship factors; likewise, the media also connects relationship factors to performances

Courtesy University of Wisconsin Women's Sports Information

described as lackluster, unfocused, and preoccupied.

Athletes, like most people, have attributions and perceptions about how changes in their relationships have (or will) impact their athletic performance. In working with athletes, understanding their perceptions or models of how relationships impact their thoughts, feelings, and behaviors as well as their athletic performance can be important. This might involve breaking through the often tough shell of self-focus and self-involvement that has typically been adaptive and successful for them in their sport involvement but has become dysfunctional in a relationship. From an early age athletes are primed to engage in self-focus and, to some degree, block out concerns of others. This focus, this drive, this all-consuming eat-drink-sleep-your-sport attitude, is associated with success; thus for some athletes, focusing on interrelationships can be difficult and is sometimes resisted. This different "other-focus" can be seen as threatening, because it might disrupt or break the focus they feel is necessary to achieve success.

Mike expresses some of these concerns. He feels that the focus on discussions of his marriage and the upset that might ensue or already be present is a distraction that is likely to interfere with achieving his athletic goal. He expresses this feeling to Denise by claiming that she is being unsupportive of him.

Most athletes must deal with relationship issues like anybody else, but in some cases media coverage makes this more difficult. With some high-profile professional or Olympic athletes, the human-interest factor can focus more media attention on relationship issues and less on athletic performance. How many times have aspects of athletes' personal or interpersonal lives been used as lead-ins to or commentary during their athletic performances? Recent Olympic athlete examples include death of a family member, estrangement or divorce from a spouse, and conflicts with teammates or coach. Unfortunately, athletes often end up dealing with not only the actual relationship issues, but also the impact of media reports of their relationships. This situation can occur at the same time they are trying to focus on training or competitive performance.

Athletes show significant variation in how they respond to public discussion of their personal or interpersonal lives. Some athletes find it extremely distracting, disorienting (the focus is not on athletic performance as they are used to), and intrusive; it might lead other athletes to increase their focusing efforts to a higher level.

Resistance to or denial of the existence of interpersonal difficulties is fairly common in athletes. Athletes can find themselves battling others' perceptions that athletes have no emotional, personal, or interpersonal problems. In professional sports the money, fame, and general prestige are thought to make athletes immune to adversity. As is becoming clearer, athletes might be, at the least, just as vulnerable to insecurities and interpersonal difficulties, drug abuse, and diseases as nonathletes. However, the possibility that highly competitive athletes are more at risk for interpersonal difficulties because of the nature of their intense training and focused lives must be considered. Heyman (1987) cites the misunderstanding of training demands, sport-related travel away from home, jealousy, infidelity possibilities, and identity questions of the spouse as possible problem areas for athlete relationships. He suggests that in some cases "the role of athletics and sport can play a unique role in maintaining the patterns that will be dysfunctional to the marriage."

DEVELOPMENTAL CONSIDERATIONS

Relationship issues have developmental differences based on factors such as age and level of athletic involvement. Sandra and Dan's relationship concerns are different in many ways from Mike and Denise's. The stage of the relationship (e.g., dating vs. marriage) is an important factor, as it often reflects the different levels of commitment and role expectation. Couples who are dating are likely to have different implicit and explicit expectations about interactive behaviors than couples who are married. Relationships that have endured over time have typically made some attempts to cope with the integration of two people and the formation of a relationship; the degree to which these attempts and strategies are functional to both the couple and the individuals generally relates to relationship satisfaction and helpfulness.

Identity Development

Different levels of personal development in the couple can yield relationship difficulties, as the developmental issues being confronted might be very discrepant. At the core of many developmental stages is the ongoing issue of identity in one's self and in connection to others and the world (Erikson, 1959). Athletes often generate identities based primarily on their athletic performance and potentially face different life crises at each stage of development (Heyman, 1987). For example, issues of intimacy or isolation face those in early adulthood (Erikson, 1963); these issues are seen in our two case studies. Sandra is struggling with her identity as a figure skater, which at this time appears to be at conflict with her developing identity as a caring person in a relationship. Mike and Denise are dealing with identities at different levels. They are trying to maintain and sustain their identity as a couple while trying to do the things they need to do to establish more secure individual identities. For Mike, a more secure personal identity emerges directly from successful athletic performance and to a lesser degree from a successful relationship.

Priorities and Sacrifice

To achieve success, athletes typically place sport training and related activities as their number-one priority. They often sacrifice social lives and experiences to pursue athletic success. Often, as mentioned earlier, they focus on themselves, rather than being other focused, except to please others by successful performances. The most negative consequences and sequelae of these sacrifices can often be seen in relationship difficulties. Age-related social immaturity, significant emotional difficulties with low self-esteem, and social evaluative anxiety are prominent factors.

With some athletes, an intense involvement in sport has deprived them of typical adolescent, young adult, or school experiences; these players might display a sort of developmental gap in the ability to relate to others. In some cases, athletes relate to others almost exclusively by using their physical bodies, leaving other relating skills to develop more slowly. For other athletes the physical (often intimidating) skills that have served them well in sport are brought or generalized to their relationship interactions. Perhaps, on a speculative note, the focus on using the physical body in highly stressful and competitive environments even desensitizes athletes or lowers the threshold to physical action during, for example, marital arguments.

Social Life and Relationships

May and Veach (1987) indicate that interpersonal issues such as relationships with girlfriends, boyfriends, spouses, and parents are frequent focuses in their work with the United States Alpine ski team. Some of the emotional symptoms seen in athletes might be associated with their efforts to maintain meaningful personal relationships.

Harris (1987) suggests that the lack of opportunity for a social life creates "conflict and discontentment among the female athletic population." She also states that sustaining a relationship with another person is problematic due to travel demands and training; this parallels Sandra's situation as she experiences the conflicts between her relationship with Dan and the time and concentration demands of her training.

Like most people in marital or relationship counseling, athletes can bring a wide range of family-of-origin issues to their adult relationships. Sometimes the intense involvement of the parents and family in the athlete's support over the years can delay the onset of individuation and independence activities. The relationships that athletes are involved in often reflect the expectations and behaviors found in their own family-of-origin experiences. From a clinical standpoint, it is probably extremely helpful, if not crucial, to explore and gain information about the families of origin in relationship counseling. This allows one to look for systems factors (Aylmer, 1986) as well as origins of socially learned behavior and cognitions (Jacobson & Holtzworth-Munroe, 1986).

POTENTIAL PROBLEM AREAS IN ATHLETES' RELATIONSHIPS

The most common problem areas athletes must face in their relationships are related to sport demands, priority issues, and power.

Sport Demands

Sport demands have been mentioned earlier in this chapter as being a significant detriment, not only to the establishment of relationships but also to their maintenance. In some instances, spouses or significant others might not realize the time required for training as well as competing; they might hope for a change over time or, in some cases, that their presence will create change in these training patterns. Some athletes use sport demands as a way out of confronting relationship issues.

Priority Issues

Priority issues are usually expressed by spouses, girlfriends, and boyfriends in the statement, You care more about the sport than me. This is a corollary to the sport-demand issue, but typically goes deeper, because it relates to how loved, how special, or how important a partner feels in the relationship. Spouses can feel rejected if most energy, enthusiasm, and excitement is oriented to sport, with very little experienced in relationship time. Sometimes athletes are preoccupied with a coming competition and are not as attentive to the communications of others; this further contributes to the feelings of lower priority or even devaluation.

Power

Athletes' relationships often emerge out of their athletic status or prestige; people relate to them because of who they are athletically. It should be noted that this can also be the origin of many athletes' insecurities about others' motives and their own abilities to relate (Why can't people like me for me, not just me the athlete?). It also establishes, for some, the belief that relationships are dependent on successful athletic performance; thus after a perceived poor performance some athletes fear rejection.

Power and control can be exerted by the degree to which relationships are centered on the athlete's sport involvement. These power and control (and probably priority) issues are seen in the conditions Mike put on his involvement in therapy, namely, that it not interfere with his training and travel. Athletes who are used to getting what they want (they set goals and achieve them) and getting special allowances or accommodations because of who they are typically enter into relationships with a sense of entitlement and expectation. This can create difficulties in communication, activities, and problem solving. A sense of equality in the relationship might be further undermined if income discrepancies are a factor.

INTERVENTION STRATEGIES AND CONSIDERATIONS

There are many models and approaches to working with relationships (Jacobson & Gurman, 1986), each generating intervention strategies focused on how relationship problems are conceptualized. A social-learning–cognitive-behavioral framework (Jacobson & Holtzworth-Munroe, 1986) focuses primarily on interventions designed to impact the couple's behavior together: perceptions, expectations, communication skills, and problem-solving skills. Systems-oriented approaches see relationship conflict emerging out of "interactive influences in the self-system, extended-family system (families of origin), and the couple–nuclear family system" (Aylmer, 1986).

Recognition of the influence of family-of-origin experiences on current relationship interactions and emotional patterns can make a significant impact for couples in distress (Framo, 1981). Other approaches and models emphasize emotional expression experiences, which allow for vulnerability and acceptance sequences, followed by new solutions and responses (Greenberg & Johnson, 1987).

Social learning approaches tend to focus on social or environmental determinants and patterns of behavior in marital interaction (the idea that action and reaction successively influence each other). Behavior marital therapy (Jacobson & Margolin, 1979) focuses on behavior exchange principles and the notion that spouses can change behaviors of their partners by changing their own behaviors and achieving some reciprocity arrangements. In this way they can create new behavior patterns that are more satisfying to each person and the relationship.

Beck (1988) presents a marital therapy model based on his cognitive therapy. In this model the nature of marital problems is found in the self-defeating and dysfunctional attitudes and distortions in thinking and communicating of the couple. Examining the couple's negative or distorted thinking and generating alternative, more accurate thinking is one way to improve communication. Communication based on distorted thinking produces greater distortion and more negativity in the relationship. For example, the assumptions that Mike and Denise have about each other's motives in the relationship provide a negative lens for each of them to interpret subsequent behavior and comments.

GENERAL STRUCTURE AND PROCEDURES

Relationship, or marital, therapy often consists of an initial joint consultation session, then an individual session with each person, followed by a return to joint sessions. Some therapists collect information in the form of questionnaires or inventories; this helps specify problem areas or aspects of the partners or the relationship that might impact the process or course of therapy. It is important that the therapist know about high-risk behaviors, such as spouse abuse, domestic violence activity or threats, alcoholism, or drug abuse. For example, in the athletic world relationship difficulties are often found in athletes involved in steroid abuse due to the "roid rage" responses, general irritability, and aggressiveness that can be present.

Creating a Safe Environment

As with most therapy approaches, creating a safe environment for couples becomes a crucial component. In the cognitive-behavioral models (Beck, 1988; Jacobson & Holtzworth-Munroe, 1986), focusing on positive aspects of the relationship can be important. This shifts and changes the generally negative focus of distress and might offer some cognitive perspective for the couple. Helping the couple to generate behaviors and pleasant activities they can do together is also a component. Some couples have gotten out of the habit of doing what they enjoyed together or have forgotten about common interests; thus returning to some of the patterns that contributed to mutual attraction earlier in the relationship can be helpful.

Changing Behavior

Jacobson and Holtzworth-Munroe (1986) discuss behavior exchange as a way to overcome the negative perceptual bias and counteract the feelings of helplessness that the couple might express. It also serves to show the couple's connectiveness and might restructure their efforts to improve their relationship. Typically, the couple is told to focus on their own individual behaviors, i.e., what each can do to improve the relationship, and increase the frequency of these behaviors. Effort in changing or increasing behaviors can be appreciated by partners and provide a more positive platform to explore the interactive and process aspects of the relationship.

Teaching Communication Skills

Helping couples to improve communication is usually a large component of relationship work. Communication-skills training allows couples to become more aware of their communication process (both functional and dysfunctional). Learning more about the way words, tone, volume, or body language are used and the way these aspects are perceived by the couple can be revealing. For example, understanding that being loud might not mean that one is angry or on the verge of violence can change the feeling of threat and escape that might occur in a communication exchange.

Often couples' communication behavior patterns have become so presumptive (mind reading or, I know what they are thinking) that partners feel unheard or misunderstood. The teaching of basic communication skills such as listening, paraphrasing, and clarifying is extremely useful. These communication-skills training components have been used with great success in my consultation with doubles tennis partners, ice dancers, and pair skaters to improve their ability to communicate and to reduce chances of misunderstanding that would directly impact their tandem performances.

Developing Problem-Solving Skills

In addition to communication skills, specific problem-solving skills are typically included in therapy to aid couples in communication about conflict areas and help them engage in some structured attempts at problem solving and resolution. Briefly, couples are asked to spend time on problem definition so that they are ultimately solving the same problem. Problems are discussed in specific, behaviorally referenced terms, which include direct expression of feelings. Most important in the process of problem definition and solution is the validation of the problem (hearing and understanding) and the assumption of a collaborative problem-solving set.

Courtesy University of Wisconsin Women's Sports Information

Problem solution involves generating solutions in a brainstorming procedure and forming *contracts* or agreements to attempt to solve the defined problem. For a detailed description of problem-solving and communication-skills training, see Jacobson and Margolin (1979).

Providing Neutrality

For some couples, it is important that they have a neutral place to discuss and express their feelings. They have typically been focused on blaming each other for the problems and have strong beliefs and ideas about how the other person can change to improve the relationship. If the relationship difficulties have continued over a long time, couples have usually developed patterns in their thinking and behavior that perpetuate both their positions and the distress. Interventions in relationship therapies are aimed at increasing awareness or bringing about better understanding of these patterns. With this new understanding, along with generating and trying alternative approaches (interpersonally and intrapersonally), a different and more mutually-satisfying relationship can emerge.

CASE STUDIES FOLLOW-UP

Mike and Denise entered into couples therapy after several cancellations due to Mike's sport commitments. Their communication skills and problem-solving attempts were based on blame and apparent misunderstanding, which further alienated each of them. Structured communication training and problem solving gave them a common language and structure to connect with each other. Over the course of therapy, Mike and Denise began to share some of the assumptions and beliefs they had about each other and about marriage that related to their frustrations.

Denise expressed concern over her feelings of helplessness and dependency in the relationship. She revealed feeling that she was repeating her mother's marital experience. She was also able to express her own anxiety and insecurity about pursuing a career. She assumed Mike would reject her if she failed as an interior designer. Mike was initially quiet and absorbed Denise's anger and upset. When he finally shared his feelings with Denise about failing as a professional athlete and his sense of having nothing else he could do in life, Denise's anger was reduced.

They worked out agreements concerning time together and began to plan activities they both enjoyed. They appeared to achieve an increased sense of mutual understanding and support. They reaffirmed their basic acceptance of each other, not as an athlete or interior designer, but as people. In addition, they were able to support each other in changing some of the basic assumptions concerning their self-worth, confronting their fears of rejection, and forging a new comfort and nurturance in their relationship.

Reframing—suggesting to Mike that if his marital and home life is more positive, he is more likely to improve his sport performance and would be less distracted—was an important shift. Mike could now commit to working on the marriage and still feel he was working on his performance. Denise and Mike were seen for approximately 7 months; over that time their marital relationship improved, Mike's sport performance reached last year's strong level, and Denise successfully completed several interior design courses.

Sandra and Dan were seen for five sessions. A time-limited structure was established to preserve the individual consultative relationship initially started with Sandra. If further relationship work was needed a referral would have been given. Sandra and Dan were quite apprehensive about the first meeting. Dan felt it was a cut-and-dried issue of Sandra having to choose skating or him; Sandra felt that a compromise should be reached. In the background, mother and coach felt more aligned with Dan's either-or approach but could not let go of their investment and entitlement issues. Sandra and Dan were able to talk about what they liked about each other.

It was noted that communication about disagreements and conflicts was very frustrating for Dan, and anxiety provoking for Sandra. Dan was challenging of Sandra's goals and dreams in skating; this attitude was apparently rooted in his negative experience in the sport. Rather than being a source of empathy and commonality for the relationship, his skating history became the venue for his frustrations. Sandra expressed her belief that if she focused on her skating she would lose Dan and, as she later revealed, her chance to be happy in a relationship. Skating was Sandra's main source of self-esteem, and she held it tightly. Dan backed away from his threatened breakup as he heard Sandra becoming more focused on wanting to make her "wholehearted" skating efforts.

When Sandra realized Dan would not break up with her, she felt even more confident about her choice to skate. Dan's threat and ultimatum had made her think that perhaps he wasn't as sensitive or supportive as she expected in a relationship partner. Sandra and Dan had to come to some understanding and arrangement concerning time together, so some problem-solving techniques were implemented. Agreements were reached that limited time together, and skating demands were designated as the top priority. Sandra and Dan eventually concluded that they were too young for their relationship to be top priority. Sandra's skating immediately improved and she described that a "weight was off my shoulders" (a weight that apparently had been throwing off her double axel). Following the competitive season, Sandra and Dan continued to date, but 3 or 4 months later, as training for the new season was about to begin, they broke up with only short-lived upset for Sandra.

ETHICAL ISSUES

When working with athletes and their relationships, one can be faced with numerous ethical or practice-related issues. Sometimes the exploration of an important relationship issue is likely to have an emotional or distracting effect on the athlete, who might be in the middle of training or competing. Do you pursue the issue for the benefit of the relationship or wait until the competition is over? Generally, this is an issue that can be brought up to the couple so that choices to explore or not explore are explicit, not implicit; in this way, you also protect yourself as a therapist from alienating the nonathlete spouse as you would by seeming to buy into the idea that the relationship is a lower priority than sport involvement is.

It is also important to be clear about confidentiality issues and policies in relationship therapy. This is especially important if an individual consultative relationship previously had been established. If you want to maintain the individual consultative relationship, it seems prudent to either limit the number of sessions with a collateral or make a referral to another therapist.

Awareness of cultural and sex-role issues is important, as ethical issues can arise out of these factors. Further discussion of ethical issues in marital therapy can be found in Margolin (1986).

CONCLUSION

Relationships play an important role in the lives of most people, including athletes. The bidirectional arrow between relationships and sport performance and involvement seems well established but has been explored only minimally. On an anecdotal basis, relationships among athletes are seen as sources of support as well as sources of upset and distraction.

Little research is available on relationship issues among athletes. This appears to be an area that warrants exploration. Relationship enrichment might indeed prove to be a strong influence on level of performance or effort. The other arrow direction deals with the impact of both sport and sport-related behavior and attitudes on the development of relationships—in terms of quality and quantity, problem areas, and suggestions for enrichment. Retrospective interviewing of athletes might explore how they came to understand the role of relationships in their sport goals. These perceptions might be helpful in understanding current relationship patterns or problems.

Monitoring aspects of social networks and relationship functioning among athletes might prove to be important in suggesting focuses for interventions designed to improve general personal adjustment, sport adjustment, and sport performance.

Further research into the relationship difficulties facing athletes is crucial. Exploring how their involvement in sport influences their relationship behavior patterns, both positive and negative, would make a significant contribution to sport psychology.

REFERENCES

Aylmer, R. (1986). Bowen family systems marital therapy. In N. Jacobson & A. Gurman (Eds.), *Clinical handbook of marital therapy* (pp. 107-148). New York: Guilford Press.

Baillie, P., & Danish, S. (1992). Understanding the career transition of athletes. *Sport Psychologist*, **6**, 77-98.

Beck, A.T. (1988). *Love is never enough*. New York: Harper & Row.

Botterill, C. (1990). Sport psychology and professional hockey. *Sport Psychologist*, **4**, 358-368.

Erikson, E. (1959). Identity and life cycle. *Psychological Issues*, **1**, 1-171.

Erikson, E. (1963). *Childhood and society* (2nd ed.). New York: Norton.

Framo, J. (1981). The integration of marital therapy with sessions with family of origin. In A. Gurman & D. Kniskern (Eds.), *Handbook of family therapy* (pp. 133-186). New York: Brunner/Mazel.

Golding, J., & Ungerleider, S. (1991). Social resources and mood among masters track and field athletes. *Journal of Applied Sport Psychology*, **3**, 142-159.

Greenberg, L., & Johnson, S. (1987). Emotionally focused couples therapy. In N. Jacobson & A. Gurman (Eds.), *Clinical handbook of marital therapy* (pp. 253-276). New York: Guilford Press.

Greendorfer, S., & Lewko, J. (1978). Role of family members in sport socialization of children. *Research Quarterly*, **49**, 146-152.

Hardy, C., Richman, J., & Rosenfield, L. (1992). The role of social support in life stress/injury relationship. *Sport Psychologist*, **5**, 128-139.

Harris, D. (1987). The female athlete. In J. May & M. Asken (Eds.), *Sport psychology: The psychological health of the athlete* (pp. 99-116). New York: PMA.

Heyman, S. (1987). Counseling and psychotherapy with athletes: Special considerations. In J. May & M. Asken (Eds.), *Sport psychology: The psychological health of the athlete* (pp. 135-156). New York: PMA.

Jacobson, N., & Gurman, A. (Eds.) (1986). *Clinical handbook of marital therapy*. New York: Guilford Press.

Jacobson, N., & Holtzworth-Munroe, A. (1986). Marital therapy: A social learning-cognitive perspective. In N. Jacobson & A. Gurman (Eds.), *Clinical handbook of marital therapy* (pp. 29-70). New York: Guilford Press.

Jacobson, N., & Margolin, G. (1979). *Marital therapy*. New York: Brunner/Mazel.

Margolin, G. (1986). Ethical issues in marital therapy. In N. Jacobson & A. Gurman (Eds.), *Clinical handbook of marital therapy* (pp. 621-638). New York: Guilford Press.

May, J., & Veach, T. (1987). The U.S. Alpine ski team psychology program: A proposed consultation model. In J. May and M. Asken (Eds.), *Sport psychology: The psychological health of the athlete* (pp. 19-39). New York: PMA.

McElroy, M., & Kirkendall, D. (1980). Significant others and professionalized sport attitudes. *Research Quarterly for Exercise and Sport*, **51**, 645-653.

Rosenfield, L., Richman, J., & Hardy, C. (1989). Examining social support networks among athletes: Description and relationship to stress. *Sport Psychologist*, **3**, 23-33.

Smith, R. (1986). Athletic stress and burnout: Conceptual models and intervention strategies. In D. Hackfort & C. Spielberger (Eds.), *Anxiety in sports: An international perspective* (pp. 183-201). New York: Hemisphere.

Smith, R., Smoll, F., & Ptacek, J. (1990). Conjunctive moderator variables in vulnerability and resiliency research: Life stress, social support and coping skills, and adolescent sport injuries. *Journal of Personality and Social Psychology*, **58**, 360-370.

CHAPTER 9

GENDER ISSUES: A SOCIAL-EDUCATIONAL PERSPECTIVE

Diane L. Gill, PhD
University of North Carolina at Greensboro

Gender as an issue in sport psychology is relatively recent. Gender was not an issue in the sport psychology of Coleman Griffith's day. From Griffith's time in the 1920s up to the 1970s when sport psychology emerged as an identifiable area, *athlete* meant *male athlete*. Women were active in sport and physical activity much earlier, as historians of women's sport note (e.g., Spears, 1978), but women entered the modern athletic world in significant numbers only with the passage in 1972 of Title IX of the Educational Amendments Act and the related social changes of the early 1970s. Modern sport science, particularly sport psychology, also emerged in the 1970s, with the more professionally oriented applied sport psychology following in the 1980s. Given the short history of women's sport participation, we should not be surprised to find that the history of gender issues in sport psychology is short. What is surprising, though, is that despite the tremendous influx of females into athletics over the past 20 years and the increasing popularity of applied sport psychology over the last 10 years, we have little research or professional writing on gender issues in applied sport psychology. This is a particularly striking void because even a moment's reflection or a glance at the popular media reveals many gender issues. The Billie Jean King–Bobby Riggs Battle of the Sexes tennis match captured public attention in the early 1970s. Women athletes gained prominence through Olympic coverage in the 1970s and 1980s; in the 1992 Winter Olympics, the female contingent of the United States team garnered most of the country's medals. In the 1990s the NCAA, the major governing body of intercollegiate sports, grapples with the issue of gender equity. Sport psychologists have contributed little to these discussions, and we seldom consider the implications of gender in our work.

By definition, psychology focuses on individual behavior, thoughts, and feelings. But we cannot fully understand the person without considering the larger world, that is, social context. Social context is important for all our work—no behavior takes place in isolation—and social context is critical in gender issues. Thus this chapter's title contains the word *social*. I follow a social approach easily, as nearly all my sport and exercise psychology work takes a social-psychological perspective. The second part of the title, educational, is a bigger stretch for me. I have reviewed the sport psychology work on gender elsewhere (Gill, 1992a), but not with the applied emphasis of this chapter.

As noted in the introduction, this book is intended for practicing sport psychologists. I purposely used *educational* rather than *clinical* in this chapter's title for several reasons. I do not have clinical training or experience and could not legitimately claim that perspective. Indeed, I do little educational sport psychology practice, although I have consulted with teams in the past on psychological skills. Primarily, I am an academic sport and exercise psychologist researching and writing on social-psychological aspects of physical activity and attempting to draw implications for those who work more directly with men and women, girls and boys, as teachers, coaches, or practicing sport psychologists.

For this chapter's topic, gender, this social-educational approach seems appropriate. Gender is not a special issue; it is an issue for everything we do in sport psychology. Gender is not a psychological disorder or problem that calls for therapy. Rather, gender influences all other issues, practices, problems, and experiences that are discussed in other chapters of this book. This chapter's point is that gender makes a difference. Sport psychologists who are aware of gender influences on athletes, the athletic world, and sport psychology practice will better serve athletes and society.

To better understand this issue, consider the following cases. These are not clinical cases, and I will not offer a solution to them either here or later in this chapter. Instead, these brief scenarios represent situations that a practicing sport psychologist might encounter. At the end of the chapter we will return to these cases to discuss gender implications. But for now, consider how you would interpret the situation and respond as well as what approaches you might take if you were to encounter these situations. If you have already encountered such cases, consider your reactions.

■ *THE CASE OF TERRY* ■

Terry, a 16-year-old figure skater, has been referred to you because the coach is concerned about a possible eating disorder. Terry says, "There's no problem. I need to stay trim to keep that 'line' the judges look for. I've always had trouble keeping extra pounds off, but I need to work at it to be at my best, make it to nationals, and eventually get endorsements."

■ *THE CASE OF A.J.* ■

A.J. is an 18-year-old freshman on the intercollegiate soccer team. A.J. is given to angry outbursts and temper tantrums and has already been thrown out of two games. A.J. says, "I know I need to stay in the game for my coach and teammates, but I play better when I'm on the edge. I need to be really up for the game and sometimes I just lose it." The coach is concerned about A.J.'s lack of control and further reports that A.J. shows a similar lack of control by skipping the team study hall to drink and party.

■ *THE CASE OF CHRIS* ■

In contrast to A.J., Chris, starting forward on the basketball team, never gets angry or loses control. Chris has talent and size but plays tentatively and seems to lack confidence. The coach not only wants 100% from Chris but also is concerned that the other players, who look to Chris for leadership, might be affected. Chris says, "I can't do what the coach wants. I can't get mad at my opponent, and it doesn't seem right to me to throw elbows or try to hurt someone. And I'm no good at being a leader, I don't like telling others what to do; I want to be a teacher, not a coach."

■ *THE CASE OF PAT* ■

Pat's the third-ranked singles player on the tennis team. Normally a solid, consistent player, lately Pat's play has been off. After some discussion Pat says, "I'm worried about the assistant coach. Although nothing has been said or done directly, I think the coach likes me and hints at wanting more of a relationship. I'm not at all interested, but I don't want to hurt the coach's feelings. I used to stay after practice and do extra work, but now I don't hang around or ask for any help because I'm avoiding the coach. I want the extra practice and coaching, and I know I'm not concentrating, but I don't know what to do."

Consider how gender influences your interpretations and responses. I did not identify the athletes by gender, but in imagining the scenarios you probably did. (To develop a vivid image you probably also imagined athletes of a particular race and with other characteristics; we'll get back to some of those issues later.) Consider the gender implications. Terry could be a male figure skater, but chances are much greater that a female skater would exhibit those behaviors. Perhaps you were tuned in to gender issues by the title and introduction and tried to be nonsexist, assuming that you should treat females and males the same way. But if you tried to do that, you likely had difficulty. Gender indeed makes a difference. Take any of the scenarios and try to imagine the situation with the other gender (e.g., if you imagined a male A.J., imagine a female and see if you still have the same interpretations and responses). Does athlete gender influence your immediate reactions, your expectations, or the options and approaches you would consider? I suspect that gender influences all of these and, moreover, I believe that gender *should* have an influence. If you try to assume a gender-neutral approach and treat everyone the same, I believe you'll do a disservice to the athletes. Again, gender makes a difference.

Of course I am not arguing for an approach based on biases and stereotypes. Indeed, the literature indicates that even trained therapists and educational professionals hold many stereotypes and that we should consciously try to avoid acting on such biases. However, misguided attempts to treat everyone the same go against current practice in sport psychology. Specifically, one of the strongest guidelines in most discussions of educational and clinical sport psychology is individualization. Each athlete has individual characteristics, experiences, and preferences, and gender is a salient individual characteristic.

However, in this chapter I do not wish to emphasize gender as an individual characteristic, but rather as a social characteristic and one of the most salient and powerful aspects of the social context. For example, Terry is more likely to be a female figure skater not simply because females are more likely to have eating disorders but because society expects and values thinness more in women than in men and communicates that message in many ways. You might consider different options for Christine or Christopher, not because of gender biases or stereotypes but because you know that their situations are different because of gender. For example, media coverage, social support systems, future opportunities, and teammate and coach expectations all vary with gender, even if both are talented players in competitive programs. Pat's scenario seems the most directly tied to biological sex. Yet even here with a change of gender of Pat or the coach your responses might change dramatically because of the social connotations of gender and sexuality.

Before continuing with a review of the literature related to gender and sport, go back through the scenarios and try to imagine each one with both male and female athletes. Consider how your reactions, interpretations, or approaches might change. Consider how a change of gender for others (e.g., coaches, parents) might influence you. Lastly, consider how your own gender influences your views and approaches. When you are actually dealing with cases such as these, does your gender have an influence? Do you do anything, or not do anything, because you are a man or a woman? No doubt you can think of some ways that gender influences your behavior. Still, it's probably impossible for any of us to really identify all the ways that gender affects us. From birth our world has been shaped by gender. Our parents, teachers, peers, and coaches reacted to us as girls or boys. Our images of athletes have been shaped by gendered media portrayals. Gender is such a pervasive influence in society that it's nearly impossible to pinpoint. Sport is no exception, and sport psychologists should be aware of gender influences in the larger society and in the sport world.

REVIEWING THE LITERATURE

Neither psychology nor sport and exercise science provides conclusive answers to our many questions about gender, but we can draw on both areas to develop our sport psychology literature. Gender is a recent topic for sport and exercise science, but some scholars are beginning to build a knowledge base. Given that most research has been done with men, the phrase *considering gender* implies that issues specific to women will now be incorporated. For example, exercise physiologists have studied specific training responses, injury patterns, and nutritional issues for women, and journals often include articles on exercise during pregnancy, athletic amenorrhea, and other issues of special concern to women (see Wells, 1991, for a review). As some of the biological scientists in sport and exercise are examining gender issues, the most prominent gender scholarship is being conducted by sociocultural sport scholars (see Birrell, 1988, for a review). Sport has a social and historical context; individual differences and psychological processes operate in this context, and to understand gender and behavior sport psychologists should be aware of this sociocultural scholarship as well as biological research.

The sociohistorical context of competitive athletics for women, the setting most sport psychologists work with, is particularly relevant. Sport psychologists today will find a vastly different athletic world than they themselves might have experienced 25, 15, or even 5 years ago. In 1967, Kathy Switzer created a stir when she defied the rules barring women and sneaked into the Boston Marathon; today (after much prodding) we have an Olympic marathon for women. I grew up as an avid backyard baseball player, but was left with few options when most of my teammates moved into Little League; today two girls are the star players on my 9-year-old nephew's soccer team.

The landmark beginning for this turnaround in women's sports was the 1972 passage of Title IX of the Educational Amendments Act. This law emerged from the civil rights and women's movements, when actions such as those of Switzer and several young women who tried to break into all-male athletic programs helped highlight larger discrimination issues. Title IX is a broad ban on sex discrimination in all educational programs receiving federal assistance, including educational sport programs. Most educational programs quickly moved to eliminate discrimination, but athletic programs took a defensive posture. Discrimination persists and Title IX challenges continue today, but women and girls have taken giant steps into the sport world.

The number of girls in interscholastic athletics and women in intercollegiate athletic programs has increased about 6- to 10-fold from pre-Title IX days. Mariah Burton Nelson illustrates some of these changes in describing her experiences at Stanford:

> Between 1974 and 1978, I played varsity basketball at Stanford. Those years bridged the transition from female-controlled to male-controlled women's sports. For the first two years, we played in the "women's" (read: old, tiny) gym. We wore plain red shorts and white blouses; over those we tied "pinnies," a word only women seem to know. My teammates and I spent our spare time in the athletic department, begging the male athletic director to enforce Title IX. In my junior year, we finally received uniforms, a more experienced coach, and playing time in the men's gym. In 1978, my senior year, Stanford offered its first women's basketball scholarship. In 1990, Stanford won its first national championship. (Nelson, 1991, p. 6)

Women have gained a place in the sport world and now constitute about a third of high-school, college, and Olympic athletes. But, a third is not a half, and in other ways women have failed to gain or actually have lost a place. Most noticeably, the competitive sport world is hierarchical, and women are clustered at the bottom. The glass ceiling is lower and more impervious than in other domains, and women have not broken through in significant numbers to become coaches, administrators, sports writers, or sports medicine personnel. Vivian Acosta and Linda Carpenter have followed the status of women in athletics for several years, and the trends are clear. Before Title IX (1972) nearly all (more than 90%) women's athletic teams were coached by women and had a

Courtesy USOC

woman heading the program. Today less than half of women's intercollegiate teams are coached by a woman and just 16% of women's programs have a woman director, usually as an associate athletic director (e.g., Carpenter & Acosta, 1993; Nelson, 1991; Uhlir, 1987). Of course, no parallel change has occurred for men's athletics, which were and continue to be coached and administered nearly entirely (more than 99%) by men.

Other changes are less noticeable—but just as notable—for gender implications. Although women have moved into previously all-male competitive athletic programs, other sport programs with more emphasis on participation, skill development, cooperation, and recreation have been lost to both men and women. And the implications extend beyond participation numbers. Safrit (1984) noted declining numbers of women in university physical education and exercise science departments, particularly in research-oriented programs, and a continuing low percentage of women as authors and editors in the professional literature. Duda (1991) specifically noted that most articles in the *Journal of Sport & Exercise Psychology*, our main research journal, from 1979 to 1986 were by male authors, about male athletes, and focused on competitive sports. In summarizing the journal's articles during my editorial term (1985 to 1990), I (Gill, 1992b) noted that most samples included both males and females and that although we had more male than female authors, proportions were closer to equal. Still, my observations of conferences, journals, and organizations suggest that males (definitely white males) dominate research and professional practice in sport psychology as well as competitive athletics, and sport psychologists should be aware of potential gender bias because of this pattern.

Like sport and exercise science, psychology is male dominated, although the numbers are not as striking. Psychology programs attract more female than male students, and the American Psychological Association (APA) has a task force exploring the implications of this gender shift. Still, as with other fields, organizational leadership, research journals, and university faculties are male dominated. The psychology of women and gender is more peripheral than central to psychology, but the area is active and sport psychologists can look to that literature to help understand gender and sport.

As with sport and exercise science, psychologists have approached gender by studying women and women's issues. Division 35 (psychology of women) is active in the APA, and several journals focus on the psychology of women. Psychologists as well as women's studies scholars are beginning to focus more on gender rather than on women, recognizing that gender issues apply to both women and men and that *gender* means more than simply *gender differences*. In the following review I focus on this work from psychology and incorporate the related sport-specific psychology work.

Sex Differences

Generally, psychology work on women and gender has progressed from a sex-differences approach, to an emphasis on gender role as a personality orientation, to more current social-psychological models that emphasize social context and processes. Before reviewing that work, though, I should clarify terminology. Typically, *sex* differences refers to biologically-based differences between males and females, whereas *gender* refers to social and psychological characteristics and behaviors associated with females and males. The early sex-differences work assumed dichotomous biologically-based psychological differences that paralleled and, indeed, stemmed from biological male–female differences. Today, consensus holds that psychological characteristics and behaviors associated with females and males are neither dichotomous nor biologically based. Indeed, even most biological factors that are relevant to sport and exercise are not dichotomously divided between males and females, but are normally distributed in both females and males. For example, considering NCAA tournament basketball teams, the average male center is taller than the average female center, but the average female center is taller than most men. For social-psychological characteristics and behaviors, average differences are elusive, no evidence supports a biological basis, and no dichotomous sex-linked connections are evident.

The most widely cited sex-differences work is Eleanor Maccoby and Carol Jacklin's 1974 compilation of the existing research. Although they cautioned that few conclusions could be drawn, most subsequent discussions ignored that caution and their suggested "possible" sex differences quickly became accepted as established fact. Most people assume that males are more aggressive and have greater math and visuospatial ability, whereas females have greater verbal ability; these sex differences are sometimes cited as a reason for males' presumed superiority in sport.

Despite many attempts to identify sex differences and their biological correlates, the bulk of the research casts doubt even on the possible differences cited by Maccoby and Jacklin (1974). Several reviews, and most notably the meta-analytic reviews by Eagley (1987) and Hyde and Linn (1986), indicate that sex differences in ability are minimal, inconsistent, and not biologically based and that interactions are common. For example, boys might complete a timed math test faster than girls, but do no better on math accuracy with unlimited time. In general, overlap and similarities are much more apparent than differences.

Ashmore (1990) summarized the meta-analyses and research on sex differences and concluded that sex differences are large for certain physical abilities (e.g., throwing velocity, body use, posturing), more modest for other abilities and social behaviors (e.g., math, aggression), and negligible for all other domains (e.g., leadership, attitudes, such physical abilities as reaction time and balance). Even the larger sex differences are confounded with nonbiological influences. Ashmore as well as Maccoby (1990) and Jacklin (1989) advocate abandoning sex-differences approaches for more multifaceted and social approaches. Jacklin states that although researchers have been preoccupied with the search for sex differences, the tentative 1974 conclusions cannot be supported. Maccoby suggests that behavioral sex differences emerge mainly in social situations and vary with the gender composition of the group. Most psychologists who have reviewed this topic suggest that a sex-differences approach assumes an underlying, unidimensional cause (biological sex) and ignores the rich and complex variations in gender-related behavior.

In response to criticisms of the sex-differences approach and its failure to shed any light on gender-related behavior, psychologists turned to personality and individual differences for explanations.

Personality and Gender-Role Orientation

Psychologists have focused on gender-role orientation as the relevant personality construct to explain gender-related behavior. Specifically, Sandra Bem's (1974, 1978) work and her Bem Sex Role Inventory (BSRI) served as the major impetus for a large body of research and brought the constructs of masculinity, femininity, and androgyny to public attention and debate. Janet Spence and Bob Helmreich (1978) developed their parallel measure of gender-role orientation, the Personality Attributes Questionnaire (PAQ).

Both the BSRI and PAQ assess masculinity (or instrumentality) and femininity (or expressiveness) as separate, independent constructs. Most sport psychology research on gender uses the constructs and measures developed by Bem or by Spence and Helmreich. Helmreich and Spence (1977) sampled intercollegiate athletes and reported that most female athletes were either androgynous or masculine, in contrast to their nonathlete college female sample, who were most often classified as feminine.

Several subsequent studies with female athletes yielded similar findings. Harris and Jennings (1977) surveyed female distance runners and reported that most were androgynous or masculine. Both Del Rey and Sheppard (1981) and Colker and Widom (1980) found that most intercollegiate athletes were classified as androgynous or masculine. Myers and Lips (1978) reported that most female racquetball players were androgynous whereas most males were masculine.

Many more studies have surveyed women athletes using the BSRI or PAQ, but listing them would not tell us more about women's sport and exercise behavior. Moreover, both the methodology and underlying assumptions of this line of research have been widely criticized (e.g., Locksley & Colten, 1979; Pedhazur & Tetenbaum, 1979; Taylor & Hall, 1982). Most investigators accept the separate masculinity–instrumentality and femininity–expressiveness dimensions but question the meaning of the underlying constructs and the implications for other gender-related constructs and behaviors. Deaux (1985) concluded that the BSRI and PAQ seem to measure self-assertion and nurturance and do predict specific assertive and nurturant behaviors but do not relate very well to other gender-related attributes and behaviors.

Overall, then, the sport and exercise psychology research on gender-role orientation suggests that female athletes possess more masculine–instrumental personality characteristics than do female nonathletes. This is not particularly enlightening. Sport, especially competitive athletics, is an achievement activity that demands instrumental, assertive behaviors. Both the BSRI and PAQ include *competitive* as a masculine item, and the higher masculine scores of female athletes probably reflect an overlap with competitiveness. Competitive orientation can be measured directly (e.g., Gill & Deeter, 1988; Gill & Dzewaltowski, 1988), so we need not invoke more indirect, controversial measures.

Perhaps even more important, athlete–nonathlete status is an indirect and nonspecific measure of behavior. If instrumental and expressive personality characteristics predict instrumental and expressive behaviors, we should examine those instrumental and expressive behaviors in sport. Even in highly competitive sports, expressive behaviors might be advantageous. Creative, expressive actions might be the key to success for a gymnast; supportive behaviors of teammates might be critical on a soccer team; and sensitivity to others might help an Olympic coach (not to mention a sport psychologist) communicate with each athlete.

Even if we recognize cautions and limits, gender-role orientation raises concerns. Ann Hall (1988), one of the first sport sociologists to take a feminist approach, charges that using the gender-role constructs and measures reifies abstract masculine–feminine dichotomous constructs. Hall (1990) also cautions that this gender-role approach encourages a focus on "role conflict," (i.e., that the role of athlete conflicts with the female role.) Del Rey (1978) and Harris (1980), for example, discussed the conflicting demands of sport and femininity as problems for athletes. Today that role-conflict approach has been largely discounted. Female athletes typically do not express role conflict as defined in this literature, and both Hall (1990) and Allison (1991) summarize this work by concluding that the notion of role conflict has not been helpful and should be abandoned.

Although this early role-conflict work is not credible today, athletes might experience role conflict in which gender plays a role. Blinde and Greendorfer (1992) summarized five previous studies and concluded that athletes experience four types of conflict:

- Value alienation (conflict of athletic values with personal values)
- Role strain (difficulty meeting others' varied expectations of the athlete role, such as coach and professor expectations of the athlete)
- Role conflict (difficulty meeting expectations of multiple roles, such as athlete and student)
- Exploitation (dominance of the athlete role such that other roles cannot be fulfilled)

Although both male and female athletes might experience any of these conflicts, they might be gender-related. For example, values of intercollegiate coaches and programs might well be more alien to a freshman female recruit than to her male counterpart, or the demands of the male-athlete role in a big-time basketball program might more likely lead to exploitation. Blinde and Greendorfer (1992) noted fewer conflicts for female athletes in pre-Title IX and post-Title IX Division III programs than for post-Title IX female athletes in Division I who are moving into the male sport model. Importantly, for most female athletes the sport experience was not negative but worthwhile and challenging. Thus sport psychologists should not assume role conflict for female athletes, but should be aware that some female or male athletes might experience conflicts in which gender might play a role.

Overall, the sport and exercise psychology research on gender-role orientation has all the drawbacks of early sport personality research wrapped up with limiting gender stereotypes and biases. Most psychologists now recognize the limits of the earlier sex-differences and gender-role approaches and look beyond the simple male–female and masculine–feminine dichotomies.

Gender and Sport Achievement

For example, research on achievement has progressed from early sex differences through gender roles to more current social-cognitive models. Achievement is a prominent topic in the psychology research on gender, as well as a clear concern of sport psychologists. Most sport and exercise activities involve achievement behavior and particularly competitive achievement. Gender differences were ignored in the early achievement research (McClelland, Atkinson, Clark, & Lowell, 1953), and researchers simply took male behavior as the norm until Matina Horner's (1972) doctoral work focused attention on gender. Horner suggested that success has negative consequences for women, because success requires competitive achievement behaviors that conflict with the traditional feminine image. This conflict arouses a motive to avoid success, popularly termed the fear of success (FOS), and leads to anxiety and avoidance. Horner provided some evidence, and her work was widely publicized, but critics (e.g., Condry & Dyer, 1975; Tresemer, 1977) noted that FOS imagery was prevalent in men as well as women, the FOS measure confused stereotyped attitudes with motives, and the research failed to link FOS directly to achievement behaviors. McElroy and Willis (1979), who specifically considered women's achievement conflicts in sport contexts, concluded that no evidence supports a FOS in female athletes and that achievement attitudes of female athletes are similar to those of male athletes.

Current scholars have replaced global achievement motives with multidimensional constructs and an emphasis on achievement

Courtesy Tim McKinney

cognitions. Spence and Helmreich (1978, 1983) developed a multidimensional measure with separate dimensions of mastery, work, and competitiveness; they found that males score higher than females on mastery and competitiveness, whereas females score higher than males on work. Gender differences on mastery and work diminish for athletes, but males score higher than females on competitiveness. Also, masculinity scores relate positively to all three achievement dimensions, whereas femininity scores relate slightly positively to work and negatively to competitiveness. Generally, gender influence is strongest and most consistent for competitiveness.

My work (Gill, 1988, 1993) with the Sport Orientation Questionnaire (SOQ) (Gill & Deeter, 1988) that assesses competitiveness (an achievement orientation to enter and strive for success in competitive sport), win orientation (a desire to win and avoid losing), and goal orientation (an emphasis on achieving personal goals) also suggests that gender influences vary across dimensions. Males typically score higher than females on competitiveness and win orientation, whereas females typically score slightly higher than males on goal orientation. Comparing females and males who participated in competitive sport, noncompetitive sport, and nonsport achievement activities revealed that, overall, males consistently scored higher than females on sport competitiveness and win orientation, and males also reported more competitive sport activity and experience. However, females were just as high as males, and sometimes higher, on sport-goal orientation and general achievement. Also, females were just as likely as males to participate in noncompetitive sport and nonsport achievement activities. Thus the gender differences do not seem to reflect either general achievement orientation or interest in sport and exercise activities per se. Instead, gender is related to an emphasis on social comparison and winning in sport.

Other researchers report similar gender influences on reactions to competitive sport. When McNally and Orlick (1975) introduced a cooperative broomball game to children in urban Canada and in the Northwest Territories, they found girls were more receptive to the cooperative rules than boys were. They also noted cultural differences, with northern children more receptive, but the gender influence held in both cultures. Duda (1986) similarly reported both gender and cultural influences on competitiveness with Anglo and Navajo children in the southwestern United States. Male Anglo children were the most win oriented and placed the most emphasis on athletic ability. Weinberg and Jackson (1979) found that males were more affected by success and failure than were females, and in a related study Weinberg and Ragan (1979) reported that males were more interested in a competitive activity whereas females preferred a noncompetitive activity.

Although several lines of research suggest gender influences on competitive sport achievement, the research does not point to any unique gender-related personality construct as an explanation. Instead, most investigators are turning to socialization, societal influences, and social-cognitive models for explanations.

Cognitive approaches currently dominate research on achievement. The concept underlying these approaches is that what the person *thinks* is important, *is* important. For example, if you expect to do well at volleyball, you probably will. Research consistently indicates that expectations are good predictors of achievement behavior and performance (e.g., Bandura, 1977, 1986; Crandall, 1969; Eccles et al., 1983; Feltz, 1988), and research also suggests gender influences. Typically, females report lower expectations of success and make fewer achievement-oriented attributions than males do. However, gender differences are not completely consistent. In her review of the self-confidence literature, Lenney (1977) concluded that gender differences in confidence are more likely to occur in achievement situations that

- involve tasks perceived as masculine,
- provide only ambiguous feedback or ability information, and
- emphasize social comparison.

In sport and exercise psychology, Corbin and his colleagues (Corbin, 1981; Corbin, Landers, Feltz, & Senior, 1983; Corbin & Nix, 1979; Corbin, Stewart, & Blair, 1981; Petruzzello & Corbin, 1988; Stewart & Corbin, 1988) have conducted a series of experimental studies that confirm Lenney's propositions. Specifically, Corbin and his colleagues demonstrated that females do not lack confidence with a gender-neutral, non-socially-evaluative task and that performance feedback can improve the confidence of low-confidence females; the researchers also suggested lack of experience as an additional factor affecting female self-confidence. In our lab (Gill, Gross, Huddleston, & Shifflett, 1984) we matched female and male competitors of similar ability on a pegboard task. Males were slightly more likely than females to predict a win, but performance expectations were similar; females performed slightly better in competition than males did, and females generally had more positive achievement cognitions (higher perceived ability, more effort attributions).

Thus females and males display similar levels of confidence when tasks are appropriate for females, when females and males have similar experiences and capabilities, and when clear evaluation criteria and feedback are present. Importantly, though, the confirming research involves experimental studies in controlled settings. We cannot so easily equate task appropriateness, experience, and social influence in the real world of sport. We must consider socialization and social context.

Jacquelynne Eccles's (1985, 1987; Eccles et al., 1983) model incorporates such sociocultural factors along with achievement cognitions. Eccles recognizes that both expectations and importance or value determine achievement choices and behaviors. As discussed earlier, gender differences in expectations are common, and gender also influences the value of sport achievement. Eccles further notes that gender differences in expectations and value develop over time and are influenced by gender-role socialization, stereotyped expectations of others, and sociocultural norms, as well as individual characteristics and experiences. Recently, Eccles and Harold (1991) summarized existing work and provided new evidence showing that her model holds for sport achievement, that gender influences children's sport achievement perceptions and behaviors at a very young age, and that these gender differences seem to be the product of gender-role socialization.

Physical Activity and Self-Perceptions

Before moving away from personality and individual differences I want to consider the role of sport and exercise on self-perceptions, particularly body image and self-esteem. As just noted, females tend to lack confidence in their sport and exercise capabilities. Thus sport has a tremendous potential to enhance women's sense of competence and control. Many women who begin activity programs report such enhanced self-esteem and a sense of physical competence that often carries over into other aspects of their lives. A few studies add some support to these testimonials. Holloway, Beuter, and Duda (1988), Brown and Harrison (1986), and Trujillo (1983) all report that exercise programs, particularly weight and strength training, enhance the self-concepts of women participants.

As well as developing feelings of physical strength and confidence, sport offers the opportunity to strive for excellence, the chance to accomplish a goal through effort and training, and the psychological challenge of testing oneself in competition. Marathon swimmer Diana Nyad expressed this:

> When asked why, I say that marathon swimming is the most difficult physical, intellectual, and emotional battleground I have encountered, and each time I win, each time I reach the other shore, I feel worthy of any other challenge life has to offer. (1978, p. 152)

The values expressed by Nyad should be gained in competitive athletics, but too often we lose these real benefits when we focus on competitive outcomes. Research clearly shows that overemphasizing extrinsic rewards detracts from intrinsic interest, other psychological benefits, and even performance achievements. Focusing on intrinsic standards for both performance and nonperformance goals should benefit all athletes and especially help women enhance their sense of physical competence and confidence.

Sport psychologists should take particular note of the work on gender and the relationship of body image to individual perceptions and attitudes about physical activity and to participation and behavior in sport and exercise settings. For example, *The Bodywise Woman* (Melpomene Institute, 1990) and Rodin, Silberstein, and Streigel-Moore's (1985) symposium contribution "Women and Weight" provide excellent reviews and discussion. This information clearly points to a strong sociocultural influence on body image. Our images of the ideal body, and particularly the ideal female body, have changed through history and across social contexts. Today's ideal is a slender, lean female body, and most women recognize and strive for that ideal—which is much less than ideal in terms of physical and mental health. Boys and men also have concerns about body image, but the literature indicates that girls and women are much more negative about their bodies. Moreover, these concerns are gender related. Girls are particularly concerned with physical beauty and maintaining the ideal thin shape, whereas boys are more concerned with size, strength, and power. Research indicates that most adult women perceive an underweight body as ideal and tend to see themselves as overweight even though most fall within normal weight ranges. We could simply encourage young women to ignore media images, but unfortunately our obsession with body image and particularly weight loss has justification in our society. Studies indicate that people who don't match the ideal, especially overweight, obese people, and more especially overweight, obese women, are evaluated negatively and discriminated against. Thus society shapes body image; this societal pressure for a body image that is not particularly healthy nor attainable for many women likely has a negative influence on self-esteem and psychological well-being as well as on physical health.

We must also note here that biology plays an important role in body image, particularly when we consider overweight and obese women. Obese people do not necessarily lack willpower, and they cannot lose weight merely by "really" wanting to. Metabolic rates and processes vary greatly among people and are largely genetically determined; some of the assumed links between obesity and health might reflect psychological and social problems rather than medical problems; and the constant dieting, especially with a yo-yo pattern of weight gains and losses, might be more detrimental to health than remaining consistently overweight.

Concerns about body image affect all women, but we should be especially mindful of how such body concerns influence women in sport. Athletes are just as susceptible as other women to the general societal pressure toward eating disorders and unrealistic, unhealthy thinness. Sport psychologists need to be aware of this possibility. Pressures toward thinness, and thus unhealthy eating behaviors, are of most concern in the thin-body sports, such as gymnastics, dance, and running. Coaches in such sports should be especially sensitive to what they communicate about ideal and realistic body shapes to their athletes. For example, one athlete reported:

> At age 14 my cycling coach told me I was "fat" in front of my entire team . . . At 5 ft, 5 in., 124 lb [56 kg], I was not fat, but my self-esteem was so low that I simply believed him. After all, he was the coach." (Melpomene Institute, 1990, p. 36)

Coaches and teachers should know that pressuring an athlete, who already has tremendous societal pressure to lose weight, is not a desirable approach. Most enlightened coaches and instructors follow nutritional guidelines and emphasize healthy eating rather than weight standards.

Gender and Social Processes

As Deaux (1984) reported, gender research in the 1980s moved away from studying sex differences and individual differences to regarding gender as a social category. Even Bem moved away from her early focus on personality to a broader, more social gender-schema theory (1985). Gender-schema theory suggests that sex-typed people (masculine males and feminine females) are more likely than non-sex-typed people to classify sports as gender-appropriate and to restrict their participation to gender-appropriate activities. Matteo (1986, 1988) and Csizma, Wittig, and Schurr (1988) confirmed that sports are indeed sex-typed (mostly as masculine). Matteo further reported that sex-typing influenced sport choice and that sex-typed people did not participate in gender-inappropriate sports.

Gender Beliefs and Stereotypes

Deaux (1984, 1985; Deaux & Kite, 1987) focuses on social categories and social context, suggesting that how people think males and females differ is more important than actual differences. As discussed earlier, psychological differences between females and males are small and inconsistent. Nevertheless, we maintain our beliefs in gender differences. Deaux proposes that our gender stereotypes are pervasive and exert a major influence on social interactions. Considerable evidence supports the existence of gender stereotypes. From their often-cited research, Broverman, Rosenkrantz, and their colleagues (Broverman, Vogel, Broverman, Clarkson, & Rosenkrantz, 1972; Rosenkrantz, Vogel, Bee, Broverman, & Broverman, 1968) found that people believe males and females differ on a large number of characteristics and behaviors (e.g., women are more emotional and sensitive, whereas men are more forceful and independent). More relevant to clinical practice, I.K. Broverman and her colleagues asked therapists to judge the healthy man, healthy woman, and healthy adult on these characteristics. Therapists held gender stereotypes, and their ratings of the healthy adult more closely resembled their ratings of the healthy man than of the healthy woman.

More recent work (Deaux & Kite, 1987; Deaux & Lewis, 1984; Eagley & Kite, 1987) suggests that bipolar stereotypes persist and that gender stereotypes have multiple components. We not only hold gender stereotypes about personality traits but also about role behaviors, occupations, physical appearance, and sexuality. For example, we tend to picture construction workers as men and secretaries as women; if women are construction workers we picture them as looking like men in physical appearance. Deaux suggests that these multiple components are interrelated and that the relationships and implications for gender-related behavior might vary with the social context. For example, Deaux and Lewis found that people weigh physical appearance heavily and infer other gender-related traits and behaviors (e.g., personality, sexuality) from physical characteristics. Such multidimensional gender stereotypes certainly have counterparts in sport. We expect men with athletic body types to be athletes and, moreover, to be aggressive, competitive, independent, and of course heterosexual. Coaches seldom encourage a smaller young man, or one with artistic talents, to try out for football. We also tend to assume that women with athletic body builds or talents are aggressive, competitive, independent, and lesbian. Such stereotypes are prominent and have far-reaching implications for women and men in sport.

Considerable research suggests a gender bias in the evaluation of female and male performance. In a provocative study, Goldberg (1968) reported a bias favoring male authors when women judged articles that were equivalent except for sex of author. Subsequent studies confirmed a male bias, but suggest that the bias varies with information and situational characteristics (e.g., Pheterson, Kiesler, & Goldberg, 1971; Wallston & O'Leary, 1981). A series of studies that adopted the Goldberg approach to examine gender bias in attitudes toward hypothetical female and male coaches (Parkhouse & Williams, 1986; Weinberg, Reveles, & Jackson, 1984; Williams & Parkhouse, 1988) revealed a bias favoring male coaches. However, Williams and Parkhouse reported that female basketball players coached by a successful female did not exhibit the male bias, suggesting more complex influences on gender stereotypes and evaluations.

Although sport psychologists have not examined multidimensional gender stereotypes and interrelationships, gender stereotypes and gender bias in evaluations certainly exist in sport. Eleanor Metheny (1965) identified gender stereotypes in her classic analysis of the social acceptability of various sports. For example, Metheny concluded that it is not appropriate for women to engage in contests in which

- the resistance of the opponent is overcome by bodily contact,
- the resistance of a heavy object is overcome by direct application of bodily force, or
- the body is projected into or through space over long distances or for extended periods of time.

According to Metheny, acceptable sports for women (e.g., gymnastics, swimming, tennis) emphasize aesthetic qualities and often are individual activities in contrast to direct competition and team sports. Although Metheny offered her analysis more than 25 years ago, our gender stereotypes have not faded away with the implementation of Title IX. Gender stereotypes persist, and they seem more persistent in sport than in other social contexts. For example, Kane and Snyder (1989) recently confirmed gender stereotyping of sports, as suggested by Metheny, and more explicitly identified physicality as the central feature.

Not only do gender beliefs persist in sport and exercise, but socialization pressures toward such gender beliefs are pervasive, strong (although often subtle), and begin early (e.g., see Greendorfer, 1987). Gendered beliefs and behaviors are apparent even in infants, and parents, schools, and other socializers convey gendered beliefs in many direct and indirect ways. For example, in a text on women and gender, Unger and Crawford (1992) summarized the literature by noting that toys (boys have more vehicles and active toys, whereas girls have more dolls), clothes (colors, ruffles even on play suits of girls), and play (stories, activities) are powerful sources of gender stereotyping in early childhood and that by school age children's social networks are sex-segregated. Overall, differential treatment is consistent with producing independence and efficacy in boys and emotional sensitivity, nurturance, and helplessness in girls. Pressures for gender-role conformity are stronger for boys, and, of particular interest for this chapter, many girls resist typing to be active in sports. Although both girls and boys participate, sport psychologists should expect subtle but pervasive gender pressures; an understanding of gender socialization provides the basis for understanding individual gender-related behavior in sport and exercise.

One prominent source of gender stereotyping that has been investigated by sport scholars is the media. Investigations of television, newspaper, and popular magazine coverage of female and male athletes reveal clear gender bias (e.g., Kane, 1989; Kane & Parks, 1992; Messner, Duncan, & Jensen, 1993). Females receive little media coverage (less than 10%) whether considering TV air time, newspaper space, feature articles, or photographs. Moreover, female and male athletes receive different coverage that reflects gender hierarchy. Generally, athletic ability and accomplishments are emphasized for men, but femininity and physical attractiveness are emphasized for women athletes. Kane (1989) described one graphic example with a photograph on the cover of the 1987-88 Northwest Louisiana State women's basketball media guide showing the team members wearing Playboy bunny ears and tails, captioned "These girls can Play, boy!" Gender bias in the sport media also occurs in more subtle ways. Eitzen and Baca Zinn (1993) reported that a majority of colleges had sexist nicknames or symbols (e.g., adding "elle" or "ette," Lady) that gender marked the women athletes as different from and less than the men athletes.

In a study of 1989 NCAA basketball tournaments and U.S. Open tennis coverage, Messner et al. (1993) noted less stereotyping than in previous studies, but still found considerable

- gender marking (e.g., *Women's* Final Four but Final Four for men), and
- gendered hierarchy of naming (e.g., females referred to as *girls*, *young ladies*, or *women*; men never referred to as *boys*).

Gender marking might be appropriate and useful when it's symmetrical or similar for women and men, as it was for most of the tennis coverage, but asymmetrical marking labels females as other than the norm or real athletes. Gendered language was also apparent in comments about success, failure, and strength. Comments about strength and weakness were ambivalent for women, but clearly about strength for men, and emotional reasons for failure (e.g., nerves, lack of confidence) were cited more often for women. Messner et al. noted that "dominants" in society typically are referred to by last names and subordinates by first names. They found first names used more than 50% of the time to refer to females but only 10% of the time to refer to males. Also, the few male athletes referred to by first names were black male basketball players. No race differences were observed for females; gender seemed to be more prominent.

My own observations of the most recent Olympic and NCAA tournaments suggests improvement with less stereotyping and trivialization of female athletes, but institutional change is slow and the sports media does not reflect current female sport participation. Overall, gendered beliefs seem alive and well in the sport world. Sport activities are gender stereotyped, and the sex-typing of sport activities seems linked with other gender beliefs (e.g., physicality). Gender beliefs influence social processes, and the research on gender bias in evaluation of coaches suggests that influence is at least as likely in sport as in other social interactions. Overt discrimination is unlikely, and participants might not recognize the influence of gendered beliefs in themselves or others. For example, many sport administrators and participants fail to recognize gender beliefs operating when athletic programs developed by and for men, stressing male-linked values and characteristics, are opened to girls and women.

Gender and Social Context

Not only should we consider gender stereotypes and beliefs, but as Deaux and Major (1987) state, we must consider the immediate social context and understand gender-related behavior in a given situation. Like Deaux, who has moved from her earlier gender work on attributions and individual characteristics to emphasize social context, Bem (1993) has moved beyond gender-schema and strictly psychological approaches to a more encompassing gender perspective. Bem now offers a more comprehensive analysis and proposes that the three gender lenses of

- gender polarization (the view that male–female differences are an organizing principle for social life),
- androcentrism (the view that the male is the norm), and
- biological essentialism (the view that these differences are the inevitable consequence of biological nature)

interact in historical context to perpetuate male dominance, particularly wealthy, white, heterosexual male dominance.

Deaux and Major, as well as Bem, advocate moving beyond traditional psychology boundaries to incorporate broader sociocultural perspectives on gender. Those recent calls echo Carolyn Sherif's (1976, 1982) earlier prolific and provocative social psychology work and her early advocacy for women and gender issues in psychology. Sherif, a persistent advocate for social psychology, emphasized social context and process in all her work and extended her discussions to sport and competition (e.g., Sherif, 1976). Unfortunately, sport and exercise psychologists have not adopted Sherif's suggestions or other current social-psychological approaches. Indeed, our research and practice seems narrower and more oblivious to social context and process than ever before. To break out of this isolation, sport psychologists might incorporate some of the sociology work on gender.

In *The Female World*, Jessie Bernard (1981) points out that social experiences and contexts for females and males are different, even when they appear similar on the surface. Indeed, male and female worlds are different. In the early days of organized sport, from the 1920s to Title IX in 1972, we intentionally established and maintained separate sport worlds for females and males. These separate sport worlds have not disappeared with legal and organizational changes. The social world differs for female and male members of intercollegiate basketball teams, for male and female joggers, and for girls and boys pitching a youth baseball game. In sport and exercise science, sport psychologists can look to the work of sport sociologists, who are doing the most prominent and innovative work on gender. Sport psychologists familiar with the work of such scholars as Ann Hall (1988), Susan Birrell (1988), Alison Dewar (1987), Nancy Theberge (1987), and Michael Messner (1992) could develop a fuller understanding of gender and sport. I particularly recommend Helen Lenskyj's (1986) coherent and provocative analysis of sexuality and gender, which emphasizes the historical and sociocultural pressures toward compulsory heterosexuality that influence women's sport and exercise participation and behaviors.

The work of these feminist sport scholars suggests that gender is pervasive in society, and specifically in sport society; that gender beliefs, relations, and processes are multifaceted; and that an understanding of the historical–cultural context and immediate social context is necessary to understand women's sport and exercise experiences.

Diversity in Social Context

Not only should we adopt more encompassing conceptual frameworks, but we should look into a wider range of issues and behaviors with more diverse women and men. Gender influences are just as prominent in youth sports, physical education classes, and exercise settings as in competitive athletics. Moreover, sport is not only male, but white, middle class, and heterosexual. Gender is one of several social identities and we should consider gender relations across varying social groups.

Duda and Allison (1990) point out the striking void in the field of sport and exercise psychology on race and ethnicity. Most of the issues raised for gender have parallels in race and ethnicity. That is, stereotypes are pervasive and multifaceted; racial and ethnic socialization, self-perceptions, and social context influence sport and exercise behavior; and a grounding in sociocultural history would enhance our understanding of race and ethnicity in sport. Although parallel issues arise, race and class are qualitatively different from gender; moreover we do not even have the limited work on racial or ethnic stereotypes and individual characteristics to parallel the gender research. More important for this chapter, gender likely interacts with race and class in many complex ways. For example, the experiences of a black, female tennis player are not simply a combination of the experiences of white female and black male players. Althea Gibson (1979) described her experiences in a personal account that highlights some of the complex interactions of race and gender and illustrates some of the influences of both social history and the immediate social situation in her development as a tennis player and as a person.

Significant numbers of athletes are not white and middle class, yet power in sport remains solidly white and middle class. As noted earlier for women, sport's glass ceiling keeps all but white middle-class athletes clustered at the bottom. The popular media and some sport scholars have discussed such practices as "stacking" (e.g., playing African-Americans in certain positions such as football running back or baseball outfield but not in central quarterback or pitching roles) and the nearly exclusive white male dominance of coaching and management positions. To date, few of these reports have included in-depth or critical analysis of race or socioeconomic class in sport.

Thus the sport experience varies with race and socioeconomic class, as it does with gender. Majors (1990) added more critical analysis to the literature with his discussion of the "cool pose" (a set of expressive lifestyle behaviors) used by black males to counter racism. Majors noted that although a few black males escape limits and express pride, power, and control, the emphasis on the cool pose in sport is self-defeating for the majority because it comes at the expense of education and other opportunities for advancement. Moreover, Majors notes that the cool pose uses sexist oppression to counter racist oppression, rather than encouraging more empowering strategies. Majors's discussion begins to tie together analyses of race and gender, but few others have done so. Smith (1992) drew together literature on women of color in sport and society with the primary conclusion that we have a deafening silence on diverse ethnic women in sport.

Recently, Brooks and Althouse (1993) edited a volume on racism in college athletics focusing on the African-American athlete's experience. Not only does this volume draw together needed scholarship on race and sport, but it includes a welcome section on gender and race. In one chapter Corbett and Johnson (1993) drew on the limited research and their own insights to focus on African-American women in college sport. They noted that society holds different stereotypes and treats African-American women differently than white women. African-American women in America have a social-historical context of sexual exploitation, low wages, and substandard education; they are stereotyped as independent, loud, and dominating. Also, Corbett and Johnson noted that our popular myth that African-American women gravitate to track is not supported. African-American women have had more opportunities in track than in some other activities, and some talented athletes from Wilma Rudolph to Jackie Joyner-Kersee are widely recognized, but the limited survey data indicates that track is not a particularly popular activity for African-American students, and both formal and informal opportunities likely are limited by social stereotypes and constraints. In another chapter Tina Sloan Green (1993) optimistically discusses such opportunities as Girls Clubs, YWCA, PGM golf and the NCAA's national Youth Sport Program as strategies that might help overcome barriers and encourage more young African-American women to participate and develop their full potential in sports and athletics.

We can extend considerations further to incorporate other ethnic groups and other social categories such as socioeconomic class, age, and physical attributes. The lack of sport and exercise research on any such categories precludes conclusions. Clearly, though, we should move to consider diversity within gender in our gender research.

Not only should we consider greater social diversity within gender, but we should consider gender issues for both men and women in sport and exercise. Given that most sport and exercise psychology research (like most research) focuses on men, research aimed at understanding women's sport is essential. The recent influx of women into the traditional male sport world has brought gender issues to light for men as well as for women. Messner and Sabo (1990) edited a volume on sport, men, and gender, and Messner (1992) has followed that with an insightful analysis of sport and masculinity in *Power at Play*.

As discussed by Messner (1992), sport is a powerful force that socializes boys and men into a restricted masculine identity. Messner cites the major forces in sport as

- competitive hierarchical structure with conditional self-worth that enforces the must-win style and
- homophobia.

Messner describes the extent of homophobia in sport as staggering, and states that homophobia leads all boys and men regardless of sexual orientation to conform to a narrow definition of masculinity. Real men compete and, above all, avoid anything feminine that might lead one to be branded a sissy. Messner interviewed one successful elite athlete who noted that he was interested in dance as a child, but instead threw himself into athletics as a football and track jock. He reflected that he probably would have been a dancer except that he wanted the athlete's macho image. Messner ties this masculine identity to sport violence, because using violence to achieve a goal is acceptable and encouraged in this identity. Notably, female athletes are less comfortable with aggression in sport. Messner further notes that homophobia in athletics is closely linked with misogyny; that is, sport bonds men together as superior to women.

Messner's linking of homophobia and misogyny reflects Lenskyj's (1986, 1991) analysis citing compulsory heterosexuality as the root of sexist sport practices and Bem's (1993) contention that sexism, heterosexism, and homophobia all are related consequences of the same gender lenses in society. We expect to see men dominate women, and we are uncomfortable with bigger, stronger women who take the active, dominant roles that we expect in athletes.

Homophobia in sport has been discussed most often as a problem for lesbians, with good reason. Nelson (1991), in her chapter "A Silence So Loud, It Screams," illustrates restrictions and barriers for lesbians by describing one LPGA tour player who remains closeted to protect her status with friends, family, sponsors, tour personnel, and the general public. A few years ago Penn State women's basketball coach Renee Portland made headlines by declaring that she did not allow lesbians on her team. Few other coaches or administrators are as blatantly discriminatory, but more subtle discrimination is widespread. In a *Village Voice* article, Solomon (1991) cites several incidents of athletes or coaches losing jobs, positions, or roles on teams, as well as the use of accusations of lesbianism as scare tactics in recruiting or to keep women in line. Not surprisingly, those involved with women's athletics often go out of the way to avoid any appearance of lesbianism, like the golfer in Nelson's chapter, or deny a lesbian presence in sport. Pat Griffin, who has written and conducted workshops on homophobia in sport and physical education, describes this state as people "tip-toeing around a lavender elephant in the locker room and pretending that it's just not there." As Griffin notes (1987, 1992), lesbians are not the problem; homophobia is the problem. Homophobia manifests itself in women's sports as

- silence,
- denial,
- apology,
- promotion of a "heterosexy" image,
- attacks on lesbians, and
- preference for male coaches.

We stereotypically assume that sport attracts lesbians (but not gay men); however, there is no inherent relationship between sexual orientation and sport (no "gay gene" will turn a woman into a softball player or a man into a figure skater). No doubt, homophobia has kept more heterosexual women than lesbians out of sports, and homophobia restricts the behavior of all women in sport. Moreover, as the analyses of Messner (1992) and Ponger (1990) suggest, homophobia probably restricts men in sport even more than it restricts women.

Homophobia is not likely to bring gay or lesbian athletes to sport psychologists. As Rotella and Murray (1991) note in their discussion of the ramifications of homophobia for sport psychology practice, most problem issues are brought up by heterosexual athletes. Homosexual athletes are more reluctant to trust and discuss sexual issues. Sport psychologists would do well to check themselves for homophobia or heterosexist assumptions and approach sexuality as an issue of diversity calling for education rather than therapy. As with race and other gender-related issues discussed earlier, sexuality and sexual orientation are largely socially constructed and context-dependent. Sport psychologists must look beyond the individual and immediate issue to understand and deal with diversity and gender-related issues with a social-educational approach.

A Note on Biology

Now that I've taken a giant step in the social direction, I'll drag my feet just a bit to caution that sport psychologists should not dismiss biology. Sport and exercise are physical activities. Biological factors are not unidirectional determinants of behavior, and we should not fall into the old trap of assuming that biological factors necessarily dominate or underlie social and behavioral influences. As Birke and Vines (1987) suggest, biological factors are not static and absolute, but rather are dynamic processes that can interact with social-psychological influences in varied, complex ways. Thus we should incorporate biology into our social psychological models to develop a *biopsychosocial* perspective. Consideration of physical characteristics along with related social beliefs, self-perceptions, and social processes might add insight to research on youth sport and health behavior, body image, exercise behavior, and competitive sport behavior. Now, after a lengthy discussion of the literature, let's return to the cases presented at this chapter's beginning to try to more directly tie some of this work to sport psychology practice.

INTERVENTION ISSUES AND CASE DISCUSSION

Before considering specific gender-related cases and issues, let's consider how gender affects sport psychology practice in general. Given the pervasiveness of gender influence and the inextricable linking of gender with everything we do, as illustrated by the previous review, an understanding of the gender literature is likely to lead sport psychologists to adopt more feminist or at least more enlightened nonsexist approaches.

A great deal has been written and discussed in clinical psychology about feminist approaches to practice. Psychoanalysis and other more popular current approaches have been criticized for sexist assumptions and practices. Current clinical and counseling literature typically advocates nonsexist practice, but we still find considerable gender bias in diagnosis, labeling, prescriptions, and treatment strategies (e.g., Travis, 1988; Unger & Crawford, 1992). A sizable contingent of (mostly) women in clinical psychology have moved beyond nonsexist practices to advocate more actively feminist approaches. In general, feminist practice incorporates gender scholarship, emphasizes neglected women's experiences (e.g., sexual

Courtesy University of Wisconsin Women's Sports Information

harassment), and takes a more nonhierarchical, empowering, process-oriented approach that shifts emphasis from personal change to social change. Because sport is more sexist, heterosexist, and homophobic than the larger society, I'm not optimistic that sport psychology, as a field, will turn to a feminist approach—but if some sport psychologists adopt a feminist approach, both individual athletes and sport will be better off. At the least all sport psychologists can educate themselves about gender, look beyond superficial gender differences, and stay aware of gender in the social context of their practice.

First, sport psychologists might consider gender influences on interactions with athletes. A recent special issue of the *Sport Psychologist* highlighted gender issues for female consultants working with male athletes (Yambor & Connelly, 1991), male consultants working with female athletes (Henschen, 1991), and issues for consultants working with other diverse groups. Considerable research (e.g., Hall, 1987; Tannen, 1990) indicates that gender influences communication and interaction, and this may affect sport psychology practice. For example, although we stereotype females as more talkative, men talk more, interrupt more, and take more space and dominant postures. Tannen proposes that women and men speak different languages, and that suggests special concern for cross-sex consulting. Moreover, when a male sport psychologist consults with female athletes, the situation reflects the sexual power hierarchy of society, raising further potential barriers. Sport psychologists with training in communication and interpersonal skills, as well as in gender issues, might adjust. Still, the larger world is different for female and male athletes, and gender influences both the issues athletes present and their options.

Gender influences clinical disorders, as categorized in DSM-III-R (American Psychiatric Association, 1987), because women are more likely to present certain disorders, such as anxiety and depression, whereas men are more likely to exhibit antisocial or substance-abuse disorders. The largest gender gap, by far, appears for eating disorders, with females nine times more likely than males to exhibit either anorexia or bulimia. Terry, the 16-year-old figure skater in the case study who was referred because of a possible eating disorder, is much more likely to be a female, particularly a white, middle- to upper-class adolescent female, than a male. The relevant psychology literature not only indicates that females are more likely to exhibit eating disorders, but also that body image plays a major role. Eating disorders might also pose unique concerns with athletes. Female athletes are not necessarily more prone to identified associated factors of dysfunctional family background or compulsive desire for control, but female athletes in certain sports might be more prone to body-image concerns related to appearance and performance in their sports. Indeed, many poor eating behaviors in athletes might not be clinical eating disorders but misguided attempts to improve performance. For such cases an educational approach stressing proper nutrition without discounting the athlete's understandable concern for body image might be effective. A team approach including medical and nutritional experts as well as psychologists is preferable if an athlete lacks information and critical if an athlete presents more pathological eating behaviors. Perhaps most important for feminist sport psychologists would be to educate the coach and significant others and to try to change the system that leads athletes to pursue an unhealthy body image.

The case studies of both A.J. and Chris represent cases more likely to fall in the realm of the educational sport consultant focusing on performance enhancement. Both could be either male or female, but given gender socialization and context, A.J. is more likely a male athlete who has grown up in a world that reinforces aggressive behavior. Moreover, a male athlete is more likely to continue to have such behaviors reinforced (e.g., teammates cheer; the coach encourages related behaviors only slightly less dramatic than those that draw penalties).

Chris presents a less aggressive, more tentative approach generally typical of female athletes. Even talented, competitive female athletes are socialized to keep quiet, be good, and let others take the lead. Moreover, chances are good that a female athlete will have a male coach, trainer, athletic director, and professor and that she will see males in most other power positions. To be sure, overly aggressive, uncontrolled behavior is not exclusively male, nor is a tentative style exclusively female. Still, sport psychologists will work more effectively with such athletes if they recognize gender influences in the athlete's background and situation.

Pat's case study reflects sexual harassment, an issue with clear gender connotations that's prevalent and likely to emerge yet one that's been neglected in sport psychology. Research and writing on violence toward women has expanded greatly in the past few years, and this is a major contribution of the gender scholarship to the field of psychology. Given the prevalence of sexual harassment and sexual assault (discussed in following paragraphs), especially for college women, female athletes are much more likely to present problems related to these issues than eating disorders or any other potentially clinical issues. Yet, despite the relevance of sexual harassment and assault for female athletes, and the growing related psychology work, I have seen virtually nothing in the sport psychology research or professional literature on this topic.

Recently, several studies as well as more public attention have demonstrated the prevalence of sexual harassment and assault (e.g., Matlin, 1993 or Unger & Crawford, 1992). In mid-1993 a media release reported a study on sexual harassment in Grade 8 through 11 students indicating that the majority of both boys and girls reported being harassed. Girls reported more harassment in all categories except being called gay or lesbian; however, boys reported being called gay or homosexual more often. Also, girls were much more likely to report negative emotional impact. About one third of college women report being sexually harassed, and when jokes and discriminatory remarks are included, the number goes to more than 50%. Recent work also indicates that sexual assault is much more prevalent than previously assumed, and recent attention to acquaintance rape reveals that most assaults are not committed by strangers. Koss (1990; Koss, Gidycz, & Wisniewski, 1987) has done considerable research on sexual assault, and her findings indicate that 38 of 1,000 college women experience rape or attempted rape in one year, that 85% of sexual assaults are by acquaintances, and that men and women define and interpret sexual situations and behaviors differently. All women are at risk, and no particular psychological pattern characterizes victims, although college students are more at risk and alcohol is often involved. Given that most sport psychologists work with college athletes, we should be particularly familiar with this work. Sexual harassment can be a tremendous barrier to educational and athletic achievement, and rape can be a devastating experience. Many rape victims remain anxious and depressed months later, and some experience severe substance abuse, eating disorders, major depression, or other symptoms, in some cases years later (e.g., Gordon & Riger, 1989; Koss, 1990; Murphy et al., 1988).

Although I know of no sport research, some authors have started to discuss these issues for athletes. Nelson (1991), in her aptly titled chapter "Running Scared," notes (and any woman jogger can confirm) that harassment is almost routine and expected by women runners. Women cannot run without harassment any time, any place. Lenskyj (1992) recently discussed sexual harassment in sport, drawing ties to power relations and ideology of male sports. Lenskyj notes that sexual harassment raises some unique concerns for female athletes, in addition to the concerns of all women: sport (as a nonfeminine activity) might elicit derisive comments; clothes are revealing; male coaches are often fit and conventionally attractive; female athletes might have spent much time training and less in general social activity; coaches are authoritarian and rule much of athletes' lives; for some sports, merit is equated with heterosexual attractiveness.

Of course, the gender socialization and social context that holds for everyone else also holds for athletes, and Pat is much more likely to be a female athlete harassed by a male coach than any other combination. Given that virtually no females coach male athletes, we can eliminate that, although with that combination the social male-over-female hierarchy could counter the coach-over-athlete hierarchy. Sexual harassment could occur with same-sex athletes and coaches. Writings on homophobia suggest that fears of lesbian harassment are often invoked, but reality clearly is otherwise. Overwhelmingly, sexual harassment is males harassing females, even in less gender-structured settings than sport. As Lenskyj (1992) notes, and earlier discussions of homophobia suggest, lesbians and gay men are more likely to be the targets than perpetrators of sexual harassment. Lenskyj notes that allegations of lesbianism might deter female athletes (regardless of sexual orientation) from rejecting male advances or complaining about harassment. A student in my women and sport class interviewed female coaches about lesbianism and to her surprise found the married female coach more open and willing to discuss these issues than single coaches (lesbian or heterosexual). Given the sport climate, we should not be surprised that female coaches are so worried about charges of lesbianism that they refrain from complaining about harassment or seeking equity for their programs. Sexual harassment (heterosexual or homophobic harassment) intimidates women and maintains traditional power structures.

Sexual harassment and assault have recently been brought to public attention as a concern for male athletes as well as female athletes. Recent accounts (e.g., Neimark, 1993) suggest that male athletes are particularly prone to sexual assault. These popular media reports, as well as more theoretical work (e.g., Lenskyj, 1992; Messner, 1992), suggest that male bonding, the privileged status of athletes, and the macho image of sport are contributing factors.

Pat's case probably occurs much more often than we recognize, and many athletes in Pat's situation would not discuss the problem with a sport psychologist or anyone else. Sport psychologists who are aware of the sport and gender dynamics that can lead to such situations might be quicker to recognize such issues and help athletes deal with the situation. As well as educating athletes, sport psychologists can take steps to change the situation by educating coaches and administrators. Most universities have developed counseling and educational programs on sexual harassment and assault and have established policies and procedures to deal with incidents. Sport psychologists can use these resources (e.g., refer victims, incorporate workshops) but also can develop programs targeted to athletes. As previously noted, some female athletes might be more susceptible to harassment or assault because of the situation unique to sport. Athletes often train both in isolated locations and during late hours; they also travel and might be placed in vulnerable situations more so than other students. Female athletes must be aware of sexual harassment and assault and concerns related to the particular demands of athletes.

Male athletes must also be aware of these issues, and male administrators must support such educational efforts. As Guernsey (1993) reports, several rape-prevention programs have been designed for male athletes. Such programs as those now operating at Cornell University and The University of Arkansas are supported by athletic coaches and administrators and aim to prevent the aggression needed on the field from affecting personal lives. With carefully planned programs developed with the athletic administration and relevant university resources, sport psychologists could educate female and male athletes, coaches, and others and go far toward preventing sexual harassment and assault. Again, to take a more feminist approach, sport psychologists could attempt to change the social situation as well as educate individuals—perhaps by demanding safe lighting, secure facilities, and clear, enforceable policies.

CONCLUSION

Gender makes a difference. Gender is a pervasive social force in society, and the sport world reflects in the extreme society's gender hierarchy. Gender is so ingrained in our sport structure and practice that we cannot simply treat all athletes the same. But neither can we assume that male and female athletes are dichotomous opposites and thus treat all males one way and all females another. Gender is a dynamic influence that varies with the individual, situation, and time. Sport psychologists should be aware of the many overt and subtle ways that gender affects athletes, the sport setting, and sport psychologists themselves and attempt to turn that awareness into action in their practice.

REFERENCES

Allison, M.T. (1991). Role conflict and the female athlete: Preoccupation with little grounding. *Journal of Applied Sport Psychology*, **3**, 49-60.

American Psychiatric Association. (1987). *Diagnostic and statistical manual of mental disorders* (3rd ed., rev.). Washington, DC: Author.

Ashmore, R.D. (1990). Sex, gender, and the individual. In L.A. Pervin (Ed.), *Handbook of personality theory and research* (pp. 486-526). New York: Guilford.

Bandura, A. (1977). Self-efficacy: Toward a unifying theory of behavior change. *Psychological Review*, **84**, 191-215.

Bandura, A. (1986). *Social foundations of thought and action*. Englewood Cliffs, NJ: Prentice Hall.

Bem, S.L. (1974). The measurement of psychological androgyny. *Journal of Consulting and Clinical Psychology*, **42**, 155-162.

Bem, S.L. (1978). Beyond androgyny: Some presumptuous prescriptions for a liberated sexual identity. In J. Sherman & F. Denmark (Eds.), *Psychology of women: Future directions for research* (pp. 1-23). New York: Psychological Dimensions.

Bem, S.L. (1985). Androgyny and gender schema theory: A conceptual and empirical integration. In T.B. Sonderegger (Ed.), *Nebraska Symposium on Motivation, 1984: Psychology and Gender* (pp. 179-226). Lincoln, NE: University of Nebraska Press.

Bem, S.L. (1993). *The lenses of gender*. New Haven: Yale University Press.

Bernard, J. (1981). *The female world*. New York: Free Press.

Birke, L.I.A., & Vines, G. (1987). A sporting chance: The anatomy of destiny. *Women's Studies International Forum*, **10**, 337-347.

Birrell, S.J. (1988). Discourses on the gender/sport relationship: From women in sport to gender relations. In K. Pandolf (Ed.), *Exercise and Sport Science Reviews: Vol. 16* (pp. 459-502). New York: Macmillan.

Blinde, E.M., & Greendorfer, S.L. (1992). Conflict and the college sport experience of women athletes. *Women in Sport and Physical Activity Journal*, **1**, 97-113.

Brooks, D., & Althouse, R. (1993). *Racism in college athletics: The African-American athlete's experience*. Morgantown, WV: Fitness Information Technology.

Broverman, I.K., Vogel, S.R., Broverman, D.M., Clarkson, F.E., & Rosenkrantz, P.S. (1972). Sex role stereotypes: A current appraisal. *Journal of Social Issues*, **28**, 59-78.

Brown, R.D., & Harrison, J.M. (1986). The effects of a strength training program on the strength and self-concept of two female age groups. *Research Quarterly for Exercise and Sport*, **57**, 315-320.

Carpenter, L.J., & Acosta, R.V. (1993). Back to the future: Reform with a woman's voice. In D.S. Eitzen (Ed.), *Sport in contemporary society: An anthology* (4th ed.) (pp. 388-398). New York: St. Martin's Press.

Colker, R., & Widom, C.S. (1980). Correlates of female athletic participation. *Sex Roles*, **6**, 47-53.

Condry, J., & Dyer, S. (1976). Fear of success: Attribution of cause to the victim. *Journal of Social Issues*, **32**, 63-83.

Corbett, D., & Johnson, W. (1993). The African-American female in collegiate sport: Sexism and racism. In D. Brooks & R. Althouse (Eds.), *Racism in college athletics: The African-American athlete's experience* (pp. 179-204). Morgantown, WV: Fitness Information Technology.

Corbin, C.B. (1981). Sex of subject, sex of opponent, and opponent ability as factors affecting self-confidence in a competitive situation. *Journal of Sport Psychology*, **3**, 265-270.

Corbin, C.B., Landers, D.M., Feltz, D.L., & Senior, K. (1983). Sex differences in performance estimates: Female lack of confidence vs. male boastfulness. *Research Quarterly for Exercise and Sport*, **54**, 407-410.

Corbin, C.B., & Nix, C. (1979). Sex-typing of physical activities and success predictions of children before and after cross-sex competition. *Journal of Sport Psychology*, **1**, 43-52.

Corbin, C.B., Stewart, M.J., & Blair, W.O. (1981). Self-confidence and motor performance of preadolescent boys and girls in different feedback situations. *Journal of Sport Psychology*, **3**, 30-34.

Crandall, V.C. (1969). Sex differences in expectancy of intellectual and academic reinforcement. In C.P. Smith (Ed.), *Achievement-related motives in children* (pp. 11-45). New York: Russell Sage.

Csizma, K.A., Wittig, A.F., & Schurr, K.T. (1988). Sport stereotypes and gender. *Journal of Sport & Exercise Psychology*, **10**, 62-74.

Deaux, K. (1984). From individual differences to social categories: Analysis of a decade's research on gender. *American Psychologist*, **39**, 105-116.

Deaux, K. (1985). Sex and gender. *Annual Review of Psychology*, **36**, 49-81.

Deaux, K., & Kite, M.E. (1987). Thinking about gender. In B.B. Hess & M.M. Ferree (Eds.), *Analyzing gender* (pp. 92-117). Beverly Hills, CA: Sage.

Deaux, K., & Lewis, L.L. (1984). The structure of gender stereotypes: Interrelationships among components and gender label. *Journal of Personality and Social Psychology*, **46**, 991-1004.

Deaux, K., & Major, B. (1987). Putting gender into context: An interactive model of gender-related behavior. *Psychological Review*, **94**, 369-389.

Del Rey, P. (1978). The apologetic and women in sport. In C. Oglesby (Ed.), *Women and sport: From myth to reality* (pp. 107-111). Philadelphia: Lea & Febiger.

Del Rey, P., & Sheppard, S. (1981). Relationship of psychological androgyny in female athletes to self-esteem. *International Journal of Sport Psychology*, **12**, 165-175.

Dewar, A.M. (1987). The social construction of gender in physical education. *Women's Studies International Forum*, **10**, 453-465.

Duda, J.L. (1986). A cross-cultural analysis of achievement motivation in sport and the classroom. In L. VanderVelden & J. Humphrey (Eds.), *Current selected research in the psychology and sociology of sport* (pp. 115-132). New York: AMS Press.

Duda, J.L. (1991). Editorial comment: Perspectives on gender roles in physical activity. *Journal of Applied Sport Psychology*, **3**, 1-6.

Duda, J.L., & Allison, M.T. (1990). Cross-cultural analysis in exercise and sport psychology: A void in the field. *Journal of Sport & Exercise Psychology*, **12**, 114-131.

Eagley, A.H. (1987). *Sex differences in social behavior: A social-role interpretation*. Hillsdale, NJ: Erlbaum.

Eagley, A.H., & Kite, M.E. (1987). Are stereotypes of nationalities applied to both women and men? *Journal of Personality and Social Psychology*, **53**, 451-462.

Eccles, J.S. (1985). Sex differences in achievement patterns. In T. Sonderegger (Ed.), *Nebraska Symposium of Motivation, 1984: Psychology and Gender* (pp. 97-132). Lincoln, NE: University of Nebraska Press.

Eccles, J.S. (1987). Gender roles and women's achievement-related decisions. *Psychology of Women Quarterly*, **11**, 135-172.

Eccles, J.S., Adler, T.F., Futterman, R., Goff, S.B., Kaczala, C.M., Meece, J.L., & Midgley, C. (1983). Expectations, values and academic behaviors. In J. Spence

(Ed.), *Achievement and achievement motives* (pp. 75-146). San Francisco: Freeman.

Eccles, J.S., & Harold, R.D. (1991). Gender differences in sport involvement: Applying the Eccles expectancy-value model. *Journal of Applied Sport Psychology*, **3**, 7-35.

Eitzen, D.S., & Baca Zinn, M. (1993). The deathleticization of women: The naming and gender marking of collegiate sports teams. In D.S. Eitzen (Ed.), *Sport in contemporary society: An anthology* (4th ed.) (pp. 396-405). New York: St. Martin's Press.

Feltz, D.L. (1988). Self-confidence and sports performance. In K. Pandolf (Ed.), *Exercise and Sport Sciences Reviews: Vol. 16* (pp. 423-457). New York: Macmillan.

Gibson, A. (1979). I always wanted to be somebody. In S.L. Twin (Ed.), *Out of the bleachers* (pp. 130-142). Old Westbury, NY: Feminist Press.

Gill, D.L. (1988). Gender differences in competitive orientation and sport participation. *International Journal of Sport Psychology*, **19**, 145-159.

Gill, D.L. (1992a). Gender and sport behavior. In T.S. Horn (Ed.), *Advances in sport psychology* (pp. 143-160). Champaign, IL: Human Kinetics.

Gill, D.L. (1992b). Status of the *Journal of Sport & Exercise Psychology*, 1985-1990. *Journal of Sport & Exercise Psychology*, **14**, 1-12.

Gill, D.L. (1993). Competitiveness and competitive orientation in sport. In R.N. Singer, M. Murphey, & L.K. Tennant (Eds.), *Handbook on research in sport psychology* (pp. 314-327). New York: Macmillan.

Gill, D.L., & Deeter, T.E. (1988). Development of the Sport Orientation Questionnaire. *Research Quarterly for Exercise and Sport*, **59**, 191-202.

Gill, D.L., & Dzewaltowski, D.A. (1988). Competitive orientations among intercollegiate athletes: Is winning the only thing? *Sport Psychologist*, **2**, 212-221.

Gill, D.L., Gross, J.B., Huddleston, S., & Shifflett, B. (1984). Sex differences in achievement cognitions and performance in competition. *Research Quarterly for Exercise and Sport*, **55**, 340-346.

Goldberg, P. (1968). Are women prejudiced against women? *Transaction*, **5**, 28-30.

Gordon, M.T., & Riger, S. (1989). *The female fear: The social cost of rape*. New York: Free Press.

Green, T.S. (1993). The future of African-American female athletes. In D. Brooks & R. Althouse (Eds.), *Racism in college athletics: The African-American athlete's experience* (pp. 205-223). Morgantown, WV: Fitness Information Technology.

Greendorfer, S.L. (1987). Gender bias in theoretical perspectives: The case of female socialization into sport. *Psychology of Women Quarterly*, **11**, 327-340.

Griffin, P.S. (1987, August). *Homophobia, lesbians, and women's sports: An exploratory analysis*. Paper presented at the APA convention, New York.

Griffin, P. (1992). Changing the game: Homophobia, sexism, and lesbians in sport. *Quest*, **44**, 251-265.

Guernsey, L. (1993, February 10). More campuses offer rape-prevention programs for male athletes. *Chronicle of Higher Education*, pp. A35, A37.

Hall, J.A. (1987). On explaining sex differences: The case of nonverbal communication. In P. Shaver & C. Hendrick (Eds.), *Sex and gender* (pp. 177-200). Newbury Park, CA: Sage.

Hall, M.A. (1988). The discourse of gender and sport: From femininity to feminism. *Sociology of Sport Journal*, **5**, 330-340.

Hall, M.A. (1990). How should we theorize gender in the context of sport? In M.A. Messner & D.F. Sabo (Eds.), *Sport, men, and the gender order* (pp. 223-239). Champaign, IL: Human Kinetics.

Harris, D.V. (1980). Femininity and athleticism: Conflict of consonance? In D.F. Sabo & R. Runfola (Eds.), *Jock: Sports and male identity* (pp. 222-239). Englewood Cliffs, NJ: Prentice Hall.

Harris, D.V., & Jennings, S.E. (1977). Self-perceptions of female distance runners. *Annals of the New York Academy of Sciences*, **301**, 808-815.

Helmreich, R.L., & Spence, J.T. (1977). Sex roles and achievement. In R.W. Christina & D.M. Landers (Eds.), *Psychology of motor behavior and sport—1976: Vol. 2* (pp. 33-46). Champaign, IL: Human Kinetics.

Henschen, K. (1991). Critical issues involving male consultants and female athletes. *Sport Psychologist*, **5**, 313-321.

Holloway, J.B., Beuter, A., & Duda, J.L. (1988). Self-efficacy and training for strength in adolescent girls. *Journal of Applied Social Psychology*, **18**, 699-719.

Horner, M.S. (1972). Toward an understanding of achievement-related conflicts in women. *Journal of Social Issues*, **28**, 157-176.

Hyde, J.S., & Linn, M.C. (Eds.) (1986). *The psychology of gender: Advances through meta-analysis*. Baltimore: Johns Hopkins University Press.

Jacklin, C.N. (1989). Female and male: Issues of gender. *American Psychologist*, **44**, 127-133.

Kane, M.J. (1989). The post Title IX female athlete in the media. *Journal of Physical Education, Recreation and Dance*, **60**(3), 58-62.

Kane, M.J., & Parks, J.B. (1992). The social construction of gender difference and hierarchy in sport journalism—Few new twists on very old themes. *Women in Sport & Physical Activity Journal*, **1**, 49-83.

Kane, M.J., & Snyder, E. (1989). Sport typing: The social "containment" of women. *Arena Review*, **13**, 77-96.

Koss, M.P. (1990). The women's mental health research agenda. *American Psychologist*, **45**, 374-380.

Koss, M.P., Gidycz, C.A., & Wisniewski, N. (1987). The scope of rape: Incidence and prevalence of sexual aggression and victimization in a national sample of higher education students. *Journal of Consulting and Clinical Psychology*, **55**, 162-170.

Lenney, E. (1977). Women's self-confidence in achievement settings. *Psychological Bulletin*, **84**, 1-13.

Lenskyj, H. (1986). *Out of bounds: Women, sport and sexuality*. Toronto: Women's Press.

Lenskyj, H. (1991). Combatting homophobia in sport and physical education. *Sociology of Sport Journal*, **8**, 61-69.

Lenskyj, H. (1992). Unsafe at home base: Women's experiences of sexual harassment in university sport and physical education. *Women in Sport & Physical Activity Journal*, **1**, 19-33.

Locksley, A., & Colten, M.E. (1979). Psychological androgyny: A case of mistaken identity? *Journal of Personality and Social Psychology*, **37**, 1017-1031.

Maccoby, E.E. (1990). Gender and relationships. *American Psychologist*, **45**, 513-520.

Maccoby, E., & Jacklin, C. (1974). *The psychology of sex differences*. Stanford, CA: Stanford University Press.

Majors, R. (1990). Cool pose: Black masculinity and sports. In M.A. Messner & D.F. Sabo (Eds.), *Sport, men, and the gender order* (pp. 109-114). Champaign, IL: Human Kinetics.

Matlin, M.W. (1993). *The psychology of women* (2nd ed.). Fort Worth: Harcourt Brace Jovanovich.

Matteo, S. (1986). The effect of sex and gender-schematic processing on sport participation. *Sex Roles*, **15**, 417-432.

Matteo, S. (1988). The effect of gender-schematic processing on decisions about sex-inappropriate sport behavior. *Sex Roles*, **18**, 41-58.

McClelland, D.C., Atkinson, J.W., Clark, R.A., & Lowell, E.C. (1953). *The achievement motive*. New York: Appleton-Century-Crofts.

McElroy, M.A., & Willis, J.D. (1979). Women and the achievement conflict in sport: A preliminary study. *Journal of Sport Psychology*, **1**, 241-247.

McNally, J., & Orlick, T. (1975). Cooperative sport structures: A preliminary analysis. *Mouvement*, **7**, 267-271.

Melpomene Institute. (1990). *The bodywise woman*. Champaign, IL: Human Kinetics.

Messner, M.A. (1992). *Power at play: Sports and the problem of masculinity*. Boston: Beacon Press.

Messner, M.A., Duncan, M.C., & Jensen, K. (1993). Separating the men from the girls: The gendered language of televised sports. In D.S. Eitzen (Ed.), *Sport in contemporary society: An anthology* (4th ed.) (pp. 219-233). New York: St. Martin's Press.

Messner, M.A., & Sabo, D.F. (1990). *Sport, men, and the gender order*. Champaign, IL: Human Kinetics.

Metheny, E. (1965). Symbolic forms of movement: The feminine image in sports. In E. Metheny (Ed.), *Connotations of movement in sport and dance* (pp. 43-56). Dubuque, IA: Brown.

Murphy, S.M., Kilpatrick, D.G., Amick-McMullen, A., Veronen, L., Best, C.L., Villeponteaux, L.A., & Saunders, B.E. (1988). Current psychological functioning of child sexual assault survivors: A community study. *Journal of Interpersonal Violence*, **3**, 55-79.

Myers, A.E., & Lips, H.M. (1978). Participation in competitive amateur sports as a function of psychological androgyny. *Sex Roles*, **4**, 571-578.

Neimark, J. (1993). Out of bounds: The truth about athletes and rape. In D.S. Eitzen (Ed.), *Sport in contemporary society: An anthology* (4th ed.) (pp. 130-137). New York: St. Martin's Press.

Nelson, M.B. (1991). *Are we winning yet: How women are changing sports and sports are changing women*. New York: Random House.

Nyad, D. (1978). *Other shores*. New York: Random House.

Parkhouse, B.L., & Williams, J.M. (1986). Differential effects of sex and status on evaluation of coaching ability. *Research Quarterly for Exercise and Sport*, **57**, 53-59.

Pedhazur, E.J., & Tetenbaum, T.J. (1979). BSRI: A theoretical and methodological critique. *Journal of Personality and Social Psychology*, **37**, 996-1016.

Petruzzello, S.J., & Corbin, C.B. (1988). The effects of performance feedback on female self-confidence. *Journal of Sport & Exercise Psychology*, **10**, 174-183.

Pheterson, G.I., Kiesler, S.B., & Goldberg, P.A. (1971). Evaluation of the performance of women as a function of their sex, achievement, and personal history. *Journal of Personality and Social Psychology*, **19**, 114-118.

Ponger, B. (1990). Gay jocks: A phenomenology of gay men in athletics. In M.A. Messner & D.F. Sabo (Eds.), *Sport, men, and the gender order* (pp. 141-152). Champaign, IL: Human Kinetics.

Rodin, J., Silberstein, L., & Streigel-Moore, R. (1985). Women and weight: A normative discontent. In T.B. Sonderegger (Eds.), *Nebraska Symposium on Motivation, 1984: Psychology and Gender* (pp. 267-307). Lincoln, NE: University of Nebraska Press.

Rosenkrantz, P., Vogel, S., Bee, H., Broverman, I., & Broverman, D.M. (1968). Sex-role stereotypes and self-concepts in college students. *Journal of Consulting and Clinical Psychology*, **32**, 286-295.

Rotella, R.J., & Murray, M. (1991). Homophobia, the world of sport, and sport psychology consulting. *Sport Psychologist*, **5**, 355-364.

Safrit, M.J. (1984). Women in research in physical education: A 1984 update. *Quest*, **36**, 104-114.

Sherif, C.W. (1976). The social context of competition. In D. Landers (Ed.), *Social problems in athletics* (pp. 18-36). Champaign, IL: Human Kinetics.

Sherif, C.W. (1982). Needed concepts in the study of gender identity. *Psychology of Women Quarterly*, **6**, 375-398.

Smith, Y.R. (1992). Women of color in society and sport. *Quest*, **44**, 228-250.

Solomon, A. (1991, March 20). Passing game. *Village Voice*, p. 92.

Spears, B. (1978). Prologue: The myth. In C. Oglesby (Ed.), *Women in sport: From myth to reality* (pp. 3-15). Philadelphia: Lea & Febiger.

Spence, J.T., & Helmreich, R.L. (1978). *Masculinity and femininity*. Austin, TX: University of Texas Press.

Spence, J.T., & Helmreich, R.L. (1983). Achievement-related motives and behaviors. In J.T. Spence (Ed.), *Achievement and achievement motives: Psychological and sociological approaches* (pp. 7-74). San Francisco: Freeman.

Stewart, M.J., & Corbin, C.B. (1988). Feedback dependence among low confidence preadolescent boys and girls. *Research Quarterly for Exercise and Sport*, **59**, 160-164.

Tannen, D. (1990). *You just don't understand*. New York: Morrow.

Taylor, M.C., & Hall, J.A. (1982). Psychological androgyny: Theories, methods and conclusions. *Psychological Bulletin*, **92**, 347-366.

Theberge, N. (1987). Sport and women's empowerment. *Women's Studies International Forum*, **10**, 387-393.

Travis, C.B. (1988). *Women and health psychology: Mental health issues*. Hillsdale, NJ: Erlbaum.

Tresemer, D.W. (1977). *Fear of success*. New York: Plenum Press.

Trujillo, C. (1983). The effect of weight training and running exercise intervention on the self-esteem of college women. *International Journal of Sport Psychology*, **14**, 162-173.

Uhlir, G.A. (1987). Athletics and the university: The post-women's era. *Academe*, **73**, 25-29.

Unger, R., & Crawford, M. (1992). *Women and gender: A feminist psychology*. New York: McGraw-Hill.

Wallston, B.S., & O'Leary, V.E. (1981). Sex and gender make a difference: The differential perceptions of women and men. *Review of Personality and Social Psychology*, **2**, 9-41.

Weinberg, R.S., & Jackson, A. (1979). Competition and extrinsic rewards: Effect on intrinsic motivation. *Research Quarterly*, **50**, 494-502.

Weinberg, R.S., & Ragan, J. (1979). Effects of competition, success/failure, and sex on intrinsic motivation. *Research Quarterly*, **50**, 503-510.

Weinberg, R., Reveles, M., & Jackson, A. (1984). Attitudes of male and female athletes toward male and female coaches. *Journal of Sport Psychology*, **6**, 448-453.

Wells, C.L. (1991). *Women, sport, and performance: A physiological perspective* (2nd ed.). Champaign, IL: Human Kinetics.

Williams, J.M., & Parkhouse, B.L. (1988). Social learning theory as a foundation for examining sex bias in evaluation of coaches. *Journal of Sport & Exercise Psychology*, **10**, 322-333.

Yambor, J., & Connelly, D. (1991). Issues confronting female sport psychology consultants working with male student-athletes. *Sport Psychologist*, **5**, 304-312.

CHAPTER 10

CONSULTATIONS WITH SPORT ORGANIZATIONS: A COGNITIVE-BEHAVIORAL MODEL

Frank Perna, EdD, Megan Neyer, PhD, Shane M. Murphy, PhD
United States Olympic Committee
Bruce C. Ogilvie, PhD
Los Gatos, California
Annemarie Murphy, PhD
AimCare Clinic, Colorado

The psychology professional wishing to consult for a sport organization faces an often daunting and confusing task. There are few areas where psychological consultation presents the challenges that are to be found in the sport world. The goal of this chapter is to describe a process that clarifies the consultation role with a sport organization and offers a model of consultancy that has proven effective in a variety of situations.

As Gardner points out in chapter 6 of this book, one of the principal challenges that often faces the potential sport psychology consultant is an unfamiliarity with the milieu of the professional sport world (see also Ravizza, 1990). Typically, sport psychology consultants have come from academic institutions and clinical settings but are asked to function in a business atmosphere. Also, members of the professional sport world are not accustomed to having psychologists, psychiatrists, or educators interact with their teams on an ongoing basis. Thus the partners in the prospective consultation relationship are unfamiliar with their respective roles, responsibilities, and generally accepted rules of interaction. This unfamiliarity can contribute to mutual uncertainty and the potential for a perceived lack of consultant credibility. This chapter emphasizes that a critical aspect of all sport consultations is the process of clarifying expectations on the part of clients, so that consultation can proceed with both parties agreeing on the criteria by which the efficacy of consultation will be evaluated.

At present, no standard model exists to guide interactions between professional sport teams and the sport psychology consultant (McKelvain, 1988). However, it is crucial for consultants to develop a philosophy of service delivery defining the scope of practice, structure of interaction, and professional limits. By addressing these issues consultants will be in a better position to decrease ambiguity and to clarify expectations of consultation. This chapter presents the currently prominent philosophies and approaches of sport psychology consultation, identifies critical issues in the sport consultation process, presents a comprehensive cognitive-behavioral model for consultation in sport psychology, and demonstrates the model through a case-study illustration.

■ *THE CASE OF LI-WU* ■

Li-Wu is a 16-year-old elite gymnast. At the end of the last competitive season, Li-Wu was seriously injured while performing on the vault. Her hands slipped on the horse, and she landed on her neck, causing a minor concussion and temporary numbness throughout her body. She was removed from the competition site on a backboard and taken to the hospital, where she was admitted for neurological testing and observation. It was determined that she had sprained ligaments and strained muscles in the cervical region of the spinal cord. Li-Wu was instructed to take a month off from gymnastics and report for injury rehabilitation three times a week.

After diligently following the prescribed regime of the sports medicine team for 2 months, Li-Wu was permitted to return to full training. Although she seemed to be progressing well with the floor exercise and with her difficult moves on the uneven bars and the balance beam, it was clear she was reluctant to attempt her difficult vaulting exercises. Li-Wu was frustrated with herself; she was unable to manage her fear of vaulting and considered quitting gymnastics. At this point she was referred to a sport psychology consultant by her coach.

CHOOSING A CONSULTATION MODEL

Two important questions must be answered in choosing a consultation model that will best fit the philosophy and training of the consultant: (a) Who is the client? and (b) What services are provided? Identifying the client clarifies the consultant's primary allegiance, which in turn determines the limits of confidentiality existing in the consultation relationship. Deciding which services will be offered clarifies expectations and helps define the boundaries of the consultation relationship. Leading sport psychology consultants vary in their opinions both as to whom they view as the primary client and as to the scope of services they provide to professional and elite sport organizations (see the December 1990 special issue of the *Sport Psychologist*). The consultant must decide these issues prior to initial contact with the sport organization. By comprehensively answering these initial questions, the consultant is in the best position to clarify client expectations.

Identifying the Client

The primary client potentially includes the coach(es), general manager, sports medicine staff, athletes, and parents (in situations where the athlete is a minor). Unlike in some other consulting relationships, the party requesting and paying for services is not necessarily the client. The sport organization typically pays the consultant's salary, although, as will be seen, the sport organization is often not the client in the consulting relationship (Biddle, Bull, & Seheult, 1992). This situation most closely resembles one that often exists in corporate settings, where the corporation pays for the consultant's services but the employees are the primary clients.

Although the range of potential clients is wide, the essential decision is to identify the athlete(s) or a member of the sport organization as the primary client. Defining the primary client is essential for two reasons.

- For psychologists, legal and professional obligations regarding limits of confidentiality are determined by the client's identity.
- Defining the client is essential for clarifying expectations and the professional role of the consultant with the sport organization.

One potential model is that all services, decisions, and interventions must first be processed with the head coach, thus defining a sport organization official as the primary client (Ogilvie, 1977). Ogilvie contends that the commitment to the head coach can be maintained without diminishing the professional responsibilities to others in the organization. Adherence to this model places the consultant in the role of deciding what information will or will not be shared about interactions with players. This model also carries the expectation that coaches and management are privy to discussions and information pertaining to the athlete. In this model the consultant has the burden of notifying the athlete that a coach or team official might request information from the consultant (e.g., case summaries and test result interpretations). Operating from this philosophy, the consultant might more readily be granted access to players but might not find athletes to be totally forthcoming.

Other consultants view the athlete(s) as the primary client and seek assurances from coaches and management that the consultant will not be expected to disclose information without the athlete's permission (Ravizza, 1990; Rotella, 1990). The materials (e.g., notes or test results) derived from consultation are the property of the athlete rather than the organization. A subtle but important shift from the first model has occurred that directly influences the services that ethically can be offered. For example, testing or interview

Courtesy USOC

information regarding an athlete ethically could not be provided to the organization unless an athlete releases the information. To facilitate the strongest client-consultant bond, some consultants who identify the athlete as the primary client either specify that they will not become involved in player selection (Rotella) or clarify the conditions by which athlete information can be released.

When working with adult athletes the consultant has a choice in specifying who is the primary client, the athlete or an outside agent (e.g., coach or management). However, in cases where the athlete is a minor, consultant psychologists are obligated to obtain permission from parents, who are the legal clients, since minors are legally incapable of providing informed consent (American Psychological Association, 1990). In this situation another shift in the right to information has occurred. When working with minors, the consultant psychologist is obligated to protect the minor's best interests; however, case summaries and written test interpretations must be provided to parents on request.

Three important points emerge from a discussion of identifying the client in sport psychology consultation.

- Identifying the primary client in the consultation process determines the flow of information and concomitantly restricts the range of services that may be ethically provided.
- The consultant has a responsibility to communicate to sport organization officials and to athletes at the outset the conditions of consultation. By clarifying client status and limits of service delivery, consultants can avoid misperceptions as well as provide guidelines to direct behavior. For example, the sport organization, having been provided a clear statement of what to expect from the consultant, may not expect nor ask for confidential player information; thus the consultant and the sport organization are saved from potentially awkward situations.
- Although recent debate continues regarding appropriate practice requirements of sport psychology consultants (Anshel, 1992; Gardner, 1991; Silva, 1989; Zaichkowsky & Perna, 1992), consultants who are psychologists have clear legal and professional responsibilities. Sport psychology consultants who are psychologists must align their consultation practice to conform with state licensing and American Psychological Association guidelines (Gardner). It appears, however, that non-psychologist-consultants will also be encouraged by major sport psychology bodies such as the Association for the Advancement of Applied Sport Psychology (AAASP) to incorporate APA ethical guidelines into their practice.

Consultation Models

Four models of consultation are examined in this section: educational, clinical, supervisory, and cognitive-behavioral.

The Educational Consultation Model

Educational approaches to sport psychology consultation conceptualize the purpose of consultation as optimizing the use of mental skills by the athlete client (Botterill, 1990; Halliwell, 1990; LaRose, 1988; Loehr, 1990; McKelvain, 1988; Ravizza, 1990; Rotella, 1990). This approach seeks to teach people how to further develop existing skills or to teach athletes new skills appropriate for managing performance in competition. Frequently used mental skills in training or actual competition include goal-setting strategies, arousal control techniques, visualization procedures, attention and refocusing training, and cognitive restructuring (self-talk). A typical consultation might include a series of group presentations by the consultant, who explains and demonstrates the potential of mental-skills training, followed by individual conferences, on request, with athletes and coaches. Crucial to the educational approach is the sport specificity of examples and an explanation of how skills can be applied in a competitive pressure situation or built into a precompetitive routine (Ravizza, 1988). Additionally, LaRose (1988) highlights that the success of the educational approach with athletes largely hinges on reinforcement of techniques by coaches. That is, although some success might accrue to athletes using mental-skills training, maximal benefit occurs when coaches become thoroughly versed in and reinforce the use and development of these skills in the practice setting.

The educational approach requires the consultant to spend considerable time at the practice field observing situations and implementing on-the-spot interventions. Ravizza (1988) comments that immediate interventions and visibility of the consultant on the field hastens rapport, facilitates "teachable moments," and lowers barriers to effective consultation.

The Clinical Consultation Model

The clinical approach to consultation (Dorfman, 1990; Neff, 1990; Nideffer, 1981; Ogilvie, 1979), in contrast to the educational approach, focuses on the special stressors affecting athletes in elite sports and does not automatically assume that athletes possess all the coping resources necessary to deal with these. The clinical consultation model involves interventions designed to help athletes function more effectively in their special roles and can involve interventions at the organizational, team, or individual level. However, interventions at the individual level have most commonly been described in the literature (Murphy, 1988; Murphy and Ferrante, 1989). In the clinical approach, the organization often approaches the consultant with a specific issue, and the consultant's main task is to assess the problem and recommend a solution (McKelvain, 1988).

The clinical model stresses that cost effectiveness is the standard by which all services are measured in professional and elite sport (Ogilvie, 1992; Ravizza, 1988, 1990; Rotella, 1990). Some clinical consultants contend that identifying athletes with serious emotional reactions that could intrude upon their performance is the service most valued by the elite sport organization (Ogilvie, 1992). Consultants using the clinical approach argue that early recognition and design of an appropriate support system for the athlete is a service that receives high priority and increases the consultant's credibility with players and management, because these services are intended to prevent loss of talent that was acquired at considerable cost to the organization.

Dorfman (1990) draws an analogy between traditional employee assistance programs (EAP) and his clinical consulting approach with professional sports teams. In an employee assistance program, direct services are offered, but the consultant's primary role is to provide diagnostic services and coordinate appropriate interventions. Dorfman suggests offering a range of services to the team, including traditional diagnostic assessment and mental-skills training as well as educational presentations. However, assessment and intervention-planning skills are highlighted as those most valued by organizations.

Consultants using the clinical approach can function in a manner similar to their educational colleagues, operating from an outreach perspective and maintaining frequent contact with the team throughout the preseason and the regular season. It is also possible to use a consultation approach that is more typical of mainstream clinical psychology, involving a very low profile with the team and serving primarily as a referral source for athletes identified as needing services. In either mode the consultant must determine whether a performance problem is confined to the athletic field or also affects other life spheres. When problems occur, clinical consultants might intervene directly, but they often refer when long-term or inpatient treatment is required, such as for substance abuse counseling and eating disorders. The consultant then assumes the role of liaison between the sport organization and the primary treatment provider (Thompson & Sherman, 1993). Depending on training, it is possible for educational consultants to also perform liaison functions. However, identification and management of clinical concerns is not the primary focus of consultation, and some consultants who use the educational model specify at the outset that they will not become involved in any clinical matters (Rotella, 1990).

As a caution, consultants wishing to use the clinical approach with elite sports teams should be aware that the clinical approach has been criticized by clinical as well as educational consultants as being at times inappropriate and contributing to a negative stereotype of sport psychology (Halliwell, 1990; Murphy & Murphy, 1992; Rotella, 1990; Smith & Johnson, 1990). Additionally, Ravizza (1988) and Gordon (1990) have claimed that even identifying oneself as a clinical consultant raises barriers to effective consultation with elite sport organizations.

The Supervisory Consultation Model

A third approach used with competitive sports teams involves the consultant acting as a supervisor to a staff member of the organization (Smith & Johnson, 1990). In this paradigm, the consultant and the management officers of the team select a trainee—ideally a former player or coach with a counseling background in the organization—to receive specific training and ongoing supervision from the consultant. Although the consultant initially spends a large block of time on-site teaching and demonstrating mental-skills training applications to the trainee, the consultant steadily decreases on-site involvement with the team. The trainee, however, maintains regular contact with the supervisor and daily contact with the team.

The supervisory approach addresses many of the barriers that arise for a consultant initially gaining access to the sport organization (Ravizza, 1988). Because trainees are selected from existing sport organization personnel, they have sport-specific experiences to draw on and understand the political climate of the team environment. Smith and Johnson (1990) recommend that the trainee be instructed in a cognitive-behavioral orientation to counseling that meshes well with an educational-skills-building approach.

The supervisory model is an appealing consultation approach offering many benefits to the sport organization as well as minimizing potential barriers to effective entry and intervention. However, few teams have available potential trainees with adequate counseling or sport-science backgrounds to receive supervision. In addition, those trainees who have the requisite background might not wish to change their current status with the team. Trainees who do make a shift into a sport-psychology role with their teams might find difficult the adjustment to new roles and changing relationships with players and coaches.

The Cognitive-Behavioral Consultation Model

Murphy and Murphy (1992) have outlined a comprehensive eight-step cognitive-behavioral consultation model that they use to structure initial contacts and subsequent interactions with the national governing bodies or administrative organizations of various sports. Murphy and Murphy highlight the importance of the initial contact with the sport organization. The primary objective of the initial contact is to determine if consultation is desirable and possible and to derive an agreement outlining consultation parameters. Coaches' and athletes' needs and expectations are identified before beginning consultation, and the philosophy of the cognitive-behavioral model is explained to the client. Murphy and Murphy recommend drawing up a contract that specifies client and consultant behaviors and expectations and includes a prearranged evaluation meeting after a specified period to determine if consultation should be continued.

The cognitive-behavioral consultation model espouses an educational approach with a focus on mental-skills training; however, evaluation and assessment of the athlete's functioning in multiple contexts is crucial. An emphasis is placed on viewing the athlete as a person, not just a performer, and assessments of the athlete's functioning in sport, in relationships, and in work and academic settings are all part of a comprehensive evaluation. A comprehensive view of the athlete's experience is emphasized.

The cognitive-behavioral model represents a hybrid of the educational and clinical approaches. Assessment, diagnosis of problems, and intervention planning, characteristic functions of a clinical approach, figure prominently. Sport familiarization and mental-skills training—elements of an educational approach—are also key characteristics of the cognitive-behavioral approach. Essential to the consulting process is establishing a "collaborative empiricism" so that the athlete and consultant (or coach and consultant) experience assessment as a process in which they are involved rather than one in which they are passive. The assessment process is focused primarily on determining the pertinence of specific mental skills to the sport situation, the mastery level of mental skills, the use of skills, and obstacles that interfere with the use of mental skills. The assessment and evaluation process drives interventions that are carried out in both group and individual settings.

Athletes and coaches supply data regarding both baseline and postintervention functioning; therefore, they determine their needs and evaluate the efficacy of interventions. Furthermore, there is no assumption of pathology. Collaborative assessment helps athletes and coaches identify specific areas that they determine would benefit from improvement.

The eight steps of the Murphy and Murphy (1992) model are

1. consultation orientation,
2. sport familiarization,
3. evaluation and assessment,
4. goal identification,
5. group intervention,
6. individual intervention,
7. outcome evaluation, and
8. reassessment of goals.

These steps are presented here in some detail to help professionals working in a sport setting or with athletic populations. A great amount of trial-and-error learning has gone into the development of this model, and it is hoped that the suggestions that are offered will help others avoid making some of the mistakes made in developing the model. Figures 10.1 through 10.8 present the cognitive-behavioral model in an easily accessible graphic manner. In each step, the objective of that phase of consultation is described, followed by a list of bullet points describing the methods developed to reach that objective.

A CONSULTATION PROCESS FOR LI-WU

A comprehensive description follows of a consultation process for Li-Wu using the cognitive-behavioral model. This case is presented in sufficient detail to clarify the issues and steps involved in working with an athlete in the framework of the cognitive-behavioral

Objective

To determine if consultation is desirable and possible; to come up with an agreement outlining the parameters of the consultation

Methods

- Set up initial meeting with coach; determine coach's expectations; clarify nature of consultation relationship
- Meet with athlete and determine athlete's wants and needs; is consultation appropriate?
- Meet with appropriate parties; explain philosophy and approach; set realistic expectations
- Set up preliminary contract specifying only *parameters* of the consultation. Specify
  - Goals of consultation
  - Amount and length of consultation (suggest evaluation of progress after a specific time)
  - Payment

Figure 10.1 Step 1. Consultation orientation.

Objective

To become familiar with athlete's sport so effective communication is possible; to identify key sport-specific factors impacting athlete's performance

Methods

- Attend practices and competitions to learn about sport and build trust with athlete
- Ask many questions; don't let technical details go over your head
- Talk to athlete; ask athlete to explain the sport
- Read up on athlete's sport (both technical and historical details will aid in consultation)
- Try out athlete's sport yourself; if possible, participate in an event to learn about performance demands but don't become a fan to clients
- Go to a competition; talk to competitors (other than clients)

Figure 10.2 Step 2. Sport familiarization.

model described above. The case material has been altered to represent a composite person.

Assessment of Li-Wu

The BASIC ID format (see Figure 10.3), designed by Lazarus (1981), was used to evaluate Li-Wu to determine the most effective intervention plan. Following is a description of the assessment in each of the key component areas.

Behavior

An examination of Li-Wu's behaviors revealed an absence of vaulting behavior during her practice sessions. In particular, it was noted that she avoided her difficult vaulting skills, such as the one that resulted in her injury. Instead, she spent more time practicing other events.

Affect

Li-Wu's affect included anxiety, frustration, fear, anger, and a loss of pleasure in activities that previously produced enjoyment. Li-Wu was administered the Competitive State Anxiety Inventory-2 (CSAI-2) (Martens, Burton, Vealey, Bump, & Smith, 1990) to assess the dimensions of her anxiety. Although the results indicated she was experiencing high levels of cognitive and somatic anxiety, it was determined that most of Li-Wu's anxiety originated in cognitive concerns.

Sensations

Li-Wu reported experiencing nervousness, sweaty palms (a particular concern given the

Objective

To obtain all information necessary to identify

- Key mental skills for sport
- Reasons for performance blocks
- Potential intervention targets

Methods

Assess		*By*
B	Behavior (performance)	Self-report, observation, video
A	Affect	Self-report, observation, testing
S	Sensations (attentional focus)	Self-report, testing, self-monitoring
I	Imagery	Self-report, testing, guided imagery
C	Cognitions (self-talk)	Self-report, self-monitoring, video (watch with client)
I	Interpersonal (coach, team, family)	Self-report, interviews
D	Drugs (training, diet)	Self-report, medical evaluation

Testing Instruments

SAS: Trait anxiety scale (Smith, Smoll, & Schutz, 1990)

CSAI-2: State anxiety scale (Martens et al., 1990)

SIMS: Sports inventory of mental skills (Murphy, Hardy, Thomas, & Bond, 1993)

POMS: State emotional inventory (McNair, Lorr, & Droppleman, 1971)

Note. In Step 3, Lazarus's (1981) BASIC-ID assessment paradigm has been adopted for sport settings and guides the evaluation process.

Figure 10.3 Step 3. Evaluation and assessment.

circumstances of her accident), feeling "sick to her stomach," and an inability to focus her attention. An interview revealed that Li-Wu did not believe she had the confidence or correct frame of mind to perform on the vaulting apparatus.

Imagery

Li-Wu's imaging involved seeing herself slip and land on her neck again. Although she had tried to visualize herself successfully completing the vault, she was unable to do so.

Cognitions

Li-Wu's self-talk was dominated by negative beliefs about herself, her abilities, her future as an Olympian, and specifically her ability to complete the vaulting routine that resulted in her injury. For example, she reported she was "certain" she could not perform the vault and that there was "no way" she could make the Olympic team.

Interpersonal

Li-Wu and her coach reported having a positive working relationship. However, Li-Wu

Objective

To identify in specific terms the nature of the mental–performance relationship; to suggest specific interventions based on this analysis to improve athlete's coping skills

Methods

- For team education
  - Describe key mental skills for sport
  - Identify interventions to enhance skills
  - Generate curriculum; explain key skills and set agenda for how relevant techniques will be taught
- For individual consults
  - Generate summary of athlete's current mental strategies; identify strengths and weaknesses
  - Identify the critical areas appropriate for intervention
  - Map out the mental–performance relationship in detail for critical areas
  - Devise plans for improving athlete's coping skills in weak areas; use athlete's strengths if possible; identify intervention techniques, using approaches taught in group sessions
  - Discuss plans with athlete: get feedback from the athlete and use in your plans
  - Devise method for evaluating progress toward goals (in what specific areas do you expect to see change?)

Figure 10.4 Step 4. Goal identification.

stated that her coach's anxiety about her difficulties performing on the vault have not helped her in coping effectively with her fears. Although Li-Wu does not live with her family (she moved away from home to train at an elite gymnasium), the relationship appears to have been appropriately supportive.

Objective

To expand and strengthen coping resources of athlete with respect to sport performance

Methods

- Adopt an educational approach; explain rationale of techniques to athlete; teach athlete how to apply techniques in relevant contexts
- Encourage use of mental skills in athletic situations; if needed, visit appropriate facility (gym, pool, track, rink, etc.)
- Be systematic in developing a rationale for importance of mental skills and showing how these assist in developing sport skills; this involves
  - Course curriculum
  - Teaching exercises
  - Methods for encouraging athlete participation
  - Follow-up and feedback strategies
  - Coach feedback

Experience indicates that athletes learn more and derive more enjoyment from participatory learning rather than didactic exercises.

Figure 10.5 Step 5. Group intervention.

Drugs and Biology

Li-Wu must spend a considerable amount of time caring for her injury. For example, she must thoroughly warm up and stretch her neck muscles before each workout and apply ice to these same muscles afterwards to prevent swelling. Additionally, she continues to take anti-inflammatory medication although she reports it makes her feel groggy and upsets her stomach.

Li-Wu appears to be inappropriately concerned about her weight. She reported that she worries about her weight a great deal and believes she is not thin enough for her

Objective

To help individuals develop and practice a mental routine for performance that will help with consistency and self-control. This routine will use coping techniques learned in group sessions. Individual sessions allow athlete to share unique ideas, thoughts, perspective; to discuss personal issues athlete brings up.

Methods

- Stick to plan developed in Step 4; be flexible and adjust where necessary
- Devise a mental routine for competition; include specific preparations day before, morning of, 30 min before, immediately before, during, and after competition, if necessary; include cues for use of coping skills
- Have athlete practice mental routine during workouts and at competitions
- Identify potential obstacles and ways to refocus if encountered
- Build toward problem resolution; don't try to take care of everything at once; prioritize interventions
- Deal with athlete's personal issues (this is important, and in many cases counseling will be appropriate); be aware of any limitations in your own expertise, make these clear to athlete, and have support available if athlete wants to discuss issues outside of your expertise; be firm in limiting inappropriate discussion of such issues
- If counseling and mental skills training are concurrent, give separate time to each; help athlete focus on single issues

Figure 10.6 Step 6. Individual intervention.

sport. To determine if her diet was too restrictive, Li-Wu was referred to a nutritionist. It was reported that she had no indications of an eating disorder, but several further consultations with the nutritionist were scheduled

Objective

To assess how well goals of Step 4 (goal identification) have been met; if goals not met, to identify reasons

Methods

- Use evaluation method devised when intervention plans were made. Evaluation should include
  - Feedback from athlete regarding satisfaction with consultation
  - Measurable feedback regarding relevant performance goals
  - Feedback from coach
- Include a variety of criteria in the evaluation, such as
  - Performance
  - Attitude
  - Commitment to sport
  - Life balance
  - Personal development
- Provide feedback on mental-skills training progress to both coaches and athletes

Figure 10.7 Step 7. Outcome evaluation.

to help her select and maintain a more well balanced diet that would meet her nutritional and caloric needs.

Conceptualization of the Case

A cognitive-behavioral approach suggested that each of the affective, cognitive, and behavioral systems be addressed to most effectively help the client. According to Mahoney and Meyers (1989), the experience of anxiety creates an interaction among systems (muscular, respiratory, cardiac, attention, etc.) in anticipation of danger or pain, which in turn leads to an attempt to avoid or control the

Objective

To reassess goals if necessary; to modify plans as needed

Methods

- Be prepared for the unexpected; especially in group sessions, group dynamics can change dramatically
- Be prepared to focus on new issues as they arise; a team might unexpectedly fail to qualify for a competition, an athlete might be severely injured, a coach might be fired—all can greatly impact the program
- Use athlete's progress in individual sessions as an indicator of pace you should maintain with athlete
- Use constructive feedback in an effort to improve your program (our programs have placed more and more emphasis on individual sessions based on feedback from coaches and athletes; also, we have tried harder to get the teaching out of the classroom and into the gym)

Figure 10.8 Step 8. Reassessment of goals.

experience. Anxiety is the result of the memories or anticipation of an experience and whether that experience was good or bad. Anxiety is also determined by the sense of efficacy the individual has about the experience (Bandura, 1977, 1982, 1986; Beck, Emery, & Greenberg, 1985).

Ellis's (1975) Rational-Emotive Therapy (RET) approach was utilized in the management of Li-Wu's worries. His A-B-C principle can be applied with Li-Wu.

- The **a**ctivating event is the difficult trick on the vault.
- The **c**onsequence is Li-Wu's anxiety level.
- Her **b**elief about the vault is what causes Li-Wu anxiety, not the difficult vault itself.

The intervention suggested is that by utilizing positive self-statements, Li-Wu must dispute her irrational belief that she is definitely going to be injured again and instead create new emotional affects, such as confidence, strength, and positive feelings that she will, indeed, be able to efficiently do the difficult vault.

Intervention With Li-Wu

Intervention began with teaching Li-Wu some relaxation exercises to help manage her anxiety. Progressive relaxation (Jacobson, 1974) is based on the notion that the body responds with muscle tension to anxiety-provoking thoughts and events. This physiological tension then increases the subjective experience of anxiety. Deep muscle relaxation reduces physiological tension and is incompatible with anxiety. By alternately tensing and relaxing her muscles, she learned where she "holds" her tension and how to release it and relax. Li-Wu had a high level of shoulder tension, preventing her from moving her arms freely when she was anxious. Deep diaphragmatic breathing was also incorporated in this exercise, as it is an easy-to-use way to produce a relaxed state.

The positive effects of these exercises help the consultant build trust with the client. At the same time, the consultant teaches the client about both anxiety and self-control of anxiety. After some practice, progressive relaxation can be a 10-second exercise that can be done at any time, even during a competition.

The next intervention step with Li-Wu was cognitive restructuring (Davis, Eschelman, & McKay, 1988). This treatment method is based on the assumption that emotional problems result from maladaptive thought patterns (Ellis, 1975). The task of therapy is to alter these faulty cognitions (Wilson, 1984). An assumption of cognitive restructuring is that reorganizing and restructuring verbal statements about oneself and one's world will result in a corresponding reorganization of behavior with respect to one's world (Risley & Hart, 1968). Li-Wu was taught to become aware of her maladaptive thoughts and learn to modify them with more positive, rational ones. Several frequently expressed self-statements, identified through self-monitoring, such as I'm going to wipe out on the vault and get injured again or I can't do this vault, were increasing her anxiety levels. A list of positive, coping self-statements were then developed to replace these negative cognitions:

- I am calm and at peace.
- I am a good gymnast.
- I am able to do difficult tricks.
- I am able to do difficult tricks on the vault.
- I am confident and strong.
- I am in control of my body and mind.
- I can meet this challenge.

Li-Wu was able to transform her self-talk through practice with these self-statements, which resulted in increased self-confidence and more adaptive coping behaviors in the gym.

Another problem identified in the assessment phase was that Li-Wu was unable to imagine herself successfully completing the vault trick and consistently saw herself getting hurt again. The first step to enabling Li-Wu to visualize completing the vault trick was to find some videos of her doing the trick successfully. Her coach had some footage of her doing the vault well. Li-Wu was instructed to watch these successful vaults repeatedly to gain a clear image of herself doing that vault effectively. The goal was to readopt a vision of herself performing the behavior successfully (a self-modeling exercise). Bandura (1977) suggested that modeling is effective in changing behaviors, as it teaches new skills and assists in disinhibiting the anxiety associated with the feared behavior. Rushall (1988) has suggested that covert modeling can progress from imaging others to imaging oneself. This self-modeling procedure enabled Li-Wu to start imaging herself completing the trick without anxiety.

However, Li-Wu found that she could begin the image appropriately but then suddenly see herself crashing to the floor, injured once again. Li-Wu was instructed to utilize a "freeze-frame" technique to control the image. When imaging the difficult trick, Li-Wu was told to stop the image by using the "freeze-frame buttons, just as if you were watching it on a VCR." She could then move the image frame by frame in order to see herself complete the image successfully. Li-Wu was encouraged to visualize the element from an internal perspective, although the research literature suggests that both internal and external imagery can be used effectively for mental rehearsal (Murphy & Jowdy, 1992).

Suinn's (1980) visuomotor behavior rehearsal (VMBR) combines several coping skills that involve total reintegration of experience, including visual, auditory, tactile, kinesthetic, and emotional cues (Murphy, 1990). When Li-Wu was told to visualize "vividly," she was encouraged to use all of her senses to more closely assimilate the actual experience of doing the vault. Li-Wu was asked to visually put herself in the gym, smell the chalk in the air, hear the music of someone else doing a floor routine, hear her coach giving her instructions, feel the chalk on her hands, feel the horse under her hands when attempting the skill, taste the dryness in her mouth and chalk particles floating in the air, feel her body running down the runway and flying through the air to and over the vault, and experience landing the skill successfully. If she is able to recreate this experience and manage her anxiety about it, she will be more likely to feel self-efficacious and, therefore, more likely to attempt the skill without balking.

A variant of systematic desensitization (Wolpe, 1958) was used to help Li-Wu start approaching the actual vault with conviction. A stimulus hierarchy was constructed in which the aspects of the situation the client fears (in Li-Wu's case, approaching the vault on her difficult trick) are ordered along a continuum from mildly stressful to very threatening. The client is instructed to conjure a clear and vivid image of each item on the hierarchy while deeply relaxed (Wilson, 1984). Progressive relaxation can be used to produce deep relaxation. As Li-Wu moved through the levels of the hierarchy, she was instructed to cease visualization and utilize progressive relaxation whenever she began to feel anxious. The item was then repeated until Li-Wu could visualize doing that behavior on the hierarchy without feeling anxious. The entire hierarchy was completed in this fashion until Li-Wu was able to successfully imagine the difficult vault without fear. Then Li-Wu was taken into the gym to complete an in vivo experience similar to the one she was able to achieve by visualization. A new step in the hierarchy was completed each day until she was able to execute the skill. This hierarchy was used by Li-Wu:

- Go to the gym and sit by the vault.
- Walk down the runway to the vault.
- Turn around at the end of the runway to the vault.
- Look down the runway to the vault.
- Visualize doing a simple vault at the end of the runway.
- Run down the vault runway.
- Run down the runway and execute a simple vault.
- Visualize a difficult vault at the end of the runway.
- Run down the runway toward the vault.
- Run down the runway and execute the difficult vault.

It is important to be aware that elite athletes might want to rush the desensitization process, but this can lead to setbacks. Encourage the athlete to be patient and take only one step at a time.

Courtesy University of Illinois Sports Information

A meeting was conducted with Li-Wu, her coach, and the sport psychology consultant to encourage Li-Wu to share her feelings about the coach's behaviors and how they were affecting her. A separate meeting between the coach and sport psychology consultant involved discussion of the coach's feedback style and ideas to more effectively work with a fearful gymnast. The coach was receptive to the meeting with the consultant and was willing to make changes.

The case of Li-Wu demonstrates that even a specific, well-defined athletic issue (in this case, return from injury) can involve a variety of interventions in several modalities. The consultant must be flexible to be able to adapt to the specific needs of the athlete and the sport situation. There are several combinations of cognitive-behavioral interventions that can be used effectively with athletes experiencing anxiety-related or confidence problems. The combination could include a relaxation exercise (see Davis et al., 1988 for a variety of both relaxation and cognitive restructuring ideas), cognitive restructuring, and imagery. A review of the literature on psychological interventions with competitive athletes by Greenspan & Feltz (1989) indicated that educational relaxation-based interventions and remedial cognitive-restructuring interventions with individual athletes are generally effective.

Additional Case Management Considerations

Li-Wu's case demonstrates how traditional cognitive-behavioral interventions can be successful with managing many performance issues. However, there are several other issues in such cases to which the sport psychology consultant must be sensitive. In any case involving athlete injury, the consultant must obtain information from medical and other personnel concerning the likely postinjury level of athletic functioning, which is often extremely difficult to predict. Even if the injury is not career ending, it is possible nevertheless that the athlete will be unable to return to the previous training and competition level. Preparing in advance for such issues can help the athlete's adaptation to rehabilitation. For many athletes, rehabilitation can be a long and arduous process, often accompanied by depression. Injuries can have a profound impact on an athlete's sense of identity and self-esteem, particularly if it is likely that the athlete will not be able to perform at the previous level. Athletes often derive a certain amount of their identity from sport and athletes at any level can experience an identity crisis when forced to relinquish their sport. Elite athletes generally structure their lives to be compatible with athletic advancement (Brewer, Van Raalte, & Lindner, 1993; Ogilvie & Howe, 1986). Injuries can completely alter an athlete's lifestyle and socialization patterns, so there is a need to be sensitive to the potential problems that can occur when working with this kind of situation.

The coach also plays a critical part in managing such a situation as Li-Wu's. Li-Wu's coach was amenable to consultation and implemented suggestions made by the consultant, but this does not always happen. Coaches can feel threatened by consultants, whom they might view as coming in to tell them what to do with their athletes. Good rapport with the coach is necessary to provide the most effective intervention with an athlete. It is important for the sport psychology consultant to get out of the office and into the gym to become familiar with the sport and its jargon, the training and competition environment, and the dynamics between the athletes and coach. It is best to observe the environment before offering any interventions. If a consultant does not become familiar with the sport (see Figure 10.2), know the coach, and learn about the training and competition environment, the probability of success with the consultancy is low.

Transfer of Cognitive-Behavioral Skills to Nonsport Areas

Cognitive-behavioral interventions teach skills to the client that can be generalized across a broad variety of situations, which means that once the client has learned the skills specifically for one area of life, the skills can be adapted to other life areas. For instance, goal setting, stress management, and cognitive restructuring can be used in academic or work environments to manage many anxiety-provoking situations. Behavioral medicine has utilized many cognitive-behavioral techniques over the years in an attempt to facilitate preventive medicine efforts in patients and to help the chronically ill manage their illnesses and reduce pain (see Turk, Meichenbaum, & Genest, 1983). Therefore, these techniques are not situation specific, but can be viewed as techniques that facilitate healthy and effective coping behaviors in life (see the discussion of this issue by Danish and colleagues in chapter 2).

CONSULTATION AND INTERVENTION GUIDELINES

Adopt an educational, coping-skills approach.

Performance enhancement is achieved in personal development.

Never take credit for the athlete's performance. Adopt the approach, Look at what you can do with your new skills!

Set realistic expectations. If the coach or athlete has unreasonable expectations, educate them right at the beginning as to what you can and can't do.

Be careful of boundaries in the sport consultation setting. By the nature of the process, it is easy to become friendly with your clients (going to practices, going to competitions, etc.). However, you need to retain consultant–client boundaries.

Help athletes realize that they must practice skills for them to be effective. Athletes should not try out a new mental skill for the first time in competition. Skills and mental routines must be gradually built into the repertoire.

CONCLUSION

In this chapter we have examined existing models of psychology consultancy with sport organizations and offered a cognitive-behavioral model that has been effective in a variety of sport situations. The cognitive-behavioral approach presented here offers the advantages both of being based on educational and coping skills and also of viewing the athlete in the context of her life situation. It thus avoids the medical-model drawbacks often associated with the clinical approach and minimizes the overly narrow emphasis on performance concerns typically associated with the educational model.

We close this chapter with some important guidelines for sport consultants, no matter what the level of assistance offered sport organizations. By observing these principles, helping professionals can avoid common pitfalls in their work as consultants. A key to successful interventions is a coherent outlook, and this chapter has shown you how to develop such a model.

REFERENCES

American Psychological Association. (1990). Ethical principles of psychologists. *American Psychologist*, **45**, 390-395.

Anshel, M. (1992). The case against the certification of sport psychologists: In search of the phantom expert. *Sport Psychologist*, **6**, 265-286.

Bandura, A. (1977). Self-efficacy: Toward a unifying theory of behavior change. *Psychological Review*, **84**, 191-215.

Bandura, A. (1982). Self-efficacy in human agency. *American Psychologist*, **37**, 122-147.

Bandura, A. (1986). *Social foundations of thought and action*. Englewood Cliffs, NJ: Prentice Hall.

Beck, A.T., Emery, G., & Greenberg, R.L. (1985). *Anxiety disorders and phobias: A cognitive perspective*. New York: Basic Books.

Biddle, S.J.H., Bull, S.J., & Seheult, C.L. (1992). Ethical and professional issues in contemporary British sport psychology. *Sport Psychologist*, **6**, 66-76.

Botterill, C. (1990). Sport psychology and professional hockey. *Sport Psychologist*, **4**, 358-367.

Brewer, B., Van Raalte, J., & Lindner, D. (1993). Athletic identity: Hercules' muscle or Achilles' heel? *International Journal of Sport Psychology*, **24**, 237-254.

Davis, M., Eschelman, E.R., & McKay, M. (1988). *The relaxation and stress reduction workbook* (3rd ed.). Oakland, CA: New Harbinger.

Dorfman, H.A. (1990). Reflections on providing personal performance enhancement consulting services in professional baseball. *Sport Psychologist*, **4**, 341-346.

Ellis, A. (1975). *Humanistic psychotherapy: The rational-emotive approach*. New York: McGraw-Hill.

Gardner, F.L. (1991). Professionalization of sport psychology: A reply to Silva. *Sport Psychologist*, **5**, 55-60.

Gordon, S. (1990). A mental skills training program for the Western Australian cricket team. *Sport Psychologist*, **4**, 386-399.

Greenspan, M.J., & Feltz, D.L. (1989). Psychological interventions with athletes in competitive situations: A review. *Sport Psychologist*, **3**, 219-236.

Halliwell, W. (1990). Providing sport psychology consulting services in professional hockey. *Sport Psychologist*, **4**, 369-377.

Jacobson, P. (1974). *Progressive relaxation*. Chicago: University of Chicago Press.

LaRose, B. (1988). What can the sport psychology consultant learn from the educational consultant? *Sport Psychologist*, **2**, 141-153.

Lazarus, A.A. (1981). *The practice of multimodal therapy*. New York: McGraw-Hill.

Loehr, J.E. (1990). Providing sport psychology consultation services to professional tennis players. *Sport Psychologist*, **4**, 400-408.

Mahoney, M., & Meyers, A. (1989). Anxiety and athletic performance: Traditional and cognitive-behavioral perspectives. In D. Hackfort (Ed.), *Anxiety in sports: An international perspective* (pp. 77-94). Washington, DC: Hemisphere.

Martens, R., Burton, D., Vealey, R., Bump, L., & Smith, D. (1990). Development and validation of the Competitive State Anxiety Inventory-2 (CSAI-2). In R. Martens, R. Vealey, & D. Burton (Eds.), *Competitive anxiety in sport* (pp. 117-190). Champaign, IL: Human Kinetics.

McKelvain, R. (1988, October). *Consulting effectively with national governing bodies*. Paper presented at the Annual Conference of the Association for the Advancement of Applied Sport Psychology, Nashua, NH.

McNair, D., Lorr, M., & Droppleman, L. (1971). *Profile of mood states manual*. San Diego: Educational and Testing Service.

Murphy, S.M. (1988). The on-site provision of sport psychology services at the 1987 U.S. Olympic Festival. *Sport Psychologist*, **2**, 337-350.

Murphy, S.M. (1990). Models of imagery in sport psychology: A review. *Journal of Mental Imagery*, **14**, 153-172.

Murphy, S.M., & Ferrante, A.P. (1989). Provision of sport psychology services to the U.S. Team at the 1988 Summer Olympic Games. *Sport Psychologist*, **3**, 374-385.

Murphy, S.M., Hardy, L., Thomas, P., & Bond, J. (1993). *The Sports Inventory of Mental Skills*. Unpublished manuscript, U.S. Olympic Committee, Colorado Springs.

Murphy, S.M., & Jowdy, D. (1992). Imagery and mental practice. In T. Horn (Ed.),

Advances in sport psychology (pp. 221-250). Champaign, IL: Human Kinetics.

Murphy, S.M., & Murphy, A.I. (1992, August). *Sport psychology: Performance enhancement for athletes.* Workshop presented at the Annual Meeting of the American Psychological Association, Washington, DC.

Neff, F. (1990). Delivering sport psychology services to a professional sport organization. *Sport Psychologist*, **4**, 378-385.

Nideffer, R. (1981). *The ethics and practice of applied sport psychology.* Ithaca, NY: Mouvement.

Ogilvie, B.C. (1977). Walking the perilous path of the team psychologist. *Physician & Sportsmedicine*, **5**(4), 63-67.

Ogilvie, B.C. (1979). The sport psychologist and his professional credibility. In P.H. Klavora & J.V. Daniel (Eds.), *Coach, athlete, and the sport psychologist* (pp. 45-55). Toronto: University of Toronto Press.

Ogilvie, B.C. (1992). *Consultation issues within professional sport.* Unpublished manuscript, U.S. Olympic Committee, Colorado Springs.

Ogilvie, B.C., & Howe, M. (1986). The trauma of termination from athletics. In J.M. Williams (Ed.), *Applied sport psychology: Personal growth to peak performance* (pp. 365-382). Palo Alto, CA: Mayfield Press.

Ravizza, K. (1988). Gaining entry with athletic personnel for season-long consulting. *Sport Psychologist*, **2**, 243-254.

Ravizza, K. (1990). Sportpsych consultation issues in professional baseball. *Sport Psychologist*, **4**, 330-340.

Risley, T., & Hart, B. (1968). Developing correspondence between the nonverbal and verbal behavior of preschool children. *Journal of Applied Behavior Analysis*, **1**, 267-281.

Rotella, R.J. (1990). Providing sport psychology consulting services to professional athletes. *Sport Psychologist*, **4**, 409-417.

Rushall, B. (1988). Covert modeling as a procedure for altering an athlete's psychological state. *Sport Psychologist*, **2**, 131-140.

Silva, J.M. (1989). Toward the professionalization of sport psychology. *Sport Psychologist*, **3**, 265-273.

Smith, R.E., & Johnson, J. (1990). An organizational empowerment approach to consultation in professional baseball. *Sport Psychologist*, **4**, 347-357.

Smith, R.E., Smoll, F.L., & Schutz, R.W. (1990). Measurement and correlates of sport specific cognitive and somatic trait anxiety: The Sport Anxiety Scale. *Anxiety Research*, **2**, 263-280.

Suinn, R. (1980). Psychology and sports performance: Principles and application. In R. Suinn (Ed.), *Psychology in sports: Methods and applications* (pp. 26-36). Minneapolis: Burgess.

Thompson, R., & Sherman, R. (1993). *Helping athletes with eating disorders.* Champaign, IL: Human Kinetics.

Turk, D.C., Meichenbaum, D., & Genest, M. (1983). *Pain and behavioral medicine: A cognitive-behavioral perspective.* New York: Guilford Press.

Wilson, T.E. (1984). Behavior therapy. In R.J. Corsini (Ed.), *Current psychotherapies* (3rd ed.). Itasca, IL: Peacock.

Wolpe, J. (1958). *Psychotherapy by reciprocal inhibition.* Stanford, CA: Stanford University Press.

Zaichkowsky, L.D., & Perna, F.M. (1992). Certification of consultants in sport psychology: A rebuttal to Anshel. *Sport Psychologist*, **6**, 287-296.

PART II

SPECIAL ISSUES IN COUNSELING ATHLETES

CHAPTER 11

CARING FOR INJURED ATHLETES

Al Petitpas, EdD
Springfield College
Steven J. Danish, PhD
Virginia Commonwealth University

Traditionally, physicians and sports medicine professionals have focused most of their attention on the physical aspects of athletic injuries. This emphasis has spurred others to develop marked improvements in sports equipment, conditioning, and training methods, yet incidence of athletic injury have at best remained constant (Yaffe, 1983). With the recent emphasis on psychobiological relationships, it is not surprising that researchers have turned their attention to the impact of psychological variables on the sports injury process. In fact, several practitioners have suggested that adverse psychological factors are instrumental in predicting sports injury, prolonging the rehabilitative process, and causing subsequent performance decrements, emotional problems, and even suicide in certain athletes.

This chapter examines some psychological factors that affect athletes with injuries, emphasizing the psychological rehabilitative process. The chapter's five sections explore the following questions:

- How do sports injuries affect athletes psychologically?
- What are some warning signs of a potentially difficult adjustment?
- What are some psychological factors to consider in treatment planning?
- What would be a typical treatment protocol?
- What are some practical and ethical issues sport psychologists face in the sports medicine setting?

Critical psychological considerations can be present in the full range of athletic injuries. From sprains and strains to overuse and knee injuries, many athletes have found psychological interventions a necessary component of their rehabilitation. The following case studies might help to illustrate some of the psychological dynamics to be explored and underscore material that will be presented later in the chapter. The outcome of these cases will be presented in the chapter's conclusion.

■ *THE CASE OF JANE* ■

Jane is a 30-year-old mother of two children. She met her husband while competing in the NCAA National Gymnastics Championships.

They married shortly after her graduation 3 years later. After a 2-year stint as an assistant gymnastics coach, Jane decided to open her own gymnastics school. With her reputation as an all-American collegiate athlete and excellent coach, her school thrived.

Jane's injury problems began with a stress fracture of her left foot. This was quickly followed by a badly sprained neck, sustained while demonstrating a dismount, and a back injury resulting from a car accident. After more than 2 years of hard work in physical therapy and a demanding home rehabilitation program, Jane was able to resume a full work schedule. However, within a month she began to experience pain in her heel. Her physician explained it as pain referred from her neck and suggested that she stop working and refrain from exercise. Within 2 days, Jane reported that she had lost most of the stability she had gained during the previous 2 years of physical therapy. She quickly found another physician who gave her the green light to resume physical therapy and light exercise. Jane decided to stop working and concentrate on her rehabilitation. She returned to work two months later only to find herself becoming "extremely fatigued and feeling overwhelmed" each time she attempted to demonstrate her routines to her students. She has since had three additional setbacks with chronic pain, numbness, and tingling. She has crying spells, depression, difficulty sleeping, and is unable "to feel my body working correctly." A complete neurological workup proved negative.

Jane's husband has been very supportive as she has struggled with each successive injury. However, recently he has begun to lose his patience with her crying spells and inability to do anything around the house.

■ *THE CASE OF MIKE* ■

Mike, an 18-year-old straight-*A* high-school senior, was a two-time captain and all-state performer on the state championship football team. He had been contacted by more than 200 colleges with various scholarship offers and was the odds-on favorite to win the prestigious scholar-athlete award for his region.

Mike had always stood out. From youth league through high school, he was the biggest, fastest, and toughest player. His father, a highly successful college player, had been grooming Mike to follow in his footsteps. Mike had not been a disappointment.

After a preseason scrimmage game, Mike complained of discomfort in his stomach and lower back. The pain grew progressively worse and Mike went to his physician for a complete examination. To everyone's amazement, it was discovered that Mike had only one kidney, located in the abdominal area. He underwent surgery to extract the kidney stone that had caused his discomfort.

Although Mike was declared healthy, he was advised to avoid contact sports. Mike could not believe it. He and his father spent the next few weeks contacting sports medicine professionals from around the country about special protective gear, but the risk of serious injury was too great. After a couple of weeks of angry outbursts and moodiness, Mike was forced to accept the decision to terminate his football career. He appeared to handle the loss of football remarkably well. In fact, he was the first person to admit that "football is only a game." He seemed more concerned with how his father was handling the situation and suggested that his father "needs some help in dealing with it."

Mike continued to stay active with the team. He went to every practice and every game. He represented his team at the coin toss before every game and was appointed as an unofficial coach to assist the underclassmen during practices. Academically, Mike decided to work even harder on his studies in the hope of getting an academic scholarship. Instead of socializing with his teammates after practice as he had been accustomed, he went directly home and hit the books.

As a tribute to Mike's courage and dedication, he was awarded a trophy at the annual December football dinner. This trophy recognized his inspiration, courage, and contributions to the team. Mike accepted the trophy by honoring his coaches and most importantly his father "for making me what I am today."

PSYCHOLOGICAL EFFECTS OF ATHLETIC INJURY

For many people physical injury and the accompanying treatment and rehabilitation process can be extremely stressful. For athletes who might derive significant amounts of self-esteem and personal competence from their ability to perform, the injury process can be emotionally devastating.

The impact of athletic injury is dependent on a number of factors, including the nature and severity of the injury, the importance of sport in the athlete's life, and the reaction of the athlete's support network to the injury. The complexity of these and other factors makes predicting individual reactions difficult at best. To complicate matters, research efforts have concentrated on injury prediction rather than the rehabilitation process. Thus most of what is reported about psychological effects of athletic injury is based on the experience of a small number of practitioners. Despite these limitations, a few reactions have been reported consistently enough to warrant further discussion.

Grief Reaction

Suinn (1967) was one of the first sport psychologists to suggest that athletes cope with injuries in essentially the same manner as any person faced with disablement or significant loss. He proposed a sequence of reactions including shock, denial, depression or anxiety, and partial or complete acceptance. Others (Astle, 1986; Rotella, 1984; Rotella & Heyman, 1986; Weiss & Troxel, 1986) have suggested that athletes frequently undergo a grieving process for the temporary or permanent loss of athletic self. This process follows Kubler-Ross's (1969) familiar stages of denial, anger, bargaining, depression, and acceptance.

Recent studies have suggested that these stage models might not accurately reflect athletes' affective responses to injuries that result in temporary impairment. It appears that athletes experience a brief period of mood disturbance (increased tension, depression, and anger with decreased levels of vigor) following an injury but return to normal when they perceive they are making progress toward recovery (McDonald & Hardy, 1990; Smith, Scott, O'Fallon, & Young, 1990). It might be that a grief reaction occurs in athletes who experience career-ending injuries, but so far we have only anecdotal evidence for this assumption.

It is clear that the severity of emotional reaction is dependent on numerous factors, not the least of which is the athlete's own coping skills. However, awareness of these possible reactions can help professionals identify potential warning signs for those athletes who might need more specialized assistance. In some situations the lack of an emotional reaction can signal potential problems. This might be seen in the case of Mike, the high-school football player, where his denial and anger were not as surprising as the suddenness of his public acceptance of the loss of football. Based on the centrality of sport in Mike's life, a longer and more emotional adjustment period might have been expected.

Identity Loss

Injured athletes might also experience a threat to personal identity. Elkin (1981) contends that athletes who have made premature or exaggerated commitments to sport are most vulnerable to ego-identity loss and subsequent depression. Little (1969) labeled this syndrome *athletic neurosis* and described it as

> a bereavement reaction to the loss of a part of the self, the overvalued physical prowess. Athleticism may not be neurotic in itself; but, like exclusive and excessive emotional dependence on work, intellectual pursuits, physical beauty or any other overvalued attribute or activity, athleticism can place the subject in a vulnerable pre-neurotic state leading to manifest neurotic illness in the event of an appropriate threat, or actual enforced deprivation, especially if it is abrupt or unexpected. (p. 195)

If Little's observations are accurate, overidentification with athletics could lead to emotional upset in people who are forced to disengage from sport roles. This notion has received some support in the literature (Chartrand & Lent, 1987; Haerle, 1975; Hill & Lowe, 1974; Ogilvie & Howe, 1986). Others (Orlick, 1980; Svoboda & Vanek, 1982) view disengagement from sport roles as a life transition similar to leaving a job or becoming a parent. (See chapter 14, where Murphy discusses at length transition issues faced by athletes retiring from sport.) Each transition offers an opportunity for self-evaluation and growth. The levels of emotional upset would be a function of people's coping abilities coupled with the quality and availability of their social supports (Pearson & Petitpas, 1990).

Kleiber and Greendorfer (1983) conducted one of the few studies of the impact of sport participation on college athletes. Their survey of former Big Ten Conference athletes found that most of their sample expressed some sense of loss over the termination of the college athletic experience. For most, the bereavement centered on either a loss of identity and friendship or regrets about unmet goals and lost opportunities. The disengagement process was not as traumatic as some other writers (Haerle, 1975; Ogilvie & Howe, 1986) would have predicted. Kleiber and Greendorfer suggested that the athletes might have been able to adjust their priorities by moving sport to a lesser status or that perhaps these athletes were not unidimensional and had other activities in which they were invested.

Kleiber, Greendorfer, Blinde, and Samdahl (1987) reexamined these same athletes to learn about their level of life satisfaction 3 to 8 years after college graduation. Those athletes who suffered a career-ending injury expressed significantly lower levels of life satisfaction than their noninjured counterparts.

Courtesy University of Illinois Sports Information

The authors speculated that this reaction could be a result of "unfinished business" or unfulfilled dreams. Regardless of the reason for the feelings, injuries are significant events in the lives of athletes. This link has received some empirical support from Brewer (1991), who found that a strong and exclusive athletic identity is a risk factor for depressive reactions among injured athletes.

Numerous cases of college, Olympic, and professional athletes who have suffered acute depression or abused alcohol or other drugs as a result of a sudden career-ending injury have been described in the literature (Hill & Lowe, 1974; Mihovilovic, 1968; Ogilvie & Howe, 1986). Recreational runners have been found to experience guilt, irritability, and depression after they stop exercising for a few days (Sacks & Sachs, 1981). Danish (1986) cited several other effects of athletic injury including threats to self-concept, belief systems, values, commitments, emotional equilibrium, and social and emotional functioning. All of these reactions could be influenced by the level of personal identification with sport roles. The potential impact of injuries on role identity should not be underestimated.

Separation and Loneliness

Sport psychologists have suggested that feelings of separation and loneliness can also result from athletic injury (Crossman & Jamieson, 1985; Lewis-Griffith, 1982). If injured athletes can no longer practice or participate on the team, they can lose an important element of their social support system. Many sport psychologists recognize the importance of social interactions with teammates and encourage injured players to remain actively involved with the team in some capacity. Some athletes, however, will purposely avoid contact with the team when they are unable to play because they feel guilt at letting down their teammates and coaches. Others find watching practice or a game highly stressful and "a painful reminder of all I'm missing."

Some injured athletes find it easier to withdraw from their support system rather than deal with their feelings. At the same time, some teammates might ignore injured athletes because they feel they are bad luck. Other teammates and friends might not know how to respond to the injured athlete. This is particularly true if their primary connections and identifications are through athletic roles and the injury is severe. Feeling inadequate to help, friends might avoid the athlete (Rotella & Heyman, 1986). The result of this interaction can be a withdrawal of social support at a time when it is most needed.

Injured athletes are also faced with a dramatic increase in their amount of unstructured time. The 3 to 5 hr per day of practice or game time is now devoid of activity. As one injured athlete put it, "I used to go down to the gym and get my fix every day; now I sit in my room staring at my books or daydreaming of what it used to be like."

Helping athletes plan strategies to cope with their unstructured time is often critical to the success of the psychological intervention. Some athletes need continued active involvement with the team through activities such as scouting, charting, or practice coaching. Other athletes need to get their exercise "fix" through alternative sports or activities. Still others might need assistance in coping with coaches or teammates who do not want injured players hanging around the team for fear that they might distract players or encourage less aggressive play. Helping professionals need to be aware of these individual differences in planning appropriate interventions.

Fear and Anxiety

Injured athletes face uncertain futures and potentially diminished social support. Many athletes begin to question their ability to cope with everything that is happening to them. The loss of a daily routine, the pain and discomfort of the injury, and the threats to future plans all can lead to anxiety and fear.

With more free time and uncertainty about the immediate future, it is not surprising that many athletes begin to have self-doubts. They question: Will I recover? What if I am reinjured? Will I be strong enough to regain my starting position? What if I can never play again? In many cases these doubts lead to behaviors that adversely affect the healing process (Rotella & Heyman, 1986). Athletes push too hard. They attempt shortcuts in their rehabilitation programs. They lose hope if they do not make continuous progress. In each of these examples, an athlete's behavior can become self-defeating and prolong the recovery process. As rehabilitation time increases, so does the fear and anxiety.

The emotional reactions to injury can consume a person's life. Feeling helpless in the face of stress and uncertainty, athletes can become externally controlled by the injury itself (Weiss & Troxel, 1986). This occurred in the case of Jane, which began the chapter. The multiple injuries and protracted rehabilitation eroded her confidence and increased her self-doubt. Soon the injury assumed an existence of its own. Even Jane's language reflected this, as she would insist that her "foot would not allow her to participate" or "I have to wait to see how the pain is before I go out." Helping injured athletes regain a sense of control often becomes the primary counseling goal.

Loss of Confidence and Performance Decrements

With all the physical and emotional changes with which some injured athletes must cope, it is not surprising that many of them lose confidence in their athletic skills as well. Athletes often feel that they are indestructible (Rotella, 1984). They learn to push their bodies to the limit, often taking major physical risks.

Once hurt, they begin to question their invulnerability, and many return to competition before they are psychologically ready. This is seen in athletes who become much more tentative in their play or protective of the injured area. They often lose the spontaneity and assertiveness that allowed them to excel. Their cautious play translates into performance decrements, which can further erode their confidence and lead to more stress and frustration. The end result of this process can be reinjury, injury to another area of the body, temporary or permanent performance problems, or emotional upsets that further drain motivation and the desire to compete (Rotella & Heyman, 1986).

Athletes can be affected by injuries in numerous ways. Depending on the severity of the injury, ego-involvement with sport, and the person's and support network's coping skills, athletes can experience significant psychological trauma, including emotional upheaval, identity loss, fear, anxiety, and decrements in athletic performance and self-confidence. Health-care professionals need to be sensitive to these potential psychological reactions to insure an optimal recovery process. Failure to do so can lead to tragic consequences.

WARNING SIGNS OF A POOR ADJUSTMENT

Health-care professionals can be in an excellent position to identify those athletes who are having difficulty adjusting to an injury. Ryde (1977) suggested that physicians and other professionals need to spend more time understanding what the injury means to the athlete. Without an understanding of the psychological aspects of the injury, there is a greater risk of missing important diagnostic material; this could lead to prolonged recoveries or greatly exacerbated symptoms.

Professionals who are able to establish rapport with injured athletes are better able to recognize potential warning signs of a poor adjustment. If athletes feel understood, there is a much greater chance that they will share their fears and insecurities. Based on our clinical experience, some of the signs of a potential problematic adjustment are

- evidence of anger, depression, confusion, or apathy;
- obsession with the question, When will I be able to play again?;
- denial, reflected in remarks such as, "Things are going great," "The injury is no big deal," or other remarks that lead you to believe that the athlete is making an extraordinary effort to convince you that the injury does not really matter;
- a history of coming back too fast from injuries;
- exaggerated storytelling or bragging about accomplishments in or out of sport;
- dwelling on minor somatic complaints;
- remarks about letting the team down or feeling guilty about not being able to contribute;
- dependence on the therapist or the therapy process or "just hanging around the training room" too much;
- withdrawal from teammates, coaches, friends, family, or therapist;
- rapid mood swings or striking changes in affect or behavior; and
- statements that indicate a feeling of helplessness to impact recovery.

The presence of several of these warning signs might indicate that the athlete is in need of assistance in adjusting to the injury. Attending simultaneously to both the physical and psychological aspects of the injury can greatly enhance the establishment of therapeutic rapport and facilitate the development of a comprehensive treatment plan.

In those facilities where a sport psychologist or athletic counselor is a member of the treatment team, psychological aspects of injury are addressed routinely as part of intake and evaluation. In other cases, various health-care professionals could assess the situation and where appropriate enlist the services of a trained counselor or psychologist.

Much care is needed in making psychological referrals. Face-saving is important for most people. For athletes, it might be even more critical (Kane, 1984). For people who are already questioning their own abilities, being told that they need to see a psychologist can be harmful. It might be more therapeutic to introduce psychological services as education or skill-building activities. More will be said about this later in the chapter.

Attending to the person and not just the injury should be the goal of the intervention. Once initial trust is established and the athlete feels somewhat understood, it might be easier to detect areas of concern and plan more appropriate multimodal treatments.

PSYCHOLOGICAL FACTORS IN TREATMENT PLANNING

The adage that you need to understand a problem before you can fix it is clearly indicated when treating injured athletes. In these situations professionals are faced with a complex picture of psychological factors (see Figure 11.1). Their initial goals should be to understand the athlete, build rapport, and assess the specifics of the case. Assessment requires consideration of a number of intrapsychic, interpersonal, and situational factors.

Ego-Involvement in Sport

The threat of identity loss for athletes with severe injuries has been discussed earlier. In

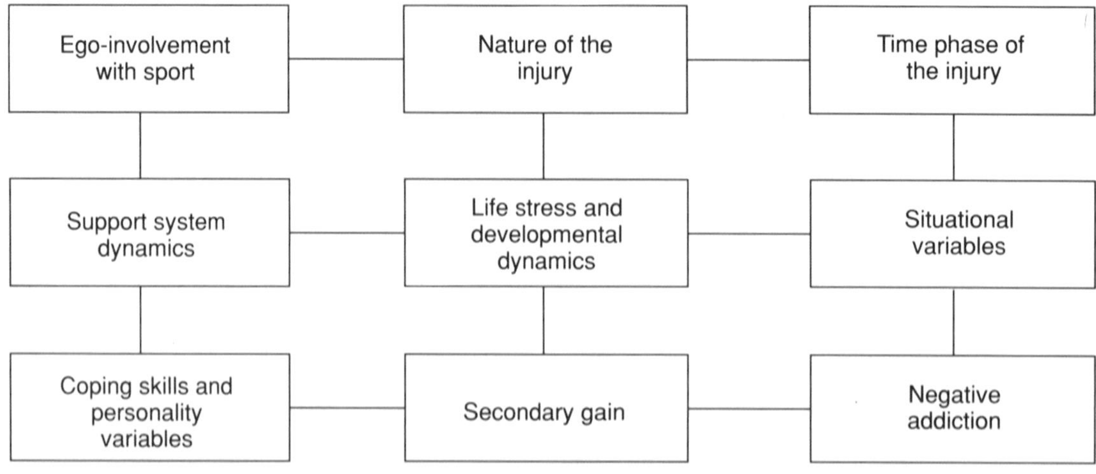

Figure 11.1 Factors in treatment planning.

assessment it is important to evaluate the degree to which players' identities are tied up in their sport roles.

Studies have suggested that involvement in high-level athletics might require athletes to focus their energies on a limited number of activities (Blann, 1985; Petitpas, 1981; Sowa & Gressard, 1983). Danish has called this process *selective optimization* and contends that "athletes invest maximal effort both physically and emotionally on behaviors judged to be essential for optimal athletic performance because this is where they believe their skills lie" (1983, p. 13). The more they continue through the sport system, the more committed athletes become to that role (Chartrand & Lent, 1987). For some athletes, sport can become the prime source of their identity.

Commitment to sport roles has the potential to be both positive and negative. It provides athletes with numerous opportunities to demonstrate their skills, interact with others, and measure their personal abilities. This is particularly valuable for young athletes who need to develop a sense of industry and competence. Sport experiences can enhance self-esteem and build confidence (Danish, Petitpas, & Hale, 1990). However, these experiences can also be harmful to young athletes, especially in situations where winning is promoted as the only measure of personal success. For example, Kozar and Lord (1983) found that a large number of overuse injuries were found in children and young adolescents who participated on teams that stressed winning rather than learning and fun. Emphasis on winning has also been cited as the chief cause of burnout in young athletes (Feigley, 1984; Henschen, 1986; Rowland, 1986).

The pressure to win can come not only from coaches and the sport system but also from parents. Noakes and Schomer (1983) found that parental pressure to win resulted in fictive injuries in some young athletes. They labeled this process *eager parent syndrome* and suggested that some young athletes found injury their only escape from the pressures imposed on them.

Sport participation can also impact the developmental process of college-age athletes. At a time when these athletes should be exploring career and ideological alternatives, many find themselves caught up in a system that demands exclusive devotion to their sport (Petitpas & Champagne, 1988; Remer,

Tongate, & Watson, 1978). The conflict between student versus athletic expectations often causes role strain (Chartrand & Lent, 1987). Many athletes will opt to forgo opportunities to expand the student role and commit more to sport as a source of identity. The process of making role commitments without adequate experimentation has been labeled *identity foreclosure* (Marcia, 1966).

It is important to understand that premature foreclosure is not in itself harmful. Many of our most respected careers necessitate early commitments of exclusive time and energy. Foreclosure becomes problematic only when people fail to develop adequate life skills. In bypassing the exploration of alternatives, foreclosed people miss opportunities to learn about their strengths and weaknesses. They avoid an identity crisis, but they do so at the expense of self-knowledge. The ultimate cost of foreclosure might become apparent only when people are faced with the threat of role loss due to a career-ending injury, the selection process, or other forced disengagement from sport (Petitpas, 1978).

In treatment planning, it is necessary to evaluate the degree to which a person's identity is based solely on athletic roles. If foreclosure is present, it is important to distinguish between psychological and situational types (Henry & Renaud, 1972). (See the highlight box on this page.)

Athletes in a state of psychological foreclosure typically require more intense treatment options than those in the situational type. For this reason, it is important to give athletes opportunities to disclose what sport means to them and what part it has played in their lives. In situations where the injury is career threatening, the psychologically foreclosed athlete is more likely to display denial and hostility.

Psychological and Situational Foreclosure

Psychological Foreclosure

In psychological foreclosure people rigidly adhere to their identities to maintain security or to cope with intrapsychic anxiety. This might be seen in athletes who are adult children of an alcoholic parent. They may be resistant to change and more vulnerable to threats of identity loss because their method of coping with their life situations is to seek approval through their athletic successes. The loss of their athletic role would compromise their entire defensive structure.

Situational Foreclosure

In situational foreclosure people might initially appear resistant to change, but this is due to a lack of exposure to new ideas and options. Their commitment to athletic roles is not defensive but rather a function of selective optimization. In the words of one situationally foreclosed athlete, "I went to college because that was the next league, not to get an education."

Athletes' Coping Skills

There is some evidence that athletes with fewer coping skills tend to have more injuries and more difficulty during the rehabilitation process (Williams, Tonyman, & Wadsworth, 1986). In assessing coping skills, it is critical to differentiate practical (problem-focused) and affective (emotion-focused) problem-solving skills (Smith, Scott, & Wiese, 1990). Some athletes can manage all the practical aspects of treatment. They keep all their medical appointments and adhere to their physical therapy and home exercise programs. However, they might have difficulty dealing with their anger or loss. Their interpersonal relationships might become strained, and they might isolate from their support system.

Other athletes become so involved in putting up a good emotional front that they neglect the practical aspects of treatment. They do not adhere to their therapy protocols. They push themselves beyond prescribed physical therapy limits or fail to comply with treatment at all.

Related to coping skills is the athlete's belief system concerning the injury and the rehabilitation process. One of the effects of injury outlined earlier was the loss of a sense of control. Athletes who feel powerless to impact their own recovery can impede rehabilitation. They often blame themselves for the injury, citing a careless warm-up or their own "stupid mistake" as the cause. Now filled with guilt, they fail to invest in their own recovery and, instead, rely solely on external agents, such as God or physicians.

It is also important to determine the athlete's attitudes before the injury. Some athletes have adopted sport-specific learning that can sabotage their physical or psychological recovery. Rotella and Heyman (1986) have suggested that such learned attitudes ("Injured athletes are worthless," "Act tough and give 110%") can sabotage the athlete's recovery. Many athletes feel that they can never allow themselves to be vulnerable; this attitude prevents them from using available sources of social support.

Assessment of the coping skills and the belief system of injured athletes provides insight for planning cognitive interventions. These interventions might be required to assist athletes in gaining confidence in their own ability to impact their recovery or adjust to their level of disability.

Life Stress and Developmental Dynamics

A growing body of research shows a correlation between life stress and athletic injury (e.g., Coddington & Troxell, 1980; Cryan & Alles, 1983). Although this relationship might account for only a small portion of the injuries (Lysens, VandenAuweele, & Ostyn, 1986), it remains an important consideration in treatment planning. It is obvious that a person who is coping with large amounts of life stress might be more susceptible to breaking down under the additional weight of an injury. The amount of life stress experienced is affected by the personal meaning that a person places on the event. For example, a divorce can be stress reducing for some and catastrophic for others.

Investigating other sources of stress in an injured athlete's life can uncover potentially exacerbating situations and provide insight into the athlete's coping skills. It also provides opportunities to teach stress management techniques in life areas that might be less sensitive to the athlete. For an athlete who is presenting a brave front, indirect intervention might be the only viable course of action.

In addition, individual and family-life-cycle tasks and dynamics warrant consideration. The college football player who is undergoing a developmental identity crisis might be feeling additional pressure from a father in mid-life transition. A young gymnast reported that injury was her only escape from the incredible family pressures she felt to exceed the athletic accomplishments of her recently deceased older sister. Developmental and family-life-cycle dynamics can significantly affect rehabilitation. In some cases, these considerations demand primary therapeutic emphasis.

Secondary Gain

As with other injuries, it is important to consider whether the athlete seems to derive any benefits from the injury. Sanderson (1977) outlined a number of these potential benefits, including face-saving, escape, passive-aggressiveness against parental pressure, and avoidance of training. An injury can provide struggling athletes with a socially acceptable reason for leaving a team or for playing poorly. Rather than quit or accept a reserve role, some athletes find injury a face-saving mechanism.

The number of athletes who use injury to avoid competition has been reported as small (Kane, 1984). Some athletes discover the benefits of being injured while dealing with minor ailments. While hurt, they may receive extra attention from friends, teammates, coaches, or trainers. If this occurs at the same time that their playing time is diminishing or they are not performing well, they might find a prolonged recovery period an attractive escape route.

The adage "Never underestimate the power of secondary gain," often used in conjunction with conversion reactions, may also hold true for injured athletes. In planning treatment, it might become necessary to acknowledge the benefits of the injury and develop a strategy that will provide the same advantages without some of the ensuing costs. Exploring transferable skills and building self-confidence are examples of these strategies (Danish et al., 1990).

Social Support Systems

As with the athlete, it is important to explore the practical problem-solving skills and emotional responses of a person's support system. Family, friends, and teammates can have difficulty dealing with an injured athlete's affect. If the injury is severe enough to threaten full recovery, support system members might feel uncomfortable talking about sport. They often focus on the practical aspects of rehabilitation and avoid the athlete's feelings. In these cases, the athlete is denied the support needed to facilitate psychological adjustment.

In addition there is evidence that the attitudes and beliefs of a person's social support system can have considerable impact on the recovery process (Rolland, 1984). If significant others have doubts about an athlete's ability to get well, they can unconsciously sabotage rehabilitation. This has been shown in studies of males recuperating from uncomplicated heart attacks. O'Leary (1985) found that if the patients' wives took treadmill tests along with their spouses, they were less likely to misinterpret fatigue or heavy breathing as heart attack related. Convinced that the patients have sturdy hearts, their spouses were more likely to encourage normal physical activities, which in turn strengthen the heart.

Family and friends can unwittingly foster doubts in an injured athlete's mind by overprotecting, acting frightened, or purposely avoiding all talk about either the injury or sport. Coaches and teammates can impact rehabilitation by indirectly causing stress or guilt if they apply pressure to return too quickly or threaten playing status.

Often, social support system members play a substantial role in the recovery process. For example, working with a coach on an athlete's psychological readiness to return to competition can help avoid reinjury, injury to another body part, or performance decrements (Rotella & Heyman, 1986). For instance, an athlete's reentry into game situations might need to be a gradual process. This might be indicated in situations where an athlete is experiencing internal or external pressure to rescue the season. Rushed back into a starting position, an athlete can force action at the expense of injury or poor performance.

In treatment planning it is often necessary to understand the types of support an injured athlete might be receiving. Rosenfeld, Richman, & Hardy (1989) identified six distinct types of social support:

listening
technical appreciation
technical challenge
emotional support
emotional challenge
shared social reality

They also found that coaches, parents, friends, and teammates differed in the types of support they offered. For example, coaches and teammates were not good sources of emotional support. This could present a major deficit to athletes who are physically separated from their families; for example, college athletes and athletes attending Olympic training centers who are too proud to share emotional issues with friends.

Another area of concern is the density of the social support network. In the sport environment, athletes tend to be highly interactive with a limited set of similar peers. This can be problematic because it tends to restrict the range of information, skills, and knowledge available to assist people in developing alternative coping responses (Mitchell, 1974; Pearson & Petitpas, 1990).

Assessment of social support concerns is often necessary to plan the concurrent interventions that are often required. For example, the helping professional might need to work with parents or coaches on how to cope with an athlete's withdrawal or intense emotions.

The Nature of the Injury

At least five main considerations describe the nature of the injury. These are severity, onset, course, history, and type.

Severity

Whether an injury causes permanent or temporary impairment is clearly a fundamental consideration in treatment planning. Athletes with high levels of ego-involvement in sport might face a perceived total loss of identity in the face of a career-ending injury. Their reactions might be more severe and protracted than those of athletes whose prognosis for full recovery is more favorable. The same might be true for injured athletes who face an extended or uncertain rehabilitation (Smith et al., 1990). A protracted recovery process with an unpredictable outcome can seriously test the coping resources of an athlete who is used to a highly regimented, structured life. Severity is often linked with control and predictability, two factors that clearly impact on the levels of anxiety experienced.

Onset

Athletes can experience the onset of an injury in either an acute or gradual manner. This differentiation does not reflect biological onset, but rather the athlete's subjective experience of the injury. A sudden, unexpected injury can find a person's social support system as well as the person ill prepared to cope. Yet crisis management skills are typically quickly mobilized and support becomes readily available. This can contrast markedly from the more solitary experience of an injured athlete coping with a gradual onset.

The emotional process for an athlete with a gradual-onset injury can take a much different form from that of an athlete with an acute injury. Athletes often live with physical discomfort. They learn to manage or ignore pain. Yet for some a nagging injury might gradually progress to a point where they can no longer tough it out. These athletes reach pain levels where they must give in. For an athlete who has learned to act tough and give 110%, admitting that the pain is affecting performance can add guilt or anxiety and further erode self-confidence.

Course

Rolland's (1984) typology of illness suggests that chronic diseases essentially follow three general courses: progressive, constant, or episodic. The same holds true for athletic injuries.

In a progressive-course injury, there is a continual stepwise progression toward either recovery or permanent disability. The speed of the progression might vary, but the course

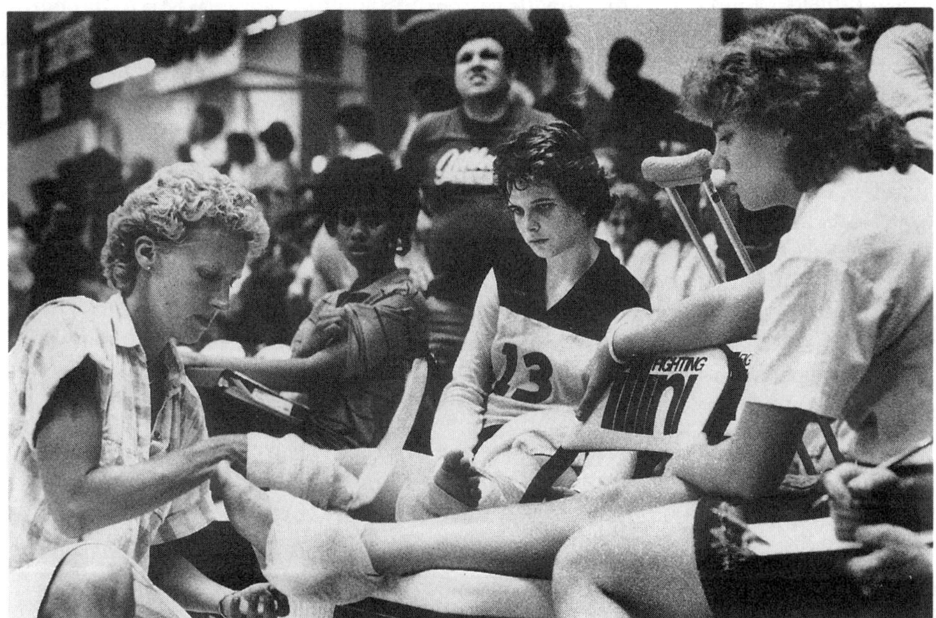

Courtesy University of Illinois Sports Information

would be predictable and gradual, with few surprises or unknowns. Athletes and their support systems would need to make a series of adaptations and role changes in response to the different levels of health or incapacitation.

For example, Thomas, an intercollegiate basketball player, had suffered an ankle injury that was to sideline him for 3 to 4 weeks. He was the only black player on the team and was the leading scorer and assist man. He was described as "a cocky kid who did everything his way." During the first week of physical therapy, Thomas's athletic trainer was surprised by his openness and self-disclosures of fear that he would not recover. The trainer assured him that his injury was common and full recovery was a sure bet, but Thomas continued to express doubts and spent considerable time sharing his concerns with the trainer.

As he began to see himself make measurable progress during the latter part of the second week, Thomas returned to his preinjury interpersonal style. His initial dependence on his athletic trainer was replaced by arrogance and disdain. The athletic trainer was not prepared for this sudden turnaround in behavior. He felt used and stated that he was "not thrilled to have to treat that jerk."

In the previous example, the sports medicine professional had difficulty adapting to the changing needs of the injured athlete. In progressive-course injuries, where full recovery is expected, it is not uncommon for athletes to return to their preinjury personality style after a brief period of fear, self-doubt, or confusion. In cases where permanent disability is evident, athletes are much more likely to experience the grief process outlined previously.

In constant-course injuries, athletes are required to adapt to a biological condition that remains stable. Athletes are faced with a clear-cut prognosis of permanent physical change. Although the course of the injury is stable and predictable, athletes and their support systems need to adapt to and accept a new level of physical ability. This may mean adjusting to life without sport, changing sports, or adjusting one's game based on physical limitations. The latter can be seen in examples of baseball players who had to learn to be pitchers instead of just throwers because of an arm injury that inhibited their throwing velocity.

Injuries can also be characterized as episodic-, or relapsing-course injuries. In these cases, athletes are faced with adapting to physical conditions that can flare up at any time, as in the cases of a golfer with a back problem or a tennis player with tendinitis. Symptom-free periods alternate with relapses. Athletes and their support systems are constantly faced with the uncertainty of when the injury will flare up again. Being overcautious when competing can cause declines in performance; this can lead to additional stress. These situations require adaptation to the unpredictability of the injury. Athletes often need assistance in accepting their condition without abandoning the physical style that gave them their competitive edge.

History

An exploration of the history of previous injuries can provide insight into the athlete's coping skills, beliefs about injury, levels of stress, and supports from their social network. Athletes who are injured for the first time might require much more initial information and understanding. Without a track record, injured athletes might not know what to expect. They might be too frightened or too proud to ask for help. In these cases, it is often more difficult to predict an athlete's response to the injury or the types of support that might be required.

Type

Injuries that require a cast or other visible sign of impairment often involve a much different experience for an athlete when compared to injuries that are not obvious. For example, in the case of Mike, the high-school football player, his internal injury did not provide him with a visible badge of courage. He was forced to field numerous questions as to why he was not playing. If he had a cast on his leg or arm, there would have been no question as to why he was not playing, and he would probably have received more support from his social system.

Phases in the Injury Process

Athletic injuries have three distinct phases that necessitate consideration in treatment planning. These can be described as the crisis period, the rehabilitation phase, and the recovery target date.

The crisis period includes the time immediately after a sudden onset or the point at which an athlete becomes concerned with the nagging injury that won't go away. It is important to initiate treatment as soon as possible following the onset of the injury to alleviate fears and handle denial (Danish, 1986; May & Seib, 1987; Rotella & Heyman, 1986). During this phase it is important to help an athlete feel understood and evaluate an injury in a realistic manner.

The rehabilitation phase follows the crisis period; the athlete has accepted the reality of the injury and is now focused on the recovery process. This phase can last from a few weeks to several years and is distinguished by feelings of resignation, calm, mood swings, relief, or growth. During this phase it is essential to help the athlete cope with the ups and downs of rehabilitation, teach new coping skills, and support and encourage an athlete's efforts to manage frustrations.

The recovery target date is the phase during which an athlete must test the injured area under game conditions or accept the loss of that valued activity because of the permanency of the impairment. It is often a time marked by a reactivation of earlier fears and doubts. This period is characterized by the need to assist the athlete to work with coaches, parents, spouse, or teammates in preparing for the reentry process or to help the athlete readjust to life without sport.

Rolland (1984) suggests that movement from one phase of the injury process to the next can be similar to a life transition. In such situations, unfinished business from an earlier phase can hinder the adaptation to the new time period. For example, individuals who deal with the crisis of an athletic injury by using denial might have difficulty taking responsibility for their own recovery during the rehabilitation process.

Situational Variables

A number of situational variables also come into play in developing a treatment plan. Among these are the type of sport, the duration of the sport season, the amount of playing time the injured athlete is receiving, the performance of the athlete, the team or individual record at the time of the injury, and the player's age or career stage. For example, an Olympic-medal-winning athlete, who was in the midst of preparation for the 1994 Winter Olympics, expressed initial relief when he experienced a potential career-ending injury. He said "winning the medal in 1992 was my goal, but competing in 1994 was for everyone else." Helping him cope with his injury required a different emphasis from working with two other similarly injured athletes who had not yet reached their goals. One needed to "get back in control of my life." He had to decide if competing was something that he wanted to do, or, instead, was doing for family, friends, and the media. The other felt cheated out of the opportunity to reach a goal. In these cases, treatment focused much more on managing anger and depression.

Situational variables often play into face-saving concerns. A senior collegiate football player who is not getting much playing time is likely to cope with an injury quite differently than a freshman superstar player.

In treatment planning, it is important to understand how these situational factors are interpreted by an injured athlete. One athlete who was "finally living up to my potential" experienced an early-season injury as "Murphy's Law—just when things are going well I get hurt, and I'm never going to make it now." This athlete had struggled for years to prove her abilities. She was a classic practice superstar who could never produce in a game. Just as her play was coming all together, she injured her shooting hand. Her initial reaction of frustration and anger quickly turned to despair and hopelessness. Ironically, 2 years earlier this same athlete had described a similar injury as "a godsend, I needed to get away from the game to get my head on straight."

Negative Addiction

The last psychological factor in treatment planning that we address in this chapter is negative addiction. Morgan contends that an increasing number of people have become addicted to exercise and manifest many negative physical and psychological symptoms. "A hard-core exercise addict can't live without daily running, manifests withdrawal symptoms if deprived of exercise, and runs even when his physician says he shouldn't" (1979, p. 57). What begins as a positive and healthy endeavor for the vast majority of exercisers can become a negative addiction. The classic symptoms of this syndrome might best be illustrated by the following case.

■ *THE CASE OF RICHARD* ■

Richard is a 40-year-old regional sales manager for a large northeastern company. In high school he was an outstanding basketball player and continued in the sport until 8 years ago, at which time the "roughness of the city-league games" and his lack of playing time led him to seek an alternative activity. Richard always had run to stay in shape for basketball, but now decided to take running more seriously. He quickly progressed from 2 to 6 mi per run. He entered local road races. Eventually, basketball became no match for the competition, the trophies, the positive feelings, and "the cardiovascular rush and endorphin highs" that running provided. He was now averaging 85 to 95 mi a week. Often he ran twice a day. He purchased a treadmill and an exercise bike for home. He "never felt better."

At work, Richard was extremely successful. He became the youngest regional sales manager in the company's history. His social life "could be a little better" since he broke up with his long-time girlfriend about a year ago, but his style had always been long-term relationships (2 to 4 years) with highly successful women. "Unfortunately, things never seemed to work out," he commented.

Although Richard reported that his life was going well, he had become increasingly more frustrated with the nagging foot, ankle, and back problems that he had suffered through over the last 3 years. He often found himself struggling to run through the pain, only to find it worse the next day. On the advice of a friend, Richard decided he needed to cross train for triathlons. He enrolled in an individualized fitness program, purchased an expensive racing bike, and took advanced swimming lessons. The resulting 3.5 to 5 hr of exercise per day put Richard in "the best shape of my life."

Unfortunately, the increased time commitment to working out began to affect Richard's work productivity and his social life was "at an all-time low." On the advice of his fitness instructor, Richard decided to consult an athletic counselor for some life-work planning so he could "fit in everything."

Initially, running had served many positive functions for Richard. It had given him a replacement for basketball. It gave him a new source of competence, feelings of fitness, and filled a void created by his slumping social life. Unfortunately, Richard increased his workouts to a point where overuse injuries and work decrements began to take a toll.

In treatment planning it is helpful to understand the dynamics of negative addiction. For example, direct challenges to the efficacy of intensive exercise are usually ineffective. Often indirect strategies prove to be more viable. More will be said about this when a suggested treatment protocol is examined.

PSYCHOLOGICAL TREATMENT FOR INJURED ATHLETES

Much of the literature on psychological treatment for injured athletes focuses on specific techniques (see a list of some of these techniques in the highlight box on page 271). Rather than reiterate these approaches, we will now outline a protocol for managing psychological treatment. The protocol suggests progressing through four phases and concurrently working with the injured athlete's social support network. Although these phases are presented as discrete, in practice they are interdependent and not absolutely differentiated.

Rapport-Building Phase

The initial task is to understand the injury from the athlete's perspective. Use basic attending skills to gather information in a manner that allows an athlete to feel understood. The goal is to explore also the various intrapsychic, interpersonal, and situational variables related to an athlete's injury. Although emotional support is often needed during this process, it is critical to insure that the

Psychological Treatments for Injured Athletes

1. *Attention control training* (Nideffer, 1983)
2. *Biofeedback* (Gordon, 1986; Nideffer, 1983)
3. *Cognitive strategies*—modification of self-talk, rational-emotive psychotherapy, reframing, restructuring, time projection, thought stoppage (Gordon, 1986; Rotella, 1984; Wiese & Weiss, 1987)
4. *Communication-skills training* (Wiese & Weiss, 1987)
5. *Crisis intervention* (Rotella & Heyman, 1986)
6. *Goal setting* (Danish, 1986; Wiese & Weiss, 1987)
7. *Grief counseling* (Astle, 1986; Wehlage, 1980)
8. *Imagery*—coping rehearsal, emotive rehearsal, mastery rehearsal, task-oriented rehearsal, visual rehearsal (Gordon, 1986; King & Cook, 1987; Rotella, 1984; Rotella & Heyman, 1986; Samples, 1987)
9. *Progressive relaxation* (Gordon, 1986; Nideffer, 1983; Weiss & Troxel, 1986)
10. *Psychological-skills training* (Ievleva & Orlick, 1991; Weiss & Troxel, 1986)
11. *Psychotherapy* (Eldridge, 1983; Scott, 1984)
12. *Stress inoculation training* (Meichenbaum, 1985)
13. *Systematic desensitization* (King & Cook, 1987; Rotella & Campbell, 1983)
14. *Support system interventions* (Wiese & Weiss, 1987)

athlete feels understood and accepted. Premature attempts at encouragement can cause an athlete to feel discounted.

Many athletes feel particularly vulnerable during the initial time after an injury. They often feel out of control and confused as to how to react to their injuries. In some cases they turn to potentially self-defeating methods, such as withdrawal or substance abuse, in an attempt to cope. It is critical to validate the intent of these attempts at self-cure. Acknowledging the short-term efficacy of withdrawal can allow an athlete to maintain self-respect and may enhance the rapport between athlete and helper. Conversely, premature confrontations over these behaviors might jeopardize the counseling relationship and further erode the athlete's confidence. Confrontations about self-defeating behaviors are often better addressed under the guise of skill acquisition, which occurs later in the counseling process. In the example of Richard, the negatively addicted runner, direct confrontations of the efficacy of running would test the strength of the counseling relationship and probably would lead to premature termination of therapy.

Once initial rapport is established, enlist the injured athlete as a collaborator in the planning and implementation of the treatment strategy. This usually enhances the athlete's sense of control and continues the process of rebuilding the athlete's confidence in being able to impact recovery.

Education Phase

The counselor should insure that an injured athlete has as much accurate information as possible about the injury and the recovery process. This helps the athlete become a collaborator in the treatment and reduces exaggerated worry or fear of the unknown. Danish (1986) suggests that injured athletes want information on specific topics:

- The nature of the injury and the medical reasons for initiating particular treatments
- The goals of treatment

- Details of medical procedures that will be performed
- Possible sensations or side effects
- Coping strategies for adjusting to the upcoming treatment

This phase is also an appropriate time to discuss the change process. Athletes, especially those who have been injured for the first time, might not be aware that change—whether psychological or physical—usually does not occur along a smooth continuum. This knowledge can help athletes cope with setbacks or plateaus in rehabilitation.

Educating athletes about their injuries and the change process can eliminate some surprises that might otherwise occur during treatment. This educating process also sets the stage for athletes to acquire new coping skills during the next phase of treatment.

Skill-Development Phase

The goals of the skill-development phase are to help athletes acquire new coping strategies and build confidence in their problem-solving abilities. It is important to assess and utilize the athlete's learned coping skills before introducing any new strategies. Many athletes have learned to use goal setting, relaxation techniques, guided imagery, deep breathing, and other strategies to enhance athletic performance. Building on proven skills enables athletes to gain confidence and feel more in control.

When an injury raises fear and self-doubts, an athlete may "catastrophize" about the future (Gordon, 1986). Introducing complicated treatment options at this time can exacerbate the feelings of worry and of being overwhelmed. Counselors who adopt a philosophy of using the least-involved intervention possible can better help to quell these exaggerated fears by creating some doubts in the doubts of the athlete.

Counselors and athletes should evaluate possible advantages and disadvantages of various self-help strategies, concentrating on those skills already familiar to the athlete. Once the most promising primary options have been identified, an implementation plan should be agreed on. While determining the appropriate choices, evaluate both the strategies and the implementation plan. In some cases, athletes report that a selected strategy did not help, even though in reality the failure developed from an implementation plan that did not allow sufficient time to practice new skills or did not provide ways in which to measure (and note) progress.

Establishing short-term and long-term goals greatly facilitates measuring skill attainment levels and planning implementation strategies. Although many goal-setting formats are available, Danish (1986) has developed a model (Life Development Intervention, or LDI) that is readily adaptable to injury rehabilitation. This approach begins with a three-part goal assessment: goal identification, goal importance, and goal roadblocks.

In goal identification, injured athletes are assisted in specifying intended actions in positive, behavioral terms. This helps an athlete avoid focusing on negative thoughts and provides observable criteria for measuring progress. This process also allows a counselor to sense how realistic an athlete is concerning physical aspects of rehabilitation and the recovery target date.

Investigating goal importance helps to determine whether goals are more important to the athlete or to coach, teammates, family, or friends. The Olympic athlete who felt initial relief after a potential career-ending injury (outlined earlier in this chapter) was not achieving his early rehabilitation goals because they were not his own. It was only when the goals became important to him that he was able to put out the commitment and concentration necessary to recover fully.

The final stage in the goal-setting model is to identify potential roadblocks to goal attainment. Four major blocks to goal achievement identified by Danish (1986) are

- lack of knowledge,
- lack of skill,
- lack of risk-taking ability, and
- lack of social supports.

Consideration of the level of importance for each of these roadblocks is critical to establishing the implementation plan.

If the selected strategies were already part of the athlete's repertoire, short-term goals need to be established to measure progress. If new skills are to be introduced, they should be taught systematically. Such a format might include these steps (Danish & Hale, 1983):

1. Describe the skill in behavioral terms
2. Give a rationale for the new skill
3. Specify a skill-attainment level
4. Demonstrate effective and ineffective uses of the skill
5. Provide opportunities to practice the new skill with supervision and feedback
6. Assign homework to promote generalization of the skill
7. Evaluate the skill-attainment level

Although building confidence and learning new coping strategies are the stated goals of the skill-development phase, the importance of the interaction between counselor and athlete should not be underestimated. By initially limiting the number of strategies to test out and enlisting the athlete as a collaborator in the helping process, adherence to the treatment regimen is greatly enhanced (Genest & Genest, 1987). It also places greater responsibility for a successful rehabilitation in the athlete's hands. Once injured athletes have assumed some ownership for their role in the recovery process and have learned some coping skills, the stage is set for the next phase of treatment.

Practice and Evaluation Phase

The goals for the practice and evaluation phase are

1. to provide opportunities for injured athletes to practice their coping skills with continuous feedback,
2. to evaluate goal-attainment levels,
3. to plan strategies to cope with setbacks in rehabilitation,
4. to prepare for the recovery target date, and
5. to terminate the counseling relationship.

The success of this phase is dependent on the counselor's proficiency during the rapport-building, education, and skill-development phases of treatment.

During the practice phase, injured athletes test out their coping skills in vivo. The counselor monitors progress and provides feedback and encouragement to help the athletes stay actively involved with their own recovery process. As goal-attainment levels are evaluated, the athlete is assisted in coping with plateaus or setbacks in rehabilitation. At times athletes might become impatient with the speed of recovery and begin to question the effectiveness of the coping skills they are employing. In these situations, a counselor who has established good rapport can assist athletes in facing realistic barriers and encourage them to allow adequate time for their coping skills to work. A well-developed short-term-goal-setting plan would allow athletes to see measurable progress and help lessen their doubts. At other times, situational problems or outside stressors might make it necessary to recycle through the skill-development phase to further expand the range of coping skills available to the athlete.

Beyond the monitoring process that takes place during this phase, it is also important to assist the athletes in developing a strategy to deal with setbacks in rehabilitation. This process serves two functions. It enables the athletes to understand that both physical and psychological setbacks are common during the recovery process. This can help prevent the athletes from interpreting setbacks as failures due to their own inadequacies (Meichenbaum, 1985). This is particularly important for athletes who display a tendency toward self-doubt and hopelessness during the initial crisis period of the injury experience. In addition, developing a strategy to deal with setbacks reinforces the concept that the counseling process is directed at teaching injured athletes to become more self-reliant. It provides a plan to directly utilize coping skills at a time when many athletes can get bogged down in negative self-talk or other self-defeating behaviors.

Another goal of this phase is to help injured athletes prepare for their recovery target date. As mentioned earlier, this is the period of time when athletes must test out their rehabilitation in game situations or else face the fact that they will not be able to continue to participate in their sport at their preinjury ability level. This period can be extremely anxiety provoking for athletes even though most do not show their concerns outwardly. It can also come at the heels of a relatively uneventful rehabilitation period in which the athlete seems to have everything under control. The sudden resurgence of doubts and fears can catch an athlete and the treatment team off guard. The athlete can be prepared for this transitional period by examining the reentry into competition from both intrapsychic and interpersonal perspectives. Once an athlete has received the OK to return to competition, counselors can be in a position to assess the athlete's readiness from a psychological standpoint. An athlete who is filled with exaggerated fears might benefit more from a slow, gradual reentry into competition than from being thrust directly into a starting role (Rotella & Campbell, 1983).

It is more difficult to prepare athletes to cope with the loss of their ability to perform. Ideally, regular contact with athletes is planned throughout the entire recovery period. As a result, contact with athletes is maintained at a time when they still might be denying or grieving the loss of sport. If an athlete continues to deny the permanency of an injury, it might be more helpful to develop contingency plans than to challenge the denial head-on.

The final goal of this phase is the termination of the counseling relationship. For those few athletes who become highly dependent on their counselors, this is the most critical part of treatment. It is not unusual for these athletes to hold on to the counseling relationship by developing new symptoms as the termination date approaches. In these situations, a modified time-limited psychotherapy model (Mann, 1973) has proven helpful by teaching athletes how to separate from relationships and find their own unique identities. This situation is most likely to occur with career-ending injuries or when athletes lack the physical skills to compete at their desired level.

In all counseling relationships with injured athletes, the termination phase is an opportunity to review and reinforce the range of skills that have been learned, to self-disclose what the relationship has meant, to share ambivalence about ending, and to discuss the transferability of acquired skills and knowledge to other areas of life. For some athletes this process can be critical to the success of the entire treatment and can take many sessions.

Social Support System Interventions

So far, the treatment protocol has focused on the individual athlete. In practice, successful treatment often necessitates concurrent work with the athlete's social support (family, friends, teammates, coaches) and sports medicine systems (athletic trainers, physical therapists, physicians).

Without presenting a long discourse on confidentiality, it must be noted that an athlete's permission must be obtained before information can be disclosed to others. This important caveat notwithstanding, involving significant members of the injured athlete's support system can create a positive environment to facilitate the recovery process. For example, family members can be instructed on how to listen to the athlete's concerns rather than trying to fix them. Coaches can be informed about the athlete's psychological readiness to return to competition and alternative methods of reentry can be explored. Physical therapists can be assisted in individualizing treatment programs to enhance adherence.

Helping the support network understand the importance of listening to the athlete when feelings are being expressed cannot be overstated. If social support and sports medicine systems are skillful at helping an injured athlete feel understood, the physical and emotional rehabilitation process will be greatly enhanced.

Working with the social support network can also help lessen an athlete's tendency to isolate or withdraw following a severe injury. Whether it is a problem with members of the support system not knowing how to interact with an injured athlete or an athlete's own attempt at getting away from the hurt, withdrawal will be less likely to occur if the support system understands what to expect and how to respond.

Incorporating a family systems perspective, in which the entire family becomes the treatment unit, is often indicated in situations where face-saving inhibits the recovery process. This would be the case in situations like the eager parent syndrome outlined earlier. Family-life-cycle dynamics and interactions might dictate a systemic counseling approach.

Whatever the case, developing a positive social support system can become an important aspect of the intervention. A counselor can help athletes understand what types of support are provided by their support network and what types are lacking. Learning to identify support needs and to develop new sources of support are important life skills.

THE PSYCHOLOGIST IN THE SPORTS MEDICINE CLINIC

Although the importance of psychological factors in athletic injury rehabilitation has been well documented (Crossman, 1985; Eldridge, 1983; Feigley, 1984; Hair, 1977; King & Cook, 1987), the inclusion of sport psychologists on sports medicine treatment teams has been slow to develop. Some of the probable reasons for this are a lack of understanding of the role of sport psychology in injury rehabilitation, financial considerations, insurance reimbursement policies, and issues of medical or psychological hegemony.

Not all people who identify themselves as *sport psychologists* have the training or the interest to function on a sports medicine team. In general, the ideal professional would have a background in both psychology and the sport sciences, possess an understanding of the sport experience, and have solid counseling skills. Throughout the chapter, the term *counselor* has been used in place of *sport psychologist* to signify such a professional.

Involving sport psychologists as integral members of the sports injury team is gaining increased support in the medical literature (Lombardo, 1985; Murphy, 1991; Samples, 1987; Yukelson & Murphy, 1992). Utilization of a sport psychologist often allows an injured athlete to bypass additional losses in self-confidence and control. Sports medicine teams that include a sport psychologist provide athletes with an opportunity to be introduced to sport psychology skills as a normal part of rehabilitation. The connection between mind and body healing is reinforced and the athlete learns additional life skills as part of the treatment process.

Some sports medicine clinics have chosen to use a different title to describe the sport psychologist to spare athletes any stigma or loss of face as a result of needing to see a psychologist. Titles such as athletic counselor, self-help skills specialist, and mental training specialist are being used to get around the word *psychologist*. Whatever the title, the key is to provide quality services.

Beyond providing direct services to injured athletes, sport psychologists must also spend considerable time and energy building credibility with the sports medicine staff. This is accomplished through educating the medical team about the services that are available and documenting progress through well-designed evaluation and follow-up studies. Great care must be exercised to avoid "stepping on the toes" of the medical staff during this process. The sport psychologist must be perceived as an ally, not an adversary or competitor.

Clinics that choose to utilize sport psychology services on a consultant basis must devote ample time during in-service training to educate staff members on how to make effective referrals. For example, referring to the sport psychologist as the "person who teaches self-help skills" sends a different message to injured athletes than telling them they "need to see a psychologist."

Sport psychologists can train sports medicine personnel to use basic counseling skills. This can help the staff create psychologically safe environments where injured athletes feel free to express their fears or concerns. Patients who feel understood are more likely to adhere to both physical and psychological treatments (Genest & Genest, 1987).

In addition, sport psychologists who have expertise in process consultation can provide a sports medicine clinic with valuable resources to handle communication problems, conflict management, problem solving, motivation, burnout prevention, or other employee concerns. It is important for a sport psychologist to be particularly sensitive to the frustrations and politics of a sports medicine clinic. Direct services to staff members assist in building credibility and demystifying the helping process. Indeed, sport psychologists can make major contributions to a sports medicine clinic in direct patient care, consultation with the medical staff, or employee assistance.

Along with playing multiple roles in a sports medicine clinic comes the potential burden of ethical problems. It is imperative to always be clear about who is the client and who is the patient. For example, if a softball coach contacts you about a player, the coach is the client. Ethically, the coach should also be your patient. You can assist the coach in managing the situation, but you must be clear that changing the coach's behavior is the focus of your interventions, not changing the player.

In addition, confidentiality and record-keeping practices should be addressed early in staff training, and it is advisable to maintain a separate record-keeping system. Often sport psychologists in the sports medicine clinic setting get caught up in the dilemma of needing to justify their existence based on the number of contacts, while at the same time maintaining the confidentiality of athletes, coaches, and support system members. Evaluation procedures, confidentiality, and record keeping are but a few of the concerns that should be addressed before a sport psychologist accepts a position in a sports medicine clinic.

CONCLUSION

Before closing, we think it helpful to follow up on the three cases presented earlier in the chapter. Jane, the gymnastics instructor, eventually came to understand that she had allowed her pain to control her life. Early in her injury process she was able to "tough it out," but the cumulative effects of the stress and frustrations surrounding her injuries eroded her confidence and prompted depressive episodes. The final straw was her husband's refusal "to cover for me anymore." His withdrawal of emotional and physical support forced her to seek psychological help.

In counseling, the therapist assisted Jane in getting back in control of her life. This was accomplished through building on her experience with mental imagery to distinguish between "injury" pain and "getting into shape" pain. The ability to differentiate the two elements placed the responsibility for choosing to perform in Jane's control. Other sport skills that she had learned, such as goal setting and progressive relaxation, were utilized to help her gain confidence in her own coping behaviors. Family counseling allowed her husband to continue to refrain without guilt from enabling behaviors. Jane's ability to manage the psychological aspects of her injury soon translated into physical and emotional gains. Her symptoms dissipated and she was able to resume her demonstrations. Ironically, Jane now has less need to demonstrate and spends more time on staff training and motivation.

Mike was the high-school football star who suffered a career-ending diagnosis. Unfortunately, Mike's story does not end on a positive note. Following his award at the football dinner, Mike committed suicide. The case material came from Mike's father, who sought counseling to deal with "guilt over not recognizing Mike's pain." Although this is an extreme case, it is an important reminder of the significance of sport in the identity of some people. For a few athletes, sport becomes more than just a game and disengagement from it can be traumatic. Greater sensitivity to the importance of football in Mike's life might have raised some concerns about his rather cavalier attitude toward not being able to play. His withdrawal from his social supports and projections about his father's needs might have been warning signs. Whatever the case, professionals need to pay particular attention to the psychological aspects of athletic injuries.

Richard, the runner who illustrated some of the classic symptoms of negative addiction, continued to push himself until the frequency of his injuries and work-related problems prompted him to seek professional counseling for stress management. The therapist was clear not to challenge the efficacy of Richard's physical activities. Instead, the initial meetings focused on building rapport and exploring the range of Richard's coping skills. This process validated Richard's physical efforts and set the stage for more in-depth exploration of potential sources of job, interpersonal, and physical stress.

Eventually, Richard was able to identify his level of diminishing physical returns and acknowledge that his increased time commitments to working out had allowed him to avoid certain fears, such as "being alone for the rest of my life."

The therapist worked with Richard and his exercise trainer to find a comfortable and appropriate level of physical activity and time involvement for workouts. Richard began to address his fears of social rejection and was better able to "just be myself" and "focus on enjoying" when he went out socially.

This chapter's purpose has been to focus on the psychological aspects of athletic injuries and to offer suggestions for designing and implementing comprehensive rehabilitation strategies. The most important consideration is to understand injured athletes as individuals. Numerous intrapsychic, interpersonal, and situational variables impact the recovery process. We hope the information outlined in this chapter provides a departure point for researchers to investigate the weight of these factors and the effectiveness of various intervention strategies.

REFERENCES

Astle, S.J. (1986). The experience of loss in athletes. *Journal of Sports Medicine and Physical Fitness*, **26**, 279-284.

Blann, F.W. (1985). Intercollegiate athletic competition and students' educational and career plans. *Journal of College Student Personnel*, **26**, 115-119.

Brewer, B.W. (1991). Athletic identity as a risk factor for depressive reactions to athletic injury. Unpublished doctoral dissertation, Arizona State University, Tempe, AZ.

Chartrand, J.M., & Lent, R. (1987). Sports counseling: Enhancing the development of the student-athlete. *Journal of Counseling and Development*, **66**, 164-167.

Coddington, R.D., & Troxell, J.R. (1980). The effect of emotional factors on football injury rates: A pilot study. *Journal of Human Stress*, **6**(4), 3-5.

Crossman, J. (1985). Psychosocial factors and athletic injury. *Journal of Sports Medicine and Physical Fitness*, **25**, 151-154.

Crossman, J., & Jamieson, J. (1985). Differences in perceptions of seriousness and disrupting effects of athletic injury as viewed by athletes and their trainers. *Perceptual and Motor Skills*, **61**, 1131-1134.

Cryan, P.D., & Alles, W.F. (1983). The relationship between stress and college football injuries. *Journal of Sports Medicine*, **23**, 52-58.

Danish, S.J. (1983). Musings about personal competence: The contributions of sport, health, and fitness. *American Journal of Community Psychology*, **11**, 221-240.

Danish, S.J. (1986). Psychological aspects in the care and treatment of athletic injuries. In P.E. Vinger & E.F. Hoerner (Eds.), *Sports injuries: The unthwarted epidemic* (2nd ed.). Boston: Wright.

Danish, S.J., & Hale, B. (1983). Teaching psychological skills to athletes and coaches. *Journal of Physical Education, Recreation, and Dance*, **54**(8), 11-12, 80-81.

Danish, S.J., Petitpas, A.J., & Hale, B.D. (1990). Sport as a context for developing competence. In T. Gullotta, G. Adams, & R. Montemayor (Eds.), *Developing social competence in adolescence: Vol. 3* (pp. 169-194). Newberry Park, CA: Sage.

Eldridge, W.D. (1983). The importance of psychotherapy for athletic related orthopedic injuries among adults. *Comprehensive Psychiatry*, **24**, 271-277.

Elkin, D. (1981). *The hurried child*. Reading, MA: Addison-Wesley.

Feigley, D.A. (1984). Psychological burnout in high level athletes. *Physician and Sportsmedicine*, **12**, 109-114.

Genest, M., & Genest, S. (1987). *Psychology and health*. Champaign, IL: Research Press.

Gordon, S. (1986). Sport psychology and the injured athlete: A cognitive-behavioral approach to injury response and injury rehabilitation. *Science Periodical on Research and Technology in Sports*, **3**, 1-10.

Haerle, K.K. (1975). Athletic scholarships and the occupational career of the professional athlete. *Sociology of Occupations*, **2**, 373-403.

Hair, J.E. (1977). Intangibles in evaluating athletic injuries. *Journal of the American College of Health*, **25**, 228-231.

Henry, M., & Renaud, H. (1972). Examined and unexamined lives. *Research Reporter*, **7**(1), 5.

Henschen, K.P. (1986). Athletic staleness and burnout: Diagnosis, prevention, and treatment. In J.M. Williams (Ed.), *Applied sport psychology: Personal growth to peak experience* (pp. 327-342). Palo Alto, CA: Mayfield.

Hill, P., & Lowe, B. (1974). The inevitable metathesis of the retiring athlete. *International Review of Sport Sociology*, **9**, 5-29.

Ievleva, L., & Orlick, T. (1991). Mental links to enhanced healing: An exploratory study. *Sport Psychologist*, **5**, 25-40.

Kane, B. (1984). Trainer counseling to avoid three face saving maneuvers. *Athletic Training*, **18**, 171-174.

King, N.J., & Cook, D.L. (1987). Helping injured athletes cope and recover. *First Aider*, **3**, 10-11.

Kleiber, D.A., & Greendorfer, S.L. (1983). *Social reintegration of former college athletes: Male football and basketball players from 1970-1980*. (Report No. 3). Unpublished manuscript.

Kleiber, D.A., Greendorfer, S.L., Blinde, E., & Samdahl, D. (1987). Quality of exit from university sports and subsequent life satisfaction. *Sociology of Sport Journal*, **4**, 28-36.

Kozar, B., & Lord, R.M. (1983). Overuse injuries in the young athlete: Reasons for concern. *Physician and Sportsmedicine*, **11**, 221-226.

Kubler-Ross, E. (1969). *On death and dying*. New York: Macmillan.

Lewis-Griffith, L. (1982). Athletic injuries can be a pain in the head too. *Women's Sports*, **4**, 44.

Little, J.C. (1969). The athletic neurosis: A deprivation crisis. *Acta Psychiatrica*, **45**, 187-197.

Lombardo, J.A. (1985). Sports medicine: A team approach. *Physician and Sportsmedicine*, **13**, 70-74.

Lysens, R., VandenAuweele, Y., & Ostyn, M. (1986). The relationship between psychosocial factors and sports injuries. *Journal of Sports Medicine and Physical Fitness*, **26**, 77-84.

Mann, J. (1973). *Time-limited psychotherapy*. Cambridge, MA: Harvard University Press.

Marcia, J.E. (1966). Development and validation of ego-identity status. *Journal of Personality and Social Psychology*, **3**, 551-558.

May, J.R., & Seib, G.E. (1987). Athletic injuries: Psychosocial factors in the onset, sequelae, rehabilitation, and prevention. In J.R. May & M.J. Asken (Eds.), *Sport psychology: The psychological health of the athlete* (pp. 157-186). New York: PMA.

McDonald, S.A., & Hardy, C.J. (1990). Affective response patterns of the injured athlete: An exploratory analysis. *Sport Psychologist*, **4**, 261-274.

Meichenbaum, D. (1985). *Stress inoculation training*. Elmford, NY: Pergamon Press.

Mihovilovic, M.A. (1968). The status of former sportsmen. *International Review of Sport Sociology*, **3**, 73-96.

Mitchell, J.C. (1974). Social networks. *Annual Review of Anthropology*, **3**, 279-300.

Morgan, W.P. (1979). Negative addiction in runners. *Physician and Sportsmedicine*, **7**(2), 57-70.

Murphy, S.M. (1991). Behavioral considerations. In R.C. Cantu & L.J. Micheli (Eds.), *ACSM's guidelines for the team physician* (pp. 252-265). Malvern, PA: Lea & Febiger.

Nideffer, R.M. (1983). The injured athlete: Psychological factors in treatment. *Orthopedic Clinics of North America*, **14**, 373-385.

Noakes, T.D., & Schomer, H. (1983). The eager parent syndrome and schoolboy injuries. *South African Medical Journal*, **63**, 956-968.

Ogilvie, B.C., & Howe, M. (1986). The trauma of termination from athletics. In J.M. Williams (Ed.), *Applied sport psychology: Personal growth to peak performance* (pp. 365-382). Palo Alto, CA: Mayfield.

O'Leary, A. (1985). Self efficacy and health. *Behavior Research and Therapy*, **23**, 437-441.

Orlick, T.D. (1980). *In pursuit of excellence*. Champaign, IL: Human Kinetics.

Pearson, R., & Petitpas, A. (1990). Transitions of athletes: Pitfalls and prevention. *Journal of Counseling and Development*, **69**, 7-10.

Petitpas, A. (1978). Identity foreclosure: A unique challenge. *Personnel and Guidance Journal*, **56**, 558-561.

Petitpas, A. (1981). The identity development of the male intercollegiate athlete (Doctoral dissertation, Boston University, 1981). *Dissertation Abstracts International*, **42**, 2508A.

Petitpas, A., & Champagne, D.E. (1988). Developmental programming for intercollegiate athletes. *Journal of College Student Development*, **29**, 454-460.

Remer, R., Tongate, R.A., & Watson, J. (1978). Athletes: Counseling the overprivileged minority. *Personnel and Guidance Journal*, **56**, 616-629.

Rolland, J.S. (1984). Toward a psychosocial typology of chronic and life threatening illness. *Family Systems Medicine*, **2**, 245-251.

Rosenfeld, L.B., Richman, J.M., & Hardy, C.J. (1989). Examining social support networks among athletes: Description and relationship to stress. *Sport Psychologist*, **3**, 23-33.

Rotella, R.J. (1984). Psychological care of the injured athlete. In L. Bunker, R.J. Rotella, & A.S. Reilly (Eds.), *Sports psychology: Psychological considerations in maximizing sport performance* (pp. 273-288). Ithaca, NY: Mouvement.

Rotella, R.J., & Campbell, M.S. (1983). Systematic desensitization in the psychological rehabilitation of the injured athlete. *Athletic Training*, **18**, 140-142.

Rotella, R.J., & Heyman, S.R. (1986). Stress, injury, and the psychological rehabilitation of athletes. In J.M. Williams (Ed.), *Applied sport psychology: Personal growth to peak performance* (pp. 343-364). Palo Alto, CA: Mayfield.

Rowland, T.W. (1986). Exercise fatigue in adolescents: Diagnosis of athletic burnout. *Physician and Sportsmedicine*, **14**, 69-75.

Ryde, A. (1977). The role of the physician in sport injury prevention: Some psychological factors in sport injuries. *Journal of Sports Medicine and Physical Fitness*, **17**, 187-194.

Sacks, M.H., & Sachs, M.L. (1981). *Psychology of running*. Champaign, IL: Human Kinetics.

Samples, P. (1987). Mind over muscle: Returning the injured athlete to play. *Physician and Sportsmedicine*, **15**, 172-180.

Sanderson, F.H. (1977). The psychology of the injury prone athlete. *British Journal of Sports Medicine*, **11**, 56-57.

Scott, S.G. (1984). Current concepts in the rehabilitation of the injured athlete. *Mayo Clinic Proceedings*, **59**, 83-90.

Smith, A.M., Scott, S.G., O'Fallon, W., & Young, M.L. (1990). The emotional responses of athletes to injury. *Mayo Clinic Proceedings*, **65**, 38-50.

Smith, A.M., Scott, S.G., & Wiese, D.M. (1990). The psychological effects of sports injuries coping. *Sports Medicine*, **9**(6), 352-369.

Sowa, C.J., & Gressard, C.F. (1983). Athletic participation: Its relationship to student development. *Journal of College Student Personnel*, **24**, 236-239.

Suinn, R.M. (1967). Psychological reactions to physical disability. *Journal of the Association for Physical and Mental Rehabilitation*, **21**, 13-15.

Svoboda, B., & Vanek, M. (1982). Retirement from high level competition. In T. Orlick, J. Partington, & J. Salmela (Eds.), *Mental training: For coaches and athletes* (pp. 166-175). Ottawa, ON: Coaching Association of Canada and Sport in Perspective.

Wehlage, D.F. (1980). Managing the emotional reaction to loss in athletics. *Athletic Training*, **15**, 144-146.

Weiss, M.R., & Troxel, R.K. (1986). Psychology of the injured athlete. *Athletic Training*, **2**, 104-109, 154.

Wiese, D.M., & Weiss, M.R. (1987). Psychological rehabilitation and physical injury: Implications for the sportsmedicine team. *Sport Psychologist*, **1**, 318-330.

Williams, J., Tonyman, P., & Wadsworth, W. (1986). Relationship of life stress to injury in intercollegiate volleyball. *Journal of Human Stress*, **12**, 38-43.

Yaffe, M. (1983). Sports injuries: Psychological aspects. *British Journal of Hospital Medicine*, **29**, 224-230.

Yukelson, D., & Murphy, S. (1992). Psychological considerations in the prevention of sport injuries. In P. Renstrom (Ed.), *Sport injuries: Basic principles of prevention and care* (pp. 321-333). Cambridge, MA: Blackwell Scientific Publications.

CHAPTER 12

ALCOHOL AND DRUGS IN SPORT

Chris M. Carr, PhD
Washington State University
Shane M. Murphy, PhD
United States Olympic Committee

Alcohol and drug use in athletics has been present since the 3rd century B.C., when Greek athletes experimented with many types of psychoactive substances to improve performance (Chappel, 1987). The saga of drug use for performance enhancement has continued into the modern Olympic Games, most notably with Canadian sprinter Ben Johnson's disqualification and loss of a 1988 Olympic gold medal because of his anabolic steroid use. The role of alcohol in sport, although less identified in the media, has been just as significant. The alcohol-related driving death of Philadelphia Flyer goalie Pelle Lindbergh represents the often tragic consequences of excessive alcohol use. Ryne Duren, a former New York Yankees pitcher and recovering alcoholic, describes his experience combining alcohol use with athletic performance:

> . . . Alcohol was bombarding my central nervous system to the point where I was never able to control my eye/hand coordination sufficiently. I was lucky to be there. . . . I was a very vulnerable person on the mound, in spite of the fact that I put together some pretty impressive innings pitched. (Wholey, 1984).

All drugs, including alcohol, represent a risk of danger for athletes. From the Little Leaguer to the major leaguer, participants in all levels of age and competition in sport suffer consequences from the use and abuse of alcohol and other drugs. This chapter defines the various types of drugs used in the athletic community. An examination of some possible sociological explanations for alcohol and drug-using behaviors will be presented. Specifically for the clinical sport psychologist who might provide counseling services for athletes, we discuss assessment, intervention, and prevention measures in cases of substance use and abuse. This information is intended to provide an overview of the sociological and psychological issues related to the use and abuse of alcohol and other drugs in sport. The following case example might be typical of identification and intervention issues confronting the clinical sport psychologist in an athletic setting.

■ *THE CASE OF SHEILA* ■

Sheila first sought professional help at the insistence of her partner, Mary. Sheila, a bright, outgoing 25-year-old, had been a world-class synchronized swimmer for 4 years. She and Mary were the current world champions in the pairs event. But with the Olympics just 11 months away, Mary refused to practice with Sheila unless she sought counseling. Sheila visited a clinical psychologist in a nearby city, someone recommended by the sport psychology consultant who worked with her coach.

In the initial sessions Sheila revealed a long history of drinking, although she attempted to minimize the seriousness of the problem. She first experimented with alcohol in junior high with some friends, but began to get drunk on an "occasional basis" during high school. Sheila said she drank to forget about her "worries"—including her parents, who were constantly fighting, and school, which she found difficult and boring. She was a good high-school swimmer and became involved in synchronized swimming through a friend who took her to some coaching sessions at an area pool.

In synchronized swimming, Sheila found the success and excitement that had eluded her in other life areas. She had great talent, and after 18 months in the sport her coach paired her up with Mary, a successful competitor who had recently broken up with a partner. They trained long and hard together, and after 3 years broke into the national rankings. Now rewarded with international trips and competitions, they performed well at the world level and soon became the second-ranked pair in the U.S. They came in second at the U.S. Nationals three years in a row, until the first-ranked pair broke up after a series of injuries. Last year they not only won the U.S. title for the first time but the world championship as well. Now they are aiming at the Olympics.

Sheila reported her drinking became less of a problem once she attained success in synchronized swimming. Her main problems apparently occurred on trips to competitions, when she hung out with friends after competition and "occasionally had a few too many." Sheila's partner, Mary, requested to come to the next session, and Sheila agreed. The clinical psychologist first met alone with Mary and heard a very different account of Sheila's situation. According to Mary, Sheila showed up drunk to morning practices at least three times a week. Mary always knew if Sheila had drunk heavily the previous night by the smell of alcohol on Sheila's breath. Sheila's drinking had seemingly become more frequent over the past year, since the world championship. Mary believed that Sheila was hanging out with "a bad crowd," and that she was getting too much attention for their recent successes. Practices were going poorly because of Sheila's poor coordination. Mary felt totally frustrated and eventually coerced Sheila into counseling by refusing to practice with her until counseling was initiated. When Sheila joined Mary in the session, she did not refute Mary's accusations, but instead began complaining about Mary's "weight problem," saying that Mary had gained 10 lb (4.5 kg) over the past 2 years. Sheila told the psychologist that performing routines with Mary was difficult because of Mary's weight.

Realizing that many issues were involved and that Sheila was still in some denial about the severity of her problem, the psychologist arranged to meet with both athletes in the next session to discuss some inpatient treatment possibilities for Sheila. Only 3 days later, the psychologist received an urgent phone call from Mary. Sheila had missed a morning practice session, and when she visited Sheila's apartment, Mary found the door locked and was unable to get an answer to the doorbell. She called the police, and when they entered the apartment they found Sheila on the bedroom floor in a drunken stupor. The psychologist arranged for Sheila to be admitted that afternoon to a 30-day inpatient residential treatment program for alcoholics.

SOCIOLOGICAL ISSUES

For the practitioner working with athletes, a relevant question is: Do athletes (at various levels of participation) use alcohol more often than their nonathletic peers? Previous research by Hayes and Tevis (1977) found that high-school athletes used less alcohol than nonathletes. Rooney (1984) found that there were no differences at the secondary level between athletes and nonathletes. More recent survey data suggests that athletic involvement might reinforce the social use of alcohol for males at the high-school level. In a survey of 1,700 high-school students, Carr, Kennedy, and Dimick (1990) found that male athletes reported significantly more alcohol use behaviors as compared to male nonathletes. In the same study, it was found that there were no differences between female athletes and female nonathletes. In an NCAA study of collegiate student athletes in 1985, it was found that 88% of respondents reported alcohol use in the past year, with 37% reporting marijuana use and 17% reporting cocaine use (National Collegiate Athletic Association Drug Education Committee, 1985). Table 12.1 demonstrates the reported use of alcohol by athletes at the secondary, collegiate, and elite level.

Table 12.1 Use of Alcohol by Athletes

Athletic level	Used alcohol during past year	*N*
Secondary and high school (Carr et al., 1990)	92.3%	1,713
Collegiate (College of Human Medicine, Michigan State University, 1985)	88.0%	2,048
Elite (Carr, 1992)	90.4%	70

In a nonscientific poll of professional athletes by *USA Today*, 50.7% of 278 respondents surveyed indicated that they believed that alcohol and drug abuse problems with professional athletes had worsened. Just 10.4% believed that the problem had gotten better (*USA Today*, 1992). The facts remain inconclusive; however, these data indicate that the risk for potential problems with alcohol and drug abuse might exist in the athletic population. In a survey of 1,713 high-school students, Carr et al. (1990) found that male athletes not only consumed more alcohol than male nonathletes, but also drank to intoxication significantly more often. The data in this study also supported Duda's findings (1986), which indicate no differences between female athletes and female nonathletes. These findings suggest that male athletes might be one of the greatest at-risk groups for alcohol abuse problems at the high-school level.

Very few universities offer specific alcohol and drug education to combat this problem. In a review of 71 university athletic departments, Tricker and Cook found that athletic trainers reported that most college programs do not offer drug education as a drug-abuse prevention strategy. The results of the study, according to the authors, "strengthened the assumption that drug education programs for college athletes continue to remain largely unexplored" (1989, p. 45).

The data in Table 12.1 reflect the alcohol usage patterns of a specific social group: athletes. Denial might play a major role in the abuse of alcohol in this social microcosm. Athletes represent a distinct social group in local high schools, on university campuses, and in major communities. In order to understand alcohol abuse by athletes, it is essential to understand the norms and standards of the athletic social group. An understanding of the unique stressors experienced by athletes is also important in designing interventions for athletes.

Peer Pressure and Sensation Seeking

Heyman (1986) suggests that there are two social factors that might be relevant to the use of alcohol and other drugs by athletes: peer pressure and sensation seeking. Pressure from peers to engage in experimental risk-taking behaviors is common in the developmental stages of adolescence and early adulthood. When the association between alcohol use and athletics is so strongly identified in the print and electronic media (e.g., beer commercials in sport contexts), the external pressure might be transmitted even more strongly by the sport group. Males might be at greater risk to engage in macho drinking behaviors, such as chugging beer or having contests to see who can drink the most alcohol in a certain period of time. The study by Carr et al. (1990) found that male athletes drank to intoxication significantly more often than male nonathletes; this might suggest that male athletes engage in the previously mentioned behaviors.

Sensation-seeking behaviors might be represented by the use of cocaine or other illicit stimulants to heighten stimulation and sensory input (Heyman, 1986). The nature of sport, where the athlete stretches the physical limitations of endurance, might promote similar nonsport behaviors. The use of anabolic steroids (discussed later in this chapter) among athletes at all levels suggests pushing the limits of the human body. Both of these factors, in addition to other sport-related social norms, must be studied by clinical sport psychology researchers to ascertain the relevance for effective prevention and treatment of potential problems.

Clinical sport psychologists must not only be able to identify and provide intervention and counseling for the athlete abusing alcohol and other drugs but also must be aware of the social pressures and norms demonstrated by the athletic group they serve. It is advisable before beginning consulting with any sport team to discuss with coaches, trainers, and athletes themselves the social climate regarding the use of alcohol and other drugs. This information will allow the consulting sport psychologist to provide complete and effective education, intervention, and treatment recommendations for the sport team. Thomas Griffin (1985), a substance-abuse specialist with the Hazelden Foundation, identifies several key societal variables that might place risks on the student athlete.

One of these issues is the social demands that fans might place on athletes in addition to the athletic demands. At all levels of competition (high school, collegiate, and professional), athletes are expected to be available to the public via the media, public appearances, or speaking engagements. An athlete who might be too tired or unwilling to commit to these due to family or other relationships might be perceived as snobbish or too egocentric. These expectations are often unrealistic and place additional stressors on the athlete. Another societal pressure includes the media, which monitor the movements and activities of athletes, especially at the professional level. Most people from the general population who experience substance abuse problems will impact only a limited number of others and will most likely obtain confidential treatment. However, when an athlete, whether it be at the collegiate or professional level, experiences a problem with alcohol or drugs, many people become involved. The much-publicized substance-abuse treatments of athletes such as Dwight Gooden, Dexter Manley, Steve Howe, and Chris Mullin lent little room for confidentiality. Societal expectation is a stressor that today's athlete must acknowledge. Both personal and athletic endeavors are likely to be evaluated and judged by the wide audience reached by today's media.

The Advertising Media Influence

Another societal factor that must be identified is a clear connection between sports and alcohol use (Griffin, 1985). It is difficult to observe a televised sporting event without also seeing advertisements for alcohol (usually beer). As a billion-dollar industry, the sale of alcoholic beverages is clearly connected with sport. Sport teams, sporting events, and even individual athletes are sponsored by brewing companies. It is not just alcohol that is problematic, because a person must first make the choice to drink alcohol before any problems can develop. However, this connection can be confusing in the development of coping skills and stress-reduction techniques for the student athlete. The study of advertising media influence on individual drinking behaviors has received little attention in the literature. It is important, however, that clinical sport psychologists be attentive to the messages that are heard by the athletes they consult with. Providing athletes with alternative methods of coping and stress management, for example, might replace the belief that one or two beers before bed helps one relax. In and of itself, such alcohol use might not be harmful. Yet the message that alcohol must be consumed to relax is wrong. Open and knowledgeable communication with athletes regarding the societal messages they receive about drugs and sport must be facilitated by the consulting sport psychologist. Beyond the societal norms and expectations that must be identified, specific assessment and intervention skills must be addressed. The next section addresses clinical issues relevant to substance-abuse assessment, intervention, and treatment.

CLINICAL ISSUES

As a consultant for a high school, college, or professional sports team, coaches, trainers, managers, teachers, or athletes themselves might be referred to you with the question: Do I have any alcohol [and/or drug] problem? This section identifies diagnostic symptoms of alcohol and other drug abuse and dependence according to the *Diagnostic and Statistical Manual of Mental Disorders* (3rd Edition, Revised) (American Psychiatric Association, 1987). Familiarity with the criteria specified by the DSM-III-R is essential in the diagnosis of abuse of alcohol and other drugs. In addition, the specific sport-related context of alcohol-abuse symptoms is presented. It is important to note that not all classes of drugs will be discussed; for further review, readers should refer to the DSM-III-R.

This chapter will present relevant symptoms and diagnostic categories regarding abuse of and dependence on various substances. The focus of this section is to familiarize clinical sport psychologists with information related to observing symptoms of substance abuse and substance dependence among people whom they might consult with in an athletic arena.

Substance Abuse

According to the DSM-III-R (American Psychiatric Association, 1987), the prevalence of drinking alcohol is highest and abstention is lowest in people ages 21 to 34. Among all ages, males are two to five times more likely than females to be heavy drinkers. Among athletes, particularly at the high-school level, male athletes have been found to drink to intoxication significantly more often than female athletes (Carr et al., 1990). The consulting sport psychologist should be aware of this information, especially if working with an all-male team. On an individual level, it is important for the psychologist to be able to recognize and intervene with patterns of abusive drinking or drugging behaviors.

The consulting sport psychologist should be aware that the DSM-III-R provides a list of identifying behaviors that might be observed when a person is abusing substances, including alcohol and other drugs. The DSM-III-R criteria serve as the reference for clinical diagnosis and intervention or treatment recommendations in many substance-abuse treatment agencies. The diagnostic criteria for psychoactive substance abuse is as follows:

A. A maladaptive pattern of psychoactive substance use indicated by at least one of the following:
   (1) continued use despite knowledge of having a persistent or recurrent social, occupational, psychological, or physical problem that is caused or exacerbated by use of the psychoactive substance
   (2) recurrent use in situations in which use is physically hazardous (e.g., driving while intoxicated);
B. Some symptoms of the disturbance have persisted for at least one month, or have occurred repeatedly over a longer period of time;
C. Never met the criteria for Psychoactive Substance Dependence for this substance. (American Psychiatric Association, 1987, p. 169)

Any psychoactive substance, including alcohol, marijuana, cocaine, amphetamines, and hallucinogens, can be included in this diagnostic criteria. For example, if a college athlete demonstrates continued use of alcohol despite academic difficulties due to drinking behavior and this has been prevalent since high school, the clinical sport psychologist can substantiate an evaluation of alcohol abuse and seek appropriate referral and intervention.

Abuse Symptoms With Athletes

Maladaptive patterns of drinking or drugging behaviors might lead to a diagnosis of psychoactive substance abuse. In the athletic community some of these symptoms might be readily visible, and some might be more covert. The clinical sport psychologist must be attentive to the persistent and recurring issues present in the assessment of a student athlete for alcohol or drug abuse. For example, if an athlete has identified repeatedly driving while intoxicated, the criteria for "recurrent use in situations in which substance use is physically hazardous" would be met. It is also important to assess the length and persistence of the symptoms, particularly if the athlete has identified specific symptoms lasting longer than a few months.

Social problems due to alcohol and drug abuse are often more visible and easily identified. For example, if an athlete has been involved in a physical confrontation at a social gathering, a coach is likely to be informed, particularly if the police are involved. Assessing the athlete's social support system will also help to identify potential problems. The team itself represents a significant social network, and internal confrontations often take place when a team member demonstrates inappropriate behaviors that reflect on the team as a whole. For example, such a confrontation might take place when an athlete involved in a social altercation is identified in the media. The resulting messages from fans, peers, faculty, and family members might be negative and indicting. The clinical sport psychologist should be aware of and attentive to the team dynamics if such an incident were to occur; in particular, observation of locker-room, practice, and team-meeting behaviors can often detect interpersonal conflicts. These conflicts might be focused on one specific athlete who might have a substance-abuse problem.

If a student athlete is being seen for individual counseling, another area of assessment should be the person's academic progress. Student athletes face stress in balancing academics and athletics; however, as identified by Finn and O'Gorman (1989), decreased academic performance (particularly among adolescents) is often attributable to the abuse of alcohol and other drugs. Sudden declines in such academic markers as grades are special warning signs.

Assessing the individual athlete's coping and stress management skills is crucial. Athletes at all levels of competition might turn to the use of alcohol and other drugs to cope with the stress of pressures from athletic injury, dejection, exhaustion, and other related stressors (Ogilvie, 1981). Given the frequent media messages that alcohol is a great relaxant and social elixir, it is not surprising that some young athletes learn to manage stress and self-confidence through chemical use (Ryan, 1984).

As a clinical sport psychologist, identifying how the athlete copes with the stress of academics, friends, and rejection (e.g., losing starting position, being yelled at by coaches) is important. If an athlete has experienced an injury, particularly one that prohibits further sport activity, assessment of coping strategies is again relevant. Research on athletes and injury (May & Seib, 1987) has identified frustration and impatience as specific emotional consequences of injury. The use of alcohol and other drugs might be deemed by the athlete as an effective release of pressure, anxiety, and depression associated with lack of sports participation due to injury.

Specific symptoms of psychoactive substance abuse that may be observed in the athlete population include

- drinking or drugging in secrecy (either alone or with others);
- feelings of guilt about drinking or drugging;
- lying about drinking or drugging behavior when confronted by others;
- needing increased intake to produce the desired effects (i.e., increased tolerance); and
- the experience of alcohol-induced amnesia or blackouts (Carroll, 1989).

In the athletic environment, specific team rules often regulate the use of alcohol and other drugs. Violation of these rules can lead to suspension or removal from the team. It is most likely that when confronted, athletes will not risk their future participation if they have violated team rules regarding substance use or abuse. The clinical sport psychologist must be attentive to this complex dynamic and must be aware of confidentiality issues during the assessment process. If athletes believe that reports of alcohol use will be shared with coaches, they most likely will not report such behavior. However, if the athletic policy includes a supportive condition for self-referral, the chances for acknowledgment of symptoms might be enhanced. Later in this chapter we will discuss the role of the clinical sport psychologist as a policy consultant.

Symptoms of alcohol and drug abuse are often difficult to detect. If, as a consulting sport psychologist, you assess your own knowledge of substance-abuse issues as limited, a referral to a chemical dependency agency or specialist is warranted. Being aware of local agencies that provide assessment of substance-abuse problems is ethical and competent consultant behavior, particularly considering the psychological welfare of the athletes. Once abuse symptoms are identified, appropriate interventions must be implemented. We will discuss these later in this chapter.

Substance Dependence

The issue of psychoactive substance dependence, whether it concerns alcohol, cocaine, or amphetamines, is of great importance for the clinical sport psychologist involved with the individual counseling of athletes. The DSM-III-R identifies that 13% of the adult population has had alcohol-abuse or dependence problems at some time in their lives (American Psychiatric Association, 1987). That 10% of the total population experiences problems with alcohol abuse and dependence is frequently referenced (e.g., Carroll, 1989; Finn & O'Gorman, 1989). If this means that only one member of a team of 15 has a problem, there will surely be residual effects on each team member and individual intervention will be a necessity. The issue of dependence on substances is indeed a touchy subject, for the label *drunk, addict, alcoholic,* or *doper* often seems permanent. What must be identified is the insidious aspect of the problem of psychoactive substance dependence and, yet, the treatable nature of this disorder.

The DSM-III-R (American Psychiatric Association, 1987) identifies the following diagnostic criteria for psychoactive substance dependence:

A. At least *three* of the following:
   (1) substance often taken in larger amounts or over a longer period than the person intended
   (2) persistent desire or one or more unsuccessful efforts to cut down or control substance use
   (3) a great deal of time spent in activities necessary to get the substance (e.g., theft), taking the substance (e.g., chain smoking), or recovering from its effects
   (4) frequent intoxication or withdrawal symptoms when expected to fulfill major role obligations at work, school, or home (e.g., does not go to work because hung over, goes to school or work "high," intoxicated while taking care of his or her children), or when substance use is physically hazardous (e.g., drives when intoxicated)
   (5) important social, occupational, or recreational activities given up or reduced because of substance use
   (6) continued substance use despite knowledge of having a persistent or recurrent social, psychological, or physical problem that is caused or exacerbated by the use of the substance (e.g., cocaine-induced depression, or having an ulcer made worse by drinking)
   (7) marked tolerance: need for markedly increased amounts of the substance (i.e., at least a 50% increase) in order to achieve intoxication or desired effect, or markedly diminished effect with continued use of the same amount

   Note: The following items may not apply to cannabis, hallucinogens, or phencyclidine (PCP):

   (8) characteristic withdrawal symptoms
   (9) substance often taken to relieve or avoid withdrawal symptoms

B. Some symptoms of the disturbance have persisted for at least one month, or have occurred repeatedly over a longer period of time.

These criteria assist in establishing the baseline symptoms in assessing whether or not an athlete might be dependent on any psychoactive substance, including alcohol. Whether or not treatment should be differential for abusers and for those who are dependent will be discussed later in the chapter. It is important that the clinical sport psychologist be either competent in the assessment of psychoactive substance abuse and dependence or knowledgeable about the local referral sources that we will discuss later in this chapter. The bottom line is ultimately the responsibility of the clinical sport psychologist whose assessment must provide the athlete with the optimal treatment intervention to alleviate this debilitating disorder.

Dependence Issues With Athletes

Specific symptoms related to alcohol dependence include

- preoccupation with drinking behavior;
- rapid intake behaviors, such as gulping and guzzling;
- an inability to abstain from alcohol use;
- the loss of control phenomenon, where the individual is unable to control the use of alcohol once it has begun;
- withdrawal symptoms, including involuntary shakes, insomnia, loss of appetite, mental confusion, and restlessness; and
- an inability to predict behavior once drinking has begun (for example, people who are alcohol dependent go to a social event unable to predict if they will have only a couple of drinks) (Carroll, 1989).

Most of these symptoms will be observed outside of the athletic arena. If an athlete comes to a practice or competition under the influence of alcohol or other drugs, however, it is important that immediate intervention take place. My (CC) previous assessment experience has found that substance-abuse behaviors observed at practice or competition are always symptomatic of more severe abuse or dependence issues. Although the signs and symptoms of psychoactive substance dependence vary greatly among people, the most common and shared features include psychological dependence (e.g., alcohol use as stress management), tissue tolerance, physical dependence, loss of control over use, and withdrawal symptoms (Carroll, 1989). Referral to a chemical dependency treatment program is the intervention of choice for an athlete who demonstrates symptoms of alcohol or drug dependence. In most cases, the clinical sport psychologist will serve as the catalyst for referral for the addicted athlete.

Other Assessment Issues

The previous sections focused on the essential diagnostic features of psychoactive substance abuse and dependence. As discussed in other chapters in this book, a key factor in being an effective clinical sport psychologist is the skill of observational analysis. Being able to observe the athlete's environment is essential to understanding that person's view of life as an athlete, whether it be at the collegiate level or at the elite level (e.g., Olympic). Each level of athletic participation presents a variety of external stressors and situations where the symptoms of alcohol and drug abuse or dependence might be observed.

Perhaps most relevant to understanding potential substance abuse problems is that most athletes begin using alcohol and drugs, with the exception of cocaine, in high school or earlier (College of Human Medicine, Michigan State University, 1985). This fact bears direct relevance for the clinical sport psychologist who may be consulting with a local high-school team. The attainment of age 21 appears to have little relevance as to whether athletes will or will not use alcohol or any other drug. If the clinical sport psychologist is working in a university setting or with an older group of athletes, the second diagnostic criterion for psychoactive substance abuse (repetition of symptoms over time) might already be met. Persistence of symptoms might be more marked if the athlete began use of substances in high school or earlier. A thorough assessment of the athlete's previous substance-use history is warranted. This history should include an examination of the athlete's peer group and peer-group activities. There is a social factor to alcohol and drug use; the literature indicates that most athletes use these substances with other teammates in a social setting (College of Human Medicine, Michigan State University; Heyman, 1986). The consulting sport psychologist should be aware of the social affiliations where alcohol or other drugs appear to be the main source of interest.

Another nonperformance factor to consider is the athlete's family history of psychoactive substance abuse and dependence. The literature in chemical dependency research demonstrates a familial pattern of substance-abuse tendencies (Ward, 1980). Research has demonstrated a familial pattern of alcohol dependence; for example, studies have found that people whose biological parents (one or both) display alcoholism and who were adopted as children by nonalcoholic parents have a significantly higher incidence of alcoholism than adoptees whose biological parents were not alcoholics (Cloninger, 1987; Vaillant & Milofsky, 1982). Readers interested in assessment and treatment of dependence should familiarize themselves with the literature regarding substance abuse and family dynamics, such as the book *Another Chance* by Sharon Wegscheider (1981).

Gender Differences: Issues in Assessment

As indicated on page 285, high-school male athletes were found to consume alcohol significantly more often than male nonathletes (Carr et al., 1990). Among collegiate athletes, no differences have been observed between males and females in the usage patterns of alcohol and other drugs, except that males were more likely to use steroids (Bell & Doege, 1987; College of Human Medicine, Michigan State University, 1985). There were no observed differences between female athletes and female nonathletes; however, research has shown that at the high-school level male athletes drink to intoxication significantly more often than female athletes (Carr et al.).

In our society, there are differences in the perceived social acceptance of alcohol use behavior by men or women. For example, women tend to drink alone or in the privacy of their homes more often than men (Sandmaier, 1980). The stigma of drinking secretly or alone often encourages females to hide their problems rather than to seek help (Carroll, 1989). This stigma plays itself out in relationships, as research has found that men are more likely to leave their alcoholic spouses than are women (Bourne & Light, 1979).

Some specific gender differences in alcohol dependence are that women usually begin both drinking and problem drinking at a later age than men; women progress from abuse to dependence more rapidly than men; females more often than males cite a specific stressor or traumatic event as the beginning reason for problem drinking; and alcohol-dependent women more often than alcohol-dependent men are described as feeling guilty, anxious, or depressed (Bourne & Light, 1979; Sandmaier, 1980). These differences are important to acknowledge, especially in sport psychology consulting. Often, clinical sport psychologists consult with both men's and women's teams and therefore must be attentive to the gender differences regarding not only performance issues but also psychological development issues.

The Team-as-Family Dynamic

Theories identifying family systems dynamics have proven to be extremely useful in the assessment and treatment of family dysfunctions, including substance abuse. The literature on the dynamics of alcoholism in families includes work by such authors as Claudia Black, Sharon Wegscheider-Cruise, and John Bradshaw, to name a few. This section provides a brief analysis of the athletic team as a family. The resultant dynamics of health and dysfunction in teams can be examined utilizing this analogue.

Wegscheider identifies four broad functions of the family system:

1. To establish attitudes, expectations, values, and goals for the family
2. To determine who will hold the power and authority, how they will be used,

and how members are expected to respond to them

3. To anticipate how the family will deal with change—in itself as a unit, in its members, and in the outside world
4. To dictate how members may communicate with one another and what they may communicate about (1981, p. 47)

Similarly, an athletic team might be observed to maintain similar functions. There are certain attitudes (1979 Pittsburgh Pirates theme We are Family), expectations (e.g., practice attendance, NCAA rules, grade point average), values (e.g., team unity, discipline in training, etc.), and goals (e.g., conference championship, Olympic medal) that are demonstrated in the athletic realm. The role of power and authority is clearly represented by coaches, administrators, and team captains. As well, all athletic teams are confronted with change. Each athletic season represents the potential for change, whether it be the first winning season or defense of a national championship. With team members changing consistently, change is a constant in athletics and sport. Lastly, each team develops communication lines and style. Viewing the team as a family and examining the team (family) functions can help us understand the effect of substance abuse and dependence on the team system.

When family system rules are rigid, enforced, and closed, they are often unhealthy and facilitate dysfunction (Wegscheider, 1981). In alcoholic families, symptoms shared by family members include denial of the problem, acute pain and stress regarding the family pattern, highly developed defenses to protect family members from even greater pain and lower self-worth, a predictable and fixed pattern of defensive roles, limited access to healthy communication, and lack of trust in members of the family (Wegscheider). The clinical sport psychologist might see patterns of enmeshment, detachment, and dysfunction with athletic teams in which members have substance abuse problems.

An unhealthy behavior manifested in alcoholic (dysfunctional) families is *enabling*. One can enable an alcoholic (or drug dependent person) by preventing the person from understanding the consequences of dysfunctional behaviors. For example, teammates may continually bail out a team member who has a pattern of getting drunk at social events. Although motivated by care, the enabling behaviors allow the dependent person to become more pathological. Although there are benefits to this enabling behavior (e.g., coach doesn't find out, so there is no threat to status on the team), the potential damage is more severe. The goal of intervention is to ensure that the dependent person not only receives help but also understands individual responsibility. In addition, it is important that the enablers receive help in understanding the process of healthy and nonenabling communication and behavior. Helping team members understand how they might unwillingly be playing enabling roles can be a primary goal of preventive education programs.

Specific interventions are required when a member of an athletic team suffers from alcohol or other drug problems. Effective sport psychology consultants will utilize extra resources when their own seem limited. The key feature is understanding the complex dynamics of the team as a family. Recent work by Oglesby and Hill (1990) explores sport psychology interventions, utilizing family systems theory. Regarding the intervention of abuse and dependency issues among athletes, it is important to recognize the role of the team in conjunction with the individual. As an effective clinician and consultant, one should be able to identify dysfunctional family behaviors and implement or suggest alternative methods of communication and intervention. This requires that the entire family is treated; thus it is recommended that when an athlete is treated or counseled for substance-abuse or dependence issues, the whole team (e.g., coaches, teammates, trainers) also receive some type of intervention.

For example, in the case study presented at this chapter's beginning it would be helpful to involve Mary (Sheila's partner) and their coach for follow-up counseling on Sheila's discharge from the treatment center. (The psychologist should obtain a release from Sheila approving such an intervention.) In this manner both Mary and the coach (and other teammates who have been involved) can learn about the process of recovery and aftercare for Sheila. They can be taught what to expect and how to react and, most importantly, they can be given an opportunity to seek counsel to discuss how Sheila's drinking behavior had affected them. If this type of intervention were not provided, resentment and frustration might develop among the family. This can jeopardize the individual's recovery from abuse or dependence problems. Although the focus of intervention and treatment is on the athlete who is abusing or dependent on alcohol and other drugs, it is important to consider intervention at a systems level. This allows for all affected members to have an opportunity to discuss their own feelings and learn about how to best support their teammate on return. Specific interventions for the athlete who is abusing alcohol and other drugs are discussed in the following section.

TREATMENT ISSUES

Once an athlete has been identified as having a substance-abuse or dependence problem, it is important that appropriate intervention and treatment steps be implemented. The goal of the initial intervention is for the person to acknowledge the possibility of having a substance-abuse problem and of further treatment proving helpful. The focus of this section is to identify specific types of treatment and briefly discuss the implications of treatment for the athlete with a substance-abuse or dependence problem (see Figure 12.1). The following treatment modalities are discussed: inpatient treatment, aftercare, outpatient treatment, and Alcoholics Anonymous (AA).

Inpatient Treatment

When an athlete is diagnosed with psychoactive substance dependence (whether alcohol or other drugs), it is important that inpatient treatment be explored. It is often necessary for a person who has demonstrated symptoms of dependency to be removed from the current environment so that the recovery process can begin. If detoxification is

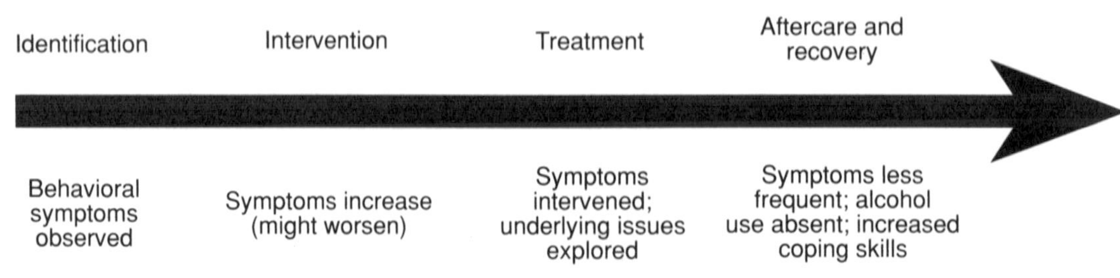

Figure 12.1 Symptoms change during the course of treatment.

necessary, inpatient programs often provide the environment to monitor for withdrawal symptoms and provide medical assistance. During the 4- to 6-week inpatient stay, the patient usually receives both individual and group psychotherapy. The groups and assigned counselors remain intact throughout treatment, and the patient experiences learning and growth via exploration of emotions, cognitions, and behaviors related to the drug-use pattern (Mann, 1979).

Typically, individuals are introduced to Alcoholics Anonymous during their inpatient stay. In addition, family members are usually involved in the treatment process by attending their own family treatment and receiving education on the salient issues of alcohol and drug addiction. Most inpatient programs involve family members from the beginning to end of treatment, due to family members' significant role in the recovery process.

Aftercare

Aftercare is a program of outpatient care for people who have completed inpatient treatment. This program usually lasts anywhere from 3 months to 2 years after treatment (Mann, 1979). Aftercare usually focuses on reentry into the person's environment; this includes family, occupation, and social network and, for athletes, their teams. The clinical sport psychologist must be attentive to the dynamics that occur when an athlete returns to the team from chemical dependency treatment. Often, teammates are unsure as to how to respond or what to say to their teammate. By facilitating normal communication and honest disclosure (e.g., "I'm not sure how to respond—can you help me?"), the clinical sport psychologist can assist the difficult process of reentry for the recovering athlete.

Typically, involvement in AA is an essential component of aftercare. In addition, family members usually attend aftercare sessions for their own recovery (from enabling behaviors) and transition. The focus of aftercare is to provide support and encouragement for personal responsibility and change.

Outpatient Treatment

The purpose of outpatient therapy is to provide intensive substance abuse treatment while at the same time allowing continuation of other occupational, family, and personal pursuits. This type of treatment is often unsuccessful if the patient continues to use alcohol and other drugs. St. Mary's Adult Chemical Dependency Center, Minneapolis, requires that the patient comply with three conditions to be admitted to outpatient therapy: (a) the maintenance of sobriety (abstinence from mood-altering substances), (b) the ability to continue employment without disruption, and (c) the ability to sustain home life and personal life (Mann, 1979). A patient's inability to comply with these conditions is seen as loss of control necessitating a recommendation for inpatient therapy.

It is important that the clinical sport psychologist be aware of local substance-abuse treatment agencies that provide both inpatient and outpatient care. Arranging tours and meeting personnel can help consultants to increase not only their own understanding, but often that of coaches, trainers, and sports-medicine personnel who might be able to attend. These local treatment groups can often serve as a resource for speakers for educational and prevention programs, discussed later in this chapter.

Alcoholics Anonymous

> I never believed I was an alcoholic. I never believed I couldn't handle my

> alcohol. All the problems I had—bankruptcy, loss of career, the end of my first marriage after 13 years, the fact that my current wife was going to divorce me—were just a part of my life, I thought. I never attributed it to my alcoholism. . . . Eighteen years ago, I didn't know anything about AA, and I wasn't ready to admit that I was an alcoholic. . . . Now I do what Don Newcombe wants to do. . . . You've got peace of mind when you are in control of your own well-being. . . . (Newcombe, in Wholey, 1984)

One of the most widely accepted approaches to recovery from alcoholism is Alcoholics Anonymous (AA), a fellowship of problem drinkers who together seek help in maintaining abstinence from alcohol and other drug use. Voluntary membership in AA involves the admission that a person, alone, is powerless over alcohol. Using the "Twelve Steps" of AA, members strive to maintain their sobriety through emotional self-exploration and a philosophy of basic goals including a searching personal moral inventory, a public admission of personal wrongs, a willingness to make amends to those who have been harmed by one's drinking behavior, and an attempt to carry AA's message to alcoholics who are still suffering (Carroll, 1989).

Various groups have been patterned after AA, including Al-Anon (for family members of alcoholics), CA (Cocaine Anonymous, for those who have abused cocaine), NA (Narcotics Anonymous, for those whose drug of abuse is heroin, opium, or morphine), and Alateen (for children of alcoholics). All of these groups operate without therapists as facilitators and are true self-help groups, in that the only membership requirement is a desire to quit using alcohol or other drugs.

For the clinical sport psychologist, a listing of local AA and other support group meetings is usually available through local mental health agencies. There are both open and closed meetings; open meetings are typically designed for people who might be struggling with whether or not they have a problem, whereas closed meetings are usually attended by persons who identify themselves as alcoholic and are in the day-to-day process of recovery. AA is a recommended referral option, as research has shown that a supportive social network is an essential element of long-term behavior change (Carroll, 1989). At the same time, by listening to others share their history, the people can confront their own denial systems and pursue further counseling.

Treatment Goals

The development and course of psychoactive substance abuse and dependence are based largely on unique individual and family processes. Treatment goals can be selected based on the therapist's specific theoretical orientation (e.g., client-centered, gestalt, behavioral, etc.). Additional treatment goals will be influenced by the focus of treatment (individual, group, or family).

The following three goal areas must be addressed in the treatment of the chemically abusive or dependent athlete client.

Awareness

Clients must become aware of not only the chronic and damaging effects of mood-altering drugs (basic drug education), but they must also be aware of how their own use has disrupted such life areas as

- family (including spouse, children, parents, siblings, and other nuclear-family members);
- social life, including relationships with peers;
- employment or academic performance;

- athletic performance (which may be the least-recognized effect);
- and, most importantly, their sense of self-esteem.

Clients should be informed about the disease concept of alcoholism so they can begin to formulate recovery philosophies.

Implementation of Change

Awareness should lead to action. This concept usually works well with people who develop an athletic lifestyle of practice, practice, practice, and performance. Often, practice time is spent in developing awareness of an opponent's abilities. This awareness helps the athlete to develop a more proficient game plan for success. If this plan is practiced successfully, the chances for performance success are optimized. Using this metaphor with the chemically dependent athlete might enhance implementation of treatment goals. Once athletes are aware of the dynamics of their addiction, they must practice the following skills: (a) increase self-knowledge through therapy by examining personal strengths and attributes that can assist in developing a healthy lifestyle; (b) learn skills of stress management, decision-making, and assertiveness to facilitate independence (vs. dependence); and (c) develop healthy communication skills that can be practiced with supportive family members and friends. Family therapy is often a necessary adjunctive process to reestablish positive relationships and to explore the damaging effects of the client's behaviors. Especially in chronic cases, there is considerable anger toward the abusing person, often expressed indirectly.

Process of Healing

For the chemically dependent person to heal and fully recover from alcoholism and drug dependency, self-esteem enhancement and self-awareness must continue over the long term. In fact, this must become a lifelong goal. It is important for the client to recognize that recovery happens one day at a time. Many athletes must confront this same dynamic as they prepare for a long competitive season leading to a higher goal, such as NCAA competitions or the Olympic games. Again, relevant sporting metaphors may assist in adherence to treatment goals. The therapist must continue to help people recognize their personal strengths and limitations.

The following factors should be considered by the therapist and client in the treatment of a substance-abusing athlete:

- The effect of the clash of self-images between that of the healthy athlete and the sick patient
- The impact of public exposure on the treatment process (Some athletes are celebrities and their entire treatment will be open to public scrutiny.)
- The role of exercise in treatment (There has been some debate as to whether exercise can serve as a positive replacement addiction for the client.)
- The effect of organizational policy on treatment (Many sports organizations react to substance abuse with a punishment, rather than a treatment, philosophy.)
- The likelihood of a return to competition (Often the high stress levels associated with the sport contributed to the abuse problems, and return to competition must be considered in a context of an athlete's developing the coping skills necessary to survive in a stressful environment.)

This is not an exhaustive description of the treatment process. It does not take into consideration the unique individual issues that confront the athlete with a substance-abuse or dependence problem. However, it provides a basic guide to the process of recovery and attainment of a chemical-free lifestyle.

An important goal for the sport psychology consultant involved in alcohol education is to create a supportive and receptive attitude towards treatment within the athletic community. In an interview with *USA Today*, Thomas "Hollywood" Henderson, a former NFL player with the Dallas Cowboys and recovering alcoholic, responded to the question of how sports administrators should attend to helping athletes with alcohol and drug problems:

> They need to understand, rather than be understood. They need to understand the disease. . . It's not just willpower. They need to believe in treatment (*USA Today*, 1992).

The sport psychologist is in a unique and influential position in providing such information not only to athletes, but to coaches, trainers, sports medicine personnel, and administrators. The team physician is an important potential ally in this process. The next section of this chapter will discuss the education and prevention issues related to substance abuse and dependency with athletes. Ryan (1984) emphasized the need for athletes to have a better awareness of the myths and risks associated with alcohol and drug use than they have received from many drug education programs.

PREVENTION AND EDUCATION ISSUES

The role of the sport psychology consultant in substance-abuse education has received increased attention in recent years. Tricker, Cook, and McGuire (1989) identify the significant role of the sport psychologist in the planning, preparation, facilitation, and presentation of substance-abuse education. Chappell (1987) identifies education as the cornerstone of drug abuse prevention programs for athletes. Yet the frequency and quality of drug education programs for athletes at all levels of competition might be inadequate. In a survey of 71 collegiate athletic departments, Tricker and Cook found that 95% of respondents identified their drug education programs as infrequently organized and holding from no meetings at all to one or two per year. The most frequent substance-abuse education meetings for athletes occurred once a month and were primarily informational (1989). With the high incidence of reported alcohol use by athletes at the secondary, collegiate, and elite levels, it appears that substance-abuse education would be a priority; rather, at the collegiate level the incidence of this type of programming is minimal, based on the literature.

It is premature to say that all athletic systems are negligent in providing substance-abuse education programs for their athletes; however, some data suggest that more extensive education is warranted. The clinical sport psychologist might be able to facilitate substance-abuse education through contacts with local chemical-dependency treatment centers, university counseling center staffs, and other outreach contacts. This section reviews the essential components of substance-abuse education for athletes. Literature on effective and ineffective methods of prevention are discussed, and a model of substance-abuse education used with resident athletes at the United States Olympic Training Center will be presented. This model is not intended to represent the ideal program; rather, it is presented as a demonstration of a multimodal education program specifically designed for athletes.

What Works in Education?

The effectiveness of substance-abuse education has been debated for the past 20 years.

In most education and prevention literature, the stated goal for substance-abuse education is to decrease substance-abuse behaviors and to facilitate more healthy and nonusing attitudes and beliefs. It is at this cognitive and behavioral level of functioning that substance-abuse education with athletes must minimally be targeted. In a large meta-analytic study of 143 adolescent drug prevention programs, Tobler (1986) was able to ascertain the significant and nonsignificant factors related to outcome. She found that peer programs (drug prevention facilitated by same-age peers) were the most effective substance-abuse education models; these peer programs produced the most significant decrease in drug use behaviors from pretest to posttest measures. Results in the same study indicate that the least effective programs at changing drug use attitudes and behaviors are information-only and affective-only (experiential) programs. Information-only programs focus on the sharing of drug abuse statistics and symptoms, whereas affective programs focus on role plays and self-awareness (e.g., values clarification). Subsequent research has demonstrated that effective substance abuse prevention programs must be multimodal to assist the transfer of knowledge to attitudes and to subsequent behavior changes (e.g., Botvin, Baker, Renick, Filazzolla, & Botvin, 1984; Rozelle, 1980).

Courtesy Jeff Miller and the University of Wisconsin

Utilizing a multimodal substance-abuse education model, Marcello, Danish, and Stolberg (1989) assessed the efficacy of such a program with university-student athletes. The program, developed out of the life skills training model designed by Botvin et al. (1984), incorporates four separate components; education, decision-making skills, interpersonal and communication skills, and alternative coping methods. Presented over a 6-hr format, the results demonstrated no differences between the treatment group and the control group. Due to questions concerning the motivation of the participants, limited time, and the small sample size, the researchers viewed the study as exploratory. However, it represented the first study of multifaceted substance-abuse education specifically for athletes to be presented in the literature.

Chapter 2 discusses the utility of counseling athletes via a life skills through sport model. This model emphasizes the various facets of athletic involvement at the cognitive, behavioral, and affective level of the athlete. In the same manner, an effective substance-abuse education model with athletes must incorporate a multifaceted approach to the athlete as a person; such a model stresses substance abuse information as integrally, but not solely, connected to the athlete's physical and psychological well-being. Tricker et al. (1989) postulate that individual progress can be achieved by developing the precursors to behavior change, including heightened awareness, improved attitudes, and decision-making skills.

Performance-Enhancing Versus Social Drug Use

The focus of this chapter has not been on the identification of pharmacological components of various classes of drugs (e.g., depressants, narcotics, stimulants) or on the specific differences between recreational drug use and performance-enhancing drug use. Rather, the focus has been on identifying the psychological symptoms, treatments, and prevention modalities of psychoactive substance abuse and dependence. It is assumed that health-care professionals who read this chapter will seek additional references when implementing their own intervention, prevention, or education strategies. However, there are some differences between the recreational use of drugs, such as alcohol and marijuana, and the use of performance-enhancing drugs, such as anabolic steroids and growth hormone. This section identifies some factors related to differences between the use of drugs to enhance performance and for recreational purposes.

A truly comprehensive substance-abuse education program will include information on performance-enhancing drugs such as steroids. Tricker and Cook (1989) found that 66% of surveyed collegiate athletic departments tested athletes for anabolic steroid use. In a survey of 2,048 collegiate student athletes, 4% reported steroid use (College of Human Medicine, Michigan State University, 1985). The sports medicine community has become increasingly aware of the harmful effects of steroid use among young athletes, and physicians are being encouraged to refrain from prescribing steroids unless medically warranted (Bell & Doege, 1987). Wagner (1989) identifies that athletes seeking a competitive edge might turn to drugs that risk serious adverse effects; he encourages other pharmacists to work toward ensuring that athletes do not abuse drugs, whatever the reason.

Although athletes might recognize that the use of alcohol and other illicit drugs does not enhance performance, the fact is that some performance-enhancing drugs (e.g., anabolic steroids) increase strength and performance (Wagner, 1989). The athlete's ego-involvement often has been identified as strongly attached to athletic performance (Ogilvie, 1987). Involvement of ego and self-worth in athletic success might blind the athlete to negative effects of performance-enhancing drug use. Effective substance-abuse education must address this conflict; the athlete works many hard and long hours to achieve success and might view drug use as an adjunct of training. Particularly if the family system enables this type of behavior, the athlete might not view steroid use as negative. Jay Coakley and Robert Hughes, sport sociologists at the University of Colorado in Colorado Springs, have identified this type of behavior as "positive deviance" (Hughes & Coakley, 1991).

In brief, positive deviance involves over-compliance to the norms and values embodied in the sport ethic, such as Win at all Cost, No Pain, No Gain, and Sacrifice for the Team (Hughes & Coakley, 1991). This sport ethic emphasizes positive norms; however, the ethic itself might become the vehicle by which athletes participate in deviant behaviors (e.g., steroid use) as a means of over-conformity. Some of Hughes and Coakley's recommendations in addressing this issue include trying to develop team norms emphasizing an awareness of one's limits (physical and psychological), not allowing athletes to play while injured, and a reframing of sport science goals to emphasize the growth and enhancement of the athlete through the expansion and continuation of the sport experience for athletes at all levels.

Additional information on performance-enhancing drugs is available in much of the sports medicine literature. Including a physician or pharmacist who is knowledgeable about anabolic steroids, growth hormone, and blood doping can be valuable in a multifaceted substance-abuse education program for athletes. The significant point is acknowledging and discussing decision-making skills when athletes examine performance-enhancing drugs.

United States Olympic Committee's Alcohol Education Model

Based on the literature concerning the efficacy of substance-abuse education among adolescents and young adults, combined with a study of previous programs used with athletes, a multimodal substance-abuse program was developed for resident athletes at the United States Olympic Training Center in Colorado Springs. The program was administered in three separate sections, each representing the essential components of substance-abuse education for athletes, based on the existing literature. The sections included (a) an education component; (b) a decision-making and coping skills component; and (c) a social skills and self-esteem component (Carr, 1992). As we present this program, we will discuss each section both theoretically and pragmatically.

Each separate component of the model includes lecture presentations, group discussions, role-play exercises, and written materials. The program uses a cognitive-behavioral framework. As a theoretical construct, this framework represents the most empirically supported prevention model. This theoretical approach suggests that substance-use behavior, like other behaviors, is learned through a process of modeling and reinforcement and is mediated by intrapersonal factors, such as cognitions, attitudes, expectations, and personality attributes. Each of the components of this model were presented based on this theoretical paradigm, and examples were demonstrated in a similar manner.

Education Component

The purpose of the education component was to present factual and updated information on the prevalence of alcohol and drug abuse in athletics, as well as to provide information on the pharmacological effects of alcohol and other drugs on the human system. Today's athlete is much more attuned to the effects of nutrition and physical preparation on the physiological processes of training. Therefore, it is important that relevant and updated information on the effects of alcohol, performance-enhancing drugs, and other drugs be included.

Definitions of the terms *use, abuse,* and *addiction* were presented and discussed. The DSM-III-R guidelines were used to define abuse and dependency (addiction) with various drugs, including alcohol. Symptoms of abuse and dependency were discussed and various treatment alternatives were presented. A group discussion on responsible attitudes and drug use behaviors was facilitated; included in this process were ethical dilemmas confronted by athletes who use psychoactive substances.

Decision-Making and Coping Skills Component

As indicated by various researchers (e.g., Botvin et al., 1984; Tobler, 1986), peer-resistance training is essential in effective substance-abuse education programs. The focus of this component was on discussing stress-management techniques as alternatives to alcohol and drug use, communication-skills (assertiveness) training, and general decision-making strategies using a cognitive-behavioral approach. Identifying sport-specific stressors was extremely relevant in this section, and subsequent group discussion focused on stressors similar to those discussed earlier in this chapter. Role-play scenarios allowed for the participants to demonstrate alternative coping responses to stressful situations. An example of a scenario related to coping behaviors and alcohol use follows:

> An athlete does not make the final selection for a national team. He/she goes out with friends and drinks to intoxication. Is it OK for him/her to get drunk this night? The next two nights? Why or why not? (Carr, 1992)

The work of Finn and O'Gorman (1989) assisted in the development and creation of athlete-specific scenarios that facilitated group discussion among participants. This specific component also allows for the clinical sport psychologist to discuss psychological techniques such as relaxation training and imagery training as alternative interventions for stress (e.g., competitive training stress). Trained sport psychologists might find this opportunity significant in identifying the utility of mental training techniques as necessary components for optimal performance. Concurrently, these techniques can assist the athlete in coping with stressors that might otherwise be managed through the use of alcohol and other drugs.

Social Skills and Self-Esteem Component

During the program for resident athletes at the Olympic Training Center, the theme of social responsibility was adopted by the participants in group discussion. The athletes identified the incongruent societal values attached to alcohol and sport (e.g., in the media). Regarding responsibility for self and the team, small groups discussed the choices of alcohol- and drug-use behavior during preseason, in-season, and postseason time frames.

A discussion of the positive benefits of sports participation was used in this component. Values clarification exercises were used to explore the role of drug use and the personal conflicts that arise when drug-use consequences interfere with self-selected personal values. One area of discussion that would have benefited from more time was the influence of others on usage behaviors and attitudes. As identified by Marcello et al. (1989), substance-use behaviors and attitudes are influenced by parental modeling, media advertising, cultural, ethnic, and religious factors, and peer influence prior to an athlete's arrival at college (or even high school, or the Olympic Training Center).

Upon completion of the 8-hr program (three separate components about 2-1/2 hr long), the participants evaluated the program contents. In addition, pretest (before beginning the program), posttest (immediately following completion of the program), and follow-up (7 weeks after completion of the program) data were collected on both participants and control-group athletes (who were offered the opportunity to attend the substance-abuse program that was scheduled after collection of follow-up measures). Although the evaluation of the program by participants was positive—participants rated the organization, presenter receptivity, participation allowed, and presentation style as good to excellent—the outcome data was disappointing.

The outcome results of this program (Carr, 1992) demonstrated no posttest or follow-up differences between the initial participants and control-group members on measures of substance-abuse knowledge, attitudes, or self-esteem. The author submitted some possible reasons for consideration. Perhaps the longitudinal effects of substance-abuse education are difficult to measure with current inventories; in the future, we hope that more sensitive attitudinal and self-report measures will be developed. Another potential problem with analyzing this type of study is the low baseline of reported use of other drugs (besides alcohol). This might make any actual changes in behavior and attitudes difficult to measure due to the lack of statistical sensitivity. Future research efforts will benefit from studies using such models as the Olympic Training Center's and other sport-specific models (e.g., Marcello et al., 1989).

Education and Prevention Recommendations

Again, the multifaceted model we have discussed is not all inclusive. It is intended as representative of a multidimensional (cognitive-behavioral-affective) prevention program for athletes. Clinical sport psychologists might be able to creatively implement similar programs; however, the literature indicates that inclusion of the previously mentioned components is essential. Perhaps of even more impact, particularly based on the results of Tobler (1986), would be the development of a peer-based prevention model.

The clinical sport psychologist involved with secondary or collegiate student athletes might be in a unique position to develop a peer model of substance-abuse prevention. After requesting volunteers, specific substance-abuse prevention training that includes presentation style, group facilitation, and role-play skills could be developed for potential peer leaders. For example, a list of volunteer athletes from the resident training program was developed. Athletes who participated in the training were asked to speak at local high schools. This experience was both challenging and rewarding, according to reports of the athletes involved. The potential benefits of peer programs with athletes as a group have yet to be studied in the literature; however, the previous literature on peer programs in substance-abuse education in general is promising.

We hope the roles of the clinical sport psychologist as consultant, counselor, and educator with substance-abuse issues have been made clearer during this chapter. An additional component of effective consultation includes policy (substance abuse and dependence) consultation and implementation in athletic organizations.

Policy Issues

The guiding force for substance-abuse education in athletic communities is athletic policy. Overall, such policies dictate the athlete's required grade point average, practice hours, athletic eligibility status, rules concerning recruitment, and other external variables. The adoption of substance-abuse education as a policy issue ensures its implementation and effective growth. Often, a consulting sport psychologist might have the opportunity to suggest policy changes or adoptions. Given this potential, the role of the sport psychologist in enhancing the potential for effective substance-abuse education is encouraging.

The NCAA Drug Education Committee has developed a set of minimum guidelines for policy consideration at its member institutions. These guidelines might be successful for athletes at the secondary as well as the elite (national governing body) level. A partial description of the program guidelines follows:

1. Schedule at the beginning of the school year a course on drug and alcohol awareness for all men and women athletes. It is suggested that each institution utilize the expert resources available on its campus or in its community. . . .

2. Each member institution should develop and have in place a plan for treatment of student-athletes with drug or alcohol-related problems. Such plans might utilize treatment centers and programs available in the local community and should emphasize

rehabilitation rather than punishment. It obviously is more prudent to have such a plan in place before rather than after a problem develops.

3. Coaches should become more aware of potential drug-related problems in student-athletes, and specifically should be an available source of support in the identification and treatment of such problems.

4. In relation to Recommendation #3, the athletics department at each member institution should schedule training sessions for all coaches, trainers, and team physicians as to how to recognize and handle drug and alcohol-related problems. (NCAA Drug Education Committee, n.d.)

Although clearly not all inclusive, these guidelines provide support for the process of identification, treatment, and prevention of substance abuse in athletes. The NCAA recommends a minimum of three sessions, but based on a review of the literature, we recommend more sessions of a longer format and with more specific content material guidelines. The goal of effective policy implementation is to reinforce intervention, treatment, and education; even in its brief form, the NCAA guidelines identify each of the essential issues. The clinical sport psychologist might serve as a catalyst to ensure the implementation of effective and realistic programs.

CONCLUSION

This chapter focused on substance-abuse and dependence issues relevant to the assessment of, intervention with, treatment of, and education of athletes at various levels of competition. Specific stressors for athletes were identified; the subsequent risk factors associated with alcohol and other drug use were discussed. Although pharmacological information on various drugs, including performance-enhancing drugs, was not presented here, there are many references for this information.

The authors do not expect that, having read this chapter, readers will feel proficient enough to be chemical dependency counselors; rather, we hope that previously unidentified clinical issues are now salient. More importantly, issues of treatment options and suggestions for educational alternatives have been presented. As a reference guide, this chapter is intended to answer questions that might arise for a sport psychologist in any athletic setting, be it with high-school, collegiate, or elite-level teams.

The authors suggest that additional resources be consulted for information on the disease concept of alcoholism and other specific concerns regarding behavioral pharmacology. In addition, local chemical dependency hospitals might be able to provide sport psychologists with handouts, assessment materials, or speakers for substance-abuse education programs. A complete copy of the model presented in this chapter is available directly from the first author. A key component of effective consulting is knowing where local resources exist; often, substance-abuse specialists can be found in mental health directories. For sport psychologists in university settings, contact the university student-counseling center and student health service for information. At some universities, substance-abuse counselors or coordinators exist through the division of student affairs. Sport psychologists who consult with national governing bodies or other national sport organizations can contact the sports medicine and sport science programs of the United States Olympic Committee in Colorado Springs.

The multifaceted role of the clinical sport psychologist requires basic knowledge about alcohol and drug abuse and dependence. The psychological concerns of athletes can be exacerbated by the abuse of alcohol and other psychoactive substances; appropriate intervention and treatment referral is necessary and can be facilitated by the sport psychologist. In addition, the sport psychologist can share insights and techniques that help athletes to deal with the pressures of sport. Non-clinicians can play a valuable role in promoting and coordinating substance-abuse education programs with sport organizations. Although not the most popular subject to discuss, the devastating effects of alcohol and drug abuse and dependence can create permanent consequences for the athlete, the coach, teammates, and the family. The effective sport psychology consultant will be able to assist athletes in recognizing, treating, and preventing substance-abuse problems, thereby allowing each athlete to strive for and achieve their optimal performance potential as athletes and as people.

REFERENCES

American Psychiatric Association. (1987). *Diagnostic and statistical manual of mental health disorders* (3rd ed. rev.). Washington, DC: Author.

Bell, J.A., & Doege, T.C. (1987). Athlete's use and abuse of drugs. *Physician and Sportsmedicine*, **15**(3), 99-108.

Botvin, G.J., Baker, E., Renick, N.L., Filazzola, A.D., & Botvin, E.M. (1984). A cognitive-behavioral approach to substance abuse prevention. *Addictive Behaviors*, **9**, 139-147.

Bourne, P.G., & Light, E. (1979). Alcohol problems in blacks and women. In J.H. Mendelson & N.K. Mello (Eds.), *The diagnosis and treatment of alcoholism* (pp. 110-115). New York: McGraw-Hill.

Carr, C.M. (1992). *Substance abuse education with athletes*. University Microfilms: Ann Arbor, MI.

Carr, C.M., Kennedy, S.R., & Dimick, K.M. (1990). Alcohol use and abuse among high school athletes: A comparison of alcohol use and intoxication in male and female high school athletes and non-athletes. *Journal of Alcohol and Drug Education*, **36**(1), 39-45.

Carroll, C.R. (1989). *Drugs in modern society* (2nd ed.). Dubuque, IA: Brown.

Chappel, J.N. (1987). Drug use and abuse in the athlete. In J.R. May & M.J. Asken (Eds.), *Sport psychology: The psychological health of the athlete* (pp. 187-211). New York: PMA.

Cloninger, C.R. (1987). Neurogenetic adaptive mechanisms in alcoholism. *Science*, **236**, 410-416.

College of Human Medicine, Michigan State University. (1985, June). *The substance use and abuse habits of college student-athletes*. Presented to NCAA Drug Education Committee, Michigan State University.

Duda, M. (1986). Female athletes: Targets for drug abuse. *Physician and Sportsmedicine*, **14**(4), 142-146.

Finn, P., & O'Gorman, P.A. (1989). *Teaching about alcohol*. Dubuque, IA: Brown.

Griffin, T.M. (1985). *Paying the price*. Hazelden Foundation: Minneapolis, MN.

Hayes, R.W., & Tevis, B.W. (1977). A comparison of attitudes and behavior of high school athletes and non-athletes with respect to alcohol use and abuse. *Journal of Alcohol and Drug Education*, **23**(1), 20-28.

Heyman, S.R. (1986). Psychological problem patterns found with athletes. *The Clinical Psychologist, Summer*, 68-71.

Hughes, R., & Coakley, J.J. (1991). *Positive deviance among athletes: The implications of overcommitment to the sport ethic*. Unpublished manuscript.

Mann, G.A. (1979). *Recovery of reality: Overcoming chemical dependency*. New York: Harper & Row.

Marcello, R.J., Danish, S.J., & Stolberg, A.L. (1989). An evaluation of strategies developed to prevent substance abuse among student-athletes. *Sport Psychologist*, **3**, 196-211.

May, J.R., & Seib, G.E. (1987). Athletic injuries: Psychosocial factors in the onset, sequelae, rehabilitation, and prevention. In J.R. May & M.J. Asken (Eds.), *Sport psychology: The psychological health of the athlete* (pp. 157-187). New York: PMA.

National Collegiate Athletic Association. (n.d.) Drug Education Committee. *Drugs, the coach, and the athlete*: Author.

Ogilvie, B.C. (1981). The emotionally disturbed athlete: A round table. *Physician and Sportsmedicine*, **9**(7), 68-74.

Ogilvie, B.C. (1987). Counseling for sports career termination. In J.R. May & M.L. Asken (Eds.), *Sport psychology: The psychological health of the athlete* (pp. 213-230). New York: PMA.

Oglesby, C.A., & Hill, K. (1990). *Family systems approaches: A new methodology for work with athletic teams*. Colloquium presentation at Association for the Advancement of Applied Sport Psychology Annual Conference, San Antonio.

Rooney, J.F. (1984). Sports and clean living: A useful myth. *Drug and Alcohol Dependency*, **13**, 75-87.

Rozelle, G.R. (1980). Experiential and cognitive small group approaches to alcohol education for college students. *Journal of Alcohol and Drug Education*, **26**(1), 40-54.

Ryan, A.J. (1984). Drugs and self-confidence. *Physician and Sportsmedicine*, **11**(1), 42.

Sandmaier, M. (1980). *The invisible alcoholics: Women and alcohol abuse in America*. New York: McGraw-Hill.

Staff. (1992, January 23). Drugs, alcohol and professional athletes: Special article. *USA Today*.

Tobler, N.S. (1986). Meta-analysis of 143 adolescent drug prevention programs: Quantitative outcome results of program participants compared to a control or comparison group. *Journal of Drug Issues*, **16**, 537-567.

Tricker, R., & Cook, D.L. (1989). The current status of drug intervention and prevention in college athletic programs. *Journal of Alcohol and Drug Education*, **34**(2), 38-45.

Tricker, R., Cook, D.L., & McGuire, R. (1989). Issues related to drug abuse in college athletics: Athletes at risk. *Sport Psychologist*, **3**, 155-165.

Vaillant, G.E., & Milofsky, E.S. (1982). The etiology of alcoholism. *American Psychologist*, **37**, 494-503.

Wagner, J.C. (1989). Abuse of drugs to enhance athletic performance. *American Journal of Hospital Pharmacy*, **46**, 2059-2067.

Ward, D.A. (1980). *Alcoholism: Introduction to theory and treatment*. Dubuque, IA: Kendall/Hunt.

Wegscheider, S. (1981). *Another chance: Hope and help for the alcoholic family*. Palo Alto: Science and Behavior Books.

Wholey, D. (1984). *The courage to change*. Boston: Houghton Mifflin.

CHAPTER 13

EATING DISORDERS AND WEIGHT MANAGEMENT IN ATHLETES

Robert A. Swoap, PhD and Shane M. Murphy, PhD
United States Olympic Committee

It is likely that most competitive athletes have been concerned with weight control at one time or another. There are many reasons why serious athletes self-monitor weight and diet, such as making weight, appearing attractive in front of judges, or trying to reach ultimate performance potential. Weight management is a necessary part of most athletes' training. For some athletes, however, weight management goes awry and becomes a serious problem. These athletes, having become obsessed about their weight, begin using harmful methods, such as severe dehydration, to lose weight; some cases progress to clinical eating disorders. Because weight management is a prevalent issue in competitive sport and because there can be severe consequences for eating-disordered people, it is critical for the helping professional working with athletes to understand how to recognize and treat eating disorders. More generally, it is greatly beneficial for the helping professional in sport to be able to inform athletes about safe and effective methods of weight management.

Why so much concern about weight management in sport? From a purely performance perspective, athletes can experience compromised competitive ability due to poor weight-management practices. For example, rapid weight reduction often results in loss of lean-body mass but unsustained weight loss (Blackburn et al., 1989; Stuart, Mitchell, & Jensen, 1981). The loss of lean-body mass and carbohydrate stores can be exceptionally harmful to athletes who participate in a demanding athletic training regimen (Porcello, 1984). The rapid weight loss associated with some techniques (e.g., fasting, long steam baths) comes primarily from water depletion, and dehydration is an unfavorable state in which to compete. The American College of Sports Medicine (ACSM) has recognized that female athletes might be at special risk for a triad of related health issues: eating disorders, amenorrhea, and osteoporosis (Otis, 1993; Yeager, Agostini, Nattiv, & Drinkwater, 1993).

In addition to the deleterious effects that poor weight-management techniques have on performance, it is probably the case that when athletes engage in medically unsafe weight-loss practices, they place themselves at higher risk for developing eating disorders. The following case history illustrates how a focus on weight loss in sport can become unhealthy and self-destructive.

■ *THE CASE OF KARL* ■

The following case is from the second author's files. It represents elements of case histories of several athletes and does not portray any one person.

I first met Karl at a multisport competitive event in Florida. He was a competitor in the diving competition. I was a sport psychologist assigned to the medical team providing services at the event. Karl asked to see me before his competition, and we met in an office in the medical center. He was worried about his upcoming competition and described symptoms of lack of sleep and disturbed appetite. Only 2 years before, at age 25, Karl had won a bronze medal in a World Cup competition in his event. He had appeared destined for a stellar career, but the 2 years after his win were described by Karl as "a nightmare." His competitive performances had deteriorated, his confidence was low, and he was struggling just to make international teams. Karl asked for help in dealing with his nerves. He described a pattern of losing focus in the moments leading up to his dive. He described being distracted and feeling physically weak as he stood on the board. Karl attributed his poor performances to predive anxiety. We worked on finding a way to deal with his anxiety; I taught Karl a simple relaxation method to use a few minutes before his dives. He tried to identify his negative precompetition cognitions (e.g., If I mess up on this dive, I'll drop out of the top five) and constructed positive coping statements to substitute (I'm nervous, but I only need to focus on a good takeoff and good position on the board. The rest will follow). We met twice before Karl's competition began.

Karl finished fourth in his competition. The top three divers qualified for an overseas trip to compete in several world competitions. I did not see Karl the next day but encountered him at breakfast in the competitor's dining hall the following morning. I asked Karl if he wished to meet again, and he set up an appointment for that afternoon. As we began, Karl stated that his career was "finished." He seemed greatly upset and began crying as he struggled to describe his competition. He mentioned that his "starvation diet" had left him feeling so weak that he felt physically unable to perform his best. I asked Karl about this diet, and he began to describe a pattern of self-injurious eating behaviors that spanned 7 years.

Karl began his diving career at age 17. Over the next 3 years he progressed steadily, and at age 20 he was offered a chance to train with one of the country's top coaches. This coach was famous for his strict work ethic, which Karl eagerly embraced. All athletes on the team weighed in twice a week and their levels of body fat were closely monitored. Karl became obsessed with his weight and with the idea that losing 15 lb (about 7 kg) was the key to his becoming a top diver. At this time he began the habit of purging, forcing himself to vomit after any meal he regarded as self-indulgent. He used laxatives regularly in an attempt to control his weight, especially before competitions. After 2 years with his new coach, Karl had tried a variety of weight-control approaches, including many different diets, subliminal tapes, fasting before competitions, and using diuretics. His weight frequently fluctuated, but he could never seem to keep that 15 lb off for any length of time.

After finishing college, Karl left his coach to train in a new program near where his girlfriend lived. His new coach soon took him aside for a frank discussion about Karl's weight-loss efforts. He told Karl that his current weight was acceptable and that he wanted Karl to stop dieting. "You need to be strong to be a great diver," he told Karl. Over time, Karl began to gain confidence in his body image and stopped his purging and fasting behaviors. Two years later, he broke onto the world scene with his third-place finish in a major international competition. Karl made the United States team to go to the world championships. The national coach was his old college mentor. When Karl arrived, the coach commented that he looked "heavy" and asked Karl if he had gained weight recently. The coach told Karl that weight control was essential for diving success and suggested that Karl drop a few pounds. Karl was devastated. His confidence plummeted, and he had a miserable competition. When he returned home, Karl found himself returning to his old habits. Scared that his coach would find out, Karl became extremely secretive about his dieting and eating. He noticed that his mood fluctuated rapidly, from exhilaration one day to deep depression the next. Over the next 2 years his good performances became more and more infrequent. His coach tried to talk to him about it, but Karl felt that he had to work things out on his own. After finishing his story, Karl began crying again. "I tried to tell my parents about this last Christmas," said Karl, "but they just told me that I was a great athlete and that things would work out. I feel like nobody cares."

This chapter has two main goals: (a) to promote an understanding among helping professionals of the special issues related to weight management in the sporting community and (b) to educate those concerned people in the sporting community about major issues in identifying and treating eating disorders and to encourage healthy weight-management behaviors. It is not necessary in this chapter to deal extensively with the literature on eating disorders in general, as this has been done thoroughly in other texts. Indeed, two excellent texts dealing with eating and weight-loss issues in sport have been published recently (Brownell, Rodin, & Wilmore, 1992; Thompson & Sherman, 1993). This chapter is organized to examine and provide information on the prevalence of eating disorders in the athletic population, promote an understanding of predisposing factors to the development of eating disorders in sport, indicate how to recognize an eating or weight-loss problem, discuss treatment issues with athletes, and provide a brief guide to the prevention of eating disorders in sport, with an emphasis on healthy weight-management techniques for athletes and their coaches.

PREVALENCE

Some basic definitions and classifications are necessary to examine the prevalence of eating disorders in athletes. According to the *Diagnostic and Statistical Manual of Mental Disorders* (3rd Edition, Revised) (American Psychiatric Association, 1987), the diagnostic criteria for anorexia nervosa include the following:

- Refusal to maintain body weight over a minimal normal weight for age and height, e.g., weight loss leading to maintenance of body weight 15% below that expected; or failure to make expected weight gain during period of growth, leading to body weight 15% below that expected
- Intense fear of gaining weight or becoming fat, even though underweight
- Disturbance in the way in which one's body weight, size, or shape is experienced (e.g., the person claims to "feel fat" even when emaciated, believes that one area of the body is "too fat" even when obviously underweight)
- In females, absence of at least three consecutive menstrual cycles when otherwise expected to occur (primary or secondary amenorrhea) (A woman is considered to have amenorrhea if her

periods occur only following hormone, e.g., estrogen, administration.)

The DSM-III-R diagnostic criteria for bulimia nervosa include these:

- Recurrent episodes of binge eating (rapid consumption of a large amount of food in a discrete period of time)
- A feeling of lack of control over eating behavior during the eating binges
- The person regularly engages in either self-induced vomiting, use of laxative or diuretics, strict dieting or fasting, or vigorous exercise in order to prevent weight gain
- A minimum average of two binge-eating episodes a week for at least 3 months
- Persistent overconcern with body shape and weight

An accurate assessment of the prevalence of bulimia and anorexia nervosa in any population is difficult to achieve, due to the secretive nature of these disorders. In the athletic domain, discovery might lead to serious repercussions for an athlete who has this type of problem, including being dropped from a team or program. Jack Wilmore states that "even the roommates and parents of those who have a problem often don't know what's going on. Sometimes they don't find out until it becomes almost catastrophic and professional help is a necessity. So we may be seeing just the tip of the iceberg" (Thornton, 1990, p. 118). Researchers and clinicians who examine eating disorders in sport must take into account the perceived threat of their assessments.

The accuracy of most studies purporting to measure the prevalence of eating disorders in sport is uncertain. Part of this uncertainty is due to the secretive nature of the disorder. However, part of the lack of confidence in current findings is due to the assessment techniques (paper-and-pencil self-report surveys) used in the majority of these studies. As Brownell, Rodin, and Wilmore point out, ". . . self-reports have questionable validity, at least with certain athletes under some circumstances [therefore] prevalence figures from existing studies might underestimate the extent of the problem" (1992, p. 138). Alternative methodologies, such as clinical interviews, randomized telephone surveys, admission records in sports medicine clinics, and representative population sample surveys with follow-up interviews, have been used infrequently. In addition, many investigators have not specifically determined the prevalence of clinical eating disorders but instead have focused on describing the frequency of eating-disordered behaviors. Although the prevalence of subclinical eating problems (i.e., pathogenic weight loss techniques) in athletics is also very important to determine, it should not be construed as an estimate of eating disorders. Because of these assessment problems, current prevalence findings must be interpreted cautiously.

Burckes-Miller and Black (1988b) surveyed 695 male and female athletes and reported that 3% met DSM-III-R criteria for anorexia nervosa (4.2% female, 1.6% male), and that 21% met the criteria for bulimia nervosa (39.2% female, 14.3% male). They also found that several techniques were used to lose weight (see Figure 13.1). Dick (1991) found that there is a sport-specific prevalence for eating disorder conditions, but cautioned that no sport should be considered "exempt" from having individuals susceptible to eating disorders (p. 139) (see Figure 13.2.).

To ascertain the prevalence of subclinical eating problems, Rosen, McKeag, Hough, and Curley (1986) surveyed 182 female collegiate athletes and reported that 32% practiced at least one pathogenic weight-control behavior (e.g., self-induced vomiting; use of laxatives, diet pills, or diuretics). They also found these behaviors to be sport-related, as 74% of gymnasts and 47% of distance runners

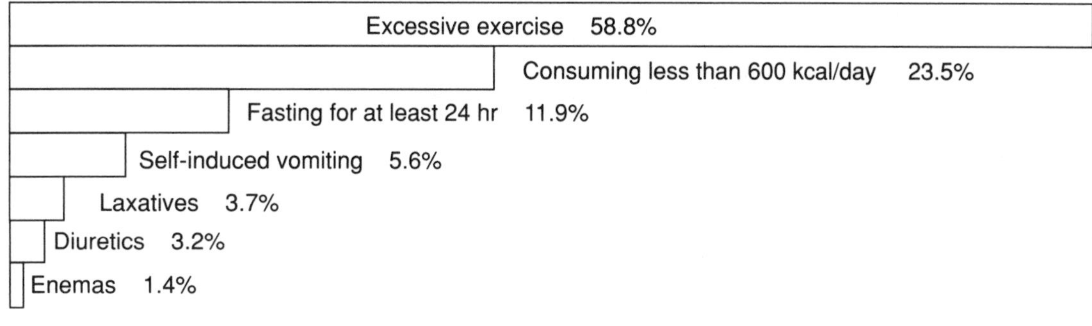

Figure 13.1 Common weight-loss techniques used by athletes.
Note. From "Male and Female College Athletes: Prevalence of Anorexia Nervosa and Bulimia Nervosa" by M.E. Burckes-Miller and D.R. Black, 1988, *Athletic Training*, **23** (pp. 137-140). Copyright 1988 by the National Athletic Trainers Association. Adapted by permission.

practiced pathogenic weight-control behavior. A subsample of the athletes (N = 30) indicated that 83% used pathogenic weight-control behavior to improve athletic performance and only 7% did so to improve appearance. In a follow-up study, Rosen and Hough (1988) found that of 42 gymnasts, all were attempting to lose weight and 62% used at least one pathogenic method. Furthermore, of the 42 gymnasts, 67% reported that they had been told by coaches that they were too heavy, and 75% of these then resorted to pathogenic weight-control behavior. Gustafson (1989) examined attitudes and behaviors about weight in surveying 227 female collegiate athletes. Of these, 71% believed they were at least 5 lb (about 2 kg) overweight, 53% were not satisfied with their body weight, and 37% reported bingeing behavior. In these studies, athletes with some of these behaviors might or might not meet the DSM-III-R criteria for diagnosis of eating disorders. In any event, it is important to remember that these studies did not use clinical interviews and standardized reports to determine prevalence according to current diagnostic standards.

These and other prevalence studies (Black & Burckes-Miller, 1988; Burckes-Miller & Black, 1988a; Clark, Nelson, & Evans, 1988; Klesges, 1983; Pasman & Thompson, 1988; Thornton, 1990; Zuckerman, Colby, Ware, & Lazerson, 1986) demonstrate a number of patterns in the prevalence of eating disorders in athletes.

- Clinical eating disorders appear to occur more often in athletes than in the general population.
- A significant percentage of athletes engage in pathogenic eating or weight-loss behaviors, which, although subclinical, are important to examine.
- Eating disorders and use of pathogenic weight-loss techniques in athletics tend to have a sport-specific prevalence (e.g., they occur more frequently in gymnastics and in wrestling than in archery and football).

Brownell and Rodin (1992), in their review of the prevalence of eating disorders in athletes, call for more epidemiological research to identify prevalence rates in the athletic population. Such research is required, and we propose that it address critical questions for athletes and coaches. Such questions include the following:

- Do the conditions in which athletes participate in sports make it more likely that

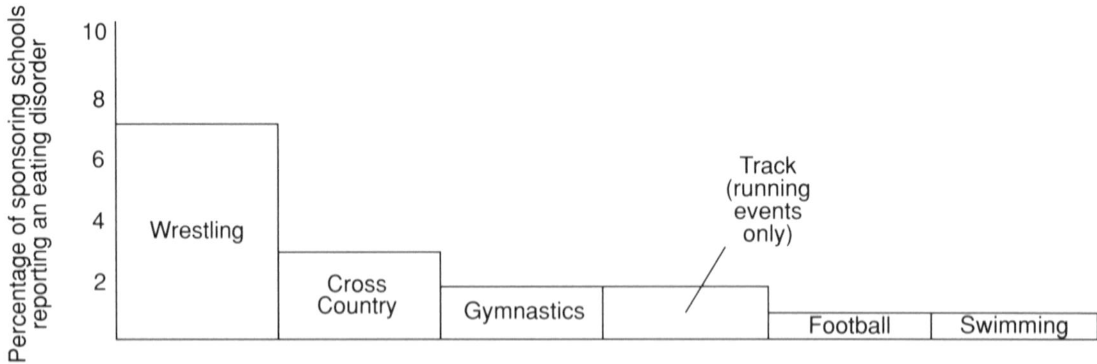

Figure 13.2a Prevalence of eating disorders in men's collegiate sports.
Note. From "Eating Disorders in NCAA Athletics Programs" by R.W. Dick, 1991, *Athletic Training*, **26** (pp. 137-140). Copyright 1991 by the National Athletic Trainers Association. Adapted by permission.

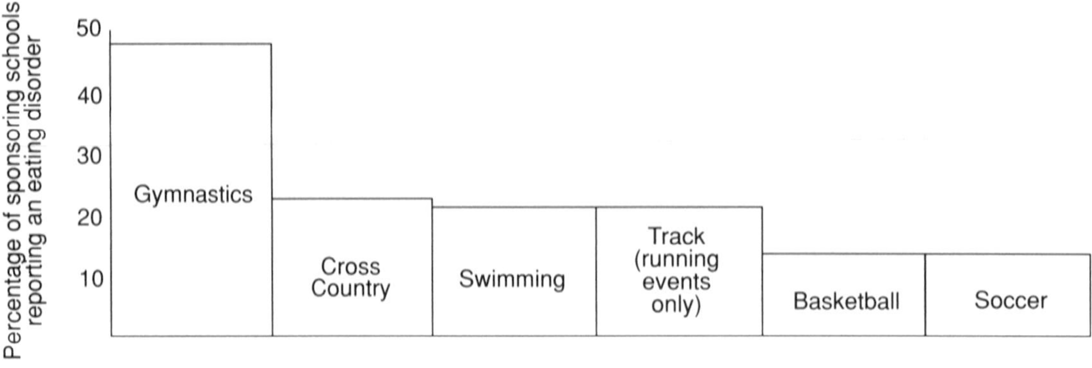

Figure 13.2b Prevalence of eating disorders in women's collegiate sports.
Note. From "Eating Disorders in NCAA Athletics Programs" by R.W. Dick, 1991, *Athletic Training*, **26** (pp. 137-140). Copyright 1991 by the National Athletic Trainers Association. Adapted by permission.

they might resort to eating-disordered behaviors?

- If a person is predisposed to an eating disorder (family history, metabolic rate), does athletic participation increase the disorder's risk of occurring?
- Are the behaviors of sport personnel (coaches, officials, judges) sometimes instrumental in the onset of an eating disorder? Can such behaviors be changed?
- If an athlete adopts pathogenic weight-loss techniques while participating in sport, do such behaviors persist when competitive participation has ended?

These issues have received little attention in the literature, but experience indicates that they are critical to a complete understanding of the sport–eating disorders relationship. Answers to these questions have crucial implications for prevention and treatment efforts.

PREDISPOSING FACTORS

As emphasized at this chapter's beginning, one of the potential problems in modern sports is that leanness has become equated with performance to such a degree that there is an almost obsessive preoccupation with maintaining low body weight. The following accounts from the *Austin American-Statesman* illustrate how serious the ramifications of an unhealthy focus on weight in a sports program can be.

> During the past 18 months, more than a dozen university women athletes, including some of the best swimmers in the world, have been diagnosed as having severe eating disorders traceable in most cases to the pressures of their sport and the training method of their coaches. One of every 10 female athletes at the university has been diagnosed as having an eating disorder and referred to a specialist for treatment, according to university documents and officials. Another 20 to 30% show signs of a disorder. (Halliburton & Sanford, 1989b, D1)

> She did not want to come into workouts overweight, so she started resorting to drastic measures. Her swimming began to falter, so she would try to forget her sorrows by indulging in food. But that made more of the drastic measures necessary to keep the pounds off. Soon she was trapped in the bulimic cycle of binges and purges. . . . "It was hard for me to tell him [coach]," she said. "He said 'You have to take care of it.' That was it. He never brought it up again. It was still real hard. I still felt pressure. And he would say to me, 'Work on your weight.'" (Halliburton & Sanford, 1989a, D8)

It was indicated that the coach

> emphasized weight in training and competition and insisted that his swimmers remain under maximum weight limits. Those who failed to do so were required to participate in special workouts. According to current and former university swimmers . . . the pressure to meet those guidelines was so intense that many routinely fasted, induced vomiting, used laxatives and diuretics, or exercised in addition to workouts. They did not want to be relegated to the group they called "The Fat Club." "Primarily the pressure came from the coach, until you started to internalize it. Then it became self-inflicted—torture almost—where some people would weigh themselves three or four times a day." (Halliburton & Sanford, 1989c, D1, D7)

> "Weighing in is a constant reminder of your weight," [a former swimmer] said. "I remember being at the swim center at 5:30 in the morning and being on that stupid freight scale and looking at everybody else and looking at . . . the reaction on their faces, and it was just non-stop. You became obsessive with it. I'm talking to the pound—that's how fanatical it makes you." (Sanford & Halliburton, 1989, D7)

The sports environment does not necessarily facilitate an unhealthy focus on weight concerns, but as shown in this section, many aspects of various sports promote a focus on weight. This can be especially dangerous to a person who, for whatever reason (genetic or familial factors or unusual stress level), is predisposed to an eating disorder or weight-management problem. It is plausible that the extra pressure of such an intense focus on weight might precipitate an eating disorder in a predisposed person.

Factors commonly encountered in sport that encourage this strong focus on weight issues are as follows:

- Weight restrictions
- Judging criteria that emphasize thin and stereotypically attractive body build
- Performance demands encouraging very low percent body fat
- Coach-applied pressure to lose weight
- Peer pressure to try pathogenic weight-loss techniques

Weight Restrictions

The following sports in the Olympic program have weight classifications that determine in which group an athlete competes:

- Boxing
- Wrestling (Greco-Roman and freestyle)
- Weightlifting
- Judo
- Tae kwon do

Other sports, such as rowing, also commonly use weight classifications, such as *lightweight*, to subdivide competitors based on body weight. In professional sports, jockeys always perform under weight restrictions and have been identified as a high-risk group (Thompson & Sherman, 1993). Weight classifications become a problem when a desire to perform and win at high levels influences athletes to compete at below their natural body weight, hoping that by competing against lighter opponents they will be more successful. Often, this results in athletes resorting to unusual and dangerous practices in an effort to drop several pounds immediately before competition and weigh-in (the practice of "cutting weight"). Weight-loss techniques typically encountered in such sports as boxing and wrestling are

- dehydration (sauna, sweat box, heat-restrictive clothing),
- use of laxatives,
- use of diuretics,
- use of diet pills,
- fasting,
- crash dieting,
- purging (self-induced vomiting), and
- fluid restriction.

Rapid dehydration is the end result of many of these practices; paradoxically, the athlete intent on winning typically does not have sufficient time to fully rehydrate before competition and thus competes in a weakened state. Although the practice of cutting weight has the goal of improving performance, two factors militate against improvement: (a) Many other athletes of larger body type are also losing weight to compete at lower weight classes and (b) the dehydration experience weakens the athlete and typically results in poorer performance.

In addition to such performance concerns, the medical literature shows that rapid dehydration is a dangerous behavior in terms of impact on the body, particularly if carried out repeatedly (Webster, Rutt, & Weltman, 1990). In addition, as mentioned previously, concerns are growing over long-term health effects, including osteoporosis, for female athletes who maintain low body weight and suffer chronic amenorrhea.

Judging Criteria

The following Olympic sports depend on judging to determine performance outcome; physical attractiveness, especially for women, is considered by participants to be a determining factor in the final score.

- Diving
- Figure skating
- Gymnastics (artistic and rhythmic)
- Synchronized swimming

It is difficult to describe the powerful influence that perceived judging biases have on the attitudes of young athletes participating in such sports. Research in this area is lacking, but our personal experience with divers and figure skaters indicate that there is frequently open communication between judges, coaches, and athletes about the perceived body weight (and often, the need to lose weight) of the competitors. An athlete might receive feedback such as, "If you lose ten pounds, you will do much better in competition this year." Such a message has a powerful influence on the competitive adolescent who fiercely desires success in sport and whose parents may have spent between $30,000 and $50,000 in the previous year to support training. Helping professionals working with athletes in this area must be alert to the variety of pressures on the athlete and to the gender-specific issues often involved (see chapter 9). Education of all those involved in the process, including athletes, coaches, judges, parents, and administrators, is essential.

An unknown is whether losing weight to meet stereotypic notions of attractiveness results in higher marks from judges. At this time, no research on this topic exists. Observation, however, indicates that frequently such weight losses have either no effect or a deleterious effect on performance, particularly when weight loss comes at the expense of muscle development. Strong muscular development is a necessity among both male and female athletes in these sports to accomplish the difficult maneuvers that result in high scores.

Performance Demands

One of the consequences of the increasing application of science to sport performance (Wilmore, 1992) is that coaches and athletes have become increasingly aware of the statistical relationship between various physical factors and sport performance. In some sports, research has indicated that there is a correlation between low percent body fat and high levels of performance (swimming, speedskating, long-distance running, cross-country skiing). Problems arise when this information is applied in individual cases without a full understanding of the body type–performance relationship. For example, a male runner might assume that if he is able to lower his percent body fat from 10% to 8%, he will increase his running times. But if such a change proves beneficial, is it possible to predict that lowering percent body fat from 8% to 5% will have a similar effect on performance? In the sports under discussion, a commonly encountered belief is that Lean Equals Mean, or that the leaner the body, the better the performance. Research, however, provides no evidence for such an all-encompassing relationship.

Problems can begin when the desire for success is married to the perceived need to lose weight to achieve success. Unhealthy weight-management practices are often employed because young athletes have no knowledge of effective and safe nutrition and exercise principles. If coaches also lack knowledge of nutrition and exercise principles, young athletes have few options for sources of information. A runner stated that

> she went to the coach and said, "How can I improve my times?" And he said, "Well, I think you have to knock off some weight." He was right. She was overweight. And she said, "It's really very difficult for me." And he said, "Well, a lot of the kids vomit after they eat and use that as a means of weight control." She took him up on this suggestion. ("Eating disorders," 1985, p. 96)

Coach-Applied Pressure

In the situations discussed, in which the perception exists that weight loss results in more athletic success, the coach can play a critical role in shaping the attitude and behaviors of athletes. The greatest danger to an athlete's health exists when pressure is applied to lose weight in the absence of knowledge concerning safe and effective weight-management procedures. Harris and Greco (1990) studied 28 female gymnasts who believed that their current weight was significantly more than they or their coach would like. Fifty-six percent experienced pressure from the coach to lose weight. Team weigh-ins averaged 6 a month and individual weigh-ins, 14 a month. Also, it has been suggested that some coaches might suspect that an athlete working with a therapist for treatment of an eating disorder might either be encouraged to abandon the sport or return to their event with a lower competitive drive ("Eating disorders," 1985).

Peer Pressure

Another factor in many sport situations that is not as common in other life areas is the close and shared experience of people who train together, compete together, and often travel together on competitive trips. This increases the possibility of peer modeling of pathogenic weight-loss techniques. Chiodo and Latimer (1983), for example, found that most bulimic patients could identify specific incidents associated with the onset of vomiting and that many developed the problem after learning from someone else or the media about the behavior. To the extent that athletes are likely to spend a greater amount of time than their nonathletic peers in close proximity to other people who might have an intense focus on weight and might be using pathogenic weight-loss techniques, this is likely to be a greater problem in sport than in other life areas.

These sport-specific factors, then, must be understood by the helping professional intervening in a case involving an eating-disordered athlete or, indeed, when education efforts are called for. In a survey of 384 intercollegiate athletes, Guthrie (1986) found that their top self-reported reasons for weight loss were as follows:

1. Required for performance excellence
2. Required to reach aesthetic ideals of beauty
3. Remark by a member of athletic staff concerning need to lose weight
4. Required to meet a lower weight category

Guthrie also found that other contributing factors were identified by the athletes:

- Peer pressures (e.g., engage in bingeing and purging as a form of ritualistic behavior after a meet)
- Poor travel diets
- Public ridicule of overweight athlete's body
- Fear of not being able to participate in a particular match if weight loss did not occur (1986)

RECOGNIZING EATING DISORDERS IN ATHLETES

Although athletes might use pathogenic weight-loss methods frequently and experience eating disorders occasionally, these problems are not always obvious, and many cases are unrecognized and untreated. How does one recognize and identify a problem? With clinical eating disorders in athletes, early detection (and early intervention) is associated with better outcome (Thompson, 1987). For a sport psychologist or consultant, the ability to identify both the eating-disordered and at-risk athlete is vital. In some situations, e.g., life-threatening anorexia nervosa, there is a need for immediate treatment. In other cases, especially with bulimia nervosa, the athlete's problems are not so readily observed. This section discusses the signs and symptoms that might indicate the presence of an eating problem.

Standardized Assessment

It is important to take a multimodal approach to the assessment of eating disorders in athletes. Standardized assessment tools should be used in initial assessment stages. For example, the Diagnostic Survey for Eating Disorders—Revised (DSED) (Johnson & Pure, 1986) can be used as a self-report inventory or in a semistructured interview. It provides information in eight areas: demographic factors, weight history and body image, dieting behavior, binge eating and purging behavior, related behaviors, menstruation and sexual functioning, medical and psychiatric history for patient (athlete) and family, and life adjustment. Additional self-report inventories often of use are (a) the Eating Disorders Inventory (EDI) (Garner, Olmsted, & Polivy, 1983), a self-report scaled instrument that provides information regarding individual eating attitudes and behaviors (i.e., drive for thinness, bulimic tendencies, body dissatisfaction, ineffectiveness, perfectionism, interpersonal distrust, interoceptive awareness, and maturity fears), and (b) the Eating Attitudes Test (EAT) (Garner & Garfinkel, 1979), a test of disordered eating symptoms associated with anorexia nervosa. It should be stressed that for diagnostic purposes, these tools should be administered and interpreted by a licensed psychologist and followed up with a clinical interview as indicated.

Behavioral and Personality Assessment

Another important source of information is behavioral observations, either directly or as reported by the athlete's coaches or teammates. The use of behavioral assessment to validate self-report or test data can help to clarify the nature of the problem. Some behavioral signs of eating disorders include weight loss, eating alone, preoccupation with food, mood changes, and body distortion statements. Weight loss is by definition a characteristic of the anorexic, i.e., at least 15% below expected body weight. Individuals with bulimia can be normal weight, overweight, or somewhat below expected weight. Thus, body weight is an inadequate predictor of bulimia. However, frequent fluctuations in weight might be an indication of bulimia or a bulimic-type weight-management style.

Eating alone might be a sign of either anorexia nervosa or bulimia. Anorexics are often involved in food preparation, but might only eat their small portion after everyone else has finished. Bulimics might eat alone, making it easier to engage in purging after the meal. However, in a bulimic athlete who is required to attend team training meals, other signs might emerge (e.g., frequent trips to the bathroom; returning from the bathroom with bloodshot eyes, due to the strain of vomiting; much talk of and preoccupation with the composition and caloric content of the meal).

Changes in mood and personality styles are additional factors helpful in detecting eating disorders. For example, depression, irritability, and wide fluctuations in mood are often associated with the eating-disordered athlete (Thompson, 1987). Self-worth issues might be salient, with some athletes using "athletics as a vehicle to be accepted" (Bickelhaupt, 1989, p. 80). An intense drive for being thin, dissatisfaction with one's body, feelings of ineffectiveness, interpersonal distrust, maturity fears, and perfectionism are also factors associated with many eating-disordered people (Garner et al., 1983).

It is important to note both that an eating-disordered athlete might have some or none of the personality characteristics previously described and that a non-eating-disordered athlete might have some of these characteristics. For example, although perfectionistic tendencies are a hallmark of anorexic patients, perfectionistic tendencies are also common in many athletes, eating-disordered or not. Indeed, the emerging consensus appears to be that "there is no one personality structure characteristic of either anorexia nervosa or bulimia. . . . [instead these] are multidetermined and multidimensional syndromes; they develop in different people at different times for different reasons" (Garner, Rockert, Olmsted, Johnson, & Coscina, 1985, p. 561). This might be true especially in athletes where, as discussed in the section on predispositions, a variety of environmental factors might contribute to the onset of a disorder. However, if taken with other information, emotional and personality characteristics can be useful in understanding and treating the eating-disordered athlete.

Medical Assessment

A thorough medical evaluation is a necessary part of the detection and diagnosis of an eating disorder. Recognition of the common medical symptoms of eating disorders can assist the sport psychology consultant in understanding the nature of the disorder. Medical symptoms of eating disorders might include the following: anemia, leukopenia, osteopenia, renal and liver problems, peripheral edema, electrolyte imbalance, cardiac problems (e.g., bradycardia), dental problems, and gastrointestinal problems. Some medical problems (e.g., anemia, leukopenia) have overt signs (e.g., fatigue, increased susceptibility to infection) that a coach or psychologist can detect and use for additional validation of a suspicion of an eating problem.

In attempting to identify eating disorders in athletes, it is important to distinguish between dieting and anorexia nervosa. Many researchers believe that anorexia is not simply an extreme point in a continuum of dieting, but is qualitatively different (e.g., psychological manifestations such as ineffectiveness and interpersonal distrust occur more frequently in eating-disordered people than in dieters). "In a weight-preoccupied culture, this distinction is important in distinguishing illness from overvalued social attitudes" (Garfinkel, Garner, & Goldbloom, 1987, p. 627). This is especially important in assessing athletes, because effective weight control (including reasonable diets) is essential in sport. Often, a distorted body image is a sign that a more serious problem exists. Self-critical references to one's body (e.g., "I think my stomach is too big," or "My hips are much too large") can be associated with eating disorders or weight-management problems. Evidence of a body image that is widely discrepant with an objective viewpoint is cause for serious concern; for example, a very thin, 90-lb (41 kg) 19-year-old woman saying that she is "a fat blob."

Treatment Referral Issues

Knowing when and how to refer an athlete for treatment is crucial. As mentioned previously, early referral and intervention is associated with better outcome. In such cases as an 80-lb (36 kg) anorexic, immediate referral and treatment is vital. For coaches and staff, when a serious question exists as to the presence or the absence of an eating disorder, referral for a more extensive assessment is necessary. Athletes in general, and in particular those with eating disorders, often have perfectionistic tendencies (including considerable desires to please others) and thus often have difficulty admitting that a problem exists. This perfectionistic tendency, along with the fear of possibly losing a spot on the team or suffering reduced playing time, contributes to the athlete's resistance to any referral. Tact, respect, and awareness of these issues is paramount to a successful referral.

Because many athletes might be hesitant to seek treatment for their problem, certain guidelines can be helpful. Thompson (1987) recommends that the coach or sport psychologist approach the athlete with an emphasis on feelings, rather than directly focusing on eating behaviors. Focusing on eating behaviors and attempting to exert control in this area can be counterproductive, because eating is often the only thing over which the athlete feels control. Targeting feelings might facilitate the athlete to confide in the referring person. In the case of Karl, presented at the chapter's beginning, the initial focus of assessment was on performance, and a strong message was sent to the athlete that the psychologist cared about Karl and his diving. Karl was able to describe his eating and weight problems at a subsequent session.

We also suggest that referrals be made to specific persons or clinics. A clear and explicit referral will more likely produce compliance with seeking treatment than will a vague "you should seek help." Thompson suggests that "if the athlete is hesitant about seeking professional assistance, suggest to her that she see the referral person for an 'assessment' to determine if there is a problem" (1987, p. 118). This request is often easier for the athlete to comply with than is going to "therapy." It is additionally recommended that as soon as the referral is accepted the athlete be encouraged to call immediately to schedule the initial consultation. In all cases, a concerned, not confrontational, style is advisable.

TREATMENT ISSUES

Although there is an abundance of information on treating the eating-disordered patient, there is little information on treating the eating-disordered athlete. Furthermore, some of the information addressed to coaches and other athletic staff is incorrect. For example, an assistant athletic director wrote that the coach should provide the primary

Courtesy K R Maier

assistance to the athlete and "make up a diet and a schedule of workouts. He/she should explain the balance of caloric intake and expenditure, set a specific weight goal, and coordinate the intake and expenditure to meet that goal in a specific time frame" (Bickford, 1990, p. 87). This is simply not appropriate or feasible in most cases. Few coaches have the training, knowledge, or time to be nutritional counselors and dieticians. In fact, some athletes have reported that unreasonable weight goals set by their coaches contributed to their eating disorders (Guthrie, 1986; Halliburton & Sanford, 1989c).

This section gives an overview of treatment for the eating-disordered athlete. A general guide to treatment modalities in the management of eating disorders or pathogenic weight-loss techniques is provided. In this context, the special needs of an athlete undergoing treatment are addressed. The reader interested in a more detailed presentation of treatment is referred to the *Handbook of Psychotherapy for Anorexia Nervosa and Bulimia* (Garner & Garfinkel, 1985). This edited book has discussions of cognitive, behavioral, and cognitive-behavioral therapy, response prevention treatment, group therapy, family therapy, inpatient and residential treatment, self-help and support groups, and psychoeducational therapy. Additional guides that address treatment issues are also widely available (Blinder, Chaitin, & Goldstein, 1988; Brownell & Foreyt, 1986; Gross, 1986; Johnson, 1991; Johnson & Connors, 1987; Reece & Gross, 1982; Thompson & Sherman, 1993).

Individual Therapy

Some therapists suggest that during individual therapy, the focus should be on the patient as a person and not on eating habits or weight. It has been suggested that "if the therapist gets stuck on issues of weight or food, it will only reinforce the patient's game and allow the patient to avoid dealing with the underlying causes of the disorder" (Gross, 1986, p. 4). This may or may not be true with the athlete client. In some cases the athlete in individual therapy may need an outlet to discuss the pressure to compete at a low body weight. Thus the therapist might well focus on weight issues, in an educational and supportive manner.

In addition to educating and supporting an athlete in individual therapy, other aspects of treatment might include reality-oriented cognitive feedback (to challenge all-or-nothing thinking, personalization, superstitious thinking, and underlying assumptions). Also, improving affective expression—guiding the patient to identify a range of feelings to learn how to tolerate uncomfortable affect—will often prove useful. Similarly, enhancing body image perception (e.g., through movement therapy, relaxation) might assist in the task of freeing self-esteem from weight, shape, and familial or societal expectations.

Group Therapy

Group therapy is a mode of treatment that has been effective for eating-disordered patients, usually as an adjunct to other therapies (Davis, Olmsted, & Rockert, 1990; Fernandez, 1984; Huerta, 1982; Maher, 1984). Although there has been little information regarding its efficacy with athletes, a group setting appears to provide advantages with this population. A group setting could provide support, for example, by allowing the opportunity for members to share their experiences of competitive pressure, demanding coaches, perfectionistic strivings, and so forth. It would also provide a forum for the sharing of information, interpersonal learning, instillation of hope, and development of socializing techniques (Yalom, 1985). Group therapy should primarily be used in the treatment of eating disorders in combination with other treatment modalities. Group interventions might be the most useful in education efforts, which will be discussed later in this chapter.

Family Therapy

In working with athletes, traditional family therapy is a viable treatment option (cf. Miller, 1984; Minuchin & Fishman, 1981). Interestingly, family therapy in sport might be conducted by bringing together the athlete's "family" (i.e., athlete, coach, nutritionist, and closest teammates) and working with them as a family structure. In this setting, the members of the athlete's family would be encouraged to share in a supportive fashion their concern for the athlete. In addition, educational information could be imparted to the whole competitive group in a consistent way. Lastly, understanding the influences that the behaviors of these people have on one another (e.g., interpersonal relationships) can be examined in this context. According to Garfinkel (1991), family therapy is especially useful with patients under age 19 who have had an eating disorder less than 3 years.

Inpatient Treatment

Ideally, pathogenic weight-loss behaviors in athletes are discovered and addressed before the problem becomes severe. However, if the eating disorder has become critical, inpatient hospitalization might be necessary. Inpatient treatment must always be carefully considered as an option and will usually be chosen if the medical risk to the athlete is great. The factors that suggest consideration of inpatient treatment for anorexia and bulimia are shown in Table 13.1.

Due to factors related to sports participation issues or to interpersonal factors, an athlete might resist hospitalization. However, a joint and cooperative decision with the athlete and the athlete's family, physician, and coaches is most productive for treatment success.

Table 13.1 Major Considerations in the Decision to Provide Inpatient Treatment for Anorexia and Bulimia

Anorexia nervosa

- Weight loss of more than 25% of ideal body weight
- Weight loss of more than 15% with a lack of control
- Failure of outpatient treatment
- Medical and psychiatric complications (e.g, gastrointestinal consequences, suicidal ideation)
- Persistent substance abuse

Bulimia nervosa

- Failure of outpatient treatment
- Medical complications
- Uncontrolled insulin dependent diabetes mellitus
- Pregnancy
- Concomitant depression
- Persistent substance abuse

Note. From "Treatment Issues in Eating Disorders" by P. Garfinkel (paper presented at the Second Annual Rocky Mountain Conference on Eating Disorders, Colorado Springs, CO); and from "Multidisciplinary Approach to Treatment and Evaluation" by P.S. Powers, in *Current Treatment of Anorexia Nervosa and Bulimia* by P.S. Powers and R.C. Fernandez (Eds.), 1984, New York: Karger. Table 13.1 is adapted from both sources with permission.

Psychoactive Medication

Medication has a secondary but often useful role in the treatment of eating disorders. Because of drug-use standards and restrictions in sports, the physician who is considering pharmacological treatment of an athlete must be extremely sensitive to and knowledgeable of these issues. Medications to avoid include thyroid hormones, insulin, diuretics, laxatives, or benzodiazepines (for bulimics who might abuse this class of potent psychotropic drugs). Benzodiazepines for the nonbulimic anorexic restrictor might be useful if given premeal. Tricyclic antidepressants might be indicated as an adjunct treatment for bulimics.

In all modes of psychotherapy (e.g., group, family, individual therapy), a multimodal approach is recommended. Components of an effective intervention might include a combination of psychoeducation, cognitive therapy (e.g., challenging irrational beliefs), behavior therapy (e.g., response prevention), and interpersonal and individual therapy (cf. Johnson, 1991). Also, the assistance of a dietician or nutritionist is recommended. In each case, keeping the athlete's coach generally informed as to the progress of treatment is vital. Many coaches might fear that treatment providers are steering the athlete in an unproductive direction. It is the sport psychologist's duty to reassure the coach that you both have the athlete's best interests in mind and that the athlete will continue to participate in sport if it can be done safely and the athlete so desires. Lastly, an overall goal is to sequence and individualize treatments. This involves starting with the least intrusive intervention and working up as necessary and as appropriate for the individual athlete.

Many athletes might not have any idea that help is available. The pressures to maintain or lose weight can be intense, and attempts at seeking help might be viewed as a sign of weakness. In all cases, the issue of sensitivity to the athlete's fears (real or imagined) is significant in a successful intervention. An athlete may fear that disclosing the problem is a sure way of losing a spot on the team. This is not an unfounded fear because, as we have seen, extreme weight-loss methods are often not only tolerated, but encouraged.

Lastly, it is helpful to keep in mind that the course of recovery from anorexia is gradual. Current estimates are that approximately one third recover in the first 3 years after onset, one third by 6 years, and one third do not recover. Treatment outcome for bulimics, whose symptoms often wax and wane throughout and beyond the treatment period, is more difficult to assess. However, there are some factors related to prognosis:

- Age of onset—A younger onset is associated with a better outcome.
- Gender—There is some evidence that males do worse in treatment. They might have more severe underlying pathology, because cultural factors are less involved. This might be less true in sports, where pathogenic weight-loss behavior in male athletes is often culturally determined (e.g., the wrestling culture).
- Marriage—Onset after marriage is related to poorer prognosis.
- Chronicity—Delay of treatment carries a poor prognosis.

Treatment in the Case of Karl

Karl, the diver described earlier, illustrates a typical pattern or course in the development of an eating disorder. Several factors common in the sport context are evident, including a history of self-initiated efforts to overcome the eating disorder followed by a relapse, the critical role of coaches in promoting healthy or unhealthy attitudes and behaviors, and the severe negative impact of the disorder on performance. This section on treatment issues concludes with a discussion of a treatment scenario for Karl.

Treatment in this case involved several subsequent sessions between the sport psychologist and Karl that helped Karl identify the fact that he was suffering from bulimia. Reading materials were provided that described the similar experiences of other athletes. When he understood more about the nature of his problem, he was more committed to taking the necessary steps to return to an optimal state of functioning.

Next, Karl identified for the psychologist his whereabouts during the upcoming summer training and competition season. Athletes often live a semi-nomadic existence, and their busy travel schedules often increase the difficulty in arranging for consistent outpatient treatment. Fortunately, Karl was planning to stay in a large West-Coast city for 4 months over the summer, and Karl was referred to a weight-management and eating-disorder treatment program there. He signed a release of information so the sport psychologist was able to contact the program staff, make the referral, and provide background information on Karl's situation. Karl entered into treatment in the program and was exposed to an interdisciplinary intervention approach that involved a medical evaluation, individual counseling, group therapy, nutritional counseling, and behavioral contracting involving homework assignments and extensive self-monitoring. After 4 months of intensive intervention, Karl had made considerable progress and was asked to regularly attend a self-help group. He also received further individual counseling every 2 months. At follow-up a year after the referral, Karl was still attending the self-help group and had made excellent progress toward adopting and maintaining a healthy lifestyle and a balanced and productive approach toward weight management. He had cut back on his diving involvement, although he still competed and had even won a national-level meet. But the majority of his efforts were devoted toward establishing the business career he had always dreamed of, and he was attending night school while working at a financial-management company.

PREVENTING EATING DISORDERS IN ATHLETES

Perhaps one of the most important services we can provide as health care professionals is promoting the prevention of a problem. This is the case with eating disorders and pathogenic weight-loss techniques in sports. Communicating knowledge about eating, weight, health, and sport performance to the appropriate populations is vital. This can be done through educational workshops (e.g., through a university counseling center), interviews with the media, discussions with coaches, and consultations with teams or individual athletes. Because of the high incidence of eating disorders in adolescents, an efficient prevention program might target high-school or junior-high athletes. The factors that should be considered in proactive sport education programs include de-emphasizing body weight, providing nutritional education, promoting sensitivity to weight issues, and facilitating healthy weight management.

De-Emphasize Body Weight

One concept to emphasize is fitness rather than body-weight ideals. Many athletes and coaches become obsessed with setting and obtaining a certain weight. However, body weight is often insignificantly related to athletic outcome. Despite many efforts to alter athletes' and coaches' beliefs about ideal weights in sport, many athletes at all competitive levels continue to rely on pathogenic weight-loss methods, which are both dangerous and deleterious to performance. It is important to discuss with coaches and athletes that there is no ideal body composition or weight for an athlete. Guidelines exist for sports and participants, but these can fluctuate greatly, depending on the athlete's specialty (e.g., long-distance vs. sprinter); natural variations in both body composition (e.g., lean-body vs. fat mass) and metabolic rate; and patterns of eating and exercise. For an analysis of metabolic and health effects of weight-regulation practices in athletes, see Brownell, Steen, and Wilmore (1987). Ultimately, the decision to strive for an ideal range must be individually determined, preferably with the assistance of an exercise physiologist and the coach.

Provide Nutritional Education

Similarly, nutritional education and counseling are important aspects of athletes' training. This knowledge has been improving among the athletic world such that most competitors no longer eat steak and eggs a few hours before a competition. However, there is much more to be learned: "It has been said that there is no area of nutrition where faddism, misconceptions, and ignorance are more obvious than in athletics" (Leaf & Frisa, 1989, p. 1066). An abundance of research indicates that many athletes and coaches have limited or incorrect views on proper sport nutrition (Bedgood & Tuck, 1983; Benadat, Schwartz, & Wertzenfeld-Heller, 1989; Clark et al., 1988; Douglas & Douglas, 1984; Koszewski & Strong, 1991; Perron & Endres, 1985; Tilgner & Schiller, 1989; Wolf, Wirth, & Lohman, 1979).

Although accurate and useful information can be obtained from a variety of sources (e.g., nutritionists, dieticians, and written materials), Koszeski and Strong (1991) found that most athletes unsuccessfully turn to their peers or coaches for nutritional advice. It is imperative that the consulting sport psychologist working with eating and weight-management strategies be knowledgeable of general nutritional principles, sport nutrition, and weight management and, as well, have a good working relationship with a qualified nutritionist. The sport psychologist should not be expected to work with the individual athlete to plan dietary intake. However, the consultant should be able to refer a coach or athlete to the proper source for this information; for example, a nutritionist or the *Coaches Guide to Nutrition and Weight Control* (Eisenman, Johnson, & Benson, 1990). Athletic personnel and athletes would also benefit greatly from attending a workshop on sport nutrition and weight control. This could include such topics as carbohydrate loading, precompetition meals, water and electrolyte replacement, and so on.

Promote Sensitivity to Weight Issues

In the prevention of pathogenic weight-loss practices and eating disorders in athletes, it is important to help athletic personnel become more sensitive to issues of weight control and dieting. This might involve working with them to be more tactful about weight issues (e.g., eliminating statements such as "You're looking a little heavy today"). The coach and staff must understand that they have a powerful influence on athletes: Some athletes will go to extremes to please coaches. Therefore, it is useful to present to the coach and staff some examples of unhelpful and potentially dangerous weight-management practices, including

- group weigh-ins,
- arbitrary weight or body-composition goals,
- punishment for not making weight,
- careless or unfeeling remarks about weight issues,
- always associating weight loss with enhanced performance, and
- minimizing the detrimental and unhealthy effects of rapid weight gain or loss.

Facilitate Healthy Weight Management

Attention has increased recently on eating disorders in sport, and there has been a corresponding increase in the availability of educational resources. For example, the NCAA has produced an informative set of three videos and supporting educational information on eating disorders in sport (National Collegiate Athletic Association, 1989). Ron Thompson and Roberta Sherman from the Bloomington Center for Counseling and Human Development recently wrote a volume on *Helping Athletes with Eating Disorders* (1993), and other authors have presented a variety of model systems for managing eating problems in athletic settings (Grandjean, 1992; Ryan, 1992). Much has been learned about behavioral approaches to the management of weight and the effectiveness of a variety of weight-management strategies (Kirschenbaum, 1992). Perhaps most important for education efforts aimed at changing attitudes, much has been learned about the effects of unhealthy weight-loss methods on sporting performance (Thompson & Sherman, 1993, chapter 4).

It will probably take some time to change ingrained and perhaps institutionalized attitudes toward weight in the sport setting (Lopiano & Zotos, 1992), but health-care professionals must take the lead in emphasizing the relationship between body type and weight, the realities of optimal body composition and weight for effective performance, and the nature of healthy and effective weight-management strategies that can be employed by athletes and coaches. Only through such efforts will negative examples (like the cases of Karl and the university team described earlier) become rarities rather than all-too-common encounters.

CONCLUSION

Eating disorders and their subclinical manifestations exist all too frequently in the sport environment. Given this fact, in-service training regarding eating disorders is essential for athletic personnel. In the case of Karl, many problems might have been prevented if his coach had displayed more awareness of the impact of his weight-related comments on the athlete. Because early detection and referral is associated with a more successful treatment outcome, the importance of increasing the awareness of sport personnel concerning these issues cannot be overemphasized. It might be particularly important for male coaches of female athletes to understand the relevant issues that have been raised in this chapter. The training program should be for the entire athletic and support staff (coaches, trainers, physicians, weight coaches, psychologists, and all other associates), and should have as its emphasis prevention, recognition, and referral. As Murphy (1991) has described, a critical ingredient for successful interventions in the sport world is the presence of a clear plan of action and the readiness of a team of qualified personnel to respond to problems. The coach's active involvement is, from experience, probably the most critical ingredient in the success of any such program. The coach's influence in the sport environment is such that a clear communication to athletes that "this is important" will result in active participation, whereas the opposite message that "this should be ignored" will ensure the program's failure. Education and prevention efforts should also include a realization that information alone will probably not change attitudes or behaviors. The inclusion of other behavior-change methods (such as athlete involvement in education, mentor programs, and peer counseling involvement) should be considered in efforts to prevent eating disorders in sports.

There is still much that is not known about the development and maintenance of eating disorders in the sport setting. We hope that research efforts will continue to address these issues as a matter of urgency for the health, well-being, and safety of athletes everywhere.

REFERENCES

American Psychiatric Association. (1987). *Diagnostic and statistical manual of mental disorders* (3rd ed., rev.). Author: Washington, DC.

Bedgood, B.L., & Tuck, M.B. (1983). Nutrition knowledge of high school athletic coaches in Texas. *Journal of the American Dietetic Association*, **83**, 672-677.

Benadat, D., Schwartz, M., & Wertzenfeld-Heller, D. (1989). Nutrient intake in young, highly competitive gymnasts. *Journal of the American Dietetic Association*, **89**, 401-403.

Bickelhaupt, S. (1989, September 13). The thin game. *Boston Globe*, 73.

Bickford, B. (1990). Eating disorders: Treatment and prevention. *Scholastic Coach*, **59**, 86-88.

Black, D.R., & Burckes-Miller, M.E. (1988). Male and female college students: Use of anorexia nervosa and bulimia nervosa weight loss methods. *Research Quarterly for Exercise and Sport*, **59**, 252-256.

Blackburn, G.L., Wilson, G.T., Kanders, B.S., Stein, L.J., Lavin, P.T., Adler, J., & Brownell, K.D. (1989). Weight cycling: The experience of human dieters. *American Journal of Clinical Nutrition*, **49**, 1105-1109.

Blinder, B.J., Chaitin, B.F., & Goldstein, R. (1988). *The eating disorders: Medical and psychological bases of diagnosis and treatment*. New York: PMA.

Brownell, K.D., & Foreyt, J.P. (1986). *Handbook of eating disorders: Physiology, psychology, and treatment*. New York: Basic Books.

Brownell, K.D., & Rodin, J. (1992). *Prevalence of eating disorders in athletes*. In K.D. Brownell, J. Rodin, & J.H. Wilmore (Eds.), *Eating, body weight, and performance in athletes* (pp. 128-145). Malvern, PA: Lea & Febiger.

Brownell, K.D., Rodin, J., & Wilmore, J.H. (Eds.) (1992). *Eating, body weight, and performance in athletes*. Malvern, PA: Lea & Febiger.

Brownell, K.D., Steen, S.N., & Wilmore, J.H. (1987). Weight regulation practices in athletes: Analysis of metabolic and health effects. *Medicine and Science in Sports and Exercise*, **19**(6), 546-556.

Burckes-Miller, M.E., & Black, D.R. (1988a). Eating disorders: A problem in athletics? *Health Education*, 22-25.

Burckes-Miller, M.E., & Black, D.R. (1988b). Male and female college athletes: Prevalence of anorexia nervosa and bulimia nervosa. *Athletic Training*, **23**, 137-140.

Chiodo, J., & Latimer, P.R. (1983). Vomiting as a learned weight-control technique in bulimia. *Journal of Behavior Therapy and Experimental Psychiatry*, **14**, 131-135.

Clark, N., Nelson, M., & Evans, W. (1988). Nutrition education for elite female runners. *Physician and Sportsmedicine*, **16**, 124-136.

Davis, R., Olmsted, M.P., & Rockert, W. (1990). Brief group psychoeducation for bulimia nervosa: Assessing the clinical significance of change. *Journal of Consulting and Clinical Psychology*, **58**, 882-885.

Dick, R.W. (1993). Eating disorders in NCAA athletics programs: Replication of a 1990 study. *NCAA Sports Sciences Education Newsletter*, 3-4.

Douglas, P.D., & Douglas, J.G. (1984). Nutrition knowledge and food practices of high school athletes. *Journal of the American Dietetic Association*, **84**, 1198-1202.

Eating disorders in young athletes: A round table (1985). *Physician and Sportsmedicine*, **13**, 88-106.

Eisenman, P.A., Johnson, S.C., & Benson, J.E. (1990). *Coaches guide to nutrition and weight control* (2nd ed.). Champaign, IL: Leisure Press.

Fernandez, R.C. (1984). Group therapy of bulimia. In P.S. Powers & R.C. Fernandez (Eds.), *Current treatment of anorexia nervosa and bulimia* (pp. 277-291). New York: Karger.

Garfinkel, P. (1991, May). *Treatment issues in eating disorders*. Invited address presented at the Second Annual Rocky Mountain Conference on Eating Disorders, Colorado Springs.

Garfinkel, P.E., Garner, D.M., & Goldbloom, D.S. (1987). Eating disorders: Implications for the 1990's. *Canadian Journal of Psychiatry*, **32**, 624-631.

Garner, D.M., & Garfinkel, P.E. (1979). The eating attitudes test: An index of the symptoms of anorexia nervosa. *Psychological Medicine*, **9**, 273-279.

Garner, D.M., & Garfinkel, P. (1985). *Handbook of psychotherapy for anorexia nervosa and bulimia*. New York: Guilford Press.

Garner, D.M., Olmsted, M.P., & Polivy, J. (1983). *Eating Disorders Inventory*. Odessa, FL: Psychological Assessment Resources.

Garner, D.M., Rockert, W., Olmsted, M.P., Johnson, C., & Coscina, D.V. (1985). Psychoeducational principles in the treatment of bulimia and anorexia nervosa. In D.M. Garner & P.E. Garfinkel (Eds.), *Handbook of psychotherapy for anorexia nervosa and bulimia* (pp. 513-572). New York: Guilford Press.

Grandjean, A.C. (1992). The dilemma of making weight. *The U.S. Olympic Team Experience: A Model for Sports Medicine*. Brochure published by the United States Olympic Committee, Colorado Springs, CO.

Gross, M. (1986). Anorexia nervosa: Treatment perspectives. In F.E. Larocca (Ed.), *Eating disorders: Effective care and treatment* (pp. 1-10). St. Louis: Ishiyaku Euro-America.

Gustafson, D. (1989). Eating behaviors of women college athletes. *Melpomene*, **8**(3), 11-13.

Guthrie, S.R. (1986). The prevalence and development of eating disorders within a selected intercollegiate athlete population (Doctoral dissertation, Ohio State University, 1985). *Dissertation Abstracts International*, **46**, 3649A.

Halliburton, S., & Sanford, S. (1989a, July 30). Battle with bulimia tarnishes Cohen's golden world. *Austin American-Statesman*, pp. D1, D8.

Halliburton, S., & Sanford, S. (1989b, July 30). Being thin turns grim at Texas. *Austin American-Statesman*, pp. D1, D8.

Halliburton, S., & Sanford, S. (1989c, July 31). Making weight becomes torture for UT swimmers. *Austin American-Statesman*, pp. D1, D7.

Harris, M.B., & Greco, D. (1990). Weight control and weight concern in competitive female gymnasts. *Journal of Sport and Exercise Psychology*, **12**, 427-433.

Huerta, E. (1982). Group therapy for anorexia patients. In M. Gross (Ed.), *Anorexia nervosa: A comprehensive approach* (pp. 111-118). Lexington, MA: Collamore Press.

Johnson, C. (1991). *Psychodynamic treatment of anorexia nervosa and bulimia*. New York: Guilford Press.

Johnson, C., & Connors, M. (1987). *The etiology and treatment of bulimia nervosa: A biopsychosocial perspective*. New York: Basic Books.

Johnson, C., & Pure, D.L. (1986). Assessment of bulimia: A multidimensional model. In K.D. Brownell & J.P. Foreyt (Eds.), *Handbook of eating disorders: Physiology, psychology, and treatment* (pp. 405-449). New York: Basic Books.

Kirschenbaum, D.S. (1992). Elements of effective weight control programs: Implications for exercise and sport psychology. *Journal of Applied Sport Psychology*, **4**, 77-93.

Klesges, R.C. (1983). An analysis of body image distortions in a nonpatient population. *International Journal of Eating Disorders*, **2**, 35-41.

Koszewski, W.M., & Strong, D. (1991). *Dietary beliefs and practices among college student athletes*. Unpublished manuscript.

Leaf, A., & Frisa, K.B. (1989). Eating for health or for athletic performance. *American Journal of Clinical Nutrition*, **49**, 1066-1069.

Lopiano, D.A., & Zotos, C. (1992). Modern athletics: The pressure to perform. In K.D. Brownell, J. Rodin, & J.H. Wilmore (Eds.), *Eating, body weight, and performance in athletes* (pp. 275-292). Malvern, PA: Lea & Febiger.

Maher, M.S. (1984). Group therapy for anorexia nervosa. In P.S. Powers & R.C. Fernandez (Eds.), *Current treatment of anorexia nervosa and bulimia* (pp. 265-276). New York: Karger.

Miller, S.G. (1984). Family therapy of the eating disorders. In P.S. Powers & R.C. Fernandez (Eds.), *Current treatment of anorexia nervosa and bulimia* (pp. 92-112). New York: Karger.

Minuchin, S., & Fishman, M. (1981). *Family therapy techniques*. Cambridge, MA: Harvard University Press.

Murphy, S.M. (1991). Behavioral considerations. In R.C. Cantu & L.J. Micheli (Eds.), *ACSM's guidelines for the team physician* (pp. 252-265). Malvern, PA: Lea & Febiger.

National Collegiate Athletic Association. (1989). *Nutrition and eating disorder in collegiate athletics* (Video). Author: Kansas City, MO.

Otis, C.L. (1993, March). *The active woman: Special concerns*. Paper presented at the American College of Sports Medicine Team Physician Course, Lake Buena Vista, FL.

Pasman, L., & Thompson, J.K. (1988). Body image and eating disturbance in obligatory runners, obligatory weightlifters, and sedentary individuals. *International Journal of Eating Disorders*, **7**, 759-769.

Perron, M.S., & Endres, J. (1985). Knowledge, attitudes and dietary practices of female athletes. *Journal of the American Dietetic Association*, **85**, 573.

Porcello, L.A. (1984). A practical guide to fad diets. *Clinical Sports Medicine*, **3**, 723-729.

Powers, P.S. (1984). Multidisciplinary approach to treatment and evaluation. In P.S. Powers & R.C. Fernandez (Eds.), *Current treatment of anorexia nervosa and bulimia* (pp. 166-179). New York: Karger.

Reece, B.A., & Gross, M. (1982). A comprehensive milieu program for treatment of anorexia nervosa. In M. Gross (Ed.), *Anorexia nervosa: A comprehensive approach* (pp. 103-109). Lexington, MA: Collamore Press.

Rosen, L.W., & Hough, D.O. (1988). Pathogenic weight-control behaviors of female college gymnasts. *Physician and Sportsmedicine*, **16**, 141-144.

Rosen, L.W., McKeag, D.B., Hough, D.O., & Curley, V. (1986). Pathogenic weight-control behavior in female athletes. *Physician and Sportsmedicine*, **14**, 79-86.

Ryan, R. (1992). Management of eating problems in athletic settings. In K.D. Brownell, J. Rodin, & J.H. Wilmore (Eds.), *Eating, body weight, and performance in athletes* (pp. 344-362). Malvern, PA: Lea & Febiger.

Sanford, S., & Halliburton, S. (1989, July 31). Rhodenbaugh's path winds through secret world of bulimia. *Austin American-Statesman*, pp. D1, D7.

Stuart, R.B., Mitchell, C., & Jensen, J.A. (1981). Therapeutic options in the management of obesity. In L.A. Bradley & C.K. Prokop (Eds.), *Medical psychology: A new perspective* (pp. 321-353). New York: Academic Press.

Thompson, R.A. (1987). Management of the athlete with an eating disorder: Implications for the sport management team. *Sport Psychologist*, **1**, 114-126.

Thompson, R., & Sherman, R. (1993). *Helping athletes with eating disorders*. Champaign, IL: Human Kinetics.

Thornton, J.S. (1990). Feast or famine: Eating disorders in athletes. *Physician and Sportsmedicine*, **18**, 116-122.

Tilgner, S.A., & Schiller, M.R. (1989). Dietary intakes of female college athletes: The need for nutrition education. *Journal of the American Dietetic Association*, **89**, 967-969.

Webster, S., Rutt, R., & Weltman, A. (1990). Physiological effects of a weight loss regimen practiced by college wrestlers. *Medicine and Science in Sports and Exercise*, **22**, 229.

Wilmore, J.H. (1992). Body weight and body composition. In K.D. Brownell, J. Rodin, & J.H. Wilmore (Eds.), *Eating, body weight, and performance in athletes* (pp. 77-93). Malvern, PA: Lea & Febiger.

Wolf, E.M., Wirth, J.C., & Lohman, T.G. (1979). Nutritional practices of coaches in the Big Ten. *Physician and Sportsmedicine*, **7**, 112-124.

Yalom, I.D. (1985). *The theory and practice of group psychotherapy*. New York: Basic Books.

Yeager, K.K., Agostini, R., Nattiv, A., & Drinkwater, B. (1993). The female athlete triad: Disordered eating, amenorrhea, osteoporosis. *Medicine and Science in Sports and Exercise*, **25**, 775-777.

Zuckerman, D.M., Colby, A., Ware, N.C., & Lazerson, J.S. (1986). The prevalence of bulimia among college students. *American Journal of Public Health*, **76**, 1135-1137.

CHAPTER 14

TRANSITIONS IN COMPETITIVE SPORT: MAXIMIZING INDIVIDUAL POTENTIAL

Shane M. Murphy, PhD
United States Olympic Committee

The issue that helping professionals most commonly encounter in the sport setting is how athletes will plan for and cope with life after competitive sport. Unlike such issues as injury or drug use, which many athletes avoid, all athletes must consider the prospect of ending their competitive athletic careers. The helping professional might encounter this issue in a variety of forms, often depending on the athlete's developmental stage. A teenage athlete might face the decision of whether to enter college or to put academic aspirations on hold while spending 2 intensively athletic years trying to make an Olympic team. A young adult might struggle with a relationship, facing conflicting input from his spouse, who wants to begin a family and structure some stability in their relationship, and from his own desires to chase his dream of professional baseball, even though it means an almost nomadic existence with a low income level. A young tennis player might be faced with a variety of choices about what career path to follow after a knee injury forces abandonment of a lucrative career as a tennis professional on the tour. Difficult choices in the career area are universally encountered by athletes, but they are not always acknowledged and they are not dealt with in the same way by everyone. The following case examples offer two styles of coping with career transition issues.

■ *THE CASE OF DARIUS* ■

Darius grew up in a suburb of Los Angeles, the son of middle-class parents who encouraged his natural athletic interests. Blessed with great speed and excellent hand-eye coordination, Darius excelled at a variety of sports, but his lack of size prevented him from a long career in his two favorite activities, football and basketball. By age 16, he had played competitive baseball, basketball, football, tennis, and soccer and had tried out such sports as surfing, golf, bowling, cycling, and skiing. In his junior year at high school, a friend of his father encouraged him to attend a local field hockey club, where Darius's rapid skill development brought him to the attention of a national-level development coach. Darius was offered a spot at a national coaching clinic on the East Coast and subsequently was selected for a national junior development squad.

In his senior year, Darius was offered the chance to enroll in an exchange program with an Australian high school; this included a place on a local Australian hockey-club team. He made the trip, played a lot of field hockey, and made many contacts in the Australian field-hockey community. When he returned to the United States, he again attended a national training camp, and this time the national coach selected him for one of four scholarship spots with the national team, whose members lived and trained at the Olympic Training Center in San Diego. Once again, Darius took advantage of the opportunity and moved to San Diego. He enrolled part-time in a local college, studying engineering, and in his second year got a part-time job as an assistant with a local construction firm.

From the time he moved to San Diego, Darius impressed coaches and officials with his aggressive approach to career development. As he traveled around the country on competition trips, Darius handed out his personal card to many people he came in contact with, including sponsors, supporters, and sport officials. The inexpensive card simply read Darius McKee, Member of the U.S. National Field-Hockey Team, and gave his address and telephone number. He also collected hundreds of business cards from these contacts and stored them alphabetically in a plastic folder. Those who met him at after-game dinners or sponsor-related functions remember that he was never afraid to ask questions and that he showed a great interest in the careers of those he met, often questioning them at length about the type of work they did and how they got started in their businesses.

After 3 years of hard work, Darius won a spot on the United States Olympic team, one of just 18 athletes to earn that honor in field hockey. The team played hard at the Games, but lost four matches and tied one, finishing 11th in the field of 12. The coach, full of praise for Darius, who scored four goals in the tournament, told the press that "if I had another 10 who worked as hard as Darius, we would have won a couple of those close games." Taking 2 months off after the Olympics, Darius, after a long talk with the national coach, decided to end his national team career in field hockey. Darius believed that he had reached the level of excellence he had aimed for in the sport and that his Olympic experience had been a tremendous bonus for him. His coach asked him to stay on for 4 years, but supported Darius's decision to go back to school full-time and complete his engineering degree.

The job market was tight when Darius finished his degree, but he landed a good job with the second company he interviewed with. A deciding factor in his final interview with the company was his response to a question posed to all three final candidates. Minutes before a meeting with the selection panel, Darius was given a blank piece of paper and asked to "fill up this sheet by writing down as much about yourself as you can." After completing sections about his education, job experience, and career goals, Darius was still faced with a blank two inches at the bottom of the paper. For a moment he was stuck, but then he wrote down the name of every state and country he had visited during his extensive field-hockey tours. When he sat down to meet with the panel, the first questions they asked were about some of the more exotic locales he had mentioned on his interview sheet.

After 6 productive years with that firm, Darius, now married, left to start his own consulting business with a colleague in Los Angeles. After a rough start-up year, they experienced great success and Darius displayed many of the hard-work skills he had shown in field hockey years before. He was very proud of his hockey career and at the bottom of his business card was a line that read Member of the USA 1976 Olympic Team, Field Hockey.

As he and his partner expanded their business, many of the contacts Darius had made in his field-hockey years and had kept in touch with proved to be valuable sources of information about a variety of business opportunities. Darius became a well-known, active member of his local community, and after the birth of his first child he successfully ran for mayor of the suburb in which he lived, becoming the first black mayor of that community. When young people ask him for advice on how to get started in a career, he tells them to "pay attention to all the great lessons you learn in sport. My sporting career helped me out a great deal, and it can help you out, too, if you keep your eyes and ears open."

■ *THE CASE OF ELEANOR* ■

Eleanor began her figure skating career at age 6, after she had watched a graceful young American win the gold medal at Grenoble. She showed remarkable aptitude on the ice, and her coach encouraged her parents to enroll her in individual lessons in addition to the group classes in which she had started. By age 10, she was competing successfully at the national level in novice competitions, and her coach admitted to her parents that for Eleanor's skating career to advance, she would need a more experienced coach. Eleanor and her mother moved to a city in the Rocky Mountains that was home to a prestigious international figure skating coach, while her father and two siblings stayed in the large midwestern city she had grown up in.

In high school, Eleanor's skating goals took precedence over everything else. Her school allowed her to design a special school day so she could practice in the morning, attend 3 hours of concentrated schooling, and get 4 hours of practice in during the afternoon. Because Eleanor could not take enough credits on this schedule, she fell behind her age-group peers in grade level, but her skating career continued to rocket. At age 15, she became national junior champion, and the next year found her competing with the other senior women for a spot on the Olympic team in two years.

The year before the Olympics, Eleanor stopped going to school completely and kept up her education with only some correspondence classes. She had very few friends outside of skating, but her national success had taken her on trips to such faraway places as Australia and Belgium, and she was very satisfied at the outcome of her choices. Then, in the first major international competition of the Olympic season, she fell on a triple axel and broke a bone in her ankle. She had to undergo extensive rehabilitation to make it back on the ice for the Olympic trials 4 months later, but she showed her usual tenacity and entered the competition. She was in first place after the figures section of the competition, but in the short program, she fell to sixth place after falling on her weak ankle three times. Devastated, Eleanor withdrew from competition and scarcely noticed the Olympics 3 weeks later as her competitors proudly represented their country at the brand-new Olympic skating facility.

After 6 months of indecision, Eleanor turned professional, deciding that 4 years was too long to wait for the uncertainty of another chance at an Olympic team. As an attractive and exciting skater, Eleanor was popular at ice shows across the country, and she earned more than $100,000 in her first year as a professional. Yet 2 years after breaking her ankle, she still felt confused and depressed. She experimented with a variety of drugs and often used cocaine at the parties following the ice shows. Because she had gained 10 lb (4.5 kg) over the 2 years, she underwent liposuction to restore her "original" figure. Eleanor believed that she might be attracted to a career as a professional in law or health care, but without even her high school diploma she didn't know where to begin. When she confided in her old coach at a tour stop in her city, the coach recommended a local psychologist who had helped several skaters in the community. It took Eleanor another 6 months before she telephoned the psychologist and made her first appointment.

These two case studies illustrate how the same basic process, transferring from a competitive sport career to another career area, can be experienced in different ways. Many of the issues raised in these case studies will be addressed later in this chapter. The case of Darius, in particular, shows how high-level sports participation can play an important role in optimizing career opportunities. This chapter examines from a number of perspectives the transition process when leaving high-level competitive sport and analyzes ways in which helping professionals can assist athletes in making such transitions effectively.

The chapter is organized into four main sections. First, an attempt is made to understand the motivation of elite athletes. To help athletes who are leaving elite competition, it is necessary to understand what this transition means to them and what they feel they are leaving behind. Next, the nature of the transition process in sport is examined, and typical transition scenarios are presented. Then, factors related to optimal transition are presented. Lastly, several alternatives for assisting athletes in making effective transitions in sport are offered.

PARTICIPATION MOTIVATION IN ELITE ATHLETES

Elite athletes have an extensive history of socialization into the sport role (Ames, 1984), and during their competitive careers most have as their central identity the role of athlete. Leaving competitive sport means that they must adapt to viewing themselves in other roles and realizing that they will no longer be identified as athletes (although many develop an identity of ex-athlete). In helping athletes who are undergoing transition from sport, it is important to understand the athlete identity and the changes that result when this identity is altered.

A large part of the athlete identity can be understood in terms of the motivation of elite athletes. That is, what reasons lead athletes to devote so many resources to developing excellence in sport, and what factors continue to encourage them to participate in high-level sports when many of their cohort have left competition? A large literature exists on participation motivation in sport, and a consistently clear picture has emerged of the motivation of athletes (Gould, 1987a). One of the more thorough studies of elite athletes and their participation motivation was conducted by Kesend and Murphy (1989). They studied athletes in training for the Olympic Games and used an interview-and-qualitative-analysis methodology to identify the major motivational themes expressed by these elite athletes (Kesend, Perna, & Murphy, 1993). These are the main motives these athletes identified as encouraging them to participate in sport during their careers:

1. Perceived competence
   - Measurement of skill
   - Improvement of skill
2. Intrinsic motivation
   - Fun
   - Drive to achieve
3. Recognition
4. The sport
5. Self-development
6. Affiliation and life opportunities
7. Health, fitness, and activity
8. Overcoming adversity
9. Turning points in life
10. Altruism or idealism

Similar participation motivation themes have been identified in other research studies (Scanlan, Stein, & Ravizza, 1989). An examination of these themes indicates the central place of sport in the elite athlete's life and suggests the difficulty in leaving this high-level participation behind. If sport is satisfying because it enables a person to develop and demonstrate competence, because it provides a high level of intrinsic motivation, because it offers the athlete opportunities for social recognition, because is it fun, and because it provides many opportunities to develop satisfying social relationships, then it is likely that the athlete will seek to satisfy these motivational needs in other life areas, including work, on cessation of competitive sport involvement. People who can plan career alternatives that are also motivating are likely to better adjust to competitive sport cessation than those who cannot find ways to replace the role of sport in their lives.

A large literature exists on career counseling (Bolles, 1992; Sinetar, 1987), but much less has been published on the career counseling that might be provided to athletes in transition (Baillie, 1993; Petitpas, Danish, McKelvain, & Murphy, 1992). The career counselor or helping professional who is assisting athletes in transition must first understand the athletes' perspectives and the role sport has played in their lives. Motivational issues that are likely to impact the transition process must be identified. A rich literature exists to help the consultant understand the drives and motivations of elite athletes, but each individual has unique issues in the transition process.

Society has an ambivalent attitude toward the superstar gymnast who retires at age 18 with lucrative endorsement opportunities, or the professional athlete who retires at age 30 after earning many millions playing a sport that most people participate in for fun. Until recently, there has been little to guide us in understanding these unique experiences. The next section examines the literature that has attempted to describe the nature of the transition experience for athletes.

THE NATURE OF THE TRANSITION PROCESS

Two extremes of the reaction to leaving sport are provided in a study by Baillie (1992), who surveyed 260 elite and professional athletes concerning their experiences in leaving sport. The responses of two United States Olympians clearly demonstrate the wide range of possible responses to leaving high-level competition:

> . . . you assume that once the athlete has retired from *their* sport they have retired from *all* sport. I haven't touched an oar since retirement, but I do a zillion other sports, some competitively, and I work on a program that takes athletes overseas to coach in black townships in South Africa. I doubt any athlete ever retires from sport, just from *their* sport.
>
> Retirement from competition was . . . frustrating because 1988 was to be my best year, but illness prevented that (and an injury). . . . The only thing I truly regret is that I did not jump off the building in Seoul as I had contemplated every night. All I had to do was slide six inches further forward, but didn't. (Baillie, 1992, p. 157)

On the one hand, leaving high-level competitive sport can be an experience that opens up many avenues for athletes, allowing them to try new career paths and explore new opportunities. As the first athlete points out, sport can still play an important role in the athlete's life even when elite competition has ended. On the other hand, leaving elite competition can be a confusing and depressing experience, especially when the athlete has unfinished business in sport or when the future is filled with doubt and uncertainty. Sinclair and Orlick (1993) surveyed 200 retired Canadian athletes and found that athletes who had achieved their sport-related goals tended to feel more satisfied with their present life than those who had not accomplished their goals. Pearson and Petitpas (1990) examined the transition process and predicted that six factors would make the process most difficult for athletes:

- identity strongly and exclusively based on athletic performance
- a great gap between level of aspiration and level of ability
- little experience with the same or similar transitions
- behavioral or emotional deficits that limit the ability to adapt to change
- limited supportive relationships
- the need to deal with the transition in a context that lacks the emotional and material resources that could be helpful

Other writers who have tried to predict the natural course of the transition experience from elite sport have had a difficult time because the experience is unlike other experiences to which it has commonly been compared, such as the retirement from work or the experience of loss from a death (Rosenberg, 1981). Unlike the typical retirement from work, the athlete who retires from competitive sport still has many productive career years left. And although the loss of the athlete identity might be compared to the loss of someone close through death, the athlete still has time to forge a new identity by building on the old one, a process dissimilar to the experience of loss through a death. Such differences have led theorists to criticize attempts to use social gerontological or thanatological theories to describe the sport transition process (Blinde & Greendorfer, 1985). They argue that such theories are too limiting and that attempts to explain the sport transition process must be developmentally based, focusing on the socialization experience of the athlete, the nature of the transition, the reaction of others, the development of coping resources to handle the transition, and the development of new individual roles.

The effects of the transition out of sport on elite or very competitive athletes have been examined in many studies. If this process is indeed difficult for athletes, then it can be hypothesized that they will show signs of psychological distress after retiring from sport or that their adjustment to new careers will not be effective. One of the first studies to examine this question was conducted by Mihovilovic (1968). He surveyed 44 former first-league players from the Yugoslavian soccer league about the end of their soccer careers and subsequent adjustment. His results indicated that 95% of the athletes ended their careers involuntarily, due to age, injury, or other factors. In 52% of cases, players reported that their career end was sudden. Mihovilovic found that if a player had no other profession on retirement, then the career ending was painful, marked by feelings of frustration and conflict. He also found that for many of the players, their circle of friends diminished after retirement. Mihovilovic concluded with several suggestions from these players as to how their retirement process could have been structured to lessen the negative aspects. These include giving players increased responsibilities during their playing careers and continuing to participate in sports on a recreational basis.

A variety of other researchers since Mihovilovic have studied other groups of athletes undergoing transition out of sport (Allison & Meyer, 1988; Blann & Zaichowsky, 1986; Haerle, 1975; Koukouris, 1991; Reynolds, 1981). Ogilvie and Taylor (1992) provide an excellent summary of the literature on career transitions in sport. Several of these studies demonstrate that the transition process is not automatically distressing. Allison and Meyer, for example, found that 50% of the 28 retired female tennis professionals they surveyed expressed relief at being off the tour. All the studies, however, indicated that at least some of the elite athletes experienced difficulties at some stage of the transition process, such as Allison and Meyer's finding that 30% of the tennis professionals described feeling a loss of identity after cessation of tour play. Most of the researchers described changes that the athletes would like to see in the transition process, such as more organizational support from the sporting body involved (Blann & Zaichowsky, 1986) or a more gradually phased retirement process, such as that described by Mihovilovic (1968). In the comprehensive study mentioned earlier of 260 elite and professional athletes (Baillie, 1992), adjustment to the transition from competition was measured by such variables as level of family disruption, feelings of loss, acceptance of the situation, valuing new pursuits, and self-rated satisfaction with the transition process. Using these criteria, Baillie found that athletes tended to adjust better to the end of their sports career when they had

- retired by choice,
- accomplished their goals,
- been able to remain as involved in their sports as they would like,
- completed college undergraduate programs, and
- been able to disengage from their sports at or shortly after the peak of their careers (1992, p. 78).

These factors suggest that certain aspects of the way the transition is structured have a large impact on the adjustment of the athlete. Some of the ways in which the transition process is structured are examined next.

STRUCTURAL FACTORS IN SPORT TRANSITIONS

A variety of circumstances might initiate the athlete's transition out of elite-level competitive sport. Some of the most common reasons for leaving high-level sport are choice, being cut, injury, and age.

Choice

Although the Mihovilovic (1968) study found that just 5% of the sample retired "voluntarily" (no desire to continue sport practice), the present author has found that many athletes make a decision at some stage of participation that the expected benefits of pursuing some other life activity outweigh the advantages of continued sporting involvement and so decide to leave. In a study of British teenagers participating in a fitness and sports campaign, White and Coakley (1986) argue that the term *dropout* is an inaccurate one when applied to youth sports participants. Instead of dropping out, most teenagers have simply decided that they want to do other things with their limited time than play sports. Elsewhere, Coakley has suggested that "one should not assume that retirement from competitive sport automatically creates problems until the experiences of former athletes are compared with the experiences of similar nonathletes" (1983, p. 9).

The case of Darius shows that making the choice to leave high-level sports participation can lead to great satisfaction and fulfillment in other areas. On the other hand, however, the case of Eleanor shows that a voluntary decision to make the transition out of elite sport can be a confusing and troubling one. Two important factors, gender and ethnicity, must be considered by the helping professional working with athletes in transition. Experience and preliminary research suggest that both factors can have a significant impact on the experience of the transition process, but little research exists clarifying the role of either factor.

The findings of Lee (1983) suggest that there are differences in the career expectations of athletes with different ethnic backgrounds. Specifically, Lee found that a significantly higher percentage of black high-school athletes than white high-school athletes expected to pursue a career in sports. Such differences might be a reflection of the promotion of different role models by society for blacks, whites, Asians, Hispanics, and others. Insufficient research exists to understand possible differences in career expectations for athletes from varying ethnic and cultural backgrounds, but such differences in this area should be kept in mind by the helping professional.

Gender issues also undoubtedly impact the transition experiences of athletes, particularly women. As documented by Diane Gill in chapter 9, many fewer professional career opportunities exist in sport for women than for men. Far fewer women than men are employed in intercollegiate athletic programs as coaches or administrators. This inequitable situation impacts women even earlier during their athletic careers, because there are many fewer athletic roles for women in sport, despite the passage of Title IX. As an example, an elite male basketball player can expect to make a financially rewarding career from basketball, but few opportunities exist in her sport for the elite female basketball star graduating from college. The issue of gender equity is being seriously examined by the NCAA and might have far-reaching consequences for collegiate and high-school athletics. The dearth of female coaches in elite coaching positions is so severe that the United States Olympic Committee is exploring institutional changes that might be implemented to enhance the quality and status of coaching, encouraging more female athletes to enter the coaching profession upon completion of their sport careers. Consultants working with female athletes should be especially aware of these issues concerning transition processes in sport.

Courtesy University of Illinois Daily Illini

Being Cut

In this author's experience, a common reason for an athlete to leave sport is being cut from a team or failing to progress to the next higher level of competition. Studies have indicated that the loss rate of young athletes from organized sport is about 35% in any one year (Gould, 1987b). It is probable that the greatest problems arise when high expectations for continued athletic success clash with the reality of not moving forward to the next level of participation. For example, in the study mentioned earlier, Lee (1983) found that 36% of black and 14% of white high-school starting team athletes expected a career in sport. Contrast this figure with findings that in football, for example, less than 5% of high-school players receive college scholarships to play and, of these, only 1% ever have a chance to play in the National Football League (Ogilvie & Howe, 1986). If alternative plans are not made for the development of a career in an area other than sport, transition problems are likely to arise.

Athletes who have been unexpectedly cut and whose performance goals were never met in the sport are most likely to have negative emotions toward the transition process and perhaps develop bitterness or frustration toward the sporting groups with which they were involved. Such attitudes of frustration toward the political system in sport have been a common encounter in my experience with athletes who are having trouble adjusting to a transition. Another athlete from the Baillie study describes this attitude well:

> The most difficult part of retirement was the strange way your sport treats you. One minute everyone involved loves you and includes you. Then, you make a decision to leave the team and they don't even say goodbye. At least at university, they have a graduation ceremony. As an athlete we give a lot to the sport. They dictate all you do. . . . A happy retired athlete does a lot more good than a bitter one! (1992, p. 152)

Injury

Another factor that might lead to the unexpected and sudden transition out of sport for an athlete is illness or injury. Chapter 11 in this book describes the experience of injury for an athlete and discusses in some detail the possible emotional ramifications of the injury experience. If the injury is severe enough to force the athlete out of high-level competition or to raise doubts about the possibility of continued participation, then the athlete must begin to deal with the transition from sport in addition to coping with the process of rehabilitation from the injury. Unless the athlete has excellent coping resources, this dual challenge is likely to tax the athlete's ability to adjust. In a follow-up study of elite-level college athletes, Kleiber, Greendorfer, Blinde, and Samdahl (1987) found that athletes who had left sport as the result of an injury had significantly lower ratings of current life satisfaction than other athletes.

Although in the case of Eleanor her injury did not lead directly to her retirement from skating, we can hypothesize that if she had had a chance to fulfill her Olympic dream her subsequent decisions and experiences might have been different. Thus injuries can impact later career adjustment in a variety of ways, not merely through sports cessation.

Age

The final reason to be considered here for sport termination is the decline in sport skills and capabilities that inevitably accompanies advancing years. Depending on the sport, this point might occur at a wide variety of ages. In women's gymnastics, for example, the onset of maturation and the rigors of years of training usually lead top-level competitors to quit around age 20 or earlier. International competitors can still be found achieving great success in their 40s in some sports, such as shooting or golf. Again, the reason for career transition is not as important as a person's reaction to that situation. Some athletes accept the decline in skills as obvious, make other plans, and complete a successful transition to another career. Others, however, fight the process, perhaps by training harder or more scientifically and, feeling that they have been betrayed by officials and coaches who do not recognize their continued skill level, might eventually be forced out of the sport by younger competitors.

Helping professionals should understand the transition experience from the athlete's viewpoint and recognize the variety of transition experiences commonly encountered by athletes. To help athletes achieve optimal transitions, it is also important to understand the change process in human behavior. Methods for achieving positive change are discussed next.

HELPING ATHLETES ACHIEVE OPTIMAL TRANSITIONS

As professional sports leagues have grown in size and popularity, as opportunities for elite athletes have increased, and as popular participation in many forms of organized sport has grown, there has been a development of interest in helping athletes refocus their lives in other areas once their competitive careers are finished. A variety of perspectives has been offered to help athletes in transition (Baillie, 1993; Chartrand & Lent, 1985; Danish, Petitpas, & Hale, 1990; Pearson & Petitpas, 1990; Skovholt, Morgan, & Negron-Cunningham, 1989). The perspective taken in both this chapter and in this book is that athletes can manage their sporting experience to achieve optimal satisfaction and that the role of helping professionals is to assist athletes maximize their potential and help those who are having difficulty with some aspect of the sport experience.

The author has had the opportunity to be involved in the process of helping elite athletes at all stages of transition through his participation in the United States Olympic Committee's Career Assistance Program for Athletes (CAPA), which has been described elsewhere (Petitpas et al., 1992). The author has participated in more than 20 career-planning workshops offered by CAPA and has personally counseled several hundred athletes struggling with transition in his role as sport psychologist at the Olympic Training Center in Colorado Springs. These experiences have led to the formulation of the model of transition assistance that is offered here. This model draws on the thoughts of many career guidance experts who have been involved in CAPA and has as its basic philosophy the goal of enabling athletes to develop the skills necessary to gain a feeling of control over the transition process. Effective strategies to help athletes with transition are described next.

Career Planning Assistance

Athletes differ from most of their college-age peers in that their career planning must involve sports participation as their primary focus, whereas most of their cohort are focused primarily on education or work. As discussed previously, elite-level sports participation usually lasts a decade or less (although in some sports, such as golf, top-level participation can be lifelong) and can be abruptly terminated through injury or selection decisions. Thus education and work-related decisions are often put on hold until the sporting career is completed. This often leads athletes to feel that they have fallen behind their peers in the career development area, as they are often making critical education and work decisions in the mid-20s or later.

> Unfortunately, hockey was what I knew best, am most competent at, my 'job' since ten years old. To be like a 21-year-old entry-level business person with 34-, 35-, 36-year-olds is very difficult. The lack of preparation, training to succeed in difficult economic environments is a problem I am still overcoming. (Baillie, 1992, p. 166)

A common theme expressed by many athletes is that they desire to somehow make use of their sport experiences in their future careers. In a survey of career needs of 531 Olympic athletes, Hilliard (1988) found that 67% of respondents endorsed the statement, I would like to learn how to emphasize my special qualifications obtained through sports, whereas only 24% endorsed the statement, I need help preparing my resume. Athletes realize that they are special in their career needs and they desire this to be acknowledged in the transition process. The basics of career guidance planning are the same for athletes as for nonathletes, but the issues both of active sports participation interfering with education and work planning and of athletes' special experiences must be taken into account in helping athletes with career planning. The five major steps in career planning assistance are briefly described next.

Understanding the Career Process

At any point in their athletic careers, athletes can benefit from an understanding of the career process and the necessary steps involved in making well-informed career decisions. During many CAPA seminars, the concern has been expressed that planning for a life after sport will somehow distract the athlete from a focus on high-level achievement. Instead, many athletes have told us that planning for another career after sport lessens their anxiety about the transition process and allows them to concentrate more fully on sporting goals. As the case of Darius illustrates, such simple steps as making contacts throughout a sport career, making up business cards, and taking advantage of corporate sponsorship opportunities can set the stage for an easier transition when sport involvement ends.

Developing Job-Relevant Skills

A common concern heard from athletes at CAPA seminars is, "I'm just an athlete, I don't know how to do anything else." Actually, athletes learn many job-relevant skills during their years of sports participation. Skills learned in one area that can be used in another are called *transferable skills* by career counselors. A large segment of the CAPA seminars is devoted to helping athletes realize the variety of skills they have learned through sports participation and how these skills can be targeted at potential employers in new career areas. Some examples of transferable skills commonly gained by playing sports are as follows:

- Performing optimally under pressure
- Communicating effectively with a team to reach group goals
- Setting weekly goals that lead to long-range goal attainment
- Accepting criticism and using it effectively
- Adhering to a strict schedule
- Competitiveness

Identifying Personal Career Needs

Self-knowledge is emphasized by career counselors as a critical aspect of developing a satisfying career (Bolles, 1992). Elite athletes often realize the special nature of their passionate involvement in sport and wonder about replacing it with another career.

• . . . The toughest part of the transition was finding a replacement for the challenge and the stimulation, not to mention financial security, that baseball afforded (Baillie, 1992, p. 162).

• . . . I really do believe that it's hard for all athletes to retire from a pro sport because [you miss] the thrill of playing in front of large crowds and the ego strokes of people wanting your autograph. It's very difficult to replace that rush of scoring a goal, blocking a shot to save a goal, or just being part of a winning team. It would be very difficult to replace that, no matter what we did afterwards (Baillie, 1992, p. 166).

Like others dealing with transition, athletes must identify their own skills and interests, the values they hold most strongly, and understand the influence their personality would have on a job. Then they can plan to develop new skills or try to find a career that they will find satisfying and fulfilling. It might be important to emphasize to elite athletes in transition that a job alone might not replace sport in satisfying all their needs, but that a career is made up of many elements besides a job (e.g., family, recreation, friends, community service). The combination of these various elements should provide the satisfaction and fulfillment athletes seek after transition.

Identifying Job-Related Opportunities

A critical reason that many people seek help from professional career counselors is that they do not understand the job marketplace or the many opportunities that exist there. Some athletes, like Darius, make use of their sporting careers to widen their exposure to various jobs and career possibilities. Others, like Eleanor, are so focused on their sport career that when it ends they feel ignorant about other opportunities that might exist. A critical ingredient of the CAPA seminars is providing training to athletes in such skills as informational interviewing, which they can apply in seeking information about new career possibilities.

Setting Career Goals

At some point, career guidance offered to athletes must move from the advice-giving stage to the action-oriented stage. Athletes are, in general, very goal oriented, so it is natural for them to set career-related goals that help them follow through on their objectives. However, because athletes are often very results-oriented, it can be helpful to emphasize that career management is a gradual process, and that often many opportunities must be pursued before a satisfying career after sport is developed. Some of the individual counseling strategies discussed in the next section can help in dealing with the common frustrations encountered in the job-finding or career-building stage of the transition.

Individual Counseling

Along with the special career needs of athletes just described, an optimal transition experience might depend on dealing with some of the emotional issues described earlier in this chapter. Athletes not only need to know how to find and get a job after sport, but they must also develop the skills and resources to manage the transition experience effectively. The helping professional working with the athlete in transition can be a great support by providing individual counseling concerning the following four issues.

Expansion of Self-Identity

The process of making an early commitment to a career identity and not exploring other alternatives has been called "identity foreclosure" by some writers (Marcia, 1978). Identity foreclosure can cause problems in adjustment if that identity is lost and the person has few alternatives for structuring a new identity. This process might be a common one for athletes, who are often rewarded for athletic excellence at an early age and are sometimes encouraged to de-emphasize educational and work opportunities in favor of developing athletic excellence. The case of Eleanor illustrates how confusing the end of a high-level career can be when a person has invested a great deal in developing an identity that is no longer functional. Eleanor thought of herself almost exclusively as a figure skater and found it difficult to even begin the sort of career planning (described above) necessary to move on to a new stage of her life.

When counseling the athlete who has a strong investment in the athlete identity, emphasizing the special qualities that the person has developed through sports experiences is a good way of building rapport and understanding. Counseling with Eleanor, for example, was a gradual process, as she saw herself as an overachiever who accomplished things on her own, without much support. It was, therefore, difficult for her to see herself as in need of counseling. Instead, it was emphasized that Eleanor had been a star in one field and would need to plan just as carefully and work just as hard to achieve success in another area. This approach paid off, as Eleanor became committed to the development of a new career and got her high-school diploma and enrolled in night school. Although she still skated occasionally to earn money, she felt confident enough to start a serious relationship and was able to kick the drug habit that she had found so egodystonic.

Emotional and Social Support

As is the case when dealing with other sources of stress, having support during the transition period can be the key to a successful career change. Athletes experiencing transition have emphasized the importance of support from their family and friends.

> Retirement is not an easy experience but I truly believe that my family and close friends made the difference for me. They really supported me. (Baillie, 1992, p. 152)
>
> Getting married sure made retirement easier for me. (Baillie, 1992, p. 157)

Some authors have argued that the very nature of sport makes it unlikely that athletes will seek emotional support themselves (Petitpas et al., 1992). This viewpoint contends that the athletic system reinforces individuals who can tough it out, so many athletes do not disclose their fears or vulnerabilities to others. Emotional support is often a major lack for such people. A counselor who encourages these people to share their feelings, providing a safe and supportive environment for the disclosure of emotions, can be a great source of support. In the CAPA seminars conducted by the USOC, it is striking how many participants commented on the relief they felt when they heard other athletes disclose feelings of insecurity and doubt about the transition process. Many athletes said they felt "alone" or "unique" in experiencing negative emotions associated with the transition.

There is often such a strong social network connected with sports participation that the athlete contemplating transition might be drawn back to sport because such social support exists. Many athletes interviewed by the author say they have retired several times during their sport career before making a final break with elite-level participation. The counselor can help the athlete identify and develop other sources of social support away from the sporting area. From the author's experience, athletes often feel better about their posttransition career if they have at least had the chance to explore other nonsport career possibilities.

Enhancement of Coping Skills

A person-environment relational view of stress sees the amount of stress experienced by a person as a product of the severity of the stressor and the extent of coping resources possessed by the person (Lazarus & Folkman, 1984). People high in coping resources will experience less stress than people with few coping strategies. Thus, whatever the cause of the transition experience, for elite athletes, the greater the variety of coping strategies at their disposal the less stress they will experience. An important part of the assistance the helping professional can provide athletes in transition is identifying athletes' coping skills, helping athletes apply their skills to the transition situation, and teaching athletes appropriate new coping skills.

Development of a Sense of Control

The major reasons identified for the cessation of an elite sport career are often outside the athlete's control (selection, injury, age). Even when they have voluntarily decided to retire from high-level sport, athletes might feel that the process is one over which they have little control. This sensed loss of control can be a frightening impediment to an optimal transition.

> Suddenly my life went from a structured, organized lifestyle where goals were predetermined to no structure and feeling at a loss as to which way to turn—a support system of guidance would have been very helpful. The decision to retire was my own and I have NO regrets. Nevertheless, there was a profound sense of loss and a feeling of being forgotten quickly. (Baillie, 1992, p. 150)

The feeling that you are in control of events, rather than events controlling you, has been called having an internal locus of control (Rotter, 1975), a feeling of competence (White, 1959), or having a sense of self-efficacy (Bandura, 1977). Experience with the CAPA seminars indicates that athletes who perceive themselves as having control are more likely to initiate actions that are likely to help their posttransition career development (e.g., prepare a resume, go on job interviews, actively build a network). The counselor can promote this sense of control in athletes by explaining the career development process, showing them the variety of transferable skills they possess, and helping them develop a plan for managing the transition process.

CONCLUSION

In this chapter I examined in detail the transition experience for the elite athlete. Helping professionals who offer guidance to athletes in this situation are encouraged to understand what sports participation and the transition out of sport mean to the elite athlete. The causes of transition from sport were described, as were the factors that have been identified as relating to optimal transition experiences. Lastly, ways were suggested to help athletes achieve optimal transitions to new careers.

Many athletes make the transition from high-level sport to the next stage of their lives with few problems and little distress. However, the opportunity to make an effective and satisfying transition to a new career should be afforded to all athletes. It is hoped that this chapter will help those professionals working with athletes to assist them in structuring an optimal transition experience. We can all benefit from helping such a high-achieving group of people use their extraordinary capabilities to the fullest.

REFERENCES

Allison, M.T., & Meyer, C. (1988). Career problems and retirement among elite athletes: The female tennis professional. *Sociology of Sport Journal*, **5**, 212-222.

Ames, N.R. (1984, Winter). The socialization of women into and out of sports. *Journal of NAWDAC*, pp. 3-8.

Baillie, P. (1992). *Career transition in elite and professional athletes: A study of individuals in their preparation for and adjustment to retirement from competitive sports.* Unpublished doctoral dissertation, Virginia Commonwealth University, Richmond, VA.

Baillie, P. (1993). Understanding retirement from sports: Therapeutic ideas for helping athletes in transition. *The Counseling Psychologist*, **21**, 399-410.

Bandura, A. (1977). Self-efficacy: Toward a unifying theory of behavioral change. *Psychological Review*, **84**, 191-215.

Blann, W., & Zaichowsky, L. (1986). *Career/life transition needs of National Hockey League players.* Report prepared for the National Hockey League Players Association, Boston.

Blinde, E., & Greendorfer, S. (1985). A reconceptualization of the process of leaving the role of competitive athlete. *International Review of Sport Sociology*, **20**, 87-94.

Bolles, R.N. (1992). *The 1992 what color is your parachute.* Berkeley, CA: Ten Speed Press.

Coakley, J. (1983). Leaving competitive sport: Retirement or rebirth? *Quest*, **35**, 1-11.

Chartrand, J., & Lent, R. (1985). Sports counseling: Enhancing the development of the student-athlete. *Journal of Counseling & Development*, **66**, 164-167.

Danish, S., Petitpas, A., & Hale, B. (1990). Sport as a context for developing competence. In T. Gullota, G. Adams, and R. Monteymar (Eds.), *Adolescent development: Interpersonal competence.* Elmsford, NY: Plenum Press.

Dubois, P.E. (1981). The youth sport coach as an agent of socialization: An exploratory study. *Journal of Sport Behavior*, **4**, 95-107.

Gould, D. (1987a). Promoting positive sport experiences for children. In J. May & M. Asken (Eds.), *Sport psychology: The psychological health of the athlete.* New York: PMA.

Gould, D. (1987b). Understanding attrition in youth sports. In D. Gould & M. Weiss (Eds.), *Advances in pediatric sport sciences: Vol. 2. Behavioral issues* (pp. 61-85). Champaign, IL: Human Kinetics.

Haerle, R. (1975). Career patterns and career contingencies of professional baseball players: An occupational analysis. In D.W. Ball & J.W. Loy (Eds.), *Sport and social order* (pp. 461-519). Reading, MA: Addison-Wesley.

Hilliard, N. (1988). *The career counseling needs of Olympic and Pan-American athletes: A needs assessment survey.* Unpublished survey conducted for the United States Olympic Committee, Colorado Springs.

Kesend, O., & Murphy, S.M. (1989, August). *Participation motivation in elite athletes: A developmental perspective.* Paper presented at the 7th World Congress in Sport Psychology, Singapore.

Kesend, O., Perna, F., & Murphy, S. (1993). *The development of participation motivation in elite athletes.* Paper submitted for publication.

Kleiber, D., Greendorfer, S., Blinde, E., & Samdahl, D. (1987). Quality of exit from university sports and subsequent life satisfaction. *Sociology of Sport Journal*, **4**, 28-36.

Koukouris, K. (1991). Disengagement of advanced and elite Greek male athletes from organized competitive sport. *International Review for the Sociology of Sport*, **26**, 289-306.

Lazarus, R.S., & Folkman, S. (1984). *Stress, appraisal and coping*. New York: Springer.

Lee, C. (1983). An investigation of the athletic career expectations of high school student athletes. *Personnel and Guidance Journal*, **61**, 544-547.

Marcia, J.E. (1978). Identity foreclosure: A unique challenge. *Personnel and Guidance Journal*, **56**, 558-561.

Mihovilovic, M. (1968). The status of former sportsmen. *International Review of Sport Sociology*, **3**, 73-96.

Ogilvie, B., & Howe, M. (1986). The trauma of termination from athletics. In J.M. Williams (Ed.), *Applied sport psychology: Personal growth to peak performance* (pp. 365-382). Palo Alto, CA: Mayfield.

Ogilvie, B., & Taylor, J. (1992). Career termination issues among elite athletes. In R.N. Singer, M. Murphy, & L.K. Tennant (Eds.), *Handbook of research on sport psychology* (pp. 761-775). New York: Macmillan.

Pearson, R., & Petitpas, A. (1990). Transitions of athletes: Developmental and preventive perspectives. *Journal of Counseling & Development*, **69**, 7-10.

Petitpas, A., Danish, S., McKelvain, R., & Murphy, S. (1992). A career assistance program for elite athletes. *Journal of Counseling and Development*, **70**, 383-386.

Reynolds, M.J. (1981). The effects of sports retirement on the job satisfaction of the former football player. In S.L. Greendorfer & A. Yiannakis (Eds.), *Sociology of sport: Diverse perspectives* (pp. 127-137). Champaign, IL: Leisure Press.

Rosenberg, E. (1981). Gerontological theory and athletic retirement. In S.L. Greendorfer & A. Yiannakis (Eds.), *Sociology of sport: Diverse perspectives* (pp. 119-126). Champaign, IL: Leisure Press.

Rotter, J. (1975). Some problems and misconceptions related to the construct of internal versus external control of reinforcement. *Journal of Consulting and Clinical Psychology*, **43**, 56-57.

Scanlan, T.K., Stein, G.L., & Ravizza, K. (1989). An in-depth study of former elite figure skaters: II. Sources of enjoyment. *Journal of Sport and Exercise Psychology*, **11**, 65-83.

Sinclair, D.A., & Orlick, T. (1993). Positive transitions from high-performance sport. *The Sport Psychologist*, **7**, 138-150.

Sinetar, M. (1987). *Do what you love, the money will follow*. New York: Dell.

Skovholt, T.M., Morgan, J.I., & Negron-Cunningham, H. (1989). Mental imagery in career counseling and life planning: A review of research and intervention methods. *Journal of Counseling and Development*, **67**, 287-292.

White, A., & Coakley, J. (1986). *Making decisions: The response of young people in the Medway towns to the "Ever Thought of Sport?" campaign*. West Sussex Institute of Higher Education Sports Council, Greater London and Southeast Region, London.

White, R.W. (1959). Motivation reconsidered: The concept of competence. *Psychological Review*, **66**, 297-333.

CHAPTER 15

OVERTRAINING AND BURNOUT

Sean McCann, PhD
United States Olympic Committee

Virtually every issue facing a sport psychologist working with elite athletes in today's sport environment involves questions of training. Diverse problem areas (such as sport performance difficulties, coach-athlete conflicts, drug use, emotional stress, and athlete career-choice anxiety), are all intensified by the incredible training pressures and demands facing the modern elite athlete. Although much attention is paid to competition performance, little in the sport psychology literature focuses on the preparation leading to competitions. This emphasis on competition performance is often misplaced, because in many cases, most of the sport psychologist's job is to help athletes successfully cope with training—getting them to, rather than through, competition.

This less-than-glamorous truth is old news for elite athletes themselves. Practices and training sessions always have accounted for most of the time a top athlete works at a sport. What has changed, however, is the nature of training time. At the elite sport level, in response to increasing rewards for success and increasing pressures on athletes and coaches, there has been a marked increase in the stress of training. In attempts to maximize performance at competitions, many athletes and coaches have experimented with increases in the duration and intensity of training time. Many of these experiments have been organized attempts to capitalize on knowledge gained from recent studies in sport science, whereas others have been based on the simple notion that more is better. These studies suggest that large increases in training stress can have both obvious and subtle effects, many of which are detrimental to athlete performance. This chapter focuses on the negative psychological and physiological responses, collectively referred to as *overtraining*, that result from overwhelming training stress. After defining terms and briefly reviewing the literature on overtraining and athlete burnout, I discuss intervention and ethical issues for the consulting sport psychologist.

■ *THE CASE OF CINDY* ■

Cindy is an elite bicycle racer in her late teens. She quickly rose in earlier years to elite status, showing talent and, even more markedly, an amazing work ethic and an ability to train harder than everyone else. Cindy felt more confident when she knew she had ridden more miles and had done more high-intensity training than her competitors. Now at the senior elite level, she has found that her improvement has slowed considerably, to only gradual, incremental increases in performance. Even more disturbing, Cindy has discovered that everyone trains hard at this level. Unsatisfied with her rate of progress and fearful that her lack of rapid improvement might threaten her national-team status, she began extra evening training rides without her coach's knowledge to gain an edge over other competitors.

Despite Cindy's efforts to hasten her improvement, she and her coaches began noticing significant negative changes in her performance during the current training season. Cindy appeared sluggish and slow to respond to attacks in training rides. Always an aggressive rider in the past, Cindy began to ride defensively and cautiously. In sprint and interval sessions, Cindy was losing ground to riders she had earlier beaten easily. She began to complain of chronic knee pain and developed a cough that wouldn't go away. Perhaps even more disturbing to the coaches were changes in Cindy's personality. Always the first to arrive at training sessions, she often arrived late and appeared sleepy. Previously a positive and exuberant athlete, Cindy began to complain about minor equipment problems and other team members. As the training season progressed, Cindy began expressing doubts about her ability and on two occasions quit training sessions in tears. After she missed an important training race due to oversleeping and missing a ride, her coaches called a conference to discuss Cindy's attitude and to determine if she belonged in the elite cycling program. The team's consulting sport psychologist was asked to attend.

DEFINITIONS

A clear definition of terms is essential to reviewing work in overtraining. One difficulty encountered when reviewing the literature is a tendency for authors to use a variety of terms to describe similar concepts. ***Overtraining*** refers to a maladaptive response to training stress, often due to chronically high training stress levels without periods of lower training loads. The end result of this chronic stress can be an ***overtraining syndrome*** with a variety of psychophysiological signs and symptoms. ***Staleness*** is another term used to describe the negative results of excessive training stress (Morgan, Brown, Raglin, O'Connor, & Ellickson, 1987), and authors have variously described it as the end result of overtraining (Hackney, Pearman, & Nowacki, 1990) or a stage in the development of the overtraining syndrome (Silva, 1990). In this chapter I will not distinguish staleness from overtraining.

In addition to using different terms for similar concepts, authors have also used similar terms to convey different concepts. Some reasons for this inconsistency are that training stress can impact athletes both positively and negatively and that terms describing training stress have been used to describe both positive and negative results. In contrast to ***overtraining***, the terms ***overload*** or ***overwork*** typically refer to a short-term increase in an athlete's training load that can result in a short-term performance decrease. Overload, often a well-planned phase of an athlete's training program, is based on sport physiology research showing that this short-term decrease in performance can be followed by increased future performance. This phenomenon is often used in a program of ***periodization*** (Bompa, 1983; Matveyev, 1981), in which a period of lower training loads (known as the rest or taper stage) follows the overload phase, ideally resulting in a peak physical state at competition.

OVERTRAINING RESEARCH

The search for an ideal training approach is not new; it has always been the central focus

Courtesy USOC

for coaches and athletes attempting to improve competitive performance. At the elite level, even the most gifted athletes cannot afford to be undertrained. The fear of being undertrained and unprepared often produces a more-is-better training philosophy. Where athletes are free to make sport a full-time occupation, significant increases in training load length and intensity have been attempted. In many cases, these have been at a significant cost. Just as undertraining can spell defeat for athletes, too-high and too-long training loads can negatively impact performance (Levin, 1991). The impact can be seen in physiological and psychological effects or, perhaps more accurately, in a combined *psychophysiological* effect.

Many studies of athletes' responses to high training loads use methodologies developed in generalized studies of response to stress. Following the early work of Hans Selye (1946), who saw stress as the body's reaction to a noxious stimulus, many researchers studied hormonal and other physiological changes in humans and other organisms in response to *stressors*. As stress research expanded from purely physiological studies to the study of psychological stress, researchers developed a growing awareness of the interaction between psychological and physiological stress reactions (Lazarus & Folkman, 1984). A similar realization recently occurred in overtraining research, but for the purpose of review, I will discuss research findings on the physiological effects of overtraining separately from the psychological effects before considering the interconnection of the psychological and physiological effects.

Specific Areas of Physiological Impact

Physiological research on overtraining has built on Selye's early work on hormonal changes in response to increased training stress, and additional studies have included cardiovascular changes, neuromuscular changes, performance changes, and immune system changes (Hackney et al., 1990). A common theme throughout much of the recent literature is the search for a physiological marker indicating the approach of overtraining (Callister, Callister, Fleck, & Dudley, 1989; Kuipers & Keizer, 1988; Levin, 1991).

The efforts to search for a physiological marker, or warning sign, of overtraining have generally begun with a recognition that athletes who have reached a full-blown overtraining syndrome exhibit characteristic physiological symptoms. These include hormonal changes (such as increased serum cortisol levels and decreased testosterone), higher resting heart rates and blood pressure (according to some reports), loss of body weight and percent body fat, and chronic muscle soreness (Callister et al., 1989; Costill et al., 1988; Dressendorfer and Wade, 1983; Hackney et al., 1990; Kirwin et al., 1988). In addition, athletes experiencing an overtraining syndrome appear to be at significantly greater risk for injuries and illnesses, with concomitant changes in the immune system (Costill, 1986; Hackney et al., 1990). Most applied research has monitored one or more of these physiological signs while tracking or modifying training loads.

Unfortunately, short-term physiological studies, using varying methods, have produced inconsistent findings (Hackney et al., 1990). Also, individual differences in ability to tolerate increased training stresses might mask results in studies using group designs (Levin, 1991; Morgan, 1991). As well, individual differences might exist in symptom expression of an overtraining syndrome. Lastly, comparing results from studies with athletes of various abilities is difficult, because elite athlete programs might, by their very nature, select for athletes who can tolerate higher training loads (Callister et al., 1989). Thus, despite some interesting and suggestive findings, early physiological markers for overtraining have not been clearly established. It appears that physiological symptoms accompanying overtraining are evident primarily after a fully developed overtraining syndrome exists (Hackney et al.; Levin); at this point, rest or greatly reduced training load is the preferred intervention.

Psychological Impact of Overtraining

Much of the work on the psychological impact of overtraining has focused on emotional and mood states in response to large training demands. The most comprehensive efforts to document this impact have been by Bill Morgan and his co-workers at the University of Wisconsin (Morgan et al., 1987; Morgan, 1991). Much of this work has utilized the Profile of Mood States (POMS), (McNair, Lorr, & Droppleman, 1971), a measure of mood states with six subscales, to characterize the psychological functioning of athletes across time and various training and competitive situations.

Early in Morgan's work, he found that active individuals and elite athletes have a positive mood profile on the POMS, which he labeled the *Iceberg Profile* (1985). This name was derived from the shape of this characteristic profile: a higher than average score on the *Vigor* scale, and lower than average scores on the five other negative mood scales (*Tension, Depression, Anger, Fatigue,* and *Confusion*). The strength of the relationship between POMS scores and elite-athlete status led to a theoretical hypothesis that elite athletes might be emotionally healthier than non-elite athletes and that mental health is correlated with sport success (1985, 1991).

In addition to Morgan's characterization of the iceberg profile, his research team performed a 10-year longitudinal study of competitive college swimmers, using the POMS and other means to monitor the swimmers' psychological states during training periods of various intensity (Morgan et al., 1987). The researchers found that with ever-increasing training levels, the iceberg profile disappeared and that an overall negative mood disturbance increased in conjunction with increased training levels. The authors described the relationship as following a *dose–response* pattern, with training levels being the dosage level and mood disturbance being the response. At the highest training levels, the iceberg profile actually inverted, with the *Vigor* subscale falling below negative mood subscale levels. Morgan (1991) notes that, despite the clear group results, there were significant individual differences in response to various training loads.

In a companion study, which monitored the physiological status and performance levels of the swimmers (Costill et al., 1988), there was a correspondence between mood disturbance and physiological signs of lower functioning. This pattern of psychological and physiological disturbances in response to higher levels of training was described as a state of "staleness," the product of intense training levels (Morgan et al., 1987). Interestingly, mood disturbances on the athlete's POMS scores fell to a preovertrained baseline following a period of rest or reduced training load (tapering).

Interaction of Psychological and Physiological Effects

Recent research on overtraining has focused on the interaction of psychological, physiological, and general performance effects in response to training. This focus is due to two major factors, one being recognition on a theoretical level of the problems of attempting to separate mind from body when describing the effects of stress (Lazarus & Folkman, 1984; Yukelson & Murphy, 1993). Another factor in the trend toward studying physiological and psychological effects together is the need for cross-validating data on the impact of overtraining (Levin, 1991; Murphy, Fleck, Dudley, & Callister, 1990).

On the theoretical level, recent work from the field of psychoneuroimmunology (PNI) has influenced thinking on the connections between physiological and psychological systems (Ader, 1981). The work in this area has interesting implications for overtraining research as well as for sport psychology in general. PNI research focuses on the interaction of the body's three major information systems: the nervous system, the endocrine system, and the immune system (Hall, 1989). Although molecular connections between these systems have been charted, research on their mechanisms of communication is just beginning. Perhaps PNI's greatest utility at this time is its use as a theoretical model to explain what has been suspected for some time: that behavioral factors as well as environment and genetic predisposition have an impact on disease and health (Borysenko, 1984). PNI research might also be useful as a heuristic for understanding the relationship between training levels, mood states, and immune-system functioning in overtrained athletes.

In addition to increasing the research's theoretical sophistication, monitoring the interaction of psychological and physiological effects when studying overtraining increases the ability to accurately document the impact of very high training levels (Morgan, Brown, et al., 1987). For example, considering physiological and psychological data simultaneously has shown that the impact of overload can occur at different times for different systems (Murphy et al., 1990). Thus the timing of an overload training period and accompanying taper for competition might be appropriate for maximizing physical capacity for competition, but not for maximizing emotional readiness for competition.

An interdisciplinary study with elite judo athletes at the United States Olympic Training Center systematically controlled training levels over a 10-week period while monitoring psychological states, physical performance variables, and physiological markers of overtraining, such as resting heart rates and resting blood pressure levels (Callister et al., 1989; Murphy et al., 1990). Following a protocol suggested by Matveyev (1981) to optimize performance at the end of the training period, the athletes in the study participated in baseline, increased conditioning, and increased sport-specific skill-training periods, in that order.

Interestingly, the results of the Murphy et al. (1990) study differed in some respects from earlier studies. The performance data indicated that decreases in strength and speed occurred despite the absence of physiological markers. Psychological results revealed (unlike those of earlier studies also using the POMS) a lack of overall mood disturbance on the POMS, but the POMS *Anger* scale was significantly higher at the end of the 10-week period. In addition, general anxiety and somatic competitive anxiety also increased over the course of the study. Psychological indices and performance measures showed similar patterns in response to training load, despite the absence of physiological markers. These results as well as other studies showing a link between psychological state and performance in the absence of clear early physiological markers (Morgan, Costill, Flynn, Raglin, & O'Connor, 1988) have led some authors to advocate that coaches pay closer attention to individual athletes' self-reports of effort and psychological state when there is a concern about a potential overtraining syndrome (Levin, 1991; Morgan, 1991). This emphasis on a person's psychological state might be even more important in the burnout syndrome, which is of recent interest to sport psychologists studying training stress.

BURNOUT RESEARCH

Burnout is a psychological term that first appeared in the 1970s but is now a frequent subject of popular-magazine articles and television talk shows. Like many popularized terms or phrases that originated as psychological constructs, the word *burnout* now means many things to many people. Much of the early research on burnout focused on the stress and stress reactions of people working in "helping professions." From an initial focus on a job-related syndrome (Maslach, 1976), the definition of burnout syndrome has now been broadened to include many situations where characteristic signs of burnout are present. In a recent review, Dale and Weinberg (1990) summarize the classic characteristics of burnout: exhaustion, negative responses to others, and low self-esteem and depression. In addition, most definitions of burnout emphasize the presence of chronic stressors (Dale & Weinberg; Silva, 1990; Smith, 1986).

Based on these definitions, the characteristics of burnout are in some ways similar to those of an overtraining syndrome. For this reason, overtraining and burnout are often included together in discussions of athlete stress. Before discussing burnout in further detail, it is useful to determine how these concepts differ and how they overlap. Some authors have argued that overtraining and burnout are on a continuum, burnout being the product of chronic overtraining (Silva, 1990), whereas others have noted parallels and interactions between these syndromes (Dale & Weinberg, 1990; Henschen, 1986; Smith, 1986).

Perhaps the most obvious overlap between the overtraining and burnout syndromes is that stress appears to play a major role in the etiology of each. A salient difference between the two syndromes as typically defined is the specific theoretical role of cognitive factors posited for burnout (see Figure 15.1). As in Selye's early stress studies, research on overtraining has generally focused on a stressor (training load) and a reaction (overtraining

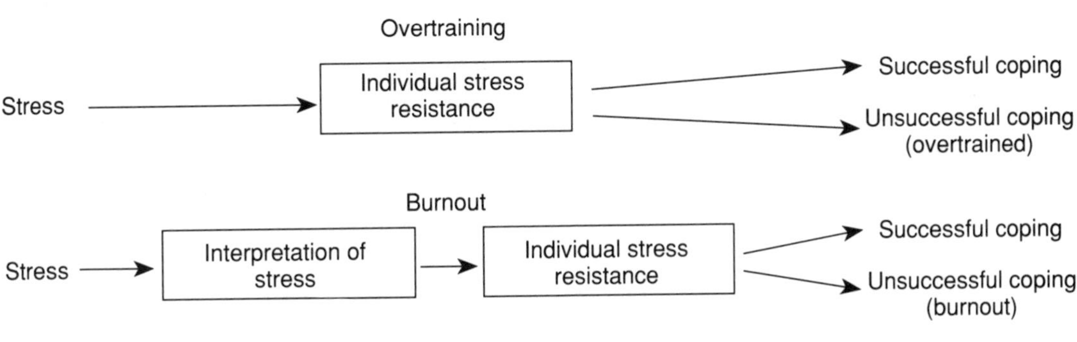

Figure 15.1 The role of stress in overtraining and burnout models.

symptoms), omitting an athlete's interpretation of the stressor. Research on burnout, begun in the midst of the cognitive-behavioral era, pays a great deal of attention to the cognitions of persons suffering from burnout. This introduction of cognitive factors in burnout research mirrors developments in the stress-coping literature (Lazarus & Folkman, 1984), and adds a level of complexity and subtlety that might also be an important part of future overtraining research.

The application of burnout concepts to the sporting world is a fairly recent development, and the earliest work focused on burnout in coaches (Caccese & Mayerberg, 1984; Dale & Weinberg, 1990; Wilson & Bird, 1984) and athletic trainers (Capel, 1986; Gieck, Brown, & Shank, 1982). One reason for the focus on these populations is the similarity of job requirements of previously studied helping professions (nurses, teachers, mental health workers) and those of coaches and trainers.

The topic of burnout in athlete populations was advanced and given a theoretical focus in an article by Smith (1986), who proposed a model to explain athlete burnout. Smith used the social exchange model of Thibault and Kelly (1959), which suggests that humans behave logically to maximize or approach positive experiences and minimize or avoid negative experiences. Smith emphasizes that burnout is a kind of withdrawal and that athletes with burnout syndrome withdraw, either physically or psychologically, from sport participation.

Smith (1986) makes many theoretical points that have relevance for both research on and intervention in athlete burnout. He notes that sport might have distinct causal burnout factors and cautions against over-reliance on work-based models. He argues, as well, for development of sport-specific burnout scales and behavior-based ratings of burnout effects and causal variables. Another important observation is Smith's distinction between dropping out of sport versus burnout; he makes the point that people stop participating in sports for many reasons other than burnout.

For sport psychologists, perhaps the most important contribution of Smith's article was its integration of ideas from the general stress-coping literature into the study of burnout and overtraining. In particular, the addition of individual cognitive factors and individual differences in personal resources suggests that burnout and overtraining are not simple and inevitable responses to stimuli like increased training load or competitive stress. By emphasizing the importance of individual interpretation, Smith's model of burnout suggests avenues of intervention for sport psychologists. Because addressing the levels of training load might not be possible or appropriate for a consulting sport psychologist, working to develop the personal resources or choices of an athlete might at times be the only viable avenue of clinical intervention.

INTERVENTION ISSUES

Before proceeding with an intervention in burnout or overtraining, the sport psychologist must be clear about role and value issues. As is emphasized in chapter 7 with respect to student athletes, a lack of specificity of roles can lead to uncomfortable and occasionally untenable positions for a sport psychology consultant. Clarity of roles is especially critical in overtraining, where role conflicts can be exacerbated by value clashes over training practices and philosophy. Consultants must know whether they are acting as psychologists or whether their opinions are straying into the areas of coaching, competitive career planning, physiological consulting, nutritional consulting, or even athlete decision making.

Although these roles initially might seem clear, exposure to training issues reveals the complexity and value-laden nature of consulting in this area. Consider these examples:

- How does the sport psychologist feel about a 12-year-old gymnast's chronic use of ice packs and anti-inflammatory medicine?
- Should a figure skater compete in the national championships with stress fractures in one leg?
- Is a coach ignoring signs of overtraining due to a desire for a world-championship medal?

When the responsibilities and potential limits of a consultant role are clear, questions of boundaries are less frequent. By communicating these boundaries to coaches, organizations, and athletes, the consultant should be able to impact the complex subject of overtraining by working cooperatively with other disciplines. Difficult moral and ethical decisions will, however, inevitably be encountered.

Diagnosing Overtraining

Recognizing or diagnosing an overtraining syndrome is one role in which the sport psychologist might be particularly useful. As with other interventions discussed in this book, not all problems are immediately apparent to athletes and coaches, so a psychologist's training in assessment can be invaluable. In diagnosing overtraining, the consultant should use multimodal assessment methods wherever possible. As in the case example of Cindy, the young cyclist, at the beginning of this chapter, indications of overtraining can come from a variety of data. Sources of information for the sport psychologist include

- physiological symptoms,
- psychological symptoms,
- decreased performance indicators,
- results of medical testing,
- athletes' reports,
- psychological test data, and
- the reports of coaches and significant others.

Overtraining Symptoms

A first step for consultants wishing to assess overtraining syndrome is to be familiar with the symptoms documented in the literature. As previously described, symptoms can be divided into physiological, psychological, and general performance effects, although authors generally agree that these symptoms interact (Morgan, Costill, et al., 1988). Physiological symptoms described in the literature include

- elevated resting heart rate and blood pressure,
- muscle soreness,
- weight loss and loss of body fat,
- changes in serum hormonal levels,
- sleep disturbance, and
- increased incidence of sickness and injury (Callister et al., 1989; Costill et al., 1988; Hackney, et al., 1990).

Given the importance of these symptoms, developing a good working relationship with physicians or exercise physiologists for teams or athletes can be critical to a consultant's successful interventions. Trainers for athletes or teams are useful but often neglected sources of information. The degree to which ice-packs, aspirin, and ultrasound are used might give a good indication of athlete stress levels. Often trainers are the first to hear of physical and emotional complaints from athletes. Developing a working relationship with athletic trainers can be a key step in prevention of training-stress-related problems (Heil, 1993).

The search for a purely physiological marker for overtraining has met with mixed success, due to individual differences and to the appearance of most physiological signs late in the course of a syndrome (Hackney et al., 1990; Levin, 1991). There is recent evidence that performance measures might reflect signs of overtraining before physiological signs appear (Callister et al., 1989). Close communication with a coach can help a consultant be aware of important performance areas, including strength and speed measures, longer recovery times after exertion, and decreasing performance despite increased training (when this is an unplanned consequence of the training load).

Psychological symptoms might be the most sensitive measures of overtraining (Levin, 1991). Signs of apathy, fatigue, anger, and depression should be carefully monitored. When working with teams, it should be emphasized that individual differences might result in these signs appearing in some athletes and not others. Occasionally, these individual differences can result in an overtrained athlete's being perceived as having an attitude problem, as was the case with Cindy in the case example at the beginning of this chapter. When present, however, these signs should prompt a consultant to gather further information, such as physiological and performance data.

Athlete Report

Perhaps the most powerful source of information about overtraining is an athlete's direct report to a consultant. An athlete's self-report of feelings of overtraining should always be taken seriously. In this author's experience, athletes in a proper state of training are generally the most positive and energetic of clients. Thus, athlete reports of fatigue, feelings of amotivation, increases in perceived exertion, anger, or distress are unusual and should be carefully heeded. In addition to anecdotal and subjective evidence of the novelty of athlete self-reports of negative mood, the body of Morgan's work at the University of Wisconsin is strongly supportive of the notion that successful competitive athletes generally possess greater energy and less negative affect than the population as a whole (Morgan, 1985, 1991; Morgan and Pollock, 1977; Morgan et al., 1987). As has been noted in many recent articles, athletes are often aware of the affective and behavioral symptoms of overtraining before the physiological signs of overtraining are present (Levin, 1991). Thus an athlete's self-report might be the only early-warning signal of an impending overtraining syndrome.

When listening to an athlete's self-report, a consultant can gain a great deal of information about an athlete's interpretation of the training environment. As mentioned previously in the discussion of Smith's (1986) model of burnout, the introduction of a cognitive-behavioral perspective to the problems of burnout and overtraining emphasizes the importance of an athlete's perspective. Subjective self-reports of stress might reflect individual differences in the ability to cope with certain training pressures and might be much more informative than objective reports of training loads. These individual interpretations of the training environment might also provide a critical opportunity for psychological intervention.

One very practical method for gathering athletes' self-report data is through the use of training logbooks (see Figure 15.2) that record an athlete's thoughts, feelings, and behaviors in training and competition. The structure and use of this method can vary greatly across settings. Many athletes use logbooks as a private method of better understanding their reactions to various training and competition settings. Other athletes might feel comfortable using logbooks as a method to communicate with their coach or sport psychologist about mental training issues. Physical training logbooks are used by athletes in a number of sports, and space for recording moods, self-talk, goals, and behaviors can be easily added. After a brief period of monitoring these factors, an athlete can more directly see the interaction of mental and physical states and more easily spot early signs of overtraining.

Psychometric Devices

The psychological research data on overtraining collected by Morgan and his coworkers (1987) is a convincing argument for the use of psychometric testing to identify overtraining problems. In addition, the classic work by Meehl (1954) on the increased accuracy of clinical decision making when using psychometric testing is a reminder of the importance of using the science of psychology whenever possible. The question for the consulting sport psychologist, therefore, should be, Is it possible to effectively use psychometric testing in the competitive sport setting? In some sport settings, the use of any formal psychological test data can meet with resistance, whereas in other settings coaches and athletes welcome psychological data. This is especially true when feedback from the testing is rapid and useful.

Using the POMS as a specific tool for monitoring athlete training responses generally requires the cooperation of a coach who is interested in psychological feedback and who will not feel threatened by this method. A theoretical discussion of overtraining and the POMS might be a useful part of early discussions with a coaching staff. At this time, the consultant might suggest specific nonintrusive data collection and feedback points throughout a season. Also important is a clear understanding among athletes as to the use of the POMS and the level of confidentiality or disclosure to coaches. Cooperative efforts with coaches and athletes toward the goal of preventing overtraining will reduce the likelihood that a consultant will identify an overtraining problem through the use of testing, only to find out that the athlete does not want this information shared.

Coaches Report

Although the case example of Cindy suggested that her coaches were unaware of her overtraining problem, coaches often are in the best position to identify potential overtraining situations. At elite sport levels, there appears to be a growing awareness of the problems of overtraining (Levin, 1991). In endurance sports in particular, programs designed to produce peaking for major races typically are monitored carefully by coaches and are often individualized based on athletes' differences in response to planned training stress (Carmichael, 1992). Most elite coaches in endurance sports have worked

Training Logbook for Cycling

Date ____________

Hr sleep ____________ Resting pulse ____________

Appetite ____________ Muscles feel ____________

Preride plan

Miles ____________

Pace ____________

Specific tasks ____________

Preride attitude: How motivated are you?

1	2	3	4	5
Don't want to ride		Average motivation		Can't wait to get riding

Mental goals for the ride

1 ____________

2 ____________

Postpractice comments

Energy level: How much energy did you have?

1	2	3	4	5
Very low energy				Very high energy

Why? ____________

Performance: How was your riding, recovery from effort, sense of how hard it was?

____

____

Self-talk: What were you saying to yourself during the ride?

____

Goals: Did you meet your mental goals for the ride?

1	2	3	4	5
Met no goals		Met 50% goals		Met 100% goals

Name at least **one positive accomplishment** from today's ride:

____

____

Figure 15.2 A training logbook for cycling.

with overtrained athletes and understand how devastating the impact on performance can be. In these situations, coaches often have a keen eye for early signs of overtraining and can also act as powerful change agents when problems are identified.

Goals of an Overtraining Intervention

The potential goals of an overtraining intervention are

- performance focus,
- psychological well-being,
- education of coaches and athletes,
- protecting the physical health of the athlete,
- increasing coach–athlete communication, and
- developing athlete resources to cope with training.

Although at first glance the goals of intervention in overtraining might seem obvious—eliminate or prevent it—in reality the intervention goals for a consulting sport psychologist can be varied, subtle, and potentially conflicting.

One reason for this is the contrast between the role of a sport psychologist and the role of a psychologist not involved in working with athletes. For example, when a clinical psychologist works with a person who has a stress-related disorder, one goal might be to eliminate or reduce the level of the stressor. A sport psychologist, however, is typically asked to optimize the level of the stressor for the athlete's benefit. As mentioned previously, determining optimal stress and determining optimal benefit are value questions and at times might become ethical questions. This will be discussed more fully later in this chapter. Because stress is a fact of life at elite levels of sport, a sport psychologist working at elite levels needs to be attentive to the goals of any overtraining intervention.

Performance Focus

One potential goal for an overtraining intervention is improved performance. Athletes and coaches are comfortable with performance as a focus, and thus discussing the problems of overtraining as a performance issue might allow a consultant to have immediate access to participants and information about their training levels. Ability to effect change might also be aided by a performance focus. There are, however, potential pitfalls.

One potential problem with a performance focus is a consultant's lack of expertise and credibility. Consider the consultant's answers to the following questions:

- What does the consultant know about planned overload and periodization?
- Does the consultant understand the importance of peaking for particular meets or competition?
- Which performance is the focus, short-term or long-term?

These legitimate questions are critical to athletes whose entire career might be significantly affected by one performance in a single competition. Unless a consultant has established a strong working relationship with an interdisciplinary group that can monitor and plan for performance (coach, athlete, exercise physiologist, trainer, team physician), intervening solely with the goal of performance enhancement not only is difficult but is likely inappropriate.

A second problem with making performance enhancement a goal of intervention is a general issue in applied sport psychology. Should a consultant take credit or blame for an athlete's performance? Although the temptation to take pride in the performance of a client athlete is great, are consultants also willing to take responsibility for poor performance? It is important to note that there are many valid goals for overtraining interventions besides performance enhancement. An alternative focus, based on developing an athlete's coping resources, can also take performance-enhancement goals into account; this will be described later in this chapter.

Psychological Well-Being

Unlike in performance issues, sport psychologists typically have special expertise and training in psychological assessment and treatment. This knowledge can be usefully shared during an intervention and can give a consulting sport psychologist a special and important role in an athletic context, even though the psychological health of an athlete might not always be a priority or focus in an athletic setting.

Even in this more familiar area, it is necessary to consider the importance of temporal and sport-specific factors. One question might be whether the level of negative emotional response to a current period of planned overload is worth it if it means that athletes will compete at their best and succeed at a critical competition 1 month later. Another relevant question might be whether coaches are ignoring the human need for short-term reinforcement in an effort to concentrate solely on peaking for a later competition. By emphasizing the importance of enjoyment of sport by athletes and coaches, even in the high-stress world of elite athletics, a consultant can help contribute an awareness of the need for balance in training.

Educating Coaches and Athletes About Overtraining

In addition to special training in psychological assessment and treatment, many consulting sport psychologists have expertise as educators and information specialists. Although more and more elite coaches and athletes in endurance sports are highly knowledgeable about overtraining, many less-experienced coaches and athletes are not. Often, the sport psychologist might have the most current information available about overtraining, thanks to access to current sport science journals. Providing general knowledge about overtraining and specifying the potential impact for individuals being consulted can be useful.

Occasionally, a prime benefit of this education can be the relabeling of a "bad attitude" as simply one facet of an overtraining syndrome. This might be true in the chapter's case example of Cindy, where overtraining symptoms might have been mislabeled.

In addition to the potential benefits of education for a specific individual or situation, the education process can work as a proactive mechanism to prevent further cases of overtraining. For athletes, this education might be their first detailed discussion of overtraining, and it might give them an explanation for present or past performance and training problems. For some coaches, education on overtraining might act to challenge long-held More is Good—Much More is Very Good notions about training.

Physical Health

Although physical health is not often thought to be a focus of psychological consultation, one goal of an overtraining intervention can be to indirectly impact the physical health of athletes. Advances in health psychology or behavioral medicine as well as the PNI research described previously provide evidence that behavior can have a significant impact on health. By discussing the research on overtraining, with specific mention of the relationship between overtraining and increased potential for injury and illness, a sport psychologist can add a useful and unique voice in discussions about training levels. By using connections with team physicians and athletic trainers and coaches, a consultant with an understanding of health and behavior can sometimes recognize patterns of overtraining behavior that might otherwise be missed.

Increasing Coach-Athlete Communication

Although more communication might seem to be a particularly indirect method of addressing overtraining, communication enhancement can be a critical intervention goal. In the case example of Cindy, her lack of openness about actual training levels and the resultant lack of coaching awareness was a prime factor in her development of overtraining symptoms.

Cindy's story is common in endurance sports, where highly motivated young athletes who have seen benefits from increased training add private workouts in an attempt to increase these benefits. Even at the national-team level, athletes might sometimes choose not to disclose actual training levels to coaches for a variety of reasons.

Athletes also might be unwilling to disclose symptoms of overtraining to coaches in situations where training levels are fairly well controlled and uniform, for fear of losing playing time or losing the coach's respect. This might be especially true in team sports where individual differences in the ability to tolerate increased training stress can result in the labeling of some athletes as tough and others as weak. A sport psychology consultant who can facilitate structured discussions about training levels and athlete responses can provide a useful service for a team that needs all its athletes to be fit and ready to play a long season. Ideally, this sort of structured discussion would allow athletes to understand coaching philosophy and coaches to understand athletes' differing resources in response to increased training stress. This information is critical, given the growing awareness that individualized training regimens are critical, even in team sport settings (Levin, 1991).

Developing Athlete Resources

A good deal of the sport psychology services provided at the United States Olympic Training Center in Colorado Springs falls into the category of stress-management work with athletes. This work attempts to develop an athlete's resources in managing the stress of elite athletics. Of all the intervention goals in overtraining, building an athlete's resources might be the most universally applicable. One advantage of this intervention goal is that it focuses on elements potentially in the athlete's control. Many of the stressors involved in elite athletics are simply not controllable by the participants, athletes, or coaches. In Olympic sport, training levels inevitably are high, competition is intense, and public and private pressures to perform are unavoidable. By developing resources, or "inoculating" against stress (Meichenbaum, 1985), a consultant shifts focus to those elements athletes and coaches can purposefully work on. The development of personal coping skills is the focus of a number of recent applied sport psychology studies.

As Smith's (1986) article on athlete burnout suggests, variations in personal cognitive and affective resources can result in greatly differing responses to similar stressors. In developing personal resources, a consultant can help athletes determine areas of strength and weakness, including time-management skills, relaxation ability (Davis, 1991), personal social-support networks (Smith, Smoll, & Ptacek, 1990), useful goal setting for training (Yukelson & Murphy, 1993), and self-reinforcing ability (Heiby & Campos, 1986).

Recent work by Davis (1991), who taught athletes relaxation skills to impact injury rates, is an example of proactively building personal resources in anticipation of training stress. This research and clinical trend is encouraging, as often the ability to relax is addressed in the context of enhancing competition performance, although the vast majority of an athlete's time, which is spent training, is ignored.

Another area receiving much research attention is social support and its relationship to injuries and illnesses. Many researchers have found evidence to argue for a model of social support as a "buffer" to reduce the impact of stress on injury rates (Andersen & Williams, 1988; Billings & Moos, 1981; Hardy, Richman, & Rosenfeld, 1991; Sarason, Sarason, & Pierce, 1990). These studies suggest that helping athletes identify, build, and utilize social-support systems might help reduce the impact of training-stress problems.

Borysenko (1984) argues for a model of disease susceptibility with three factors acting alone and in concert: genetic predisposition, environmental factors, and behavioral factors. This model, developed from research in PNI, might be usefully applied as well to susceptibility to overtraining and burnout (see Figure 15.3). In the case of overtraining, behavioral factors can encompass the range of personal resources and stress-coping responses available to an athlete. Building an athlete's resources for dealing with training stress might help reduce the tendency in elite athlete selection to rely on a survival-of-the-fittest test (with fittest being those most genetically hardy rather than most talented).

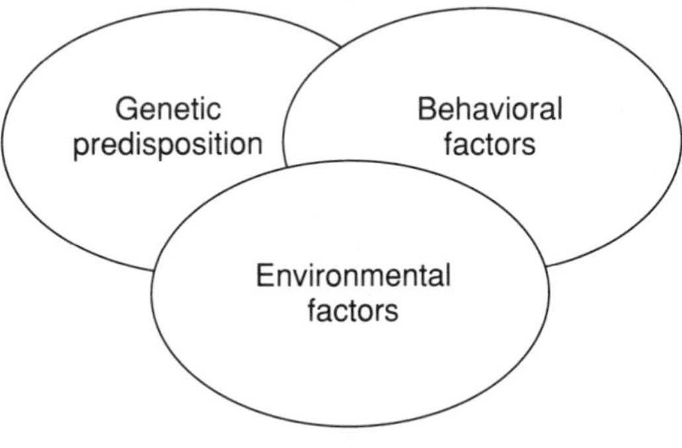

Figure 15.3 Factors that can impact vulnerability to overtraining.

Determining the Success of Interventions

Determining the success of any psychological intervention can be difficult, and the large literature on evaluating the success of therapy suggests that the process can be controversial as well (Eysenck, 1979; Smith & Glass, 1981). Having specific intervention goals, as previously discussed, can be helpful in the determination of success. If intervention goals are well specified, then the measurement of outcome becomes clearer.

- Are athletes performing better?
- Do athletes feel psychologically stronger?
- Are athletes and coaches better educated about overtraining?
- Are athletes healthier and less injury-prone?
- Do coaches and athletes communicate more completely about training issues?
- Do athletes have more resources to cope with the stress of training?

The measurement of coping resources in athletes to determine the success of an intervention is not well developed, and measurement accuracy will likely benefit from a standardized psychometric device. Hardy, Richman, and Rosenfeld (1991) describe the use of the Support Functions Questionnaire (SFQ) (Pines, Aronson, & Kafry, 1981), a social support questionnaire modified for use with athletes, as one formal measure of athletes' social support resources.

In an athletic context where participants' performances are measured regularly and

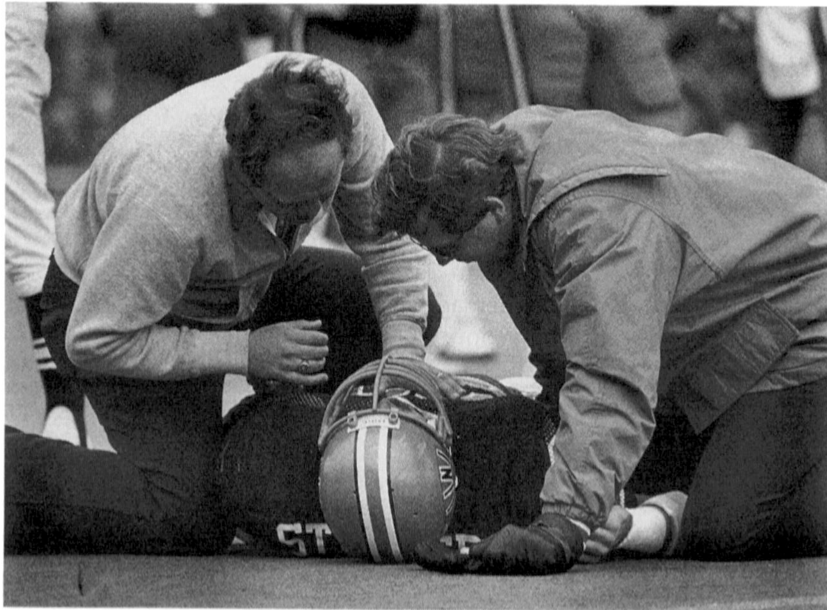

Courtesy University of Illinois Sports Information

objectively, sport psychologists should objectively review their own effectiveness. As the field is still developing a basic research base, there is a need for applied data, and a number of creative dependent variables are available for use by applied researchers (Murphy, 1991). For the practitioner, these same variables can be used as documentation of practitioner effectiveness for employers (e.g., coaches, professional and amateur sport organizations). The need of practitioners and researchers for an objective review of effectiveness is especially apparent with training stress, which is often neglected due to emphasis on competition outcomes.

Intervention in the Case of Cindy

Cindy, the young bicycle racer described at this chapter's beginning, had many characteristics of an overtraining syndrome, apparently a result of her self-imposed extra training rides in addition to an already intense team-training schedule. Her case highlights many issues this chapter discusses. Cindy's coaches called a meeting at which a consulting sport psychologist was asked to attend. The first step for a sport psychologist in addressing overtraining issues is to establish a role that allows the opportunity to intervene. Building a clearly defined role and relationships with coaches, athletes, and administrators was the crucial first step in Cindy's case.

Once at the meeting, the psychologist's expertise in assessment was very important. Recognition of the signs and results of overtraining, collected from the various areas of Cindy's performance, physical condition, and psychological condition, were used to suggest that Cindy's problems might stem from something other than a bad attitude. A psychologist aware of the overtraining symptoms might suggest psychological testing and further interdisciplinary assessment, including physiological testing.

In Cindy's case, the intervention included individual work to increase her understanding of overtraining issues. Through discussion of the psychological impact of an overtraining syndrome, Cindy was able to reinterpret her own feelings and behavior and move productively toward recovery. Individual sessions also focused on other issues that might have contributed to her desire to speed up her rate of progress, such as unrealistic expectations for competitive progress.

Additionally, Cindy needed to understand that training stress results from more than just physical training load. Teaching her a model of stress that describes the interaction of psychological and physical factors allowed her to recognize that training levels are not independent of the rest of her life. Cindy used a logbook to record both physical and psychological factors in her training, giving her a better understanding of her reactions to various training loads. A review of this logbook with a sport psychologist was combined with periodic use of the POMS to provide Cindy with more data about herself. Although not necessary in Cindy's case, another area of individual intervention could be a referral to the team physiologist or team physician to detail the physiological manifestations of an overtraining syndrome.

An especially important area in Cindy's case is communication between coaches and athlete. If the expectations of Cindy and her coaches regarding her performance were made clear to each other, Cindy might not have initiated the secret workouts on her own. With a better understanding of training theory and the underlying physiological theory, Cindy was better able to understand her training program as designed by her coaches. Perhaps the most useful intervention the psychologist arranged was a facilitated discussion between Cindy and her coaches to clarify future training and competitive goals.

ETHICAL ISSUES

In applied sport psychology, some ethical issues that arise are common to other areas of psychology, whereas others are particular to sport consultation. Using the latest revision of the American Psychological Association's Ethical Principles (American Psychological Association, 1992), issues can be grouped under three of the APA's general principles: competence, professional and scientific responsibility, and integrity (see Figure 15.4).

Competence
- Experience with sport-training issues
- Adequate access to information
- Awareness of diagnostic issues

Professional responsibility
- Relationships with experts

Integrity
- Role clarity—who is the client?
- Awareness of own values

Figure 15.4 Ethical issues the sport psychologist must consider.

Competence

Competence in the area of overtraining comprises many factors that address the central question: Is the sport psychologist qualified to give consulting advice about training issues? Although there are no established guidelines, efforts of the Association for the Advancement of Applied Sport Psychology (AAASP) to set educational and training guidelines for certified consultants have helped clarify this issue. A specific element especially important for the area of overtraining is education in exercise physiology and modern training methods. Specialized knowledge of planned overwork, periodization of training cycles, and planned peaking also are particularly useful.

The potential for misdiagnosis of overtraining and burnout should be recognized as a significant issue. Due to overtraining's impact on multiple facets of an athlete's life, it is important to rule out differential diagnoses. The question of potential depression should be addressed, as a number of symptoms of a major depressive episode listed in the DSM-III-R (American Psychiatric Association, 1987) have also been used to describe symptoms of overtraining (e.g., depressed mood, weight loss, sleep disturbance, fatigue, inability to concentrate). Of course, one might argue that overtraining could be an etiological factor in depression; this is an interesting counterpoint to the literature on the beneficial impact of moderate exercise on mood.

Another obvious and important possible alternative diagnosis is a physical disorder. If an athlete has not seen a physician about feelings of fatigue, muscle soreness, or the need for more sleep, for example, then a referral to rule out any physical problem should be a part of any planned intervention. As previously described, PNI research suggests that overtraining might have a role in the etiology of illnesses. Because vulnerability to injury and illness can be a sign of overtraining, awareness of an athlete's physical condition and contact with team health personnel is important.

Professional and Scientific Responsibility

The responsibility to "consult with, refer to, or cooperate with other professionals and institutions" (American Psychological Association, 1992) falls under APA's general principle of professional and scientific responsibility. Perhaps even more important than the psychologist's acquisition of knowledge about training and overtraining is ongoing access to experts. Given the interaction of physiological, psychological, and performance factors in overtraining, contact with trainers, coaches, and team physicians is critical in making responsible decisions. Interdisciplinary resources appear to be a necessary condition for successfully intervening in overtraining.

Integrity

The need for interaction with other experts brings up the issue of professional relationships. As was emphasized in the section on role issues, consulting sport psychologists must be clear regarding their place in the sport environment to maintain boundaries and avoid uncomfortable and unethical relationships. APA's general ethical principle of integrity specifically calls for psychologists to clarify the roles they are performing and to identify their own value systems.

One specific question that might arise is, Who is the client—athlete, coach, or team? Although in some situations (such as in the professional sports world) where the consultant is clearly hired by the team organization, there might be less clarity in other consulting environments.

At the United States Olympic Training Center in Colorado Springs, for example, an athlete might come to the sport psychology department singly and present indications of overtraining to the psychologist. Should the psychologist work individually with the athlete to build personal resources to deal with the training load or should the psychologist attempt to intervene with the coach (within the bounds of confidentiality)? What if large numbers of athletes all present with symptoms of overtraining? Does the psychologist have a responsibility to intervene at the team or national governing body level to eliminate the overtraining? These systemic or professional relationship issues are highly relevant in training. Ideally, consultants should establish good relationships with all levels of an organization to ensure maximum freedom to intervene as appropriate.

Personal values about sport participation might be the most difficult ethical issue for a consulting sport psychologist. In particular, a consultant needs to recognize personal values about playing with injury or training under severe stress. When a consultant sees that training stress is having a negative impact on other facets of an athlete's life (whether or not the athlete has an overtraining syndrome), the dilemma of choosing an appropriate course of action exists. If the training load is necessary for a long-term goal of national or international success, should the consultant attempt to continue to build an athlete's personal resources, or does there come a point when the consultant recommends that an athlete avoid the stress? Does it matter how old the athlete is? Does it make a difference whether daily ice packs are used by a 30-year-old professional baseball player or a 13-year-old figure skater?

Most sport psychologists have a positive orientation toward sport and despite the stress of elite sports see genuine benefits for participants. Given this viewpoint and the organizational and social pressures for continuing in sport when success at an elite level is near, consultants must be aware of their own biases when attempting to help an athlete concerned about training stress. One possible bias is the tendency to treat star athletes differently. Does a realistic opportunity at a professional contract or an Olympic gold medal outweigh the risk of altered moods, chronic fatigue, loss of family support, loss of life outside of sport, and loss of positive marital interactions that might result because of the training time required for success? These questions might need to be addressed individually, based on personal circumstances, but they are not merely philosophical queries. They are real issues likely to be faced by a sport psychologist involved with athletes in training.

Although athletes make personal choices about sport participation, does a sport psychology consultant have a professional obligation to advise against sport participation based on the negative impact of training stress? I believe that a sport psychologist can and should give this advice at times. Although the development of psychological conditions, such as depression, disordered eating, or anxiety disorders might be obvious signals that training stress can be a negative moderator or etiological variable, other impacts of training stress might be more subtle.

CONCLUSION

This chapter's major premise is that sport psychologists must understand the stress of training for elite athletic competition. This understanding begins with the recognition that the elite athlete's life is dominated by training as well as by competition and that an athlete's ability to master intense training loads is a necessary step in reaching elite status. Currently, however, sport psychology consultations typically focus more on competition preparation than on training issues. Increasing the attention given to and research on training issues remains a challenge for the field.

There are some encouraging signs of greater interest in the area of training and overtraining. For example, there is an increase in psychological research in the area of overtraining and burnout. A recent special issue of the *Journal of Applied Sport Psychology* was devoted entirely to studies of training stress (Association for the Advancement of Applied Sport Psychology, 1990) and summary literature reviews have appeared in other recent publications (Morgan, 1991).

Individual sport psychologists face the challenge of becoming familiar and comfortable with basic knowledge in exercise physiology. Recent reviews of overtraining suggest that psychological and physiological elements are clearly interrelated and that both should be considered in assessment and interventions in this area (Callister et al., 1989; Morgan, 1991). Currently, sport psychologists might have greater familiarity with the psychological signs of overtraining than with physiological signs or symptoms. For psychologists to better recognize physiological warning signs of an overtraining syndrome, it is important to understand and recognize a well-planned training program. For sport psychologists without a background in exercise physiology, obtaining knowledge in this area might greatly increase their ability to understand the training stress of elite athletes. An encouraging trend for the future of the field is a strong emphasis on physiological aspects of psychology in the proposed certification criteria for AAASP consultants (Association for the Advancement of Applied Sport Psychology, 1990).

Training stress is a reality for athletes at many competitive levels, and adapting to high training loads is a chronic concern for elite athletes. Helping athletes cope with training stress can be a critical step in reducing or preventing the ill effects of an overtraining syndrome or athlete burnout. The role of a sport psychologist presents a special opportunity to positively impact the bulk of an athlete's life, that portion spent in training.

REFERENCES

Ader, R. (1981). *Psychoneuroimmunology*. New York: Academic Press.

American Psychiatric Association. (1987). *Diagnostic and statistical manual of mental disorders* (3rd ed., rev.). Washington, DC: American Psychiatric Association.

American Psychological Association. (1992). Ethical principles of psychologists and code of conduct. *American Psychologist*, **47**, 1597-1611.

Andersen, M.B., & Williams, J.M. (1988). A model of stress and athletic injury: Prediction and prevention. *Journal of Sport and Exercise Psychology*, **10**, 294-306.

Association for the Advancement of Applied Sport Psychology (1990). Criteria for AAASP certification. *AAASP Newsletter*, **6**, p. 4.

Billings, A.G., & Moos, R.H. (1981). The role of coping responses and social resources in attenuating the stress of life events. *Journal of Behavioral Medicine*, **4**, 139-157.

Bompa, T.O. (1983). *Theory and methodology of training*. Dubuque, IA: Kendall/Hunt.

Borysenko, J. (1984). Stress, coping, and the immune system. In J.D. Matarazzo, S.M. Wiss, J.A. Herd, N.E. Miller, & S.H. Weiss (Eds.), *Behavioral health: A handbook of health enhancement and disease prevention* (pp. 241-260). New York: Wiley.

Caccese, T.M., & Mayerberg, C.K. (1984). Gender differences in perceived burnout of college coaches. *Journal of Sport Psychology*, **6**, 279-288.

Callister, R., Callister, R.J., Fleck, S.J., & Dudley, G.A. (1989). Physiological and performance responses to overtraining in elite judo athletes. *Medicine and Science in Sports and Exercise*, **22**, 816-824.

Capel, S.A. (1986). Psychological and organizational factors related to burnout in athletic trainers. *Research Quarterly for Exercise & Sport*, **57**, 321-328.

Carmichael, C. (1992). Yearly periodization training program for the elite level cyclist. *Cycling USA*, **4**(3), 8.

Costill, D.L. (1986). Detection of overtraining. *Sportsmedicine Digest*, **8**, 4-5.

Costill, D.L., Flynn, M.G., Kirwin, J.P., Houmard, J.A., Mitchell, J.B., Thomas, R., & Park, S.H. (1988). Effects of repeated days of intensified training on muscle glycogen and swimming performance. *Medicine and Science in Sports and Exercise*, **20**, 249-254.

Dale, J., & Weinberg, R. (1990). Burnout in sport: A review and critique. *Journal of Applied Sport Psychology*, **2**, 67-83.

Davis, J.O. (1991). Sports injuries and stress management: An opportunity for research. *The Sport Psychologist*, **5**, 175-182.

Dressendorfer, R.H., & Wade, C.E. (1983). The muscular overuse syndrome in long-distance runners. *Physician and Sportsmedicine*, **11**, 116-130.

Eysenck, H.J. (1979). Behavior therapy and the philosophers. *Behavior Research and Therapy*, **17**, 511-514.

Gieck, J., Brown, R.S., & Shank, R.H. (1982). The burnout syndrome among athletic trainers. *Athletic Training*, **17**(1), 36-41.

Hackney, A.C., Pearman, S.N., & Nowacki, J.M. (1990). Physiological profiles of overtrained and stale athletes: A review. *Applied Sport Psychology*, **2**, 21-33.

Hall, S.S. (1989). A molecular code links emotions, mind and health. *Science*, 62-71.

Hardy, C.J., Richman, J.M., & Rosenfeld, J.M. (1991). The role of social support in the life stress/injury relationship. *Sport Psychologist*, **5**, 128-139.

Heiby, E.M., & Campos, P.E. (1986). Measurement of individual differences in self-reinforcement. *Psychological Assessment*, **2**, 57-69.

Heil, J. (1993). Sport psychology, the athlete at risk, and the sports medicine team. In J. Heil (Ed.), *Psychology of sport injury* (pp. 1-15). Champaign, IL: Human Kinetics.

Henschen, K.P. (1986). Athletic staleness and burnout: Diagnosis, prevention, and treatment. In J.M. Williams (Ed.), *Applied sport psychology* (pp. 327-342). Palo Alto, CA: Mayfield.

Kirwin, J.P., Costill, D.L., Flynn, M.G., Mitchell, J.B., Fink, W.J., Neufer, P.D., & Houmard, J.A. (1988). Physiological responses to successive days of intense training in competitive swimmers. *Medicine and Science in Sports and Exercise*, **20**, 255-259.

Kuipers, H., & Keizer, H.A. (1988). Overtraining in elite athletes: Review and directions for the future. *Sports Medicine*, **6**, 79-92.

Lazarus, R.S., & Folkman, S. (1984). *Stress, appraisal and coping*. New York: Springer.

Levin, S. (1991). Overtraining causes Olympic-sized problems. *Physician and Sportsmedicine*, **19**, 112-118.

Maslach, C. (1976). Burned-out. *Human Behavior*, **5**, 16-22.

Matveyev, L. (1981). *Fundamentals of sports training*. USSR: Progress.

McNair, D.M., Lorr, M., & Droppleman, L.F. (1971). *Profile of Mood States manual*. Educational and Industrial Testing Service: San Diego, CA.

Meehl, P. (1954). *Clinical versus statistical procedures: A theoretical analysis and review of the evidence*. Minneapolis, MN: University of Minnesota Press.

Meichenbaum, D. (1985). *Stress inoculation training*. New York: Pergamon Press.

Morgan, W.P. (1985). Selected psychological factors limiting performance: A mental health model. In D.H. Clarke & H.M. Eckert (Eds.), *Limits of human performance* Champaign, IL: Human Kinetics.

Morgan, W.P. (October, 1991). *Monitoring and prevention of the staleness syndrome*. Invited lecture presented at the IOC World Congress on Sport Sciences, Barcelona.

(Sport Psychology Lab Report Number 150).

Morgan, W.P., Brown, D.R., Raglin, J.S., O'Connor, P.J., & Ellickson, K.A. (1987). Psychological monitoring of overtraining and staleness. *British Journal of Sports Medicine*, **21**, 107-114.

Morgan, W.P., Costill, D.L., Flynn, M.G., Raglin, J.S., & O'Connor, P.J. (1988). Mood disturbance following increased training in swimmers. *Medicine and Science in Sports and Exercise*, **20**, 408-414.

Morgan, W.P., & Pollock, M. (1977). Psychological characterization of the elite distance runner. *Annals of the New York Academy of Science*, **301**, 382-403.

Murphy, S.M. (1991, October). Intervention research, the good. In J.W. Whelan (chair), *Intervention research, the good the bad and the ugly*. Symposium presented to the Association for the Advancement of Applied Sport Psychology, Savannah, GA.

Murphy, S.M., Fleck, S.J., Dudley, G., & Callister, R. (1990). Psychological and performance concomitants of increased volume training in elite athletes. *Journal of Applied Sport Psychology*, **2**, 34-50.

Pines, A.M., Aronson, E., & Kafry, D. (1981). *Burnout*. New York: Free Press.

Sarason, I.G., Sarason, B.R., & Pierce, G.R. (1990). Social support, personality, and performance. *Journal of Applied Sport Psychology*, **2**, 117-127.

Selye, H. (1946). The general adaptation syndrome and the disease process. *Journal of Clinical Endocrinology*, **6**, 117-230.

Silva, J.M. (1990). An analysis of the training stress syndrome in competitive athletics. *Journal of Applied Sport Psychology*, **2**, 5-20.

Smith, R.E. (1986). Toward a cognitive-affective model of athletic burnout. *Journal of Sport Psychology*, **8**, 36-50.

Smith, R.E., Smoll, F.J., & Ptacek, J.T. (1990). Conjunctive moderator variables in vulnerability and resiliency research: Life stress, social support and coping skills, and adolescent sport injuries. *Journal of Personality and Social Psychology*, **58**, 360-370.

Thibault, J.W., & Kelly, H.H. (1959). *The social psychology of groups*. New York: Wiley.

Wilson, V., & Bird, E. (1984). *Teacher-coach burnout*. Paper presented at the Annual Convention of the Northwest District Alliance for Health, Physical Education, Recreation, and Dance, Eugene, OR.

Yukelson, D., & Murphy, S.M. (1993). Psychological considerations in the prevention of sports injuries. In P. Renstrom (Ed.), *Sports injuries: Basic principles of prevention and care* (pp. 321-333). New York: Blackwell Scientific.

EPILOGUE

Looking back at the material in this book, I feel a great sense of enthusiasm at the new and exciting research and experiences described. To assemble the chapters in this book 10 years ago would not have been possible. The field has changed rapidly in the last decade, and we have learned much about sport psychology interventions. I would have wanted to read the chapters in this book if they had existed when I first studied sport psychology in the early 1980s. I'm glad and proud to have been able to assemble them here.

As I read this book as editor, I am impressed by the quantity and quality of research. As documented in chapter 1, it often has been difficult for researchers studying the psychology of sport and exercise to receive serious recognition for their work. Despite the fact that these pioneers have had to swim against the stream, they have accomplished a tremendous amount of varied, vigorous, and significant research. Today, when it is easy to specialize in only one or two areas, it is refreshing to read what has been accomplished in the diverse areas described by the chapter authors. The study of sport psychology has come of age and has reached a level of maturity that few of us might have realized it possessed.

Although a feeling of pride is justified, another strong impression is gained from reviewing the literature cited in this book. Much remains to be done. In many critical areas that demand understanding, little has been accomplished. In areas such as performance-enhancing drug use in sport, ethnicity and cultural issues, aggression in sport, and sexuality issues, little research exists. This emphasizes how critical is research to our understanding of such complex issues and how much can and should be done in understanding the impact of sport and athletic participation in our society. Perhaps we can publish a second edition of this book in the next few years and include chapters containing vigorous new research on these topics. I hope so and I look forward to it.

A book about interventions is a book about making a difference. Interventions promote change, and, guided by existing research, the potential exists for helping professionals to use sport psychology knowledge to promote positive change in sport. If we begin with the individual, change *is* possible. My hope is that the knowledge contained in this book will empower helping professionals to make a positive difference in the lives of the athletes they encounter.

Shane Murphy

CONTRIBUTORS

Throughout his career, **Shane M. Murphy, PhD**, has helped hundreds of elite athletes with performance and personal concerns. From 1987 to 1994 he served as the sport psychologist for the United States Olympic Committee (USOC). While with USOC, Dr. Murphy began a career-counseling program for elite athletes, initiated a counseling program available to all athletes at the Olympic Training Center in Colorado Springs, organized a national conference on alcohol abuse education in sport, and produced a variety of educational programs in sport psychology for coaches and athletes. In 1992 he was appointed associate director of USOC's Division of Sport Science and Technology, a position he held until 1994, when he left the organization to pursue his writing and consulting interests.

Shane Murphy, PhD, Editor

Dr. Murphy was the U.S. team sport psychologist at the Olympic Games in Seoul and Albertville and at the 1987 U.S. Olympic Festival. He is a certified consultant of the Association for the Advancement of Applied Sport Psychology and has served on the editorial board of *The Sport Psychologist* since 1989. He has also published numerous articles and chapters on sport psychology.

Born and reared in Australia, Dr. Murphy earned his doctorate in clinical psychology from Rutgers University in 1985. He and his wife, Annemarie, have two children, Bryan and Theresa. He is an avid sports fan—baseball, football, soccer, rugby, cricket, and Australian football rank among his favorites—and participant, preferring a competitive game of tennis or golf.

Mark B. Andersen, PhD, is a licensed psychologist at the Victoria University of Technology in Melbourne, Australia. He has instructed in the psychology, sociology, and philosophy of sport. Dr. Andersen's recent work involves the psychosocial aspects of injury and inquiries into the delivery of psychological services to athletic populations. He has worked with high-school, college, professional, and Olympic athletes on a one-to-one basis for 9 years. He is an AAASP-certified consultant and is listed in the USOC sport psychology registry.

Chris M. Carr, PhD, is the psychologist for athletics at Washington State University. He coordinates and directs counseling and sport psychology services for student athletes, athletic trainers, and coaching staff at WSU. He also is a faculty member for the counseling services, provides supervision for graduate students, teaches courses in applied sport psychology, and coordinates the eating disorder education and drug education programs for the athletic department. Dr. Carr received his PhD in counseling psychology with a minor in sport psychology from Ball State University. He played football at Wabash College, was a graduate assistant football coach at Ball State, and spent a year in the U.S. Olympic Committee's sport psychology department as a clinical research assistant.

David B. Coppel, PhD, is a clinical psychologist and sport psychologist in private practice in Seattle, Washington. He is a clinical associate professor in the Department of Psychiatry and Behavioral Sciences at the University of Washington Medical School, where he consults in neuropsychology. Dr. Coppel has been involved in clinical sport psychology consultation with athletes from numerous sports at all levels of competition, including high school, college, Olympic, and professional. He has consulted with numerous Olympic athletes and served as sport psychologist at the 1990 Goodwill Games. Currently he is the sport psychologist on the Sports Medicine Committee for the United States Figure Skating Association and is involved in elite-athlete and outreach training programs. Dr. Coppel has published more than 30 papers in scientific journals.

Steven J. Danish, PhD, is Director of the Life Skills Center and professor of psychology and preventive medicine at Virginia Commonwealth University. He is a licensed psychologist, a diplomate in counseling psychology, and a registered sport psychologist of the USOC. He is a Fellow of both the American Psychological Association and the Association for the Advancement of Applied Sport Psychology (AAASP). He is the author of more than 80 articles and eight books in the areas of counseling, community, and life span development psychology; health and nutrition; substance abuse prevention; and sport psychology. Dr. Danish has coached basketball at the high-school and college levels. He is the developer of the Going for the Goal Program, and was involved in the development and implementation of the Career Assistance Program for Athletes (CAPA) for the USOC and the Youth Education through Sports (YES) program for the National Collegiate Athletic Association (NCAA).

Charlene Donovan, MA graduated with honors from Rockhurst College in 1989 with a bachelor of arts in psychology and earned her master's degree in psychology from the University of Memphis, where she is now a doctoral student in clinical psychology. She has worked in a variety of clinical settings, including inpatient, chronic care, and outpatient. Her clinical interest centers on systemic therapies and health promotion. Ms. Donovan's research includes evaluations of therapy techniques, psychotherapy effectiveness, and the psychology of teaching. To apply her training as both a social scientist and a clinical psychologist, Ms. Donovan intends to pursue an academic position that involves research, teaching, and clinical psychology training.

Diane L. Gill, PhD is a professor in the Department of Exercise and Sport Science and associate dean of the School of Health and Human Performance at the University of North Carolina at Greensboro. She has published more than 50 research articles, several book chapters, and the book *Psychological Dynamics of Sport*. Her teaching and research focuses on the social psychological aspects of sport and exercise. She is former editor of the *Journal of Sport & Exercise Psychology*, past president of the North American Society for Psychology of Sport and Physical Activity (NASPSPA), and a Fellow of the AAASP, American Academy of Kinesiology and Physical Education, and Division 47 of the American Psychological Association (APA).

Frank Gardner, PhD, is in private practice in East Hills, NY.

Michael Greenspan, PhD, is a senior consultant with Kiddy and Partners, an organizational consulting firm in London, England. Prior to joining Kiddy and Partners, he spent four years as a licensed psychologist in the Arizona State University counseling center and was the head of Sport Psychology Services at ASU for three years. In addition to his work at the university, Dr. Greenspan provided outpatient psychological services, clinical sport psychology services, and performance enhancement services as a private practitioner. Most of his work was with student-athletes and amateur and professional golfers. Dr. Greenspan received his doctorate from Michigan State University in counseling psychology with a cognate in sport psychology.

Bruce D. Hale, PhD, is a principal lecturer in the Division of Sport, Health and Science at Staffordshire University in Stoke-on-Trent, UK. He contributed to this book while an affiliate assistant professor in exercise and sport science at The Pennsylvania State University. Dr. Hale received his doctorate from Penn State in physical education with an emphasis in sport psychology. He currently is registered as an educational sport psychologist with the Sports Medicine Committee of the USOC and is a certified consultant of the Association for the Advancement of Applied Sport Psychology and the British Association of Sport and Exercise Sciences. He has consulted with hundreds of college and elite athletes in performance-enhancement strategies and is a sport psychologist consultant for USAC Roller Skating, USA Wrestling, US Rugby, and the British Olympic Association.

Jon C. Hellstedt, PhD, is professor of psychology at the University of Massachusetts-Lowell. In addition to teaching and conducting research, Dr. Hellstedt is a practicing psychotherapist who specializes in marital and family therapy. He is a frequent speaker and workshop leader and has conducted seminars for coaches and parents of young athletes sponsored by regional and national sport organizations. Dr. Hellstedt has coauthored the book *On the Sidelines: Decisions, Skills and Training in Youth Sport* and has written more than 13 articles on parent involvement and young athletes' perceptions of parental pressure in the youth sport environment.

Sean McCann, PhD, is a sport psychologist with the Sport Science and Technology Division at the U.S. Olympic Training Center in Colorado Springs. He received his bachelor's degree in psychology from Brown University and his PhD in clinical psychology from the University of Hawaii; he completed his postdoctoral fellowship at the University of Washington. Dr. McCann works directly with Olympic athletes and coaches on stress management, performance enhancement, and counseling issues and supervises clinical research assistants working with resident athlete teams. Dr. McCann has published articles and presented papers on anxiety and performance, stress in athletes, and cognitive pain-management strategies in endurance sports.

Andrew W. Meyers, PhD, is professor of psychology and chairman of the Department of Psychology at The University of Memphis. Dr. Meyers received his doctorate from Pennsylvania State University in 1974. He has published extensively in the areas of sport psychology, behavioral medicine, and children's problem solving. He is a Fellow of both the AAASP and Division 47 of the APA. Dr. Meyers is currently on the editorial boards of the *Sport Psychologist*, *Journal of Sport and Exercise Psychology*, and the *Journal of Applied Sport*.

Annemarie Infantino Murphy, PhD, is a licensed clinical psychologist in private practice with the AIM Care clinic in Colorado Springs, Colorado. She specializes in rehabilitation psychology and has an extensive background in neuropsychological testing. In her clinical practice Dr. Murphy has been involved with a number of athletes in their rehabilitation from injury. Dr. Murphy received her PhD in clinical psychology from Rutgers University with a focus on behavioral medicine and her undergraduate training at the State University of New York in Albany, where she worked with Dr. David Barlow. She completed her internship at the Medical University of South Carolina in Charleston.

Megan Neyer, PhD, is completing her doctoral work at the University of Florida in counselor education with an emphasis in sport and health psychology. She is the assistant director for the human performance lab at the U.S. Air Force Academy, primarily in charge of sport psychology programs for the 27 intercollegiate teams. She is a former competitive elite athlete in diving, her accomplishments including being an Olympian, world champion, 15-time U.S. national diving champion, and 8-time NCAA champion. Her research interests include career and identity development, psychological aspects of injury rehabilitation, stress-injury relationship, eating disorders, and issues in psychoneuroimmunology.

Bruce C. Ogilvie, PhD, is a professor emeritus of psychology at San Jose State University and a member of the United States Olympic Committee's Sport Psychologist registry. His practice extends to professional, national, university, and recreational athletes. Since 1954, his interest has been in the discovery and application of mental training methods for the enhancement of performance. His recent endeavors have been the dissemination of psychological principles and methods as means for reinforcing general wellness. Dr. Ogilvie is a team consultant to the U.S. Figure Skating Association, and a consultant to business and international medical health organizations. He also is a Fellow in the American College of Sports Medicine, the AAASP, the International Society for Sport Psychology (ISSP), and Division 47 of the APA.

Frank M. Perna, EdD, was a former clinical sport psychology fellow with the U.S. Olympic Training Center and health psychologist at Harvard University. Dr. Perna currently holds a research appointment in the Behavioral Medicine department at the University of Miami, and he maintains a consulting practice with professional athletes and with the national governing body of several sports. Dr. Perna received his undergraduate psychology degree from East Stroudsburg State University, and a counseling psychology doctoral degree from Boston University. Dr. Perna's research has examined psychological variables affecting physiological recovery from exercise and athletic injury, transition out of sport, and the adoption of health behavior (exercise, stress management, and smoking cessation) for chronically ill populations. He also is an avid runner who formerly competed at the national level.

Al Petitpas, EdD, is a professor in the Department of Psychology at Springfield College, where he directs the graduate training program in athletic counseling. He maintains a private practice at S.T.A.R.T. Sport Medicine Clinic in Springfield, Massachusetts, and served as consultant for the 1990 Olympic Festival and the USOC's Career Assistance Program for Athletes and Alcohol Education Program. His research interests include psychological concerns related to athletic injury and to career and personal development in athletes.

Robert A. Swoap, PhD, is a clinical associate and postdoctoral Fellow in Behavioral Medicine at Duke University, where he works in clinical psychology, conducts health psychology research, teaches, and consults with the athletic department. Dr. Swoap is a member of Division 47 of the APA, the AAASP, and the Society of Behavioral Medicine. He completed his doctorate degree in clinical and health psychology at the University of Florida, examining the effects of anxiety on swimming performance. His clinical and research interests include performance enhancement in athletics and in the workplace, developmental sport psychology, and health psychology. Earlier in his career, Dr. Swoap worked at the U.S. Olympic Training Center in the sport psychology department.

Maureen R. Weiss, PhD, is a professor in the Department of Exercise and Movement Science at the University of Oregon. Her research has focused primarily on the psychological and social development of children and adolescents through sport participation. She has published 56 journal articles, 8 book chapters, and coedited two Human Kinetics books, *Competitive Sport for Children and Youths and Advances in Pediatric Sport Sciences, Vol. 2: Behavioral Issues*. She also is editor for the *Research Quarterly for Exercise and Sport*. In addition, Dr. Weiss has given more than 110 professional or research presentations and 85 clinics and workshops for coaches, administrators, and teachers. In addition to her other responsibilities, Dr. Weiss directs the Children's Summer Sports program and has been an invited scholar and lecturer for numerous universities and professional organizations across the United States and in several other nations.

James P. Whelan, PhD, is an assistant professor and director of the psychological services center in the Department of Psychology at The University of Memphis, from which he received his PhD in 1989. The psychological services center is a training clinic for clinical psychology doctoral students and the setting for Dr. Whelan's psychotherapy-outcome research. His sport psychology interests focus on athletic performance-enhancement issues and the role of sport and exercise involvement on psychological well-being. He has published on the topics of treatment of child abuse and neglect, children's adjustment to disabilities, and health psychology. He also is actively involved with defining legal and professional practice standards for psychologists.

INDEX

W